LITERACY IN THE EARLY GRADES

A Successful Start for PreK–4 Readers and Writers

THIRD EDITION

Gail E. Tompkins

California State University, Fresno

PEARSON

Boston • Columbus • Indianapolis • New York • San Francisco
Upper Saddle River • Amsterdam • Cape Town • Dubai • London • Madrid
Munich • Paris • Montreal • Toronto • Delhi • Mexico City • Sao Paulo
Sydney • Hong Kong • Seoul • Singapore • Taipei • Tokyo

Vice President, Editor-in-Chief: Aurora Martínez Ramos
Senior Development Editor: Hope Madden
Editorial Assistant: Meagan French
Vice President, Director of Marketing: Quinn Perkson
Executive Marketing Manager: Krista Clark
Production Editor: Janet Domingo
Editorial Production Service: Nesbitt Graphics, Inc.

Composition Buyer: Linda Cox
Manufacturing Buyer: Megan Cochran
Electronic Composition: Nesbitt Graphics, Inc.
Interior Design: Carol Somberg
Cover Designer: Susan Swan
Cover Administrator: Linda Knowles

For related titles and support materials, visit our online catalog at www.pearsonhighered.com

Printed in the United States of America

10 9 8 7 6 5 4 3 2   [WEB] 14 13 12 11 10

www.pearsonhighered.com

ISBN-10: 0-13-702787-7
ISBN-13: 978-0-13-702787-3

DEDICATION

About The Author

I'm a teacher, first and foremost. I began my career as a first-grade teacher in Virginia in the 1970s. I remember one first grader who cried as the first day of school was ending. When I tried to comfort him, he sobbed accusingly, "I came to first grade to learn to read and write and you forgot to teach me." The next day, I taught that child and his classmates to read and write! We made a small patterned book about one of the stuffed animals in the classroom. I wrote some of the words and the students supplied the others, and I duplicated copies of the book for each child. We practiced reading it until everyone memorized our little book. The children proudly took their books home to read to their parents. I've never forgotten that child's comment and what it taught me: Teachers must understand their students and meet their expectations.

My first few years of teaching left me with more questions than answers, and I wanted to become a more effective teacher so I started taking graduate courses. In time I earned a master's degree and then a doctorate in Reading/Language Arts, both from Virginia Tech. Through my graduate studies, I learned a lot of answers, but more importantly, I learned to keep on asking questions.

Then I began teaching at the university level. First I taught at Miami University in Ohio, then at the University of Oklahoma, and finally at California State University, Fresno. I've taught preservice teachers and practicing teachers working on master's degrees, and I've directed doctoral dissertations. I've received awards for my teaching, including the Provost's Award for Excellence in Teaching at California State University, Fresno, and I was inducted into the California Reading Association's Reading Hall of Fame. Throughout the years, my students have taught me as much as I taught them. I'm grateful to all of them for what I've learned.

I've been writing college textbooks for more than 20 years, and I think of the books I write as teaching, too. I'll be teaching you as you read this text. As I write a book, I try to anticipate the questions you might ask and provide that information.

BRIEF CONTENTS

CONTENTS

Chapter 7 Building Children's Word Knowledge   170

Chapter 8 Facilitating Children's Comprehension: Reader Factors   198

Chapter 9 Facilitating Children's Comprehension: Text Factors   226

Chapter 10 Scaffolding Children's Reading Development   256

Chapter 11   Scaffolding Children's Writing Development   288

Chapter 12   Integrating Literacy Into Thematic Units   320

Compendium of Instructional Procedures   345

SPECIAL FEATURES

Literacy Portraits: VIEWING GUIDE

Assessment Tools

DEVELOPMENTAL CONTINUUM

Minilesson

PreK Practices

Be Strategic!

PREFACE

My goal is for all young children to make a successful start in reading and writing, and I believe the key is a balanced approach that combines explicit instruction, guided practice, and authentic application. Effective teachers know their students and their individual learning needs, and they apply their understanding of how students develop from emergent to beginning to fluent readers and writers to guide their teaching. In this third edition of *Literacy in the Early Grades: A Successful Start for PreK-4 Readers and Writers*, I provide the knowledge, modeling, and tools to help teachers in the early grades ensure that their students meet grade level standards and become fluent readers and writers.

NEW TO THIS EDITION

These brand new special features, discussed in more depth on the pages that follow, add dimension to the chapters:

- **Literacy Portraits: Viewing Guides**
- **If Children Struggle . . .**
- **PreK Practices**
- **Be Strategic!**
- **Reality Check: Time Management**
- **MyEducationLab margin notes**

Through these features, preservice teachers connect with the world of classroom practice, learn how to link instruction and assessment, adapt instruction, and intervene when preK-4 students aren't successful.

Along with the new features, I've added and expanded content in nearly every chapter:

- **Chapter 1: Becoming an Effective Teacher of Reading** presents a thoroughly revised principle on learning theories and a brand new principle on differentiation, including information about Response to Intervention.
- **Chapter 2: Examining Children's Literacy Development** includes a new section on children's oral language development.
- **Chapter 3: Assessing Children's Literacy Development** has an expanded section on diagnostic assessment plus new material on preparing children for high-stakes assessments.
- **Chapter 4: Cracking the Alphabetic Code** offers more information on how to intervene with children who struggle with phonemic awareness and phonics.
- **Chapter 6: Developing Fluent Readers and Writers** has been completely revised, and I've updated the content, especially on writing fluency.
- **Chapter 7: Building Children's Word Knowledge** presents an updated organization with new information about the 3 tiers of vocabulary development.
- **Chapter 8: Facilitating Children's Comprehension: Reader Factors** has an expanded section on comprehension activities, including story retelling.

- ◆ **Chapter 9: Facilitating Children's Comprehension: Text Factors** offers new sections that examine the text features in a story, an informational book, and a book of poetry plus increased emphasis on books for prekindergartners.
- ◆ **Chapter 11: Scaffolding Children's Writing Development** has a new organization and the latest material on writing strategies and genres.
- ◆ **Chapter 12: Integrating Literacy into Thematic Units** includes new information on oral presentations plus an increased emphasis on differentiation and assessment in thematic units.

This comprehensive third edition is as committed as ever to supplying the research-based knowledge, teaching tools, and assessment materials, plus the authentic classroom experience that preservice teachers need to learn to get preK-4 students off to a successful start in literacy.

CONNECTING TO THE CLASSROOM

My texts have always been grounded in real classroom teaching and learning. I want preservice teachers to connect research-based information and theory about teaching reading and writing to classroom practice so I provide many classroom examples to model best practice and teacher decision-making to help new teachers understand the needs of young readers and writers. Emphasizing these connections is essential so that preservice teachers will be prepared to begin their teaching careers.

Introducing Ms. Janusz and Her Second Graders

Classrooms are different today; they've become communities of learners. There's a hum as children read together, share their writing, and work in small groups. Children are more culturally and linguistically diverse, and many are English learners. Teachers guide and nurture learning through their instructional programs. Here's what teachers do:

- ▶ Balance explicit instruction with authentic application
- ▶ Integrate reading and writing
- ▶ Teach with trade books as well as textbooks
- ▶ Differentiate instruction so every child can succeed
- ▶ Link assessment and instruction

To show what literacy in looks like in a real classroom, Ms. Janusz and five of her second graders are featured in the Literacy Portraits on MyEducationLab at www.myeducationlab.com. You can track these children's literacy development by viewing their monthly video clips. Four began second grade not meeting grade-level expectations, but Jimmy exemplifies second-grade standards and provides a grade-level comparison. All of the children have shown tremendous growth this year, becoming more capable readers and writers.

Rakie

A minte leter I opened the door and Jojo was foze in a ice cobe.

Rakie's favorite color is pink, and she loves her cat, JoJo. She came to America from Africa when she was very young, and she's currently enrolled in the school's pull-out ESL program. Rakie enjoys reading books with her friends in the library area. Her favorite book is Doreen Cronin's *Click Clack Moo: Cows That Type* because she appreciates that troublesome duck. Rakie's a fluent reader, but she has difficulty understanding what she reads, mainly because of unfamiliar vocabulary, a common problem for English learners. Rakie's bright, and Ms. Janusz is pleased that she's making great strides!

NEW! Literacy Portraits

Beginning with a multi-page introduction just prior to Chapter 1 and Viewing Guide feature boxes that appear throughout the chapters, preservice teachers will meet five second graders who are learning to read and write and the remarkable teacher who guides their learning.

Introducing Ms. Janusz and Her Second Graders. In this three-page section, preservice teachers step into a thriving second grade classroom to see how Ms. Janusz supports her students as they become successful readers and writers. They'll meet five wonderful children—Curt'Lynn, Jimmy, Rhiannon, Rakie, and Michael—and find out a little about each one.

Literacy Portraits: Viewing Guide features help preservice teachers use the year long case study videos of Jimmy, English learner Rakie, struggling readers Rhiannon and Curt'Lynn, and bilingual reader Michael to apply chapter concepts in a real-world setting. I've included features on these topics:

- Community of Learners
- Assessment
- Phonics
- Reading Fluency
- Vocabulary
- Comprehension: Reader Factors
- Comprehension: Text Factors
- Writing

You're invited to go to the Literacy Portraits section of the MyEducationLab website for the literacy methods course to watch these children and their inspiring teacher. There you'll examine classroom footage and student artifacts that document a year-long study of literacy learning.

LITERACY PORTRAITS
Viewing Guide
Ms. Janusz spent the first month of the school year creating a community of learners in her classroom. She taught the second graders how to participate in reading and writing workshop, including procedures for choosing books, reading with a buddy, and keeping a writer's notebook. They learned to work cooperatively, take responsibility for their work and behavior, and show respect to their classmates. Ms. Janusz continues to build on this foundation so that the classroom functions effectively and everyone is a contributing member. Go to the Literacy Portraits section of the MyEducationLab for the literacy course to view Curt'Lynn's March video clip to see her buddy read with a classmate, and Jimmy's October video clip to watch him participate in a writing conference with Michael. Which of the characteristics of a community of learners described in the third principle do you notice in the video clips?

New! PreK Practices

PreK Practices features are placed in chapters to draw preservice teachers' attention to the particular needs of four-year-olds. These notes point to the most appropriate instruction for the youngest literacy learners. I've created *PreK Practices* on the following topics:

PreK Practices

Which reading activities are best for young children?
Interactive read-alouds are the single most important reading activity for young children (Vukelich & Christie, 2009). As teachers read aloud picture books and involve children in a variety of participation activities, they model what good readers do. The children acquire positive attitudes about reading, develop concepts about print, build background knowledge, and expand their vocabulary. In addition to reading aloud at least two times daily, teachers read big books using shared reading procedures, encourage children to look at books that have been read aloud, and have children read calendars, signs, children's names, and other environmental print in the classroom.

- Literacy Practices in Preschool
- Interactive Read-Alouds
- Assessing Young Children
- Phonemic Awareness
- Spelling
- Vocabulary
- Comprehension
- Shared Reading
- Writing
- Thematic Units

Nurturing English Learners

Nurturing English Learners sections in most chapters focus on how teachers scaffold children who are learning to read and write at the same time they're learning to speak English. Your preservice teachers will learn ways to adapt instruction and assessment so young English learners can be successful through these topics:

NURTURING ENGLISH LEARNERS

Teachers assess English learners' developing language proficiency as well as their progress in learning to read and write. It's more challenging to assess ELs than native English speakers, because when children aren't proficient in English, their scores don't accurately reflect what they know (Peregoy & Boyle, 2008). Their cultural and experiential backgrounds also contribute to making it more difficult to assure that assessment tools being used aren't biased.

- Differentiation
- Oral Language
- Assessment
- Phonemic Awareness
- Spelling Development

- Reading and Writing Fluency
- 3 Tiers of Vocabulary Words
- Comprehension
- Writing
- Thematic Units

Spotlights

Spotlight features in Chapter 2 provide in-depth information about the 3 stages of early literacy development featuring children from one multi-age classroom. Preservice teachers will read about a five-year-old *emergent* reader and writer, a seven-year-old *beginning* reader and writer, and a nine-year-old *fluent* reader and writer. The spotlight features look closely at individual learners, using student artifacts and an analysis of each learner's strengths and weaknesses, and I've highlighted the best teaching practices for children at each stage.

Authentic Classroom Vignettes

Authentic classroom vignettes introduce each chapter to help new teachers see how chapter concepts play out successfully with early learners. Starting with Chapter 2, I begin each chapter with a vignette in which your preservice teachers will see how a real teacher teaches the topic addressed in that chapter. These vignettes are rich and detailed, with photos, dialogue, student writing samples, and illustrations. They'll be drawn into these stories of literacy instruction in real classrooms as they build background information and activate prior knowledge about the chapter's topic. Then during the chapter, I refer to the vignette so that new teachers can make connections to the world of practice.

PREPARING NEW TEACHERS FOR THEIR CLASSROOMS

The best way to teach reading and writing in the early grades is to build balanced, comprehensive literacy instruction. As I wrote this text, I built in several features that would help preservice teachers examine the components of a balanced literacy program and prepare them to create balance in their own classrooms.

New! Reality Check: Time Management

Reality Check: Time Management sections take into account the monumental task of devising a balanced instructional program and fitting explicit instruction, guided practice, and authentic application into it. These chapter sections help new teachers manage their instructional time so that young readers and writers get off to a successful start.

REALITY CHECK!
Managing Literature Circles

Developmental Continuums

The Developmental Continuum features describe children's literacy accomplishments at each grade level, prekindergarten through fourth grade. I created this feature to help new teachers understand how children grow as readers and writers and appreciate grade level expectations so they'll implement chapter concepts appropriately. I've prepared developmental continuums on these topics:

◆ Reading Development
◆ Writing Development
◆ Phonemic Awareness
◆ Phonics
◆ Spelling
◆ Reading Fluency
◆ Writing Fluency
◆ Vocabulary
◆ Comprehension: Reader Features
◆ Comprehension: Text Features

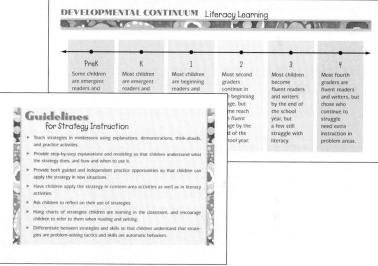

Guidelines

Guideline features throughout the text present the important, detailed implementation guidance your preservice teachers will need to put chapter concepts into action in their classrooms. These features pinpoint the most important things teachers need to know about teaching phonics, word identification, vocabulary, comprehension, and writing, for example.

New! MyEducationLab Margin Notes

MyEducationLab margin notes draw preservice teachers' attention to online, video-based assignments and lessons that deepen their comprehension, as well as other online resources that will enrich their understanding of chapter concepts.

◆ They will be directed to online Assignments and Activities that use authentic classroom video footage to help answer questions that will deepen their understanding of chapter concepts.
◆ Other notes lead to online learning units to help new teachers develop instructional strategies and dispositions to take directly into their early literacy classrooms.

Go to the Assignments and Activities section of the Topic *Organization and Management* in the MyEducationLab for the literacy course and complete the activity entitled *Planning and Managing Learning Centers*.

TOOLS TO USE

I want this text to be a rich resource for new teachers even after they begin teaching. Within these chapters preservice teachers will find features that not only illustrate the concepts they're learning, but become valuable classroom tools once they're teaching.

The Compendium of Instructional Procedures

This incredibly popular bank of procedures offers new teachers a robust resource of step-by-step instructional methods designed to get them up and running quickly in their own preK-4 classrooms. The easily accessible Compendium on the orange-edged pages at the back of the book offers clearly articulated instructional procedures. It's an invaluable resource and quick reference.

Compendium of Instructional Procedures

◆ Look for notes in chapter margins, and orange terms highlighted throughout the chapters, that connect chapter content with a fully crafted procedure in the Compendium.

ook talks are brief teasers that teachers give to introduce books and interest children reading them. Teachers show the book, summarize it without giving away the end-g, and read a short excerpt aloud to hook children's interest. Then they pass the book f to an interested reader or place it in the classroom library. Children use the same eps when they give book talks to share the books they've read during reading work-op. Here's a transcript of a third grader's book talk about Paula Danziger's *Amber own Is Not a Crayon* (2006):

Book Talks

This is my book: *Amber Brown Is Not a Crayon.* It's about these two kids—Amber Brown, who is a girl, and Justin Daniels, who is a boy. See? Here is their picture. They are in third grade, too, and their teacher—his name is Mr. Cohen—pretends to take them on airplane trips to the places they study. They move their chairs so that it is like they are on an airplane and Amber and Justin always put their chairs side by side. I'm going to read you the very beginning of the book. [She reads the first three pages aloud to the class.] This story is really funny and when you are reading you think the author is telling you the story instead of you reading it. And there are more stories about Amber Brown. This is the one I'm reading now—*You Can't Eat Your Chicken Pox, Amber Brown* (1995).

here are several reasons why this child and others in her class are so successful in giv-g book talks. The teacher has modeled how to give a book talk, and children are read-g books that they've chosen—books they really like. In addition, these children are xperienced in talking with their classmates about books.

rocedure. Teachers follow these steps in conducting a book talk:

1. Select a book to share. Teachers choose a new book to introduce to children a book that children haven't shown much interest in. They familiarize themselves ith the book by reading or rereading it.

2. Plan a brief presentation. Teachers plan how t children in reading it. They usually begin with the tit ention the genre or topic and briefly summarize the p eachers also decide why they liked the book and think sted in it. Sometimes they choose a short excerpt to re

3. Show the book and present the planned ook talk and show the book. Their comments are u hild will ask to borrow the book to read.

Assessment Tools

Assessment Tools throughout chapters recommend specific tests and informal assessments to screen, diagnose, and monitor children's progress. I've included assessment tools on these topics:

◆ Oral Language
◆ Concepts About Written Language
◆ Reading Levels
◆ Diagnostic Assessments
◆ Phonemic Awareness
◆ Phonics
◆ Spelling
◆ Reading Fluency
◆ Vocabulary
◆ Comprehension
◆ Writing

Assessment Tools

Concepts About Written Language

Teachers monitor children's growing awareness of written language as they observe them during shared reading and other literacy activities. The most widely used assessment is Marie Clay's Concepts About Print Test:

◆ **Concepts About Print Test (CAP)** (Clay, 2007a)
The CAP Test assesses young children's understanding of three concepts about written language: book-orientation concepts, directionality concepts, and letter and word concepts. The test has 24 items and is administered individually in about 10 minutes. The teacher reads a short book aloud while a child looks on. The child is asked to open the book, turn pages, and point out particular print features as the text is read. Four forms of the CAP Test booklet are available: *Sand* (Clay, 2007c), *Stones* (Clay, 2007d), *Follow Me, Moon* (Clay, 2000b), and *No Shoes* (Clay, 2007b), as well as a Spanish version. Teachers carefully observe children as they respond, and then mark their responses on a scoring sheet. Directions for administering the CAP Test are included in *Observation Survey of Early Literacy Achievement* (Clay, 2007a), which is available for purchase from Heinemann Books.

Instead of using the test booklets, teachers can also administer the test using books available in the classroom the scoring sheet below.

NEW! If Children Struggle . . .

If Children Struggle . . . sections help new teachers decide how to intervene after an assessment indicates that children aren't making adequate progress or meeting grade level standards. I've offered intervention recommendations on these topics:

- ◆ Phonemic Awareness
- ◆ Phonics
- ◆ Spelling
- ◆ Reading Fluency
- ◆ Writing Fluency
- ◆ Vocabulary
- ◆ Comprehension
- ◆ Writing

IF CHILDREN STRUGGLE . . .

When children aren't making adequate progress in writing, teachers step in to determine the problem and then intervene to address it. Emergent, beginning, and fluent writers exhibit different problems that reflect what they know about writing, so teachers start by identifying children's stage of writing dev[...] write independently and with classmates, exa[...]

Be Strategic!

Beginning Reading Strategies

These are the first reading strategies that young children learn:

- ▶ Cross-check
- ▶ Predict
- ▶ Connect
- ▶ Monitor
- ▶ Repair

Children learn these reading strategies as they participate in shared and guided reading activities and interactive read-alouds.

NEW! Be Strategic!

Be Strategic! features highlight the literacy strategies that young learners need to develop to become successful readers and writers. I've explained these cognitive and metacognitive strategies that children learn in the primary grades:

- ◆ Beginning Reading
- ◆ Test Taking
- ◆ Phonemic Awareness
- ◆ Phonics
- ◆ Spelling
- ◆ Word Identification
- ◆ Word Learning
- ◆ Comprehension: Reader Factors
- ◆ Comprehension: Text Factors
- ◆ Writing

Minilessons

Minilessons offer ready-to-use reading and writing strategy and skill instruction designed specifically for use in PreK–4 classrooms. The lessons follow the same research-based procedure to teach children about these topics:

- ◆ CVC words
- ◆ Word families
- ◆ High-frequency words
- ◆ Word sorts
- ◆ Self-questions
- ◆ Beginning, middle, and end of stories

Minilesson

TOPIC: Blending Sounds Into Words
GRADE: Kindergarten
TIME: One 20-minute period

Ms. Lewis regularly includes a 20-minute lesson on phonemic awareness in her literacy block. She usually rereads a familiar wordplay book and plays a phonemic awareness game with the kindergartners that emphasizes one of the phonemic awareness strategies.

❶ Introduce the Topic
Ms. Lewis brings her 19 kindergartners together on the rug and explains that she's going to reread Dr. Seuss's *Fox in Socks* (1965). It's one of their favorite books, and they clap their pleasure. She explains that afterward, they're going to play a word game.

❷ Share Examples
Ms. Lewis reads aloud *Fox in Socks*, showing the pictures on each page as she reads. She encourages the children to read along. Sometimes she stops and invites the children to fill in the last rhyming word in a sentence or to echo read (repeating after her like an echo) the alliterative sentences. After they finish reading, she asks what they like best about the book. Pearl replies, "It's just a really funny book. That's why it's so good." "What makes it funny?" Ms. Lewis asks. Teri explains, "The words are funny. They make my tongue laugh. You know—*fox–socks–box–Knox*. That's funny on my tongue!" "Oh," Ms. Lewis clarifies, "your tongue likes to say rhyming words. I like to say them, too." Other children recall these rhyming words from the book: *clocks–tocks–blocks–box*, *noodle–poodle*, and *new–do–blue–goo*.

❸ Provide Information
"Let me tell you about our game," Ms. Lewis explains. "I'm going to say some of the words from the book, but I'll say them sound by sound, and I want you to blend the sounds together and guess the word." "Are they rhyming words?" Teri asks. "Sure," the teacher agrees. "I'll say two words that rhyme, sound by sound, for you to guess." She says the sounds /f/ /ŏ/ /x/ and /b/ /ŏ/ /x/ and the children correctly blend the sounds and say the words *fox* and *box*. She repeats the procedure for *clock–tock*, *come–dumb*, *big–pig*, *new–blue*, *rose–hose*, *game–lame*, and *slow–crow*. Ms. Lewis stops and talks about how to "bump" or blend the sounds to figure out the words. She models how she blends the sounds to form the word. "Make the words harder," several children say, and Ms. Lewis offers several more-difficult pairs of rhyming words, including *chick–trick* and *beetle–tweedle*.

❹ Guide Practice
Ms. Lewis continues playing the guessing game, but now she segments individual words. As each child correctly identifies a word, that child leaves the group and goes to work with the aide. Finally, six children remain who need additional practice. They continue blending *do*, *new*, and other two-sound words and some of the easier three-sound words, including *box*, *come*, and *like*.

❺ Assess Learning
Through the guided practice part of the lesson, Ms. Lewis informally checks to see which children need more practice blending sounds into words and provides additional practice for them.

GET TO KNOW THE SERIES

This book is designed for a literacy methods course that covers pre-kindergarten through fourth grade. For your course covering fourth through eighth grades, consider *Literacy in the Middle Grades*, Second Edition (2010). Both books are based on my best-selling text for K–8 Literacy Methods, *Literacy for the 21st Century: A Balanced Approach*, Fifth Edition (2010). To learn more about these titles, please contact your Pearson representative, or visit www.pearsonhighered.com/literacy.

SUPPLEMENTS

PEARSON **myeducationlab**
The Power of Classroom Practice
www.myeducationlab.com

The power of classroom practice.

"Teacher educators who are developing pedagogies for the analysis of teaching and learning contend that analyzing teaching artifacts has three advantages: it enables new teachers time for reflection while still using the real materials of practice; it provides new teachers with experience thinking about and approaching the complexity of the classroom; and in some cases, it can help new teachers and teacher educators develop a shared understanding and common language about teaching. . . ."[1]

As Linda Darling-Hammond and her colleagues point out, grounding teacher education in real classrooms—among real teachers and students and among actual examples of students' and teachers' work—is an important and perhaps even an essential, part of training teachers for the complexities of teaching in today's classrooms. For this reason, we have created a valuable, time-saving website—MyEducationLab—that provides the context of real classrooms and artifacts that research on teacher education says is so important. The authentic in-class video footage, interactive skill-building exercises and other resources available on MyEducationLab offers a uniquely valuable teacher education tool.

MyEducationLab is easy to use and integrate into assignments and courses. Whenever the MyEducationLab logo appears in the text, follow the simple instructions to access the interactive assignments, activities, and learning units on MyEducationLab. For each topic covered in the course you will find most or all of the following resources:

Connection to National Standards Now it's easier than ever to see how coursework is connected to national standards. Each topic on MyEducationLab lists intended learning outcomes connected to the appropriate national standards. And all of the Assignments and Activities and Building Teaching Skills and Dispositions in MyEducationLab are mapped to the appropriate national standards and learning outcomes as well.

---

[1]Darling-Hammond, l., & Bransford, J., Eds.(2005). Preparing Teachers for a Changing World. San Francisco: John Wiley & Sons.

Literacy Portraits Year-long case studies of second graders—complete with student artifacts accompanying each video clip, teacher commentary, and student and teacher interviews—track the month-by-month literacy growth of five second graders. You'll meet English learner Rakie, struggling readers Rhiannon and Curt'Lynn, bilingual learner Michael, and grade-level reader Jimmy, and travel with them through a year of assessments, word study instruction, reading groups, writing activities, partner reading, and more.

Assignments and Activities Designed to save preparation time and enhance new teachers' understanding, these assignable exercises show concepts in action (through video, cases, and/or student and teacher artifacts). They synthesize and apply concepts and strategies your preservice teachers read about in the book.

Building Teaching Skills and Dispositions These learning units help new teachers practice and strengthen strategies and skills that are essential to quality teaching. They're presented with the core concept and then your preservice teachers are given opportunities to practice their understanding of this concept multiple times by watching video footage (or interacting with other media) and then critically analyzing the strategy or skill being presented.

General Resources on Your MyEducationLab Course The Resources section on MyEducationLab is designed to help preservice teachers pass their licensure exams, put together effective portfolios and lesson plans, prepare for and navigate the first year of their teaching careers, and understand key educational standards, policies, and laws. This section includes:

◆ *Licensure Exams*: Contains guidelines for passing the Praxis exam. The *Practice Test Exam* includes practice multiple-choice questions, case study questions, and video case studies with sample questions.
◆ *Lesson Plan Builder*: Helps preservice teachers create and share lesson plans.
◆ *Licensure and Standards*: Provides links to state licensure standards and national standards.
◆ *Beginning Your Career*: Offers tips, advice, and valuable information on:
  • Resume Writing and Interviewing: Expert advice on how to write impressive resumes and prepare for job interviews.
  • Your First Year of Teaching: Practical tips on setting up a classroom, managing student behavior, and planning for instruction and assessment.
  • Law and Public Policies: Includes specific directives and requirements teachers need to understand under the No Child Left Behind Act and the Individuals with Disabilities Education Improvement Act of 2004.

Visit www.myeducationlab.com for a demonstration of this exciting new online teaching resource.

Instructor Resource Center

The Instructor Resource Center at www.pearsonhighered.com has a variety of print and media resources available in downloadable, digital format—all in one location. As a registered faculty member, you can access and download pass code–protected resource files, course-management content, and other premium online content directly to your computer.

Digital resources available for *Literacy in the Early Grades: A Successful Start for PreK–4 Readers and Writers*, 3e, include the following:

◆ A test bank of multiple choice and essay tests.
◆ PowerPoints presentations specifically designed for each chapter.
◆ Chapter-by-chapter materials, including objectives, suggested readings, discussion questions, and in-class activities, and guidance on how to use the vignettes meaningfully in your instruction.
◆ A MyEducationLab guide to help you make the best use of MyEducationLab in your classes.

To access these items online, go to www.pearsonhighered.com and click on the Instructor option. You'll find an Instructor Resource Center option in the top navigation bar. There you'll be able to log in or complete a one-time registration for a user name and password. If you have any questions regarding this process or the materials available online, please contact your local Pearson sales representative.

ACKNOWLEDGMENTS

Many people encouraged me as I developed and revised this text. My heartfelt thanks go to the teachers who welcomed me into their classrooms, showed me how they work with preschool through fourth grade students, and allowed me to learn from them and their students. In particular, I want to express my appreciation to the teachers and students who appear in the vignettes and video clips at MyEducationLab: Kendra Chase, Susan McCloskey, Kristi McNeal, Nicki Paniccia McNeal, Gay Ockey, Leah Scheitrum, Darcy Williams, and Susan Zumwalt. In addition, special thanks to Lisa Janusz who welcomed us into her second grade classroom every month while we videotaped her literacy instruction, collected writing samples, and interviewed students. She's a remarkable teacher who uses her knowledge of how children learn to propel her second graders toward high levels of achievement.

Thanks to the professors who reviewed this text for their insightful comments: Bonnie Armbruster, University of Illinois at Urbana-Champaign; Stacey A. Dudley, Bowling Green State University; and Porfirio Lozza, California State University, Sacramento.

Also, I want to express sincere appreciation to my team at Pearson for their dedication and hard work: Aurora Martínez, my new acquisitions editor, for her support; Hope Madden, my cheerleader who encourages me every step of the way and spurs me toward impossible deadlines; Janet Domingo, my accommodating production editor who has skillfully supervised the production of this book; Melissa Gruzs, who expertly copyedited my manuscript, asking all the right questions and nudging me to become a better writer; and Kimberly Lundy, who graciously took over the proofreading duties at the last minute.

A special thank you to Linda Bishop for her inspired idea that led to the Literacy Profiles project in Lisa Janusz's classroom and to Hope Madden for her year-long supervision of the project and expert editing of the video clips. It's a very valuable resource for both preservice teachers and professors.

Introducing
Ms. Janusz and Her Second Graders

Classrooms are different today; they've become communities of learners. There's a hum as children read together, share their writing, and work in small groups. Children are more culturally and linguistically diverse, and many are English learners. Teachers guide and nurture learning through their instructional programs. Here's what teachers do:

▶ Balance explicit instruction with authentic application

▶ Integrate reading and writing

▶ Teach with trade books as well as textbooks

▶ Differentiate instruction so every child can succeed

▶ Link assessment and instruction

To show what literacy looks like in a real classroom, Ms. Janusz and five of her second graders are featured in the Literacy Portraits on MyEducationLab for the Literacy Course. You can track these children's literacy development by viewing their monthly video clips. Four began second grade not meeting grade-level expectations, but Jimmy exemplifies second-grade standards and provides a grade-level comparison. All of the children have shown tremendous growth this year, becoming more capable readers and writers.

 Rakie

A minte leter I opened the door and Jojo was foze in a ice cobe.

Rakie's favorite color is pink, and she loves her cat, JoJo. She came to America from Africa when she was very young, and she's currently enrolled in the school's pull-out ESL program. Rakie enjoys reading books with her friends in the library area. Her favorite book is Doreen Cronin's *Click Clack Moo: Cows That Type* because she appreciates that troublesome duck. Rakie's a fluent reader, but she has difficulty understanding what she reads, mainly because of unfamiliar vocabulary, a common problem for English learners. Rakie's bright, and Ms. Janusz is pleased that she's making great strides!

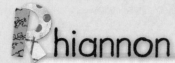hiannon

Rhiannon, the youngest in Ms. Janusz's class, is a charmer. Her gusto for life is contagious! In September, she held books upside down, but she's made tremendous progress since then. Mo Willems is her favorite author; she loves his stories, including *Don't Let the Pigeon Drive the Bus!* She struggles to decode unfamiliar words, usually depending on the "sound it out" strategy. Rhiannon is passionate about writing. She creates inventive stories about her dogs, Taco and Tequila, and gets very animated when sharing them with classmates, but abbreviated spellings make her writing difficult to read.

I SOD it to my DaD. B u D up! SO I pot Logr CLOS onanD pas anD soD It to my DaD. B u D u p!

TRANSLATION:
I showed it to my Dad. BUNDLE UP! So I put longer clothes on and pants and showed it to my Dad. BUNDLE UP!

ichael

Michael is gregarious and loves fun in any size or shape. He takes karate lessons, and his Xbox video gaming system is a prized possession. In September, Michael, who is bilingual, was reading below grade level and couldn't stay on task, but after Ms. Janusz encouraged him to choose books that he wanted to read and to identify topics for writing, his motivation began to grow. Now, he's making rapid progress! He's not crazy about reading except for The Magic Tree House series of chapter books, but he really enjoys writing. He says that his stories are good because he uses wordplay effectively.

Beep beep beep beep it was 9:00 am. I new I had to wacke up. I toock my first step, Slip the flors were frozen Solid.

 immy

It was a haunted house! The door creKed opin. "BOO!" said a ghost. And Lady was gone! "AAAA!" said Jim.

Jimmy's a big sports fan—he likes the Cleveland Indians and the Ohio State Buckeyes, in particular—but his real passion is World War II. He likes to play Army with his best friend, Sam. Jimmy often chooses nonfiction books on varied topics to read; recently, he read a biography about rock-and-roll idol Elvis Presley. Jimmy's a bright student who achieves at or above grade level in all subjects. He's eager to please and worries about making a mistake when he's sharing his writing or reading aloud. In September, Jimmy had trouble with comprehension, but now he's a confident, strategic reader.

urt'Lynn

When I was just 4 years old, I was a CherLeedre Because I rill Wueted to be a cherLeedre.

Curt'Lynn enjoys playing with her buddies Leah and Audri at recess and spending time with her Granny. Her reading was at early-first-grade level at the beginning of second grade. She often "read" books to herself, telling the story through the illustrations. Now Curt'Lynn loves to read Dr. Seuss books because they're funny. Her focus is on decoding words, but she's beginning to think about whether the words she's reading make sense. Curt'Lynn recognizes that her reading has been improving this year because, as she explains, it's becoming easier to get the words right.

Go to the Literacy Portraits in the MyEducationLab for the literacy course to meet these five remarkable young learners and examine their progress over a year of literacy learning with Ms. Janusz.

Chapter 1

Becoming an Effective Teacher of Reading

Literacy is the ability to use reading and writing for a variety of tasks at school and outside of school. *Reading* is a complex process of understanding written text. Readers interpret meaning in a way that's appropriate to the genre and their purpose. Similarly, *writing* is a complex process of producing text. Writers create meaning in a way that's appropriate to the genre and their purpose. Peter Afflerbach (2007b) describes reading as a dynamic, strategic, and goal-oriented process. The same is true of writing. *Dynamic* means that readers and writers are actively involved in reading and writing. *Strategic* means that readers and writers consciously monitor their learning. *Goal-oriented* means that reading and writing are purposeful; readers and writers have a plan in mind.

Gambrell, Malloy, and Mazzoni (2007) recommend that teachers develop a vision of what they hope to achieve with the children they teach and then work to accomplish their plans. The goal of literacy instruction is to ensure that all children achieve their full literacy potential, and in that light, this chapter introduces eight principles of balanced literacy instruction.

PRINCIPLE 1: EFFECTIVE TEACHERS UNDERSTAND HOW CHILDREN LEARN

Understanding how children learn influences how teachers teach. Until the 1960s, behaviorism, a teacher-centered theory, was the dominant view; since then, child-centered theories that advocate children's active engagement in authentic literacy activities have become more influential. The three most important theories are constructivism, sociolinguistics, and information processing. In the last few years, however, behaviorism has begun a resurgence as evidenced by the federal No Child Left Behind Act, renewed popularity of textbook programs, current emphasis on curriculum standards, and mandated high-stakes testing. Tracey and Morrow (2006) argue that multiple theoretical perspectives improve the quality of literacy instruction, and the stance presented in this text is that instruction should represent a realistic balance between teacher- and child-centered theories. Figure 1–1 summarizes these theories.

Behaviorism

Behaviorists focus on the observable and measurable aspects of children's behavior. They believe that behavior can be learned or unlearned as the result of stimulus-and-response actions (O'Donohue & Kitchener, 1998). Reading is viewed as a conditioned response. This theory is described as teacher centered because it focuses on the teacher's role as a dispenser of knowledge. Skinner (1974) explained that children learn to read by mastering a series of discrete skills and subskills; teachers use explicit instruction to teach skills in a planned, sequential order. Information is presented in small steps and reinforced through practice activities until children achieve mastery because each step is built on the previous one. Children practice skills by completing fill-in-the-blank worksheets, and they usually work individually, not in small groups or with a classmate. Behavior modification is another key feature: Behaviorists believe that teachers control and motivate children through a combination of rewards and punishments.

Constructivism

Constructivist theorists describe children as active and engaged learners who construct their own knowledge. Learning occurs when children integrate new information with their existing knowledge. This theory is child centered because teachers engage children with experiences so that they can construct their own knowledge.

Schema Theory. Knowledge is organized into cognitive structures called *schemas*, and schema theory describes how children learn. Piaget (1969) explained that learning is the modification of schemas as children actively interact with their environment.

Imagine that the brain is a mental filing cabinet, and that new information is organized with existing knowledge in the filing system. When children are already familiar with a topic, the new information is added to a mental file, or schema, in a revision process called *assimilation*, but when children study a new topic, they create a mental file and place the information in it; this more difficult construction process is *accommodation*. Everyone's cognitive structure is different, reflecting their knowledge and past experiences.

Inquiry Learning. Dewey (1997) advocated an inquiry approach to develop citizens who could participate fully in democracy (Tracey & Morrow, 2006). He theorized that learners are innately curious and actively create their own knowledge and concluded that collaboration, not competition, is more conducive to learning. Children collaborate to conduct investigations in which they ask questions, seek information, and create new knowledge to solve problems.

Figure 1-1 ◆ Overview of the Learning Theories

Orientation	Theory	Characteristics	Applications
Teacher-Centered	Behaviorism	• Focuses on observable changes in behavior • Views the teacher's role as providing information and supervising practice • Describes learning as the result of stimulus–response actions • Employs incentives and rewards for motivation	• Basal readers • Minilessons
Child-Centered	Constructivism	• Describes learning as the active construction of knowledge • Recognizes the importance of background knowledge • Views learners as innately curious • Suggests ways to engage children so they can be successful	• Literature focus units • K-W-L charts • Thematic units • Word sorts
	Sociolinguistics	• Emphasizes the importance of language and social interaction on learning • Views reading and writing as social and cultural activities • Explains that children learn best through authentic activities • Describes the teacher's role as scaffolding children's learning	• Literature circles • Shared reading • Reading and writing workshop • Author's chair
	Information Processing	• Recommends integrating reading and writing • Views reading and writing as meaning-making processes • Explains that readers' interpretations are individualized • Describes children as strategic readers and writers	• Guided reading • Graphic organizers • Grand conversations • Interactive writing

Engagement Theory. Theorists examined children's interest in reading and writing, and they found that engaged learners are intrinsically motivated. They do more reading and writing, enjoy these activities, and reach higher levels of achievement (Guthrie & Wigfield, 2000). Engaged learners have self-efficacy, or confidence that they will reach their goals (Bandura, 1997). Children with high self-efficacy are resilient and persistent, despite obstacles that get in the way of their success. These theorists believe that children are more engaged when they participate in authentic literacy activities with classmates in a nurturing classroom community.

Sociolinguistics

Vygotsky (1978, 1986) theorized that language organizes thought and is a learning tool. He recommended that teachers incorporate opportunities for children to talk with classmates as part of the learning process. Vygotsky realized that children can accomplish more challenging tasks in collaboration with adults than on their own but that they learn very little by performing easy tasks that they can already do independently; he recommended that teachers focus instruction on children's *zone of proximal development*, the level between their actual development and their potential development. As children learn, teachers gradually withdraw their support so that children eventually perform the task independently. Then the cycle begins again.

Sociocultural Theory. Reading and writing are viewed as social activities that reflect the culture and community in which children live (Moll & Gonzales, 2004). Sociocultural theorists explain that children from varied cultures have different expectations about literacy and preferred ways of learning. Teachers apply this theory as they create culturally responsive classrooms that empower everyone, including those from marginalized groups, to become successful readers and writers (Gay, 2000). Teachers are respectful of all children and confident in their ability to learn.

Teachers often use powerful multicultural literature to develop children's cross-cultural awareness, including *Goin' Somewhere Special* (McKissack, 2001), a story about the mistreatment of black children in the segregated South; *Esperanza Rising* (Ryan, 2002), a story about a Mexican American girl who creates a new future for herself in a migrant camp; and *Happy Birthday, Mr. Kang* (Roth, 2001), a story about a Chinese American grandfather who learns a lesson about freedom.

Culturally responsive teaching acknowledges the legitimacy of all children's cultures and social customs and teaches children to appreciate their classmates' diverse heritages. This theory emphasizes that teachers are responsive to their students' instructional needs. When children aren't successful, teachers examine their instructional practices and make changes so that all children become capable readers and writers.

Situated Learning Theory. Learning is a function of the activity, context, and culture in which it occurs (Lave & Wenger, 1991). Situated learning theory rejects the notion of separating learning to do something from actually doing it and emphasizes the concept of apprenticeship, where beginners move from the edge of a learning community to its center as they develop expertise (Brown, Collins, & Duguid, 1989). For example, to become a chef, you could go to cooking school or learn as you work in a restaurant; situated learning theory suggests that working in a restaurant is more effective. In the same way, children learn best through authentic and meaningful activities. They join a community of learners and become more expert readers and writers through interaction with classmates. The teacher serves as an expert model, much like a chef does.

Figure 1–2 ◆ Books That Foster Critical Literacy

Bridges, R. (1999). *Through my eyes*. New York: Scholastic. (grades 3–4)

Bunting, E. (1997). *A day's work*. New York: Clarion Books. (K–2)

Bunting, E. (1999). *Smoky night*. San Diego: Voyager. (K–3)

Bunting, E. (2006). *One green apple*. New York: Clarion Books. (1–3)

Choi, Y. (2003). *The name jar*. New York: Dragonfly. (preK–2)

Coleman, E. (1999). *White socks only*. New York: Whitman. (3–4)

DiSalvo, D. (2001). *A castle on Viola Street*. New York: HarperCollins. (K–2)

DiSalvo-Ryan, D. (1994). *City green*. New York: HarperCollins. (K–2)

Golenbock, P. (1992). *Teammates*. San Diego: Voyager. (1–4)

Gunning, M. (2004). *A shelter in our car*. San Francisco: Children's Book Press. (1–3)

McGovern, A. (1999). *The lady in the box*. New York: Turtle Books. (1–3)

Pinkney, A. D. (2003). *Fishing day*. New York: Hyperion Books. (K–2)

Recorvits, H. (2003). *My name is Yoon*. New York: Farrar, Straus & Giroux. (preK–1)

Ringgold, F. (2003). *If a bus could talk: The story of Rosa Parks*. New York: Aladdin Books. (1–3)

Ryan, P. M. (2002). *Esperanza rising*. New York: Blue Sky Press. (3–4)

Tamar, E. (1996). *The garden of happiness*. Orlando: Harcourt. (1–3)

Uchida, Y. (1996). *The bracelet*. New York: Putnam. (1–3)

Weatherford, C. B. (2007). *Freedom on the menu: The Greensboro sit-ins*. New York: Puffin Books. (3–4)

Wiles, D. (2005). *Freedom summer*. New York: Aladdin Books. (1–2)

Winter, J. (2008). *Wangari's trees of peace: A true story from Africa*. San Diego: Harcourt. (1–4)

Woodson, J. (2001). *The other side*. New York: Putnam. (preK–1)

Wyeth, S. D. (2002). *Something beautiful*. New York: Dragonfly. (K–4)

Critical Literacy. Freire (2000) called for sweeping educational change so that students examine fundamental questions about justice and equity. Critical literacy theorists view language as a means for social action and advocate that students become agents of social change (Johnson & Freedman, 2005). This theory has a political agenda, and the increasing social and cultural diversity in American society adds urgency to resolving inequities and injustices. One way that children examine social issues is by reading books such as *Smoky Night* (Bunting, 1999), a Caldecott Medal–winning story about overcoming racism set during the Los Angeles riots. This story and others listed in Figure 1–2 describe injustices that children can understand and discuss (Lewison, Leland, & Harste, 2008).

Information Processing

Information-processing theory compares the mind to a computer and describes how information moves through a series of processing units—sensory register, short-term memory, and long-term memory—as it's stored (Tracey & Morrow, 2006). There's a control mechanism, too, that oversees learning. Theorists create models of the reading and writing processes to describe the complicated, interactive workings of the mind (Hayes, 2004; Kintsch, 2004; Rumelhart, 2004). They believe that reading and writing are related, and their models describe a two-way flow of information between what readers and writers know and the words written on the page.

Interactive Models. Reading and writing are interactive processes of meaning-making. The interactive model of reading emphasizes that readers focus on comprehension and construct meaning using a combination of reader-based and text-based information. This model also includes an executive monitor that oversees children's attention, determines whether what they're reading makes sense, and takes action when problems arise (Ruddell & Unrau, 2004).

Hayes's (2004) model of writing describes what writers do as they write. It emphasizes that writing is also an interactive, meaning-making process. Children move through a series of stages as they plan, draft, revise, and edit their writing to ensure that readers will understand what they've written. Writers use the same control mechanism that readers do to make plans, select strategies, and solve problems.

Transactive Theory. Rosenblatt's transactive theory (2004) explains how readers create meaning. She describes comprehension, which she calls *interpretation*, as the result of a two-way transaction between the reader and the text. Instead of trying to figure out the author's meaning, readers negotiate an interpretation based on the text and their knowledge about literature and the world. Interpretations are individualized because each child brings different knowledge and experiences to the reading event. Even though interpretations vary, they can always be substantiated by the text.

Strategic Behaviors. Children employ strategic or goal-oriented behaviors to direct their thinking. Cognitive strategies, such as visualizing, organizing, and revising, are used to achieve a goal, and metacognitive strategies, such as monitoring and repairing, determine whether that goal is reached (Dean, 2006; Pressley, 2002a). The word *metacognition* is often defined as "thinking about your own thinking," but more accurately, it refers to a sophisticated level of thought that people use to control their thinking (Baker, 2002). Metacognition is a control mechanism; it involves both children's active control of thinking and their awareness of their thinking.

PRINCIPLE 2: EFFECTIVE TEACHERS SUPPORT CHILDREN'S USE OF THE CUEING SYSTEMS

Language is a complex system for creating meaning through socially shared conventions (Halliday, 1978). English, like other languages, involves four cueing systems:

- ◆ The phonological, or sound, system
- ◆ The syntactic, or structural, system
- ◆ The semantic, or meaning, system
- ◆ The pragmatic, or social and cultural use, system

Together, these systems make communication possible; children and adults use all four systems simultaneously as they read, write, listen, and talk. The priority people place on the cueing systems varies; however, the phonological system is especially important for beginning readers and writers as they use phonics to decode and spell words. Information about the four cueing systems is summarized in Figure 1–3.

The Phonological System

There are approximately 44 speech sounds in English. Children learn to pronounce these sounds as they learn to talk, and they associate the sounds with letters as they learn to read and write. Sounds are called *phonemes*, and they are represented in print with diagonal lines to differentiate them from graphemes (letters or letter combinations).

Thus, the first grapheme in *mother* is *m*, and the phoneme is /m/. The phoneme in *soap* that is represented by the grapheme *oa* is called "long *o*" and is written /ō/.

The phonological system is important for both oral and written language. Regional differences exist in the way people pronounce phonemes; for example, New Yorkers pronounce sounds differently from Georgians. English learners learn to pronounce the sounds in English, and not surprisingly, sounds that differ from those in their native language are harder to learn. For example, because Spanish doesn't have /th/, native Spanish speakers have difficulty pronouncing this sound, often substituting /d/ for /th/ because the sounds are articulated in similar ways. Younger children usually learn to pronounce unfamiliar sounds more easily than do older children and adults.

This system plays a crucial role in early literacy instruction. In a purely phonetic language, a one-to-one correspondence would exist between letters and sounds, and teaching children to decode words would be simple. But English is not a purely phonetic language because there are 26 letters and 44 sounds and many ways to combine the letters to spell some of the sounds, especially vowels. Consider these ways to spell

Figure 1-3 ◆ Relationships Among the Four Cueing Systems

System	Terms	Applications
Phonological System The sound system with approximately 44 sounds and more than 500 ways to spell them	• Phoneme (the smallest unit of sound) • Grapheme (the written representation of a phoneme using one or more letters) • Phonological awareness (knowledge about the sound structure of words) • Phonemic awareness (the ability to orally manipulate phonemes in words) • Phonics (knowledge about phoneme–grapheme correspondences and rules)	• Decoding words • Using invented spelling • Noticing rhyming words • Dividing words into syllables
Syntactic System The structural system that governs how words are combined into sentences	• Syntax (the structure or grammar of a sentence) • Morpheme (the smallest meaningful unit of language) • Free morpheme (a morpheme that can stand alone as a word) • Bound morpheme (a morpheme that must be attached to a free morpheme)	• Forming compound words • Adding prefixes and suffixes to root words • Using capitalization and punctuation • Writing simple, compound, and complex sentences
Semantic System The meaning system that focuses on vocabulary	• Semantics (meaning) • Synonyms (words that mean the same or nearly the same thing) • Antonyms (opposites) • Homonyms (words that sound alike but are spelled differently)	• Discovering that many words have multiple meanings • Studying synonyms, antonyms, and homonyms • Using a dictionary and a thesaurus
Pragmatic System The social and cultural use system that explains how language varies	• Standard English (the form of English used in textbooks and by television newscasters) • Nonstandard English (other forms of English)	• Varying language to fit specific purposes • Comparing standard and nonstandard forms of English

long *e: sea, green, Pete, me,* and *people.* And the patterns used to spell long *e* don't always work—*head* and *great* are exceptions. Phonics, which describes the phoneme–grapheme correspondences and related spelling rules, is an important component of reading instruction. Children use phonics to decode words, but it isn't a complete reading program because many common words can't be decoded easily and because reading involves more than just decoding.

The Syntactic System

The syntactic system is the structural organization of English. This system is the grammar that regulates how words are combined into sentences; the word *grammar* here means the rules governing how words are combined in sentences, not parts of speech. Children use the syntactic system as they combine words to form sentences. Word order is important in English, and English speakers must arrange words into a sequence that makes sense. Young Spanish speakers who are learning English, for example, learn to say "This is my red sweater," not "This is my sweater red," the literal translation from Spanish.

Children use their knowledge of the syntactic system as they read: They expect that the words they're reading have been strung together into sentences. When they come to an unfamiliar word, they recognize its role in the sentence even if they don't know the terms for parts of speech. In the sentence "The horses galloped through the gate and out into the field," children may not know the word *through,* but they can easily substitute a reasonable word or phrase, such as *out of* or *past.*

Another component of syntax is word forms. Words such as *dog* and *play* are morphemes, the smallest meaningful units in language. Word parts that change the meaning of a word are also morphemes; when the plural marker *-s* is added to *dog* to make *dogs,* for instance, or the past-tense marker *-ed* is added to *play* to make *played,* these words now have two morphemes because the inflectional endings change the meaning of the words. The words *dog* and *play* are free morphemes because they convey meaning while standing alone; the endings *-s* and *-ed* are bound morphemes because they must be attached to free morphemes to convey meaning. Compound words are two or more morphemes combined to create a new word: *Birthday,* for example, is a compound word made up of two free morphemes.

The Semantic System

The semantic system focuses on meaning. Vocabulary is the key component of this system: Researchers estimate that children have a vocabulary of 5,000 words by the time they enter school, and they continue to acquire 3,000 to 4,000 words each year; by the time they graduate from high school, their vocabularies reach 50,000 words (Stahl & Nagy, 2006)! Children learn some words through instruction, but they acquire many more words informally through reading and through social studies and science units. Their depth of knowledge about words increases, too, from knowing one meaning for a word to knowing how to use it in many ways. The word *fire,* for example, has more than a dozen meanings; the most common are related to combustion, but others deal with an intense feeling, discharging a gun, or dismissing someone.

The Pragmatic System

Pragmatics deals with the social aspects of language use. People use language for many purposes; how they talk and write varies according to their purpose and audience. Language use also varies among social classes, ethnic groups, and geographic regions;

PreK Practices

Why involve prekindergartners with literacy?

Bennett-Armistead, Duke, and Moses (2005) list these reasons to explain why it's important to provide a literacy-rich environment for young children and to involve them in literacy activities:

▶ Children learn about different uses of literacy.

▶ Children discover that reading and writing are fun.

▶ Children acquire knowledge about the world through book experiences.

▶ Children prepare for kindergarten and the primary grades as they learn letters of the alphabet and concepts about print.

▶ Children build their vocabularies and expand the ways they construct sentences.

In this text, you'll read about ways to involve prekindergartners in reading and writing using a combination of embedded instruction that's developmentally appropriate as well as explicit instruction that builds skills, including phonemic awareness (McGee, 2007).

these varieties are known as *dialects*. School is one cultural community, and the language of school is Standard English. This dialect is formal—the one used in textbooks, newspapers, and magazines and by television newscasters. Other forms, including those spoken in urban ghettos or in Appalachia, are generally classified as nonstandard English. These nonstandard forms of English are alternatives in which the phonology, syntax, and semantics differ from those of Standard English. They're neither inferior nor substandard; instead, they reflect the communities of the speakers, and the speakers communicate as effectively as those who use Standard English. The goal is for children to add Standard English to their repertoire of language registers, not to replace their home dialect with Standard English.

Teachers understand that children use all four cueing systems as they read and write. For example, when children read the sentence "Jimmy is playing ball with his father" correctly, they are probably using information from all four systems. When a child substitutes *dad* for *father* and reads "Jimmy is playing ball with his dad," he might be focusing on the semantic or pragmatic system rather than on the phonological system. When a child substitutes *basketball* for *ball* and reads "Jimmy is playing basketball with his father," he might be relying on an illustration or his own experience. Or, because both *basketball* and *ball* begin with *b*, he might have used the beginning sound as an aid in decoding, but he apparently didn't consider how long the word *basketball* is compared with the word *ball*. When the child changes the syntax, as in "Jimmy, he play ball with his father," he may speak a nonstandard dialect. Sometimes a child reads the sentence as "Jump is play boat with his father," so that it doesn't make sense: The child chooses words with the correct beginning sound, but there's no comprehension. This becomes a serious problem because the child doesn't seem to understand that what he reads must make sense.

 ## RINCIPLE 3: EFFECTIVE TEACHERS CREATE A COMMUNITY OF LEARNERS

Classrooms are social settings. Together, children and their teacher create a classroom community, and the environment strongly influences the learning that takes place (Angelillo, 2008). The classroom community should be inviting, supportive, and safe so learners will participate actively in reading and writing activities. Perhaps the most striking quality is the partnership between the teacher and children: They become a "family" in which all members respect one another and support each other's learning. Children value culturally and linguistically diverse classmates and recognize that everyone makes important contributions.

Think about the differences between renting and owning a home. In a classroom community, children and the teacher are joint "owners" where they assume responsibility for their behavior and learning, work collaboratively with classmates, complete assignments, and care for the classroom. In contrast, the classroom belongs to the teacher in traditional classrooms, and children are "renters" for the school year. This doesn't mean that teachers abdicate their responsibility; on the contrary, they are the guides, instructors, coaches, and evaluators.

Characteristics of a Classroom Community

A successful classroom community has specific, identifiable characteristics that are conducive to learning:

Safety. The classroom is a safe place that promotes in-depth learning and nurtures children's physical and emotional well-being.

Respect. Children and the teacher are respectful of each other. Harassment, bullying, and verbal abuse aren't tolerated. Cultural, linguistic, and learning differences are respected so that children feel comfortable and valued.

High Expectations. Teachers set high expectations and emphasize that all children can be successful. Their expectations promote a positive classroom environment where children behave appropriately and develop self-confidence.

Risk-Taking. Teachers encourage children to explore new topics, try unfamiliar activities, and develop higher-level thinking skills.

Collaboration. Children work with classmates on literacy activities and other projects. Working together provides scaffolding and enhances their achievement.

Choice. Children make choices about books they read, topics they write about, and projects they pursue within parameters set by the teacher. When children make choices, they're more motivated to succeed, and they value the activity.

Family Involvement. Teachers involve parents in classroom activities and develop home–school links through special programs and regular communication because when parents are involved, children's achievement increases (Edwards, 2004).

These characteristics emphasize the teacher's role in creating an inviting, supportive, and safe classroom climate.

How to Create the Classroom Culture

Teachers are more successful when they take the first 2 weeks of the school year to establish the classroom climate and their expectations; it's unrealistic to assume that children will instinctively be cooperative, responsible, and respectful. Teachers explicitly explain classroom routines, such as how to get supplies out and put them away and how to work with classmates in a small group, and they set the expectation that everyone will adhere to the routines. They demonstrate literacy procedures, including how to choose

LITERACY PORTRAITS
Viewing Guide

Ms. Janusz spent the first month of the school year creating a community of learners in her classroom. She taught the second graders how to participate in reading and writing workshop, including procedures for choosing books, reading with a buddy, and keeping a writer's notebook. They learned to work cooperatively, take responsibility for their work and behavior, and show respect to their classmates. Ms. Janusz continues to build on this foundation so that the classroom functions effectively and everyone is a contributing member. Go to the Literacy Portraits section of the MyEducationLab for the Literacy Course to view Curt'Lynn's March video clip to see her buddy read with a classmate, and Jimmy's October video clip to watch him participate in a writing conference with Michael. Which of the characteristics of a community of learners described in the third principle do you notice in the video clips?

myeducationlab

Check the Compendium of Instructional Procedures, which follows Chapter 12, for more information on highlighted terms.

a book, how to provide feedback about a classmate's writing, and how to participate in a **grand conversation**. Third, teachers model ways of interacting with classmates and assisting them with reading and writing projects.

Teachers are the classroom managers: They set expectations and clearly explain to children what's expected of them and what's valued in the classroom. The classroom rules are specific and consistent, and teachers also set limits. Children can talk quietly with classmates when they're working together, for example, but they're not allowed to shout across the classroom or talk when the teacher's talking or when classmates are presenting to the class. Teachers also model classroom rules themselves as they interact with children. This process of socialization at the beginning of the school year is crucial to the success of the literacy program.

Not everything can be accomplished during the first 2 weeks, however; teachers continue to reinforce classroom routines and literacy procedures. One way is to have student leaders model the desired routines and behaviors; this way, classmates are likely to follow the lead. Teachers also continue to teach additional literacy procedures as children become involved in new activities. The classroom evolves, but the foundation is laid at the beginning of the school year.

The classroom environment is predictable, with familiar routines and literacy procedures. Children feel comfortable, safe, and more willing to take risks in a predictable environment. This is especially true for children from varied cultures, English learners, and struggling readers and writers (Fay & Whaley, 2004).

PRINCIPLE 4: EFFECTIVE TEACHERS ADOPT A BALANCED APPROACH TO INSTRUCTION

The balanced approach to instruction is based on a comprehensive view of literacy that combines explicit instruction, guided practice, collaborative learning, and independent reading and writing. It's grown out of the "reading wars" of the late 20th century in which teachers and researchers argued for either teacher-centered or child-centered instruction. Cunningham and Allington (2007) compare the balanced approach to a multivitamin, suggesting that it brings together the best of teacher- and child-centered learning theories. Even though balanced programs vary, they usually embody these characteristics:

Literacy. Literacy involves both reading and writing; in fact, linking the two facilitates children's learning.

 Explicit Instruction. Teachers provide explicit instruction to develop children's knowledge about reading and writing according to grade-level standards.

Authentic Application. Children have regular opportunities to practice what they're learning by reading trade books and writing compositions.

Reading and Writing Strategies. Children become strategic readers and writers by learning to apply cognitive and metacognitive strategies.

Oral Language. Opportunities for children to talk and listen are integrated with reading and writing activities.

Tools for Learning. Children use reading, talking, and writing as tools for content-area learning.

Pearson, Raphael, Benson, and Madda (2007) explain that "achieving balance is a complex process that requires flexibility and artful orchestration of literacy's various contextual and conceptual aspects" (p. 33).

The characteristics of the balanced approach are embodied in an instructional program that includes these components:

- Reading
- Phonemic awareness and phonics
- Literacy strategies and skills
- Vocabulary
- Comprehension

- Literature
- Content-area study
- Oral language
- Writing
- Spelling

These components are described in Figure 1–4. Creating a balance is essential, because when one component is over- or underemphasized, the development of the others suffers. A balanced literacy program integrating these components is recommended for all children, including those in high-poverty urban schools, struggling readers, and English learners (Braunger & Lewis, 2006).

Preventing Reading and Writing Difficulties. Excellent instruction is the best way to prevent reading problems (Snow, Burns, & Griffin, 1998). But what is excellent instruction? Even though there's a great deal of debate about what constitutes excellent instruction for young children, the consensus is that it involves a combination of systematic phonics instruction and meaningful reading and writing experiences. This combination is the balanced approach that's advocated in this text. Forty years ago, Chall (1967) advocated what's now known as the balanced approach, and more recently, Adams (1990) reached the same conclusion. She identified these components:

- Explicit instruction in phonemic awareness and phonics
- Exposure to a variety of reading materials
- Opportunities to read interesting books

Before first grade, teachers read aloud to children; invite children to read and explore predictable books; use the Language Experience and interactive writing approaches to record children's language, encourage children to write using invented spelling, involve children in dramatic activities related to literature and thematic units, and present more structured activities to teach phonemic awareness, alphabet knowledge, and high-frequency words. In this way, children explore concepts of print and discover the alphabetic principle. Knowing about letters is important, because it's a good predictor of success in learning to read.

No matter whether teachers use trade books or basal readers, children benefit from these activities:

- Explicit instruction in phonemic awareness, phonics, and spelling concepts
- Practice recognizing and spelling high-frequency words
- Explicit instruction on comprehension strategies
- Daily opportunities to read books independently

The goal is for children to read and write fluently by the time they reach fourth grade.

Figure 1-4 ◆ Components of the Balanced Literacy Approach

Component	Description
Reading	Children participate in a variety of reading experiences using picture-book stories and novels, informational books, books of poetry, textbooks, and Internet materials.
Phonemic Awareness and Phonics	Children learn to manipulate sounds in words and apply the alphabetic principle and phonics rules to decode words.
Literacy Strategies and Skills	Children learn to use problem-solving and monitoring behaviors called *strategies* and automatic actions called *skills* as they read and write.
Vocabulary	Children learn the meaning of words through listening to books teachers read aloud and from content-area study.
Comprehension	Children learn to use reader factors, including comprehension strategies, and text factors, including text structures, to understand what they're reading.
Literature	Children become engaged readers who enjoy literature through reading and responding to books and learning about genres, text structures, and literary features.
Content-Area Study	Children use reading and writing as tools to learn about social studies and science topics in thematic units.
Oral Language	Children use talk and listening as they work with classmates, participate in grand conversations, give oral presentations, and listen to the teacher read aloud.
Writing	Children learn to use the writing process to draft and refine stories, poems, reports, and other compositions.
Spelling	Children apply what they're learning about English orthography to spell words, and their spellings gradually become conventional.

 # PRINCIPLE 5: EFFECTIVE TEACHERS SCAFFOLD CHILDREN'S READING AND WRITING

Teachers scaffold children's literacy development as they demonstrate, guide, and teach, and they vary the amount of support they provide according to the instructional purpose and children's needs. Sometimes teachers model how experienced readers read or record children's dictation when the writing's too difficult for them to do on their own. At other times, they guide children as they read a leveled book or proofread their writing. Teachers use five levels of support, moving from more to less as children assume responsibility (Fountas & Pinnell, 1996). Figure 1–5 summarizes these levels of support—modeled, shared, interactive, guided, and independent—for literacy activities.

Modeled Reading and Writing

Teachers provide the greatest amount of support when they model how expert readers read and expert writers write. When teachers read aloud, they're modeling: They read fluently and with expression, and they talk about their thoughts and the strategies they're using. When they model writing, teachers write a composition on chart paper or an interactive whiteboard so that everyone can see what the teacher does and how it's being written. Teachers use this support level to demonstrate procedures, such as choosing a book to read or doing a word sort, and to introduce new writing genres, such as "I am . . . " poems. Teachers often do a think-aloud to share what they're thinking as they read or write, the decisions they make and the strategies they use. Teachers use modeling for these purposes:

- Demonstrate fluent reading and writing
- Explain how to use reading and writing strategies, such as predicting, using context clues, and revising
- Teach the procedure for a literacy activity
- Show how reading and writing conventions work

Shared Reading and Writing

Teachers "share" reading and writing tasks with children at this level. Probably the best-known shared activity is shared reading, which teachers use to read big books with

Figure 1–5 ◆ A Continuum of Teacher Support		
Level of Support	**Reading**	**Writing**
High *Modeled*	Teacher reads aloud, modeling how capable readers read fluently and with expression. Books too difficult for children to read themselves are used. Examples: interactive read-alouds and listening centers.	Teacher writes in front of children, creating the text, doing the writing, and thinking aloud about writing strategies and skills. Examples: demonstrations and morning messages.
Shared	Teacher and children read books together, with children following as the teacher reads and then repeating familiar refrains. Books children can't read by themselves are used. Examples: big books, buddy reading.	Teacher and children create the text together; then the teacher does the actual writing. Children may assist by spelling familiar or high-frequency words. Example: Language Experience Approach.
Interactive	Teacher and children read together and take turns doing the reading. The teacher helps children read fluently and with expression. Instructional-level books are used. Examples: choral reading and readers theatre.	Teacher and children create the text and share the pen to do the writing. Teacher and children talk about writing conventions. Example: interactive writing.
Guided	Teacher teaches reading lessons to small, homogeneous groups using instructional-level books. Example: guided reading lessons.	Teacher teaches a lesson on a writing procedure, strategy, or skill, and children participate in supervised practice activities. Example: class collaborations.
Low *Independent*	Children choose and read self-selected books independently. Teacher conferences with children to monitor their progress. Examples: reading workshop and reading centers.	Children use the writing process to write stories, informational books, and other compositions. Teacher monitors children's progress. Examples: writing workshop and writing centers.

young children. The teacher does most of the reading, but children join in to read familiar and predictable words and phrases. Teachers use the Language Experience Approach to write children's dictation on paintings and brainstorm lists of words on the chalkboard, make K-W-L charts, draw graphic organizers, and write collaborative books.

Sharing differs from modeling in that children actually participate in the activity rather than simply observing the teacher. In shared reading, children follow along as the teacher reads, and in shared writing, they suggest the words and sentences for the teacher to write. Teachers use shared reading and writing for these purposes:

- Involve children in literacy activities they can't do independently
- Create opportunities for children to experience success in reading and writing
- Provide practice before children read and write independently

Interactive Reading and Writing

Children assume an increasingly important role in interactive reading and writing. They no longer observe the teacher reading or writing, repeat familiar words, or suggest words for the teacher to write; instead, they're actively involved in reading and writing. They support classmates by sharing the reading and writing responsibilities, and their teacher provides assistance when needed. Choral reading and readers theatre are two examples of interactive reading. In interactive writing, children and the teacher create a text and write a message (Button, Johnson, & Furgerson, 1996; Tompkins & Collom, 2004). In these activities, classmates support each other by sharing the work.

Figure 1–6 shows a piece of interactive writing done by a group of kindergartners after reading Eric Carle's repetitive book *Does a Kangaroo Have a Mother, Too?* (2000). The teacher wrote the title and the author's name, and the kindergartners created the sentence *Animals have mothers just like me and you*. The children took turns writing the letters they knew in red, and the teacher wrote the letters unfamiliar sounds in black. The boxes around four of the letters represent correction tape the teacher placed over an incorrectly formed letter before the child tried again to print the letter conventionally.

Teachers use interactive reading and writing for these purposes:

- Practice reading and writing high-frequency words
- Apply phonics and spelling skills
- Read and write texts that children can't do independently
- Have children share their literacy expertise with classmates

Guided Reading and Writing

Even though teachers continue to support children, they now do the actual reading and writing themselves. In guided reading, small, homogeneous groups meet with the teacher to read a book at their instructional level. The teacher introduces the book and guides children as they begin reading. Then children continue reading on their own while the teacher supervises. Afterward, they discuss the book, review vocabulary words, and practice skills. In guided writing, teachers plan structured writing activities and then supervise children as they write. For example, when they make

Figure 1-6 ◆ A Kindergarten Interactive Writing Chart

pages for a collaborative book, it's guided writing because the teacher organizes the activity and supervises children as they work. Teachers also provide guidance as they conference with children about their writing.

Teachers use guided reading and writing to provide instruction as children actually read and write. Guided reading and writing have these purposes:

- Support children's reading in appropriate instructional-level materials
- Teach literacy strategies and skills
- Involve children in collaborative writing projects
- Teach children to use the writing process—in particular, how to revise and edit

Independent Reading and Writing

Children do the reading and writing themselves at the independent level, applying the strategies and skills they've learned in authentic literacy activities. During independent reading, children usually choose their own books and work at their own pace as they read and respond to books. Similarly, during independent writing, children usually choose their own topics and move at their own pace as they develop and refine their writing. It would be wrong to suggest, however, that teachers don't play a role in independent-level activities because they continue to monitor children, but they provide much less guidance at this level.

Through independent reading, children learn how pleasurable reading is and, teachers hope, become lifelong readers, and as they write, children come to view themselves as authors. Teachers use independent reading and writing for these purposes:

- Create opportunities for children to practice the reading and writing strategies and skills they've learned
- Provide authentic literacy experiences in which children choose their own topics, purposes, and materials
- Develop lifelong readers and writers

Teachers working with prekindergartners through fourth graders use all of these levels. When teachers introduce a reading strategy, for instance, they model how to apply it. And, when teachers want children to practice a strategy they've already introduced, they guide them through an activity, slowly releasing more responsibility to them. Once children can apply the strategy easily, they're encouraged to use it independently. The purpose of the activity, not the activity itself, determines the level of support. Teachers are less actively involved during independent reading and writing, but the quality of instruction that children have received is clearest because they're applying what they've learned.

Figure 1-7 ◆ Instructional Programs

	Basal Reading Programs	Literature Focus Units
Description	Children read textbooks containing stories, informational articles, and poems that are sequenced according to grade level. Teachers follow directions in the teacher's guide to teach word identification, vocabulary, comprehension, grammar, and writing lessons. Directions are also provided for working with English learners and struggling readers.	Teachers and children read and respond to a book together as a class. They choose high-quality literature that is appropriate for the grade level and children's interests. The book may be too difficult for some children to read on their own, so teachers read it aloud or use shared reading. After reading, children usually create projects.
Strengths	• Textbooks are aligned with grade-level standards. • Children read selections at their grade level. • Teachers teach strategies and skills and provide structured practice opportunities. • Teachers reteach strategies and skills as needed. • The teacher's guide provides detailed instructions. • Assessment materials are included in the program.	• Teachers choose picture-book stories, novels, or informational books for units. • Teachers scaffold reading instruction as they read with the whole class or small groups. • Teachers teach minilessons on reading strategies and skills. • Children study vocabulary. • Children develop projects to extend their reading.
Limitations	• Selections may be too difficult for some children. • Selections may lack the authenticity of good literature. • Programs include many worksheets. • Most of the instruction is presented to the whole class.	• Everyone reads the same book whether or not it's interesting or appropriate. • Many of the activities are teacher directed.

RINCIPLE 6: EFFECTIVE TEACHERS ORGANIZE FOR LITERACY INSTRUCTION

No single instructional program best represents the balanced approach to literacy; instead, teachers organize for instruction by creating their own program that fits their students' needs and their school's grade-level standards and curricular guidelines. Instructional programs should reflect these principles:

- Teachers create a community of learners in their classroom.
- Teachers incorporate the components of the balanced approach.
- Teachers scaffold children's reading and writing experiences.

Four of the most popular programs are basal reading programs, literature focus units, literature circles, and reading and writing workshop, and they're compared in Figure 1–7.

Basal Reading Programs

Commercially produced reading programs are known as *basal readers*. These programs feature a textbook containing reading selections with accompanying workbooks, supplemental books, and related instructional materials at each grade level. Phonics,

Literature Circles	Reading and Writing Workshop
Teachers choose five or six books and collect multiple copies of each one. Children each choose the book they want to read and form groups or "book clubs" to read the book. They develop a reading and discussion schedule and assume roles for the discussion. Teachers sometimes participate in the discussions.	Children choose books and read them independently during reading workshop and write books on self-selected topics during writing workshop. Teachers monitor children's work through conferences. During sharing, children share with classmates the books they read and those they write. Teachers also teach minilessons.
• Teachers differentiate instruction by providing books at varied reading levels. • Children are more strongly motivated because they choose the books they read. • Children work with their classmates. • Children participate in authentic literacy experiences. • Teachers may participate in discussions to help children think more deeply about the book.	• Children read books appropriate for their reading levels. • Children choose the books they read. • Children work through the stages of the writing process during writing workshop. • Children work at their own pace. • Teachers have opportunities to work individually with children during conferences.
• Teachers often feel a loss of control because children are reading different books. • Children must learn to be task oriented and to use time wisely. • Sometimes children choose books that are too difficult or too easy.	• Teachers often feel a loss of control because children are reading different books and working at different stages of the writing process. • Children must learn to be task oriented and to use time wisely.

vocabulary, comprehension, and spelling instruction is coordinated with the reading selections and aligned with grade-level standards. The teacher's guide provides detailed procedures for teaching the selections and related strategies and skills. Instruction is typically presented to the whole class, with reteaching to small groups of struggling students. Testing materials are also included so that teachers can monitor children's progress. Publishers tout basal readers as a complete literacy program, but effective teachers realize that they aren't.

Literature Focus Units

Teachers create literature focus units featuring high-quality picture-book stories and novels. The books are usually included in a district- or state-approved list of award-winning books that all children are expected to read at a particular grade level. These books include classics such as *The Very Hungry Caterpillar* (Carle, 1994) and *Charlotte's Web* (White, 2006) and award winners such as *Officer Buckle and Gloria* (Rathmann, 1995). Everyone in the class reads and responds to the same book, and the teacher supports children's learning through a combination of explicit instruction and reading and writing activities. Through these units, teachers teach about literary genres and authors and develop children's interest in literature.

Literature Circles

Small groups of children get together in literature circles or book clubs to read a story or other book. To begin, teachers select five or six books at varying reading levels. Often, the books are related in some way—representing the same theme or written by the same author, for instance. They collect multiple copies of each book and give a book talk to introduce them. Then children choose a book and form a group to read and respond to it. They set a reading and discussion schedule and work independently, although teachers sometimes sit in on the discussions. Through the experience of reading and discussing a book together, children learn more about how to respond to books and develop responsibility for completing assignments.

Reading and Writing Workshop

Children do authentic reading and writing in workshop programs. They select books, read independently, and conference with the teacher about their reading; and they write books on topics that they choose and conference with the teacher about their writing. Teachers set aside a time for reading and writing workshop, and children read and write while the teacher conferences with small groups. Teachers also teach minilessons on reading and writing strategies and skills and read books aloud to the whole class. In a workshop program, children read and write more like adults do, making choices, working independently, and developing responsibility.

These programs can be divided into authentic and textbook programs. Literature focus units, literature circles, and reading and writing workshop are classified as authentic programs because they use trade books and involve children in meaningful activities. Basal readers, not surprisingly, are textbook programs that reflect the behaviorist theory. Teachers generally combine these authentic and textbook programs because children learn best through a variety of reading and writing experiences. Sometimes the books that children are reading are challenging, or teachers are introducing a new writing genre; these situations require more teacher support and guidance. Some teachers alternate literature focus units or literature circles with reading and writing workshop and a textbook program, and others use some components from each approach throughout the school year.

PRINCIPLE 7: EFFECTIVE TEACHERS DIFFERENTIATE INSTRUCTION

Effective teachers adjust their instruction because children vary in their levels of development, academic achievement, and ability. Tomlinson (2004) explains that the one-size-fits-all instructional model is obsolete, and teachers respect children by honoring both their similarities and their differences. Differentiation is based on Vygotsky's idea of a zone of proximal development. If instruction is either too difficult or too easy, it isn't effective; instead, teachers provide instruction that meets children's instructional needs.

How to Differentiate Instruction

Teachers vary instructional arrangements, choose instructional materials at children's reading levels, and modify assignments as they differentiate instruction. They monitor children's learning and make adjustments, when necessary, and assess learning in multiple ways, not just using paper-and-pencil tests. Differentiation involves adjusting the content, the process, and the products.

Differentiating the Content. Teachers identify the information that children need to learn to meet grade-level standards so that every child will be successful. They differentiate the content in these ways:

- Choose instructional materials at children's reading levels
- Consider children's developmental levels as well as their current grade placement in deciding what to teach
- Use assessment tools to determine children's instructional needs

Differentiating the Process. Teachers vary instruction and application activities to meet children's needs. They differentiate the process in these ways:

- Provide instruction to individuals, small groups, and the whole class
- Scaffold struggling readers and writers with more explicit instruction
- Challenge advanced readers and writers with activities requiring higher-level thinking
- Monitor children's learning and adjust instruction when they aren't successful

Differentiating the Products. Teachers vary how children demonstrate what they've learned. Demonstrations include both the projects that children create and the tests used to measure their academic achievement. Teachers differentiate the products in these ways:

- Have children create projects individually, with partners, or in small groups
- Design projects that engage children with literacy in meaningful ways
- Assess children using a combination of visual, oral, and written formats

These three ways to differentiate instruction are reviewed in Figure 1–8.

Figure 1-8 ◆ Ways to Differentiate Instruction

Component	Description	Instructional Procedures
Content	Teachers identify the information that children need to learn to meet grade-level standards and the instructional materials to be used.	• Choose instructional materials at children's reading levels. • Consider children's developmental levels as well as their grade placement in deciding what to teach. • Use assessment tools to determine children's instructional needs.
Process	Teachers vary instruction and application activities to meet children's needs.	• Provide instruction to individuals, small groups, and the whole class. • Scaffold struggling readers and writers with more explicit instruction. • Challenge advanced learners with activities requiring higher-level thinking.
Products	Teachers modify the ways children demonstrate what they've learned.	• Have children create projects individually or with classmates. • Design projects that engage children in meaningful ways. • Assess children using visual, oral, and written formats.

NURTURING ENGLISH LEARNERS

Children who come from language backgrounds other than English and aren't yet proficient in English are known as *English learners* (ELs). Many can converse in English but struggle with academic language. These children benefit from participating in the same instructional programs that mainstream classmates do, but teachers make adaptations to create learning contexts that respect minority students and meet their needs (Shanahan & Beck, 2006). Learning to read and write is more challenging because they're learning to speak English at the same time. Teachers scaffold ELs' oral language acquisition and literacy development in these ways:

Explicit Instruction. Teachers present more explicit instruction on literacy strategies and skills because ELs are more at risk (Genesee & Riches, 2006). They also spend more time teaching unfamiliar academic vocabulary (e.g., *homonym, paragraph, revise, summarize*).

Oral Language. Teachers provide many opportunities for children to practice speaking English comfortably and informally with partners and in small groups. Through conversations about topics they're learning, ELs develop both conversational and academic language, which in turn supports their literacy development.

Small-Group Work. Teachers provide opportunities for children to work in small groups because social interaction supports their learning. As English learners talk with classmates, they're learning the culture of literacy.

Reading Aloud to Children. Teachers read aloud a variety of stories, poems, and informational books, including some books that represent children's home cultures. In the process, teachers model fluent reading, and children build background knowledge as they become more familiar with English vocabulary and written language structures.

Background Knowledge. Teachers organize instruction into units to build children's world knowledge about grade-level-appropriate concepts, and they develop ELs' literary knowledge through minilessons and a variety of reading and writing activities.

Authentic Literacy Activities. Teachers provide daily opportunities for children to apply the strategies and skills they're learning as they read and write for authentic purposes. English learners participate in meaningful literacy activities through literature circles and reading and writing workshop.

These recommendations promote English learners' academic success.

Teachers' attitudes about minority children and their understanding of how people learn a second language play a critical role in the effectiveness of instruction (Gay, 2000). It's important that teachers understand that ELs have different cultural and linguistic backgrounds and plan instruction accordingly. Most classrooms reflect the European American middle-class culture, which differs significantly from minority children's backgrounds and how they use language. For example, some children are reluctant to volunteer answers to teachers' questions, and others may not answer if the questions are different than those their parents ask (Peregoy & Boyle, 2008). Teachers who learn about their students' home language and culture and embed what they learn into their instruction are likely to be more successful.

Partnering With Parents

Parents play a crucial role in helping their children become successful readers and writers. They support their children's learning by actively participating in literacy activities, such as reading aloud and modeling literate behaviors. Home-literacy activities profoundly influence children's academic success: Children score higher on standardized achievement tests, have better school attendance, and exhibit stronger thinking skills when parents are involved their education (Bus, van Ijzendoorn, & Pellegrini, 1995).

Most teachers recognize the importance of home-literacy activities and want to become partners with their students' parents. In some communities, parents respond enthusiastically when teachers ask them to listen to their children read aloud or invite them to participate in a home–school writing event, for example, but in other communities, there's little or no response. When partnership attempts don't work, teachers conclude that they may not get the parent support they hoped for.

Teachers' expectations have been based on middle-class parents who typically see themselves as partners with teachers, reading to their children, playing educational games, going to the public library together, and helping with homework. Other parents view their role differently (Edwards, 2004). Some are willing to attend teacher–parent conferences and support school projects such as bake sales and carnivals, but they expect teachers to do the teaching. Others feel inadequate when it comes to helping their children because of their own unsuccessful school experiences or limited ability to read and write in English.

Parents' viewpoints reflect their culture and socioeconomic status (Lareau, 2000): Middle-class parents usually work with teachers to support their children's literacy development, working-class parents believe that teachers are better qualified to teach their children, and poor, minority, and immigrant parents often feel powerless to help their children. Parents' involvement is also related to educational level; parents who didn't graduate from high school are less likely to get involved (Paratore, 2001).

Ways to Work With Parents. Not all parents understand the crucial role they play in their child's academic success, so it's up to teachers to establish collaborative relationships with parents. Edwards (2004) explains that parent–teacher collaborations "involve rethinking the relationship between home and school such that students' opportunities to learn are expanded" (p. xvii). Here are three ways that teachers create a more empowering classroom culture and improve communication with parents:

Respect the literacy activities of families. Nearly all families incorporate reading and writing activities into their daily routines, but these activities may differ from school-based literacy activities. Teachers often overlook the importance of literacy activities that differ from those they value. Because culture and learning are closely linked, some children are at risk of failing because they aren't familiar with the literacy activities and language patterns that teachers use. Nieto (2002) urges teachers to recognize the value of parents' literacy activities, even if they don't match teachers' expectations, and use them in developing a literacy program that's culturally responsive.

Reach out to families in new ways. Edwards (2004) recommends that beginning in September, teachers work together to create schoolwide programs with a year-long schedule of activities that address particular literacy goals at each grade level. Effective communication is essential: When teachers demonstrate that they want to listen to parents, giving them opportunities to share insights about their children and ask questions about how children learn to read and write, parents become more willing to work with teachers and support their children's learning.

Build parents' knowledge of literacy procedures. Too often teachers assume that parents know how support their children's literacy learning, but many parents don't know how to read aloud, respond to their children's writing, or use other literacy procedures. They tend to have more success when teachers offer specific suggestions and provide clear directions (Edwards, 2004).

When teachers accept that parents view their role in different ways and become more knowledgeable about cultural diversity and how it affects parent–teacher relationships, they're more likely to be successful.

Home-Literacy Activities. Many parent-involvement programs focus on preschoolers, but parents continue to play an important role in supporting their children's reading and writing development through elementary and high school. Parents implement home-literacy activities as well as support children's in-school literacy development through these activities:

- Reading aloud to children
- Listening to children read aloud and reading along with them
- Making time for children to read books independently a priority
- Providing books and other reading materials in the home
- Talking with children about books they're reading
- Providing materials and opportunities for children to write at home
- Taking children to the library to check out books and multimedia materials
- Giving books and magazine subscriptions as gifts

- Monitoring children as they complete homework assignments
- Emphasizing the value of literacy and the importance of school success

Creating a partnership means more than turning parents into homework monitors; instead, teachers help parents develop the tools to support their children's literacy learning, and teachers build on the knowledge and experiences families bring to their children's education.

Interventions

Schools use the results of assessments to identify low-achieving students, and they plan intervention programs to remedy children's reading and writing difficulties and accelerate their learning (Cooper, Chard, & Kiger, 2006). These programs are used in addition to regular classroom instruction, not as a replacement for it. The classroom teacher or a specially trained reading teacher meets with struggling students every day; using paraprofessionals is a widespread practice but not recommended because they aren't as effective as certified teachers (Allington, 2006). Teachers provide intensive, expert instruction to individuals or very small groups of no more than three students. Interventions take various forms: They can be provided by adding a second lesson during the regular school day, offering extra instruction in an after-school program, or holding extended-school-year programs during the summer. Figure 1–9 summarizes the recommendations for effective intervention programs.

Figure 1–9 ◆ High-Quality Interventions

Scheduling
Interventions take place daily for 30–45 minutes, depending on children's age and instructional needs. Classroom teachers often provide the interventions, but sometimes specially trained reading teachers provide them.

Grouping
Teachers work with children individually or in very small groups; larger groups, even when children exhibit the same reading or writing problems, aren't as effective.

Reading Materials
Teachers match children to books at their instructional level for lessons and to books at their independent level for voluntary reading.

Instruction
Teachers' lessons generally include rereading familiar books, reading new books, teaching phonics and reading strategies, and writing, but the content varies according to children's areas of difficulty.

Reading and Writing Practice
Teachers provide opportunities for children to practice reading and writing.

Assessment
Teachers monitor progress on an ongoing basis by observing children and collecting work samples. They also use diagnostic tests to document children's learning according to grade-level standards.

Professional Development
Teachers engage in professional development to improve teaching expertise and ensure that aides who work in their classroom are well trained.

Home–School Partnerships
Teachers keep parents informed about children's progress and encourage them to support independent reading and writing at home.

Until recently, most school-based interventions were designed for middle-grade students who were already failing; now the focus has changed to early intervention to eliminate the pattern of school failure that begins early and persists throughout some children's lives (Strickland, 2002). Three types of interventions for young children have been developed:

- Preventive programs to create more effective early-childhood programs
- Family-focused programs to develop young children's awareness of literacy, parents' literacy, and parenting skills
- Early interventions to resolve reading and writing problems and accelerate literacy development for low-achieving K–3 students

Teachers are optimistic that earlier and more intensive intervention will solve many of the difficulties that older students exhibit today.

Federal Early Interventions. To prevent literacy problems and break the cycle of poverty in the United States, the federal government directs two early-intervention programs for economically disadvantaged children and their parents. Head Start promotes the healthy development and school preparedness of young low-income children through a variety of services; it provides education, health, nutrition, and social support to children and their families. This long-running program, administered by the U.S. Department of Health and Human Services, reaches one million children and their families each year through prenatal and infant programs, preschool programs, and other services for children of migrant farm workers, Native Americans, and homeless families. Head Start began in 1965 as part of President Lyndon Johnson's War on Poverty, and as it approaches its 50th anniversary, the program remains controversial because studies evaluating its long-term effectiveness have been inconclusive.

The Even Start Family Literacy Program is a newer program for low-income children from birth to age 7 that began as part of the No Child Left Behind Act. It's designed to improve educational opportunities for low-income families through these related activities:

- An early childhood education program to prepare children for school success
- An adult literacy program to improve parents' reading and writing competencies
- A parent education program to train parents to participate more fully in children's education
- Opportunities for children and their parents to participate in literacy activities together

All four components are required in this unified family literacy program.

Reading Recovery. Reading Recovery is a first-grade intervention program for the lowest achievers (Clay, 2005a, 2005b). The intervention is a 30-minute daily one-on-one tutoring session taught by specifically trained and supervised teachers. Reading Recovery lessons involve these components:

Rereading familiar books

Independently reading the book introduced in the previous lesson

Teaching decoding and comprehension strategies

Writing sentences

Reading a new book with teacher support

The intervention continues for 12 to 30 weeks, depending on children's progress. Once children reach grade-level standards and demonstrate that they can work independently in their classroom, they leave the program. The results of this intervention program are impressive: 75% of children who complete the Reading Recovery program meet grade-level literacy standards and continue to be successful.

Response to Intervention. Response to Intervention (RTI) is a promising schoolwide initiative to identify struggling students quickly, promote effective classroom instruction, provide interventions, and increase the likelihood that children will be successful (Mellard & Johnson, 2008). It involves three tiers:

Tier 1: Screening and Prevention. Teachers provide high-quality instruction that's supported by scientifically based research, screen children to identify those at risk for academic failure, and monitor their progress. If children don't make adequate progress toward meeting grade-level standards, they move to Tier 2.

Tier 2: Early Intervention. Trained reading teachers provide enhanced, individualized instruction targeting children's specific areas of difficulty. If children's literacy problems are resolved, they return to Tier 1; if they make some progress but need additional instruction, they remain in Tier 2; and if they don't show improvement, they move to Tier 3, where the intensity of intervention increases.

Tier 3: Intensive Intervention. Special education teachers provide more intensive intervention to individual children and small groups. They focus on remedying children's problems and teaching compensatory strategies, and they monitor children's progress more frequently.

This schoolwide instruction and assessment program incorporates data-driven decision making, and special education teachers are optimistic that it will be a better way to diagnose learning-disabled students.

Improving classroom instruction, diagnosing children's specific reading and writing difficulties, and implementing intensive intervention programs to remedy children's literacy problems are three important ways that teachers work more effectively with struggling readers and writers.

PRINCIPLE 8: EFFECTIVE TEACHERS LINK INSTRUCTION AND ASSESSMENT

Assessment is an integral and ongoing part of both learning and teaching (Mariotti & Homan, 2005). Sometimes teachers equate standardized high-stakes achievement tests with assessment, but classroom assessment is much more than a once-a-year test. It's a daily part of classroom life: Teachers collect and analyze data from observations, conferences, and classroom tests, and then use the results to make decisions about children's academic achievement (Cunningham & Allington, 2007).

Purposes of Classroom Assessment

Teachers assess children's learning for these purposes:

Determining Reading Levels. Because children read at a wide range of levels, teachers determine children's reading levels so that they can plan appropriate instruction.

Monitoring Progress. Teachers regularly assess children to ensure that they're making expected progress in reading and writing, and when they're not progressing, teachers take action to get them back on track.

Diagnosing Strengths and Weaknesses. Teachers examine children's progress in specific literacy components, including phonics, fluency, comprehension, writing, and spelling, to identify their strengths and weaknesses. Diagnosis is especially important when children are struggling or aren't making expected progress.

Documenting Learning. Teachers use a combination of test results and collections of children's work to provide evidence of their academic achievement and document that they've met grade-level standards.

Go to the Assignments and Activities section of the Topic *Emergent Literacy* in the MyEducationLab for the literacy course and complete the activity entitled *Assessing Emergent Readers and Writers*.

Assessment is linked to instruction; teachers use assessment results to inform their teaching (Snow, Griffin, & Burns, 2005). As they plan, teachers use their knowledge about children's reading levels, their background knowledge, and their strategy and skill competencies to plan appropriate instruction that's neither too easy nor too difficult. Teachers monitor instruction that's in progress as they observe children, conference with them, and check their work to ensure that their instruction is effective, and they make modifications, including reteaching when necessary, to meet children's needs. Teachers also judge the effectiveness of their instruction after it's completed. It's easy to blame children when learning isn't occurring, but teachers must consider how they can make their teaching more effective so that their students will be successful.

Classroom Assessment Tools

Teachers use both a variety of informal assessment tools that they create themselves and commercially available tests. Informal assessment tools include the following:

- Observation of children participating in instructional activities
- Running records of children's oral reading to analyze their ability to solve reading problems
- Examination of children's work
- Conferences with individual children
- Checklists to monitor children's progress
- Rubrics to assess children's writing and other activities

These assessment tools support instruction, and teachers choose which one to use according to the kind of information they need. They administer commercial tests to individuals or the entire class to determine children's overall reading achievement or their proficiency in a particular component—phonemic awareness or comprehension, for example.

High-Stakes Tests

Beginning in second grade, the results of yearly, high-stakes standardized tests also provide evidence of children's literacy achievement. The usefulness of these data is limited, however, because the tests are usually administered in the spring and the results aren't released until after the school year ends. At the beginning of the next school year, teachers do examine the data and use what they learn in planning for their new class, but the impact isn't as great as it would be for the teachers who worked with those children during the previous year. Another way the results are used is in measuring the effectiveness of teachers' instruction by examining how much children grew since the previous year's test and whether they met grade-level standards.

CHAPTER Review

How Effective Teachers Teach Reading and Writing

▶ Teachers apply learning theories as they teach reading and writing.

▶ Teachers create a community of learners in their classrooms.

▶ Teachers adopt a balanced approach to literacy instruction that reflects teacher-centered and child-centered learning theories.

▶ Teachers differentiate instruction so all children will be successful.

▶ Teachers link instruction and assessment.

Chapter 2

Examining Children's Literacy Development

Ms. McCloskey's Students Become Readers and Writers

Kindergarten through third-grade students sit on the carpet for a shared reading lesson. They listen intently as Ms. McCloskey prepares to read *Make Way for Ducklings* (McCloskey, 2001), the big-book version of an award-winning story about a family of ducks living in downtown Boston. She reads the title and the author's name, and some children recognize that the author's last name is the same as hers, but she explains that they aren't related. She reads the first page and asks for predictions. During this first reading, Ms. McCloskey reads each page expressively and tracks the text, word by word, with a pointer as she reads. After she finishes, they talk about the story. Some of the English learners are initially hesitant, but others eagerly relate their own experiences to the story.

The following day, Ms. McCloskey rereads *Make Way for Ducklings*. She begins by asking for volunteers to retell the story. Children take turns retelling each page, using the illustrations as clues. Ms. McCloskey includes this oral language activity because many of her students are English learners. The class is multilingual: Approximately 45%

of the children are Asian Americans who speak Hmong, Khmer, or Lao; 45% are Hispanics who speak Spanish or English at home; and the remaining 10% are African Americans and whites who speak English.

Next, Ms. McCloskey rereads the story, stopping several times to ask the class to think about the characters, draw inferences, and reflect on the theme. Her questions include: Why did the police officer help the ducks? What would have happened to the ducks if the police officer didn't help? What was Robert McCloskey saying to us? On the third day, the teacher reads the story again, and the children take turns using the pointer to track the text and join in reading familiar words. Afterward, the children clap because rereading the now familiar story provides a sense of accomplishment.

Ms. McCloskey understands that her students are moving through three developmental stages—emergent, beginning, and fluent—as they learn to read and write. She monitors each child's development to tailor instruction to meet his or her needs. As she reads the big book aloud, she uses a pointer to show the direction of print, from left to right and top to bottom on the page. She also moves the pointer across the lines of text to demonstrate the relationship between the words on the page and the words she's reading. Emergent-stage readers are learning these concepts.

Others are beginning readers who are learning high-frequency words and to decode phonetically regular words. One day after rereading the story, Ms. McCloskey turns to one of the pages and asks these children to identify familiar high-frequency words (e.g., *don't*, *make*) and decode CVC words (e.g., *run*, *big*). She also asks children to isolate individual sentences on the page and note the capital letter at the beginning and the punctuation that marks the end of each sentence.

Ms. McCloskey addresses the needs of fluent readers, too, as she rereads a page from the story: She asks these children to identify adjectives and notice inflectional endings on verbs. She also rereads the last sentence on the page and asks a child to explain why commas are used in it.

Ms. McCloskey and her teaching partner, Mrs. Papaleo, share a large classroom and 38 students; despite the number of children, the room feels spacious. Children's desks are arranged in clusters around the large, open area in the middle where children meet for whole-class activities. An easel to display big books is placed next to the teacher's chair. Several chart racks stand nearby; one rack holds Ms. McCloskey's morning messages, a second one holds charts with poems that the children use for choral reading, and a third rack holds a pocket chart with word cards and sentence strips.

On one side of the classroom is the library with books arranged in crates by topic. One crate has frog books, and others have books about the ocean, plants, and the five senses. Other crates contain books by authors who have been featured in author studies, including Eric Carle, Kevin Henkes, and Paula Danziger. Picture books and chapter books are arranged in the crates; children take turns keeping the area neat. Sets of leveled books are arranged on a shelf above the children's reach for the teachers to use in guided reading lessons. A child-size sofa, a table and chairs, pillows, and rugs make the library area cozy. A listening center is set up at a nearby table with a tape player and headphones that accommodates six children at a time.

A word wall with high-frequency words fills a partition separating instructional areas. It's divided into sections for each letter of the alphabet. Arranged on it are nearly 100 words written on small cards cut into the shape of the words. The teachers introduce new words each week and post them on the word wall. The children often practice reading and writing the words as a center activity, and they refer to the word wall to spell words when they're writing.

A bank of computers with a printer are located on another side of the classroom. Everyone uses them, even the youngest children; those who have stronger computer skills assist their classmates. They use word processing to publish their writing during writing workshop and monitor their independent reading practice on the computer using the Accelerated Reader® program. At other times, they search the Internet to find information related to topics they're studying in science and social studies, and use software programs to learn typing skills.

Ms. McCloskey spends the morning teaching reading and writing using a variety of teacher-directed and student-choice activities. Her daily schedule is shown below. After shared reading and a minilesson, the children participate in reading and writing workshop.

Ms. McCloskey's Schedule

Time	Activity	Description
8:10–8:20	Class Meeting	Children participate in opening activities, read the morning message from their teachers, and talk about plans for the day.
8:20–8:45	Shared Reading	The teachers read big books and poems written on charts; this activity often serves as a lead-in to the minilesson.
8:45–9:00	Minilesson	The teachers teach minilessons on literacy procedures, concepts, strategies, and skills.
9:00–9:45	Writing Workshop	Children write books while the teachers confer with individual children and small groups. They also do interactive writing activities.
9:45–10:00	Recess	
10:00–11:15	Reading Workshop	Children read self-selected books independently while the teachers do guided reading lessons with small groups.
11:15–11:30	Class Meeting	Children share their writing from the author's chair, and they review the morning's activities.
11:30–12:10	Lunch	
12:10–12:30	Read-Aloud	Teachers read aloud picture books and chapter books, and children discuss them in grand conversations.

The children write books during writing workshop. While most of them are working independently, Ms. McCloskey brings together a small group for a special activity: She conducts interactive writing lessons with emergent writers and teaches the writing process and revision strategies to more fluent writers. Today she's conferencing with six children who are beginning writers. Because they're writing longer compositions, Ms. McCloskey has decided to introduce revising. After each child reads his or her rough draft aloud to the group, classmates ask questions and offer compliments, and Ms. McCloskey encourages them to make a change in their writing so that their readers will understand it better. Anthony reads aloud a story about his soccer game, and after a classmate asks a question, he realizes that he needs to add more about how he scored a goal. He moves back to his desk to revise. The group continues with children sharing their writing and beginning to make revisions. At the end of writing workshop, the children come together for author's chair. Each day, three children sit in the author's chair to share their writing.

During reading workshop, children read independently or with a partner while Ms. McCloskey and her teaching partner conduct guided reading lessons. The children have access to books in the classroom library, including predictable books for emergent readers, decodable books for beginning readers, and easy-to-read chapter books for fluent readers. The children know how to choose books that they can read successfully so they're able to spend their time really reading.

Ms. McCloskey is working with a group of four emergent readers, and today they'll read *Playing* (Prince, 1999), a seven-page predictable book with one line of text on each page that uses the pattern "I like to _____." She begins by asking children what they like to do when they're playing. Der says, "I like to play with my brother," and Ms. McCloskey writes that on a strip of paper. Some children say only a word or two, and she expands the words into a sentence for the child to repeat; then she writes the expanded sentence and reads it with the child. Next, she introduces the book and reads the title and the author's name. The teacher does a picture walk, talking about the picture on each page and naming the activity the child is doing—running, jumping, sliding, and so on. She reviews the "I like to _____" pattern, and then the children read the book independently while Ms. McCloskey supervises and provides assistance as needed. The children eagerly reread the book several times, becoming more confident with each reading.

Ms. McCloskey reviews the high-frequency words *I*, *like*, and *to*, and the children point them out on the classroom word wall. They use magnetic letters to spell the words and then write sentences that begin with *I like to* . . . on whiteboards. Then Ms. McCloskey cuts apart their sentence strips for them to sequence; afterward the children put their sentences into envelopes to practice another day. At the end of the lesson, the teacher suggests that the children might want to write "I like to _____" books during writing workshop the next day.

During the last 30 minutes before lunch, the children work at literacy centers. Ms. McCloskey and Mrs. Papaleo have set out 12 centers, and the children are free to work at any one they choose. They're familiar with the routine and know what's expected of them at each center. The two teachers circulate around the classroom, monitoring children's work and taking advantage of teachable moments to clarify misunderstandings, reinforce previous lessons, and extend children's learning. A list of the literacy centers is presented in the box on page 36.

After lunch, Ms. McCloskey reads aloud picture books and easy-to-read chapter books. Sometimes she reads books by a particular author, but at other times, she reads books related to a thematic unit. She uses these read-alouds to teach predicting, visualizing, and other comprehension strategies. This week, she's reading award-winning books, and today she reads aloud *The Stray Dog* (Simont, 2001), the story of a homeless dog that's taken in by a loving family. She uses the interactive read-aloud procedure to involve children in the book as she reads, and afterward they talk about it in a grand conversation. Ms. McCloskey asks them to share their connections to the story, which she records on a chart divided into three sections. Most comments are text-to-self connections, but several children make other types of connections.

Literacy Centers

Center	Description
Bag a Story	Children use objects in a paper bag to create a story. They draw pictures or write sentences to tell the story they've created.
Clip Boards	Children search the classroom for words beginning with a particular letter or featuring a spelling pattern and write them on paper attached to clip boards.
Games	Children play alphabet, phonics, and other literacy card and board games with classmates.
Library	Children read books related to a thematic unit and write or draw about the books in reading logs.
Listening	Children listen to a recording of a story or informational book while they follow along in a copy of the book.
Making Words	Children practice a making words activity that they've previously done together as a class with teacher guidance.
Messages	Children write notes to classmates and the teachers and post them on a special "Message Center" bulletin board.
Poetry Frames	Children arrange word cards on a chart-sized poetry frame to create a poem and then practice reading it.
Reading the Room	Children use pointers to point to and reread big books, charts, signs, and other texts posted in the classroom.
Research	Children use the Internet, informational books, photos, and realia to learn more about topics in literature focus units and thematic units.
Story Reenactment	Children use small props, finger puppets, or flannel board figures to reenact familiar stories with classmates.
Word Sort	Children categorize high-frequency or thematic word cards displayed in a pocket chart.

Rosario says, "I am thinking of a movie. It was *101 Dalmatians*. It was about dogs, too"; that's a text-to-text connection. Angelo offers a text-to-world connection: "You got to stay away from stray dogs. They can bite you, and they might have this bad disease called rabies—it can kill you."

Literacy is a process that begins in infancy and continues throughout life. It used to be that 5-year-olds came to kindergarten to be "readied" for reading and writing instruction, which formally began in first grade. The implication was that there's a point in children's development when it's time to teach them to read and write; for those not ready, a variety of "readiness" activities would prepare them. Since the 1970s, this view has been discredited because preschoolers have demonstrated that they could recognize signs and other environmental print, retell stories, scribble letters, invent printlike writing, and listen to stories read aloud (Morrow & Tracey, 2007). Some young children even teach themselves to read!

This perspective on how children learn to read and write is known as *emergent literacy,* a term that New Zealand educator Marie Clay coined. Studies from 1966 on have shaped the current outlook (McGee & Richgels, 2003). Now, researchers are looking at literacy learning from the child's point of view. Literacy development has been broadened to incorporate the cultural and social aspects of language learning, and children's experiences with and understandings about written language—both reading and writing—are included as part of emergent literacy.

URTURING CHILDREN'S ORAL LANGUAGE DEVELOPMENT

Young children develop oral language through everyday experiences and interaction with parents and others; they learn words at the grocery store, on the playground, during swimming lessons, and at the zoo, for example. Children who go fishing with their grandpas, plant gardens with their moms, or collect Thomas trains or Disney princesses learn new words along the way, too. They learn even more words listening to adults read aloud picture books and watching *Sesame Street*, *Blue's Clues*, and other television programs designed for young children.

Through these experiences, children develop expertise in all four language modes:

- **Phonology.** Preschoolers learn to produce the sounds of English and to manipulate language in playful ways.

- **Syntax.** Children learn to combine words into different types of sentences and to use irregular verb forms, pronouns, and plural markers and other inflectional endings.

- **Semantics.** Four- and five-year-olds acquire knowledge about the meanings of words and add approximately 2,000 words to their vocabularies each year.

- **Pragmatics.** Children learn to use language socially—to carry on a conversation, tell stories, and use social conventions, including "hello" and "goodbye" and "please" and "thank you."

By age 4 or 5, children have acquired the oral language of their home culture. They learn to converse with individuals and in groups, to tell stories, and to listen to and follow directions, and they acquire vocabulary related to concepts they're learning.

Oral Language Activities

Children continue to develop oral language competence at school, especially as they participate in literacy activities. Probably the most valuable activity is the instructional procedure teachers use to read stories and other books aloud that's known as interactive read-alouds. As they listen, children learn new vocabulary and acquire more sophisticated sentence structures. Figure 2–1 presents popular picture books that introduce new vocabulary and develop young children's talking and listening abilities. Afterward, they talk about the story in grand conversations and participate in story retelling and activities using story boards.

Figure 2–2 lists of literacy activities that develop children's oral language. These activities are described in the Compendium of Instructional Procedures, which follows Chapter 12. In addition, whenever children work together in small groups, they have opportunities to use new vocabulary to talk about things they're learning.

> Check the Compendium of Instructional Procedures, which follows Chapter 12, for more information on highlighted terms.

Figure 2-1 ◆ Picture Books to Develop Oral Language

Bang, M. (2004). *When Sophie gets angry—really, really angry*. New York: Scholastic.

Barton, B. (1992). *I want to be an astronaut*. New York: HarperCollins.

Carle, E. (1994). *The very hungry caterpillar*. New York: Scholastic.

Crews, D. (1998). *Night at the fair*. New York: HarperCollins.

Ehlert, L. (1990). *Growing vegetable soup*. Orlando: Voyager.

Fleming, D. (2007). *In the small, small pond*. New York: Henry Holt.

Fox, M. (1998). *Tough Boris*. Orlando: Voyager.

Henkes, K. (2000). *Wemberly worried*. New York: Greenwillow.

Hoban, T. (2008). *Over, under, and through*. New York: Aladdin Books.

Hurd, T. (2003). *Moo cow kaboom*. New York: HarperCollins.

Keats, E. J. (1998). *Peter's chair*. New York: Viking.

Martin, B., Jr., (2007). *Brown bear, brown bear, what do you see?* New York: Henry Holt.

Martin, B., Jr., & Archambault, J. (2000). *Chicka chicka boom boom*. New York: Beach Lane Books.

McCloskey, R. (2001). *Make way for ducklings*. New York: Viking.

Most, B. (1996). *Cock-a-doodle-moo!* Orlando: Harcourt.

Rathmann, P. (2000). *Good night, gorilla*. New York: Putnam.

Root, P. (2004). *Rattletrap car*. Cambridge, MA: Candlewick Press.

Taback, S. (1997). *There was an old lady who swallowed a fly*. New York: Viking.

Walsh, E. S. (1995). *Mouse count*. Orlando: Voyager.

Wells, R. (2000). *Bunny cakes*. New York: Puffin Books.

Willems, M. (2003). *Don't let the pigeon drive the bus!* New York: Hyperion Book.

Wood, A., & Wood, D. (2000). *The napping house*. Orlando: Harcourt.

Learning a Second Language

Children learn a second language much the same way they learn their first language: Both are developmental processes that require time and opportunity. Young children learn a second language best in a classroom where talk is encouraged and where the teacher and classmates serve as English language models. They hear English spoken in meaningful contexts and associated with physical actions, artifacts, and pictures. Children acquire conversational English, known as *Basic Interpersonal Communication Skills* (BICS) quickly, in 2 years or less, but academic English, known as *Cognitive Academic Language Proficiency* (CALP), can take 7 or 8 years to acquire (Cummins, 1979). Even though English learners in third or fourth grade may appear fluent in conversational settings, they may still struggle academically because they haven't learned more formal, academic English.

Language acquisition is influenced by societal and cultural factors; children's personalities, the attitudes of their cultural group, and teacher expectations all play a role (Samway & McKeon, 2007). Children's level of proficiency in their first language also affects their second language development: Those who continue to develop their first-language proficiency become better English speakers than those who stop learning their native language (Tabors, 2008).

✳ The Link Between Oral Language and Literacy

Developing children's <u>oral language</u> is essential because it provides the foundation for <u>literacy learning</u> (Roskos, Tabors, & Lenhart, 2009). Children who don't develop strong oral language before first grade have difficulty keeping pace with classmates (Hart & Risley, 2003; Snow, Burns, & Griffin, 1998). Researchers have found that <u>vocabulary</u> knowledge is an important predictor of beginning reading success (Roth, Speece, &

Cooper, 2002). Interestingly, children's ability to orally define words was found to be an important predictor of how well they'd be able to decode words and comprehend text in the primary grades. Other significant factors, such as phonemic awareness and letter knowledge, are related to children's ability to decode words, but not to their comprehension.

Assessing Children's Oral Language

Prekindergarten and kindergarten teachers monitor children's oral language development because they understand its importance for academic achievement. They check that children demonstrate these talk skills:

- Speak clearly in complete sentences
- Respond to questions
- Initiate conversations
- Take turns
- Ask questions
- Participate in discussions
- Sing songs and recite fingerplays
- Tell about experiences

Teachers also monitor that young children listen during conversations and discussions, to stories teachers are reading, and to follow directions. They notice whether children play with words (e.g., rhyming words and alliterations), connect new words to concepts they're learning, and use new words appropriately as they talk.

Teachers also use classroom tests to evaluate 4- and 5-year-olds' oral language development, especially when they suspect that a child may have receptive or expressive language difficulties. The Assessment Tools feature on page 40 describes two tests that provide normative data so teachers can compare their student's score against national benchmarks.

Figure 2-2 ◆ Literacy Activities to Develop Oral Language

Components	PreK–Kindergarten	First–Second Grades	Third–Fourth Grades
Expanding Oral Language Expressiveness	Grand conversations Interactive read-alouds Interactive writing Language Experience Approach Story boards Story retelling	Book talks Grand conversations Interactive read-alouds Interactive writing Story boards Story retelling	Book talks Grand conversations Hot seat Interactive read-alouds
Playing With Words	Interactive read-alouds Shared reading	Choral reading Interactive read-alouds Shared reading	Choral reading Interactive read-alouds
Increasing Word Knowledge	Interactive read-alouds Interactive writing	Interactive read-alouds K-W-L charts Semantic feature analysis Word sorts Word walls	Interactive read-alouds K-W-L charts Semantic feature analysis Word sorts Word walls

Assessment Tools

Oral Language

Teachers use these classroom tests to screen prekindergartners' and kindergartners' oral language development and identify children with possible language problems:

◆ **Assessment of Literacy and Language™ (ALL)**

Preschool, kindergarten, and first-grade teachers use ALL to assess children who they believe are at risk for reading difficulties because of an <u>underlying language disorder.</u> It assesses listening comprehension, semantics and syntax, phonological awareness, understanding of the alphabetic principle, and concepts about print. This test is time-consuming so teachers use it selectively; it's administered individually in 60 minutes or less. ALL is available for purchase from Pearson.

◆ **Teacher Rating of Oral Language and Literacy (TROLL)**

Prekindergarten teachers use TROLL to assess 3-, 4-, and 5-year-olds' oral language, reading, and writing. This individual assessment is easy to use and can be completed in 5 to 10 minutes. Teachers judge children's language competence using a 25-item rating scale; eight of the items focus on oral language, including asking questions, sharing personal experiences, and identifying rhyming words. TROLL is available free of charge from the Center for the Improvement of Early Reading Achievement at the University of Michigan (www.ciera.org).

These tests provide normative data so teachers can compare children against national benchmarks as well as chart their growth over the school year.

FOSTERING AN INTEREST IN LITERACY

Young children's introduction to written language begins before they come to school. Parents and other caregivers read to them, and they learn to read signs and other environmental print in their community. They experiment with writing and have their parents write messages for them; they also observe adults writing. When young children come to school, their knowledge about written language expands quickly as they learn concepts about print and participate in meaningful experiences with reading and writing.

Concepts About Written Language

Through experiences in their homes and communities, young children learn that <u>print carries meaning</u> and that reading and writing are used for a variety of purposes (Clay, 2000a). They notice menus in restaurants, write and receive postcards and letters to communicate with friends and relatives, and listen to stories read aloud for enjoyment. Children also observe parents and teachers using <u>written language </u>for all these reasons.

Preschool and kindergarten teachers demonstrate the purposes of written language and provide opportunities for children to experiment with reading and writing in many ways, including the following:

Posting signs in the classroom

Integrating reading and writing materials into literacy play centers

Exchanging messages with classmates

> Reading and writing stories
> Labeling classroom items
> Drawing and writing in journals
> Writing notes to parents

Young children learn these concepts about written language:

- **Book-Orientation Concepts.** Children learn how to hold a book and turn pages, and where to start reading on a page. They also understand that the words, not the illustrations, carry the message.

- **Directionality Concepts.** Children learn that print is written and read from left to right and from top to bottom on a page. They also match the reader's voice to print, pointing word by word to the text as it's read aloud.

- **Letter and Word Concepts.** Children acquire concepts of what a letter is, what a word is, and what a sentence is; with this understanding, they can identify letters, words, and sentences on a page of text. They also develop awareness of capital letters and punctuation marks and why they're used.

As young children develop these concepts, they apply their knowledge in both reading and writing. For instance, they open books and point to where their teachers or parents should begin reading and pick out familiar letters and words that they notice in the text. Preschoolers also begin to make letterlike forms and add a field of periods to their scribbles.

Concepts About Words

At first, young children have only vague notions of literacy terms, such as *word, letter, sound,* and *sentence,* that teachers use in talking about reading and writing, but children develop an increasingly sophisticated understanding of these terms. Papandropoulou and Sinclair (1974) identified four levels of word consciousness. At first, children don't differentiate between words and things. Next, children describe words as labels for things; they consider nouns that stand for objects as words, but they don't classify verbs and prepositions as words because words such as *go* and *with* can't be represented with objects. At the third level, children understand that words carry meaning and that stories are built with words. Finally, more fluent readers and writers describe words as autonomous elements having meanings of their own with definite semantic and syntactic relationships. Children also understand that words have different appearances: They can be spoken, listened to, read, and written. Invernizzi (2003) explains the importance of reaching the fourth level: "A concept of word allows children to hold onto the printed word in their mind's eye and scan it from left to right, noting every sound in the beginning, middle, and end" (p. 152).

Children develop concepts about words through active participation in literacy activities. They watch as teachers point to words in big books during shared reading, and they mimic the teacher and point to words as they reread familiar texts. After many shared reading experiences, children notice that word boundaries are marked with spaces, and they pick out familiar words. Their pointing becomes increasingly exact, and they become more proficient at picking out specific words in the text, noticing that words at the beginning of sentences are marked with capital letters and words at the end of sentences are followed with punctuation marks.

Environmental Print. Young children begin reading by recognizing logos on fast-food restaurants, department stores, grocery stores, and commonly used household items within familiar contexts (Harste, Woodward, & Burke, 1984). They recognize the golden arches of McDonald's and say "McDonald's," but when they're shown the word

Go to the Assignments and Activities section of the Topic *Organization and Management* in the MyEducationLab for the literacy course and complete the activity entitled *Planning and Managing Learning Centers*.

McDonald's written on a sheet of paper without the familiar sign and restaurant setting, they can't read the word. At first, they depend on context to read familiar words and memorized texts, but slowly, children develop relationships linking form and meaning as they gain more reading and writing experience.

Literacy Play Centers.   Young children learn about the purposes of reading and writing as they use written language in their play: As they construct block buildings, children write signs and tape them on the buildings; as they play doctor, children write prescriptions on slips of paper; and as they play teacher, children read stories aloud to stuffed animal "students" (McGee, 2007). Young children use these activities to reenact familiar, everyday activities and to pretend to be someone else. Through these literacy play activities, children use reading and writing for a variety of purposes.

Preschool and kindergarten teachers add literacy materials to play centers to enhance their value for literacy learning (Sluss, 2005). Housekeeping centers are probably the most common play centers; they can easily be transformed into grocery stores, post offices, or medical centers by changing the props. They become literacy play centers when materials for reading and writing are included: Food packages, price stickers, and play money are props in grocery store centers; letters, stamps, and mailboxes are props in post office centers; and appointment books, prescription pads, and folders for patient records are props in medical centers. Literacy play centers can be set up in classrooms and coordinated with literature focus units and thematic units. Ideas for eight literacy play centers are presented in Figure 2–3; each center includes authentic literacy materials that young children can experiment with to learn more about the purposes of written language.

Concepts About the Alphabet

Young children also develop concepts about the alphabet and how <u>letters are used to represent phonemes.</u> Pinnell and Fountas (1998) identified these components of letter knowledge:

- The letter's name
- The formation of the upper- and lowercase letter in <u>manuscript handwriting</u>
- The features of the letter that distinguish it from other letters
- The direction the letter must be turned to distinguish it from other letters (e.g., *b* and *d*)
- The use of the letter in known words (e.g., names and common words)
- The sound the letter represents in isolation
- The sound the letter represents in combination with others (e.g., *ch, th*)
- The sound the letter represents in the context of a word (e.g., the *c* sounds in *cat, city*, and *chair*)

Children use this knowledge to decode unfamiliar words as they read and to create spellings for words as they write.

The most basic information children learn about the alphabet is how to identify and form the letters in handwriting. They notice letters in environmental print and learn to sing the ABC song. By the time children enter kindergarten, they usually recognize some letters, especially those in their own names, in names of family members and pets, and in common words. Children also write some of these familiar letters.

Figure 2-3 ◆ Literacy Play Centers

Centers	Materials			
Bank	teller window checks	play money roll papers for coins	deposit slips money bags	signs receipts
Grocery Store	food packages artificial foods	grocery cart cash register	money grocery bags	cents-off coupons advertisements
Hairdresser	hair rollers brush and comb mirror	empty shampoo bottle towel posters of hair styles	wig and wig stand hairdryer (remove cord) curling iron (remove cord)	ribbons, barrettes, clips appointment book open/closed sign

Medical	appointment book
	white shirt/jacket
	medical bag
		hypodermic syringe (play)
		thermometer
		stethoscope
			prescription pad
			folders (for patient
			    records)
				bandages
				prescription bottles
				    and labels

Office	computer calculator paper	stapler file folders in/out boxes	pens and pencils envelopes and stamps telephone	message pad rubber stamps stamp pad
Post Office	mailboxes envelopes stamps (stickers)	pens wrapping paper tape	packages scale package seals	address labels cash register money
Restaurant	tablecloth dishes glasses	silverware napkins menus	tray order pad and pencil apron for waitress	vest for waiter hat and apron for chef
Veterinarian	stuffed animals cages (cardboard boxes) pet information cards	white shirt/jacket medical bag stethoscope	medicine bottles prescription labels bandages	popsicle stick splints hypodermic syringe (play) open/closed sign

Research suggests that children don't learn alphabet letter names in any particular order or by isolating letters from meaningful written language in skill-and-drill activities. McGee and Richgels (2008) conclude that learning letters of the alphabet requires many, many experiences with meaningful written language and recommend that teachers take these steps to encourage alphabet learning:

Capitalize on children's interests. Teachers provide letter activities that children enjoy, and they talk about letters when children are interested in talking about them. Teachers know what features to comment on because they observe children during reading and writing activities to find out which letters or features of letters they are exploring.

Talk about the role of letters in reading and writing. Teachers talk about how letters represent sounds and how letters combine to spell words and point out capital letters and lowercase letters. Teachers often talk about the role of letters as they write with children.

Provide a variety of opportunities for alphabet learning. Teachers use children's names and environmental print in literacy activities, do interactive writing, encourage children to use invented spelling, share alphabet books, and play letter games.

Teachers begin teaching letters of the alphabet using two sources of words—children's own names and environmental print. They teach the ABC song to provide children with a strategy for identifying the name of an unknown letter. Children learn to sing this song and point to each letter on an alphabet chart until they reach the unfamiliar one; this is a very useful strategy because it gives them a real sense of independence in identifying letters. Teachers also provide routines, activities, and games for talking about and manipulating letters. During these familiar, predictable activities, teachers and children say letter names, manipulate magnetic letters, and write letters on whiteboards. At first, the teacher structures and guides the activities, but with experience, the children internalize the routine and do it independently, often at a literacy center. Figure 2–4 presents 10 routines to teach the letters of the alphabet. One of the routines involves using alphabet books; Figure 2–5 presents a list of these books.

Being able to name the letters of the alphabet is a good predictor of beginning reading achievement, even though knowing the names of the letters doesn't directly affect a child's ability to read (Adams, 1990; Snow, Burns, & Griffin, 1998). A more likely explanation for this relationship is that children who have been actively involved in literacy activities before first grade know the names of the letters, and they're more likely to begin reading quickly. Simply teaching children to name the letters without the accompanying reading and writing experiences doesn't have this effect.

Figure 2-4 ◆ Routines to Teach the Letters of the Alphabet

Routine	Description
Environmental Print	Children sort food labels, toy traffic signs, store names cut from advertisements, and other environmental print to find examples of a letter being studied.
Alphabet Books	Teachers read aloud alphabet books to build vocabulary, and later, children reread the books to find words when making books about a letter.
Magnetic Letters	Children pick all examples of one letter from a collection of magnetic letters or match upper- and lowercase letterforms using magnetic letters. They also arrange the letters in alphabetical order and use them to spell familiar words.
Letter Stamps	Children use letter stamps and ink pads to print letters on paper or in booklets. They also use letter-shaped sponges to paint letters and letter-shaped cookie cutters to cut out clay letters.
Alphabet Chart	Children point to letters and pictures on the alphabet chart as they recite the alphabet and say the names of the pictures, such as "A-airplane, B-baby, C-cat," and so on.
Letter Containers	Teachers collect coffee cans or shoe boxes, one for each letter, and place several familiar objects that represent the letter in each container. Teachers use these containers to introduce the letters, and children use them for sorting and matching activities.
Letter Frames	Teachers make circle-shaped letter frames from tagboard, collect large plastic bracelets, or shape pipe cleaners or Wikki-Stix (pipe cleaners covered in wax) into circles for students to use to highlight particular letters on charts or in big books.
Letter Books and Posters	Children make letter books with pictures of objects beginning with a particular letter on each page. They add letter stamps, stickers, or pictures cut from magazines. For posters, the teacher draws a large letterform on a chart and children add pictures, stickers, and letter stamps.
Letter Sorts	Children sort objects and pictures representing two or more letters and place them in containers marked with the specific letters.
Whiteboards	Children practice writing upper- and lowercase forms of a letter and familiar words on whiteboards.

Figure 2-5 ◆ Alphabet Books

Bayer, J. E. (1992). *A, my name is Alice*. New York: Puffin Books.

Dragonwagon, C. (1992). *Alligator arrived with apples: A potluck alphabet feast*. New York: Aladdin Books.

Ehlert, L. (1993). *Eating the alphabet: Fruits and vegetables from A to Z*. Orlando: Voyager.

Elting, M., & Folsom, M. (2005). *Q is for duck*. New York: Sandpiper.

Ernst, L. C. (2004). *The turn-around, upside-down alphabet book*. New York: Simon & Schuster.

Fleming, D. (2006). *Alphabet under construction*. New York: Henry Holt.

Grover, M. (1997). *The accidental zucchini: An unexpected alphabet*. New York: Sandpiper.

Hoban, T. (1995). *26 letters and 99 cents*. New York: HarperCollins.

Johnson, S. T. (1999). *Alphabet city*. New York: Puffin Books.

Johnson, S. T. (2008). *A is for art: An abstract alphabet*. New York: Simon & Schuster.

Kirk, D. (1998). *Miss Spider's ABC book*. New York: Scholastic.

McLeod, B. (2008). *SuperHero ABC*. New York: HarperCollins.

Palotta, J. (1993). *The icky bug alphabet book*. Watertown, MA: Charlesbridge.

Palotta, J. (2002). *The jet alphabet book*. Watertown, MA: Charlesbridge.

Rose, D. L. (2000). *Into the A, B, sea: An ocean alphabet book*. New York: Scholastic.

Shannon, G. (1999). *Tomorrow's alphabet*. New York: HarperCollins.

Sobel, J. (2006). *B is for bulldozer: A construction ABC*. New York: Sandpiper.

Wood, A. (2001). *Alphabet adventure*. New York: Blue Sky Press.

Wood, A. (2003). *Alphabet mystery*. New York: Blue Sky Press.

Wood, A. (2006). *Alphabet rescue*. New York: Blue Sky Press.

Manuscript Handwriting

Children enter kindergarten with different backgrounds of handwriting experience. Some 5-year-olds have never held a pencil, but many others have written cursivelike scribbles or manuscript letterlike lines and circles. Some have learned to print their names and even a few other letters. Handwriting instruction in kindergarten typically includes developing children's ability to hold pencils, refining their fine-motor control, and focusing on letter formation. Some people might argue that kindergartners are too young to learn handwriting skills, but young children should be encouraged to write from the first day of school. They write letters and words on labels, draw and write stories, keep journals, and write other types of messages. The more children write, the greater their need becomes for instruction in handwriting. Instruction is necessary so that children don't learn bad habits that later must be broken.

To teach children how to form letters, many kindergarten and first-grade teachers create brief directions for forming letters and sing the directions using a familiar tune. For example, to form a lowercase *a*, expand the direction "All around and make a tail" into a verse and sing it to the tune of "Mary Had a Little Lamb." As teachers sing the directions, they model the formation of the letter in the air or on the chalkboard using large arm motions. Then children sing along and practice forming the letter in the air. Later, they practice writing letters using sponge paintbrushes dipped in water at the chalkboard or dry-erase pens on whiteboards.

Handwriting research suggests that moving models are much more effective than still models in teaching children how to handwrite. Therefore, worksheets on the letters aren't very useful because children may not form the letters correctly. Researchers recommend that children watch teachers form letters and then practice forming them themselves. Also, teachers supervise children as they write so that they can correct those who form letters incorrectly. It is important to write circles counterclockwise, starting from 1:00, and to form most lines from top to bottom and left to right across the page. When children follow these guidelines, they're less likely to tear their paper, and they'll have an easier transition to cursive handwriting.

Teaching Children About Written Language

Teachers develop young children's concepts about written language as they demonstrate how reading and writing work and involve children in shared and interactive reading and writing activities. In addition, teachers often use the completed texts in minilessons about written language concepts because children are already familiar with them.

Morning Message. Teachers write a brief friendly letter, called a *morning message*, each day to share with children (Payne & Schulman, 1999). Before children arrive, they write the message on chart paper about what will happen that day; then they read the message aloud at the beginning of the school day, pointing at each word as they read. Afterward, children reread it and count the letters, words, and sentences in the message. They also pick out familiar letters and words, words illustrating a particular phonics concept, or capital letters and punctuation marks, depending on children's developmental level.

Teachers usually follow a predictable pattern in their messages each day to make it easier for children to read, as these two morning messages show:

Dear Kindergartners,
Today is Monday.
We will plant seeds.
We will make books
about plants.
    Love,
     Ms. Thao

Dear Kindergartners,
Today is Thursday.
We will measure the plants.
We will write about how
plants grow.
    Love,
     Ms. Thao

The morning messages that teachers write for first and second graders become gradually more complex, as this second-grade teacher's message demonstrates:

Good Morning!
    Today is Monday, February 1, 2010.
New literature circles begin on Wednesday.
I'll tell you about the new book choices this
morning, and then you can sign up for your
favorite book. Who remembers what a
synonym is? Can you give an example?
    Love,
    Mrs. Salazar

Teachers usually choose children to take the messages home to share with their families, either day by day or at the end of each week.

Language Experience Approach. Teachers demonstrate how written language works in the Language Experience Approach (LEA) (Ashton-Warner, [1963], 1986). Children dictate sentences about an experience, and the teacher records their dictation on chart paper. As they write, teachers demonstrate how to write from left to right on a page, how to form letters and to space between words, and how to use capital letters and punctuation marks. Then the completed text becomes the reading material. Children practice rereading the text and picking out letters and words. Because the language comes from the children and because the content is based on shared experiences, the text can usually be read easily.

Teachers often use LEA to create collaborative books, where each child creates one page to be added to a class book. For example, as part of a unit on bears, a kindergarten class made a collaborative book on bears. Children each chose a fact about bears for their pages; they drew an illustration and dictated the text for their teacher to record. One page from the class book is shown in Figure 2–6. The teacher took the children's dictation because she wanted the book to be written in conventional spelling so that children and their parents could read it.

Interactive Writing. Children and the teacher create a text together using interactive writing (McCarrier, Pinnell, & Fountas, 2000; Tompkins & Collom, 2004). The children compose the message together, and then the teacher guides them as they write it word by word on chart paper. Children take turns writing known letters and familiar words, adding punctuation marks, and leaving spaces between words. Everyone participates in creating and writing the text on chart paper, and they also write the text on small whiteboards or on paper as it's written on chart paper. Afterward, children read and reread the text together with classmates and on their own.

Figure 2–6 ◆ One Page From a Class Book About Bears

Polar bears live in
ice and snow.

Jesse

Assessment Tools

Concepts About Written Language

Teachers monitor children's growing awareness of written language as they observe them during shared reading and other literacy activities. The most widely used assessment is Marie Clay's Concepts About Print Test:

◆ **Concepts About Print Test (CAP)** (Clay, 2007a)

The CAP Test assesses young children's understanding of three concepts about written language: book-orientation concepts, directionality concepts, and letter and word concepts. The test has 24 items and is administered individually in about 10 minutes. The teacher reads a short book aloud while a child looks on. The child is asked to open the book, turn pages, and point out particular print features as the text is read. Four forms of the CAP Test booklet are available: *Sand* (Clay, 2007c), *Stones* (Clay, 2007d), *Follow Me, Moon* (Clay, 2000b), and *No Shoes* (Clay, 2007b), as well as a Spanish version. Teachers carefully observe children as they respond, and then mark their responses on a scoring sheet. Directions for administering the CAP Test are included in *Observation Survey of Early Literacy Achievement* (Clay, 2007a), which is available for purchase from Heinemann Books.

Instead of using the test booklets, teachers can also administer the test using books available in the classroom the scoring sheet below.

CAP Test Scoring Sheet

Name _____   Date _____

Title of Book _____

Check the items that the child demonstrates.

1. Book-Orientation Concepts
   ☐ Shows the front of a book.
   ☐ Turns to the first page of the story.
   ☐ Shows where to start reading on a page.

2. Directionality Concepts
   ☐ Shows the direction of print across a line of text.
   ☐ Shows the direction of print on a page with more than one line of print.
   ☐ Points to track words as the teacher reads.

3. Letter and Word Concepts
   ☐ Points to any letter on a page.
   ☐ Points to a particular letter on a page.
   ☐ Puts fingers around any word on a page.
   ☐ Puts fingers around a particular word on a page.
   ☐ Puts fingers around any sentence on a page.
   ☐ Points to the first and last letters of a word.
   ☐ Points to a period or other punctuation mark.
   ☐ Points to a capital letter.

Assessing Children's Knowledge About Written Language

Teachers observe children as they look at books and reread familiar ones. They also watch as children do pretend writing and write their names and other familiar words. They notice which concepts children understand and which ones they need to continue to talk about and demonstrate during shared reading.

Teachers use Marie Clay's Concepts About Print (CAP) Test (2007a), explained in the Assessment Tools feature on page 48, to measure young children's understanding of these written language concepts. Teachers also create their own versions of the test to use with any story they're reading with a child. As they read aloud, teachers ask the child to point out book-orientation concepts, directionality concepts, and letter and word concepts. They can use the CAP Test scoring sheet shown in the Assessment Tools feature or develop one of their own to monitor children's growing knowledge about these concepts.

HOW CHILDREN DEVELOP AS READERS AND WRITERS

Children move through three stages as they learn to read and write: emergent, beginning, and fluent (Juel, 1991). During the emergent stage, young children gain an understanding of the communicative purpose of print, and they move from pretend reading to reading predictable books and from using scribbles to simulate writing to writing patterned sentences, such as *I see a bird. I see a tree. I see a car.* The focus of the second stage, beginning reading and writing, is on children's growing ability to use phonics to "crack the alphabetic code" in order to decode and spell words. Children also learn to read and write many high-frequency words and write several sentences to develop a story or other composition. In the fluent stage, children are automatic, fluent readers, and in writing, they develop good handwriting skills, spell many high-frequency words correctly, and organize their writing into multiple-paragraph compositions. Figure 2–7 summarizes children's literacy accomplishments at each stage.

Stage 1: Emergent Reading and Writing

Children gain an understanding of the communicative purpose of print and develop an interest in reading and writing. They notice environmental print and develop concepts about print as teachers read and write with them. As children dictate stories for the teacher to record, for example, they learn that their speech can be written down, and they observe how teachers write from left to right and top to bottom.

Children grow in these ways during the first stage:

- Develop an interest in reading and writing
- Acquire concepts about print
- Develop book-handling skills
- Identify the letters of the alphabet

- Develop handwriting skills
- Learn to read and write some high-frequency words

Four- and five-year olds are usually emergent readers and writers, but some children whose parents have read to them every day and provided a variety of literacy experiences do learn how to read before they come to school. Caroline, a 5-year-old emergent reader and writer in Ms. McCloskey's classroom, is presented in the Spotlight feature on pages 52–53.

Reading. Emergent readers are interested in books and are developing concepts about written language. Children develop book-orientation skills as they listen to teachers read

Figure 2-7 ◆ Children's Literacy Development

Stage	Reading	Writing
Emergent	Children: • notice environmental print • show interest in books • pretend to read • use picture cues and predictable patterns in books to retell the story • reread familiar books with predictable patterns • identify some letter names • recognize 5–20 familiar or high-frequency words	Children: • distinguish between writing and drawing • write letters and letterlike forms or scribble randomly on the page • develop an understanding of directionality • show interest in writing • write their first and last names • write 5–20 familiar or high-frequency words • use sentence frames to write a sentence
Beginning	Children: • identify letter names and sounds • match spoken words to written words • recognize 20–100 high-frequency words • use beginning, middle, and ending sounds to decode words • apply knowledge of the cueing systems to monitor reading • self-correct while reading • read slowly, word by word • read orally • point to words when reading • make reasonable predictions	Children: • write from left to right • print the upper- and lowercase letters • write one or more sentences • add a title • spell many words phonetically • spell 20–50 high-frequency words correctly • write single-draft compositions • use capital letters to begin sentences • use periods, question marks, and exclamation points to mark the end of sentences • can reread their writing
Fluent	Children: • identify most words automatically • read with expression • read at a rate of 100 words per minute or more • prefer to read silently • identify unfamiliar words using the cueing systems • recognize 100–300 high-frequency words • use a variety of strategies effectively • often read independently • use knowledge of text structure and genre to support comprehension • make inferences	Children: • use the writing process to write drafts and final copies • write compositions with more than one paragraph • indent paragraphs • spell most of the 100 high-frequency words • use sophisticated and technical vocabulary • apply vowel patterns to spell words • add inflectional endings to words • apply capitalization rules • use commas, quotation marks, and other punctuation marks

Anthony reads orally and points only when he reads challenging texts. He's beginning to chunk words into phrases as he reads, and he notices when something he's reading doesn't make sense. He uses the cross-checking strategy to make corrections and get back on track.

Anthony has read 17 books this month, according to his reading workshop log. He is increasingly choosing easy-to-read chapter books to read, including Syd Hoff's *Sammy the Seal* (2000b) and *Oliver* (2000a). After he reads, he often shares his books with his friend Angel, and they reread them together and talk about their favorite parts. He regularly uses the connecting strategy and shares his text-to-self and text-to-world connections with Angel and Ms. McCloskey. When he reads two or more books by the same author, he shares text-to-text comparisons and can explain to his teacher how these comparisons make him a better reader: "Now I think and read at the same time," he explains.

Anthony likes to write during writing workshop. He identified his "Being Sick" story as the very best one he's written, and Ms. McCloskey agrees. Anthony tells an interesting and complete story with a beginning, middle, and end. And, you can hear his voice clearly in the story. Anthony's story is shown in the box, and here is a translation of it:

> Being Sick
>
> Sometimes I go outside with no! jacket on and the air went in my ear. I went inside and stayed in the house. My ear started to hurt because I had pain. I went to see if Mom was there. I found her. I told her I have an earache. My mom put some earache stuff in my ear and it made it better.

Anthony's spelling errors are characteristic of phonetic spellers. He sounds out the spelling of many words, such as *sum tims* (*sometimes*) and *hrt* (*hurt*), and he's experimenting with final *e* markers at the end of *tolde* and *pane*, but ignores them on other words. He uses the word wall in the classroom and spells many high-frequency words correctly (e.g., *with*, *went*, *have*).

Anthony writes single-draft compositions in paragraph form, and he creates a title for his stories. He writes in sentences and includes simple, compound, and complex sentences in his writing. He correctly uses capital letters to mark the beginnings of sentences and periods to mark the ends of sentences, but he continues to randomly put capital letters at the beginnings of words.

Anthony is at the beginning stage of reading and writing development. He reads word by word, uses his finger to track text while reading, and stops to decode unfamiliar words. He's applying what he's learning about phonics to decode words when reading and to spell words when writing. He writes multisentence compositions with good sentence structure, but his phonetic spelling makes his writing difficult to read.

> Being Sick
> Sum tims I go autsid With No! JaKit on and the err went in my ere. I went insid and stad in the house. My ere Strdit to hrt becuase I had pane. I went to see if Mom Was ther. I fand her. I tolde her I have A Eer Fea. My Mom put Sum Ear Fea Stuf in My Ear. And it Mad it Betr.

- Spell 20–50 high-frequency words
- Capitalize letters to begin sentences
- Use punctuation marks to indicate the ends of sentences
- Reread their writing

Most first and second graders are beginning readers and writers, and with explicit instruction and daily opportunities to read and write, children move through this stage to reach the fluent stage. Anthony, a 6-year-old beginning reader and writer in Ms. McCloskey's classroom, is presented in the Spotlight feature on pages 54–55.

Be Strategic!

Beginning Reading Strategies

These are the first reading strategies that young children learn:

- ▶ Cross-check
- ▶ Predict
- ▶ Connect
- ▶ Monitor
- ▶ Repair

Children learn these reading strategies as they participate in shared and guided reading activities and interactive read-alouds.

Reading. Children usually read aloud slowly, word by word, stopping often to sound out unfamiliar words. They point at each word as they read, but by the end of this stage, their reading becomes smoother and more fluent, and they point at words only when the text is especially challenging.

Although the emphasis in this stage is on word identification, children also learn that reading involves comprehension. They make predictions to guide their thinking about events in stories they read, and they make connections between what they're reading and their own lives and the world around them as they personalize the reading experience. They monitor their reading to recognize when it doesn't make sense, cross-check using phonological, semantic, syntactic, and pragmatic information in the text to figure out the problem, and repair or self-correct it (Fountas & Pinnell, 1996). They also learn about story structure, particularly that stories have a beginning, middle, and end, and use this knowledge to guide their reading and retelling.

Writing. Children move from writing one or two sentences to developing longer compositions, with five, eight, or more sentences organized into paragraphs. Their writing is better developed because they're acquiring a sense of audience, and they want their classmates to like what they've written. Children continue to write single-draft compositions but begin to make a few revisions and editing corrections as they learn about the writing process.

Children apply what they're learning about phonics in spelling, and they correctly spell many of the high-frequency words that they've learned to read. They know how to spell some high-frequency words and can locate others on word walls. They learn to use capital letters to mark the beginnings of sentences and punctuation to mark the ends. Children are more adept at rereading their writing, both immediately afterward and days later, because they're able to read many of the words they've written.

Instructional Procedures. Teachers plan activities for children at the beginning stage that range from modeled to independent reading and writing activities, but the emphasis is on interactive and guided activities. Through interactive writing, choral reading, and guided reading, teachers scaffold children as they read and write and use minilessons to provide strategy and skill instruction. For example, Ms. McCloskey's students were divided into small, homogeneous groups for guided reading lessons. The children met to read books at their reading levels, and

DEVELOPMENTAL CONTINUUM   Literacy Learning

PreK	K	1	2	3	4
Some children are emergent readers and writers before coming to school, but others enter the stage as a result of school experiences.	Most children are emergent readers and writers during kindergarten, but a few reach the beginning stage during the school year.	Most children are beginning readers and writers, and through instruction, their understanding of the alphabetic principle grows.	Most second graders continue in the beginning stage, but some reach the fluent stage by the end of the school year.	Most children become fluent readers and writers by the end of the school year, but a few still struggle with literacy.	Most fourth graders are fluent readers and writers, but those who continue to struggle need extra instruction in problem areas.

Ms. McCloskey introduced new vocabulary words, taught reading strategies and skills, and assessed their comprehension.

Teachers introduce the writing process to beginning-stage writers once they develop a sense of audience and want to make their writing better. Children don't immediately begin writing rough drafts and final copies or doing both revising and editing: They often begin the writing process by rereading their compositions and adding a word or two, correcting a misspelled word, or capitalizing a lowercase letter. These changes are cosmetic, but the idea that the writing process doesn't end after the first draft is established. Next, children show interest in making a final copy that really looks good. They either recopy the composition by hand or use word processing and print out the final copy. Once children understand that writing involves a rough draft and a final copy, they're ready to learn more about revising and editing, and they usually reach this point at about the same time they become fluent writers.

Stage 3: Fluent Reading and Writing

Fluent readers and writers reach the third stage when they accomplish the following:

- Read fluently and with expression
- Recognize most one-syllable words automatically and can decode other words efficiently
- Use decoding and comprehension strategies effectively
- Write well-developed, multiparagraph compositions
- Use the writing process to draft and refine their writing
- Write stories, reports, letters, and other genres

- Spell most high-frequency and other one-syllable words correctly
- Use capital letters and punctuation marks correctly most of the time

Some second graders reach this stage, and all children should be fluent readers and writers by the end of third grade. Reaching this stage is an important milestone because it indicates that children are ready for the increased literacy demands of fourth grade, when they're expected to read longer chapter-book stories, use writing to respond to literature, read content-area textbooks, and write essays and reports. Jazmen, an 8-year-old fluent reader and writer in Ms. McCloskey's classroom, is profiled in the Spotlight feature on pages 60–61.

Reading. The distinguishing characteristic of fluent readers is that they read words accurately, rapidly, and expressively. Fluent readers automatically recognize many words and can decode unfamiliar words efficiently. Their reading rate has increased to 100 words or more per minute; in addition, they can vary their speed according to the demands of the text they're reading.

Most fluent readers prefer to read silently because they can read more quickly than when they read orally. No longer do they point at words as they read. Children can read many books independently, actively making predictions, visualizing, monitoring their understanding, and making repairs when necessary. They have a range of strategies available and use them enhance their comprehension.

Fluent readers' comprehension is stronger, and they think more deeply about their reading than emergent and beginning readers do. It's likely that children's comprehension improves at this stage because they have more cognitive energy available for comprehension now; in contrast, beginning readers use much more cognitive energy to decode words. So, as children become fluent, they use less energy for word identification and have more cognitive resources available for comprehending what they read.

Children now read longer, more sophisticated picture books and chapter books, but they generally prefer chapter books because they enjoy really getting into a story or digging deeply in an informational book. They learn more about the literary genres, their structural patterns, and literary devices, such as alliteration, personification, and symbolism. They participate in literature focus units featuring an author, genre, or book, in small-group literature circles where children read and discuss a book together, and in author studies where they read and compare several books by the same author and examine that author's writing style. They're able to explain why they liked a particular book and make recommendations to classmates.

Writing. Fluent writers understand that writing is a process, and they use the writing process stages—prewriting, drafting, revising, editing, and publishing. They make plans for writing and write both rough drafts and final copies. They reread their rough drafts and make revisions and editing changes that reflect their understanding of writing forms and their purpose for writing. They increasingly share their rough drafts with classmates and turn to them for advice on how to make their writing better.

Children get ideas for writing from books they've read and from television programs and movies they've viewed. They organize their writing into paragraphs, indent paragraphs, and focus on a single idea in each paragraph. They develop ideas more completely and use more sophisticated vocabulary to express their ideas.

Fluent writers are aware of writing genres and organize their writing into stories, reports, letters, and poems. Their stories have a beginning, middle, and end, and the reports they write are structured using sequence, comparison, or cause-and-effect structures. Their letters reflect an understanding of the parts of a letter and how they're arranged on a page. Their poems incorporate alliteration, symbolism, rhyme, or other poetic devices to create vivid impressions.

Children's writing looks more conventional. They spell most of the 100 high-frequency words correctly and use phonics to spell other one-syllable words. They add inflectional endings (e.g., -s, -ed, -ing) and experiment with spelling two-syllable and longer words. They've learned to capitalize the first word in sentences and names and to use punctuation marks correctly at the ends of sentences, although they're still experimenting with punctuation marks within sentences.

Instructional Procedures. At this stage, children can apply the reading and writing processes and are prepared to participate independently in reading and writing workshop. They're learning about genres, text structures, and literary devices and can apply this knowledge to reading and responding to literature in literature circles. Teachers have shifted their focus from teaching children to decode words to comprehending stories and informational books.

Instructional recommendations for each of the three stages of reading and writing development are presented in Figure 2–8.

Preventing Reading and Writing Difficulties

It would be so convenient to identify a single factor—such as phonics—as the key to reading success, but preventing reading and writing difficulties is more complicated than that. Young children need a strong foundation before they reach first grade. They get interested in literacy when parents and teachers demonstrate authentic purposes for reading and writing. They listen to stories and informational books read aloud and watch adults read letters, newspapers, directions, and other real-world texts. They learn about writing as they observe adults composing messages and taking their dictations and as they write messages and lists and send e-mail messages. As young children recite nursery rhymes, sing silly songs, and play word games, they learn about the structure of spoken words. These activities are important because they prepare children for reading and writing instruction. However, most children who struggle with reading and writing come to school unprepared.

Three potential stumbling blocks exist that can interfere with children becoming successful readers and writers (Snow, Burns, & Griffin, 1998). First, emergent readers and writers may have difficulty understanding the alphabetic principle—that letters represent sounds—and applying it when they read and write. Second, beginning readers may have difficulty transferring comprehension strategies (e.g., predicting, connecting) that they use when listening to books being read aloud to using them as they read. Third, fluent readers and writers may not nurture the motivation for literacy needed to become lifelong readers and writers. To prevent difficulties, teachers must ensure that children learn to use the alphabetic principle, apply reading and writing strategies effectively, and view reading and writing as interesting and worthwhile activities.

Spotlight on . . .

A Fluent Reader and Writer

Jazmen is a confident and articulate African American third grader. She's 8 years old, and she celebrated her birthday last fall with a family trip to the Magic Mountain amusement park in Southern California. She smiles easily and likes to shake her head so that her braided, beaded hair swirls around her head. Jazmen is a pro at using computers, and she often provides assistance to her classmates. When asked about her favorite school activity, Jazmen says that she likes using the computer best of all. In fact, she's interested in learning more about careers that involve computers because she knows that she always wants to work with them.

Ms. McCloskey identified Jazmen for this feature because she's made such remarkable progress this year. This is the second year that Jazmen has been in Ms. McCloskey's class. Last year, she seemed stuck in the beginning stage, not making too much progress, according to Ms. McCloskey, "but this year, it's like a lightbulb has been turned on!" She's now a fluent reader and writer.

Jazmen likes to read, and she reports that she has a lot of books at home. According to the Accelerated Reader® program, she is reading at 3.8 (third grade, eighth month) level, which means she's is reading at or slightly above grade level. She enjoys reading the Marvin Redpost (e.g., *Marvin Redpost: A Magic Crystal?*, by Louis Sachar, 2000) and Zack Files (e.g., *Never Trust a Cat Who Wears Earrings*, by Dan Greenburg, 1997) series of easy-to-read paperback chapter books. She says she enjoys these books because they're funny.

Currently she's reading Paula Danziger's series of chapter-book stories about a third grader named Amber Brown who deals with the realities of contemporary life, including adjusting to her parents' divorce. The first book in the series is *Amber Brown Is Not a Crayon* (2006), about Amber and her best friend, Justin, who moves away at the end of the book; other chapter books in the series are *Amber Brown Goes Fourth* (2007), *Amber Brown Is Feeling Blue* (1999), *Amber Brown Sees Red* (1998), and *Amber Brown Is Green With Envy* (2004).

Fluent Reader and Writer Characteristics That Jazmen Exemplifies

Reading	Writing
• Recognizes most words automatically	• Uses the writing process
• Reads with expression	• Has a sense of audience and purpose
• Reads more than 100 words per minute	• Writes a complete story with a beginning, middle, and end
• Reads independently	• Writes in paragraphs
• Uses a variety of strategies	• Indents paragraphs
• Makes connections when reading	• Uses sophisticated language
• Thinks inferentially	• Spells most words correctly
• Applies knowledge of story structure and genre when reading	• Uses capital letters and punctuation to mark sentence boundaries

Jazmen reads well. She recognizes words automatically and reads with expression. She says that when you're reading to someone, you have to be interesting, and that's why she reads the way she does. Her most outstanding achievement, according to Ms. McCloskey, is that she thinks inferentially about stories. She can juggle thinking about plot, characters, setting, and theme in order to make thoughtful connections and interpretations. She knows about various genres and literary elements, and she uses this knowledge as she reflects on her reading.

Jazmen likes to write. She gets her ideas for stories from television programs. She explains, "When I'm watching TV, I get these ideas and I draw pictures of them and that's how I think of a story." She's currently working on a story entitled "Lucky and the Color Purple," about a princess named Lucky who possesses magical qualities. Why are her stories interesting? Jazmen says, "Most important is that they are creative." She shares her stories with her classmates, and they agree that Jazmen is a good writer.

Jazmen is particularly pleased with her story "The Super Hero With the Long Hair," which is shown here. The story has a strong voice. Jazmen wanted her story to sound interesting, so she substituted *whined* and *grouched* for *said*. Ms. McCloskey explained that she likes the story because it's complete with a beginning, middle, and end, and because Jazmen uses dialogue (and quotation marks) effectively. The errors remaining on the final draft of the paper also suggest direction for future instruction. Jazmen spelled 95% of the words in her composition correctly. In particular, she appears ready to learn more about plurals and possessives and using commas within sentences.

During her third-grade year, Jazmen has become a fluent reader and writer, and she exemplifies the characteristics listed in the chart. In fact, her classmates look to her for leadership when they're working on reading and writing projects. They ask her assistance in choosing books and decoding difficult words. Jazmen's writing has become more polished this year, too. She's become a thoughtful writer, and she uses the writing process to draft and refine her writing. Her classmates ask her to respond to their writing, and they're eager to listen to her read her new stories from the author's chair.

The Super Hero With the Long Hair

One beutiful day Nancy woke up. When she realized her hair was more beutiful than ever. She started pumping n the bed.

After that she started brushing her hair. She kept on brushing and brushing and brushing. The finally her sister's got so jealous they got mad.

Then they asked, "Can we brush you're hair and give you a little S...T...Y...L...E?" "Sure," said Nancy. They brushed and brushed.

All of a sudden they started cutting her hair. "What kind of S...T...Y...L...E are you doing?" "A pretty hair style." "Of course pretty. Is it really really pretty?"

"Yes yes it's really really pretty." Kelly said in a diskusting way. Then Kelly was done-Nancy went to go look in the bathroom miror. She started to cry. Her sister's started to laugh.

Then the light started to glow on the phone. Niky answered it. It was the mayor. "Hello mayor yes we'll be right on our way. The mayor said townsvill's in trouble. There's a monster outside and he's distroying all of townsvill!" shouted Niky.

"Go without me," whined Nancy. "What?" ""We can't go without you. You're the leader." "Just go without me!" Grouched Nancy.

They left. She started to talk to her dad. She made up her mind about going. She also made up some joke's. She flew to the monster and told her joke's to him and he laughed so hard he flew all the way to Jupiter.

Her sister's said, "Are we even?" The she lazorbeeded her sister's hair and said, "Now were even."

They lived happily everaften.

Figure 2-8 ◆ Instructional Recommendations for the Stages of Reading and Writing

Stage	Reading	Writing
Emergent	• Use environmental print. • Include literacy materials in play centers. • Read aloud to children. • Read big books and poems on charts using shared reading. • Introduce the title and author of books before reading. • Teach directionality and letter and word concepts using big books. • Encourage children to make predictions and text-to-self connections. • Have children retell and dramatize stories. • Have children respond to literature through talk and drawing. • Have children manipulate sounds using phonemic awareness activities. • Use alphabet-learning routines. • Take children's dictation using the Language Experience Approach. • Teach 20–24 high-frequency words. • Post words on a word wall.	• Have children use crayons for drawing and pencils for writing. • Encourage children to use scribble writing or write random letters if they can't do more-conventional writing. • Teach handwriting skills. • Use interactive writing for whole-class and small-group writing projects. • Have children write their names on sign-in sheets each day. • Have children write their own names and names of classmates. • Have children inventory or make lists of words they know how to write. • Have children "write the classroom" by making lists of familiar words they find in the classroom. • Have children use frames such as "I like _____" and "I see a _____" to write sentences. • Encourage children to remember what they write so they can read it.
Beginning	• Read charts of poems and songs using choral reading. • Read leveled books during guided reading lessons. • Provide daily opportunities to read and reread books independently. • Teach phonics concepts and rules. • Teach children to cross-check using the cueing systems. • Teach the 100 high-frequency words. • Point out whether texts are stories, informational books, or poems. • Teach predicting, connecting, cross-checking, and other strategies. • Teach the elements of story structure, particularly beginning, middle, and end. • Have children write in reading logs and participate in grand conversations. • Have children take books home to read with parents.	• Use interactive writing to teach concepts about written language. • Provide daily opportunities to write for a variety of purposes and using different genres. • Introduce the writing process. • Teach children to develop a single idea in their compositions. • Teach children to proofread their compositions. • Teach children to spell the 100 high-frequency words. • Teach contractions. • Teach capitalization and punctuation skills. • Have children use computers to publish their writing. • Have children share their writing from the author's chair.
Fluent	• Have children participate in literature circles. • Have children participate in reading workshop. • Teach about genres and other text features. • Involve children in author and genre studies. • Teach children to make text-to-self, text-to-world, and text-to-text connections. • Expand children's ability to use comprehension strategies. • Have children respond to books through talk and writing.	• Have children participate in writing workshop. • Teach children to use the writing process. • Teach children to revise and edit their writing. • Teach paragraphing skills. • Teach spelling rules. • Teach synonyms. • Teach homonyms. • Teach root words and affixes. • Teach children to use a dictionary and a thesaurus.

CHAPTER Review

How Effective Teachers Support Children's Literacy Development

▶ Teachers nurture children's oral language development and build their vocabulary.

▶ Teachers foster young children's interest in literacy and teach concepts about written language.

▶ Teachers understand that children move through the emergent, beginning, and fluent stages of literacy development.

▶ Teachers match instructional activities to each child's stage of reading and writing development.

Chapter 3

Assessing Children's Literacy Development

Mrs. McNeal Conducts Second-Quarter Assessments

The end of the second quarter is approaching, and Mrs. McNeal is assessing her first graders. She collects data about her students' reading, writing, and spelling development. Then she uses the information to document their achievement, verify that they're meeting state and district standards, determine report card grades, and make plans for the next quarter.

Today, Mrs. McNeal assesses Seth, who is 6½ years old. He's a quiet, well-behaved child who regularly completes his work. She has a collection of Seth's writing, but she wants to assess his current reading level. At the beginning of the school year, Mrs. McNeal considered him an average student, but in the past month, his reading progress has accelerated. She's anxious to see how much progress he's made.

Assessment 1: Determining Seth's Instructional Reading Level. Mrs. McNeal regularly takes running records as she listens to children reread familiar books to monitor their ability to recognize high-frequency words, decode unfamiliar words, and use reading strategies. In addition, Mrs. McNeal assesses each child's instructional reading level at the beginning of the school year and at the end of each quarter. She uses the Developmental Reading Assessment (DRA) (Beaver, 2006), an assessment kit with 44 leveled books arranged from kindergarten to fifth-grade reading levels.

To determine a child's instructional reading level, Mrs. McNeal chooses a book that the child hasn't read before and introduces it by reading the title, examining the picture on the cover, and talking about the story. The child does a picture walk, looking through the book and talking about what's happening on each page, using the illustrations as a guide. Next, the child reads the book aloud as Mrs. McNeal takes a **running record**, checking the words the child reads correctly and noting those read incorrectly. Then the child retells the story and the teacher assesses his or her understanding, prompting with questions, if necessary. Afterward, Mrs. McNeal scores the running record to determine the child's instructional reading level.

At the beginning of the school year, most of Mrs. McNeal's first graders were reading at level 4; by midyear, they should be reading at level 8; and by the end of the school year, they're expected to reach level 18 to 20. Seth was reading at level 4 in August, like many of his classmates, and at the end of the first quarter, he was reading at level 8. Now Mrs. McNeal decides to test him at level 16 because he's reading a level 16 book in his guided reading group.

Seth reads *The Pot of Gold* (2001), a level 16 book in the DRA assessment kit. The book recounts an Irish folktale about a man named Grumble who makes an elf show him where his pot of gold is hidden. Grumble marks the spot by tying a scarf around a nearby tree branch and goes to get a shovel with which to dig up the gold. Grumble admonishes the elf not to move the scarf, and he doesn't. Instead he ties scarves on other trees so that Grumble can't find the elf's gold. Mrs. McNeal takes a running record while Seth reads; it's shown on page 66.

As indicated on the running record sheet, there are 266 words in the book. Seth makes 17 errors but self-corrects 5 of them; his accuracy rate is 95%. Mrs. McNeal analyzes Seth's errors and concludes that he overdepends on visual (or phonological) cues while ignoring semantic ones. Of the 12 errors, only one—*Grumply* for *Grumble*—makes sense in the sentence. When Seth retells the story, he shows that he understands the big idea, but his retelling isn't especially strong: He retells the beginning and the end of the story but leaves out important details in the middle. However, he does make interesting connections between the story and his own life. Mrs. McNeal concludes that level 16 is his instructional level and that his ability to read words is stronger than his comprehension.

Mrs. McNeal makes notes about Seth's instructional priorities for the next quarter. She'll focus on comprehension and teach him more about the structure of stories, including plot and setting. She'll help him use semantic cues to support the visual ones and encourage him to structure his retellings into three parts—beginning, middle, and end. She also decides to introduce Seth to easy chapter books, such as Cynthia Rylant's Henry and Mudge series about the adventures of a boy named Henry and his dog, Mudge (e.g., *Henry and Mudge and the Big Sleepover*, 2007).

A Running Record Scoring Sheet

Name **Seth** Date **Jan. 18**

Level **16** Title **The Pot of Gold** Easy (**Instructional**) Hard

Running Record

	E	SC	E	SC

2
✓✓✓✓✓✓✓✓ ✓✓
✓ grumply / Grumble |T ✓✓✓✓✓✓✓ — 1 — m s (v)
✓✓ ✓✓ always |A/T ✓✓✓✓ ✓ — 1
✓✓✓✓✓✓✓✓✓✓

3
✓✓✓✓✓✓✓✓
✓✓✓✓✓✓✓ did not / didn't | — 1 — (m)(s)v
✓✓
✓✓✓✓✓✓✓✓
✓✓✓✓✓✓✓✓
✓✓✓✓✓

4
✓✓✓✓✓✓✓✓
✓✓✓✓✓✓✓✓
✓✓✓

5
✓✓✓✓✓✓✓✓
✓✓✓✓✓ ✓ I/I'll | make/move | ✓✓ — 1 / 1 — (m)(s)(v) / m s (v)
✓✓✓✓✓✓✓✓
safr/scarf | ✓✓✓✓✓ or/of | ✓✓ — 1 / 1 — m s (v) / m s (v)

6
✓✓✓✓ ✓ ✓ me|sc self / my| scarf | — 1 — (blank) — 1 — m s (v) / (m)(s)(v)
✓✓✓ — 1 — m s (v)
✓✓✓✓✓
✓✓✓✓✓

7
✓✓✓✓✓✓✓
✓✓✓✓✓✓✓✓ ✓
✓✓✓✓✓✓

8
✓✓✓✓✓✓✓
✓✓✓✓✓✓✓✓✓
✓✓

9
✓✓✓ take/taken | ✓ scafer/scarf | ✓✓✓ — 1 / 1 — (m)s(v) / m s (v)
✓✓✓✓✓✓✓✓

10
✓✓✓✓✓✓ — 1 — m s (v) / (m)(s)(v)
✓✓✓ they|sc / that | R ✓ ✓✓✓✓✓ — m s (v)
maybe/may | sit/still | ✓✓ — 1 / 1 — m s (v) / m s (v)
✓✓✓✓

Scoring 12/266 95% accuracy	**Picture Walk** Gets gist of story
Types of Errors: M S (V) Overdependent on V cues	**Oral Reading** Reads fluently
Self-correction Rate 1:5	**Retelling/Questions** Tells BME but middle is brief

Assessment 2: Testing Seth's Knowledge of High-Frequency Words.
Mrs. McNeal's goal is for her first graders to recognize at least 75 of the 100 high-frequency words by the end of the school year. In August, most children could read at least 12 words; Seth read 16 correctly. Today, Mrs. McNeal asks Seth again to read the list of 100 high-frequency words. She expects that he'll be able to read 50 to 60 and when he misses 5 in a row, she'll stop, but Seth surprises her and reads the entire list! He misses only these 6 words: *don't, how, there, very, were,* and *would*. Seth's high score reinforces his results on the running record: He's a very good word reader.

Assessment 3: Checking Seth's Ability to Write and Spell Words. Several days ago, Mrs. McNeal administered the "Words I Know" Test to the class: She asked the children to write as many words as they could in 10 minutes without copying from classroom charts. In August, most children could spell 15 to 20 words correctly; Mrs. McNeal's goal is for them to write 50 words by the end of the school year. Seth wrote 22 words in August, and on the recent test, he wrote 50 correctly spelled words. Seth's "Words I Know" test is shown below.

Seth's "Words I Know" Test

the im a can eat look took she play so he
man what han hat bat zadl got god cat
red in meat pig pl n see need ds and
night fight dog come from sun run
ran going lettle fin will hill rat
srach ring ug fel tnees snow fun
cowboys stop get no yes hors you

Mrs. McNeal reviews the words Seth wrote and notices that most are one-syllable words with short vowels, such as *cat* and *fin,* but he's beginning to write words with more complex spellings, such as *what, come,* and *night,* words with inflectional endings, such as *going,* and two-syllable words, such as *cowboys.* She concludes that Seth is making very good progress, in both the number of words he can write and the complexity of the spelling patterns he's using.

Assessment 4: Scoring Seth's Compositions. Mrs. McNeal looks through Seth's journal and chooses several representative samples written in the past 3 weeks to score; one of the samples is shown on page 68. Here is the text with conventional spelling and punctuation:

Last night I kept waking up. My dad slept with me. Then I fell fast asleep. Then dad went to bed.

Using the school district's 6-point rubric, Mrs. McNeal scores the composition as a 4. A score of 5 is considered grade-level at the end of the school year, and Mrs. McNeal believes that Seth will reach that level before then. She notes that he's writing several sentences in an entry, even though he often omits punctuation at the ends of sentences. Seth writes fluently but sometimes omits a word or two. Mrs. McNeal plans to talk to him about the importance of rereading his writing to catch omissions, add punctuation marks, and correct misspelled words.

Seth's Journal Entry

Seth correctly spells more than two-thirds of the words he writes, and he uses invented spelling that generally represents beginning, middle, or ending sounds. In this entry, Seth wrote 21 words, spelling 13, or 71%, correctly. He reversed the order of letters in three words (*lats* for *last*, *fli* for *fell*, *ot* for *to*) but didn't make any letter-order reversals in the other two samples that Mrs. McNeal evaluated. She recognizes that many first graders form letters backward and make letter-order reversals and isn't concerned about Seth's reversals because she thinks he'll outgrow them.

Assessment 5: Measuring Seth's Phonics and Spelling Knowledge. Each week, the first graders craft two sentences for a dictation test. On Monday, they create the sentences and write them on chart paper that's displayed in the classroom. During the week, they practice writing the sentences on small whiteboards, and Mrs. McNeal uses the text for minilessons during which she draws children's attention to high-frequency words they've studied, the phonetic features of various words, and capitalization and punctuation rules applied in the sentences. Last week's sentences focused on *The Magic School Bus Lost in the Solar System* (Cole, 1993), a book Mrs. McNeal read to the class:

Their bus turned into a rocket ship. They wanted to visit all of the planets.

After practicing the sentences all week, Mrs. McNeal dictates them for the children to write on Friday. She tells them to try to spell words correctly and to write all the sounds they hear in the words they don't know how to spell. Seth wrote:

The bus turd into a rocket ship they wande to vist all of the planis.

He spelled 10 of the 15 words correctly and included 46 of 51 sounds in his writing. He omitted the period at the end of the first sentence, however, and didn't capitalize the first word in the second sentence.

Mrs. McNeal uses this test to check children's phonics knowledge and ability to spell high-frequency words. Seth spelled most of the high-frequency words correctly, except that he wrote *the* for *their*. His other errors involved the second syllable of the word or an inflectional ending. Mrs. McNeal concludes that Seth is making good progress in learning to spell high-frequency words and that he's ready to learn more about two-syllable words and inflectional endings.

Grading Seth's Reading, Writing, and Spelling Achievement.   Having collected these data, Mrs. McNeal is ready to complete Seth's report card. He and his classmates receive separate number grades in reading, writing, and spelling: The grades range from 1, not meeting grade-level standards, to 4, exceeding standards. Seth will receive a 3 in reading, writing, and spelling. A score of 3 means that he's meeting grade-level standards in all three areas. Even though his reading level is higher than average, his dependence on visual cues when decoding unfamiliar words and his weakness in comprehension keep him at level 3 in reading.

Assessment has become a priority in 21st-century schools. School districts and state and federal education agencies have increased their demands for accountability, and today, most students take annual high-stakes tests to judge their achievement. Teachers are collecting more assessment data now, doing it more frequently, and using the information to make instructional decisions, as Mrs. McNeal demonstrated in the vignette. Researchers explain that "a system of frequent assessment, coupled with strong content standards and effective reading instruction, helps ensure that teachers' . . . approaches are appropriate to each student's needs" (Kame'enui, Simmons, & Cornachione, 2000, p. 1). By linking assessment and instruction, teachers improve children's learning and their teaching.

You'll notice that the term *assessment* is used much more often than *evaluation* in this chapter. These terms are often considered interchangeable, but they're not. Assessment is formative; it's ongoing and provides immediate feedback to improve teaching and learning. It's usually authentic, based on the literacy activities children are engaged in. Observations, conferences, and children's work samples are examples of authentic assessment. In contrast, evaluation is summative; it's final, generally administered at the end of a unit or a school year, and used to judge quality. Tests are the most common type of evaluation, and they're used to compare one child's achievement against that of other children or against grade-level standards.

CLASSROOM-BASED READING ASSESSMENT

The purpose of classroom assessment is to collect meaningful information about what children know and do, and it takes many forms (Afflerbach, 2007a). Teachers use these types of assessment to monitor and examine children's learning:

♦ Kits of leveled books to determine children's reading levels
♦ Informal procedures, such as observations and conferences, to monitor children's progress
♦ Tests to diagnose children's strengths and weaknesses in specific components of reading and writing
♦ Collections of work samples to document children's learning

Each type of assessment serves a different purpose, so it's important that teachers choose assessment tools carefully. Researchers recommend that teachers use a combination of informal and formal assessment tools to improve the fairness and effectiveness of classroom literacy assessment (Kuhs, Johnson, Agruso, & Monrad, 2001).

Determining Children's Reading Levels

Teachers match children with books at appropriate levels of difficulty because children are more likely to be successful when they're reading books that aren't too easy or too difficult. Books that are too easy don't provide enough challenge, and books that are too difficult frustrate them. Researchers have identified three reading levels that take into account children's ability to recognize words automatically, read fluently, and comprehend what they're reading:

Independent Reading Level. Children can read books at this level comfortably, on their own. They recognize almost all words; their accuracy rate is 95–100%. Their reading is fluent, and they comprehend what they're reading. Books at this level are only slightly easier than those at their instructional level, and they still engage children's interest.

Instructional Reading Level. Children can read and understand books at this level with support, but not on their own. They recognize most words; their accuracy rate is 90–94%. Their reading may be fluent, but sometimes it isn't. With support from the teacher or classmates, children comprehend what they're reading, but if they're reading independently, their understanding is limited. This level reflects Vygotsky's zone of proximal development, discussed in Chapter 1.

Frustration Reading Level. Books at this level are too difficult for children to read successfully, even with assistance. Children don't recognize enough words automatically; their accuracy is less than 90%. Children's reading is choppy and word by word, and it often doesn't make sense. In addition, they show little understanding of what's been read.

Children should be assessed regularly to determine their reading levels and monitor their progress.

These reading levels have important implications for instruction. Children read independent-level books when they're reading for pleasure and instructional-level books when they're participating in guided reading or another instructional activity.

Check the Compendium of Instructional Procedures, which follows Chapter 12, for more information on highlighted terms.

They shouldn't be expected to read books at their frustration level; when it's essential that they experience grade-appropriate literature or learn content-area information, teachers should read the text aloud.

Readability Formulas.   For nearly a century, readability formulas have been used to estimate the ease with which reading materials, both trade books and textbooks, can be read. Readability scores serve as rough gauges of text difficulty and are traditionally reported as grade-level scores. If a book has a readability score of third grade, for example, teachers assume that average third graders will be able to read it. Sometimes readability scores are marked with *RL* and a grade level, such as *RL 3*, on books.

Readability scores are determined by correlating semantic and syntactic features in a text. Several passages from a text are identified for analysis, and then vocabulary sophistication is measured by counting the syllables in each word, and sentence complexity by counting the words in each sentence. The syllable and word counts from each passage are averaged, and the readability score is calculated by plotting the averages on a graph. It seems reasonable that texts with shorter words and sentences would be easier to read than those with longer words and sentences; however, readability formulas take into account only two text factors; they can't consider reader factors, including the experience and knowledge that readers bring to reading, their cognitive and linguistic backgrounds, or their motivation for reading.

One fairly quick and simple readability formula is the Fry Readability Graph, developed by Edward Fry (1968); it's presented in Figure 3–1. This graph is used to predict the grade-level score for texts. Teachers use a readability formula as an aid in evaluating textbook and trade-book selections for classroom use; however, they can't assume that materials rated as appropriate for a particular level will be appropriate for everyone because children within a class typically vary three grade levels or more in their reading levels.

Just looking at a book isn't enough to determine its readability, because books that seem quite different sometimes score at the same level. For example, *Sarah, Plain and Tall* (MacLachlan, 2004), *Tales of a Fourth Grade Nothing* (Blume, 2007), *Bunnicula: A Rabbit-Tale of Mystery* (Howe & Howe, 2006), and *The Hundred Penny Box* (Mathis, 2006) are four novels that score at the third-grade reading level according to Fry's Readability Graph, even though their topics, use of illustrations, font sizes, and page length differ significantly.

Leveled Books.   Basal readers have traditionally been leveled according to grade levels, but grade-level designations, especially in kindergarten and first grade, are too broad. Fountas and Pinnell (2006b) developed a text gradient, or classification system that arranges books along a continuum from easiest to hardest, to match children to books in grades K–8. Their system is based on these 10 variables that influence reading difficulty:

- Genre and format of the book
- Organization and use of text structures
- Familiarity with and interest level of the content
- Complexity of ideas and themes

LITERACY PORTRAITS
Viewing Guide

Ms. Janusz regularly monitors the second graders' reading achievement. Working one-on-one, she introduces a leveled book and asks the child to read the first part aloud while she takes a running record on a separate sheet of paper. Then the child reads the rest of the book silently. She also asks questions after the child finishes reading orally and again after the child reaches the end of the book. Go to the Literacy Portraits section of MyEducationLab for the Literacy Course to watch Ms. Janusz assess Jimmy's reading in his October video clip and again in his March video clip. As you watch the videos, think about how Jimmy grew as a reader during the school year. Does he decode unfamiliar words, read fluently, and comprehend what he's read orally and silently? Next, reflect on how Ms. Janusz linked instruction and assessment when she took advantage of teachable moments while she assessed his reading.

myeducationlab

Figure 3-1 ◆ The Fry Readability Graph

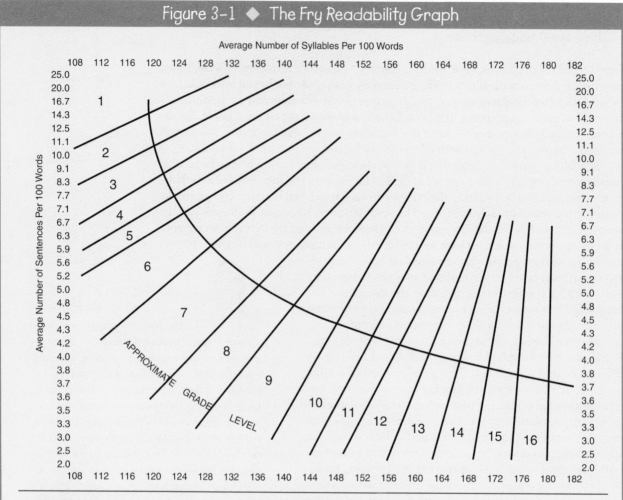

Directions:
1. Select three 100-word passages from the book or other reading material.
2. Count the number of syllables in each 100-word passage and average them.
3. Count the number of sentences in each 100-word passage and average them.
4. Plot the averages on the graph to determine the difficulty level. If the score falls outside the lined area, it isn't valid.

From "A Readability Formula That Saves Time," by E. Fry, 1968, p. 587.

- Language and literary features
- Sentence length and complexity
- Sophistication of the vocabulary
- Word length and ease of decoding
- Relationship of illustrations to the text
- Length of the book, its layout, and other text features

Fountas and Pinnell used these criteria to identify 26 levels, labeled A through Z, for their text gradient, which teachers also can use to level books in their classrooms. More than 18,000 books have been leveled according to this text gradient. A sample trade book for each level is shown in Figure 3–2; other leveled books are listed in *The Fountas and Pinnell Leveled Book List, K–8* (Fountas & Pinnell, 2006a) and are available online at www.fountasandpinnellleveledbooks.com.

The Lexile Framework.   The newest approach to matching books to readers is the Lexile Framework, developed by MetaMetrics. This approach is different because it's used to measure both children's reading levels and the difficulty level of books. Word familiarity and sentence complexity are the two factors used to determine the difficulty level. Figure 3–3 presents a list of books ranked according to the Lexile Framework.

Children's results on high-stakes tests are often linked to the Lexile Framework. Standardized achievement tests, such as the Iowa Test of Basic Skills and the Stanford Achievement Test, report test results as Lexile scores, and a number of standards-based state reading tests, including the California English-Language Arts Standards Test, the North Carolina End-of-Grade Tests, and the Texas Assessment of Knowledge and Skills, do the same. With this information, children, parents, and teachers can match

Figure 3–2 ◆ Books Leveled Using Fountas and Pinnell's Text Gradient

Level	Grade	Book
A	K	Burningham, J. (1985). *Colors*. New York: Crown.
B	K–1	Carle, E. (1997). *Have you seen my cat?* New York: Aladdin Books.
C	K–1	Martin, B., Jr. (2008). *Brown bear, brown bear, what do you see?* New York: Henry Holt.
D	1	Peek, M. (2006). *Mary wore her red dress*. New York: Clarion Books.
E	1	Hill, E. (2005). *Where's Spot?* New York: Putnam.
F	1	Hutchins, P. (2005). *Rosie's walk*. New York: Aladdin Books.
G	1	Shaw, N. (2006). *Sheep in a jeep*. Boston: Houghton Mifflin.
H	1–2	Kraus, R. (2005). *Whose mouse are you?* New York: Aladdin Books.
I	1–2	Wood, A. (2005). *The napping house*. San Diego: Harcourt.
J	2	Rylant, C. (1996). *Henry and Mudge and the bedtime thumps*. New York: Simon & Schuster.
K	2	Heller, R. (1999). *Chickens aren't the only ones*. New York: Putnam.
L	2–3	Marshall, J. (2000). *The three little pigs*. New York: Grosset & Dunlap.
M	2–3	Park, B. (2007). *Junie B. Jones and the stupid smelly bus*. New York: Random House.
N	3	Danziger, P. (2006). *Amber Brown is not a crayon*. New York: Puffin Books.
O	3–4	Cleary, B. (1992). *Ramona Quimby, age 8*. New York: HarperTrophy.
P	3–4	Mathis, S. B. (2006). *The hundred penny box*. New York: Puffin Books.
Q	4	Howe, D., & Howe, J. (2006). *Bunnicula: A rabbit-tale of mystery*. New York: Aladdin Books.
R	4	Paulsen, G. (2007). *Hatchet*. New York: Simon & Schuster.
S	4–5	Norton, M. (2003). *The borrowers*. San Diego: Odyssey Classics.
T	4–5	Curtis, C. P. (2004). *Bud, not Buddy*. New York: Laurel Leaf.
U	5	Lowry, L. (1998). *Number the stars*. New York: Yearling.
V	5–6	Sachar, L. (2008). *Holes*. New York: Farrar, Straus & Giroux.
W	5–6	Choi, S. N. (1993). *Year of impossible goodbyes*. New York: Yearling.
X	6–8	Hesse, K. (1999). *Out of the dust*. New York: Scholastic.
Y	6–8	Lowry, L. (2006). *The giver*. New York: Delacorte.
Z	7–8	Hinton, S. E. (2006). *The outsiders*. New York: Puffin Books.

Fountas & Pinnell, 2006a.

Figure 3–3 ◆ Books Ranked According to the Lexile Framework		
Level	**Grade**	**Book**
100–149	K	Willems, M. (2003). *Don't let the pigeon drive the bus!* New York: Hyperion Books.
150–199	K–1	Marshall, E. (1999). *Fox all week*. New York: Puffin Books.
200–249	1	Bridwell, N. (2002). *Clifford the big red dog*. New York: Scholastic.
250–299	1	Kellogg, S. (2002). *Pinkerton, behave!* New York: Dial Books.
300–349	1–2	Allard, H. (1985). *Miss Nelson is missing!* Boston: Houghton Mifflin.
350–399	2	Bourgeois, P. (1997). *Franklin's bad day*. New York: Scholastic.
400–449	2	Coerr, E. (1989). *The Josefina story quilt*. New York: HarperTrophy.
450–499	2–3	Bunting, E. (1998). *Going home*. New York: HarperTrophy.
500–549	3	Rathmann, P. (1995). *Officer Buckle and Gloria*. New York: Putnam.
550–599	3–4	Sobol, D. (2008). *Encyclopedia Brown saves the day*. New York: Puffin Books.
600–649	3–4	Cole, J. (1994). *The magic school bus on the ocean floor*. New York: Scholastic.
650–699	4	Lowry, L. (1998). *Number the stars*. New York: Yearling.
700–749	4	Howe, D., & Howe, J. (2006). *Bunnicula: A rabbit-tale of mystery*. New York: Aladdin Books.
750–799	4–5	Creech, S. (2005). *Walk two moons*. New York: HarperTrophy.
800–849	5	Dahl, R. (2007). *Charlie and the chocolate factory*. New York: Puffin Books.
850–899	5–6	Naylor, P. (2000). *Shiloh*. New York: Aladdin Books.
900–949	6–7	Lewis, C. S. (2005). *The lion, the witch and the wardrobe*. New York: HarperCollins.
950–999	7	O'Dell, S. (2006). *The black pearl*. Boston: Houghton Mifflin.
1000–1049	8	Philbrick, R. (2001). *Freak the mighty*. New York: Scholastic.

students to books by searching the online Lexile database to locate books at each student's reading level.

The Lexile Framework is a promising program, because the wide range of scores allows teachers to more closely match children and books. The availability of the online database with more than 44,000 leveled books makes it a very useful assessment tool; however, matching readers to books is more complicated than determining a numerical score!

The Assessment Tools feature on page 75 describes three screening tools to identify children's reading levels.

Online Book Search Systems. Teachers also consult online databases to locate books at children's reading levels so that they can match readers with appropriate books. One of the most popular search systems is the Teacher Book Wizard (http://bookwizard.scholastic.com/tbw/homePage.do), a free book search system at Scholastic's website. Teachers can search the 50,000 books in its database to locate books at a child's reading level or check the reading level of a particular book they'd like to use for a literature focus unit or a literature circle. There are three ways to access this quick and easy search system:

Quick Search. Teachers search for particular books, themed book lists, or books by an author.

Leveled Search. Teachers customize the search by children's interests, reading levels, language (English or Spanish), topic, and genre.

BookAlike Search. Teachers enter a book title to locate similar books at the same reading level or at other reading levels.

Instead of going to the Scholastic website, teachers can also download the Widget, a free version of the Teacher Book Wizard search system, to their website or their school's homepage and use it to search for books.

The search results present useful information about each book, including the title and author, a photo of the book cover, the book's interest and reading levels, the genre, a summary, and a list of topics related to the book. The reading level is expressed as a grade-level equivalent (e.g., RL 2.3 or second grade, third month) and according to both Fountas and Pinnell's levels and Lexile Framework scores. Links are also provided to author information and teaching resources.

Assessment Tools

Determining Reading Levels

Teachers use screening assessments to determine children's reading levels, monitor their progress, and document achievement through a school year and across grade levels. Here are three screening assessments:

◆ **Developmental Reading Assessment (DRA)** (Beaver, 2006)
   The DRA is available as two kits, one for grades K–3 and the other for grades 4–8, to assess reading performance using leveled fiction and nonfiction books. The K–3 kit also includes an individualized diagnostic instrument to assess phonemic awareness and phonics knowledge. Teachers use an online system to manage children's scores and group them for instruction.

◆ **Fountas and Pinnell Benchmark Assessment System** (Fountas & Pinnell, 2007)
   The Fountas and Pinnell Benchmark Assessment System is sold as two kits, one for grades K–2 and the other for grades 3–8. Each kit contains 30 leveled fiction and nonfiction books written specifically for the kit and CDs with assessment forms to manage children's scores. Teachers use the books in the kit to match children's reading levels to the Fountas and Pinnell 26-level text gradient.

For both of these assessments, teachers test children individually. The teacher selects an appropriate book for the child to read and then introduces it; the child reads the book, and the teacher takes a running record of the child's reading. Then the child retells the text and answers comprehension questions. The teacher scores and analyzes the results, and testing continues until the teacher determines the child's instructional level.

◆ **Scholastic Reading Inventory (SRI)**
   The SRI is a unique computer-adaptive assessment program that reports children's reading levels using Lexile scores. Children take this 20-minute computerized test individually. The child reads a narrative or informational passage on the computer screen and answers multiple-choice comprehension questions. This test is computer adaptive because if the child answers a question correctly, the next one will be more difficult, but if the answer is wrong, the next one will be easier. Children read passages and answer questions until their reading level is determined. They receive a customized take-home letter with their Lexile score and a personalized list of recommended books.

These assessments are usually administered at the beginning of the school year and periodically during the year to monitor children's progress. The results are also used to group children for guided reading and to identify those who need diagnostic testing.

The Scholastic website offers a variety of related literature resources for teachers:

My Book List.   Teachers make and customize book lists using the results of their Teacher Book Wizard searches.

List Exchange.   Teachers join an online community to share their book lists and collect book lists from other teachers.

All About Authors.   Teachers locate information about authors, including video clips of author interviews, lists of their books, and ideas and lesson plans for author studies.

Teaching With Books.   Teachers search for information about particular books, including lists of vocabulary words, discussion guides, extension activities, and lesson plans.

In addition, resources for prekindergartners through fourth graders are available at the website, including interactive storybooks for young children; the Flashlight Readers Club for readers who love books; information about genres; author interviews; and reading, grammar, and spelling games.

Monitoring Children's Progress

Monitoring is vital to children's success (Braunger & Lewis, 2006). Teachers monitor children's learning every day and use the results to make instructional decisions (Winograd & Arrington, 1999). As they supervise children's progress, teachers learn about their students, about themselves as teachers, and about the impact of their instructional program.

Observations.   Teachers are "kid watchers" according to Yetta Goodman (Owocki & Goodman, 2002). To be effective kid watchers, teachers must understand how children learn to read and write. The focus is on what children do as they read or write, not on whether they're behaving properly or working quietly. Of course, little learning can occur in disruptive situations, but during these observations, the focus is on literacy, not behavior. Observations should be planned. Teachers usually observe a specific group each day so that over the course of a week, they watch everyone in the class.

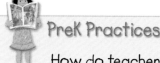

PreK Practices

How do teachers assess young children?

The two best ways to assess prekindergartners' literacy learning are by observing them and collecting samples of their reading and writing (Bennett-Armistead, Duke, & Moses, 2005; Vukelich & Christie, 2009). Teachers focus on one child at a time, carefully monitoring his or her language use and literacy behaviors, and document their observations by writing brief anecdotal notes. They also collect writing samples over time and compare them to determine growth. Assessment should be anchored in authentic reading and writing activities because young children's learning can't be measured on standardized tests. Paper-and-pencil tests aren't reliable or valid indicators of what young children can do.

Anecdotal Notes.   Teachers write brief notes in notebooks or on self-stick notes as they observe children (Boyd-Batstone, 2004). The most useful notes describe specific events, report rather than evaluate, and relate the events to other information about the child. Teachers make notes about reading and writing activities, the questions children ask, and the strategies and skills they use fluently and those they don't understand. These records monitor and document growth and pinpoint problem areas to address in future minilessons or conferences.

Conferences. Teachers talk with children to monitor their progress in reading and writing activities as well as to set goals and help them solve problems. Here are six types of conferences:

> **On-the-Spot Conferences.** The teacher visits with children at their desks to monitor some aspect of their work or to check on progress. These conferences are brief, with the teacher often spending less than a minute with each child.
>
> **Planning Conferences.** The teacher and the child make plans for reading or writing at the conference. At a prereading conference, they may talk about information related to the book, difficult concepts or vocabulary words related to the book, or the reading log the child will keep. At a prewriting conference, they may discuss possible writing topics or how to narrow a broad topic.
>
> **Revising Conferences.** A small group meets with the teacher to share their rough drafts and get specific suggestions about how to revise them.
>
> **Book Discussion Conferences.** Children meet with the teacher to discuss the book they've read. They may share reading log entries, discuss plot or characters, or compare the story to others they've read.
>
> **Editing Conferences.** The teacher reviews children's proofread compositions and helps them correct spelling, punctuation, capitalization, and other mechanical errors.
>
> **Evaluation Conferences.** The teacher meets with children after they've completed an assignment or project to talk about their growth as readers and writers. They reflect on their accomplishments and set goals.

Often these conferences are brief and impromptu, held at children's desks as the teacher moves around the classroom; at other times, however, the conferences are planned, and children meet with the teacher at a designated conference table.

Checklists. Checklists simplify assessment and enhance children's learning (Kuhs, Johnson, Agruso, & Monrad, 2001). Teachers identify the evaluation criteria in advance so children understand what's expected of them before they begin working. Grading is easier because teachers have already set the evaluation criteria, and it's fairer, too, because teachers use the same criteria to grade everyone's work. A fourth-grade checklist for giving book talks is shown in Figure 3–4. At the beginning of the school year, the teacher introduced book talks, modeled how to do one, and developed the checklist with the children. They use the checklist whenever they're preparing to give a book talk, and the teacher uses it as a rating scale to evaluate the effectiveness of their book talks.

Rubrics. Rubrics are scoring guides that evaluate children's performance in reading and writing according to specific criteria and levels of achievement (Afflerbach, 2007b). They're similar to checklists because they specify what children are expected to be able to do, but they go beyond checklists because they describe levels of achievement. A 5-level rubric for assessing second-grade writing is shown in Figure 3–5.

Work Samples. Teachers have children collect their work in folders to document their learning. Work samples might include reading logs, audiotapes of children's reading, photos of projects, videotapes of puppet shows and oral presentations, and books

Figure 3-4 ◆ Book Talk Checklist

Name _Jaime_   Date _November 12_

Title _Cockroach Cooties_

Author _Laurence Yep_

___✓___ Hold up the book to show to classmates.
___✓___ State the title and author's name.
___✓___ Interest classmates in the book by asking a question, reading an
         excerpt, or sharing some information.
_____ Summarize the book, without giving away the ending.
___✓___ Talk loud enough for everyone to hear you.
___✓___ Look at the audience.
_____ Limit the book talk to 3 minutes.

they've written. Children often choose some of these work samples to place in their portfolios.

Diagnosing Children's Strengths and Weaknesses

Teachers use diagnostic reading assessments to identify children's strengths and weaknesses, examine any area of difficulty in more detail, and decide how to modify instruction to meet their needs. They use a variety of diagnostic tests to examine children's achievement in phonemic awareness, phonics, fluency, vocabulary, comprehension, and other components of reading and writing. The Assessment Tools feature on page 80 lists the diagnostic tests recommended in this text and directs you to the chapter where you can learn more about them.

Two of the assessments that teachers commonly use are running records and informal reading inventories. They're used to determine children's reading levels as well as to diagnose difficulties in word identification, fluency, and comprehension and to monitor children's growth as readers. Mrs. McNeal used running records in the vignette at the beginning of this chapter, and as you continue reading, you'll notice that they're referred to again and again.

Go to the Assignments and Activities section of the Topic *Assessment* in the MyEducationLab for the literacy course and complete the activity entitled *Analyzing and Interpreting Running Record Data*.

Running Records. Teachers often take running records of children's oral reading to assess their word identification and reading fluency (Clay, 2007a). They calculate the percentage of words the child reads correctly and then analyze the miscues, oral responses that don't match the text. They make a series of checkmarks on a sheet of paper as the child reads words correctly and use other marks to indicate words that the child substitutes, repeats, mispronounces, or doesn't know, as Mrs. McNeal did in the vignette. Although teachers can take the running record on a blank sheet of paper, it's much easier to make a copy of the page or pages the child will read and take the running record next to or above the actual text. Using a copy of the text is especially im-

Figure 3-5 ◆ A Second-Grade Writing Rubric

5	Writing has an original title. Story shows originality, sense of humor, or cleverness. Writer uses paragraphs effectively to organize ideas. Writing contains very few spelling, capitalization, or punctuation errors. Writer varies sentence structure and word choice. Writer shows a sense of audience.
4	Writing has an appropriate title. Beginning, middle, and end of the story are well developed. A problem or goal is identified in the story. Writing includes details that support plot, characters, and setting. Writing is organized into paragraphs. Writing contains few capitalization and punctuation errors. Writer spells most high-frequency words correctly and spells unfamiliar words phonetically.
3	Writing may have a title. Writing has at least two of the three parts of a story (beginning, middle, and end). Writing shows a sequence of events. Writing is not organized into paragraphs. Spelling, grammar, capitalization, or punctuation errors may interfere with meaning.
2	Writing has at least one of the three parts of a story (beginning, middle, and end). Writing may show a partial sequence of events. Writing is brief and underdeveloped. Writing has spelling, grammar, capitalization, and punctuation errors that interfere with meaning.
1	Writing lacks a sense of story. An illustration may suggest a story. Writing is brief and may support the illustration. Some words may be recognizable, but the writing is difficult to read.

portant when assessing children who read longer texts and read them more quickly than beginning readers do.

After identifying the words the child misread, teachers calculate the percentage of words read correctly. They use this percentage to determine whether the reading material is too easy, too difficult, or appropriate. If the child reads 95% or more of the words correctly, the book is easy, or at the child's independent reading level. If the child reads 90–94% of the words correctly, the book is at his or her instructional level. If the child reads fewer than 90% of the words correctly, the book is too difficult: It's at the child's frustration level.

Teachers categorize miscues according to the semantic, graphophonic, and syntactic cueing systems to examine which word-identification strategies the child is using. As they categorize the miscues, teachers should ask themselves these questions:

- Does the reader self-correct the miscue?
- Does the miscue change the meaning of the sentence?
- Is the miscue phonologically similar to the word in the text?
- Is the miscue acceptable within the syntax (or structure) of the sentence?

Assessment Tools

Diagnostic Assessments

Component	Tests	Where to Learn More
Comprehension	Comprehension Thinking Strategies Assessment Developmental Reading Assessment Informal reading inventories	Chapter 8, Facilitating Children's Comprehension: Reader Factors, p. 223
Concepts About Written Language	Concepts About Print Test	Chapter 2, Examining Children's Literacy Development, p. 48
Fluency	Dynamic Indicators of Basic Early Literacy Skills Fluency Checks Fluency Formula Kits Observation Survey of Early Literacy Achievement Phonological Awareness Literacy Screening Reading Fluency Benchmark Assessor	Chapter 6, Developing Fluent Readers and Writers, p. 162
Oral Language	Assessment of Literacy and Language Teacher Rating of Oral Language and Literacy	Chapter 2, Examining Children's Literacy Development, p. 40
Phonemic Awareness	Dynamic Indicators of Basic Early Literacy Skills Phonological Awareness Literacy Screening Test of Phonological Awareness Yopp-Singer Test of Phonemic Segmentation	Chapter 4, Cracking the Alphabetic Code, p. 105
Phonics	Dynamic Indicators of Basic Early Literacy Skills Observation Survey of Early Literacy Achievement The Tile Test	Chapter 4, Cracking the Alphabetic Code, p. 117
Spelling	Developmental Spelling Analysis Phonological Awareness Literacy Screening Qualitative Spelling Inventory	Chapter 5, Learning to Spell, p. 143
Vocabulary	Expressive Vocabulary Test-2 Informal reading inventories Peabody Picture Vocabulary Test-4	Chapter 7, Building Children's Word Knowledge, p. 195

The miscues that interfere with meaning and those that are syntactically unacceptable are the most serious because the child doesn't realize that reading should make sense. Miscues can be classified and charted; Figure 3–6 shows the analysis of Seth's miscues on the running record in the vignette at the beginning of the chapter. Only words that the child mispronounces or substitutes can be analyzed; repetitions and omissions aren't calculated.

Informal Reading Inventories. Teachers use commercial tests called *informal reading inventories* (IRIs) to evaluate children's reading performance. They can be used in first- through eighth-grade levels, but first-grade teachers often find that IRIs don't provide as much useful information about beginning readers as running records do. These popular reading tests are often used as a screening instrument to determine whether students are reading at grade level, but they're also a valuable diagnostic tool

Go to the Building Teaching Skills and Dispositions section of the Topic *Assessment* in the MyEducationLab for the literacy course and complete the activity entitled *Administering Informal Reading Inventories*. As you work through the learning unit, consider the ways these teachers use data and observations to describe a child's strengths and needs as a reader and writer.

Figure 3–6 ◆ Miscue Analysis

Child _____ Seth _____ Date _____ Jan. 18 _____

Text _____ The Pot of Gold (Level 16) _____

WORDS			MEANING	VISUAL	SYNTAX
Text	Child	Self-corrected?	Similar meaning?	Graphophonic similarity?	Grammatically acceptable?
Grumble	Grumply			✓	
always	–				
didn't	did not		✓	✓	✓
I'll	I		✓	✓	✓
move	make			✓	✓
scarf	safr			✓	
of	or			✓	
my	me	✓		✓	
scarf	self			✓	
taken	take		✓	✓	
scarf	scafer			✓	
that	they	✓		✓	
may	maybe			✓	
still	sit			✓	

Analysis: Seth overrelies on visual cues and rarely self-corrects.

(Nilsson, 2008). Teachers can use IRIs to identify struggling children's instructional needs, particularly in the areas of word identification, oral reading fluency, and comprehension.

These individualized tests consist of two parts: graded word lists and passages ranging from first- to eighth-grade level. The word lists contain 10 to 20 words at each level, and children read the words until they become too difficult; this indicates an approximate level for children to begin reading the passages. Because children who can't read the words on their grade-level list may have a word-identification problem, teachers analyze the words children read incorrectly, looking for error patterns and deciding whether they rely on one cueing system.

The graded reading passages include both narrative and expository texts, presented in order of difficulty. Children read these passages orally or silently and then answer a series of comprehension questions. Three types of questions generally are used: They ask children to recall specific information, draw inferences, or explain the meaning of vocabulary words. When children read the passage orally, teachers assess their fluency. Fourth graders should be able to read the passages fluently; if they can't, they may have a fluency problem. Teachers also examine children's comprehension. If children can't answer the questions after reading the passage at their grade level, they may have a comprehension problem, and teachers check to see if there's a pattern to the types of questions that they miss.

Teachers use scoring sheets to record children's performance data, and they calculate children's independent, instructional, and frustration reading levels. When a child's reading level is below their grade-level placement, teachers also check their listening capacity; that is, their ability to understand passages that are read aloud to them. Knowing whether children can understand and learn from grade-level texts that are read aloud is crucial because that's a common way that teachers support struggling readers.

NURTURING ENGLISH LEARNERS

Teachers assess English learners' developing language proficiency as well as their progress in learning to read and write. It's more challenging to assess ELs than native English speakers, because when children aren't proficient in English, their scores don't accurately reflect what they know (Peregoy & Boyle, 2008). Their cultural and experiential backgrounds also contribute to making it more difficult to assure that assessment tools being used aren't biased.

Oral Language Assessment.   Teachers assess children who speak a language other than English at home to determine their English language proficiency. They typically use commercial oral language tests to determine if children are proficient in English. If they're not, teachers place them in appropriate English language development programs and monitor their progress toward English language proficiency. Two widely used tests are the Language Assessment Scales, published by CTB/McGraw-Hill, and the IDEA Language Proficiency Test, published by Ballard and Tighe; both tests assess children's oral and written language (listening, speaking, reading, and writing) proficiency in English. Individual states have developed language assessments that are aligned with their English language proficiency standards; for example, the New York State English as a Second Language Achievement Test and the California English Language Development Test.

An authentic assessment tool that many teachers use is the Student Oral Language Observation Matrix (SOLOM), developed by the San Jose (CA) Area Bilingual Consortium. It's not a test per se; rather, the SOLOM is a rating scale to assess children's command of English as they observe them talking and listening in real, day-to-day classroom activities. The SOLOM addresses five oral language components:

- **Listening.** Teachers score children along a continuum from unable to comprehend simple statements to understanding everyday conversations.
- **Fluency.** Teachers score children along a continuum from halting, fragmentary speech to fluent speech, approximating that of native speakers.
- **Vocabulary.** Teachers score children along a continuum from extremely limited word knowledge to using words and idioms skillfully.
- **Pronunciation.** Teachers score children along a continuum from virtually unintelligible speech to using pronunciation and intonation proficiently, similar to native speakers.
- **Grammar.** Teachers score children along a continuum from excessive errors that make speech unintelligible to applying word order, grammar, and usage rules effectively.

Each component has a five-point range that's scored 1 to 5; the total possible score on the matrix is 25, and a rating of 20 or higher indicates that children are fluent speakers of English. The SOLOM is available free of charge online at www.cal.org, at other websites, and in many professional books.

Reading Assessment. English learners face two challenges: They're learning to speak English at the same time they're learning to read. They learn to read the same way that native English speakers do, but they face additional challenges because their knowledge of English phonology, semantics, syntax, and pragmatics is limited and their background knowledge is different (Peregoy & Boyle, 2008). Some English learners are fluent readers in their home language (Garcia, 2000); these children already have substantial funds of knowledge about how written language works and about the reading process that they build on as they learn to read in English (Moll, 1994). Having this knowledge gives them a head start, but children also have to learn what transfers to English reading and what doesn't.

Teachers use the same assessments that they use for native English speakers to identify English learners' reading levels, monitor their growth, and document their learning. Peregoy and Boyle (2008) recommend using data from **running records** or informal reading inventories along with classroom-based informal assessments, such as observing and conferencing with children.

Because many English learners have less background knowledge about topics in books they're reading, it's important that teachers assess ELs' background knowledge before instruction so they can modify their teaching to meet children's needs. One of the best ways to accomplish this is with a **K-W-L chart**. As they work with children to complete the first two sections of the chart, teachers learn what children know about a topic and have an opportunity to build additional background knowledge and introduce related vocabulary. Later, when children complete the K-W-L chart, teachers get a clear picture of what they've learned and which vocabulary words they can use.

Another way teachers learn about ELs' development is by asking them to assess themselves as readers (Peregoy & Boyle, 2008). Teachers ask children, for example, what they do when they come to an unfamiliar word, what differences they've noticed between narrative and expository texts, which reading strategies they use, and what types of books they prefer. These quick assessments, commonly done during conferences at the end of a grading period, shed light on children's growth in a way that other assessments can't.

Writing Assessment. English learners' writing develops as their oral language grows and as they become more fluent readers (Riches & Genesee, 2006). For beginning writers, fluency is the first priority. They move from writing strings of familiar words to grouping words into short sentences that often follow a pattern, much like young native English speakers do. As they develop some writing fluency, ELs begin to stick to a single focus, often repeating words and sentences to make their writing longer. Once they become fluent writers, ELs are usually able to organize their ideas more effectively and group them into paragraphs. They incorporate more specific vocabulary and expand the length and variety of sentences. Their mechanical errors become less serious, and their writing is much easier to read. At this point, teachers begin teaching the qualities of good writing and choosing writing strategies and skills to teach based on the errors that children make.

Peregoy and Boyle (2008) explain that ELs' writing involves fluency, form, and correctness, and that teachers' assessment of children's writing should reflect these components:

- Teachers monitor children's ability to write quickly, easily, and comfortably.
- Teachers assess children's ability to apply writing genres, develop their topics, organize the presentation of ideas, and use sophisticated vocabulary and a variety of sentence structures.
- Teachers check that children control standard English grammar and usage, spell most words correctly, and use capitalization and punctuation conventions appropriately.

Teachers use rubrics to assess ELs' writing, and the rubrics address fluency, form, and correctness as well as the qualities of good writing that teachers have taught. They also conference with children about their writing and provide quick minilessons, as needed. To learn about children as writers, teachers observe them as they write, noticing how they move through the writing process, interact in writing groups, and share their writing from the author's chair. In addition, children document writing development by placing their best writing in portfolios.

Alternative Assessments. Because of the difficulties inherent in assessing English learners, it's important to use varied types of assessment that involve different language and literacy tasks and ways of demonstrating proficiency (Huerta-Macías, 1995). In addition to commercial tests, O'Malley and Pierce (1996) urge teachers to use authentic assessment tools, including oral performances, story retellings, oral interviews, writing samples, illustrations, diagrams, and projects.

Assessment is especially important for children who are learning to speak English at the same time they're learning to read and write in English. Teachers use many of the same assessment tools that they use for their native English speakers, but they also depend on alternative, more authentic assessments because it's difficult to accurately measure these children's growth. Assessment results must be valid because teachers use them to make placement decisions, modify instruction, and document learning.

Documenting Children's Learning

Teachers routinely collect children's work samples, including cassette tapes of them reading aloud, lists of books they've read, reading logs, writing samples with rubrics, and photos of projects. They also keep children's test results and the anecdotal notes they make as they observe children and meet with them in conferences. Teachers use these data to document children's progress toward meeting grade-level standards as well as to evaluate their own teaching effectiveness. Children also collect their best work in portfolios to document their own learning and accomplishments.

PORTFOLIO ASSESSMENT

Portfolios are systematic and meaningful collections of artifacts documenting children's literacy development over a period of time (Hebert, 2001). These collections are dynamic, reflecting day-to-day reading and writing activities as well as content-area activities. Children's work samples provide "windows" on the strategies they use as readers and writers. Not only do children select pieces to be placed in their portfolios, they also learn to establish criteria for their selections. Because of children's involvement in selecting pieces for their portfolios and reflecting on them, portfolio assessment respects children and their abilities. Portfolios help children, teachers, and parents see patterns of growth from one literacy milestone to another in ways that aren't possible with other types of assessment.

Collecting Work in Portfolios

Portfolios are folders, large envelopes, or boxes that hold children's work. Teachers often have children label and decorate large folders and then store them in plastic crates or cardboard boxes. Children date and label items as they place them in their portfolios, and they often attach notes to the items to explain the context for the activity and why they selected a particular item. Children's portfolios should be stored in the classroom in a place where they are readily accessible; children like to review their portfolios periodically and add new pieces to them.

Children usually choose the items to place in their portfolios within the guidelines the teacher provides. Some children submit the original piece of work; others want to keep the original, so they place a copy in the portfolio instead. In addition to the reading and writing samples that go directly into portfolios, children can record oral language and drama samples on audiotapes and videotapes to place in their portfolios. Large-size art and writing projects can be photographed, and the photographs can be placed in the portfolio. Child work might include books, story retellings on audiotapes, reading logs and learning logs, graphic organizers, open-mind portraits of characters, multigenre projects, lists of books read, and compositions. This variety of work samples reflects the children's literacy programs.

Many teachers collect children's work in folders, and they assume that portfolios are basically the same as work folders; however, the two types of collections differ in several important ways. Perhaps the most important difference is that portfolios are child oriented, but work folders are usually teachers' collections—children choose which samples will be placed in portfolios, but teachers often place all completed assignments in work folders. Next, portfolios focus on children's strengths, not their weaknesses. Because children select items for portfolios, they choose samples that best represent their literacy development. Another difference is that portfolios involve reflection (D'Aoust, 1992); through reflection, children pause and become aware of their strengths as readers and writers. They also use their work samples to identify the literacy procedures, strategies, and skills they already know and the ones they need to focus on.

Involving Children in Self-Assessment

Portfolios are a tool for engaging children in self-assessment and goal setting. Children learn to reflect on and assess their own reading and writing activities and their development as readers and writers (Stires, 1991). Teachers begin by asking children to do think-alouds about their reading and writing in terms of contrasts. For reading, children identify the books they've read that they liked most and least, and they ask themselves what these choices suggest about themselves as readers. They also identify what they do well in reading and what they need to improve. In writing, children make similar contrasts: They identify their best compositions and others that weren't as good, and they think about what they do well when they write and what to improve. By making these comparisons, children begin to reflect on their literacy development.

Teachers use minilessons and conferences to teach about the characteristics of good readers and writers. In particular, they discuss these topics:

- What fluent reading is
- Which reading strategies and skills children use
- How children demonstrate their comprehension
- What makes a good project to apply reading knowledge
- What makes an effective piece of writing
- Which writing strategies are most effective
- How to use writing rubrics
- How correcting mechanical errors is a courtesy to readers

As children learn about what it means to be effective readers and writers, they acquire the tools they need to reflect on and evaluate their own reading and writing. They learn how to think about themselves as readers and writers and acquire the vocabulary to use in their reflections, such as *goal*, *strategy*, and *rubric*.

Children write notes on items they put into their portfolios. In these self-assessments, children explain the reasons for their choices and identify strengths and accomplishments in their work. In some classrooms, children write their reflections and other comments on index cards, and in others, they design special comment sheets that they attach to the items in their portfolios.

Teachers usually collect baseline reading and writing samples at the beginning of the school year and then conduct portfolio review conferences with children at the end of each grading period. At these conferences, the teacher and the child talk about the items being placed in the portfolio and the child's self-assessments. Children also talk about what they want to improve or what they want to accomplish during the next grading period.

Showcasing Children's Portfolios

At the end of the school year, many teachers organize "Portfolio Share Days" to celebrate children's accomplishments and to provide an opportunity for them to share their portfolios with classmates and the wider community. Family members, local businesspeople, school administrators, college students, and others are invited to attend. Children and visitors form small groups, and children share their portfolios, pointing out their accomplishments and strengths. This activity is especially useful for involving community members in the school and showing them how children are becoming effective readers and writers.

These sharing days also help children accept responsibility for their own learning—especially those who haven't been as motivated as their classmates. When less motivated children listen to their classmates talk about their work and how they've grown as readers and writers, they often decide to work harder the next year.

HIGH-STAKES TESTING

Annual high-stakes testing is emphasized in American schools with the goal of improving the quality of reading instruction. These tests are designed to objectively measure children's knowledge according to grade-level standards. The current emphasis on testing and state-level standards are reform efforts that began in response to The National Commission on Excellence in Education report *A Nation at Risk* (1983), which argued that American schools were failing miserably. The report stated that American students' test scores were dropping, comparing unfavorably with students' scores in other industrialized countries, and it concluded that the United States was in jeopardy of losing its global superiority. The No Child Left Behind Act, which promoted an increased focus on reading instruction to improve children's reading performance and narrow the racial and ethnic gaps in achievement, reinforced the call for annual standardized testing.

Researchers have repeatedly refuted these arguments (Bracey, 2004; McQuillan, 1998). Allington (2006) explained that average test scores have remained stable for 30 years despite the dramatic increases in federal funding over the past decade. He goes on to explain that reporting average scores obscures important findings because it's necessary to examine subgroup data to discover that most children from middle-class families read well even though many children from low-income families lag behind. He also notes that while significant progress has been made in closing the achievement gap between white and minority children, the number of minority children has grown tremendously. Finally, he points out that grade-level standards of achievement have increased in the last 50 years so that what was considered third-grade level is now second-grade level, and older readability formulas have been renormed to reflect today's higher grade-level standards. Nonetheless, the public's perception that schools are failing persists.

High-stakes testing is different than classroom assessment. The test scores typically provide little information for making day-to-day instructional decisions, but children, teachers, administrators, and schools are judged and held accountable by the results. The scores are used to make important educational decisions—to determine school placement, for example. These scores influence administrators' evaluations of teachers' effectiveness and even their salaries in some states, and they reward or sanction administrators, schools, and school districts.

Standardized tests are comprehensive, with batteries of subtests covering decoding, vocabulary, comprehension, writing mechanics, and spelling. Most tests use multiple-choice test items, although a few are introducing open-ended questions that require children to write responses. Beginning in second grade, classroom teachers administer the tests to their students, typically in the spring. Most require multiple testing periods to administer all of the subtests.

Problems with High-Stakes Testing

A number of problems are associated with high-stakes testing (IRA, 1999). Children feel the pressure of these tests, and researchers have confirmed what many teachers have noticed: Children don't try harder because of them (Hoffman, Assaf, & Paris, 2005). Teachers complain that they feel compelled to improve children's test scores at any price, and that they lose valuable instructional time for test-taking and practice sessions (Hollingworth, 2007). Overemphasizing the test often leads teachers to abandon the balanced approach to instruction: Sometimes children spend more time completing practice tests than reading books and writing compositions. One of the most insidious side effects is that teachers are often directed to focus on certain groups of children, especially those scoring just below a cutoff point, in hopes of improving test scores.

Preparing for Standardized Tests

Standardized tests are a unique text genre, and they require readers and writers to do different things than they would normally, so teachers can't assume that children already know how to take reading tests. It's essential that teachers prepare children to take high-stakes tests without abandoning a balanced approach to instruction that's aligned to state standards. Greene and Melton (2007) agree; they maintain that teachers must prepare children for high-stakes tests without sacrificing their instructional program. Unfortunately, with the pressure to raise test scores, some teachers are having children take more multiple-choice tests while creating fewer projects.

Hollingworth (2007) recommends these five ways to prepare for high-stakes tests without sacrificing the instructional program:

- Teachers check that their state's curriculum standards align with their instructional program and make any needed adjustments to ensure that they're teaching what's going to be on the test.
- Teachers set goals with children and use informal assessments to regularly monitor their progress.
- Teachers actively engage children in authentic literacy activities so they become capable readers and writers.
- Teachers explain the purpose of the tests and how the results will be used, without making children anxious.
- Teachers stick with a balanced approach that combines explicit instruction and authentic application.

Other researchers advise that in addition to these recommendations, teachers prepare children to take standardized tests by teaching them how to read and answer test items and having them take practice tests to hone their test-taking strategies (McCabe, 2003). Preparing for tests involves explaining their purpose, examining the genre and format of multiple-choice tests, teaching the formal language of tests and test-taking strategies, and providing opportunities for children to take practice tests; but these lessons should be folded into the existing instructional program, not replace it. Greene and Melton (2007) organized test preparation into minilessons that they taught as part of reading workshop.

The Genre of Standardized Tests. Children need opportunities to examine old test forms to learn about the genre of standardized tests and how test questions are formatted. They'll notice that tests look different than other texts they've read; they're typically printed in black and white, the text is dense, and few illustrations are included. Sometimes words, phrases, and lines in the text are numbered, bolded, or underlined. Through this exploration, children begin to think about what makes one type of text harder to read than others, and with practice, they get used to how tests are formatted so that they're better able to read them.

The Language of Testing. Standardized reading tests use formal language that's unfamiliar to many children. For example, some tests use the word *passage* instead of *text* and *author's intent* instead of *big idea*. Test makers also use *locate, except, inform, in order to, provide suspense*, and other words that children may not understand. Greene and Melton (2007) call the language of testing "test talk" and explain that "students are helpless on standardized reading tests if they can't decipher test talk" (p. 8). Children need help understanding test talk so that high-stakes tests really measure what they know.

Test-Taking Strategies. Children vary the test-taking strategies they use according to the type of test they're taking. Most standardized tests employ multiple-choice questions. Here's a list of test-taking strategies that children learn to use when answering multiple-choice questions:

Read the entire question first. Children read the entire question first to make sure they understand what it's asking. For questions about a reading passage, children read the questions first to guide their reading.

Look for key words in the question. Children identify key words in the question, such as *compare, except*, and *author's intent*, that will guide them to choose the correct answer.

Read all answer choices before choosing the correct one. After children read the question, they stop and think about the answer before reading all the possible answers. Then they eliminate the unlikely answer choices and identify the correct answer.

Answer easier questions first. Children answer the questions they know, skipping the difficult ones, and then they go back and answer the questions they skipped.

Make smart guesses. When children don't know the answer to a question, they make a smart guess, unless there's a penalty for guessing. To make a smart guess, they eliminate the answer choices they're sure are wrong, think about what they know about the topic, and then pick the best remaining answer also choice. The correct answer also is often the longest one.

Stick with your first answer. Children shouldn't second-guess themselves; their first answer is probably right. They shouldn't change an answer unless they're certain that their first answer was wrong.

Be Strategic!

Test-Taking Strategies

Children use these test-taking strategies to answer multiple-choice questions on standardized tests:

- ▶ Read the entire question first
- ▶ Look for key words in the question
- ▶ Read all answer choices before choosing the correct one
- ▶ Answer easier questions first
- ▶ Make smart guesses
- ▶ Stick with your first answer
- ▶ Pace yourself
- ▶ Check your work carefully

Children learn to use these strategies through test-prep lessons and practice tests.

Pace yourself. Children budget their time wisely so they'll be able to finish the test. They don't spend too much time on any one question.

Check your work carefully. Children check that they've answered every question, if they finish early.

Children use these test-taking strategies along with reading strategies, including determining importance, questioning, and rereading, when they're taking standardized tests.

Test preparation should be embedded in literacy activities and not take up a great deal of instructional time. Teachers often teach test-taking strategies through minilessons where they explain the strategy, model its use, and provide opportunities for guided practice and discussion. Greene and Melton (2007) recommend teaching minilessons on test-taking strategies as well as the genre of tests, test formats, and the language of tests as part of reading workshop. They reported that their students, many of whom are English learners, became more confident and empowered test-takers through test-preparation minilessons, and their test scores improved.

Practice Tests. Teachers design practice tests with the same types of items found on the standardized tests children will take. They use easy-to read materials for practice tests so children can focus on practicing test-taking strategies without being challenged by the difficulty level of the text or the questions. They include a combination of unrelated narrative, poetic, and expository passages on the tests because all three types of texts appear on high-stakes tests. Teachers also provide answer sheets similar to those used on the standardized test so that children gain experience using them. So that children will be familiar with the testing conditions, teachers simulate them in the classroom or take children to where the test will be administered for practice sessions. Through these practice tests, children develop both confidence in their test-taking abilities and the stamina to persist through long tests.

Preparation for reading tests is especially important because when children aren't familiar with multiple-choice tests, they'll score lower than they otherwise would. Don't confuse test preparation with teaching to the test: Preparing for a test involves teaching children how to take a test, whereas teaching to the test is the unethical practice of drilling children on actual questions from old tests. The term "teaching to the test" is also used in a less pejorative way to describe when teachers tailor instruction to meet state-mandated standards.

The Politics of High-Stakes Testing

The debate over high-stakes testing is a politically charged issue (Casbarro, 2005). Test scores are being used as a means to reform schools, and although improving the quality of instruction and ensuring that all students have equal access to educational opportunities are essential, there are unwanted consequences for both children and teachers. Proponents claim that schools are being reformed; but, although some gains in test scores for minority groups have been reported, many teachers feel that the improvement is the result of "teaching to the test." So far, no results indicate that children have actually become better readers and writers because of standardized achievement tests.

CHAPTER Review

How Effective Teachers Assess Children's Literacy Development

▶ Teachers determine children's independent, instructional, and frustration reading levels.

▶ Teachers informally monitor children's progress in reading and writing.

▶ Teachers use diagnostic assessments to identify children's strengths and weaknesses and then provide instruction to address problem areas.

▶ Teachers have children document their learning in portfolios.

▶ Teachers prepare children for high-stakes tests without sacrificing their instructional programs.

Chapter 4

Cracking the Alphabetic Code

Mrs. Firpo Teaches Phonics

It's 8:10 on Thursday morning, and the 19 first graders in Mrs. Firpo's classroom are gathered on the carpet for their phonics lesson that the teacher calls "word work." This week's topic is the long *i* and long *e* sounds for *y*: For example, in *my* and *multiply*, the *y* is pronounced as long *i*, and in *baby* and *sunny*, the *y* is pronounced as long *e*. She shows pictures representing words that end with *y*: *fly*, *baby*, *jelly*, *bunny*, and *sky*. The children identify each object and say its name slowly to isolate the final sound. Saleena goes first. She picks up the picture of a fly and says, "It's a fly: /f/ /l/ /ī/. It ends with the ī sound." Vincent is confused when it's his turn to identify the long *e* sound at the end of *bunny*, so Mrs. Firpo demonstrates how to segment the sounds in the word: /b/ /ŭ/ /n/ /ē/. Then Vincent recognizes the long *e* sound at the end. Next, the first graders sort the picture cards according to the final sound and place them in two columns in a nearby pocket chart. They add labels to the columns: *y* = ī and *y* = ē.

Mrs. Firpo begins her phonics lessons with an oral activity because she knows it's important to integrate phonemic awareness with phonics. In the oral activities, children focus on orally segmenting and blending the sounds they hear in words—without worrying about phoneme–grapheme correspondences. Next, she introduces a set of cards with words ending in *y* for the children to read and classify. They take turns using phonics to sound out these words: *funny, my, try, happy, why, fussy, very, sticky, shy,* and *cry.* They add the word cards to the columns on the pocket chart. Then the teacher asks the children to suggest other words that end in *y;* Fernando names *yucky,* Crystal says *crunchy,* and Joel adds *dry.* Mrs. Firpo writes these words on small cards, too, and adds them to the pocket chart. Then Austin uses the pointer to point to each card in the pocket chart for the class to read aloud.

At the end of this 15-minute lesson, the children return to their desks and get out their whiteboards for spelling practice. This week's spelling words end in *y* pronounced as long *i.* Mrs. Firpo calls out each word, and the children practice writing it three times on their small whiteboards. If they need help spelling the word, they check the list of spelling words on the Focus Wall. As they write, Mrs. Firpo circulates around the classroom, modeling how to form letters, reminding Jordan and Kendra to leave a "two-finger" space between words, and checking that their spellings are correct.

Mrs. Firpo's Focus Wall is shown on page 94. Each week, Mrs. Firpo posts the strategies and skills she'll be teaching, and the vocabulary words and spelling words are listed there, too. The vocabulary words are written on cards and displayed in a pocket chart attached to the Focus Wall so that they can be rearranged and used for various activities. Mrs. Firpo uses *Houghton Mifflin Reading* (Cooper & Pikulski, 2003), a basal reading textbook series; each week's topics are identified for her in the teacher's edition. The reason why she posts these topics is to emphasize what she's teaching and what children are learning. In addition, Mrs. Firpo has her state's reading and writing standards for first grade listed on a chart next to the wall.

Next, Mrs. Firpo guides children as they complete several pages in the workbook that accompanies the basal reader. Some pages reinforce phonics and spelling concepts, and others focus on comprehension, vocabulary, grammar, and writing. Today, they begin on page 201. First the children examine the illustration at the top of the page, and then they write two sentences about the silly things they see in the picture on the lines at the bottom of the page. They talk about the illustration, identifying the silly things they see. Felicia says, "I see a bunny reading a book, and I think that's silly." Mrs. Firpo gives Felicia a "thumbs up" to compliment her. And Fernando comments, "I see something else. It's a bear up in a balloon." "Is the balloon up in the sky?" Mrs. Firpo asks because she wants to emphasize the phonics pattern of the week. Fernando agrees that it is, and he repeats, "I see a bear up in a balloon in the sky." He, too, gets a "thumbs up."

After children identify five or six silly things, they get ready to write. Mrs. Firpo reminds them to begin their sentences with capital letters and end them with periods. As they write their sentences, Alicia notices that she has written *bunny*—a word that ends in *y* and has an ē sound. Mrs. Firpo congratulates her and encourages others to point out when they write words that end in *y.* Joel waves his hand in the air, eager to report that he's written *sky*—a word that ends in *y* and has an ī sound.

Mrs. Firpo's Focus Wall

| Theme 9: Special Friends | Week: 1 | Reading Level: 1.5 |

PHONICS FOCUS: Long i and long e sounds for y

WORD PATTERN: -ay

| say | day | way | bay | stay | gray |
| pay | may | lay | ray | pray | spray |

SPELLING CONCEPT: Long i sound at the end of a word spelled with y

COMPREHENSION STRATEGY: Monitoring

COMPREHENSION SKILL: Noting Details

GRAMMAR CONCEPT: is/are

WRITING GENRE: Friendly Letters

VOCABULARY WORDS

ocean	though	by
dance	talk	my
open	else	cry
ever	around	any
	Grandaddy	

SPELLING WORDS

1. by
2. my
3. fly
4. try
5. cry
6. why
7. pry
8. multiply

Then the children move on to page 202. On this page, there's a word bank with words that end in *y* and represent the ī sound at the top and sentences with blanks at the bottom. The children practice reading the words in the word bank. After reading the words several times, Vincent volunteers, "I get it! Look at these words: They all have *y* and they say ī." Mrs. Firpo is pleased and gives him a "thumbs up." Next, the teacher reads aloud the sentences at the bottom of the page and asks children to supply the missing words. Then they work independently to reread the sentences and fill in the missing words. Mrs. Firpo moves from one group of desks to the next as the children work, monitoring their work and providing assistance as needed.

Each week, the children receive take-home books that Mrs. Firpo has duplicated and stapled together; these books reinforce the week's phonics lesson and the vocabulary introduced in the reading textbook. The first graders read the books at school and use them for a phonics activity; then they take them home to practice reading. Today's book is *I Spy*: It's eight pages long, with illustrations and text on each page. Mrs. Firpo introduces the book and reads it aloud while the children follow along in their copies. They keep their books at their desks to use for a seatwork activity, and later they put the books in book bags that they take home each day. Already they've collected more than 75 books!

During the last 40 minutes of the reading period, Mrs. Firpo conducts guided reading lessons. Her students' reading levels range from beginning first grade to the middle of second grade, with about half of them reading at grade level. She has grouped the first graders into four guided reading groups, and she meets with two groups each day. Children reading below grade level read leveled books, and those reading at and above grade level read easy-to-read chapter books, including Barbara Park's series of funny stories about a girl named Junie B. Jones (e.g., *Junie B., First Grader: Boss of Lunch* [2003]) and Mary Pope Osborne's Magic Tree House series of adventure stories (e.g., *High Tide in Hawaii* [2003]). Mrs. Firpo calls this period *differentiated instruction* because children participate in a variety of activities, based on their achievement levels.

While Mrs. Firpo does guided reading with one group, the others participate in seatwork and center activities. For the seatwork activity, children read their take-home book and highlight all the words ending in *y* pronounced as ī; they don't highlight *bunny*, *play*, and other words where the *y* isn't pronounced as ī. They also work in small groups to cut out pictures and words that end in *y*, sort them into *y = ē*, *y = ī*, and *y = other* categories, and paste them on a sheet of paper. The pictures and words for the activity include *puppy, city, they, buy, pretty, play, funny, dry, party, fifty, boy, sky, fly, today,* and *yummy*.

The first graders practice their spelling words using magnetic letters at the spelling center, practice the phonics focus and word pattern using letter cards and flip books at the phonics center, make books at the writing center, listen to the take-home books read aloud at the listening center, and read electronic books interactively at the computer center. The centers are arranged around the perimeter of the classroom; children know how to work at centers and understand what they're expected to do at each one.

After a 15-minute recess, children spend the last 55 minutes of literacy instruction in writing workshop. Each week, the class focuses on the genre specified in the basal reading program; this week's focus is on personal letters. First, Mrs. Firpo teaches a minilesson and guides children as they complete more pages in their workbooks. Today, she reviews how to use commas in a friendly letter. The children examine several letters hanging in the classroom that the class wrote earlier in the school year using interactive writing. After the class rereads each letter, Mrs. Firpo asks the children to highlight the commas used in the letters. Crystal points out that commas are used in the date, Saleena notices that a comma is used at the end of the greeting, and Luis marks the comma used after the closing. Next, children practice adding commas in the sample friendly letters on page 208 in their workbooks.

Then children spend the remaining 35 minutes of writing workshop working on the letters they're writing to their families. Mrs. Firpo works with five children on their letters while the others work independently. At the end of the writing time, Joel

---

Angelica's Letter to Her Grandmother

April 29, 2008

Dear Nanna Isabel,
I am writting you a letter. My birthday is in 35 days! Did you no that? I wud like to get a present. I want you to come to my party. It will be very funny.
Love,
Angelica

and Angelica sit in the author's chair to read their letters aloud to their classmates. Angelica's letter to her grandmother is shown on page 95.

Mrs. Firpo's students spend 3½ hours each morning involved in literacy instruction. Most of the goals, activities, and instructional materials come from the basal reading program, but Mrs. Firpo adapts some activities to meet the first graders' varied instructional needs.

English is an alphabetic language, and children crack this code as they learn about phonemes (sounds), graphemes (letters), and graphophonemic (letter–sound) relationships. They learn about phonemes as they notice rhyming words, segment words into syllables and individual sounds, and invent silly words by playing with sounds, much like Dr. Seuss did. They learn about letters as they sing the ABC song, name the letters of the alphabet, and spell their own names. They learn graphophonemic relationships as they match letters and letter combinations to sounds, blend sounds to form words, and decode and spell vowel patterns. By third grade, most children have figured out the alphabetic code, and older students apply what they've learned to decode and spell multisyllabic words. You may think of all of this as phonics, but children actually develop three separate but related abilities about the alphabetic code:

◆ **Phonemic Awareness.** Children learn to notice and manipulate the sounds of oral language. Those who are phonemically aware understand that spoken words are made up of sounds, and they can segment and blend sounds in spoken words.
◆ **Phonics.** Children learn to convert letters into sounds and blend them to recognize words. Those who can apply phonics concepts understand that there are predictable sound–symbol correspondences in English, and they can use decoding strategies to figure out unfamiliar written words.
◆ **Spelling.** Children learn to segment spoken words into sounds and convert the sounds into letters to spell words. Those who have learned to spell conventionally understand English sound–symbol correspondences and spelling patterns, and they can use spelling strategies to spell unfamiliar words.

In the vignette, Mrs. Firpo incorporated all three components into her literacy program. She began the word work lesson on the long *e* and long *i* sounds of *y* with an oral phonemic awareness activity; next, she moved to a phonics activity where children read words that ended in *y* and categorized them on a pocket chart. Later, they practiced spelling words that ended with *y* on whiteboards. Teaching these graphophonemic relationships isn't a complete reading program, but phonemic awareness, phonics, and spelling are integral to effective literacy instruction, especially for children in kindergarten through third grade (National Reading Panel, 2000).

PHONEMIC AWARENESS

Phonemic awareness is children's basic understanding that speech is composed of a series of individual sounds, and it provides the foundation for phonics and spelling (Armbruster, Lehr, & Osborn, 2001). When children can choose a duck as the animal whose name begins with /d/ from a collection of toy animals, identify *duck* and *luck* as rhyming words in a song, or blend the sounds /d/ /ŭ/ /k/ to pronounce *duck*, they are

DEVELOPMENTAL CONTINUUM Phonemic Awareness

PreK	K	1	2	3	4
Four-year-olds become aware of words as units of sound as they play with sounds and create rhymes.	Children pronounce sounds and isolate, match, and manipulate them as they learn to blend and segment.	Children use the blending strategy to decode words and the segmenting strategy to spell words.	Second graders continue to use blending and segmenting to decode and spell more challenging words.	Children apply phonemic awareness strategies to decode and spell two- and three-syllable words.	Fourth graders blend and segment sounds as they read and spell multisyllabic words with root words and affixes.

phonemically aware. Cunningham and Allington (2007) describe phonemic awareness as children's ability to "take words apart, put them back together again, and change them" (p. 37). The emphasis is on the sounds of spoken words, not on reading letters or pronouncing letter names. Developing phonemic awareness enables children to use sound–symbol correspondences to read and spell words (Gillon, 2004).

Phonemes are the smallest units of speech, and they're written as graphemes, or letters of the alphabet. In this book, phonemes are marked using diagonal lines (e.g., /d/) and graphemes are italicized (e.g., *d*). Sometimes phonemes (e.g., /k/ in *duck*) are spelled with two graphemes (*ck*).

Understanding that words are composed of smaller units—phonemes—is a significant achievement for young children because phonemes are abstract language units. Phonemes carry no meaning, and children think of words according to their meanings, not their linguistic characteristics (Griffith & Olson, 1992). When children think about ducks, for example, they think of feathered animals that swim in ponds, fly through the air, and make noises we describe as "quacks"; they don't think of "duck" as a word with three phonemes or four graphemes, or as a word beginning with /d/ and rhyming with *luck*. Phonemic awareness requires that children treat speech as an object, to shift their attention away from the meaning of words to examine the linguistic features of speech. This focus on phonemes is even more complicated because phonemes aren't discrete units in speech: Often they're slurred or clipped in speech—think about the blended initial sound in *tree* and the last sound in *eating*.

Phonemic Awareness Strategies

Children become phonemically aware by manipulating spoken language in these ways:

Identifying Sounds. Children identify a word that begins or ends with a particular sound. For example, when shown a brush, a car, and a doll, they identify *doll* as the word that ends with /l/.

Categorizing Sounds in Words. Children recognize the "odd" word in a set of three words; for example, when the teacher says *ring, rabbit,* and *sun,* they recognize that *sun* doesn't belong.

Be Strategic!

Phonemic Awareness Strategies

As children manipulate sounds orally, they learn to use these two strategies:

▸ Blend
▸ Segment

Children apply these oral strategies to written language for decoding and spelling words.

Substituting Sounds. Children remove a sound from a word and substitute a different sound. Sometimes they substitute the beginning sound, changing *bar* to *car*, for example. Or, they change the middle sound, making *tip* from *top*, or substitute the ending sound, changing *gate* to *game*.

Blending Sounds. Children blend two, three, or four individual sounds to form a word; the teacher says /b/ /ĭ/ /g/, for example, and the children repeat the sounds, blending them to form the word *big*.

Segmenting Sounds. Children break a word into its beginning, middle, and ending sounds. For example, children segment the word *feet* into /f/ /ē/ /t/ and *go* into /g/ /ō/.

Children use these strategies, especially blending and segmenting, to decode and spell words. When they use phonics to sound out a word, for example, they say the sounds represented by each letter and blend them to read the word. Similarly, to spell a word, children say the word slowly, segmenting the sounds.

Teaching Phonemic Awareness

Teachers nurture children's phonemic awareness through the language-rich environments they create in the classroom. As they sing songs, chant rhymes, read aloud wordplay books, and play games, children have many opportunities to orally match, isolate, blend, and substitute sounds and to segment words into sounds (Griffith & Olson, 1992). Teachers often incorporate phonemic awareness into other oral language and literacy activities, but it's also important to teach lessons that focus specifically on the phonemic awareness strategies.

Phonemic awareness instruction should meet three criteria. First, the activities should be appropriate for 4-, 5-, and 6-year-old children. Activities involving songs, nursery rhymes, riddles, and wordplay books are good choices because they encourage children's playful experimentation with oral language. Second, the instruction should be planned and purposeful, not just incidental: Teachers choose instructional materials and plan activities that focus children's attention on the sound structure of oral language. Third, phonemic awareness activities should be integrated with other components of a balanced literacy program. It's crucial that children perceive the connection between oral and written language (Yopp & Yopp, 2000).

Many wordplay books are available for young children. A list of books is presented in Figure 4–1. Books such as *Cock-a-Doodle-Moo!* (Most, 1996) and *Rattletrap Car* (Root, 2004) stimulate children to experiment with sounds and to create nonsense words. Teachers often read wordplay books more than once. During the first reading, children focus on comprehension and what interests them in the book. During a second reading, however, children's attention shifts to the wordplay elements, and teachers ask questions about the way the author manipulated words and sounds. For example, they ask, "Did you notice that _____ and _____ rhyme?" They encourage children to make similar comments, too.

Teachers often incorporate wordplay books, songs, and games into the minilessons they teach. The feature on page 100 presents a kindergarten teacher's minilesson on blending sounds. The teacher reread Dr. Seuss's *Fox in Socks* (1965) and then asked children to identify words from the book that she pronounced sound by sound. This book

Check the Compendium of Instructional Procedures, which follows Chapter 12, for more information on highlighted terms.

is rich in wordplay: rhyming (e.g., *do, you, goo, chew*), initial consonant substitution (e.g., *trick, quick, slick*), vowel substitution (e.g., *blabber, blibber, blubber*), and alliteration (e.g., *Luke Luck likes lakes*).

Sound-Matching Activities.   Children choose one of several words beginning with a particular sound or say a word that begins with a particular sound (Yopp, 1992). For these games, teachers use familiar objects (e.g., feather, toothbrush, book) and toys (e.g., small plastic animals, toy trucks, artificial fruits and vegetables), as well as pictures of familiar objects.

Teachers can play a sound-matching guessing game (Lewkowicz, 1994). For this game, teachers collect two boxes and pairs of objects to place in them (e.g., forks, mittens, erasers, combs, and books); one item from each pair is placed in each box. After the teacher shows children the objects in the boxes and they name them together, two children play the game. One child selects an object, holds it up, and pronounces the initial (or medial or final) sound. The second child chooses the same object from the second box and holds it up. Classmates check to see if the two players are holding the same object.

Children also identify rhyming words as part of sound-matching activities: They name a word that rhymes with a given word and identify rhyming words from familiar songs and stories. As children listen to parents and teachers read Dr. Seuss books, such as *Fox in Socks* (1965) and *Hop on Pop* (1963), and other wordplay books, they refine their understanding of rhyme.

Figure 4-1 ◆ Wordplay Books to Develop Phonemic Awareness

Crebbin, J. (1998). *Cows in the kitchen.* Cambridge, MA: Candlewick Press.

Degan, B. (1995). *Jamberry.* New York: HarperCollins.

Deming, A. G. (1994). *Who is tapping at my window?* New York: Penguin.

Downey, L. (2000). *The flea's sneeze.* New York: Henry Holt.

Ehlert, L. (1993). *Eating the alphabet: Fruits and vegetables from A to Z.* San Diego: Voyager.

Gollub, M. (2000). *The jazz fly.* Santa Rosa, CA: Tortuga Press.

Hillenbrand, W. (2002). *Fiddle-I-fee.* San Diego: Gulliver Books.

Hoberman, M. A. (1998). *Miss Mary Mack.* Boston: Little, Brown.

Hoberman, M. A. (2003). *The lady with the alligator purse.* Boston: Little, Brown.

Hoberman, M. A. (2004). *The eensy-weensy spider.* Boston: Little, Brown.

Hutchins, P. (2002). *Don't forget the bacon!* New York: Red Fox Books.

Martin, B., Jr., & Archambault, J. (2000). *Chicka chicka boom boom.* New York: Aladdin Books.

Most, B. (1991). *A dinosaur named after me.* San Diego: Harcourt Brace.

Most, B. (1996). *Cock-a-doodle-moo!* San Diego: Harcourt Brace.

Most, B. (2003). *The cow that went oink.* San Diego: Voyager.

Prelutsky, J. (1989). *The baby uggs are hatching.* New York: Mulberry Books.

Raffi. (1988). *Down by the bay.* New York: Crown.

Raffi. (1990). *The wheels on the bus.* New York: Crown.

Root, P. (2003). *One duck stuck.* Cambridge, MA: Candlewick Press.

Seuss, Dr. (1963). *Hop on pop.* New York: Random House.

Shaw, N. (2006). *Sheep in a jeep.* Boston: Houghton Mifflin.

Slate, J. (1996). *Miss Bindergarten gets ready for kindergarten.* New York: Dutton.

Slepian, J., & Seidler, A. (2001). *The hungry thing.* New York: Scholastic.

Taback, S. (1997). *There was an old lady who swallowed a fly.* New York: Viking.

Taback, S. (2004). *This is the house that Jack built.* New York: Puffin Books.

Westcott, N. B. (2003). *I know an old lady who swallowed a fly.* Boston: Little, Brown.

Wilson, K. (2003). *A frog in a bag.* New York: McElderry.

TOPIC: Blending Sounds Into Words
GRADE: Kindergarten
TIME: One 20-minute period

Ms. Lewis regularly includes a 20-minute lesson on phonemic awareness in her literacy block. She usually rereads a familiar wordplay book and plays a phonemic awareness game with the kindergartners that emphasizes one of the phonemic awareness strategies.

1 Introduce the Topic

Ms. Lewis brings her 19 kindergartners together on the rug and explains that she's going to reread Dr. Seuss's *Fox in Socks* (1965). It's one of their favorite books, and they clap their pleasure. She explains that afterward, they're going to play a word game.

2 Share Examples

Ms. Lewis reads aloud *Fox in Socks*, showing the pictures on each page as she reads. She encourages the children to read along. Sometimes she stops and invites the children to fill in the last rhyming word in a sentence or to echo read (repeating after her like an echo) the alliterative sentences. After they finish reading, she asks what they like best about the book. Pearl replies, "It's just a really funny book. That's why it's so good." "What makes it funny?" Ms. Lewis asks. Teri explains, "The words are funny. They make my tongue laugh. You know— *fox–socks–box–Knox*. That's funny on my tongue!" "Oh," Ms. Lewis clarifies, "your tongue likes to say rhyming words. I like to say them, too." Other children recall these rhyming words from the book: *clocks–tocks–blocks–box, noodle–poodle,* and *new–do–blue–goo.*

3 Provide Information

"Let me tell you about our game," Ms. Lewis explains. "I'm going to say some of the words from the book, but I'll say them sound by sound, and I want you to blend the sounds together and guess the word." "Are they rhyming words?" Teri asks. "Sure," the teacher agrees. "I'll say two words that rhyme, sound by sound, for you to guess." She says the sounds /f/ /ŏ/ /x/ and /b/ /ŏ/ /x/ and the children correctly blend the sounds and say the words *fox* and *box.* She repeats the procedure for *clock–tock, come–dumb, big–pig, new–blue, rose–hose, game–lame,* and *slow–crow.* Ms. Lewis stops and talks about how to "bump" or blend the sounds to figure out the words. She models how she blends the sounds to form the word. "Make the words harder," several children say, and Ms. Lewis offers several more difficult pairs of rhyming words, including *chick–trick* and *beetle–tweedle.*

4 Guide Practice

Ms. Lewis continues playing the guessing game, but now she segments individual words. As each child correctly identifies a word, that child leaves the group and goes to work with the aide. Finally, six children remain who need additional practice. They continue blending *do, new,* and other two-sound words and some of the easier three-sound words, including *box, come,* and *like.*

5 Assess Learning

Through the guided practice part of the lesson, Ms. Lewis informally checks to see which children need more practice blending sounds into words and provides additional practice for them.

Sound-Isolation Activities.   Teachers say a word and then children identify the sounds at the beginning, middle, or end of the word, or teachers and children isolate sounds as they sing familiar songs. Yopp (1992) created these verses to the tune of "Old MacDonald Had a Farm":

> What's the sound that starts these words:
>   Chicken, chin, and cheek?
>   (wait for response)
>
> /ch/ is the sound that starts these words:
>   Chicken, chin, and cheek.
>   With a /ch/, /ch/ here, and a /ch/, /ch/ there,
>   Here a /ch/, there a /ch/, everywhere a /ch/, /ch/.
>
> /ch/ is the sound that starts these words:
>   Chicken, chin, and cheek. (p. 700)

Teachers change the question at the beginning of the verse to focus on medial and final sounds. For example:

> What's the sound in the middle of these words?
>   Whale, game, and rain. (p. 700)

And for final sounds:

> What's the sound at the end of these words?
>   Leaf, cough, and beef. (p. 700)

Teachers also set out trays of objects and ask children to choose the one that doesn't belong because it begins with a different sound. For example, from a tray with a toy pig, a puppet, a teddy bear, and a pen, the teddy bear doesn't belong.

Sound-Blending Activities.   Children blend sounds to combine them and form a word. For example, children blend the sounds /d/ /ŭ/ /k/ to form the word *duck*. Teachers play the "What am I thinking of?" game with children by identifying several characteristics of the item and then saying its name, articulating each sound slowly and separately (Yopp, 1992). Then children blend the sounds to identify the word, using the phonological and semantic information that the teacher provided. For example:

PreK Practices

How do teachers nurture 4-year-olds' phonemic awareness?

Prekindergarten teachers develop children's attention to the sounds in oral language through these developmentally appropriate activities:

- ▶ Singing songs
- ▶ Reciting nursery rhymes
- ▶ Sharing wordplay books
- ▶ Playing word games

Through these activities, children tune into the sounds of words and develop an understanding of rhyme. They recognize and generate rhyming words, segment words into syllables, isolate beginning or ending sounds in words, substitute sounds to create new words, blend sounds into words, and segment words into sounds.

Acquiring these oral language strategies is crucial according to Strickland and Schickedanz (2009), because children apply them as they learn phonics.

> I'm thinking of a small animal that lives in a pond when it's young. When it's an adult, it lives on land. It's a /f/ /r/ /ŏ/ /g/. What is it?

The children blend the sounds to pronounce the word *frog*. Then the teacher sets out magnetic letters for children to arrange to read and spell the word *frog*. In this example, the teacher connects the game with the thematic unit to make it more meaningful.

Sound-Addition and -Substitution Activities.   Children play with words and create nonsense words as they add or substitute sounds in words in songs they sing or in books that are read aloud to them. Teachers read wordplay books such as Pat Hutchins's *Don't Forget the Bacon!* (1989), in which a boy leaves for the store with a mental list of four items to buy. As he walks, he repeats his list, substituting words each time: "A cake for tea" changes to "a cape for me" and then to "a rake for leaves." Children suggest other substitutions, such as "a game for a bee."

Students substitute sounds in refrains of songs (Yopp, 1992). For example, they can change the "Ee-igh, ee-igh, oh!" refrain in "Old MacDonald Had a Farm" to "Bee-bigh, bee-bigh, boh!" to focus on the initial /b/ sound. Teachers can choose one sound, such as /sh/, and have children substitute it for the beginning sound in their names and in words for objects in the classroom. For example, *Jimmy* becomes *Shimmy*, *José* becomes *Shosé*, and *clock* becomes *shock*.

Sound-Segmentation Activities.   One of the more difficult phonemic awareness activities is segmentation, in which children isolate the sounds in a spoken word (Yopp, 1988). An introductory segmentation activity is to draw out the beginning sound in words. Children enjoy exaggerating the initial sound in their own names and other familiar words. For example, a pet guinea pig named Popsicle lives in Mrs. Firpo's classroom, and the children exaggerate the beginning sound of her name so that it's pronounced as "P-P-P-Popsicle." Children can also pick up objects or pictures of objects and identify the initial sound; a child who picks up a toy truck says, "This is a truck and it starts with /t/."

From that beginning, children move to identifying all the sounds in a word. Using a toy truck again, the child would say, "This is a truck, /t/ /r/ /ŭ/ /k/." Yopp (1992) suggests singing a song to the tune of "Twinkle, Twinkle, Little Star" in which children segment entire words. Here is one example:

> Listen, listen
> To my word
> Then tell me all the sounds you heard: coat
> (slowly)
> /k/ is one sound
> /ō/ is two
> /t/ is last in coat
> It's true. (p. 702)

After several repetitions of the verse segmenting other words, the song ends this way:

> Thanks for listening
> To my words
> And telling all the sounds you heard! (p. 702)

Teachers also use Elkonin boxes to teach children to segment words; this activity comes from the work of Russian psychologist D. B. Elkonin (Clay, 2005a). As seen in Figure 4–2, the teacher shows an object or a picture of an object and draws a row of boxes, with one box for each sound in the name of the object or picture. Then the teacher or a child moves a marker into each box as the sound is pronounced. Children can move small markers onto cards on their desks, or the teacher can draw the boxes on the chalkboard and use tape or magnets to hold the larger markers in place. Elkonin boxes can also be used for spelling activities: When a child is trying to spell a word, such as *duck*, the teacher can draw three boxes, do the segmentation activity, and then have the child write the letters representing each sound in the boxes.

Figure 4-2 ◆ Ways to Use Elkonin Boxes

Type	Goals	Steps in the Activity
Phonemic Awareness	Segmenting sounds in a one-syllable word	1. Show children an object or a picture of an object with a one-syllable name, such as a duck, game, bee, or cup. 2. Draw a row of boxes, side-by-side, corresponding to the number of sounds heard in the object's name. For example, draw two boxes to represent the two sounds in *bee* or three boxes for the three sounds in *duck*. 3. Distribute coins, checkers, or other small items to use as markers. 4. Say the name of the object slowly, moving a marker into each box as the sound is pronounced. Then have children repeat the procedure.
	Segmenting syllables in a multisyllabic word	1. Show children an object or a picture of an object with a multisyllabic name, such as a butterfly, alligator, cowboy, or umbrella. 2. Draw a row of boxes corresponding to the number of syllables in the object's name. For example, draw four boxes to represent the four syllables in *alligator*. 3. Distribute markers. 4. Say the name of the object slowly, moving a marker into each box as the syllable is pronounced. Then have children repeat the procedure.
Spelling	Representing sounds with letters	1. Draw a row of boxes corresponding to the number of sounds heard in a word. For example, draw two boxes for *go*, three boxes for *ship*, and four boxes for *frog*. 2. Pronounce the word, pointing to each box as the corresponding sound is said. 3. Have the child write the letter or letters representing the sound in each box.
	Applying spelling patterns	1. Draw a row of boxes corresponding to the number of sounds heard in a word. For example, draw three boxes for the word *duck*, *game*, or *light*. 2. Pronounce the word, pointing to each box as the corresponding sound is said. 3. Have the child write the letter or letters representing the sound in each box. 4. Pronounce the word again and examine how each sound is spelled. Insert unpronounced letters to complete the spelling patterns.

Guidelines
for Teaching Phonemic Awareness

▶ Begin with oral activities using objects and pictures, but after children learn to identify the letters of the alphabet, add reading and writing components.

▶ Emphasize experimentation as children sing songs and play word games because these activities are intended to be fun.

▶ Read and reread wordplay books, and encourage children to experiment with rhyming words, alliteration, and other wordplay activities.

▶ Teach minilessons on manipulating words, moving from easier to more complex levels.

▶ Emphasize blending and segmenting because children need these two strategies for phonics and spelling.

▶ Use small-group activities so children can be actively involved in manipulating language.

▶ Teach phonemic awareness in the context of authentic reading and writing activities.

▶ Spend 20 hours teaching phonemic awareness strategies, but recognize that children develop phonemic awareness at different rates and that some will need more or less instruction.

Teachers stimulate children's interest in language and provide valuable experiences with books and words. Effective teachers recognize the importance of building this foundation as children are beginning to read and write. Guidelines for phonemic awareness activities are reviewed in the box above.

 ## NURTURING ENGLISH LEARNERS

It's more difficult to develop English learners' phonemic awareness than native English speakers' because they're just learning to speak English; however, this training is worthwhile as long as familiar and meaningful words are used (Riches & Genesee, 2006). Teachers create a rich literacy environment and begin by reading books and poems aloud and singing songs so children can learn to recognize and pronounce English sound patterns.

To plan effective phonemic awareness instruction, teachers need to be familiar with English learners' home languages and understand how they differ from English (Peregoy & Boyle, 2008). Instruction should begin with sounds that children can pronounce easily and that don't conflict with those in their home language. Sounds that aren't present in children's home language or those that they don't perceive as unique, such as /ch/–/sh/ or /ĕ/–/ĭ/ for Spanish speakers, are more difficult. Children may need more time to practice producing and manipulating these difficult sounds.

Researchers recommend explicit instruction on phonemic awareness and practice opportunities for English learners (Snow, Burns, & Griffin, 1998). They sing familiar songs and play language games like native speakers do, but teachers also draw ELs' attention to pronouncing English sounds and words. Teachers often integrate phonemic awareness training, vocabulary instruction, and reading and writing activities to show how oral language sounds are represented by letters in written words (Peregoy & Boyle, 2008).

Phonemic awareness is a common underlying linguistic ability that transfers from one language to another (Riches & Genesee, 2006). Children who have learned to read in their home language—if it's alphabetic—are already phonemically aware, and this knowledge supports their reading and writing development in English.

Assessing Children's Phonemic Awareness

Through phonemic awareness instruction, children learn strategies for segmenting, blending, and substituting sounds in words. Teachers monitor children's learning as they participate in phonemic awareness activities: When children sort picture cards according to beginning sounds or identify rhyming words in a familiar song, they're demonstrating their ability to manipulate sounds. Teachers also administer one of several readily

Assessment Tools

Phonemic Awareness

Kindergarten and first-grade teachers monitor children's learning by observing them during classroom activities, and they screen, monitor, diagnose, and document their growing phonemic awareness by administering these tests:

◆ **Dynamic Indicators of Basic Early Literacy Skills (DIBELS): Phoneme Segmentation Fluency Subtest** (Kaminski & Good, 1996)
This individually administered subtest assesses children's ability to segment words with two and three phonemes. Multiple forms are available so that this test can be used periodically to monitor children's progress. The test is available free of charge on the DIBELS website, but there's a fee for analyzing and reporting the test results.

◆ **Phonological Awareness Literacy Screening (PALS) System: Rhyme Awareness and Beginning Sound Subtests** (Invernizzi, Meier, & Juel, 2003)
The kindergarten level of PALS includes brief subtests to assess young children's phonemic awareness. Children look at pictures and supply rhyming words or produce the beginning sounds for picture names. The grades 1–3 tests also include phonemic awareness subtests for children who score below grade level on other tests. PALS is available from the University of Virginia; it's free for Virginia teachers, but teachers in other states pay for it.

◆ **Test of Phonological Awareness (TPA)** (Torgesen & Bryant, 2004)
This group test is designed to measure children's ability to isolate individual sounds in spoken words and understand the relationship between letters and phonemes. The TPA is administered in 40 minutes, and it's available from LinguiSystems.

◆ **Yopp-Singer Test of Phonemic Segmentation** (Yopp, 1995)
This individually administered oral test for kindergartners measures their ability to segment the phonemes in words; it contains 22 items and is administered in less than 10 minutes. The test is free; it can be found in the September 1995 issue of *The Reading Teacher* or online. A Spanish version is also available.

Information gained from classroom observations and these assessments is used to identify children who aren't yet phonemically aware, plan appropriate instruction, and monitor their progress.

available phonemic awareness tests to screen children's ability to use phonemic awareness strategies, monitor their progress, and document their learning. Four phonemic-awareness tests are described in the Assessment Tools feature on page 105.

IF CHILDREN STRUGGLE...

Some 5-year-olds can't think of a word that rhymes with *pig* or *make*, can't clap the syllables in their names or in common words (e.g., *apple*, *umbrella*), and aren't interested in wordplay activities. It's likely that these children aren't developing the phonemic awareness knowledge that they need to learn to read and write successfully. If the results of phonemic awareness tests indicate that children are struggling, teachers must take action quickly because children with lower levels of phonemic awareness are more likely to experience reading difficulties (Snow, Burns, & Griffin, 1998).

Teachers provide fun, interactive interventions that focus on the sounds of oral language for struggling children, especially during the second half of kindergarten. They work with individual children and small groups using developmentally appropriate activities that emphasize oral language but also make links to reading and writing.

The sequence in learning phonemic awareness moves from recognizing the order of sounds in words to manipulating these sounds. First, children identify and match initial and final sounds in words. Next, they count the phonemes in words, often using Elkonin boxes. Finally, children manipulate sounds in four ways—segmenting, blending, deleting, and substituting. Teachers identify the specific phonemic awareness concepts that children haven't developed and teach lessons to address these topics in order of difficulty.

Children with extremely limited understanding of phonemic awareness may lack knowledge in one or more of these prerequisite concepts:

Environmental Sounds. Do children notice sounds in their environment? Can they recognize specific sounds, such as a bird chirping, a person coughing, a car horn honking, or a door squeaking? If children are unaware of environmental sounds, teachers develop their awareness by teaching them to identify sounds and classify them according to loudness and pitch.

Concept of Rhyme. Do children understand what rhyming words are? Can they break words into onsets and rimes? If not, teachers help children understand that words rhyme when their rimes sound alike (e.g., *go–throw*, *snail–whale*) and have them identify rhyming words in poems, songs, and books.

Concept of Word. Do children understand what a word is? Can they recognize individual words in speech? If children haven't developed this concept, teachers emphasize individual words as they speak and read aloud, and they ask children to listen for specific words.

Concept of Syllable. Do children understand what a syllable is? Can they demonstrate how to count the syllables in a word? If children can't, teachers accentuate the syllables in individual words, beginning with children's names, common words (e.g., *baby*, *pizza*, *together*), and compound words (e.g., *birthday*, *airplane*). They also teach children to clap the syllables as they say a word aloud; for example, as they pronounce the word *elephant*, they clap three times.

If children haven't developed these basic understandings, teachers begin their intervention here; however, if children can demonstrate their understanding of these concepts, teachers focus on identifying and manipulating sounds.

Why Is Phonemic Awareness Important?

A clear connection exists between phonemic awareness and learning to read; researchers have concluded that phonemic awareness is a prerequisite for learning to read. As they become phonemically aware, children recognize that speech can be segmented into smaller units; this knowledge is very useful as they learn about sound–symbol correspondences and spelling patterns (Cunningham, 2007).

Children can be explicitly taught to segment and blend speech, and those who receive approximately 20 hours of training in phonemic awareness do better in both reading and spelling (Juel, Griffith, & Gough, 1986). Phonemic awareness is also nurtured in spontaneous ways by providing children with language-rich environments and emphasizing wordplay as teachers read books aloud and engage children in singing songs, chanting poems, and telling riddles.

Moreover, phonemic awareness has been shown to be the most powerful predictor of later reading achievement. Klesius, Griffith, and Zielonka (1991) found that children who began first grade with strong phonemic awareness were successful regardless of the kind of reading instruction they received, and no particular type of instruction was better for children with limited phonemic awareness at the beginning of first grade.

PHONICS

Phonics is the set of relationships between phonology (the sounds in speech) and orthography (the spelling system). The emphasis is on spelling patterns, not individual letters, because there isn't a one-to-one correspondence between phonemes and graphemes in English. Sounds are spelled in different ways. There are several reasons for this variety. One reason is that sounds, especially vowels, vary according to their location in a word (e.g., *go–got*). Adjacent letters often influence how letters are pronounced (e.g., *bed–bead*), as do vowel markers such as the final *e* (e.g., *bit–bite*) (Shefelbine, 1995).

Language origin, or etymology, of words also influences their pronunciation. For example, the *ch* digraph is pronounced in several ways; the three most common are /ch/ as in *chain* (English), /sh/ as in *chauffeur* (French), and /k/ as in *chaos* (Greek). Neither the location of the digraph within the word nor adjacent letters account for these pronunciation differences: In all three words, the *ch* digraph is at the beginning of the word and is followed by two vowels, the first of which is *a*. Some letters aren't pronounced, either. In words such as *write*, the *w* isn't pronounced, even though it probably was at one time. The same is true for the *k* in *knight*, *know*, and *knee*. "Silent" letters in words such as *sign* and *bomb* reflect their parent words, *signature* and *bombard*, and have been retained for semantic, not phonological, reasons (Venezky, 1999).

Phonics Concepts

Phonics explains the relationships between phonemes and graphemes. There are 44 phonemes in English, that are represented by the 26 letters. The alphabetic principle suggests that there should be a one-to-one correspondence between phonemes and graphemes, so that each sound is consistently represented by one letter. English, however, is an imperfect phonetic language, and there are more than 500 ways to represent the 44 phonemes using single letters or combinations of letters. Think about the

Go to the Assignments and Activities section of the Topic *Phonemic Awareness/Phonics* in the MyEducationLab for the literacy course and complete the activity entitled *Understanding the Foundations of Effective Phonics Instruction*.

DEVELOPMENTAL CONTINUUM Phonics

PreK	K	1	2	3	4
Children play with sounds and rhymes, recite the alphabet, and identify some letters, including those in their names.	Kindergartners identify the letters of the alphabet and the sounds they represent, and they decode short vowel words.	Children blend consonant and short vowel sounds to read CVC words and use phonics rules to decode long vowel words.	Second graders use consonant blends and digraphs and vowel digraphs and diphthongs to decode more challenging words.	Third graders break unfamiliar two- and three-syllable words into syllables and apply phonics to decode these words.	Most fourth graders know how to use phonics to effectively decode and spell one-syllable and longer unfamiliar words.

word *day*: The two phonemes, /d/ and /ā/, are represented by three letters. The *d* is a consonant, and *a* and *y* are vowels. Interestingly, *y* isn't always a vowel; it's a consonant at the beginning of a word and a vowel at the end. When two vowels are side by side at the end of a word, they represent a long vowel sound; in *day*, the vowel sound is long *a*. Primary-grade students learn these phonics concepts to decode unfamiliar words.

Consonants. Phonemes are classified as either consonants or vowels. The consonants are *b, c, d, f, g, h, j, k, l, m, n, p, q, r, s, t, v, w, x, y,* and *z*. Most consonants represent a single sound consistently, but there are some exceptions. *C,* for example, doesn't represent a sound of its own: When it's followed by *a, o,* or *u,* it is pronounced /k/ (e.g., *cat, coffee, cut*), and when it's followed by *e, i,* or *y,* it's pronounced /s/, as in *city. G* represents two sounds, as the word *garbage* illustrates: It's usually pronounced /g/ (e.g., *gate, go, guppy*), but when *g* is followed by *e, i,* or *y,* it's pronounced /j/, as in *giant. X* is also pronounced differently according to its location in a word. At the beginning of a word, it's often pronounced /z/, as in *xylophone,* but sometimes the letter name is used, as in *x-ray*. At the end of a word, *x* is pronounced /ks/, as in *box*. The letters *w* and *y* are particularly interesting: At the beginning of a word or a syllable, they're consonants (e.g., *wind, yard*), but when they're in the middle or at the end, they're vowels (e.g., *saw, flown, day, by*).

Two kinds of combination consonants are *blends* and *digraphs*. Consonant blends occur when two or three consonants appear next to each other in words and their individual sounds are "blended" together, as in *grass, belt,* and *spring*. Consonant digraphs are letter combinations representing single sounds that aren't represented by either letter; the four most common are *ch* as in *chair* and *each, sh* as in *shell* and *wish*, *th* as in *father* and *both*, and *wh* as in *whale*. Another consonant digraph is *ph*, as in *photo* and *graph*.

Vowels. The remaining five letters—*a*, *e*, *i*, *o*, and *u*—represent vowels, and *w* and *y* are vowels when used in the middle and at the end of syllables and words. Vowels often represent several sounds. The two most common are short (marked with the symbol ˘, called a *breve*) and long sounds (marked with the symbol ¯, called a *macron*). The short vowel sounds are /ă/ as in *cat*, /ĕ/ as in *bed*, /ĭ/ as in *win*, /ŏ/ as in *hot*, and /ŭ/ as in *cup*. The long vowel sounds—/ā/, /ē/, /ī/, /ō/, and /ū/—are the same as the letter names, and they are illustrated in the words *make*, *feet*, *bike*, *coal*, and *rule*. Long vowel sounds are usually spelled with two vowels, except when the long vowel is at the end of a one-syllable word or a syllable, as in *she* or *secret* and *try* or *tribal*. When *y* is a vowel by itself at the end of a word, it's pronounced as long *e* or long *i*, depending on the length of the word. In one-syllable words such as *by* and *cry*, the *y* is pronounced as long *i*, but in longer words such as *baby* and *happy*, the *y* is usually pronounced as long *e*.

Vowel sounds are more complicated than consonant sounds, and there are many vowel combinations representing long vowels and other vowel sounds. Consider these combinations:

ai as in *nail*	*oa* as in *soap*
au as in *laugh* and *caught*	*oi* as in *oil*
aw as in *saw*	*oo* as in *cook* and *moon*
ea as in *peach* and *bread*	*ou* as in *house* and *through*
ew as in *sew* and *few*	*ow* as in *now* and *snow*
ia as in *dial*	*oy* as in *toy*
ie as in *cookie*	

Most vowel combinations are vowel digraphs or diphthongs: When two vowels represent a single sound, the combination is a vowel digraph (e.g., *nail*, *snow*), and when the two vowels represent a glide from one sound to another, the combination is a diphthong. Two vowel combinations that are consistently diphthongs are *oi* and *oy*, but other combinations, such as *ou* as in *house* (but not in *through*) and *ow* as in *now* (but not in *snow*), are diphthongs when they represent a glided sound. In *through*, the *ou* represents the /ū/ sound as in *moon*, and in *snow*, the *ow* represents the /ō/ sound.

When one or more vowels in a word are followed by an *r*, it's called an *r-controlled vowel* because the *r* influences the pronunciation of the vowel sound. For example, say these words: *start*, *award*, *nerve*, *squirt*, *horse*, *word*, *surf*, *square*, *stairs*, *pearl*, *beard*, *cheer*, *where*, *here*, *pier*, *wire*, *board*, *floor*, *scored*, *fourth*, and *cure*. Some words have a single vowel plus *r* and others have two vowels plus *r*, or the *r* is in between the vowels. Single vowels with *r* are more predictable than the other types. The most consistent *r*-controlled vowels are *ar* as in *shark* and *or* as in *born*. The remaining single vowel + *r* combinations, *er*, *ir*, and *ur*, are difficult to spell because they're often pronounced /ûr/ in words, including *herd*, *father*, *girls*, *first*, *burn*, and *nurse*.

Three-letter spellings of *r*-controlled vowels are more complicated; they include *-are* (*care*), *-ear* (*fear*), *-ere* (*here*), *-oar* (*roar*), and *-our* (*your*). Consider these *-ear* words, in which the vowel sound is pronounced four ways: *bears*, *beard*, *cleared*, *early*, *earth*, *hear*, *heard*, *heart*, *learner*, *pear*, *pearls*, *spear*, *wearing*, *yearly*, and *yearn*. The most common pronunciation for *ear* is /ûr/, as in *earth*, *learner*, and *pearls*; this pronunciation is used when *ear* is followed by a consonant, except in *heart* and *beard*. The next most common pronunciation is found in *cleared* and *spear*, where the vowel sounds like the word *ear*. In several words, including *bear* and *wearing*, the vowel sound is pronounced as in the word *air*. Finally, in *heart*, *ear* is pronounced as in *car*. Teachers usually introduce the more predictable ways to decode *r*-controlled vowels, but children learn words with less common pronunciations, including *award*, *courage*, *flour*, *heart*, *here*, *very*, and *work*, in other ways.

The vowels in the unaccented syllables of multisyllabic words are often softened and pronounced "uh," as in the first syllable of *about* and *machine*, and the final syllable of *pencil*, *tunnel*, *zebra*, and *selection*. This vowel sound is called *schwa* and is represented in dictionaries with ə, which looks like an inverted *e*.

Blending Into Words.   Readers blend or combine sounds to decode words. Even though children may identify each sound, one by one, they must also be able to blend them together. For example, to read the short-vowel word *best*, children identify /b/ /ĕ/ /s/ /t/ and then combine them to form the word. For long-vowel words, children identify the vowel pattern as well as the surrounding letters. In *pancake*, for example, children identify /p/ /ă/ /n/ /k/ /ā/ /k/ and recognize that the *e* at the end of the word is silent and marks the preceding vowel as long. Shefelbine (1995) emphasizes the importance of blending and explains that children who have difficulty decoding words usually know the sound–symbol correspondences but can't blend the sounds into recognizable words. Blending is a phonemic awareness strategy, and children who haven't had practice blending speech sounds into words are likely to have trouble decoding unfamiliar words.

Phonograms.   One-syllable words and syllables in longer words can be divided into two parts, the onset and the rime: The *onset* is the consonant sound, if any, that precedes the vowel, and the *rime* is the vowel and any consonant sounds that follow it. For example, in *show*, *sh* is the onset and *ow* is the rime, and in *ball*, *b* is the onset and *all* is the rime. For *at* and *up*, there is no onset; the entire word is the rime. Research has

Figure 4-3 ◆ The 37 Rimes and Common Words Using Them

Rime	Examples	Rime	Examples
-ack	black, pack, quack, stack	-ide	bride, hide, ride, side
-ail	mail, nail, sail, tail	-ight	bright, fight, light, might
-ain	brain, chain, plain, rain	-ill	fill, hill, kill, will
-ake	cake, shake, take, wake	-in	chin, grin, pin, win
-ale	male, sale, tale, whale	-ine	fine, line, mine, nine
-ame	came, flame, game, name	-ing	king, sing, thing, wing
-an	can, man, pan, than	-ink	pink, sink, think, wink
-ank	bank, drank, sank, thank	-ip	drip, hip, lip, ship
-ap	cap, clap, map, slap	-it	bit, flit, quit, sit
-ash	cash, dash, flash, trash	-ock	block, clock, knock, sock
-at	bat, cat, rat, that	-oke	choke, joke, poke, woke
-ate	gate, hate, late, plate	-op	chop, drop, hop, shop
-aw	claw, draw, jaw, saw	-ore	chore, more, shore, store
-ay	day, play, say, way	-ot	dot, got, knot, trot
-eat	beat, heat, meat, wheat	-uck	duck, luck, suck, truck
-ell	bell, sell, shell, well	-ug	bug, drug, hug, rug
-est	best, chest, nest, west	-ump	bump, dump, hump, lump
-ice	mice, nice, rice, slice	-unk	bunk, dunk, junk, sunk
-ick	brick, pick, sick, thick		

Figure 4-4 ◆ Excerpt From a Word Wall of Phonograms

-ock		-oke		-old	
block	lock	broke	poke	bold	hold
clock	rock	Coke	smoke	cold	sold
dock	sock	choke	woke	fold	told
flock		joke		gold	
		*soak			

-op		-ore		-ot	
cop	pop	more	store	dot	lot
chop	plop	sore	tore	got	not
drop	shop	shore	wore	hot	shot
hop	stop	snore		knot	spot
mop	top				
		*door *pour *soar			
		*floor *your *war			

* = exceptions

shown that children make more errors decoding and spelling the rime than the onset and more errors on vowels than on consonants (Caldwell & Leslie, 2005). In fact, rimes may provide an important key to word identification.

Wylie and Durrell (1970) identified 37 rimes, including *-ay*, *-ing*, *-oke*, and *-ump*, that are found in nearly 500 common words; these rimes and some words using each one are presented in Figure 4–3. Knowing these rimes and recognizing common words made from them are very helpful for beginning readers because they can use the words to decode other words (Cunningham, 2008). For example, when children know the *-ay* rime and recognize *say*, they use this knowledge to pronounce *clay*: They identify the *-ay* rime and blend *cl* with *ay* to decode the word. This strategy is called *decoding by analogy*, which you'll read more about in Chapter 6, "Developing Fluent Readers and Writers."

Teachers refer to rimes as *phonograms* or *word families* when they teach them, even though *phonogram* is a misnomer; by definition, a *phonogram* is a letter or group of letters that represent a single sound. Two of the rimes, *-aw* and *-ay*, represent single sounds, but the other 35 don't.

Beginning readers often read and write words using each phonogram. First and second graders can read and write these words made using *-ain*: *brain, chain, drain, grain, main, pain, plain, rain, sprain, stain,* and *train*. Children must be familiar with consonant blends and digraphs to read and spell these words. Teachers often post lists of words children create using phonograms on a word wall, as shown in Figure 4–4. Each phonogram and the words made using it are written in a separate section. Teachers use the words on the word wall for a variety of phonics activities, and children refer to it to spell words when they're writing.

Phonics Rules.　Because English has an imperfect correspondence between sounds and letters, linguists have created rules to clarify English spelling patterns. One rule is that *q* is followed by *u* and pronounced /kw/, as in *queen*, *quick*, and *earthquake*; *Iraq*, *Qantas*, and other names are exceptions. Another rule that has few exceptions relates to *r*-controlled vowels: *r* influences the preceding vowels so that they're neither long nor short. Examples are *car*, *wear*, and *four*. There are exceptions, however; one is *fire*.

Many rules aren't very useful because there are more exceptions than words that conform (Clymer, 1963). A good example is this long-vowel rule: When there are two adjacent vowels, the long vowel sound of the first one is pronounced and the second is silent; teachers sometimes call this the "when two vowels go walking, the first one does the talking" rule. Examples of conforming words are *meat*, *soap*, and *each*. There are many more exceptions, however, including *food*, *said*, *head*, *chief*, *bread*, *look*, *soup*, *does*, *too*, *and again*.

Figure 4-5 ◆ The Most Useful Phonics Rules		
Pattern	**Description**	**Examples**
Two sounds of *c*	The letter *c* can be pronounced /k/ or /s/. When *c* is followed by *a*, *o*, or *u*, it's pronounced /k/—the hard *c* sound. When *c* is followed by *e*, *i*, or *y*, it's pronounced /s/—the soft *c* sound.	*cat*　*cent* *cough*　*city* *cut*　*cycle*
Two sounds of *g*	The sound associated with *g* depends on the letter following it. When *g* is followed by *a*, *o*, or *u*, it's pronounced /g/—the hard *g* sound. When *g* is followed by *e*, *i*, or *y*, it's usually pronounced /j/—the soft *g* sound. Exceptions include *get* and *give*.	*gate*　*gentle* *go*　*giant* *guess*　*gypsy*
CVC pattern	When a one-syllable word has only one vowel and the vowel comes between two consonants, it's usually short. One exception is *told*.	*bat* *cup* *land*
Final *e* or CVCe pattern	When there are two vowels in a one-syllable word and one is an *e* at the end of the word, the first vowel is long and the final *e* is silent. Three exceptions are *have*, *come*, and *love*.	*home* *safe* *cute*
CV pattern	When a vowel follows a consonant in a one-syllable word, the vowel is long. Exceptions include *the*, *to*, and *do*.	*go* *she*
r-controlled vowels	Vowels that are followed by *r* are overpowered and are neither short nor long. One exception is *fire*.	*car*　*birth* *dear*　*pair*
-igh	When *gh* follows *i*, the *i* is long and the *gh* is silent. One exception is *neighbor*.	*high* *night*
kn- and *wr-*	In words beginning with *kn-* and *wr-*, the first letter isn't pronounced.	*knee* *write*

Children should learn the rules that work most of the time because they're the most useful (Adams, 1990). Eight useful rules are listed in Figure 4–5. Even though they're fairly reliable, very few of them approach 100% utility. The rule about *r*-controlled vowels just mentioned has been calculated to be useful in 78% of words in which the letter *r* follows the vowel (Adams, 1990). Other commonly taught rules have even lower percentages of utility. The CVC pattern rule—which says that when a one-syllable word has only one vowel and the vowel comes between two consonants, it's usually short, as in *bat*, *land*, and *cup*—is estimated to work only 62% of the time. Exceptions include *told*, *fall*, *fork*, and *birth*. The CVCe pattern rule—which says that when there are two vowels in a one-syllable word and one vowel is an *e* at the end of the word, the first vowel is long and the final *e* is silent—is estimated to work in 63% of CVCe words. Examples of conforming words are *came*, *hole*, and *pipe*; but three very common words— *have*, *come*, and *love*—are exceptions.

Teaching Phonics

The best way to teach phonics is through a combination of explicit instruction and authentic application activities. The National Reading Panel (2000) reviewed the research about phonics instruction and concluded that the most effective programs were systematic; that is, the most useful phonics skills are taught in a predetermined sequence. Most teachers begin with consonants and then introduce the short vowels so that children can read and spell consonant-vowel-consonant or CVC-pattern words, such as *dig* and *cup*. Then children learn about consonant blends and diagraphs and long vowels so that they can read and spell consonant-vowel-consonant-*e* or CVCe-pattern words, such as *broke* and *white*, and consonant-vowel-vowel-consonant or CVVC-pattern words, such as *clean*, *wheel*, and *snail*. Finally, children learn about the less common vowel diagraphs and diphthongs, such as *claw*, *bought*, *shook*, and *boil*, and *r*-controlled vowels, including *square*, *hard*, *four*, and *year*. Figure 4–6 details this instructional sequence of phonics skills.

Children also learn strategies to use in identifying unfamiliar words (Mesmer & Griffith, 2005). Three of the most useful strategies are sounding out words, decoding by analogy, and applying phonics rules. When children sound out words, they convert letters and patterns of letters into sounds and blend them to pronounce the word; it's most effective when children are reading phonetically regular one-syllable words. In the second strategy, decoding by analogy, children apply their knowledge of phonograms to analyze the structure of an unfamiliar word (White, 2005); they use known words to recognize unfamiliar ones. For example, if children are familiar with *will*, they can use it to identify *grill*. They also apply phonics rules to identify unfamiliar words, such as *while* and *clean*. These strategies are especially useful when children don't recognize many words, but they become less important as readers gain more experience and can recognize most words automatically.

The second component of phonics instruction is daily opportunities for children to apply the phonics strategies and skills they're learning in authentic reading and writing activities (National Reading Panel, 2000). Cunningham and Cunningham (2002) estimate that the ratio of time spent on real reading and writing to time spent on phonics instruction should be 3 to 1. Without this meaningful application of what they're learning, phonics instruction is often ineffective (Dahl, Scharer, Lawson, & Grogan, 2001).

Phonics instruction begins in kindergarten when children learn to connect consonant and short vowel sounds to the letters, and it's

Be Strategic!

Phonics Strategies

Children apply their phonics knowledge to decode words when they use these strategies:

- ▶ Sound it out
- ▶ Decode by analogy
- ▶ Apply phonics rules

These strategies are most effective for decoding phonetically regular one-syllable words.

Figure 4-6 ◆ Sequence of Phonics Instruction

Grade	Skills	Description	Examples
K	More common consonants	Children identify consonant sounds, match sounds to letters, and substitute sounds in words.	/b/, /d/, /f/, /m/, /n/, /p/, /s/, /t/
K–1	Less common consonants	Children identify consonant sounds, match sounds to letters, and substitute sounds in words.	/g/, /h/, /j/, /k/, /l/, /q/, /v/, /w/, /x/, /y/, /z/
	Short vowels	Children identify the five short vowel sounds and match them to letters.	/ă/ = cat, /ĕ/ = bed, /ĭ/ = pig, /ŏ/ = hot, /ŭ/ = cut
	CVC pattern	Children read and spell CVC-pattern words.	dad, men, sit, hop, but
1	Consonant blends	Children identify and blend consonant sounds at the beginning and end of words.	/pl/ = plant /str/ = string
	Phonograms	Children break CVC words into onsets and rimes and use phonograms to form new words.	not: dot, shot, spot will: still, fill, drill
	Consonant diagraphs	Children identify consonant diagraphs, match sounds to letters, and read and spell words with consonant diagraphs.	/ch/ = chop /sh/ = dash /th/ = with /wh/ = when
	Long vowel sounds	Children identify the five long vowel sounds and match them to letters.	/ā/ = name, /ē/ = bee, /ī/ = ice, /ō/ = soap, /ū/ = tune
	CVCe pattern	Children read and spell CVCe-pattern words.	game, ride, stone
	Common long vowel digraphs	Children identify the vowel sound represented by common long vowel digraphs and read and spell words using them.	/ā/ = ai (rain), ay (day) /ē/ = ea (reach), ee (sweet) /ō/ = oa (soap), ow (know)
1–2	*w* and *y*	Children recognize when *w* and *y* are consonants and when they're vowels, and identify the sounds they represent.	window, yesterday y = /ī/ (by) y = /ē/ (baby)
	Phonograms	Children divide long vowel words into onsets and rimes and use phonograms to form new words.	woke: joke, broke, smoke day: gray, day, stay
	Hard and soft consonant sounds	Children identify the hard and soft sounds represented by *c* and *g*, and read and spell words using them.	g = girl (hard), gem (soft) c = cat (hard), city (soft)
2–3	Less common vowel digraphs	Children identify the sounds of less common vowel digraphs and read and spell words using them.	/ô/ = al (walk), au (caught), aw (saw), ou (bought) /ā/ = ei (weigh) /ē/ = ey (key), ie (chief) /ī/ = ie (pie) /o͞o/ = oo (good), ou (could) /ū/ = oo (moon), ew (new), ue (blue), ui (fruit)
	Vowel diphthongs	Children identify the vowel diphthongs and read and write words using them.	/oi/ = oi (boil), oy (toy) /ou/ = ou (cloud), ow (down)
	Less common consonant digraphs	Children identify the sounds of less common consonant digraphs and read and write words using them.	ph = phone ng = sing gh = laugh tch = match
	r-controlled vowels	Children identify *r*-controlled vowel patterns and read and spell words using them.	/âr/ = hair, care, bear, there, their /ar/ = heart, star /er/ = clear, deer, here /or/ = born, more, warm /ûr/ = learn, first, work, burn

Guidelines
for Teaching Phonics

▶ Teach high-utility phonics concepts that are most useful for reading unfamiliar words.

▶ Follow a developmental continuum for systematic phonics instruction, beginning with consonant sounds and ending with r-controlled vowels.

▶ Provide explicit instruction to teach phonics strategies and skills.

▶ Provide opportunities for children to apply what they're learning about phonics through word sorts, making words, interactive writing, and other literacy activities.

▶ Take advantage of teachable moments to clarify misunderstandings and infuse phonics instruction into literacy activities.

▶ Use oral activities to reinforce phonemic awareness strategies as children blend and segment written words during phonics and spelling instruction.

▶ Review phonics as part of spelling instruction.

completed by third grade because older students rarely benefit from it (Ivey & Baker, 2004; National Reading Panel, 2000). Guidelines for teaching phonics are presented above.

Explicit Instruction. Teachers present minilessons on phonics concepts to the whole class or to small groups of children, depending on the their instructional needs. They follow the minilesson format, explicitly presenting information about a phonics strategy or skill, demonstrating how to use it, and presenting words for children to use in guided practice, as Mrs. Firpo did in the vignette at the beginning of the chapter. During the minilesson, teachers use these activities to provide guided practice opportunities for children to manipulate sounds and read and write words:

- Sort objects, pictures, and word cards according to a phonics concept.
- Write letters or words on small whiteboards.
- Arrange magnetic letters or letter cards to spell words.
- Make class charts of words representing phonics concepts, such as the two sounds of *g* or the *-ore* phonogram.
- Make a poster or book of words representing a phonics concept.
- Locate other words exemplifying the spelling pattern in books children are reading.

The minilesson feature on page 116 shows how a first-grade teacher teaches a minilesson on reading and spelling CVC-pattern words using final consonant blends.

Application Activities. Children apply the phonics concepts they're learning as they read and write and participate in teacher-directed activities. In interactive writing, for example, children segment words into sounds and take turns writing letters and sometimes whole words on the chart (McCarrier, Pinnell, & Fountas, 2000; Tompkins & Collom, 2004). Teachers help children correct any errors, and they take advantage of teachable moments to review consonant and vowel sounds and spelling patterns, as well as handwriting skills and rules for capitalization and punctuation.

TOPIC: Decoding CVC Words With Final Consonant Blends
GRADE: First Grade
TIME: One 30-minute period

Mrs. Nazir is teaching her first graders about consonant blends. She introduced initial consonant blends to the class, and children practiced reading and spelling words, such as *club, drop,* and *swim,* that were chosen from the selection they were reading in their basal readers. Then, in small groups, they completed workbook pages and made words using plastic tiles with onsets and rimes printed on them. For example, using the *-ip* phonogram, they made *clip, drip, flip, skip,* and *trip.* This is the fifth whole-class lesson in the series. Today, Mrs. Nazir is introducing final consonant blends.

1 Introduce the Topic
Mrs. Nazir explains that blends are also used at the end of words. She writes these words on the chalkboard: *best, rang, hand, pink,* and *bump.* Together the children sound them out: They pronounce the initial consonant sound, the short vowel sound, and the final consonants. They blend the final consonants, then they blend the entire word and say it aloud. Children use the words in sentences to ensure that everyone understands them, and Dillon, T.J., Pauline, Cody, and Brittany circle the blends in the words on the chalkboard. The teacher points out that *st* is a familiar blend also used at the beginning of words, but that the other blends are used only at the end of words.

2 Share Examples
Mrs. Nazir says these words: *must, wing, test, band, hang, sink, bend,* and *bump.* The first graders repeat each word, isolate the blend, and identify it. Carson says, "The word is *must*—/m/ /ŭ/ /s/ /t/—and the blend is *st* at the end." Bryan points out that Ng is his last name, and everyone claps because his name is so special. Several children volunteer additional words: Dillon suggests *blast,* and Henry adds *dump* and *string.* Then the teacher passes out word cards and children read the words, including *just, lamp, went,* and *hang.* They sound out each word carefully, pronouncing the initial consonant, the short vowel, and the final consonant blend. Then they blend the sounds and say the word.

3 Provide Information
Mrs. Nazir posts a piece of chart paper, and labels it "The *-ink* Word Family." The children brainstorm these words with the *-ink* phonogram: *blink, sink, pink, rink, mink, stink,* and *wink,* and they take turns writing the words on the chart. They also suggest *twinkle* and *wrinkle,* and Mrs. Nazir adds them to the chart.

4 Guide Practice
Children create other word family charts using *-and, -ang, -ank, -end, -ent, -est, -ing, -ump,* and *-ust.* Each group brainstorms at least five words and writes them on the chart. Mrs. Nazir monitors children's work and helps them think of additional words and correct spelling errors. Then children post their word family charts and share them with the class.

5 Assess Learning
Mrs. Nazir observes the first graders as they brainstorm words, blend sounds, and spell the words. She notices several children who need more practice and will call them together for a follow-up lesson.

Teachers use activities such as making words, word ladders, and word sorts to provide opportunities for children to practice what they're learning about phoneme–grapheme correspondences, word families, and phonics rules.

Assessing Children's Phonics Knowledge

Teachers assess children's developing phonics knowledge using a combination of tests, observation, and reading and writing samples. They often use a test to screen children at the beginning of the school year, monitor their progress at midyear, and document their achievement at the end of the year. When children aren't making expected progress, teachers administer a test to diagnose the problem and plan for instruction. Three tests that assess children's phonics knowledge are described in the Assessment Tools feature below.

Teachers observe children as they participate in phonics activities and while reading and writing to see how they're applying the phonics strategies and skills they're learning. When children use magnetic letters to write words with the *-at* phonogram,

Phonics

Teachers monitor children's developing phonics knowledge by observing them during classroom activities and by administering these tests:

◆ **Observation Survey of Early Literacy Achievement (OS): Word Reading and Hearing and Recording Sounds in Words Subtests** (Clay, 2007a)

The OS consists of six subtests. The Word Reading and the Hearing and Recording Sounds in Words subtests are used to assess children's ability to apply phonics concepts to decode and spell words. The subtests are administered individually, and children's scores for each subtest can be standardized and converted to stanines. The OS is published by Heinemann Books.

◆ **Dynamic Indicators of Basic Early Literacy Skills (DIBELS): Nonsense Word Fluency Subtest** (Kaminski & Good, 1996)

This individually administered subtest assesses children's ability to apply phonics concepts to read two- and three-letter nonsense words (e.g., *ap, jid*). Multiple forms are available, so this test can be used to monitor children's progress during kindergarten and first grade. The test is available at the DIBELS website free of charge, but there's a fee for scoring tests and for reporting scores.

◆ **The Tile Test** (Norman & Calfee, 2004)

This individually administered test assesses children's knowledge of phonics. Children manipulate letter tiles to make words, and teachers also arrange tiles to spell words for them to read. The Tile Test can easily be administered in 10 to 15 minutes. It's available online, free of charge.

These tests are useful assessment tools that teachers use to screen, monitor, diagnose, and document children's phonics knowledge and to make instructional decisions.

such as *bat*, *cat*, *hat*, *mat*, *rat*, and *sat*, for example, they're demonstrating their phonics knowledge. They also show what they've learned during interactive writing, making words, and word sort activities. Similarly, as teachers listen to children read aloud or read children's writing, they analyze their errors to determine which phonics concepts children are confusing or those they don't yet understand.

IF CHILDREN STRUGGLE...

Phonics is only one component of a balanced literacy program for young children, but it's an essential part so teachers quickly take steps to assist beginning readers in overcoming their difficulties. Most children learn phoneme–grapheme correspondences (e.g., /m/ is represented in print by the letter *m*) without too many difficulties; it's more likely that they're having trouble blending sounds into words and applying phonics rules. Too often children guess at words based on the first letter or they sound out the letters, one by one, without blending the sounds or thinking about phonics patterns.

The first step is to identify the specific problem, and teachers usually analyze test results to determine children's instructional needs. Next, teachers prepare lessons to reteach the phonics concepts children haven't learned. Teachers provide explicit instruction, and then children have opportunities to apply what they're learning, first in guided practice activities and then in authentic reading and writing activities. During their lessons, teachers provide information and involve children in hands-on reading and writing activities where they build words using foam letters, read books at their instructional level, highlight words in a text they've read, sort words according to vowel patterns, and spell words on whiteboards. Struggling readers and writers often need extended guided practice before they're ready to apply the concepts and strategies independently.

What's the Role of Phonics in a Balanced Literacy Program?

Phonics is a controversial topic. Some parents and politicians, as well as even a few teachers, believe that most of our educational ills could be solved if children were taught to read using phonics. A few people still argue that phonics is a complete reading program, but that view ignores what we know about the interrelatedness of the four cueing systems. Reading is a complex process, and the phonological system works in conjunction with the semantic, syntactic, and pragmatic systems, not in isolation.

The controversy now centers on the best way to teach phonics. Marilyn Adams (1990), in her landmark review of the research on phonics instruction, recommends that phonics be taught within a balanced approach that integrates instruction in reading strategies and skills with meaningful opportunities for reading and writing. She emphasizes that phonics instruction should focus on the most useful information for identifying words, that it should be systematic and intensive, and that it should be completed by third grade.

CHAPTER Review

How Effective Teachers Assist Children in "Cracking the Code"

▶ Teachers teach children to "crack the code" through phonemic awareness and phonics instruction.

▶ Teachers understand that phonemic awareness is the foundation for phonics instruction.

▶ Teachers teach high-utility phonics concepts, rules, and phonograms.

Chapter 5

Learning to Spell

Mrs. Zumwalt Differentiates Spelling Instruction

The 21 third graders in Mrs. Zumwalt's class have different spelling needs because they're working at varying levels of spelling development. During the first week of the school year, Mrs. Zumwalt collected writing samples, analyzed children's spelling errors, and determined each child's stage of spelling development, and she continues to analyze their spelling at the end of each quarter and regroup them for instruction. According to her most recent assessment, one group of 5 children are within-word pattern spellers: They are confusing more complex consonant and vowel patterns. Nick spells *headache* as *hedakke*, *soap* as *sope*, and *heart* as *hart*; Jovana spells *wild* as *wilde*, *ears* as *erars*, and *found* as *foeund*. Another group of 13 children spell at the syllables and affixes stage: They spell most one-syllable words correctly, and their errors involve inflectional endings and the schwa sound in unaccented syllables. Maribel spells *coming* as *comeing*; Raziel spells *uncle* as *unkol* and *believed* as *beeleved*. Three others are more sophisticated spellers; Aaron, for example, spells *actor* as *acter*; *collection* as *culection*, and *pneumonia* as *newmonia*. These children are beginning to move into the derivational relations stage, where the focus is on Latin and Greek root words and affixes and etymologies of words.

Mrs. Zumwalt spends 30 minutes, every morning on spelling. On Monday, she administers the pretest for the textbook spelling program that her school uses, and on Friday, she administers the final test. On Tuesdays, Wednesdays, and Thursdays, while children practice the spelling words independently, she teaches minilessons to small groups. The topics she chooses for the lessons depend on her students' needs and the standards set out for her district.

One day, Mrs. Zumwalt teaches a minilesson to half of the class comparing plurals and possessives because the syllables-and-affixes-stage spellers are misusing apostrophes in plurals. For example, one child writes: *The boy's rode their bike's up the biggest hill in town to reach Chavez Park*. Afterward, the third graders review their writing notebooks, locate three interesting sentences using either plurals or possessives, and copy them on sentence strips. During a follow-up minilesson, they share their sentences, identify the plurals or possessives, and correct any errors. Mrs. Zumwalt notices that several children are still confused about plurals and possessives, so she'll continue to work with them.

Another day, as the children are making learning logs for a unit on astronomy, several ask Mrs. Zumwalt why there's an unnecessary *c* following the *s* in the word *science*. She explains that *science* is a Latin word and that a few very special words that have come to English from Latin are spelled with both *s* and *c*. From that exchange, Mrs. Zumwalt decides to teach a minilesson about the ways to spell /s/. To begin, the third graders collect words with the /s/ sound from books they're reading, words posted in the classroom, and other words they know. After a day of collecting words, the children each write the five most interesting words they've found on small cards. Mrs. Zumwalt sorts the words and places them in rows on a pocket chart. Most of the words are spelled with *s* or *ss*, but several children found words using *c* or *ce* to spell /s/. Mrs. Zumwalt adds several other word cards with *se* and *sc* spellings. The children examine the chart and draw some conclusions about how to spell the *s* sound. The chart they develop is shown on page 122.

Mrs. Zumwalt is teaching her third graders that good spellers think out the spellings of words; they don't just sound them out. Mrs. Zumwalt hung a "how to spell long words" chart in the classroom, and through a series of minilessons, the class develops these rules for spelling unfamiliar words:

1. Break the word into syllables.
2. Say each syllable to yourself.
3. Sound out the spelling of each syllable.
4. Think about rules for spelling vowels and endings.
5. Check to see that the word looks right.
6. Check the dictionary if you're not sure.
7. Ask a friend for help.

Third Graders' Chart of Ways to Spell /s/

Spelling	Examples		Nonexamples	Rules
s	said monsters sister	misbehave taste	shop wish	S is the most common spelling, but sh does not make the s sound. Sh has a special sound.
c	cent bicycle city decide	cereal mice circle face	cat chair cucumber	When c is followed by e, i, or y, it makes the s sound.
ce	office dance sentence prince	science fence voice juice	cent cement	Ce is used only at the end of a word.
ss	class guessed kiss	blossom fossil lesson		Ss is used in the middle and at the end of a word.
sc	scissors science	scent	scare rascal	This spelling is unusual.
se	else house		sent	This spelling is used only at the end of a word.

Mrs. Zumwalt frequently reviews the strategy chart with the children who are learning to spell two-syllable words. During this minilesson, she reads over the list of spelling strategies and models how to use them step-by-step with the word *welcome*. She breaks the word into two syllables, *wel–come*, and writes it on chart paper, spelling it this way: *wellcome*. Then she looks at the word and asks the children to look, too. She says, "I've written *well* and *come*, but the word doesn't look right, does it It looks wrong in the middle. Maybe there's only one *l* in *welcome*." She writes *welcome* under *wellcome* and asks the children if *welcome* looks better. They agree that it does, and Mrs. Zumwalt asks a child to check the spelling in the dictionary.

Then she chooses another word—*market*—and asks a child in the group to guide her through the steps. She follows the child's direction to divide *market* into two syllables—*mar–ket*—and writes the word on chart paper, spelling it *markket*. She looks at the word and tells the child that she thinks it looks correct, but the child disagrees, as do others. So Mrs. Zumwalt looks at the word again and asks for help. The child explains that only one *k* is needed. Then Mrs. Zumwalt writes the word correctly on chart paper.

Mrs. Zumwalt passes out whiteboards and pens for children to use to practice spelling two-syllable words. First, they practice the breaking words into syllables strategy with *turkey*. They follow the steps that Mrs. Zumwalt used, and she checks their spelling. Then they continue to practice the strategy using these words: *disturb, problem, number, garden, person,* and *orbit*. The group is very successful, so they ask Mrs. Zumwalt for more difficult words. They try these three-syllable words: *remember, hamburger, banana,* and *populate*.

The next day, Mrs. Zumwalt works with the group of children spelling at the within-word pattern stage. These children still confuse long- and short-vowel words, so Mrs. Zumwalt has prepared a sorting game with similar words, including *rid–ride, hop–hope, cub–cube, slid–slide, cut–cute, pet–Pete, hat–hate, not–note,* and *mad–made*. She passes out envelopes with cards on which the words have been printed. The children sort their cards, matching up the related long- and short-vowel words. They practice reading the words and then write them on whiteboards. Finally, Mrs. Zumwalt asks the children to clarify the difference between the two groups of words; they've been asked this question before, but it's a hard question. The difference, they explain, is that the three-letter words have short vowels and the four-letter words have a final *e* and they're long vowel words.

While Mrs. Zumwalt works with one group, the other children are practicing their spelling words. For each word, they spell it in their minds, write the word, and check the spelling using the procedure that Mrs. Zumwalt taught them earlier in the school year.

After they practice their spelling words, children choose spelling games to play. Some play the children's version of Boggle, and others play computer spelling games, explore the Franklin Spelling Ace®, or work at the spelling center in the classroom.

Words Made Using the Letters in *Grandfather*

Making Words

This week's word is: | g | r | a | n | d | f | a | t | h | e | r |

1	2	3	4	5	6	7	8
a	at	and	hear	grand	father		
	he	the	hate	great			
	an	her	date	after			
		are	gate				
		hat	hare				
		eat	near				
		ate	tear				
		ear	gear				
		fat	then				
		ran	than				
		fan	hand				

The spelling center has three packets of activities. One packet has 15 plastic bags with magnetic letters, which children use to spell the 15 spelling words. The second packet has word cards with inflectional endings for children to sort and arrange on the pocket chart hanging next to the center; the word cards include *bunnies*, *walked*, *cars*, *running*, *hopped*, *foxes*, and *sleeping*. Several weeks ago, children studied spelling words with inflectional endings in minilessons with Mrs. Zumwalt, so these cards have now been placed in the spelling center for extra practice and review. In the third packet are plastic letters for a making words activity. This week's word is *grandfather*. Children work in small groups to spell as many words as possible: They manipulate the letters and arrange them to spell one-, two-, three-, four-, five-, and six-letter words. A completed sheet with 30 words made using the letters in *grandfather* is shown on page 123.

On Friday, Mrs. Zumwalt administers the weekly spelling test. She reads the 15 words aloud, and children write them on their papers. Then she asks them to go back and look at each of the words and put a checkmark next to it if it looks right and circle the word if it doesn't. Some of her third graders—especially those at the within-word stage—haven't developed a visual sense of when words "look" right, and through this proofreading exercise, Mrs. Zumwalt is helping them learn to identify misspelled words in their writing. She finds that her more advanced spellers can accurately predict whether their spellings "look" right, but the others can't. As she grades their spelling tests, Mrs. Zumwalt gives extra credit to those children who accurately predict whether their words are spelled correctly.

Young children apply what they're learning about phonemic awareness and phonics when they spell words. When beginning writers want to write a word, they say the word slowly, segmenting the sounds; segmenting is a phonemic awareness strategy that writers use to spell words. Then they choose letters to represent the sounds they hear to spell the word. The letters children choose to represent sounds reflect what they've learned about phonics and spelling patterns. Many spellings are incorrect, of course: Sometimes the spellings are very abbreviated, sometimes they're strictly phonetic and ignore spelling patterns, and at other times, letters are reversed. These incorrect spellings are clear demonstrations of children's phonological knowledge. As children's knowledge of English orthography, or the spelling system, grows, their spellings increasingly approximate conventional spelling.

Consider the ways young children might spell the word *fairy*. A 4-year-old might use scribbles or random letters to write the word or, perhaps, recognize the beginning sound of the word and use the letter *F* to represent the word. A kindergartner or first grader with well-developed phonemic awareness strategies could segment the word into its three sounds—/f/ /âr/ /ê/—and spell it *FRE*, using one letter to represent each sound. By second grade, a child with more knowledge of English spelling patterns might spell the word as *FARIEY*. This child also segments the word into its three sounds, hears the *r*-controlled vowel pattern, and correctly identifies the three letters used to spell the sound but reverses their order when writing them so that *air* is spelled *ari*. The letters *ey* are used to spell the /ē/ sound, perhaps by analogy to the word *money*. Through more experiences reading and writing the word *fairy* and other words with the same sounds, third and fourth graders will learn to spell the word conventionally.

Amazingly, most children move from spelling most words phonetically to spelling most words conventionally in less than 4 years. In Mrs. Zumwalt's classroom, for instance, most of her third graders correctly spell more than 90% of the words they write. Their understanding of the alphabetic principle, that letters represent sounds, matures through a combination of many, many opportunities to read and write and explicit spelling instruction. In the past, weekly spelling tests were the main instructional strategy, but now they're only one part of a comprehensive spelling program.

Even though spelling might not seem integral to reading, it is. When children spell words, they're using phonemic awareness strategies and applying what they've learned about phonics. In addition, there's an interesting relationship between reading and spelling: Good readers tend to be good spellers.

STAGES OF SPELLING DEVELOPMENT

As young children begin to write, they create unique spellings based on their knowledge of phonology (Read, 1975). The children in Read's studies used letter names to spell words, such as *U* (*you*) and *R* (*are*), and they used consonant sounds rather consistently: *GRL* (*girl*), *TIGR* (*tiger*), and *NIT* (*night*). They used several unusual but phonetically based spelling patterns to represent affricates; for example, they replaced *tr* with *chr* (e.g., *CHRIBLES* for *troubles*) and *dr* with *jr* (e.g., *JRAGIN* for *dragon*). Words with long vowels were spelled using letter names: *MI* (*my*), *LADE* (*lady*), and *FEL* (*feel*). The children used several ingenious strategies to spell words with short vowels: The preschoolers selected letters to represent short vowels on the basis of place of articulation in the mouth. Short *i* was represented with *e*, as in *FES* (*fish*), short *e* with *a*, as in *LAFFT* (*left*), and short *o* with *i*, as in *CLIK* (*clock*). These spellings may seem odd to adults, but they reflect phonetic relationships.

Based on examinations of children's spellings, researchers have identified five stages that students move through on their way to becoming conventional spellers: emergent spelling, letter name–alphabetic spelling, within-word pattern spelling, syllables and affixes spelling, and derivational relations spelling (Bear, Invernizzi, Templeton, & Johnston, 2008). At each stage, students use different strategies and focus on particular aspects of spelling. The characteristics of the five stages are summarized in Figure 5–1.

Stage 1: Emergent Spelling

Children string scribbles, letters, and letterlike forms together, but they don't associate the marks they make with any specific phonemes. Spelling at this stage represents a natural, early expression of the alphabet and other written-language concepts. Children may write from left to right, right to left, top to bottom, or randomly across the page, but by the end of the stage, they have an understanding of directionality. Some emergent spellers have a large repertoire of letterforms to use in writing, but others repeat a small number of letters over and over. Although they use both upper- and

Figure 5-1 ◆ Stages of Spelling Development

Stage 1: Emergent Spelling

Children string scribbles, letters, and letterlike forms together, but they don't associate the marks they make with any specific phonemes. This stage is typical of 3- to 5-year-olds who learn these concepts:

- The distinction between drawing and writing
- How to make letters
- The direction of writing on a page
- Some letter–sound matches

Stage 2: Letter Name-Alphabetic Spelling

Children learn to represent phonemes in words with letters. At first, their spellings are quite abbreviated, but they learn to use consonant blends and digraphs and short vowel patterns to spell many words. Spellers are 5- to 7-year-olds, and they learn these concepts:

- The alphabetic principle
- Consonant sounds
- Short vowel sounds
- Consonant blends and digraphs

Stage 3: Within-Word Pattern Spelling

Children learn long vowel patterns and *r*-controlled vowels, but they may confuse spelling patterns and spell *meet* as *mete*, and they reverse the order of letters, such as *form* for *from* and *gril* for *girl*. Spellers are 7- to 9-year-olds who learn these concepts:

- Long vowel spelling patterns
- *r*-controlled vowels
- More complex consonant patterns
- Diphthongs and other less common vowel patterns

Stage 4: Syllables and Affixes Spelling

Students apply what they've learned about one-syllable words to spell longer words and learn to break words into syllables. They also learn to add inflectional endings (e.g., *-es*, *-ed*, *-ing*) and to differentiate between homonyms, such as *your–you're*. Spellers are 9- to 11-year-olds, and they learn these concepts:

- Inflectional endings
- Compound words
- Syllabication
- Homonyms

Stage 5: Derivational Relations Spelling

Students explore the relationship between spelling and meaning and learn that words with related meanings are often related in spelling despite changes in pronunciation (e.g., *wise–wisdom*, *sign–signal*, *nation–national*). They also learn about Latin and Greek root words and derivational affixes (e.g., *amphi-*, *pre-*, *-able*, *-tion*). Spellers are 11- to 14-year-olds who learn these concepts:

- Consonant alternations
- Vowel alternations
- Latin affixes and root words
- Greek affixes and root words
- Etymologies

Adapted from Bear, Invernizzi, Templeton, & Johnston, 2008.

lowercase letters, they show a distinct preference for uppercase letters. Toward the end of the stage, children are beginning to discover how spelling works and that letters represent sounds in words. This stage is typical of 3- to 5-year-olds. During the emergent stage, children learn these concepts:

- The distinction between drawing and writing
- How to make letters
- The direction of writing on a page
- Some letter–sound matches

Stage 2: Letter Name–Alphabetic Spelling

Children learn to represent phonemes in words with letters. They develop an understanding of the alphabetic principle, that a link exists between letters and sounds. At first, the spellings are quite abbreviated and represent only the most prominent features in words. Children use only several letters of the alphabet to represent an entire word. Examples of early Stage 2 spelling are *D* (*dog*) and *KE* (*cookie*), and children may still be writing mainly with capital letters. Children slowly pronounce the word they want to spell, listening for familiar letter names and sounds.

In the middle of the letter name-alphabetic stage, children use most beginning and ending consonants and include a vowel in most syllables; they spell *like* as *lik* and *bed* as *bad*. By the end of the stage, they use consonant blends and digraphs and short vowel patterns to spell *hat*, *get*, and *win*, but some still spell *ship* as *sep*. They can also correctly spell some CVCe words, such as *name*. Spellers at this stage are usually 5- to 7-year-olds. During the letter–name stage, children learn these concepts:

- The alphabetic principle
- Consonant sounds
- Short vowel sounds
- Consonant blends and digraphs

Stage 3: Within-Word Pattern Spelling

Children begin the within-word pattern stage when they can spell most one-syllable short vowel words, and during this stage, they learn to spell long vowel patterns and *r*-controlled vowels. They experiment with long vowel patterns and learn that words such as *come* and *bread* are exceptions that don't fit the vowel patterns. Children may confuse spelling patterns and spell *meet* as *mete*, and they reverse the order of letters, such as *form* for *from* and *gril* for *girl*. They also learn about complex consonant sounds, including *-tch* (*match*) and *-dge* (*judge*), and less frequent vowel patterns, such as *oi/oy* (*boy*), *au* (*caught*), *aw* (*saw*), *ew* (*sew, few*), *ou* (*house*), and *ow* (*cow*). Children also become aware of homophones and compare long and short vowel combinations (*hope–hop*) as they experiment with vowel patterns. Spellers at this stage are 7- to 9-year-olds, and they learn these concepts:

- Long vowel spelling patterns
- *r*-controlled vowels
- More complex consonant patterns
- Diphthongs and other less common vowel patterns

Stage 4: Syllables and Affixes Spelling

Students focus on syllables in this stage and apply what they've learned about one-syllable words to longer words, including compound words. They learn about inflectional endings (-s, -es, -ed, and -ing) and rules about consonant doubling, changing the final y to i, or dropping the final e before adding an inflectional suffix. They also learn about homonyms and are introduced to some of the more common prefixes and suffixes. Spellers in this stage are generally 9- to 11-year-olds. They learn these concepts during the syllables and affixes stage of spelling development:

- Inflectional endings (-s, -es, -ed, -ing)
- Compound words
- Syllabication
- Homonyms

Stage 5: Derivational Relations Spelling

Students explore the relationship between spelling and meaning during the derivational relations stage, and they learn that words with related meanings are often related in spelling despite changes in vowel and consonant sounds (e.g., *wise–wisdom*, *sign–signal*, *nation–national*). The focus in this stage is on morphemes, and students learn about Greek and Latin root words and affixes. They also begin to examine etymologies and the role of history in shaping how words are spelled. They learn about eponyms (words from people's names), such as *maverick* and *sandwich*. Spellers at this stage are 11- to 14-year-olds. Students learn these concepts:

- Consonant alternations (e.g., *soft–soften*, *magic–magician*)
- Vowel alternations (e.g., *please–pleasant*, *define–definition*, *explain–explanation*)
- Greek and Latin affixes and root words
- Etymologies

DEVELOPMENTAL CONTINUUM   Spelling

PreK	K	1	2	3	4
Emergent spellers print their names and use scribbles, letterlike forms, letters, and letter strings to write messages.	Children become letter–name spellers. They learn letter–sound correspondences and begin to sound out words.	First graders learn to spell many high-frequency words, short-vowel words, and words with long-vowel patterns.	Children are within-word pattern spellers who can spell one-syllable words with more complex consonant and vowel patterns.	Children reach the syllables and affixes stage and spell longer words, including words with inflectional endings.	Fourth graders recognize homonyms and use knowledge about root words and affixes to spell multisyllabic words.

Children's spelling provides evidence of their growing understanding of English orthography. The words they spell correctly show which phonics concepts, spelling patterns, and other language features they've learned to apply, and the words they invent and misspell show what they're still learning to use and those features of spelling that they haven't noticed or learned about. Invented spelling is sometimes criticized because it appears that children are learning bad habits by misspelling words, but researchers have confirmed that children grow more quickly in phonemic awareness, phonics, and spelling, when they're invented spelling, as long as they're also receiving spelling instruction (Snow, Burns, & Griffin, 1998). As children learn more about spelling, their spellings become more sophisticated to reflect their new knowledge, even if the words are still spelled incorrectly, and increasingly children spell more and more words correctly as they move through the stages of spelling development.

NURTURING ENGLISH LEARNERS

English learners move through the same five developmental stages that native English speakers do, but they move more slowly because they're less familiar with the letter–sound correspondences, spelling patterns, and grammar of English (Bear, Helman, Templeton, Invernizzi, & Johnston, 2007). Children's spelling development reflects their reading achievement, but it lags behind reading: When ELs learn a word, they begin by learning its meaning and how to pronounce it. Almost immediately, they're introduced to the word's written form, and with practice, they learn to recognize and read it. Soon they're writing the word, too. At first their spellings reflect what they know about the English spelling system, but with spelling instruction and reading and writing practice, they learn to spell words correctly. Because spelling is more demanding than reading, it's not surprising that children's knowledge about spelling grows this way.

It's essential that teachers learn about English learners' home language, especially about the ways it differs from English, and then they need to explicitly teach children about the contrasts because they're harder to learn than the similarities (Bear, Helman, Invernizzi, Templeton, & Johnston, 2007). Consider these written language differences, for example: Chinese uses syllable-length characters instead of letters; Arabic is written from right to left, and the way letters are formed varies according to their location within a word; and vowels aren't used in Croatian and Czech. Some languages, including Arabic, Spanish, Kiswahili (Swahili), and Russian, are more phonetically consistent than English; children who speak these languages are often confused by the number of ways a sound can be spelled in English. There are phonological differences, too: Many languages, including Korean, don't have the /th/ sound; there's no /p/ in Arabic, so Arabic speakers often substitute /b/ in English; and /l/ and /r/ sound alike to speakers of Asian languages. Vowels are particularly difficult for English learners because they're often pronounced differently in their home language. For example, Russian speakers don't differentiate between short and long vowels, and Spanish speakers often substitute /ĕ/ for /ā/ and /ŏ/ for /ŏ/. Many African and Asian languages, including Kiswahili, Punjabi, Chinese, and Thai, as well as Navajo, a Native American language, are tonal; in these languages, pitch, not spelling differences, is used to distinguish between words. In addition, there are syntactic differences that affect spelling: Hmong speakers don't add plural markers to nouns; Korean speakers add grammatical information to the end of verbs instead of using auxiliary verbs; and Chinese speakers aren't familiar with prefixes or suffixes because they're not used in their language.

Teachers base their instruction on English learners' stage of spelling development, and they emphasize the contrasts between children's home languages and English. At each developmental stage, teachers focus their instruction on concepts that confuse English learners, according to Bear and his colleagues (2007):

Emergent Stage. Children learn English letters, sounds, and words, and they learn that English is written from left to right and top to bottom, with spaces between words. Developing this awareness is more difficult for children whose home languages aren't alphabetic.

Letter Name–Alphabetic Stage. Children learn that letters represent sounds, and the sounds that are the same in ELs' home languages and English are the easiest to learn. They learn both consonant and vowel sounds. Those consonant sounds that are more difficult include /d/, /j/, /r/, /sh/, and /th/. English learners often have difficulty pronouncing and spelling final consonant blends (e.g., *-st* as in *fast*, *-ng* as in *king*, *-mp* as in *stomp*, and *-rd* as in *board*). Long and short vowel sounds are especially hard because they're often pronounced differently than in students' home languages.

Within-Word Pattern Stage. Children move from representing individual sounds in words to using spelling patterns. They practice CVCe and CVVC spelling patterns and words that are exceptions to these rules; *r*-controlled vowels are especially tricky because they're found in common words, and sound often doesn't predict spelling (e.g., *bear/care/hair, bird/heard/fern/burst*). English learners also learn to spell homophones (e.g., *wear–where, to–too–two*) and contractions during this stage.

Syllables and Affixes Stage. Children learn spelling and grammar concepts together as they investigate verb forms (e.g., *talk–talked, take–took–taken, think–thought*), change adjectives to adverbs (e.g., *quick–quickly*), and add inflectional endings (e.g., *walks–walked–walking*), comparatives, superlatives (e.g., *sunny–sunnier–sunniest*). They also learn to pronounce accented and unaccented syllables differently and to use the schwa sound in unaccented syllables.

Derivational Relations Stage. Children learn about Latin and Greek root words and vowel alternations in related words (e.g., *define–definition*). Some ELs use tonal changes to signal these relationships in their home languages, but they must

---

PreK Practices

How do I teach spelling to 4-year-olds?

Spelling begins as preschoolers learn to identify and print the letters in their names. Soon these letters and others appear in their drawings. Researchers have identified this sequence in preschoolers' spelling development:

- ▶ Scribbling
- ▶ Adding letters and letterlike forms to scribbles
- ▶ Using random strings of letters to represent writing
- ▶ Copying environmental print (e.g., *Kmart*)
- ▶ Writing one or more letters that represent obvious sounds in a word (e.g., *K* = *cat*, *APL* = *apple*)
- ▶ Spelling names and phrases such as "I love you" correctly (Ray & Glover, 2008; Schickedanz & Casbergue, 2009)

As children move along this sequence, it's easy to see what they understand about the alphabet, environmental print, and words.

learn that related words in English are signaled by similar spelling and changes in how the vowels are pronounced.

Spelling instruction for English learners is similar to that for native speakers: Teachers use a combination of explicit instruction, word sorts and other practice activities, and authentic reading and writing activities. The biggest difference is that ELs need more instruction on the English spelling concepts that confuse them, often because these features aren't used in their home languages.

> Check the Compendium of Instructional Procedures, which follows Chapter 12, for more information on the highlighted terms.

TEACHING SPELLING

Perhaps the best-known way to teach spelling is through weekly spelling tests, but tests should never be considered a complete spelling program. To become good spellers, children need to learn about the English orthographic system and move through the stages of spelling development. They develop strategies for spelling unknown words and gain experience in using dictionaries and other resources. A complete spelling program includes these components:

Teaching Spelling Strategies. Children learn strategies to figure out how to spell unfamiliar words. As they move through the stages of spelling development, they become increasingly more sophisticated in their use of phonological, semantic, and historical knowledge to spell words; that is, they become more strategic. They learn to use these spelling strategies:

- ◆ Segmenting the word and spelling each sound, often called *sound it out*
- ◆ Spelling unknown words by analogy to familiar words
- ◆ Applying affixes to root words
- ◆ Proofreading to locate spelling errors in a rough draft
- ◆ Locating the spelling of unfamiliar words in a dictionary

Teachers often give the traditional "sound it out" advice when young children ask how to spell an unfamiliar word, but teachers provide more useful information when they suggest a strategic "think it out" approach. This advice reminds children that spelling involves more than phonological information and encourages them to think about spelling patterns, inflectional endings, and what the word looks like.

Be Strategic!

Spelling Strategies

Children use these strategies to spell words and to verify that words they've written are spelled correctly:

- ▶ Sound it out
- ▶ Spell by analogy
- ▶ Apply affixes
- ▶ Proofread
- ▶ Check a dictionary

Sounding out spellings works best for spelling phonetically regular words in first and second grades; later, children learn more effective strategies to think out correct spellings for longer words.

Matching Instruction to Developmental Stages. Teachers provide explicit instruction on spelling concepts and strategies that are developmentally appropriate. Children who are letter-name spellers, for example, learn about consonant and short vowel sounds because these are the concepts they're attempting to represent with letters. They're also ready to learn the "sound it out" strategy. Instruction on these topics wouldn't be appropriate for stage 4 spellers because they've already learned these concepts. Figure 5–2 lists topics for developmentally appropriate spelling instruction. Sometimes teachers find that developmentally appropriate instruction conflicts with directives about focusing instruction on grade-level standards. Differentiated instruction is the best way to address children's needs while presenting lessons on grade-level topics.

Providing Daily Reading and Writing Opportunities. Two of the most important ways that children learn to spell are through daily reading and writing activities. Children who are good readers tend to be good spellers, too: As they read, children visualize words—the shape of the word and the configuration of letters within it—and they use this knowledge to spell many words correctly and to recognize when a word they've written doesn't look right. Through writing, of course, children gain valuable practice using the strategies they've learned to spell words. And, as teachers work with children to proofread and edit their writing, they learn more about spelling and other writing conventions.

Teaching High-Frequency Words. High-frequency words are common, frequently occurring words, including *the, me, said, can, to, was, like,* and *you,* that children need to be able to spell automatically. Fewer than half of the 100 most frequently used words in English are spelled phonetically, so it's essential that children learn to spell them correctly because writers use the words again and again. Of the eight high-frequency words listed as examples, only three—*can, me,* and *like*—are spelled phonetically.

When children are engaged in a spelling program that includes these components, there's evidence of their learning in their writing. Children make progressively fewer errors, but more importantly, the types of spelling errors change: They become more

Figure 5-2 ◆ Developmentally Appropriate Spelling Instruction

Stage	Topics	
Emergent Spelling	phonemic awareness left-to-right progression of text concepts of "letter" and "word"	letters of the alphabet printing children's names consonant sounds
Letter Name-Alphabetic Spelling	initial and final consonant sounds blending and segmenting sounds initial and final consonant blends	short vowel sounds "sound it out" spelling strategy high-frequency words
Within-Word Pattern Spelling	consonant digraphs more complex consonant sounds silent letters more complex blends long vowel spelling patterns	vowel digraphs vowel diphthongs *r*-controlled vowels "think it out" spelling strategy high-frequency words
Syllables and Affixes Spelling	syllables schwa sound inflectional endings common prefixes and suffixes	compound words contractions homonyms dictionary use
Derivational Relations Spelling	Latin and Greek root words prefixs and suffixes	etymologies (word histories)

sophisticated. Children move from spelling phonetically to using morphological information and spelling rules. The feature above presents guidelines for spelling instruction.

Minilessons

Teachers regularly teach children about the English orthographic system through **minilessons** on phonics, phonograms, high-frequency words, spelling strategies, and spelling rules. The minilesson feature on page 134 shows how Mr. Cheng teaches his first graders to spell words using the *-at* phonogram or word family. In addition to teaching lessons to the whole class, teachers often differentiate instruction by teaching minilessons on developmentally appropriate topics to small groups of children, as Mrs. Zumwalt did in the vignette at the beginning of the chapter.

Word Walls

Teachers use two types of **word walls** in their classrooms. One type features "important" words from books children are reading or from thematic units. Words may be written on a large sheet of paper hanging in the classroom or on word cards and placed in a large pocket chart. Then children refer to these word walls when they're writing. Seeing the words posted on word walls and other charts in the classroom and using them in their writing help children learn to spell the words.

During a science unit on plants, for example, a first-grade teacher wrote these 11 words on word cards and placed them in a pocket chart word wall: *seed, root, stem, leaf, leaves, flower, plant, grow, soil, water,* and *sunshine.* The first graders practiced reading the words and used them when they drew diagrams about how plants grow and pictures of favorite flowers and wrote in their **learning logs.** As a culminating activity, the children wrote books about plants to demonstrate what they had learned.

Minilesson

TOPIC: Spelling -*at* Family Words
GRADE: First Grade
TIME: One 10-minute period

Mr. Cheng teaches phonics during guided reading lessons. He introduces, practices, and reviews phonics concepts using words from selections his first graders are reading. The children decode and spell words using letter and word cards, magnetic letters, and small whiteboards and pens.

1 Introduce the Topic

Mr. Cheng holds up a copy of *At Home*, the small paperback level E book the children read yesterday, and asks them to reread the title. Then he asks the children to identify the first word, *at*. After they read the word, he hands a card with the word *at* written on it to each of the six children in the guided reading group. "Who can read this word?" he asks. Several children recognize it immediately, and others carefully sound out the two-letter word.

2 Share Examples

Mr. Cheng asks children to think about rhyming words: "Who knows what rhyming words are?" Mike answers that rhyming words sound alike at the end—for example, *Mike, bike*, and *like*. The teacher explains that there are many words in English that rhyme, and that today, they are going to read and write words that rhyme with *at*. "One rhyming word is *cat*," he explains. Children name rhyming words, including *hat, fat*, and *bat*. Mr. Cheng helps each child in the group to name at least three rhyming words.

3 Provide Information

Mr. Cheng explains that children can spell these *at* words by adding a consonant in front of *at*. For example, he places the foam letter *c* in front of his *at* card, and the children blend *c* to *at* to read *cat*. Then he repeats the procedure by substituting other foam letters for the *c* to spell *bat, fat, hat, mat, pat, rat*, and *sat*. He continues the activity until every child successfully reads one of the words.

4 Guide Practice

Mr. Cheng passes out small plastic trays with foam letters to each child and asks them to add one of the letters to their *at* cards to spell the words as he pronounces them. He continues the activity until children have had several opportunities to spell each word, and they can quickly choose the correct initial consonant to spell it. Then Mr. Cheng collects the *at* cards and trays with foam letters.

5 Assess Learning

Mr. Cheng passes out small whiteboards and pens. He asks the first graders to write the words as he says each one aloud: *cat, hat, mat, pat, rat, sat, bat, fat*. He carefully observes as each child segments the onset and rime to spell the word. The children hold up their boards to show him their spellings. Afterward, children erase the word and repeat the process, writing the next word. After children write all eight words, Mr. Cheng quickly jots a note about which children need additional practice with the -*at* word family before continuing with the guided reading lesson.

They drew a picture and wrote a sentence on each page, often referring to the word wall to check the spelling of plant-related words. A page from one child's book is shown in Figure 5–3. It reads: *Plants need three things to grow big and strong.* Notice that the child used conventional spelling for the science words and high-frequency words and invented spelling for other words.

The second type of word wall displays high-frequency words. Researchers have identified the most commonly used words and recommend that children learn to spell 100 of these words because of their usefulness. The most frequently used words represent more than 50% of all the words children and adults write! Figure 5–4 lists the 100 most frequently used words.

Teachers plan a variety of activities to teach children how to read and spell high-frequency words; more information about teaching children to read these words is provided in Chapter 6, "Developing Fluent Readers and Writers." As children learn to read the words, they're also learning to spell them. Because most of the words aren't spelled phonetically, children must memorize the spellings; constant repetition as they read and write the words is useful. Also, children develop a visual representation of the word so that when they write it, they can recognize that their spelling is too short or long, or that it lacks a "tall" letter. For instance, *litle* doesn't look right with only one *t*, does it? It's not long enough, and there aren't enough tall middle letters. Or, what about *houes?* Reversing the last two letters of *house* looks funny. Children learn to refer to the word wall to spell unfamiliar words when they're writing, and as children become more proficient writers, teachers should expect them to use the word wall and to spell high-frequency words correctly.

Figure 5–3 ◆ A Page From a First Grader's "All About Plants" Book

Figure 5-4 ◆ The 100 High-Frequency Words

A	B	C	D E
a and about are after around all as am at an	back be because but by	came can could	day do did don't didn't down

F G	H	I J	K L
for from get got	had his have home he house her how him	I is if it in just into	know like little

M N	O	P Q R	S
man no me not mother now my	of our on out one over or	people put	said she saw so school some see

T	U V	W X	Y Z
that think the this them time then to there too they two things	up us very	was when we who well will went with were would what	you your

Word-Study Activities

Teachers provide hands-on activities for children to practice the spelling concepts they're learning. Concepts are usually introduced as whole-class activities, and then children have additional opportunities to practice them at centers. These activities expand children's spelling knowledge and help them move through the stages of spelling development.

Making Words. Teachers choose a five- to eight-letter word (or longer words for third and fourth graders) and prepare sets of letter cards for a making words activity (Cunningham & Cunningham, 1992). Then children use the cards to practice spelling words and to review spelling patterns and rules. They arrange and rearrange the cards to spell one-letter words, two-letter words, three-letter words, and so forth, until they use all the letters to spell the original word. Second graders, for example, can create these words using the letters in *weather*: *a, at, we, he, the, are, art, ear, eat, hat, her, hear, here, hate, heart, wheat, there,* and *where.* In addition, Mrs. Zumwalt's third graders participate in a making words activity using *grandfather* in the vignette at the beginning of the chapter

Word Ladders. Children spell words and learn word meanings when they make word ladders (Rasinski, 2006). In this word-building game, teachers direct the whole class or a small group of children to write a word and then change it into another word by substituting, adding, deleting, or rearranging letters. For example, a first-grade teacher used the word ladder game shown in Figure 5–5 to practice the short vowel sounds in CVC words. This word-building game is easy for teachers to adapt to almost any phonics or spelling concept.

Word Sorts. Children use word sorts to explore, compare, and contrast word features as they sort a pack of word cards. Teachers prepare word cards for children to sort into two or more categories according to word families, spelling patterns, or other criteria (Bear et al., 2008). Sometimes teachers tell children what categories to use, which makes the sort a closed sort; when children determine the categories themselves, the sort is an open sort. Children can sort word cards and then return them to an envelope for future use, or they can glue the cards onto a sheet of paper.

Interactive Writing. Teachers use interactive writing to teach spelling concepts as well as other concepts about written language. Because correct spelling and legible handwriting are courtesies for readers, teachers emphasize correct spelling as children take turns to collaboratively write a message. It is likely that children will misspell a few words as they write, so teachers take advantage of these "teachable moments" to clarify children's misunderstandings. Through interactive writing, children learn to use a variety of resources to correct misspelled words, including classroom word walls, books, classmates, and the dictionary.

Figure 5–5 ◆ CVC Word Ladder

The teacher says:	Children write:
Let's begin with a color word. The word is *red*. Write it now.	red
First, change one letter to spell the word for the piece of furniture you sleep on. What's the word?	bed
Change one letter to spell a word that is the opposite of *good*. What's the word?	bad
Change one letter to spell the word *mad*.	mad
Finally, change one letter to spell a word that means "wet dirt". What's the word?	mud

Figure 5-6 ◆ A First Grader's Draft and Edited News

My birthday is fabboWherey fith.
It is going to be a teyPrty
MY daddys bosse givs me my
birthday. She is Nighc.

My birthday is [February] fith.
It is going to be a [tea] [Party].
MY daddys boss [gives] me my
birthday[Party]. She is [nice].

Proofreading. Proofreading is a special kind of reading that children use to locate misspelled words and other mechanical errors in rough drafts. As children learn about the writing process, they are introduced to proofreading in the editing stage. More in-depth instruction about how to use proofreading to locate spelling errors and then correct these misspelled words is part of spelling instruction (Cramer, 1998). Through a series of minilessons, children can learn to proofread sample student papers and mark misspelled words. Then, working in pairs, children can correct the misspellings.

Teachers introduce proofreading in first grade through whole-class activities. They reread group writings to identify and correct errors, and through this experience, children learn that editing is an essential part of the writing process. In one first-grade class, for example, children share daily news using interactive writing, but as they become more fluent writers, the activity becomes a proofreading exercise. One child writes his or her news independently and then shares it with classmates. An unedited sample is shown in the top part of Figure 5–6. This child wrote about her upcoming birthday. Everyone was interested in this news and asked questions about her party. Then the teacher, the child-writer, and her classmates proofread the rough draft to identify misspelled words, capitalization and punctuation errors, and missing words. They made corrections using interactive writing techniques, as shown in the bottom part of the figure. The teacher didn't correct every mistake, focusing instead on those that children noticed and those that reflected the concepts she'd taught. The rectangles represent correction tape used to covered errors. Through this exercise, the teacher modeled proofreading and took advantage of teachable moments to review spelling concepts.

Dictionary Use. Children need to learn to locate the spelling of unfamiliar words in the dictionary. Although it's relatively easy to find a "known" word in the dictionary, it's hard to locate unfamiliar words, and children need to learn what to do when they don't know how to spell a word. One approach is to predict possible spellings for unknown words, then check the most probable spellings in a dictionary.

Children should be encouraged to check the spelling of words in a dictionary as well as to use a dictionary to check multiple meanings or etymology. Too often, children consider consulting a dictionary to be a punishment; teachers must work to change this view. One way to do this is to appoint several children as dictionary checkers: These children keep dictionaries on their desks, and they're consulted whenever questions about spelling, a word's meaning, or word usage arise.

Weekly Spelling Tests

Many teachers question the usefulness of spelling tests, because research on invented spelling suggests that spelling is best learned through reading and writing (Gentry & Gillet, 1993). In addition, teachers complain that lists of spelling words are unrelated to the words children are reading and writing and that the 30 minutes of valuable instructional time spent each day in completing spelling activities is excessive. Even so, parents and school board members value spelling tests as evidence that spelling is being taught. Weekly spelling tests, when they are used,

Go to the Assignments and Activities section of the Topic *Phonemic Awareness/Phonics* in the MyEducationLab for the literacy course and complete the activity entitled *Developmentally Appropriate Spelling Instruction*. As you examine the student artifact and answer the accompanying questions, consider the usefulness of weekly spelling tests.

should be individualized so that children learn to spell the words they need for writing.

In the individualized approach to spelling instruction, children choose the words they'll study, many of which are words they use in their writing projects. Children study 5 to 10 specific words during the week using a study strategy; this approach places more responsibility on children for their own learning. Teachers develop a weekly word list of 20 or more words of varying difficulty from which children select words to study. Words for the master list include high-frequency words, words from the word wall related to literature focus units and thematic units, and words children needed for their writing projects during the previous week. Words from spelling programs can also be added to the list.

On Monday, the teacher administers a pretest using the master list of words, and children spell as many of the words as they can. Children correct their own pretests, and from the words they misspell they create individual spelling lists. They make two copies of their study list, using the numbers on the master list to make it easier to take the final test on Friday. Children use one copy of the list for study activities, and the teacher keeps the second copy.

Children spend approximately 5 to 10 minutes studying the words on their study lists each day during the week. Research shows that instead of "busy-work" activities such as using their spelling words in sentences or gluing yarn in the shape of the words, it's more effective for children to use this study strategy:

1. Look at the word and say it to yourself.
2. Say each letter in the word to yourself.
3. Close your eyes and spell the word to yourself.
4. Write the word, and check that you spelled it correctly.
5. Write the word again, and check that you spelled it correctly.

This strategy focuses on the whole word rather than on breaking the word apart into sounds or syllables. Teachers explain how to use the strategy during a minilesson at the beginning of the school year and then post a copy of it in the classroom. In addition, children often trade word lists on Wednesday to give each other a practice test.

A final test is administered on Friday. The teacher reads the master list, and children write only those words they've practiced during the week. To make the test easier to administer, children first list on their test papers the numbers of the words they've practiced from their study lists. Any words that children misspell should be included on their lists the following week.

Assessing Children's Spelling Development

The choices children make as they spell words are important indicators of their knowledge of both phonics and spelling. For example, a child who spells phonetically might spell *money* as *mune*, and others who are experimenting with long vowels might spell the word as *monye* or *monie*. Teachers classify and analyze the words children misspell in their writing to gauge their level of spelling development and to plan for instruction. The steps in determining a child's stage of spelling

Assessment Tools

Determining a Child's Spelling Stage

1. **Choose a Writing Sample**
   Teachers choose a child's writing sample to analyze. In kindergarten and first grade, the sample should total at least 50 words, and 100 words in second through fourth grades. Teachers must be able to decipher most words in the sample to analyze it.

2. **Identify Spelling Errors**
   Teachers read the writing sample to identify errors and the words the child was trying to spell. If necessary, teachers check with the writer to determine the intended word.

3. **Make a Spelling Analysis Chart**
   Teachers draw a chart with five columns, one for each stage of spelling development.

4. **Categorize the Spelling Errors**
   Teachers classify the child's spelling errors according to the stage of development. They attribute each error to one of the stages, ignoring misspelled proper nouns, capitalization errors, and grammar errors. Teachers ignore poorly formed letters or reversed letterforms in kindergarten and first grade, but these are significant errors when older children make them. To simplify the analysis, teachers write both the child's error and the correct spelling in parentheses.

5. **Tally the Errors**
   Teachers count the errors in each column, and the one with the most errors indicates the child's current stage of development.

6. **Identify Topics for Instruction**
   Teachers examine the child's errors to identify instructional priorities.

development are explained in the Assessment Tools feature above. An analysis of a first grader's spelling development is shown in Figure 5–7.

Teachers analyze the errors in children's compositions, analyze their errors on weekly spelling tests, and administer diagnostic tests. The Assessment Tools feature on page 143 lists tests that teachers use to determine their students' stage of spelling development.

IF CHILDREN STRUGGLE...

Children who struggle with spelling often exhibit one or more of these problems:

High-Frequency Words. Children don't know how to spell high-frequency words and don't refer to lists of these words that are posted in the classroom. When they don't know how to spell these common words, struggling spellers often rely on phonics, even though many high-frequency words aren't phonetically regular. For example, they spell *was* as *wuz* and *could* as *cud*.

Figure 5-7 ◆ Analyzing a First Grader's Spelling

Writing Sample

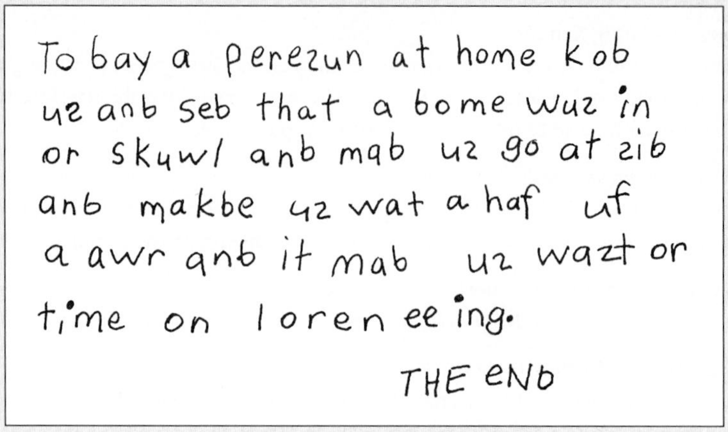

> To bay a perezun at home kob
> uz anb seb that a bome wuz in
> or skuwl anb mab uz go at zib
> anb makbe uz wat a haf uf
> a awr anb it mab uz wazt or
> time on l oren ee ing.
>   THE eNb

Translation: Today a person at home called us and said that a bomb was in our school and made us go outside and made us wait a half of an hour and it made us waste our time on learning. The end.

Spelling Analysis

Emergent	Letter Name–Alphabetic	Within-Word Patterns	Syllables and Affixes	Derivational Relations
	kod (called)	bome (bomb)	peresun (person)	
	sed (said)	or (our)	loreneeing (learning)	
	wus (was)	skuwl (school)		
	mad (made)	makde (made)		
	at (out)	uf (of)		
	sid (side)	awr (hour)		
	wat (wait)	or (our)		
	haf (half)			
	mad (made)			
	wazt (waste)			

Conclusion

The student spelled 56% of the words correctly, and most of his spelling errors were in the Letter Name–Alphabetic and Within-Word Patterns stages, which is typical of first graders' spelling.

Instructional Recommendations

- high-frequency words
- CVCe vowel pattern
- -*ed* inflectional ending

Phonics. Children continue to depend on the first phonics skills they learned, spelling words phonetically without applying phonics and spelling rules. For example, they spell *soap* as *sop*, *babies* as *babys*, and *running* as *runing*.

Handwriting. Some struggling spellers don't write legibility, or they form letters carelessly or write so quickly that they leave out letters as they spell words. It appears that they're using poor handwriting to mask misspelled words.

It's crucial that teachers determine what's causing the children's spelling problems and intervene to get them back on track for success.

The first step is diagnosis. Teachers observe struggling spellers as they write and analyze several of their writing samples. For each child, teachers determine

Assessment Tools

Spelling

Teachers assess children's spelling development by examining misspelled words in the compositions that they write. Teachers classify children's spelling errors according to the stages of spelling development and plan instruction based on their analysis. They also examine children's misspellings on weekly spelling tests and other tests. Here are three tests designed for classroom teachers to screen, monitor, diagnose, and document children's spelling development:

◆ **Developmental Spelling Analysis (DSA)** (Ganske, 2000)
   The DSA is a dictated spelling inventory with two components: a Screening Inventory for determining children's stage of spelling development, and Feature Inventories to highlight children's knowledge of specific spelling concepts. The DSA with detailed guidelines is available in Ganske's book, *Word Journeys: Assessment-Guided Phonics, Spelling, and Vocabulary Instruction* (2000).

◆ **Phonological Awareness Literacy Screening (PALS) System: Spelling Subtest** (Invernizzi, Meier, & Juel, 2003)
   The kindergarten-level battery of tests includes a brief spelling subtest in which children write the sounds they hear in CVC words. In the grades 1–3 tests, the spelling subtest includes words that exemplify phonics features that are appropriate for that grade level. Children receive credit for spelling the specific feature correctly and additional points for spelling the word correctly. The PALS test is available free for Virginia teachers from the University of Virginia, and it can be purchased by teachers in other states.

◆ **Qualitative Spelling Inventory (QSI)** (Bear et al., 2008)
   The QSI includes 20 or 25 spelling words listed according to difficulty and can easily be administered to small groups or whole classes. The QSI is available in *Words Their Way: Word Study for Phonics, Vocabulary, and Spelling Instruction* (Bear et al., 2008).

Through these tests, teachers identify children's stages of spelling development and use this information to monitor their progress and plan for instruction.

the child's stage of spelling development and examine both correctly spelled and misspelled words to identify specific problems. Teachers ask themselves these questions:

- Does the child spell most high-frequency words correctly?
- Does the child apply the phonics concepts that have been taught to spelling?
- Does the child depend on phonics for spelling almost all words?
- Does the child refer to the word wall for thematic words?
- Does the child write legibly?
- Does the child write entire words or leave out letters?

Once teachers have diagnosed each child's spelling problems, they decide how to intervene and plan for instruction.

Teachers teach minilessons and provide one-on-one and small-group instruction to address the children's identified problems. They also involve the children in practice activities, including interactive writing, making words, word ladders, and word sorts. Quick and intensive intervention is the most effective way to assist struggling spellers; otherwise, they're likely to fall further behind.

Writing is another essential component of a spelling intervention program. Typically, children who struggle with spelling don't do much writing, but they need to participate in daily writing activities to break bad habits and apply what they're learning. At first, brief and informal activities work best. Children can write a sentence or two about a book the teacher is reading aloud or about a big idea in a thematic unit. They can also write entries in personal journals about events going on in their lives. Teachers supervise children as they write and provide assistance, spelling words, demonstrating how to form letters, and locating words on word walls, as needed. Although spelling isn't usually emphasized in informal writing activities, children are expected to correctly spell high-frequency words they've been taught and words related to a book or unit that are posted on a word wall.

Teachers carefully monitor children's progress and reassess them every month or so to ensure that they're becoming more proficient spellers. If children continue to struggle, teachers repeat their diagnosis and adjust their instruction to meet children's needs.

What's the Controversy About Spelling Instruction?

The press and concerned parent groups periodically raise questions about invented spelling and the importance of weekly spelling tests. There's a misplaced public perception that today's children can't spell: Researchers who have examined the types of errors children make have noted that the number of misspellings increases in grades 1 through 4, as children write longer compositions, but that the percentage of errors decreases. The percentage continues to decline, although some children still make errors.

How Effective Teachers Teach Spelling

▶ Teachers recognize that learning to spell is a developmental process.

▶ Teachers consider each child's stage of spelling development as they plan for instruction.

▶ Teachers teach children to use strategies to "think out" the spelling of unfamiliar words.

▶ Teachers understand that a textbook is only one part of a complete spelling program.

Chapter 6

Developing Fluent Readers and Writers

Ms. Williams Teaches High-Frequency Words

The second graders in Ms. Williams's classroom are learning about hermit crabs and their tide pool environment. A plastic habitat box with a live hermit crab inside sits in the center of each group of desks. The children are learning how to care for their crustaceans, and they enjoy watching them. They've examined hermit crabs up close using magnifying glasses and identified their body parts. Ms. Williams helped them draw a diagram of a hermit crab on a large chart and label the body parts. They've also learned how to feed hermit crabs, how to get them to come out of their shells, and how they molt. Children write about their crustaceans in learning logs. One entry is shown on page 147.

Eric Carle's *A House for Hermit Crab* (2005) is the featured book for this unit. Ms. Williams has read it aloud several times, and she's also read *Moving Day* (Kaplan, 1996), *Hidden Hermit Crabs* (Doudna, 2007), and *Caring for Your Hermit Crab* (Richardson, 2006). Now the second graders are rereading these books independently or with buddies. Ms. Williams integrates many components of reading instruction into this literature focus unit, and she also conducts guided reading lessons using leveled books. Three of her second graders are fluent readers and writers; the others are at the beginning stage. They're learning high-frequency words, increasing their reading and writing speed, and becoming more expressive readers and writers.

To teach high-frequency words, Ms. Williams uses a high-frequency word wall, a brightly colored alphabet quilt with 26 letter blocks that's displayed permanently on one wall of the classroom. In September, Ms. Williams posted the 70 high-frequency words that the children already knew on the wall. Each word is written on a card, in print that's large enough for everyone to read. Then each week, Ms. Williams adds 3, 4, or 5 new words. First, she chose words from her list of the 100 high-frequency words; after finishing that list, she began choosing words from a list of the second 100 high-frequency words. She doesn't introduce the words in the order they're presented in the list; instead, she chooses words that she can connect the literature focus units or phonics lessons, as well as words children misspell in their writing.

This week, Ms. Williams adds *soon*, *house*, *your*, and *you're* to the word wall. She chooses *soon* and *house* because these words are used in *A House for Hermit Crab* and because several children have recently asked her how to spell *house*. She chooses the homophones *your* and *you're* because the second graders are confusing these two words. She's also noticed that some children don't understand contractions, so she plans to review them, using *you're* as an example.

A Child's Learning Log Entry

Ms. Williams's Literacy Centers

Library Center
Children read books about hermit crabs and reread leveled books that they've read in guided reading groups.

Listening Center
Children use headphones to listen to *A House for Hermit Crab* (Carle, 2005) and *Hermit Crab's Home* (Halfmann, 2007) as they follow along in individual copies of the books.

Retelling Center
Children sequence pictures from *A House for Hermit Crab* and use them as a guide to retell the story.

Science Center
Children observe a hermit crab and write entries in learning logs about the crustacean's physical characteristics and eating habits.

Word Sort Center
Children sort vocabulary words from *A House for Hermit Crab* into categories, including ocean animals and plants.

Word Wall Center
Children practice reading the high-frequency word wall using pointers. Then they copy familiar words from the word wall on a paper that's been divided into 10 sections with letters spelling *hermit crab* written in the sections.

Word Work Center
Children use magnetic letters to spell this week's high-frequency words and the words from the last 2 weeks. They also make a book of contractions with picture and sentence examples.

Writing Center
Children write books about hermit crabs or "I Am a Hermit Crab" poems following the model posted at the center.

The children sit on a rug in front of the word wall when Ms. Williams introduces new words. She explains that two of the new words—*house* and *soon*—are from *A House for Hermit Crab*. She uses a cookie sheet and large magnetic letters to introduce each new word, scrambling the letters at the bottom of the cookie sheet and slowly building the new word at the top of the sheet as children makes guesses. She begins with *h*, adds the *ou*, and several children call out "house." Ms. Williams continues adding letters, and when they are all in place, a chorus of voices cries, "house." It's Kari's turn to write the new word card. She carefully writes *house* and places the card in the *H* square of the word wall. The children chant and clap as they say and spell the word. Ms. Williams begins, "House, house, h-o-u-s-e," and children echo her chant. Then she calls on Enrique to lead the chant, and children echo him. Afterward, Ms. Williams repeats the procedure with the three other new words.

The next day, Ms. Williams uses interactive writing to compose sentences using each of the new words. The children write these sentences and underline the new words:

The hermit crab has a good shell for a house. He likes it but soon he will move.

"You're too small for me," he says. "I have to move, but I will always be your friend."

During the week, the children practice reading and writing the words. They do a cloze activity by filling in the missing words on sentence strips that Ms. Williams has prepared and laminated, they write words from the sentences on whiteboards as

Ms. Williams says them, and they copy the sentences in their reading logs using their best handwriting. They also cut apart word cards, arrange them to create the sentences, and then glue the cards onto a sheet of construction paper.

Ms. Williams reviews contractions in a minilesson, explaining that *you're* is a contraction of *you* and *are* and that the apostrophe indicates that a letter's been omitted. Then children volunteer other contractions. Michael identifies three: *I'm, can't,* and *don't*; Miki offers *it's* and *won't*. They make a chart, listing the contractions and the two words that make up each one. Afterward, Ms. Williams puts the chart in the word work center so the children can use the information to make books about contractions.

After this practice with high-frequency words, children participate in activities at literacy centers while Ms. Williams meets with guided reading groups. Most of the center activities integrate literacy activities with learning about hermit crabs, but children also practice reading and writing high-frequency words at two centers. Ms. Williams's literacy centers are described on page 148. Each morning, a sixth-grade student-aide comes to the classroom to monitor the children's work at the centers. Ms. Williams worked with two sixth-grade teachers to train 10 students to serve as aides, and they come to the classroom once every other week on a rotating basis.

As a culminating activity, the second graders write a retelling of *A House for Hermit Crab*. The children compose the text, and Ms. Williams uses the Language Experience Approach to write their draft on chart paper. Later the children revise their text, and then Ms. Williams types it and makes copies. Each child receives a copy of the 5-page retelling to read and illustrate. Later they'll take their booklets home to read to their families.

Ms. Williams reads their retelling aloud; afterward, the children participate in choral reading activities. The numbers on the left side indicate which group reads each sentence. As children read, they're becoming more fluent readers. Here's the last section of the class's retelling:

1	Soon it was January.
2	Hermit Crab moved out of his house and the little crab moved in.
3	"Goodbye." said Hermit Crab. Be good to my friends."
4	Soon Hermit Crab saw the perfect house.
5	It was a big, empty shell.
1	It looked a little plain but Hermit Crab didn't care.
2	He will decorate it
3	with sea urchins,
4	with sea anemones,
5	with coral,
1	with starfish,
2	with snails.
All	So many possibilities!

The blue words are posted on the word wall in Ms. Williams's classroom; of the 68 words in this excerpt, 37 are high-frequency words! Also, two of the new words for this week, *soon* and *house*, are used twice.

luency is the ability to read and write effortlessly and efficiently; becoming fluent readers and writers is a milestone in children's literacy development. Most children reach the fluent stage during second or third grade through a combination of explicit instruction and lots of authentic reading and writing. This achievement is crucial because both readers and writers must be able to focus attention on meaning, not on decoding and spelling words. Researchers have found that fluent readers do comprehend what they're reading better than less fluent readers do (National Reading Panel, 2000). The same is true about writers: Fluent writers are more successful in crafting effective compositions than less fluent writers are.

READING FLUENCY

Reading fluency is the ability to read quickly, accurately, and with expression, and to read fluently, children must recognize most words automatically and be able to identify unfamiliar words easily (Caldwell & Leslie, 2005). Pikulski and Chard (2005) explain that reading fluency is a bridge between decoding and comprehension. Fluent readers are better able to comprehend what they're reading because they automatically recognize most of the words and apply word-identification strategies to read unfamiliar words. Their reading is faster and more expressive (Kuhn & Rasinski, 2007). Reading fluency involves these three components:

Automaticity and Accuracy. Accuracy is the ability to recognize familiar words automatically, without conscious thought, and to identify unfamiliar words almost as quickly. It's crucial that children know most of the words they're reading because when they have to stop to decode words, their reading slows down. The conventional wisdom is that children can read a text successfully when they know at least 95% of the words; that's 19 of every 20 words or 95 of every 100 words. Allington (2009) challenges this notion, however, suggesting that children need to know 98 or 99% of the words to read fluently; otherwise, they're stopping too often to figure out unfamiliar words.

Speed. Fluent readers read at least 100 words per minute. Most children reach this speed by third grade, and their reading rate continues to grow each year. By eighth grade, most students read 150 words per minute, and many adults read 250 words per minute or more. In addition, fluent readers vary reading speed depending on the selection—its genre and level of difficulty—and their purpose for reading.

Prosody. The ability to read sentences expressively, with appropriate phrasing and intonation, is called *prosody*. Dowhower (1991) describes prosody as "the ability to read in expressive rhythmic and melodic patterns" (p. 166). Beginning readers read word by word with little or no expression, but with experience, they chunk words into phrases, attend to punctuation, and apply appropriate syntactic emphases. Once children become fluent readers, their oral reading approximates speech.

Too often, reading quickly is equated with fluency, and some assessment tools use speed as the only measure of fluency, but accurately identifying words and reading expressively are also critical components. Figure 6–1 summarizes the characteristics of fluent readers.

Go to the Building Teaching Skills and Dispositions section of the Topic *Fluency* in the MyEducationLab for the literacy course and complete the activity entitled *Fostering Reading Fluency*. As you work through the learning unit, note the balanced attention to the three components of fluency.

Figure 6-1 ◆ Characteristics of Fluent Readers

Component	Characteristics
Automaticity and Accuracy	Children recognize many high-frequency words. Children apply phonics knowledge to decode words. Children decode words by analogy to familiar words. Children break longer words into syllables to decode them.
Speed	Children read at least 100 words per minute. Children vary their speed depending on their purpose for reading and the difficulty of the text.
Prosody	Children read expressively. Children chunk words into phrases. Children read smoothly, with few pauses or breakdowns. Children's reading pace approximates speech.

Automatic and Accurate Reading

Children acquire a large stock of words that they recognize automatically and read correctly because it's impossible to analyze every word they encounter when reading. Through repeated reading and writing experiences, children develop automaticity, the ability to quickly recognize words (Samuels, 2004). The vital element in word recognition is learning each word's unique letter sequence.

High-Frequency Words. The most common words that readers use again and again are *high-frequency words*. There have been numerous attempts to identify these words and to calculate their frequency in reading materials. Pinnell and Fountas (1998, p. 89) identified these 24 common words that kindergartners learn to read:

a	at	he	it	no	the
am	can	I	like	see	to
an	do	in	me	she	up
and	go	is	my	so	we

They also learn to write many of these words.

The words in this list are part of the 100 high-frequency words, which account for more than half of the words people read and write. Eldredge (2005) has identified the 300 high-frequency words that make up nearly three quarters of the words people read and write; these 300 words account for 72% of the words that beginning readers read. Figure 6–2 presents Eldredge's list of 300 high-frequency words; the 100 most common ones are in red. Most children learn the majority of the 100 highest frequency words in first grade and the rest of the words during second and third grades. If fourth graders don't know these words, it's essential that they learn them to become automatic and accurate readers and writers.

Many high-frequency words are tough to learn because they can't be easily decoded (Cunningham, 2009); try sounding out the words *to*, *what*, and *could* and you'll see how difficult they are. A further complication is that many of these words are function words, so they don't carry much meaning. It's easier to learn to recognize *whale* than *what*,

Figure 6-2 ◆ The 300 High-Frequency Words

a	children	great	looking	ran	through
about	city	green	made	read	time
after	come	grow	make	red	to
again	could	had	man	ride	toad
all	couldn't	hand	many	right	together
along	cried	happy	may	road	told
always	dad	has	maybe	room	too
am	dark	hat	me	run	took
an	day	have	mom	said	top
and	did	he	more	sat	tree
animals	didn't	head	morning	saw	truck
another	do	hear	mother	say	try
any	does	heard	mouse	school	two
are	dog	help	Mr.	sea	under
around	don't	hen	Mrs.	see	until
as	door	her	much	she	up
asked	down	here	must	show	us
at	each	hill	my	sister	very
ate	eat	him	name	sky	wait
away	end	his	need	sleep	walk
baby	even	home	never	small	walked
back	ever	house	new	so	want
bad	every	how	next	some	wanted
ball	everyone	I	nice	something	was
be	eyes	I'll	night	soon	water
bear	far	I'm	no	started	way
because	fast	if	not	stay	we
bed	father	in	nothing	still	well
been	find	inside	now	stop	went
before	fine	into	of	stories	were
began	first	is	off	story	what
behind	fish	it	oh	sun	when
best	fly	it's	old	take	where
better	for	its	on	tell	while
big	found	jump	once	than	who
bird	fox	jumped	one	that	why
birds	friend	just	only	that's	will
blue	friends	keep	or	the	wind
book	frog	king	other	their	witch
books	from	know	our	them	with
box	fun	last	out	then	wizard
boy	garden	left	over	there	woman
brown	gave	let	people	these	words
but	get	let's	picture	they	work
by	girl	like	pig	thing	would
called	give	little	place	things	write
came	go	live	play	think	yes
can	going	long	pulled	this	you
can't	good	look	put	thought	your
cat	got	looked	rabbit	three	you're

From *Teach Decoding: How and Why* (2nd ed., pp. 119–120), by J. L. Eldredge, © 2005. Adapted by permission of Prentice Hall, Inc., Upper Saddle River, NJ.

*The words in red are the first 100 most frequently used words, as shown in Figure 5–4 on p. 136.

because *whale* conjures up the image of the huge aquatic mammal, but *what* is abstract; however, *what* is used much more frequently, and children must learn to read and write it.

Teachers teach the high-frequency words using explicit instruction. Each week they introduce three to five words, and then involve children in a variety of activities each day to practice reading and writing the words, as Ms. Williams did in the vignette at the beginning of the chapter. Even though the words are listed alphabetically in Figure 6–2, they aren't taught in that order; instead, teachers choose words that they can connect with literacy activities in the classroom or words that children are using but confusing.

Teachers create word walls with the high-frequency words. They prepare word walls at the beginning of the school year and then add to them as they introduce new words. Kindergarten teachers begin by listing children's names and other common words (e.g., *love*, *Mom*) and then adding the 24 highest-frequency words, 1 or 2 per week. First-grade teachers begin with the 24 words introduced in kindergarten and add new words each week. In second grade, teachers begin with the easier half of the first 100 words and introduce 100 more words during the school year. Third-grade teachers check children's knowledge of the 100 or 200 high-frequency words at the beginning of the school year, add any words they don't know, and then teach the rest of the high-frequency words so that everyone learns most of the 300 high-frequency words by the end of the year. Fourth-grade teachers continue to use high-frequency word walls if their students aren't fluent readers and writers. They test children's ability to read and write the 300 high-frequency words and teach the words they don't know.

Teaching high-frequency words isn't easy, because many of them have little or no meaning when they're used in isolation. Cunningham (2009) recommends this chant-and-clap procedure to practice the words being placed on the word wall:

1. **Introduce the word in context.** Teachers introduce the new word using a familiar book or with pictures or objects.
2. **Have children chant and clap the word.** Teachers display the word card that will be placed on the word wall. They read and spell the word and have children read and spell it. Then they begin a chant, saying the word twice and then spelling it. For the word *the*, teachers say, "The, the, t-h-e" as they clap their hands. The children repeat the chant several times.
3. **Involve children in practice activities.** Teachers provide daily opportunities for children to practice reading and writing the words:
   - Children search for the word in books they're reading and on charts posted in the classroom.
   - Children write a sentence using the word on a sentence strip, read it to classmates, and later cut the sentence apart and rearrange the words.
   - Children write the words on whiteboards.
   - Children use magnetic letters to spell the words.

   Teachers lead children in some of these activities, and children do others at centers.
4. **Provide authentic reading and writing activities.** Children read and write the word during authentic literacy activities. During sharing sessions after independent reading and writing, teachers ask children to point where they read or wrote they word. Teachers also draw attention to the word during interactive read-alouds, shared reading, and interactive writing activities.

Using this chant-and-clap procedure, teachers highlight high-frequency words, and easily confused words are clarified and practiced. A minilesson showing how a first-grade teacher teaches high-frequency words is presented on page 154.

> Check the Compendium of Instructional Procedures, which follows Chapter 12, for more information on the highlighted terms.

Minilesson

TOPIC: Teaching High-Frequency Words
GRADE: First Grade
TIME: One 15-minute period

Miss Shapiro's goal is for her first graders to learn at least 75 of the 100 high-frequency words. She has a large word wall that's divided into sections for each letter. Each week, she introduces three new words and adds them to the word wall. She chooses words from the big book she's using for shared reading. On Monday, she introduces the new words and over the next 4 days, she focuses on them and reviews those she's introduced previously. To make the word study more authentic, the children often hunt for the word in reading materials available in the classroom; sometimes they look in familiar big books, in small books they're rereading, on charts of familiar poems and songs, or on Language Experience and interactive writing charts. On other days, the children create sentences using the words, which the teacher writes on sentence strips and displays in the classroom.

1 Introduce the Topic

"Let's read the D words on the word wall," Miss Shapiro says. As she points to the words, the class reads them aloud. "Which word is new this week?" she asks. The children respond, "do." Next, they read the H words and identify *here* as a new word, and then the M words and identify *my* as a new word. She asks individual children to reread the D, H, and M words on the word wall.

2 Share Examples

"Who can come up and point to our three new words for this week?" Miss Shapiro asks. Aaron eagerly comes to the word wall to point out *do, here*, and *my*. As he points to each word, Miss Shapiro writes it on the chalkboard, pronounces it, and spells it aloud. She and Aaron lead the class as they chant and clap the words: "Do, do, d-o, do!" "Here, here, h-e-r-e, here!" "My, my, m-y, my!"

3 Provide Information

"Let's look for *do, here*, and *my* in these books," Miss Shapiro suggests as she passes out a familiar big book to the children at each table. In each group, the children reread the book, pointing out *do, here*, and *my* each time they occur. The teacher circulates around the classroom, checking that the children notice the words.

4 Guide Practice

Miss Shapiro asks Aaron to choose three classmates to come to the chalkboard to spell the words with large magnetic letters; Daniel, Elizabeth, and Wills spell the words and read them aloud. Then Aaron passes out plastic bags with small magnetic letters and word cards to each pair of children. They read the word cards and spell the three words at their desks.

5 Assess Learning

On Friday, Miss Shapiro works with the first graders in small groups, asking them to locate the words in sentences they've written and to read the words individually on word cards.

Word-Identification Strategies. Children use word-identification strategies to read unfamiliar words. Young children depend on phonics to sound out unfamiliar words, but beginning readers learn decoding by analogy and syllabic analysis as they become more fluent readers. These word-identification strategies are summarized in Figure 6–3.

Phonic Analysis. Children apply what they've learned about phoneme–grapheme correspondences and phonics rules to decode words. Even though English isn't a perfectly phonetic language, phonic analysis is a very useful strategy because almost every word has some phonetically regular parts. Researchers report that the biggest difference between children who identify words effectively and those who don't is whether they notice almost all the letters in a word and analyze the letter sequences (Stanovich, 1992). Young children often try to decode a word by guessing at it based on the beginning sound. As you might imagine, their guesses are usually wrong; sometimes they don't even make sense in the sentence.

Be Strategic!

Word-Identification Strategies

Children use these strategies to identify unfamiliar words when they're reading:

- ▶ Use phonic analysis
- ▶ Decode by analogy
- ▶ Divide into syllables
- ▶ Apply morphemic analysis

Children's choice of strategy depends on their knowledge about words and the complexity of the unfamiliar word.

Decoding by Analogy. Children identify some words by associating them with words they already know; this strategy is known as *decoding by analogy* (Cunningham, 2009). When readers come to *small*, for example, they might notice the phonogram *-all*, think of the word *ball*, and decode the word by analogy. Children learn to apply this strategy when they read and write "word families" using familiar phonograms, such as *-at*, *-ell*, *-ice*, *-own*, and *-unk*. Children must be familiar with consonant blends and digraphs and able manipulate sounds to apply this strategy. Using *-ill*, for example, children can read and spell these words: *bill, chill, fill, gill, grill, hill, kill, pill, spill, still,* and *will*. They can decode longer words, too,

Figure 6-3 ◆ Word-Identification Strategies

Strategy	Description	Examples
Phonic Analysis	Children apply their knowledge of sound–symbol correspondences, phonics rules, and spelling patterns to read or write a word.	*blaze* *chin* *peach* *spring*
Decoding by Analogy	Children use their knowledge of phonograms to deduce the pronunciation or spelling of an unfamiliar word.	*claw* from *saw* *flat* from *cat* *stone* from *cone* *think* from *pink*
Syllabic Analysis	Children break a multisyllabic word into syllables and then use their knowledge of phonics and phonograms to decode the word, syllable by syllable.	*drag-on* *fa-mous* *mul-ti-ply* *vol-ca-no*
Morphemic Analysis	Children apply their knowledge of root words and affixes to read or write an unfamiliar word.	*astro-naut* *bi-cycle* *centi-pede* *trans-port*

Go to the Assignments and Activities section of the Topic *Fluency* in the MyEducationLab for the literacy course and complete the activity entitled *Understanding the Components of Reading Fluency*.

including *hills, chilly, killers, grilling, hilltop,* and *pillow*. Teachers also share picture books that include several words representing a particular phonogram (Caldwell & Leslie, 2005). In Fleming's *In the Tall, Tall Grass* (1995), for example, children can locate these *-um* words: *drum, hum, strum*. Figure 6–4 lists additional books with words representing common phonograms. It's a big step, however, for children to move from a structured activity to using this strategy independently to identify unfamiliar words.

Syllabic Analysis. More experienced readers divide longer words, such as *angry, pioneer,* and *yogurt*, into syllables to identify them. There's one vowel sound in each syllable of a word, but sometimes there's more than one vowel letter in a syllable. Consider the two-syllable words *target* and *chimney*: *Target* has a single vowel letter representing a short vowel sound in each syllable; *chimney* has one vowel in the first syllable but two vowel letters (*ey*) representing a long vowel sound in the second syllable. The most common guidelines for dividing words into syllables are presented in Figure 6–5. The first rule about dividing syllables between two consonants is the easiest one; examples include *mer-maid* and *pic-nic*. The second rule deals with words where three consonants appear together, such as *ex-plore*: The word is divided between *x* and *p* to preserve the *pl* blend. The third and fourth rules involve the VCV pattern. Usually the syllable boundary comes after the first vowel, as in *ho-tel* and *shi-ny*; however, in words such as *riv-er*, the division comes after the consonant because *ri-ver* isn't a recognizable word. According to the fifth rule, syllables are divided between two vowels when they don't represent a digraph or diphthong. One example is *li-on*.

Figure 6-4 ◆ Books With Words Representing a Phonogram

Phonogram	Book
-ack	Shaw, N. E. (1996). *Sheep take a hike*. Boston: Houghton Mifflin.
-ail	Shaw, N. E. (1992). *Sheep on a ship*. Boston: Houghton Mifflin.
-are	Fleming, D. (1998). *In the small, small pond*. New York: Henry Holt.
-ash	Shaw, N. E. (2005). *Sheep eat out*. Boston: Houghton Mifflin.
-ay	Fleming, D. (1998). *In the small, small pond*. New York: Henry Holt.
-eep	Shaw, N. E. (1997). *Sheep in a jeep*. Boston: Houghton Mifflin.
-eet	Heiligman, D. (2005). *Fun dog, sun dog*. New York: Marshall Cavendish.
-ip	Fleming, D. (1995). *In the tall, tall grass*. New York: Henry Holt.
-og	Wood, A. (1992). *Silly Sally*. San Diego: Harcourt Brace.
-oose	Numeroff, L. J. (1991). *If you give a moose a muffin*. New York: HarperCollins.
-op	Shaw, N. E. (2005). *Sheep eat out*. Boston: Houghton Mifflin.
-ouse	Hoberman, M. A. (2007). *A house is a house for me*. New York: Puffin Books.
-own	Wood, A. (1992). *Silly Sally*. San Diego: Harcourt Brace.
-uck	Root, R. (2003). *One duck stuck*. Cambridge, MA: Candlewick Press.
-ug	Edwards, P. D. (1996). *Some smug slug*. New York: HarperCollins.
-um	Fleming, D. (1995). *In the tall, tall grass*. New York: Henry Holt.
-un	Heiligman, D. (2005). *Fun dog, sun dog*. New York: Marshall Cavendish.

Figure 6-5 ◆ Syllabication Rules

Rule	Examples
When two consonants come between two vowels in a word, divide syllables between the consonants.	mer-maid pic-nic soc-cer win-dow
When there are more than two consonants together in a word, divide the syllables keeping the blends together.	bank-rupt com-plete ex-plore mon-ster
When there is one consonant between two vowels in a word, divide the syllables after the first vowel.	bo-nus ho-tel plu-ral shi-ny
If following the previous rule doesn't make a recognizable word, divide the syllables after the consonant that comes between the vowels.	doz-en ech-o plan-et riv-er
When there are two vowels together that don't represent a long vowel sound or a diphthong, divide the syllables between the vowels.	li-ar li-on po-em qui-et

Morphemic Analysis. Children use morphemic analysis to identify multisyllabic words. They locate the root word by peeling off any affixes (prefixes or suffixes). A root word is a *morpheme*, the basic, most meaningful part of a word. Prefixes are added to the beginning of a root word, as in *replay*, and suffixes are added to the end, as in *playing*, *playful*, and *player*. Two types of suffixes are *inflectional* and *derivational*. Inflectional suffixes are endings that indicate verb tense, person, plurals, possession, and comparison:

the *-s* in *dogs*	the *-ed* in *walked*	the *-er* in *faster*
the *-es* in *beaches*	the *-s* in *eats*	the *-est* in *sunniest*
the *-'s* in *girl's*	the *-ing* in *singing*	

In contrast, derivational suffixes show the relationship of the word to its root word. Consider these words containing the root word *friend*: *friendly*, *friendship*, and *friendless*. When children recognize roots and affixes, they can more easily break apart multisyllabic words and identify them:

astronaut (astro = *star*; naut = *sailor*)	popular (pop = *people*)
bicycle (bi = *two*; cycle = *wheels*)	scribble (scrib = *write*)
equator (equa = *equal*)	superhero (super = *above*)
impossible (im = *not*)	synonym (syn = *same*; onym = *name*)

microscope (micro = *small*;
  scope = *see*)
	thermometer (therm = *heat*;
	  meter = *measure*)

multicolored (multi = *many*)	vitamin (vita = *life*)

In addition, knowing the meaning of word parts provides context and facilitates word identification.

Teaching word-identification strategies is an essential part of a balanced literacy program that helps children focus on words. Teachers choose words for mini-lessons from books children are reading, as Ms. Williams did in the vignette, or from thematic units.

Fluent readers recognize most words automatically and apply word-identification strategies effectively to decode unfamiliar words. Less fluent readers, in contrast, can't read as many words or use as many strategies for decoding words. Researchers have concluded that children who don't become fluent readers depend on explicit instruction to learn how to identify words (Gaskins, Gaskins, & Gaskins, 1991).

Reading Speed

Children need to develop an adequate reading speed so they have the cognitive resources available to focus on meaning (Allington, 2009; Rasinski & Padak, 2008). Researchers have identified target reading speeds for each grade level, and they're shown in Figure 6–6; however, teachers should use these numbers cautiously because reading speed is affected by many factors. Fountas and Pinnell (2006) identified these factors that affect reading speed:

- Children who have background knowledge about the topic can read more quickly and connect the ideas they're reading to what they already know.
- Children who are knowledgeable about the genre, text structure, and text layout can anticipate what they're reading.
- Children who speak English fluently have an advantage in developing reading speed because they know more words, are familiar with English sentence structures, and recognize metaphors and other literary features.

Children become more strategic readers as they learn to use speed appropriately and vary their reading rate depending on the text.

Teachers provide daily practice opportunities to develop children's reading speed and stamina. To increase reading volume, teachers offer a combination of teacher-guided and independent reading practice:

Figure 6-6 ◆ Oral Reading Speed by Grade Levels			
Grade	Beginning of the Year	Middle of the Year	End of the Year
1	0–10 wcpm*	10–50	30–90
2	20–80	40–100	60–130
3	60–110	70–120	80–140
4	70–120	80–130	90–150

*wcpm = words correct per minute.
From Rasinki & Padak, 2008, p. 258.

Choral Reading. Children work in small groups or together as a class for choral reading. They experiment with different ways to read poems and other short texts aloud (Rasinski, 2003). More fluent classmates serve as models and set the reading speed.

Readers Theatre. Children practice reading a story script to develop reading speed and expressiveness before performing it for classmates. Researchers have found that readers theatre significantly improves children's reading fluency (Martinez, Roser, & Strecker, 1998/1999).

Listening Center. Children read along in a book at their instructional reading level while listening to it being read aloud at a listening center (Kuhn & Stahl, 2004).

Partner Reading. Classmates read or reread books together (Griffith & Rasinski, 2004). They choose a book that interests them and decide how they'll read it; they may read aloud in unison or take turns reading aloud while the partner follows along.

To develop fluency through these practice activities, books must be appropriate; that is, children must be interested in the topics and be able to read them with 98 or 99% accuracy.

Once children become fluent readers, the focus shifts to helping them develop reading stamina so they can read for 30 minutes or more. Children develop this strength through daily opportunities to read independently for increasingly longer periods. When children's reading is limited to basal reader selections or leveled books that can be completed in 15 minutes or less, they won't develop the endurance they need. Teachers include extended opportunities each day for independent reading of self-selected texts, and children also benefit from doing additional independent reading at home.

Prosody

When children read expressively, they use their voices to add meaning to the words. Rasinski and Padak (2008) identified these components of prosody:

Expression. Children read with enthusiasm and vary their expression to match their interpretation of the text.

Phrasing. Children chunk words into phrases as they read and apply stress and intonation appropriately.

Volume. Children vary the loudness of their voices to add meaning to the text.

Smoothness. Children read with a smooth rhythm and quickly self-correct any breakdowns.

Pacing. Children read at a conversational speed.

These components seem more related to oral reading, but prosody plays an important role during silent reading, too, because children's internal voice affects comprehension.

LITERACY PORTRAITS
Viewing Guide

Most second graders move toward fluent reading, and Ms. Janusz spends a great deal of time talking about fluent reading, explaining its importance, teaching the components, and listening to her students read aloud to monitor their growth. Go to the Literacy Portraits section of the MyEducationLab for the Literacy Course and click on Rakie's December video clip to watch Ms. Janusz explain reading fluency during a guided reading lesson. Does she include the three components of fluency addressed in this chapter? Why do you think that she asks children to retell what they've just read? In this video clip, you can also listen to Rakie reading aloud. Next, click on Rakie's May button to listen to her reread *Click, Clack, Moo: Cows That Type*, by Doreen Cronin, and retell it to a classmate; it's one of her favorite books, and she's read it many times. Compare her accuracy, reading speed, and expression now with her fluency in December. Do you think that she's become a fluent reader?

myeducationlab

DEVELOPMENTAL CONTINUUM   Oral Reading Fluency

PreK	K	1	2	3	4
Four-year-olds begin to develop an understanding of fluency—accuracy, speed, and prosody—as they listen to teachers read aloud.	Children participate in fluent reading as they join in to recite refrains while teachers read aloud big books and charts.	Children learn to recognize many high-frequency words and decode others; they reach a reading speed of 50 words per minute.	Children's oral reading becomes more accurate, rapid, and expressive; their reading speed reaches 80 wpm by the end of the year.	Most third graders reach the fluency milestone where they can accurately and expressively read aloud 100 words per minute.	Fluent fourth graders can read most books successfully, but dysfluent readers struggle with grade-level reading materials.

Teachers emphasize prosody by modeling expressive reading every time they read aloud and using the think-aloud procedure to reflect on how they varied their expression, chunked words into phrases, modulated the loudness of their voice, or varied their pacing. They talk about the importance of prosody for both fluency and comprehension and show children how meaning is affected when they read in a monotone or slow down their reading speed.

Choral reading and readers theatre are two ways to develop prosody. In choral reading, children work together in small groups to read poems and other texts. They practice reading the text until they can read it smoothly, and they experiment with ways to read more expressively, including varying the loudness of their voices, their intonation patterns, and their pacing. In readers theatre, children assume the roles of characters and practice reading a script aloud without performing it. The emphasis is on reading smoothly at a conversational pace and using expression so their voices add meaning to the words.

Assessing Reading Fluency

Teachers informally monitor children's reading fluency by listening to them read aloud during guided reading lessons, reading workshop, or other reading activities. At the beginning of the school year and at the end of each month or quarter, teachers collect data about children's accuracy, speed, and prosody to document their progress and provide evidence of their growth over time:

Automaticity and Accuracy. Teachers check children's knowledge of high-frequency words and their ability to use word-identification strategies to decode other words taken from grade-level texts. Kindergartners are expected to read 24 high-frequency words, first graders 100 words, second graders 200 words, and third graders 300 words. In addition to the list of high-frequency words

Go to the Assignments and Activities section of the Topic *Fluency* in the MyEducationLab for the literacy course and complete the activity entitled *Assessing Students' Reading Fluency*. As you watch the video and answer the accompanying questions, describe effective fluency assessment and how it can be used to plan instruction.

presented in this chapter, teachers can use the Dolch list of 220 sight words and Fry's list of 300 instant words, both of which are available in *Assessment for Reading Instruction* (McKenna & Dougherty Stahl, 2009) and online.

Speed. Teachers time children as they read an instructional-level passage aloud and determine how many words they read correctly per minute. Teachers can use the speeds listed in Figure 6–6 to compare children's speeds to national norms.

Prosody. Teachers choose excerpts for children to read from both familiar and unfamiliar instructional-level texts. As they listen, teachers judge whether children read with appropriate expression. The rubric in Figure 6–7 can be used to evaluate children's prosody.

This assessment information is also useful for teachers as they make instructional decisions.

Teachers use running records, informal reading inventories, and classroom tests to document children's reading fluency. The Assessment Tools feature on page 162 lists the tests that evaluate children's oral reading fluency—their reading speed in particular. Until children become fluent readers, it's crucial that teachers regularly monitor their developing accuracy, speed, and prosody to ensure that children are making adequate progress and identify children who are struggling.

Figure 6-7 ◆ A Rubric to Assess Prosody

	1	2	3	4
Expression	Monotone	Some expressiveness	Reasonable expressiveness	Expression matches interpretation
Phrasing	Word-by-word reading	Choppy reading	Reasonable chunking and intonation	Effective phrasing
Volume	Very quiet voice	Quiet voice	Appropriate volume	Volume matches interpretation
Smoothness	Frequent extended pauses and breakdowns	Some pauses and break-downs	A few pauses or breakdowns	Smooth rhythm
Pacing	Laborious reading	Slow reading	Uneven combi-nation of fast and slow reading	Appropriate conversational pace

Adapted from Rasinski & Padak, 2008.

Assessment Tools

Oral Reading Fluency

Teachers use these assessment tools as well as running records and IRIs to monitor and document children's reading fluency:

◆ **Dynamic Indicators of Basic Early Literacy Skills (DIBELS): Oral Reading Fluency Subtest**
(Kaminski & Good, 1996)
The Oral Reading Fluency Subtest is a collection of graded passages used to measure first through third graders' reading speed. In this individually administered test, children read aloud for one minute, and teachers mark errors; children's speed is the number of words read correctly. This test is available on the DIBELS website.

◆ **Fluency Checks** (Johns & Berglund, 2006)
Teachers have children read grade-level passages to monitor their growth toward fluent reading. The authors recommend testing children several times a year. Teachers listen as children read aloud for one minute and mark errors on a scoring sheet. They also ask comprehension questions related to the part of the passage that children read. Afterward, teachers calculate children's reading speed and score it against grade-level standards, and they rate their prosody.

◆ **Fluency Formula Kits**
Teachers use these grade-level kits, developed by Scholastic, to quickly assess individual children's reading fluency three times a year and interpret their scores using national norms. Each grade-level kit (grades 1–4) contains 3 benchmark passages, 24 progress-monitoring passages, an assessment handbook, a student timer, and progress charts. The progress-monitoring passages can be used weekly to monitor struggling students' growth, and the handbook offers guidance on setting instructional goals and differentiating instruction. Scholastic sells each grade-level kit separately.

◆ **Observation Survey of Early Literacy Achievement (OS): Word Reading and Writing Vocabulary Subtests**
(Clay, 2007a)
These two OS subtests assess children's knowledge of high-frequency words. In the Word Reading Subtest, children read 15 high-frequency words, and in the Writing Vocabulary Subtest, they write all the words they know (with a 10-minute time limit). The Word Reading Subtest is administered individually, but children take the Writing Vocabulary Subtest together. The tests and directions for administering and scoring them are included in *An Observation Survey of Early Literacy Achievement* (Clay, 2007a), which is available from Heinemann.

◆ **Phonological Awareness Literacy Screening (PALS) System: Word Recognition in Isolation Subtest**
(Invernizzi, Meier, & Juel, 2003)
The Word Recognition Subtest consists of graded word lists that children read aloud; the highest level at which children read 15 words correctly is their instructional level. First- through third-grade teachers use this subtest to monitor children's automatic word recognition. The PALS test is available free for Virginia teachers from the University of Virginia, and it can be purchased by schools in other states.

◆ **Reading Fluency Benchmark Assessor (RFBA)**
Teachers use the RFBA to regularly monitor children's progress and identify those readers who aren't making adequate progress. This quick and easy-to-use assessment tool, published by Read Naturally, includes 30 fiction and nonfiction passages at each grade level, and software is available for recording data and generating reports. Teachers measure children's fluency by listening to them read a passage aloud for one minute and calculating the number of words they read correctly. The RFBA is available for purchase at the Read Naturally website.

Although many of these tests use reading speed to measure fluency, it's important to remember that fluency also requires children to recognize high-frequency words automatically, apply word-identification strategies to decode unfamiliar words, and read expressively.

IF CHILDREN STRUGGLE...

When children aren't making adequate progress toward becoming fluent readers, teachers pinpoint the problem and intervene to get children back on track. Most young struggling readers have difficulty reading words automatically. Teachers analyze the data from **running records**, informal reading inventories, or classroom tests to figure out which words children have difficulty reading. For problems with high-frequency words, teachers explicitly teach the words that children don't know and involve them in daily reading and writing activities to use the words. For problems with word-identification strategies, teachers use minilessons to teach phonic analysis, decoding by analogy, and syllabic analysis using words children are attempting to read and write. Accuracy problems often overlap with speed and prosody difficulties because children can't read quickly or expressively when they don't know the words they're trying to read.

If the problem is speed or prosody, teachers use choral reading, readers theatre, partner reading, listening centers, and other activities recommended in this chapter to develop fluency. They closely monitor children's progress and involve them in charting their own growth.

Fluency problems often reflect children's limited reading and writing experience. The amount of reading and writing that children do makes a critical difference in their literacy achievement. The most important recommendation for children who struggle with fluency is to dramatically increase the amount of reading and writing they do every day. Children need to spend at least 15 minutes reading books at their independent reading level in addition to their formal reading instruction and any intervention programs.

WRITING FLUENCY

Fluent writers spell words automatically and write quickly so that they can focus on developing their ideas. Their writing seems to flow effortlessly, and it's distinctive. Fluent writing sounds like talking—it has "voice." Fluency is as crucial for writers as it is for readers, and the components are similar:

Automaticity and Accuracy. Fluent writers write most words automatically and accurately, without having to stop and think about how to spell them. Children must know how to spell high-frequency words and be able to apply strategies to spell other words; otherwise, they get so bogged down in spelling a word that they forget the sentence they're writing or the one that comes next.

Speed and Legibility. Children need to write quickly enough to keep pace with their thinking. Researchers have examined the number of words children write per minute, compared their speed to the quality of their compositions, and concluded that children need to write 10 words per minute to be considered fluent writers (Graham, Weintraub, & Berninger, 1998). Most third graders reach this rate, and because girls usually do more writing than boys do, it isn't surprising that they write 1 or 2 words per minute faster than boys. Sometimes legibility is an issue because children can't sacrifice neatness for speed: It doesn't do any good to write quickly if readers can't decipher children's writing.

Figure 6-8 ◆ Characteristics of Fluent Writers	
Component	Characteristics
Automaticity and Accuracy	Children spell most high-frequency words correctly. Children apply spelling patterns and rules to spell words correctly. Children's spelling becomes increasingly more conventional.
Speed and Legibility	Children write quickly. Children write easily, without discomfort. Children write legibly. Children develop keyboarding skills to word process quickly.
Writer's Voice	Children make their writing distinctive.

Writer's Voice. Writers develop distinctive voices that reflect their individuality (Spandel, 2009). Voice, which is similar to prosody, is the tone or emotional feeling of a piece of writing. Writers develop their voices through the words they choose and how they string words into sentences. Each child's voice is unique, and teachers can usually identify who wrote a composition according to its voice, just as many of us can identify books written by our favorite authors by their voice.

The characteristics of fluent writers are summarized in Figure 6–8.

Automatic and Accurate Writing

To become fluent writers, children need to be able to spell most high-frequency words automatically and apply spelling strategies to write other words. Teachers teach children to write high-frequency words the same way they teach them to read the words. Each week they introduce five or six words and provide daily opportunities for children to practice reading and writing them through these activities:

- Children write the words and sentences they compose using the words on whiteboards.
- Children use letter cards or magnetic letters to spell the words.
- Children write the words in interactive writing activities.

Teachers direct some of these activities, and children participate in others at literacy centers.

At first children sound out the words they're trying to spell. They segment the word into sounds and write a letter for each sound they recognize. They might spell *baby* as *babe* or *house* as *hus*, for example, using their knowledge of phoneme–grapheme correspondences, but through phonics and spelling instruction and more experience with reading and writing, children spell words more accurately. They also learn to use the "think it out" strategy to spell words. Children apply their knowledge of phonics rules, spelling patterns, word families, syllables, and morphemes along with matching sounds to letters. They also develop a visual image of words they can read, and they're more likely to recognize when a spelling doesn't look right and ask a class-mate, check a word wall, or consult a dictionary to get the correct spelling.

Writing Speed and Legibility

For children to become fluent writers, their transcription of ideas onto paper must be automatic; that means they spell most words automatically and use legible hand-writing without thinking about how to form letters or keyboard without hunting for letter keys.

Children need to know how to hold pencils comfortably, so their hands and arms don't hurt, and they need to learn how form manuscript letters in kindergarten through second grade and cursive letters in third and fourth grades to improve their speed and legibility. Sometimes teachers require third and fourth graders to write only in cursive, but children should be allowed to use either form, as long as it's easy to read and can be written quickly for writing projects.

Left-handed writers face unique handwriting problems. The basic difference be-tween right- and left-handed writers is physical orientation: Right-handed children pull their hand and arm away from the body, but left-handed children move their left hand across what has just been written, often covering it. Too often, children adopt a "hook" position to avoid covering what they've just written. To address that problem, left-handed writers should hold pencils and pens an inch or more farther back from the tip than right-handed writers do so they can see what they've just writ-ten. The tilt of their papers is a second issue: Left-handed children should tilt their papers slightly to the right, in contrast to right-handed writers, who tilt their pa-pers to the left to more comfortably form letters. Slant is a third concern: Left-handed writers should slant their letters in a way that allows them to write comfortably. It's acceptable for them to write cursive letters vertically or even slightly backward, in contrast to right-handed children who slant cursive letters to the right.

Keyboarding is an essential 21st-century literacy skill; most schools use com-mercial tutorial programs to teach typing skills, beginning with the location of the home keys and correct fingering on the keyboard. Most programs have children prac-tice using the keys to write words and sentences, and they receive feedback about their accuracy and speed. Children usually learn keyboarding in third or fourth grade, and this instruction is critical, because when they don't know how to keyboard, they use the inefficient hunt-and-peck technique and their writing speed is very slow.

Children develop writing speed through practice. They need to use writing throughout the school day—to contribute to class charts, to make entries in read-ing logs, to write words and sentences on whiteboards, to add pages to class books, to write books at the writing center or during writing workshop, and to create proj-ects during literature focus units and thematic units, for example. When children use writing three or four times a day or write for extended periods each day, their writing speed will increase.

For children with legibility problems, teachers check that they know how to hold writing instruments and how to form manuscript or cursive letters. It may be nec-essary to have children slow down their writing at first and concentrate on forming letters carefully and including every letter in each word before they try to increase their writing speed. Interactive writing is a useful procedure for examining young children's handwriting skills and demonstrating how to form letters legibly.

DEVELOPMENTAL CONTINUUM Writing Fluency

PreK	K	1	2	3	4
Four-year-olds experiment with writing, print names, and develop a concept of fluency by watching teachers write messages.	Kindergartners learn to spell 10 high-frequency words, develop legible handwriting skills, and write patterned sentences.	Children write 50 high-frequency words, use phonics to spell other words, and develop writing speed through daily writing.	Second-grade writers become more self-reliant; they spell more words conventionally, write faster, and develop their "voice."	Many children achieve fluency by legibly writing 10 wpm, spelling words automatically, and personalizing their writing style.	Fluent writers increase writing speed and refine their writing style, but dysfluent writers struggle and try to avoid writing.

Writer's Voice

The writer's voice reflects the person doing the writing. It sounds natural, not stilted. Pulitzer prize–winning author and teacher Donald Murray (2003) says that a writer's voice is the person in the writing. As children gain experience as readers and writers, their writers' voices will emerge, especially when they're writing on topics they know well.

As children develop their writers' voices, they learn to vary their tone when they're writing to entertain, inform, or persuade. They also learn that some writing forms require a more informal or formal voice: Think about the difference when you're writing an e-mail message and a business letter. Similarly, children's voices are more casual and relaxed when they're writing for classmates than when they're writing for adults.

Doing lots of reading and writing helps children develop their voices. As they read books and listen to the teacher read others aloud, children develop an awareness of the writer's voice. Teachers highlight the lyrical tone in *Owl Moon* (Yolen, 2007) and *My Mama Had a Dancing Heart* (Gray, 2001), the lively spirit in *Barn Dance!* (Martin & Archambault, 1988), and repetition in *The Napping House* (Wood, 1984) and *Alexander and the Terrible, Horrible, No Good, Very Bad Day* (Viorst, 2009). As children become aware of these techniques, they begin applying them in their own writing.

At the same time they're examining authors' voices in books they're reading, children do lots of informal writing to develop their own voices. Children need to write every day to become fluent. Keeping a personal journal is a good way to begin, or they write in reading logs on topics they choose or on topics provided by the teacher. They can try writing from varied viewpoints to experiment with voice. For example, if children were retelling "Goldilocks and the Three Bears" from Goldilocks's viewpoint, the tone would be different than if it were from Papa Bear's perspective.

Assessing Writing Fluency

Teachers assess writing fluency as they observe children writing and examine their compositions. They consider these questions:

- Do children spell most words automatically and accurately, or do they stop to figure out how to spell many words?
- Do children write quickly enough to complete the assignment, or do they write slowly or try to avoid writing?
- Is children's writing legible?
- Do children write easily, or do they write laboriously, complaining that their hands hurt?

These questions help teachers quickly identify children who aren't fluent writers. If their observation suggests that children are struggling, teachers conduct additional testing to diagnose fluency problems:

Automaticity and Accuracy. Teachers assess children's ability to spell the high-frequency words and use strategies to spell other words with spelling tests or by examining their writing samples. Fluent writers spell most words correctly, so it's essential that children know how to spell high-frequency words automatically and efficiently figure out the spelling of most other words they want to write.

Speed and Legibility. Teachers time children as they write a paragraph or two to assess their writing speed. Children write for 1 to 5 minutes about a familiar topic and then teachers count the number of words they've written and divide the number of words written by the number of minutes to determine children's writing rates. For example, second-grader Amie writes 43 words in 5 minutes; her speed is nearly 9 words per minute, and she's almost reached the threshold fluency rate of 10 words per minute. Teachers repeat this assessment several times a year using a different, but equally familiar, topic. Each topic must be accessible because the purpose of the assessment is to monitor children's writing speed, not their knowledge about the topic. Teachers also carefully observe children as they write because their behavior may indicate handwriting problems.

Writer's Voice. Teachers reread several compositions children have written to evaluate their unique style. There aren't standards to use in assessing voice, so teachers often compare one child's writing to classmates' to rate it as comparable or above or below average.

Commercial tests aren't available to assess children's writing fluency, but these informal assessments are useful in diagnosing writers with fluency problems.

Reading fluency typically precedes writing fluency, but the two are clearly linked. The more reading children do, the sooner they'll reach writing fluency; and the more writing children do, the sooner they'll achieve reading fluency.

F CHILDREN STRUGGLE...

Most children become fluent writers by fourth grade, but if they aren't making adequate progress during the primary grades, teachers analyze assessment data to determine where the problem lies and then provide instruction and practice opportunities to resolve it. Children who aren't moving toward fluency may have problems in spelling accuracy, writing speed, or developing a writer's voice.

If the problem is accuracy, teachers determine whether children know how to spell most high-frequency words and whether they can apply strategies to spell other words. Depending on children's problems, teachers provide instruction on high-frequency words or spelling strategies and increase the amount of reading and writing children do.

If children are slow writers, teachers observe them or conference with them to figure out the problem and decide how to address it. Some children are slow writers because they have handwriting problems, and others aren't writing because they don't know what to do or lack background knowledge about the topic. Perhaps the child is being distracted by a classmate, or the child spends too much time on the illustration and runs out of time to do much writing.

If children aren't developing their writers' voices, it's likely that they haven't done much reading or writing. The best solution is to drastically increase the amount of reading and writing these children are doing. In addition, they need to listen to more books read aloud and talk about authors and how they develop their writers' voices.

Children who struggle with fluency may have a single problem, such as slow reading speed or delayed spelling development, but more often they face obstacles in both reading and writing; in this case, providing a combination of reading and writing instruction and practice is often the best solution.

NURTURING ENGLISH LEARNERS

To become fluent readers, English learners need to read words accurately, quickly, and expressively, like native English speakers do; however, it's unlikely that they'll become fluent readers until they speak English fluently because their lack of oral language proficiency limits their recognition of high-frequency words and use of word-identification strategies, and it interferes with their ability to understand word meanings, string words together into sentences, and read expressively (Peregoy & Boyle, 2008). It's also unlikely that ELs will become fluent writers before they develop oral language proficiency.

Children who are learning English are immersed in learning to read and write at the same time they're learning to speak English, and teachers help them to make connections between the oral and written language modes to accelerate their achievement and overcome the obstacles that get in the way of their becoming fluent readers and writers:

Automaticity and Accuracy. Becoming automatic and accurate readers and writers is challenging for many English learners, and the process takes longer than it does for native English speakers. High-frequency words are difficult to recognize because so many of them are abstract (*about, this, which*), and they're hard to spell because many violate spelling rules (*could, said, what, who*). Many ELs speak with a native-language accent, which makes phonic analysis more arduous, but their pronunciation differences needn't hamper their reading fluency. For example, even though some Hispanic students, especially more recent immigrants, pronounce *check* as /shĕk/ because the *ch* digraph doesn't exist in Spanish, they are reading the word accurately. Everyone has an accent, even native English speakers, so ELs shouldn't be expected to eliminate their accents to be considered fluent readers. Applying syllabic analysis to identify words that aren't in their speaking vocabularies can be a formidable task, especially if they're not familiar with cognates or related words in their native language.

Speed. English learners' limited background knowledge and lack of English vocabulary affect their reading and writing speed. By building background knowledge and introducing new words beforehand, teachers can help ELs improve their reading speed. In addition, children need opportunities to reread familiar books. To develop their writing speed, ELs need to talk about topics before writing and have available lists of words related to a topic. In addition, if teachers are overly concerned with grammatical correctness, children will stick with safe, grammatically correct sentences they already know how to write.

Expressiveness. Children's knowledge of spoken English plays a critical role in developing prosody and a writer's voice. ELs' intonation patterns usually reflect their native language. This common problem is due to their limited knowledge of English syntax, and to the fact that punctuation marks don't provide enough clues about how to chunk words (Allington, 2009). To remedy this problem, teachers teach about punctuation marks. They use echo reading, in which the teacher reads a sentence expressively and then children reread it, trying to imitate the teacher's prosody. Developing a writer's voice is just as challenging. Children need to learn to use varied sentence structures, idioms, and figurative language. Teachers highlight the authors' voices in books they're reading aloud, and ELs often use books they've read as models for their writing. For example, they can adapt the repetitive sentence structure from *Brown Bear, Brown Bear, What Do You See?* (Martin, 2008) or *If You Give a Mouse a Cookie* (Numeroff, 1985) for their writing. ELs develop expressiveness through lots of reading and writing practice.

English learners need to develop fluency because automaticity and accuracy, speed, and expressiveness are necessary to handle the demands of reading and writing in fourth grade and beyond. The same combination of explicit instruction and authentic practice activities that's recommended for native speakers works for English learners; however, ELs often require more time because they're learning to speak English at the same time they're learning to read and write.

CHAPTER Review

How Effective Teachers Develop Fluent Readers and Writers

▶ Teachers teach children to read and spell high-frequency words.

▶ Teachers teach word-identification strategies—phonic analysis, decoding by analogy, syllabic analysis, and morphemic analysis—to help children become accurate readers and writers.

▶ Teachers develop children's reading speed and prosody using lots of reading.

▶ Teachers develop children's writing speed through lots of writing.

▶ Teachers encourage children to develop their writers' voices through minilessons and authentic reading and writing activities.

Chapter 7

Building Children's Word Knowledge

Mr. Wagner Teaches Vocabulary

It's Monday morning, and the 30 fourth graders in Mr. Wagner's classroom are reading the two-page introduction to this week's featured selection, "Happy Birthday, Dr. King!" in their basal readers. Mr. Wagner reads aloud the introductory material about Martin Luther King Jr., Rosa Parks, and the civil rights movement while the children follow along in their readers.

Afterward, Mr. Wagner asks, "What do you know about the civil rights movement? Garrett offers, "Dr. King gave a famous speech in Washington, DC," and Dominique adds, "It was the 'I Have a Dream' speech." Madison says, "Black people and white people are equal, but white people used to think they were more important." "We should respect everyone," Austin emphasizes. The discussion continues as children activate their background knowledge; they talk about the discrimination that blacks faced in the South and Dr. King's sit-ins and other nonviolent protests.

Next, Mr. Wagner distributes a collection of posters about the civil rights movement to children sitting at each of the five table groups in the classroom. The children talk about the posters in table groups and then share their posters with the class, making connections with the introductory material in their basal readers. Then Mr. Wagner passes out this week's list of 10 vocabulary words and reads it aloud:

boycott	fare	protest	stupendous
civil rights	nuisance	requirement	tireless
commission	perspiration		

Most of the words come from this week's basal reader story, but a few are from the district's fourth-grade vocabulary list.

The children use a study procedure to learn the words. They divide into groups of three, and each group studies one word. The children create a poster with the word, an illustrative sentence, and a brief definition. Sometimes they locate the word in the story and copy the sentence containing it on the chart; at other times, they create their own sentence. To figure out the word's meaning, the fourth graders use what they've learned about root words, affixes, and context clues to get an idea of the meaning, and then they check the definition in the basal reader's glossary or in a dictionary. Mr. Wagner circulates around the classroom, making sure that the fourth graders write useful sentences on their posters, spell words correctly, and choose the appropriate meaning when they check the glossary or dictionary.

Next, the children take turns sharing their posters and display them in the classroom. Aaron, Spencer, and Isabella share their word: *boycott*. They present their poster, which is shown below, and read aloud the sentence and the definition. Mr. Wagner explains, "This is an important word related to the civil rights movement. Dr. King, Rosa Parks, and others were protesting when they boycotted or refused to ride in the back of buses or sit at blacks-only lunch counters. They

Vocabulary Poster for *Boycott*

WORD: boycott

SENTENCE: Dr. Martin Luther King, Jr. helped to organize a boycott.

DEFINITION: A refusal

were being treated unfairly." He also points out that *boycott* is an eponym, a word that developed from Charles Boycott's name; Mr. Boycott was a land manager in Ireland who charged unfair rents in the 1880s, which Irish tenants refused to pay.

As each group presents its chart, classmates write the word and its definition in their vocabulary journals. They use their notes to study for the Friday vocabulary test. The sharing takes about 10 minutes, and Mr. Wagner thinks that it's time well spent. The fourth graders agree: Ossanna says, "This activity helps me really learn the definitions and not just remember them for the test!"

On Tuesday, the children read the featured selection in their basal readers and confidently point out the vocabulary words they've studied. They continue with the textbook activities and workbook pages that are part of the basal reading program, and Mr. Wagner also sets out the text set of books about Martin Luther King Jr. and Rosa Parks that's shown below. The children read them during an independent reading time and mark this week's vocabulary words when they find them using small self-stick notes.

Mr. Wagner's Text Set of Books

Farris, C.K. (2005). My brother Martin: A sister remembers growing up with the Rev. Dr. Martin L. King, Jr. New York: Aladdin Books.

Farris, C.K. (2008). March on! The day my brother Martin changed the world. New York: Scholastic.

Giovanni, N. (2007). Rosa. New York: Square Fish.

Johnson, A. (2007) A sweet smell of roses. New York: Simon & Schuster.

Parks, R., & Reed, G. J. (1997). Dear Mrs. Parks. New York: Lee & Low.

Pastan, A. (2004). Martin Luther King, Jr. New York: DK Children's Books.

Rappaport, D. (2007). Martin's big words: The life of Dr. Martin Luther King, Jr. New York: Jump at the Sun/Hyperion Books.

Ringgold, F. (1998). My dream of Martin Luther King. New York: Dragonfly Books.

Ringgold, F. (1999). If a bus could talk: The story of Rosa Parks. New York: Simon & Schuster.

During the week, Mr. Wagner teaches vocabulary minilessons using these words and others they studied earlier in the school year. This week, he teaches two minilessons on how suffixes change verbs into nouns using *move/movement*, *satisfy/satisfaction*, *wreck/wreckage*, *organize/organization*, *perspire/perspiration*, *require/requirement*, and *commit/commission*. He's taught other minilessons on how to write a good definition, how to choose the appropriate meaning, how to use context clues, how to identify root words, and how affixes change the meaning of words.

On Friday, the fourth graders take down their posters before the vocabulary test. The test format varies, but children usually match words and their definitions. Most of the fourth graders score 80% or higher on the test, and Mr. Wagner thinks that they do so well because of the vocabulary-learning routine they use. Before he implemented the small-group poster-making activity, the children weren't as interested in words and didn't score as high on the weekly tests.

After they take the Friday test, the fourth graders ceremoniously add the week's words to the large word wall in the classroom. By the end of the school year, it will contain nearly 200 words. A list of the words currently on the word wall is shown on page 173.

Mr. Wagner's Class Word Wall			
AB	**C**	**DE**	**FGH**
ablaze	chamber	eager	horizon
ancestor	classical	etch	glare
attentively	conductor	experienced	fierce
bewildering	courageous	drought	flammable
blare	cordially	depot	honor
amplifier	consecutive	debut	homeland
abundance	charred	elegant	homage
aggressively	civil rights	ember	frontier
boycott	commission		fare
IJK	**LMN**	**OP**	**QR**
jazz	lure	petitioners	rugged
immense	long	oath	rhythm
jolt	landscape	persist	remind
	nervously	organization	renew
	miscalculate	plaque	reunion
	misunderstand	proud	referral
	modest	protest	requirement
	lurching	perspiration	
	nuisance		
S	**T**	**UVW**	**XYZ**
survivor	teeming	wreckage	
satchel	timid	voyage	
spawn	thermometer	unsinkable	
singe	temperature	worldwide	
shipwreck	tireless		
satisfaction	troublesome		
scavenger			
stride			
stupendous			

These fourth graders are interested in words. As they look at the class word wall, Isabella points to her favorite word, *rhythm*, explains that it means "a beat," and demonstrates by clapping a rhythm. Kaila and Erik agree that their favorite word is *bewildering*, which they say means "puzzling" or "confusing." One thing is certain: These fourth graders aren't bewildered by words!

Check the Compendium of Instructional Procedures, which follows Chapter 12, for more information on highlighted terms.

hildren learn vocabulary by being immersed in an environment that's rich with words. As they listen to teachers share books using the interactive read-aloud procedure and read other books independently, children learn more than 2,000 words each year without instruction. For example, kindergartners pick up pirate lingo as they listen to their teacher read aloud *How I Became a Pirate* (Long, 2003), about Jeremy Jacob's adventures with Braid Beard and his pirate crew:

Aargh

Ahoy, matey

Hey, ho, blow the man down

Shiver me timbers

Down the hatch

Aye, me laddies

Children repeat the phrases as they play in the blocks center, incorporate them into the Language Experience Approach stories that they dictate, and add talking balloons with them to their drawings. They also learn words as they explore social studies and science topics during thematic units. At the same time, teachers reinforce children's learning in several important ways: They explicitly teach some words and word-learning strategies, and they foster children's interest in words, as Mr. Wagner did in the vignette.

Vocabulary learning can't be left to chance because children's word knowledge affects whether they comprehend what they're reading, write effectively, and learn content-area information (Stahl & Nagy, 2006). Children come to school with varying levels of word knowledge, both in the number of words they know and in the depth of their understanding. Children from low-income homes have less than half the vocabulary of more affluent children, and some researchers estimate that they know one quarter to one fifth of the words that their classmates do. To make matters worse, this gap widens each year (Cunningham, 2009). Therefore, it's essential that teachers recognize the impact of socioeconomic level on children's vocabulary knowledge, support all children's vocabulary growth, and emphasize word learning for children who know fewer words.

HILDREN'S VOCABULARY KNOWLEDGE

Children's vocabularies grow at an astonishing rate—about 3,000 words a year, or roughly 7 to 10 new words every day. Middle-class 5-year-olds recognize 5,000 words, and by the time they graduate from high school, their vocabularies can reach 25,000 to 50,000 words or more. It seems obvious that to learn words at such a prolific rate, children learn words both in and outside of school, and they learn most words incidentally, not through explicit instruction. Reading has the greatest impact on children's vocabulary development, but other activities are important, too. For example, children learn words through family activities, hobbies, and vacations. Television also has a significant impact on vocabulary development, especially for 4- and 5-year-olds if they view educational programs and limit the amount of time they spend watching television each day. Figure 7–1 lists recommended educational television series for young children.

These series effectively combine entertainment with education, and most have interactive components that actively involve children in the learning experience. In addition, they have websites with games and other activities, DVDs of the episodes, and toys featuring the characters.

Figure 7–1 ◆ Television Programs That Build Word Knowledge

Program	Description	Ages
Backyardigans (Nick Jr.)	This animated musical series features five friends who use their imaginations to turn their backyards into fantastical settings for their adventures.	2–5
Between the Lions (PBS Kids)	This award-winning series is about a family of lions that runs a library. Children experience the magic of books while learning vocabulary, phonics, and comprehension.	4–8
Blue's Clues (Nick Jr.)	Children learn problem-solving skills in this award-winning play-along program starring a bright blue puppy named Blue. In each episode, viewers enter a storybook world to find Blue's clues and solve the puzzle.	3–5
Dora, the Explorer (Nick Jr.)	Dora, a 7-year-old Latina heroine, and her friends solve riddles and puzzles during their adventures in this interactive cartoon program that teaches Spanish words and literacy skills.	3–6
The Electric Company (PBS)	In this revival of the 1970s series, four teenage literary superheroes battle neighborhood villains. Each episode teaches four or five vocabulary words, and the program includes interactive web elements and online games.	6–8
Go, Diego, Go (Nick Jr.)	Eight-year-old Diego is an action-adventure hero who loves animals. (He's Dora the Explorer's cousin.) In each episode, he uses observation skills and scientific tools to rescue an animal in trouble.	4–6
Higglytown Heroes (Disney)	Nesting-doll characters explore their community and interact with the people in it, including firefighters, dentists, and other Higglytown heroes.	2–5
Imagination Movers (Disney)	This live-action series features Scott, Rich, Dave, and "Smitty," the members of the Imagination Movers, a rockin' New Orleans band that teaches kids to tackle challenges and solve problems while entertaining them.	4–7
Little Einsteins (Disney)	Four children and their space/air/watercraft embark on a mission in each episode to solve a problem or help a friend. This series is designed to nurture art and music appreciation and encourages viewer interaction to help the characters succeed on their missions.	3–5
Pinky Dinky Doo (NOGGIN)	Pinky, a girl who lives with her family in Great Big City, tells stories to solve problems. A great Big Fancy Word is featured several times during each episode. This animated series is dubbed in Spanish on Univision.	3–5
Sesame Street (PBS)	Since 1969, this landmark series featuring Big Bird and Elmo has combined education and entertainment using animation, puppets, and live actors to foster imagination, teach reading and math concepts, and build social skills.	2–4
Sid, the Science Kid (PBS)	In this Jim Henson Productions computer-generated series, Sid is an inquisitive 4-year-old who, with the help of his classmates and teacher, tackles questions about scientific principles and why things work the way they do.	3–5
Super Why (PBS)	Four fairy-tale friends transform into reading-powered superheroes in this interactive reading adventure series set in Storybook Village, a magical 3-D world hidden behind the bookshelves in a children's library.	3–6

Go to the Assignments and Activities section of the Topic *Vocabulary* in the MyEducationLab for the literacy course and complete the activity entitled *Choosing Tier 2 Words for Vocabulary Instruction Using a ReadAloud*. As you watch the video and answer the accompanying questions, consider the reasons teachers may want to introduce young learners to academic vocabulary.

Three Tiers of Words

Beck, McKeown, and Kucan (2002) have devised a tool to assist teachers in prioritizing words for instruction in which they recommend categorizing words into these three levels or tiers:

Tier 1: Basic Words. These common words are used socially, in informal conversation at home and on the playground. Examples include *tired*, *car*, *outside*, *spill*, and *water*. Native English speakers rarely require instruction on these words.

Tier 2: Academic Vocabulary. These words have wide application in school contexts and are used more frequently in written than in oral language. Some are related to literacy concepts, such as *sentence*, *author*, *vowel*, *question mark*, *revise*, and *character*. Other words are related to familiar ones—antonyms and synonyms, for example. Most children know the Tier 1 word *bad* and its opposite, *good*, but related words, including *naughty*, *evil*, *dangerous*, *ill*, and *trouble*, are Tier 2 words because they're less familiar.

PreK Practices

Do you teach vocabulary to 4-year-olds?

Enriching children's vocabularies must be a priority, according to Bennett-Armistead, Duke, and Moses (2005), and the best way to do this is through daily read-alouds. As they listen, preschoolers learn many, many words they wouldn't encounter through conversation, and they're exposed to more complex sentence patterns and text structures. Teachers take time to talk about the key words as they read and encourage children to use the words themselves as they talk about the book, retell the story, and participate in other response activities. McGee (2007) also recommends that teachers describe what they're doing as they demonstrate a procedure, introduce new words (e.g., *whisk*, *cash register*) as they participate in literacy play centers, and share collections of objects related to books or thematic units.

Tier 3: Specialized Terms. These technical words are content specific and often abstract. Examples include *fraction*, *explorer*, *chrysalis*, *healthy*, *amphibian*, and *equator*. They aren't used frequently enough to devote time to teaching them when they come up in texts children are reading, but they're the words that teachers explicitly teach during thematic units and math lessons.

As teachers choose words for instruction and word-study activities, they focus on Tier 2 words even though words representing all three levels are written on **word walls** and explained when necessary.

NURTURING ENGLISH LEARNERS

Young English learners often need more explicit vocabulary instruction than native English speakers do. Sometimes ELs only need to have a word translated; at other times, however, they're confused about a new meaning of a familiar word, or they don't know either the underlying concept or words that describe it, and instruction is necessary.

Tier 1 Words. These words are easiest for ELs to learn because they often know the words in their native language; what they don't know are the equivalent words in English. If teachers speak children's native language, they translate the words and help children learn the English equivalents; English-speaking teachers can use pictures and pantomime to explain them. It's often helpful for teachers to put together collections of small objects and pictures to share during literature focus units and thematic units.

Tier 2 Words. Teachers preteach some unfamiliar words, including essential Tier 2 words, before children listen to a book read aloud or read a book, and later, through explicit instruction and a variety of word-study activities, they teach other Tier 2 words. In addition, Calderon (2007) notes that ELs need to understand transition words and phrases, such as *meanwhile* and *finally*, words with multiple meanings, such as *key*, *soft*, and *ready*, and English words with cognates. Teachers point out cognates, English words that are related to words in children's native language. Many Tier 2 words are Latin based, so it's important to teach English learners who speak Spanish, Portuguese, Italian, and French to ask themselves whether an unfamiliar word is similar to a word in their native language. Examples of English/Spanish cognates include *syllable/silaba*, *triangle/tríangulo*, and *pioneer/pionero*.

Tier 3 Words. It's less important to teach these technical words because of their limited usefulness, and only a few have cognates that ELs would know. Calderon (2007) recommends that teachers translate the words or briefly explain them. During thematic units, however, teachers do teach Tier 3 words that are essential to understanding the big ideas through a combination of explicit instruction and word-study activities.

The Development of Word Knowledge

Children develop knowledge about a word gradually, through repeated oral and written exposures to it. They move from not knowing a word at all to recognizing that they've seen the word before, and then to a level of partial knowledge where they have a general sense of the word or know one meaning. Finally, children know the word fully: They know multiple meanings of the word and can use it in a variety of ways (Nagy, 1988). Here are the four levels:

> **Unknown Word.** Children don't recognize the word.
>
> **Initial Recognition.** Children have seen or heard the word or can pronounce it, but they don't know the meaning.
>
> **Partial Word Knowledge.** Children know one meaning of the word and can use it in a sentence.
>
> **Full Word Knowledge.** Children know more than one meaning of the word and can use it in several ways. (Allen, 1999)

Once children reach the third level, they can generally understand the word in context. In fact, they don't reach the fourth level with every word they learn, but when they do develop full word knowledge, they're described as flexible word users because they understand the core meaning of a word and how it changes in different contexts (Stahl & Nagy, 2006).

DEVELOPMENTAL CONTINUUM   Vocabulary

PreK	K	1	2	3	4
Children who have been read to and have developed good background knowledge possess vocabularies approaching 3,500 words; they know colors and animal names.	Kindergartners use book language to talk about stories and can name opposites for words, such as *good, day,* and *little,* and their vocabularies reach 5,000 words.	Children learn literacy-related academic language, including *consonant, sentence, predict,* and *question mark,* as their vocabularies increase by 3,000 words.	Second graders expand their knowledge base and related words through thematic units and learn more antonyms and synonyms; their vocabularies reach 10,000 words.	Children's vocabularies grow by 3,000 words, and they develop word consciousness as they notice multiple meanings of words and figurative language.	The gulf between grade-level and struggling students' vocabularies widens and becomes more obvious as literacy and content-area demands increase.

Word Consciousness

Children's interest in learning and using words is known as *word consciousness*. According to Scott and Nagy (2004), word consciousness is "essential for vocabulary growth and comprehending the language of schooling" (p. 201). Children who have word consciousness exemplify these characteristics:

- Children use words skillfully, understanding the nuances of word meanings.
- Children gain a deep appreciation of words and value them.
- Children are aware of differences between social and academic or school language.
- Children understand the power of word choice.
- Children are motivated to learn the meaning of unfamiliar words.

Word consciousness is important because vocabulary knowledge is generative—that is, it transfers to and enhances children's learning of other words (Scott & Nagy, 2004).

As children develop word consciousness, they become more aware of words, manipulate them playfully, and appreciate their power. Teachers foster word consciousness in a variety of ways. Most importantly, they model interest in words and precise use of vocabulary (Graves, 2006). To encourage children's interest in words, teachers share books about words, including *Max's Words* (Banks, 2006), *Fancy Nancy's Favorite Fancy Words: From Accessories to Zany* (O'Connor, 2008), *Miss Alaineus: A Vocabulary Disaster* (Frasier, 2007), and *Baloney (Henry P.)* (Scieszka, 2005). Next, they call children's attention to words by highlighting words of the day, posting words on word walls, and having children collect words from books they're reading. They promote wordplay by sharing riddles, jokes, puns, songs, and poems and encouraging children to experiment with words and use them in new ways.

Vocabulary Knowledge and Reading Achievement

Vocabulary knowledge and reading achievement are closely related; children with larger vocabularies are more capable readers (Graves, 2006). In the preschool years, children who listen to their parents and teachers read books aloud and talk about the books acquire larger vocabularies and are more prepared for reading instruction than children with fewer experiences. Then once children become fluent readers, reading widely is the most important way they learn new words. Better readers do more reading, both in school and out of school. The idea that capable readers learn more vocabulary because they read more is an example of the Matthew effect (Stanovich, 1986), which suggests that "the rich get richer and the poor get poorer" in vocabulary development, decoding, and other components of reading. Not only do better readers do more reading, but the books they read have more sophisticated words. The gulf separating capable and less capable readers grows larger each year because struggling readers do less reading and the easier books they read have fewer grade-level vocabulary words.

LITERACY PORTRAITS
Viewing Guide

The second graders in Ms. Janusz's class vary widely in their vocabulary knowledge. Some children have limited background knowledge and words to express ideas, but others are interested in many topics and know lots of words. Go to the Literacy Profiles section of the MyEducationLab for the Literacy Course and click on Jimmy's February video clip to watch a conference Ms. Janusz holds with him about a book he's reading during reading workshop; this informational book is about presidential elections. As they talk about the book, Jimmy uses sophisticated and technical vocabulary, including *democracy, electoral votes, snickering,* and *campaign slogan,* to discuss what he's learned. Most second graders aren't familiar with these concepts and don't use these words. How do you think Jimmy learned them? How does Ms. Janusz support his learning? Does his vocabulary knowledge correlate with his literacy level?

myeducationlab

WORD-STUDY CONCEPTS

It's not enough to memorize one definition of a word; to develop full word knowledge, children need to learn more about a word (Stahl & Nagy, 2006). Consider the word *brave*: It can be used as an adjective, a noun, or a verb. It often means "showing no fear," but it can also mean an "American Indian warrior" or "to challenge or defy." These forms are related to the first meaning: *braver, bravest, bravely,* and *bravery.* Synonyms related to the first meaning include *bold, fearless,* and *daring*; antonyms are *cowardly* and *frightened.* As children learn about *brave*, they're better able to understand the word and use it orally and in writing.

A list of synonyms, antonyms, and homonyms that are appropriate for children in the primary grades is presented in Figure 7–2.

Synonyms

Words that have nearly the same meaning as other words are *synonyms*. These related words are useful because they're more precise. Think of all the synonyms for the word *cold*: *cool, chilly, frigid, icy, frosty,* and *freezing*. Each word has a different shade of meaning: *Cool* means "moderately cold," *chilly* is "uncomfortably cold," *frigid* is "intensely cold," *icy* means "very cold," *frosty* means "covered with frost," and *freezing* is "so cold that water changes into ice." English would be limited with only the word *cold*.

Figure 7-2 ◆ Words for Word-Study Activities

Synonyms	Antonyms	Homonyms
angry–mad	add–subtract	ant–aunt
big–large	asleep–awake	ate–eight
build–construct	back–front	bare–bear
correct–right	big–little	be–bee
fast–quick	black–white	blew–blue
few–several	boy–girl	brake–break
finish–end	clean–dirty	buy–by–bye
foolish–silly	come–go	cent–scent–sent
forgive–excuse	day–night	dear–deer
funny–amusing	dog–cat	eye–I
gift–present	early–late	flew–flu
happy–glad	fast–slow	flour–flower
hard–difficult	friend–enemy	hair–hare
hurry–rush	go–stop	hear–here
joy–pleasure	happy–sad	hoarse–horse
know–understand	hot–cold	hole–whole
look–see	in–out	knew–new
mistake–error	laugh–cry	knight–night
ocean–sea	light–dark	made–maid
often–frequently	love–hate	mail–male
pain–ache	many–few	meat–meet
quiet–silent	morning–evening	one–won
rude–impolite	near–far	pair–pear
sad–unhappy	noisy–quiet	peace–piece
scare–frighten	off–on	plain–plane
sick–ill	open–close	red–read
smart–intelligent	play–work	right–write
smile–grin	remember–forget	road–rode
start–begin	rich–poor	sail–sale
steal–rob	smooth–rough	sea–see
talk–speak	strong–weak	son–sun
thin–slender	tight–loose	tail–tale
trash–garbage	truth–lie	their–there–they're
woman–lady	up–down	to–too–two
wrong–incorrect	wet–dry	wait–weight
yell–shout	young–old	wood–would

It's important to carefully articulate the differences among synonyms. Nagy (1988) emphasizes that teachers should focus on teaching concepts and related words, not just provide single-word definitions using synonyms. For example, to tell a child that *frigid* means *cold* provides only limited information. And, when a child says, "I want my sweater because it's frigid in here," it shows that he or she doesn't understand the different degrees of cold; there's a big difference between *chilly* and *frigid*.

Antonyms

Words that express opposite meanings are *antonyms*. For the word *loud*, antonyms include *soft, quiet, silent, dull,* and *colorless*. These antonyms express shades of meaning just as synonyms do, and some opposites are more appropriate for one meaning of *loud* than for another. When *loud* means *gaudy*, for instance, antonyms are *dull* and *colorless;* when it means *noisy*, the opposites are *quiet* and *silent.* Antonyms that primary graders learn are included in Figure 7–2.

Children learn to use a thesaurus to locate both synonyms and antonyms. *A First Thesaurus* (Wittels, 2001), *Scholastic Children's Thesaurus* (Bollard, 2006), and *The American Heritage Children's Thesaurus* (Hellweg, 2009) are excellent reference books. Children need to learn how to use these handy references to locate more effective words when they're revising their writing and during word-study activities.

Homonyms

Words that sound alike or are spelled alike are generally known as *homonyms*, but in fact there are three types. *Homophones* are the most common type: These words sound alike but are spelled differently, such as *ate–eight, hear–here,* and *to–too–two.* Sometimes children confuse the meanings of these words, but more often they mix up their spellings. A list of homophones is included in Figure 7–2. *Homographs* are second type: These words are spelled alike but are pronounced differently. Examples include the noun and verb forms of *wind, bow, record,* and *present;* the present and past tenses of the verb *read;* and the noun and adjective forms of *minute. Homographic homophones* are the third type: These words sound alike and are spelled alike, such as *fly, water,* and *bark.* The following words have noun and verb forms that are pronounced and spelled the same way:

A *fly* is a pesky insect. (noun)

Most birds can *fly*. (verb)

I like to drink *water*. (noun)

Did you *water* the plants? (verb)

This tree's *bark* is smooth. (noun)

Dogs *bark* at squirrels. (verb)

Homographic homophones are like words with multiple meanings because the noun and verb forms have different definitions.

Many books of homonyms are available, including Gwynne's *The King Who Rained* (2006) and *A Chocolate Moose for Dinner* (2005), Barretta's *Dear Deer: A Book of Homophones* (2007), and *Eight Ate: A Feast of Homonym Riddles* (Terban, 2007a). Sharing these books with children helps to develop their understanding of homophones and homographs. Children also make posters, as shown in Figure 7–3, to contrast homophones and other homonyms. Displaying these posters in the classroom reminds children of the differences between the words.

Multiple Meanings

Many, many words have more than one meaning. For some words, multiple meanings develop for the noun and verb forms, but sometimes meanings build in other ways, such

Figure 7-3 ◆ A Second Grader's Homophone Poster

as when new uses are created for words. The word *hot*, for example, usually means "high temperature" or "heat," but it also has these meanings:

angry	fresh
bold color	intense emotion
close to solution	popular
current	radioactive
eager	recently stolen
extreme interest	spicy
fast	unusually lucky
fiery	violent

Figure 7–4 presents a list of common words with multiple meanings that are appropriate for children in the primary grades.

Children gradually acquire additional meanings for words, and they usually learn these new meanings through reading. For instance, when children read *Tough Cookie* (Wisniewski, 1999), a delicious spoof on detective stories, they encounter the phrase "hot on the trail" and learn that *hot* in this case means "close to solution." When a familiar word is used in a new way, children often notice the new application and may be curious enough to check the meaning in a dictionary.

Figurative Meanings

Many words have both literal and figurative meanings: Literal meanings are the explicit, dictionary meanings, and figurative meanings are metaphorical. Two types are idioms and comparisons. Idioms are groups of words, such as "in the dog house" and "raining cats and dogs," that must be interpreted figuratively. There are hundreds of idioms in English, which we use every day to create word pictures that make language more colorful. Because idioms are figurative sayings, many children—and especially English learners—have difficulty understanding them. It's crucial that teachers provide explicit instruction so that children move beyond their literal meanings of phrases. Children can examine books that explain idioms, including *My Teacher Like to Say* (Brennan-Nelson, 2004), *There's a Frog in My Throat! 440 Animal Sayings a Little Bird Told Me* (Leedy & Street 2003), *Raining Cats and Dogs* (Moses, 2008), and *Mad as a Wet Hen: And Other Funny Idioms* (Terban, 2007b).

Metaphors and similes are comparisons that liken something to something else. A simile is a comparison signaled by the use of *like* or *as*; "busy as a bee" and "roaring like a lion" are two examples. In contrast, a metaphor compares two things by implying that one is the other, without using *like* or *as*; "you are my sunshine" is an example. Metaphors are stronger comparisons, as these examples show:

Simile: The dead tree looked <u>like</u> a skeleton in the moonlight. **like or as**

Metaphor: The dead tree was a skeleton in the moonlight. **Compares two things without using like or as.**

Differentiating between the terms *simile* and *metaphor* is less important than understanding the meaning of comparisons in books children read and encouraging children use comparisons to make their writing more vivid.

Children begin by learning traditional comparisons, such as "happy as a clam" and "butterflies in my stomach," and then they learn to notice and invent fresh, unexpected comparisons. Teachers often share these books to introduce comparisons: *Crazy Like a Fox: A Simile Story* (Leedy, 2009), *Quick as a Cricket* (Wood, 1997), *My Dog Is as Smelly as Dirty Socks* (Piven, 2007), and *Skin Like Milk, Hair of Silk: What Are Similes and Metaphors?* (Cleary, 2009). Once they're familiar with metaphors and similes, children point them out in books they're reading and use them in their own writing.

Figure 7-4 ◆ Words With Multiple Meanings

band	fly	open	stamp
bar	good	out	star
break	high	part	strike
check	hot	pass	tie
color	house	pick	time
cross	keep	play	trip
cut	key	ride	turn
draw	make	right	up
dry	mind	ring	wear
eye	new	roll	
face	note	run	
fall	off	slip	

TEACHING CHILDREN ABOUT WORDS

Vocabulary instruction plays an important role in balanced literacy classrooms. Baumann, Kame'enui, and Ash (2003) and Graves (2006) identified these components of vocabulary instruction:

◆ Immerse children in words through listening, talking, reading, and writing
◆ Teach specific words through active involvement and multiple encounters
◆ Teach word-learning strategies so children can figure out the meanings of unfamiliar words
◆ Develop children's word consciousness

Teachers address these components when they teach vocabulary. Too often, vocabulary instruction has emphasized only the second component, teaching specific words, without considering how to develop children's ability to learn words independently and use them effectively. The feature below lists guidelines for teaching vocabulary.

Word Walls

Teachers post word walls in the classroom; usually they're made from large sheets of butcher paper and divided into sections for each letter of the alphabet. Children and the teacher write interesting, confusing, and important words representing all three tiers on the word wall. Usually children choose the words to write on the word wall and may even do the writing themselves; teachers add other important words that children haven't chosen. Words are added to the word wall as they come up in books children are reading or during a thematic unit, not in advance. Allen (2007) says that word walls should be "a living part of the classroom with new words being added each day" (p. 120). Word walls are useful resources: Children locate words on the word wall that

Guidelines
for Teaching Vocabulary

▶ Use word walls to highlight words from books children are reading and from thematic units.

▶ Encourage children to use new words as they talk about books they're reading and during thematic units.

▶ Choose Tier 2 words—academic vocabulary—for explicit instruction.

▶ Teach minilessons about individual words and word learning strategies.

▶ Scaffold children as they develop full word knowledge by learning synonyms, antonyms, multiple meanings, and figurative uses.

▶ Engage children in word-study activities, such as word posters, word maps, and word sorts, so they can deepen their understanding of specific words.

▶ Develop children's word consciousness by demonstrating curiosity about words, teaching about words, and involving them in wordplay activities.

▶ Provide daily opportunities for children to read independently for 15–30 minutes.

Figure 7–5 ◆ A Third Grader's Wall for *Molly's Pilgrim*

AB apartment	CD clothespins dolls	EF Elizabeth freedom English	GH homework God hot as fire holiday
IJ Jewish	KL	MN Molly Miss Stickley Mama modern	OPQ pilgrim Plymouth peach
RS Russia religious freedom	TU Thanksgiving Tabernacles	VW Winter Hill	XYZ Yiddish

they want to use during a grand conversation or check the spelling of a word they're writing, and teachers use the words for word-study activities.

Some teachers use large pocket charts and word cards instead of butcher paper for their word walls; this way, the word cards can easily be used for word-study activities, and they can be sorted and rearranged on the pocket chart. After the book or unit is completed, teachers punch holes in one end of the cards and hang them on a ring. Then the collection of word cards can be placed in the writing center for children to use when they're writing.

Children also make individual word walls by dividing a sheet of paper into 20–24 boxes and labeling the boxes with the letters of the alphabet; they can put several letters together in one box. Then children write important words and phrases in the boxes as they read and discuss a book. Figure 7–5 shows a third grader's word wall for *Molly's Pilgrim* (Cohen, 1998), a story about modern-day pilgrims.

Even though 25, 50, or more words may be added to the word wall, not all of them are explicitly taught. As they plan, teachers create lists of words that will probably be written on word walls during the unit. From this list, teachers choose the words they teach—usually Tier 2 words that are critical to understanding the book or the unit.

Explicit Instruction Direct teaching time 'Modeling'

Teachers explicitly teach children about specific words, usually Tier 2 words. McKeown and Beck (2004) emphasize that instruction should be rich, deep, and extended. That means that teachers provide multiple encounters with words; present a variety of information, including definitions, contexts, examples, and related words; and involve children in word-study activities so that they have multiple opportunities to interact with words. The procedure is time consuming, but children are more successful at internalizing word meanings this way.

Minilesson

TOPIC: Word Sort
GRADE: First Grade
TIME: Two 30-minute periods

Mrs. Garcia's first graders are studying the four seasons. The teacher has read aloud several informational books about the seasons, and the children have added to the word wall more than 25 words that reflect the weather, holidays, clothes, plant and animal changes, and activities related to each season.

1 Introduce the Topic

Mrs. Garcia brings her 19 first graders together on the rug near their weather word wall. She asks children to take turns identifying familiar words. "Who can name a *spring* word?" she asks. Anthony points to *tadpoles* and reads the word aloud. Other children name *summer, autumn,* and *winter* words. Mrs. Garcia praises the children for including words representing all four seasons on their word wall.

2 Share Examples

Mrs. Garcia hangs up four narrow pocket charts (each with 10 pockets) and labels each one with the name of a season. She writes the words the children have identified on word cards and asks other children to place them in the appropriate pocket charts. The words *tadpoles* and *rain* are added to the *Spring* pocket chart, *swimming* and *crops* are added to the *Summer* pocket chart, *Halloween* and *Thanksgiving* to the *Autumn* pocket chart, and *snow* and *Christmas* to the *Winter* pocket chart. The children also identify several other words representing each season from the word wall to add to the pocket charts.

3 Provide Information

To locate additional words for each chart, the children suggest that they look in some of the books they've read or listened to Mrs. Garcia read aloud. Mrs. Garcia rereads an informational book about the seasons, and the children look through other familiar books. The teacher divides the children into four groups and asks each group to find words related to a particular season. The children identify new words, and these are written on word cards and placed in the appropriate chart.

4 Guide Practice

During the second day of the lesson, Mrs. Garcia divides the class into groups of two or three children and gives each group a packet of small word cards and a large sheet of construction paper divided into four columns with the names of the seasons written at the top of the columns; the words on the small cards are the same as the ones on the larger cards used the previous day in the large-group part of the lesson. The children practice reading the cards and sorting them according to season. Mrs. Garcia moves around the classroom, providing assistance as needed and monitoring the children's work.

5 Assess Learning

Mrs. Garcia puts several sets of the word cards and several construction paper diagrams in the word work center for the children to practice reading and sorting during center time. Later, she will have the children cut apart a list of the four seasons words and glue them in the appropriate columns on a construction paper diagram. She will assess these products.

As teachers plan for instruction, they need to consider what children already know about a word. Sometimes the word is unfamiliar, or it represents a new concept. At other times, the word is familiar and children know one meaning, but they need to learn a new meaning. A word representing an unfamiliar concept usually takes the most time to teach, and a new meaning for a familiar word, the least.

Teachers use minilessons to teach specific words and other vocabulary concepts. They provide information about words, including both definitions and contextual information, and they engage children in activities to get them to think about and use words orally and in reading and writing. Sometimes teachers present minilessons before reading; at other times, they teach them afterward. The minilesson on page 186 shows how a first-grade teacher teaches vocabulary as part of a thematic unit on the four seasons. This explicit instruction is especially important for English learners.

Word-Study Activities

Children examine words, visualize word meanings, and think more deeply about them as they participate in word-study activities (Allen, 2007). In these activities, they create visual representations of words, categorize words, or investigate related words:

Word Posters. Children choose a word and write it on a small poster; then they draw and color a picture to illustrate it and use the word in a sentence. This is one way that children visualize the meaning of word.

Word Maps. Children create a diagram to examine a word they're learning. They write the word, make a box around it, draw several lines from the box, and add information about the word in additional boxes they make at the end of each line. Three kinds of information typically included in a word map are a category for the word, examples, and characteristics or associations. Figure 7–6 shows a word map made by a first grader after reading *Rosie's Walk* (Hutchins, 2005). For the examples section, he named stories he had read about foxes.

Dramatizing Words. Children each choose a word and dramatize it for classmates, who then try to guess it. Sometimes an action explains a word more effectively than a verbal definition. For example, a teacher teaching a literature focus unit on *Chrysanthemum* (Henkes, 1996), the story of a little girl who didn't like her name, dramatized the word *wilted* for her second graders when they didn't understand how a girl could wilt. Other words in *Chrysanthemum* that can easily be acted out include *humorous, sprouted, dainty,* and *wildly.* Dramatization is an especially effective activity for English learners.

Word Sorts. Children sort a collection of words taken from the word wall into two or more categories in a **word sort** (Bear, Invernizzi, Templeton, & Johnston, 2008). Generally children choose the categories they use for the sort, but sometimes the teacher chooses them. For example, words from a story might be sorted by character, or words from a thematic unit on machines might be sorted according to type of machine. The words can be written on cards, and then children sort a pack of word cards into piles. Or, children can cut apart a list of words, sort them into categories, and then paste the grouped words together on a sheet of paper. Figure 7–7 presents a completed word sort for *Paul Bunyan* (Kellogg, 1985), a retelling of the American tall tale.

Figure 7–6 ◆ First Graders' Word Map on *Fox*

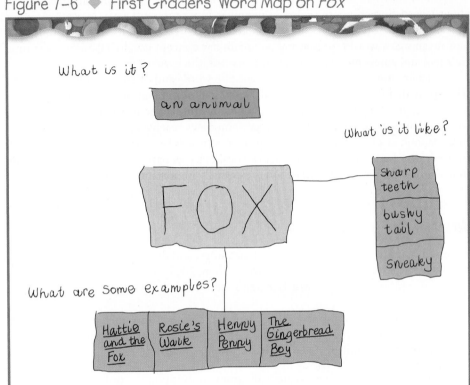

Word Chains. Children choose a word and then identify three or four words to sequence before or after it to make a chain. For example, the word *tadpole* can be chained this way: *egg, tadpole, frog*; and the word *aggravate* can be chained like this: *irritate, bother, aggravate, annoy.* Children can draw and write their word chains on a sheet of paper, or they can make a chain out of construction paper and write a word on each link.

Semantic Feature Analysis. Children learn the meanings of conceptually related words by examining their characteristics in a semantic feature analysis (Rickelman & Taylor, 2006). Teachers create a grid in which they list a group of words related to a book or a thematic unit on the left and write distinguishing characteristics across the top. Children analyze the words, characteristic by characteristic, and place a plus or minus mark in each cell to indicate whether a word represents a characteristic. In a semantic feature analysis on the solar system, for example, the planets would appear in the left column and characteristics such as "has a moon" and "life is possible" in the top row.

These word-study activities provide opportunities for children to deepen their understanding of words listed on word walls, other words related to books they're reading, and words they're learning during thematic units. Children develop concepts, learn one or more meanings of words, and make associations among words through these activities. None of them require children to simply write words and their definitions or to use the words in sentences or a contrived story.

Word-Learning Strategies

When children come across an unfamiliar word while reading, they can do several things to solve the problem: They can reread the sentence, sound out the word, look for context clues in the sentence, analyze the root word and affixes, check a dictionary, skip the word and keep reading, or ask the teacher for help, for example. Some techniques, however, work better than others. After studying the research on ways to deal with unfamiliar words, Graves (2006) identified these effective word-learning strategies:

- Using context clues
- Analyzing word parts
- Checking a dictionary

Teacher teach children to use these strategies to figure out the meaning of new words.

Children must learn what to do when they encounter an unfamiliar word. First, they notice when a word they're reading is unfamiliar and decide whether it's important to know its meaning. If it's unimportant to the text, children skip it and continue reading, but if it's important, they take action. Here's the procedure Graves (2006) recommends that children use to figure out the meaning of a new word:

1. Reread the sentence containing the word.
2. Use context clues to figure out the meaning, but if that doesn't work, go to the next step.

Be Strategic!

Word-Learning Strategies

When children are reading and come across an unfamiliar word, they use these strategies to figure out the word's meaning:

- ▶ Use context clues
- ▶ Analyze word parts
- ▶ Check a dictionary

These three strategies are effective when children know how to apply them and are interested in learning new words.

Figure 7-1 ◆ A Word Sort Using Words From *Paul Bunyan*

Words Describing Paul Bunyan	Places Paul Bunyan Created	Places Paul Bunyan Visited	Words Describing Babe
strongest	St. Lawrence River	Maine	ox calf
smartest	Grand Canyon	Texas	blue
extremely helpful	Rocky Mountains	Arizona	depressed
colossal	Great Lakes	Great Plains	sturdy
legendary		California	unusual size
extraordinary		Pacific Ocean	
		Alaska	

3. Examine the word parts, looking for familiar root words and affixes to aid in figuring out the meaning. If that's not successful, go to the next step.
4. Pronounce the word to see if they recognize it when they say it. If that doesn't work, go to the next step.
5. Check the word in a dictionary or ask the teacher for help.

This procedure has the greatest chance of success because it includes all three word-learning strategies.

Using Context Clues. The words and sentences that surround the new word offer context clues; some clues provide information about the meaning of the word. This contextual information helps children infer the word's meaning, and illustrations also provide useful information. The context clues that readers use are presented in Figure 7–8. Interestingly, two or three types of contextual information are often included in the same sentence.

Context clues rarely provide enough information to help children learn a word because typically it's only partial information, and it can be misleading. Nevertheless, Nagy, Anderson, and Herman (1987) found that grade-level readers have a 1 in 20 chance of learning the meaning of a word using context clues. Although that seems inconsequential, if children read 20,000 words a year and learn 1 of every 20 words through context, they'll learn 1,000 words, or one third of their annual vocabulary growth. That's significant! How long does it take to read 20,000 words? Nagy (1988) estimated that if teachers provide 30 minutes of daily reading time, children will learn an additional 1,000 words a year.

The best way to teach children about context clues is by modeling. When teachers read aloud, they should stop at a difficult word and talk with children about how they can use context clues to figure out its meaning. When the rest of the sentence or paragraph provides enough information, teachers use that information and continue reading, but when it doesn't, they use another strategy to figure out the meaning of the word.

Figure 7–8 ◆ Six Types of Context Clues

Clue	Description	Sample Sentence
Definition	Readers use the definition in the sentence to understand the unknown word.	Some spiders spin silk with tiny organs called *spinnerets*.
Example-Illustration	Readers use an example or illustration to understand the unknown word.	Toads, frogs, and some birds are *predators* that hunt and eat spiders.
Contrast	Readers understand the unknown word because it's compared or contrasted with another word in the sentence.	Most spiders live for about one year, but *tarantulas* sometimes live for 20 years or more!
Logic	Readers think about the rest of the sentence to understand the unknown word.	An *exoskeleton* acts like a suit of armor to protect the spider.
Root Words and Affixes	Readers use their knowledge of root words and affixes to figure out the unknown word.	People who are terrified of spiders have *arachnophobia*.
Grammar	Readers use the word's function in the sentence or its part of speech to figure out the unknown word.	Most spiders *molt* five to ten times.

Analyzing Word Parts. Children use their knowledge of prefixes, suffixes, and root words to unlock longer words when they understand how word parts function. For example, *omnivorous, carnivorous,* and *herbivorous* relate to the foods that animals eat; *omni* means "all," *carno* means "flesh," and *herb* means "vegetation." The common word part *vorous* comes from the Latin *vorare,* meaning "to swallow up." When children know *carnivorous* or *carnivore,* they use morphemic analysis to figure out the other words. Graves (2006) recommends that teachers teach morphemic analysis when non-English root words appear in books children are reading and during thematic units. Teachers break apart the words and discuss the word parts when they're posted on the word wall and through minilessons.

Checking the Dictionary. Looking up unfamiliar words in the dictionary is often frustrating because the definitions don't provide enough useful information or because words used in the definition are forms of the word being defined. Sometimes the definition that children choose—usually the first one—is the wrong one. Or, it doesn't make sense. For example, the word *pollution* is usually defined as "the act of polluting." Children could look for an entry for *polluting,* but they won't find it. They might notice an entry for *pollute,* where the first definition is "to make impure." The second definition is "to make unclean, especially with man-made waste," but it's difficult to understand. Because dictionary definitions are more useful when a reader is vaguely familiar with the word's meaning, teachers play an important role in dictionary work: They teach children how to read a dictionary entry and decide which definitions make sense, they demonstrate the strategy when they're reading aloud and come across an unfamiliar word, and they assist by explaining the definitions that children locate and comparing the word to related words.

Incidental Word Learning

Children learn words incidentally, without explicit instruction, all the time, and because children learn so many words this way, teachers know that they don't have to teach the meaning of every unfamiliar word in a book. Children learn words from many sources, but researchers report that reading is the single largest source of vocabulary growth for children, especially after third grade (Swanborn & de Glopper, 1999). In addition, the amount of time children spend reading independently in the best predictor of vocabulary growth between second and fifth grades.

Independent Reading. Children need daily opportunities for independent reading in order to learn words, and they must read books at their independent reading levels. If the books are too easy or too hard, children learn very few new words. The best way to provide opportunities for independent reading is reading workshop. Children choose books they're interested in from age-appropriate and reading-level-suitable collections in their classroom libraries, and because they're chosen the books themselves, they're more likely to keep reading.

Sustained Silent Reading (SSR) is another way to encourage wide reading. All children in a classroom or in the school spend 10 to 30 minutes silently reading appropriate books that they've chosen themselves. Even the teacher takes time to read, in the process modeling how adults who enjoy reading make it part of their daily routine. Simply providing time for independent reading, however, doesn't guarantee that children will increase their vocabulary knowledge (Stahl & Nagy, 2006); children need to know how to figure out the meaning of unfamiliar words to increase their vocabulary.

Reading Aloud to Children.   Teachers also provide for incidental word learning when they read aloud stories, poems, and informational books. Daily read-aloud activities are important for children at all grade levels, prekindergarten through fourth grade. Teachers use the interactive read-aloud procedure and focus on a few key words in the book, model how to use context clues to understand new words, and talk about the words after reading. Teachers use think-alouds when they model using context clues and other word-identification strategies. Two recent studies found that teachers enhance children's vocabulary knowledge and their comprehension when they add a focus on vocabulary to their read-alouds (Santoro, Chard, Howard, & Baker, 2008).

Cunningham (2009) recommends that teachers choose one picture book each week to read aloud and teach key vocabulary. Teachers read the book aloud one time and then present three new words from the book, each written on a word card. During the second reading, children listen for the words, and the teacher takes time to talk about each word's meaning using information available in the text and in the illustrations. Later, the teacher encourages children to practice using the new words when they talk and write about the book.

Well-written books with rich vocabulary, figurative language, and wordplay are available for reading aloud to children at every grade level. *Hey, Al* (Yorinks, 1986), for example, is an award-winning story about a man named Al and his dog, Eddie, who leave their city apartment to find happiness on a tropical island paradise, only to learn that you make your own happiness and that things that sound too good to be true usually are. These words are included in the book:

aloft	ecstasy	gorgeous	shimmering
beady	exhausted	heartbroken	shrieked
blissfully	ferried	lush	squawked
cascaded	flitted	paradise	struggling
cooed	fortunately	plumed	talented
croaked	furiously	plunged	unbelievable

In addition to learning individual words as they listen to *Hey, Al* read aloud, children also hear language that's unique to stories, more complex sentence structures, and more mature linguistic expressions, such as the following:

Unbelievable! Lush trees, rolling hills, gorgeous grass.

Birds fitted to and fro.

Waterfalls cascaded into shimmering pools.

But ripe fruit soon spoils.

Eddie, in a frenzy, was flying in circles, higher and higher. (n.p.)

As teachers read *Hey, Al* and other stories and involve children in grand conversations and other response activities, they practice using some of these words and sentence structures.

Figure 7–9 presents a list of read-aloud books with rich vocabulary. Some of these books are stories like *Hey, Al*, and others are informational books that expand children's background knowledge as well as build vocabulary. For example, as third graders listen to their teacher read aloud *The Magic School Bus Inside a Beehive*

Figure 7-9 ◆ Read-Aloud Books for Building Vocabulary

PREKINDERGARTEN

Fleming, D. (1996). *Lunch*. New York: Henry Holt.

Frasier, D. (2002). *Out of the ocean*. Boston: Houghton Mifflin.

Gibbons, G. (2009). *Dinosaurs*. New York: Holiday House.

Henkes, K. (2000). *Wemberly worried*. New York: Greenwillow.

Himmelman, J. (2006). *Chickens to the rescue*. New York: Henry Holt.

Keats, E. J. (1985). *Peter's chair*. New York: HarperCollins.

Martin, B., Jr., & Archambault, J. (1989). *Chicka chicka boom boom*. New York: Simon & Schuster.

Rockwell, A. (2001). *Bugs are insects*. New York: HarperCollins.

Schachner, J. (2005). *Skippyjon Jones*. New York: Puffin Books.

Tafuri, N. (2001). *Silly little goose*. New York: Scholastic.

Weatherford, C. B. (2006). *Jazz baby*. New York: Lee & Low.

Willems, M. (2003). *Don't let the pigeon drive the bus!* New York: Hyperion Books.

KINDERGARTEN

Bottner, B. (2003). *The scaredy cats*. New York: Simon & Schuster.

Carle, E. (2004). *Mister Seahorse*. New York: Philomel.

Cronin, D. (2005). *Diary of a spider*. New York. HarperCollins.

Frazee, M. (2006). *Roller coaster*. New York: Sandpiper.

Gibbons, G. (2008). *Ice cream: The full scoop*. New York: Holiday House.

Jenkins, E. (2004). *My favorite thing (according to Alberta)*. New York: Atheneum.

Long, M. (2003). *How I became a pirate*. Orlando: Harcourt.

Most, B. (1996). *Cock-a-doodle-moo!* New York: Harcourt Brace.

O'Connor, J. (2005). *Fancy Nancy*. New York: HarperCollins.

Walton, R. (2005). *Bullfrog pops!* Layton, UT: Gibbs Smith.

Wells, R. (1997). *McDuff comes home*. New York: Hyperion Books.

GRADE 1

Ada, A. F. (2001). *With love, Little Red Hen*. New York: Atheneum.

Heller, R. (1992). *How to hide a butterfly*. New York: Grosset & Dunlap.

Kasza, K. (1996). *The wolf's chicken stew*. New York: Paper Star.

Keats, E. J. (2001). *Pet show!* New York: Viking.

Krull, K. (2000). *Wilma unlimited: How Wilma Rudolph became the world's fastest woman*. New York: Sandpiper.

Lee, C. (2004). *Good dog, Paw!* Cambridge, MA: Candlewick Press.

Many, P. (2002). *The great pancake escape*. New York: Walker.

Munson, D. (2000). *Enemy pie*. San Francisco: Chronicle Books.

Rathmann, P. (1995). *Officer Buckle and Gloria*. New York: Putnam.

Schwartz, D. M. (2008). *How much is a million?* New York: HarperCollins.

Simont, M. (2001). *The stray dog*. New York: HarperCollins.

Yorinks, A. (1986). *Hey, Al*. New York: Farrar, Straus & Giroux.

GRADE 2

Aliki. (1996). *My trip to the aquarium*. New York: HarperCollins.

Choi, Y. (2001). *The name jar*. New York: Knopf.

Cronin, D. (2000). *Click, clack, moo: Cows that type*. New York: Simon & Schuster.

Demi. (1996). *The empty pot*. New York: Holt.

Dorros, A. (1991). *Abuela*. New York: Dutton.

LaMarche, J. (2002). *The raft*. New York: HarperCollins.

Levine, E. (2007). *Henry's freedom box*. New York: Scholastic.

Orloff, K. K. (2004). *I wanna iguana*. New York: Putnam.

Ryan, P. M. (2002). *When Marian sang: The true recital of Marian Anderson*. New York: Scholastic.

Soto, G. (1993). *Too many tamales*. New York: Putnam.

Teague, M. (1996). *The secret shortcut*. New York: Scholastic.

Yolen, J. (1987). *Owl moon*. New York: Philomel.

GRADE 3

Barrett, J. (1985). *Cloudy with a chance of meatballs*. New York: Aladdin Books.

Cherry, L. (2000). *The Great Kapok Tree*. New York: Sandpiper.

Coerr, E. (1988). *Chang's paper pony*. New York: HarperCollins.

(Contiued)

Figure 7-9 ◆ Continued

Cohen, B. (1998). *Molly's pilgrim*. New York: HarperCollins.

hooks, b. (2004). *Skin again*. New York: Hyperion Books.

Horwitz, E. L. (2004). *When the sky is like lace*. New York: Viking.

MacLachlan, P. (2004). *Sarah, plain and tall*. New York: HarperTrophy.

Pinkney, A. (2006). *Duke Ellington: The piano prince and his orchestra*. New York: Hyperion Books.

Scieszka, J. (1989). *The true story of the 3 little pigs!* New York: Viking.

Steig, W. (2006). *Sylvester and the magic pebble*. New York: Aladdin Books.

Wiesner, D. (2001). *The three pigs*. New York: Clarion Books.

Zelinsky, P. O. (1996). *Rumpelstiltskin*. New York: Puffin Books.

GRADE 4

Bunting, E. (1999). *Smoky night*. San Diego: Harcourt Brace.

Bunting, E. (2009). *So far from the sea*. New York: Sandpiper.

Dahl, R. (2007). *James and the giant peach*. New York: Puffin Books.

Dillon, L., & Dillon, D. (2007). *Jazz on a Saturday night*. New York: Blue Sky Press.

Gibbons, G. (1998). *Planet earth/inside out*. New York: HarperCollins.

Polacco, P. (1994). *Pink and Say*. New York: Philomel.

Say, A. (2004). *Music for Alice*. Boston: Houghton Mifflin.

Scieszka, J. (2001). *Baloney (Henry P.)*. New York: Viking.

Simon, S. (2007). *Our solar system* (rev. ed.). New York: Collins.

Weatherford, C. B. (2007). *Freedom on the menu: The Greensboro sit-ins*. New York: Puffin Books.

White, E. B. (2004). *Charlotte's web*. New York: HarperTrophy

Wick, W. (1997). *A drop of water*. New York: Scholastic.

(Cole, 1996), they learn about bees and are introduced to or deepen their understanding of these words:

adult	hive	pollinate
antennae	honeycombs	pupa
beekeepers	insect	queen bee
cells	larvae	social
communicate	mate	sting
drones	metamorphosis	swarming
hexagon	nectar	worker bees

Children don't learn all of these words in a single reading, of course, but through repeated experiences with the words, their level of word knowledge deepens.

Although reading aloud is important for all children, it's especially important for struggling readers who typically read fewer books themselves, and because the books at their reading level have less sophisticated vocabulary words. Researchers report that children learn as many words incidentally while listening to teachers read aloud as they do by reading themselves (Stahl & Nagy, 2006).

Assessing Children's Word Knowledge

It's difficult to assess children's vocabulary knowledge because there aren't any grade-level standards to indicate which words children should know or even how many words they need to learn. Moreover, assessing vocabulary is complicated because children learn words gradually, moving to deeper levels of "knowing" a word. Teachers typically monitor children's independent reading and use informal measures to evaluate their word knowledge, but several tests are available to measure children's vocabulary knowledge; they're described in the Assessment Tools feature below.

Teachers often choose more authentic measures of children's vocabulary knowledge because they're more useful than formal tests (Bean & Swan, 2006). These informal assessment tools show whether children have learned the words that were taught as well as the depth of their knowledge:

Observations. Teachers watch how children use new words during word-study activities, minilessons, and discussions.

Retelling Stories. Teachers listen as children participate in story retelling activities to check that they're incorporating some of the vocabulary from the book in their version and using the words appropriately.

Assessment Tools

Vocabulary

Both informal assessments and standardized tests can be used to measure children's vocabulary knowledge, but tests often equate word knowledge with recognizing or being able to state one definition of a word rather than assessing the depth of children's knowledge. Here are several norm-referenced vocabulary tests:

◆ *Peabody Picture Vocabulary Test-4 (PPVT-4) (Dunn, Dunn, & Dunn, 2006)*
The PPVT-4 is an individually administered test to screen children's word knowledge. It can be used with preK–4 children, but it's most commonly used with young children showing limited verbal fluency. The PPVT-4 measures receptive vocabulary: The teacher says a word and asks the child to identify one of four pictures that best illustrates the word's meaning. Unfortunately, this test takes 10 minutes to administer, making it too time-consuming for regular classroom use. The PPVT-4 is available from the American Guidance Service.

◆ *Expressive Vocabulary Test-2 (EVT-2) (Williams, 2006)*
The EVT-2 is also an individual test that's used to screen preK–4 children's knowledge of words. It's the expressive counterpart of the PPVT-4: The teacher points to a picture and asks the child to say a word that labels the picture or to provide a synonym for a word that's illustrated in the picture. This test, available from the American Guidance Service, is also very time-consuming for classroom teachers to use.

◆ *Informal Reading Inventories (IRIs)*
Sometimes teachers in grades 2–4 use IRIs to assess children's vocabulary knowledge. One or two comprehension questions at each grade level focus on the meaning of words selected from the passage children have read. The usefulness of this assessment is limited, however, because so few questions deal with vocabulary and because children who read below grade level aren't tested on age-appropriate words.

Even though these tests aren't very useful in classroom settings, they are valuable in diagnosing children with limited word knowledge.

Conferences. Teachers talk with children about the words they've used in word-study activities and in their writing.

Rubrics. Teachers include items about vocabulary on rubrics to emphasize its importance. For oral-presentation rubrics, teachers emphasize the use of technical words related to the topic, and for writing, they emphasize precise vocabulary.

Tests. Teachers also create a variety of paper-and-pencil tests to monitor children's vocabulary knowledge. For example, they use the cloze procedure to create a passage and then have children fill in the missing words, write a paragraph about a word's meaning, create a word map, or draw a picture to represent a word's meaning.

These informal assessments go beyond simply providing a definition or using a word in a sentence because children are using the words they're learning in meaningful ways.

IF CHILDREN STRUGGLE...

Most children pick up new words quickly. They understand their meaning and use the words in talk and writing. Some children, however, are less aware of words; they don't remember and use new words from books they're reading or from thematic units. When children aren't making adequate progress, teachers need to figure out why and provide an appropriate intervention. To begin, teachers usually talk with children about several of the words they're currently highlighting to identify the problem:

- Can children explain the meaning of these words?
- Can children locate the words on the word wall?
- Can children pronounce the words?
- Can children use the words in conversation?
- Can children use the words in writing?

Children need to understand the meaning of the words they're studying and use them expressively. They should also appreciate why it's important to learn and use new words.

Once teachers identify children's vocabulary problems, they identify intervention procedures and ways to differentiate instruction.

Emphasis on Vocabulary. When children aren't aware of vocabulary words, teachers draw their attention to new vocabulary by seating them near the word wall and enlisting their assistance in posting new words on it. They also preteach new words to these children and have them use small self-stick notes to mark vocabulary words on story boards and in books.

Word Meanings. When children aren't learning word meanings, teachers preteach vocabulary, investigate the structure of words, make packs of word cards for practice activities, and involve them in interactive games, including word ladders and word sorts.

Talk Activities. When children can't use the words orally, teachers provide a variety of informal opportunities for them to use words in conversation: They talk with partners about specific words on the word wall, collaborate with class-mates on semantic feature analysis charts, and participate in grand conversa-tions and other discussions. Children also incorporate vocabulary words during story retelling activities and complete cloze activities orally before doing them in writing.

Writing Activities. When children aren't using new words in writing, teachers have them use specific words as they draw and label pictures, write in reading logs, create word posters, and complete graphic organizers. To increase children's atten-tion to words, teachers often have them use highlighter pens to mark vocabulary words in their writing.

Teachers can help children who struggle with vocabulary by preteaching new words and providing opportunities for them to play word games, talk about words, and incorpo-rate words in writing activities.

CHAPTER Review

How Effective Teachers Build Children's Word Knowledge

▶ Teachers provide daily opportunities for children to read books independently and listen to them read aloud.

▶ Teachers categorize unfamiliar words into three tiers—basic words, academic words, and specialized words.

▶ Teachers teach Tier 2 words using explicit instruction and a variety of word-study activities.

▶ Teachers support children's development of word-learning strategies.

Chapter 8

Facilitating Children's Comprehension: Reader Factors

Third Graders Become Strategic Readers

It's reading workshop time in Mrs. Chase's third-grade classroom. The children are reading books they've selected themselves from the classroom library. Seventy-seven crates of books are set up across the counter under the windows that runs the length of the classroom. Some books are arranged by reading level; others are grouped by topics such as space and the rain forest, favorite authors, and series including Amber Brown, Magic School Bus, Lemony Snicket, and A to Z Mysteries. In addition, four crates are filled with *Cobblestones*, *National Geographic Kids*, and other magazines. As children choose reading materials, they clip a clothespin with their name on it to the crate so Mrs. Chase can easily monitor what they're reading.

The children know their reading levels and how to choose appropriate books. Aaron is reading *Flat Stanley* (Brown, 2003a) (Level N), and his friend Henry is reading *Stanley in Space* (Brown, 2003b) (Level N). These two boys read at about the same level, and they like to read related books so they can talk about them. Tanner is reading *Horrible Harry's Secret* (Kline, 1998) (Level L), which his friend Connor read recently and recommended. Jordan is reading every book in Paula Danziger's popular Amber Brown series.

Currently, she's reading *Amber Brown Is Green With Envy* (2004) (Level N), and she thinks it's the best one yet. Madison is reading *The Borrowers Aloft* (Norton, 2003b) (Level S), a sequel Mrs. Chase recommended after Madison enjoyed *The Borrowers* (Norton, 2003a).

Mrs. Chase conferences with the children sitting at one table group each day while the others are reading. Today, she meets with Jordan, Ava, Jack, William, and Grace. After the children talk briefly about the books they're reading, Mrs. Chase asks them to tell her about the strategies they're using to comprehend. Jack says, "I'm making awesome text-to-self connections because the characters are a lot like me. They do what I do—stuff like going to school, telling jokes, and riding bikes. And they get in trouble just like me, too." Jordan, who's reading the books in the Amber Brown series, says, "I'm making connections, too, but lots of mine are text-to-text connections because I'm noticing things that are the same in each book." William shares, "Predicting is my strategy. I'm wicked good at predicting what's going to happen. I'm reading faster and faster because I have to know if I'm right. That's what's different about my reading this year: I'm thinking and reading at the same time!" Grace talks about the visualizing strategy: "I'm sort of dreaming the story in my brain as I read it, and it seems like it's happening for real." After the other group members talk about their strategy use, Mrs. Chase reviews the chart on the types of comprehension strategies that the class made at the beginning of the school year. It's shown below.

The third graders learned about the comprehension strategies in first and second grades, so Mrs. Chase quickly reviewed them at the beginning of the school year. The children could identify the strategies and use them one at a time when they were directed to do so, but they weren't using them when they were reading independently. Now she's focusing on how the children can use the strategies purposefully to improve their comprehension.

Comprehension Strategies Chart	
Strategy	What Readers Do
Predicting	Readers predict what will happen next.
Connecting	Readers think about what they already know about the topic.
Visualizing	Readers make a movie in their heads.
Questioning	Readers ask questions about things that don't make sense.
Identifying Big Ideas	Readers think about the big ideas.
Summarizing	Readers combine the big ideas in a summary.
Monitoring	Readers check that they are understanding and take action if they're confused.
Evaluating	Readers reflect on the book and think about how well they read.

Third Graders' Connections With *Open Wide: Tooth School Inside*

Text-to-Self	Text-to-World	Text-to-Text
I'm thinking about all the ways tooth school is like our school. This book reminds me to take good care of my teeth. The book made me think about when I believed in the tooth fairy. My great-grandma has false teeth because she didn't take care of her teeth when she was a girl. I started thinking that my dentist would like to read this book. This book gives good advice about brushing teeth just like my dad does.	It's like my dentist told me about tooth decay. I think all dentists should have this book. There's a model of a tooth of my dentist's that's just like a picture in this book. I know there's a chemical called fluoride in our water that keeps our teeth strong.	It's a very funny book like The Scrambled States of America [Keller, 1998]. This book reminds me of Miss Alaineus [Frasier, 2007] because the pages are crowded with little pictures and lots of words and details. I'm thinking about a book called Dear Tooth Fairy [Durant, 2004] that my grandma gave me.

The third graders spend 100 minutes in three reading workshop activities: reading independently, participating in a minilesson, and listening to Mrs. Chase read aloud. Mrs. Chase also conducts guided reading lessons where she focuses her instruction to accommodate children's specific needs. After reading workshop, the third graders participate in writing workshop where they learn to use writing strategies and write books on self-selected topics.

After 15 minutes of independent reading time, Mrs. Chase brings the class together for a minilesson on the connecting strategy. "What do you remember about making connections?" Mrs. Chase begins. "It's when you connect what you know to what you're reading," Aiden answers. "There are three kinds of connections: text-to-self, text-to-world, and text-to-text," Katie continues. Children take turns explaining each type of connections. Connor explains, "Text-to-self connections are personal. You think of things in your own life that are like in the book." Madison describes text-to-world connections: "You think about what's happening in your town, what you see on the TV news, and what you know about the world; then you make connections. Sometimes they're sort of hard for me." "Text-to-text connections," Tanner says, "are connections from one book to another one that you've read." "Or one author makes you think of another author," Katie adds. Then Mrs. Chase reviews the three types of connections using the chart they made several weeks ago after reading *Open Wide: Tooth School Inside* (Keller, 2003), a hilarious picture book about tooth care. The class's chart on making connections is shown above.

Mrs. Chase uses examples from the book she's reading aloud in her minilessons. Yesterday, she read aloud the first chapter of Beverly Cleary's *Henry Huggins* (2000), a classic story about the adventures of a boy and his dog, so for today's minilesson, she's copied several paragraphs from that chapter on chart paper for everyone to reread. The first paragraph is about Henry and his new dog, Ribsy, causing an uproar as they ride home on a bus. After she reads it aloud to the class, Mrs. Chase models how she uses the connecting strategy:

> This paragraph is confusing, and the word *lurch* is a new one. I think I can make some connections to help me understand it better. I've ridden on buses, and I remember that a ride on a bus isn't as smooth as in a car. Sometimes I have to hold on so I don't slide off the seat. I'm making a text-to-self connection: I can imagine that Henry had a very hard time holding on to the box with Ribsy in it, and I'm not surprised that the frightened dog wiggled out of the box and got away from Henry.

Mrs. Chase writes about her text-to-self connection on a self-stick note. Then she places the note on the chart paper and reads it aloud: "T-S: I know buses lurch and you have to hold on."

Next, Mrs. Chase flips the page of chart paper and reads aloud a second paragraph; this one is about Henry and Ribsy being ordered off the bus. "What connections can you make to understand what's happening in this paragraph?" Mrs. Chase asks. Ava responds this way:

> I'm not surprised that the bus driver ordered them off the bus. If I was him, that's what I'd do, but I don't understand why everyone is laughing. It's not funny; it's a big mess. Now I'm making a text-to-self connection. I remember when my dad and my brother made a big mess when they were cleaning out the garage. First my mom came outside and saw the mess, and she looked real mad. Then she started laughing. I don't know why she laughed, but I think that's what the fat man was doing.

Mrs. Chase suggests that laughter releases tension, and she compliments Ava on her text-to-self connection. She hands Ava a self-stick note and a marking pen to write a note about her connection. Ava writes the note, places it on the chart paper, and reads it aloud to the class: "T-S: My mom was mad and then she laughed."

Mrs. Chase shares the third paragraph, and Tanner talks about the connection he can make to understand it better and then writes his connection on a self-stick note. Then Mrs. Chase asks, "Why does making connections help you comprehend better?" Katie responds this way: "If a part is confusing you and you think about what you know, it will help you figure it out." And Henry says, "Well, if your name is the same as the main character's name, like mine is, you think the story is about you and you think about what you would do in that situation."

At the end of the minilesson, the third graders return to their desks to continue reading in self-selected books. Mrs. Chase asks them to use the connecting strategy they practiced in the minilesson as they're reading on their own and to add small self-stick notes to show how the connection helped them understand better. While most of the children continue with independent reading, the teacher conducts guided reading lessons with small groups of children.

Sharing time is next, and Mrs. Chase brings the children together to talk about the books they've been reading. They explain the connections they've made and share the notes they've written. Aiden goes first: "I'm reading *Toliver's Secret* [Brady, 1988], and it's about the Revolutionary War, and I made a text-to-world connection to what I know because I know a lot about wars. Here's my note: 'T-W: I'm thinking about wars.'" Gillian jumps into the conversation and adds: "I'm doing it, too. My book is *Phoebe the Spy* [Griffin, 2002], and it's about the American Revolution. I'm making text-to-world connections because I know about wars. My note says 'T-W: I'm thinking about cannons and stuff.'" "I'm making text-to-text connections," Jack adds. "First I read the Marvin Redpost books, and next I read *Sideways Stories From Wayside School* [Sachar, 2004], and now I'm reading *There's a Boy in the Girls' Bathroom* [Sachar, 1988]. You can tell that the same man wrote all of these wacky stories. I really like this author!" Mrs. Chase asks about his note, and Jack reads, "T-T: This wacky book is by the great Louis Sachar!"

At 9:40, the third graders attend a 30-minute physical education class, and when they return, Mrs. Chase reads aloud while they eat a snack. Today, she's reading the second chapter in *Henry Huggins* (Cleary, 2000) using the interactive read-aloud procedure. As she picks up the book, she points out that this is the 50th anniversary edition, and the children are impressed that this story would win so many fans that it's still popular. As they review the first chapter, Henry shares that he'd been confused about something: "I thought it was weird that Henry only had 25 cents to buy an ice cream and ride the bus home. I know that ice cream costs more, and so does a bus ride. I was confused because I was making text-to-world connections, but if this book is 50 years old, I'm thinking that people way back then could buy ice cream and ride the bus for 25 cents." The teacher congratulates Henry for making connections and using them to figure out a confusing part.

After Mrs. Chase asks the children to predict what might happen in the second chapter, "Gallons of Guppies," she reads about Henry's trip to the pet store to buy fish. When she pauses partway through the chapter, Henry points out that the book says a fishbowl, guppies, and fish food cost 79 cents, but he knows that at Bailey's Pets, the pet store where he bought his goldfish, it would cost more than 5 dollars. The children agree with him, and several share their fish-buying experiences. Toward the end of the chapter, Mrs. Chase pauses again so that the children can speculate on how the chapter will end. "What will Henry do with all the baby guppies?" she asks. Ava suggests that Henry will give them away, but others think he'll sell them. Mrs. Chase reads to the end of the chapter, and the children are pleased with the conclusion: Henry takes the guppies back to the pet store and trades them for a fish tank and some tropical fish. As they talk about the chapter, several children say that they plan to write about their pets during writing workshop.

omprehension is the goal of reading instruction; it's the reason why people read. Readers must comprehend the text to learn from the experience; they must make sense of their reading to maintain interest; and they must enjoy reading to become lifelong readers. Decoding words is a relatively straightforward procedure compared to the complexity of constructing meaning after the words have been recognized (Sweet & Snow, 2003). Readers activate background knowledge and think about what they're reading; they apply cognitive and metacognitive strategies to understand the text. In the vignette, Mrs. Chase was teaching her third graders to use comprehension strategies because strategic readers are more likely to understand what they're reading.

DEVELOPMENTAL CONTINUUM Comprehension: Reader Factors

PreK	K	1	2	3	4
Young children actively engage with literature as teachers read aloud and respond through talk, drama, and drawing.	Kindergartners use strategies, including predicting and connecting, to comprehend books that teachers read aloud.	First graders transfer listening strategies they've learned to reading and use repairing to solve reading problems.	Children learn additional comprehension strategies, including questioning, visualizing, summarizing, and repairing.	Children vary how they use comprehension strategies to read and respond to stories, informational books, and poems.	Fourth graders become more adept at drawing inferences and thinking critically to understand books they're reading.

Readers use four levels of thinking—literal, inferential, critical, and evaluative—as they comprehend. The most basic level is literal comprehension. Readers pick out the big ideas, sequence details, notice similarities and differences, and identify explicitly stated reasons. The higher levels differ from this kind of thinking because readers integrate their own knowledge with the information presented in the text. In inferential comprehension, readers use clues they notice in the text, implied information, and their background knowledge to draw inferences. They make predictions, recognize cause and effect, and determine the author's purpose. Critical comprehension is the third level. Readers analyze symbolic meanings, distinguish fact from opinion, and draw conclusions. The most sophisticated level is evaluative comprehension: Readers judge the quality of texts. These levels point out the range of thinking children can do.

WHAT IS COMPREHENSION?

Comprehension is a creative, multifaceted process in which children engage with and think about the text (Tierney, 1990). The comprehension process begins as children activate their background knowledge, and it develops as they read or listen to a book read aloud and then respond to it. Readers construct a mental "picture" or representation of the text through the comprehension process (Van Den Broek & Kremer, 2000).

Judith Irwin (1991) defines comprehension as a reader's process of using prior experiences and the author's text to construct meaning that's useful to that reader for a specific purpose. This definition emphasizes that comprehension depends on two factors: the *reader* and the *text* that's being read. Whether comprehension is successful, according to Sweet and Snow (2003), depends on the interaction of reader factors and text factors.

Reader and Text Factors

Children actively engage with the text as they read or listen to it read aloud. For example, they do the following:

- Activate background knowledge
- Examine the text to uncover its organization
- Make predictions
- Connect to their own experiences
- Create mental images
- Monitor their understanding
- Solve problems that interfere with comprehension

These activities can be categorized as reader and text factors (National Reading Panel, 2000). Reader factors include the background knowledge children bring to the reading process, the strategies they use while reading, and their engagement in the reading experience. Text factors include the author's ideas, the words the author uses to express those ideas, and the organization of ideas. Children apply reader and text factors as they read, and their understanding of these factors determines whether they'll be successful. Figure 8–1 presents an overview of these two factors. This chapter focuses on reader factors, and Chapter 9 addresses text factors.

Figure 8–1 ◆ The Comprehension Factors

Type	Factors	Role in Comprehension
Reader	Background Knowledge	Children activate their world and literary knowledge to link what they know to what they're reading.
	Vocabulary	Children recognize the meaning of familiar words and apply word-learning strategies to understand what they're reading.
	Fluency	Fluent readers have cognitive resources available to understand what they're reading.
	Comprehension Strategies	Children actively direct their reading, monitor their understanding, and troubleshoot comprehension problems when they occur.
	Comprehension Skills	Children automatically note details that support big ideas, sequence events, and use other skills.
	Engagement	Children who meet the prerequisites for comprehension and apply comprehension strategies are more likely to be engaged with the text.
Text	Genres	Children's knowledge of the characteristics of genres provides a scaffold for comprehension.
	Text Structures	Children recognize the big ideas more easily when they understand how authors organize text.
	Text Features	Children apply their knowledge of literary devices to deepen their understanding and appreciate the author's use of language.

Prerequisites for Comprehension

For children to comprehend a text, they must have adequate background knowledge, understand most words in the text, and be able to read it fluently. When any of these prerequisites for comprehension are lacking, children aren't likely to understand what they're reading. Teachers can ameliorate children's difficulties through differentiated instruction, carefully matching readers to books, and using interactive read-alouds to share books with children.

> Check the Compendium of Instructional Procedures, which follows Chapter 12, for more information on highlighted terms.

Background Knowledge. Children's world and literary knowledge provides a bridge to a new text (Braunger & Lewis, 2006). World knowledge includes what children know about grocery stores, hermit crabs, deserts, and Martin Luther King Jr., for example. Recognizing the beginning, middle, and end of stories, differentiating between stories and biographies, knowing how to arrange a poem on a page, and making connections are examples of literary knowledge. For example, 4- and 5-year olds need to understand the sequential structure of *First the Egg* (Seeger, 2007) to appreciate this award-winning concept book; third graders who aren't familiar with mysteries and the clipped sentences that detectives use will have trouble understanding *Tough Cookie* (Wisniewski, 1999), an absurd crime drama that's set in a cookie jar; and fourth graders need to know about the Underground Railroad to understand *Henry's Freedom Box* (Levine, 2007), the unforgettable story of a slave's escape to freedom.

To build background knowledge, teachers determine whether readers lack world or literary knowledge and then provide experiences, visual representations, and talk to build the concepts they need for a specific book. Authentic experiences such as taking field trips, participating in dramatizations, and examining artifacts are the most effective, but photos and pictures, picture books, videos, and other visual representations also work. Talk is often the least effective way, especially for English learners, but sometimes explaining a concept or describing the characteristics of a genre provides enough information.

Vocabulary. Children's knowledge of words plays a tremendous role in comprehension because it's difficult to decode and comprehend a text that's loaded with unfamiliar words. When they don't know many words related to a topic, it's usually a sign that children don't have adequate background knowledge either. For example, children who listen to their teacher read aloud a book on plants, such as *Jack's Garden* (Cole, 1997), *Planting a Rainbow* (Ehlert, 1992), or *From Seed to Plant* (Gibbons, 1993), must be familiar with some of these words: *blossom, bloom, bud, petals, pistil, pollination, roots, seedlings, soil, sprout, stamen*, and *stem*. Those who know more of the words are likely to understand better than those who recognize fewer words.

Blachowicz and Fisher (2007) recommend creating a word-rich classroom environment to immerse children in words, organizing vocabulary instruction into concepts, and teaching word-learning strategies so readers can figure out the meaning of new words. Because of the link between background knowledge and vocabulary, teachers introduce key words at the same time they're building background knowledge. To reinforce the new vocabulary words, teachers also read aloud some books and use shared reading for others before children read them.

> Go to the Building Teaching Skills and Dispositions section of the Topic *Comprehension* in the MyEducationLab for the literacy course and complete the activity entitled *Scaffolding Reading Comprehension*. As you work through the learning unit, consider the ways teachers can address background knowledge, vocabulary, and fluency when scaffolding reading comprehension.

Fluency. Fluent readers read quickly and efficiently. Because they recognize most words automatically, their cognitive resources aren't consumed by decoding unfamiliar words, and they can devote their attention to comprehension. Developing reading fluency is an important component of reading instruction in the primary grades because children need to recognize words automatically so that they can concentrate their attention on comprehending what they're reading (Samuels, 2002).

Teachers, like Mrs. Chase in the vignette at the beginning of the chapter, often teach comprehension using the books they're reading aloud so that fluency isn't an issue. The interest-level-appropriate books that teachers read aloud provide more opportunities for children to practice higher-level thinking than predictable books and easy-to-read books do. Teachers also ensure that the books children read independently fit their reading level so they have cognitive resources available to apply what they're learning about comprehension.

Be Strategic!

Comprehension Strategies

Children apply these strategies to understand texts they're listening to or reading:

▶ Activate background knowledge	▶ Monitor
	▶ Predict
▶ Connect	▶ Question
▶ Determine importance	▶ Repair
	▶ Set a purpose
▶ Draw inferences	▶ Summarize
▶ Evaluate	▶ Visualize

These strategies emphasize what children think about as they listen or read; they're reader factors.

Comprehension Strategies

Comprehension strategies are thoughtful behaviors that readers use to facilitate their understanding (Afflerbach, Pearson, & Paris, 2008). They apply these strategies to deepen their understanding, determine whether they're comprehending successfully, and solve problems as they arise. Some strategies are *cognitive*—they involve thinking, or cognition; others are *metacognitive*—they require reflection. For example, readers make predictions about a story when they begin reading: They wonder what will happen to the characters and whether they'll enjoy the story. Predicting is a cognitive strategy because it involves thinking. Readers also monitor their reading, and monitoring is a metacognitive strategy because they reflect on their understanding; and if they get confused, they take action to solve the problem. Children are being metacognitive when they're alert to the possibility of getting confused, and they know several ways to solve the problem (Pressley, 2002b).

Children learn to apply these cognitive and metacognitive strategies to ensure that they comprehend what they're reading:

- Activating background knowledge
- Connecting
- Determining importance
- Drawing inferences
- Evaluating
- Monitoring
- Predicting
- Questioning
- Repairing
- Setting a purpose
- Summarizing
- Visualizing

Children use these comprehension strategies not only to understand what they're reading, but also to understand books teachers are reading aloud. Figure 8–2 presents an overview of the comprehension strategies and explains how readers use them.

Even preschoolers use many of these comprehension strategies as they listen to books being read aloud. Four-year-olds listening to Mo Willems's cautionary tale, *Knuffle Bunny* (2004), about a beloved stuffed animal that's left behind at the Laundromat, use these strategies:

Activating Background Knowledge. Children who live in cities recognize the book's setting and know what Laundromats are, but others wonder why Trixie's parents can't wash their clothes at home.

Connecting. Children make personal connections as they think about errands they've run with their fathers, remember their favorite stuffed animals, and recall when younger brothers and sisters were learning to talk.

Figure 8–2 ◆ Comprehension Strategies

Strategy	What Readers Do	How It Aids Comprehension
Activating Background Knowledge	Readers make connections between what they already know and the information in the text.	Readers use their background knowledge to fill in gaps in the text and enhance their comprehension.
Connecting	Readers make text-to-self, text-to-world, and text-to-text links.	Readers personalize their reading by relating what they're reading to their background knowledge.
Determining Importance	Readers notice the big ideas in the text and the relationships among them.	Readers focus on the big ideas so they don't become overwhelmed with details.
Drawing Inferences	Readers use background knowledge and clues in the text to "read between the lines."	Readers move beyond literal thinking to grasp meaning that isn't explicitly stated in the text.
Evaluating	Readers evaluate both the text itself and their reading experience.	Readers assume responsibility for their own strategy use.
Monitoring	Readers supervise their reading experience, checking that they're understanding the text.	Readers expect the text to make sense, and they recognize when it doesn't so they can take action.
Predicting	Readers make thoughtful "guesses" about what will happen and then read to confirm their predictions.	Readers become more engaged in the reading experience and want to continue reading.
Questioning	Readers ask themselves literal and higher-level questions about the text.	Readers use questions to direct their reading, clarify confusions, and make inferences.
Repairing	Readers identify a problem interfering with comprehension and then solve it.	Readers solve problems to regain comprehension and continue reading.
Setting a Purpose	Readers identify a broad focus to direct their reading through the text.	Readers focus their attention as they read according to the purpose they've set.
Summarizing	Readers paraphrase the big ideas to create a concise statement.	Readers have better recall of the big ideas when they summarize.
Visualizing	Readers create mental images of what they're reading.	Readers use the mental images to make the text more memorable.

Drawing Inferences. Children make these three inferences: First, they infer that Trixie and her daddy's errand was to take their dirty clothes to the Laundromat. In the middle of the story, children infer that Trixie's temper tantrum occurred when she realized that her stuffed animal was lost. Finally, they infer that Trixie's parents are running to the Laundromat to find Knuffle Bunny quickly.

Predicting. At the beginning of the story, children predict that Trixie and her daddy will have fun together, and in the middle, they predict that Knuffle Bunny will go into the washing machine by mistake. Finally, the predict that Trixie and her parents will find the lost stuffed animal.

Questioning. Children ask several questions about events in the story, including why Trixie's daddy wasn't more careful with Knuffle Bunny and why he didn't understand what Trixie meant when she was trying to tell him that her stuffed animal was lost.

Go to the Assignments and Activities section of the Topic *Comprehension* in the MyEducationLab for the literacy course and complete the activity entitled *Using Think-Aloud to Model Effective Reading Comprehension Strategies*. As you watch the video and answer the accompanying questions, consider the ways that predicting can help scaffold children's reading comprehension.

Teachers nurture children's use of comprehension strategies by stopping occasionally while they're reading to ask questions and by rereading books so that children can delve more deeply into them.

Activating Background Knowledge. Readers bring their background knowledge to every reading experience; in fact, they read a text differently depending on their prior experiences. Zimmermann and Hutchins (2003) explain that "the meaning you get from a piece is intertwined with the meaning you bring to it" (p. 45). Readers think about the topic before they begin reading and call up relevant information and related vocabulary to use while reading. The more background knowledge and prior experiences readers have about a topic, the more likely they are to comprehend what they're reading (Harvey & Goudvis, 2007).

Teachers rarely pick up a book and just start reading because it's essential to activate children's background knowledge first. They use a variety of prereading activities to help activate and build children's background knowledge, such as creating K-W-L charts, examining artifacts, and viewing pictures and videos. Through these activities, children think about the topic, use vocabulary related to the topic, and get interested in reading the text.

Connecting. Readers make three types of connections between a text and their background knowledge: text-to-self, text-to-world, and text-to-text connections (Harvey & Goudvis, 2007):

> **Text-to-Self Connections.** Children link the ideas they're reading about to experiences in their own lives; these are personal connections. A story event or character may remind them of something or someone in their own lives, and the facts in an informational book may remind them of a past experience or something a family member taught them.

> **Text-to-World Connections.** Children move beyond personal experience to relate what they're reading to their "world" knowledge, learned both in and out of school. For example, children who are reading a story about a stranded whale may recall a recent TV news report about a similar situation, or children reading an informational book about insects may make a connection to an animated movie they've seen about bugs.

> **Text-to-Text Connections.** Children link the text to another book they've read or to a familiar film, video, or television program. Readers often compare different versions of familiar folktales, books by the same author, and books in a series, such as Barbara Park's Junie B. Jones stories, James Preller's Jigsaw Jones mysteries, or Paula Danziger's Amber Brown chapter-book series. Text-to-text connections are often the most difficult, especially for children who know less about literature.

One way that teachers teach this strategy is by making connection charts with three columns labeled *text-to-self*, *text-to-world*, and *text-to-text*. Then children write connections that they've made on small self-stick notes and post them in the correct column of the chart. A second-grade connections chart created after reading *The Moon Over Star* (Aston, 2008), a 40th-anniversary tribute to the first moon landing, is shown in Figure 8–3. Children can also make connection charts in their reading logs and write their connections in each column. Later in the reading process, children make connections as they assume the role of a character and sit on the hot seat to be interviewed by classmates, create open-mind portraits to share the character's thinking, or write a letter or a diary entry from the viewpoint of a character, for example.

Figure 8–3 ◆ A Connections Chart About *The Moon Over Star*

Text-to-Self-Connections	Text-to-World-Connections	Text-to-Text-Connections
I've been thinking about being an astronaut. It would be an exciting job.	It's true that on July 20, 1969 the astronauts landed on the moon.	I'm reading a book called <u>Spacebusters</u>. It's about the moon landing, too.
Me and my friends have built spaceships and pretended that we were astronauts going to the moon.	Now everybody knows the words that Neil Armstrong said, "That's one small step for man, one giant leap for mankind."	This book is like <u>Team Moon</u> because they're both about how Apollo 11 changed people but one book is fiction and the other is nonfiction.
My grandma was alive then and she remembers watching the moon landing on TV.	This is a fact: The moon is 240,000 miles away from earth.	
	Both John Kennedy and Walter Cronkite are dead now, but the 3 astronauts are still alive.	

Determining Importance. Readers sift through the text to identify the important ideas as they read because it isn't possible to remember everything (Harvey & Goudvis, 2007; Keene & Zimmermann, 2007). Children learn the difference between the big ideas and the details and to recognize the more important ideas as they read and talk about the books they've read. This comprehension strategy is important because children need to be able to identify the big ideas in order to understand and summarize a story's theme.

Teachers often direct children's attention to the big ideas when they encourage them to make predictions, and the way teachers introduce the text also influences children's thinking about what's important in a book. When children read stories, they make diagrams about the plot, characters, and setting, and these graphic organizers emphasize the big ideas. Similarly, they make diagrams that reflect the structure of the text when they read informational books. Teachers usually provide the diagrams with the big ideas highlighted, but sometimes children analyze the text to determine its structure and then develop their own graphic organizers.

Drawing Inferences. Readers seem to "read between the lines" to draw inferences, but what they actually do is synthesize their background knowledge with the author's clues to ask questions that point toward inferences. Keene and Zimmermann (2007) explain that when readers draw inferences, they have "an opportunity to sense a meaning not explicit in the text, but which derives or flows from it" (p. 145). Readers make both unconscious and conscious inferences about characters in a story and its theme, the big ideas in an informational book, and the author's purpose in a poem (Pressley, 2002a).

Children often have to read or listen to a story two or three times to draw inferences because at first they focus on literal comprehension, which has to precede higher-level thinking. Sometimes children draw inferences when prompted by the teacher, but it's important to teach them how to draw inferences so that they can think more deeply when they read independently. Teachers begin by explaining what inferences are, how they differ from literal thinking, and why they're important. Then they teach these steps in drawing inferences:

1. **Activate background knowledge.** Teachers support readers as they think about topics related to the text.
2. **Look for clues.** Children notice the author's clues—unexpected information in the text—as they read.
3. **Ask questions.** Readers tie together background knowledge and the author's clues as they think of things that puzzle them about the text.
4. **Reach conclusions.** Readers draw inferences by answering the questions they posed.

Teachers comment on clues, express puzzlement, and ask "why" questions to encourage children to draw inferences.

Teachers can create inference charts to make the steps more visible as children practice drawing inferences, and readers can make their own charts to answer an inferential question. For example, after reading and discussing *The Garden of Abdul Gasazi* (Van Allsburg, 1979), the story of a magician who turns a misbehaving dog into a duck, fourth graders worked in pairs to make the inference chart shown in Figure 8–4 to answer this question: What happened to the dog? By thinking about their background knowledge, looking for clues in the story, and asking questions, the children concluded that the magician's spell didn't last long, and that after the duck flew home, it changed back into a dog.

Although drawing inferences is a difficult strategy because it requires higher-level thinking, even young children are capable of using it with teacher guidance. As teachers read aloud, they encourage preschoolers and kindergartners to use their background knowledge and clues in the illustrations as well as the words in the text to grasp the author's meaning. When preschoolers listen to David Shannon's hilarious autobiographical story, *No, David!* (1998), for example, they draw inferences on almost every page. The illustrations show a mischievous little boy tracking dirt into the house, eating with his mouth open, and letting his bath water overflow the tub, and the very brief text says "No, David, no!" "That's enough, David," "No! No! No!" and other reprimands. Children grasp the meaning and can explain the inferences.

Evaluating. Readers reflect on their reading experience and evaluate the text and what they're learning (Owocki, 2003). As with the other comprehension strategies, children use the evaluating strategy throughout the reading process. They monitor their interest in the text from the moment they pick up the book, and they judge, their success in solving reading problems each time one arises. They evaluate their reading experience, including these aspects:

- Their ease in reading the text
- The adequacy of their background knowledge
- Their use of comprehension strategies
- How they solved reading problems
- Their interest and attention in the text

Figure 8-4 ◆ Inference Chart About *The Garden of Abdul Gasazi*

Title **The Garden of Abdul Gasazi** Author **Chris Van Allsburg**

BACKGROUND KNOWLEDGE	QUESTIONS
Magicians do tricks. This story is a fantasy so magic can happen. Sometimes dogs don't behave.	Did the magician do it? How did Fritz get home? Why was Alan's hat in Miss Hester's yard?
CLUES FROM THE STORY	INFERENCES
Only time can change Fritz back into a dog. The duck was like Fritz because he took Alan's hat. Fritz the dog has Alan's hat at the end.	The magician did cast a spell and make the dog into a duck. The spell didn't last very long.

They also consider the text:

- Their assessment of the text's quality
- Their opinions about the author
- The knowledge they gained
- How they'll apply what they're learning

Children usually write about their reflections in reading log entries and talk about their evaluations in grand conversations and other discussions and conferences. Evaluating is important because it helps children assume more responsibility for their own learning.

Monitoring. Readers monitor their understanding as they read, although they may be aware that they're using this strategy only when their comprehension breaks down and they have to take action to solve their problem. Harvey and Goudvis (2007) describe monitoring as the inner conversation that children carry on in their heads with the text as they read—expressing wonder, making connections, asking questions, reacting to information, drawing conclusions, noticing confusions, for example.

Monitoring involves regulating reader and text factors at the same time. Readers often ask themselves these questions:

- What's my purpose for reading?
- Is this book too difficult for me to read on my own?

- Do I need to read the entire book or only parts of it?
- What's special about the genre of this book?
- How does the author use text structure?
- What is the author's viewpoint?
- Do I understand the meaning of the words I'm reading? (Pressley, 2002b)

Once children detect a problem, they shift into problem-solving mode to repair their comprehension.

Predicting. Readers make thoughtful "guesses" or predictions about what will happen or what they'll learn in the book they're reading. These guesses are based on what children already know about the topic and genre or on what they've read thus far. Children often make a prediction before beginning to read and several others at pivotal points in a text—no matter whether they're reading stories, informational books, or poems—and then as they read, they either confirm or revise their predictions. Predictions about nonfiction are different than for stories and poems; here children are generating questions about the topic that they would like to find answers to as they read.

When teachers read big books using shared reading, they prompt children to make predictions at the beginning of the book and again at key points during the reading. They model how to make reasonable predictions and use think-alouds to explain their thinking. When third and fourth graders are reading novels, they often write their predictions on small self-stick notes while they're reading and place them in their books to share with classmates afterward.

Questioning. Readers ask themselves questions about the text as they read (Duke & Pearson, 2002). They ask questions out of curiosity, and in the process, they become more engaged with the text and want to keep reading to find the answers (Harvey & Goudvis, 2007). These questions often lead to making predictions and drawing inferences. Children also ask themselves questions to clarify misunderstandings as they read. They use this strategy throughout the reading process—to activate background knowledge and make predictions before reading, to engage with the text and clarify confusions during reading, and to evaluate and reflect on the text and the characters' experiences after reading.

Traditionally, teachers have been the question-askers and children the question-answerers, but when children learn to generate questions about the text, their comprehension improves. In fact, children comprehend better when they generate their own questions than when teachers ask questions (Duke & Pearson, 2002). Many children don't know how to ask questions to guide their reading, so it's important that teachers teach children how. They model generating questions and then encourage children to do the same. Tovani (2000) suggests having children brainstorm a list of "I wonder" questions on a topic because they need to learn how to generate questions.

The questions children ask shape their comprehension: If they ask literal "what" and "who" questions, their comprehension will be more literal, but if children generate inferential "how" and "why" questions, their comprehension will be higher level.

Repairing. Readers use repairing to fix comprehension problems that arise while reading (Zimmermann & Hutchins, 2003). When children use the monitoring strategy and notice that they're confused or bored, they can't remember what they just read, or they're not asking questions, they need to use this strategy (Tovani, 2000).

Repairing involves figuring out the problem and taking action to solve it. Sometimes children go back and reread or skip ahead and read; sometimes they try visualizing, questioning, or another strategy that might help; and at other times, they check the meaning of an unfamiliar word, examine the structure of a confusing sentence, use picture clues, learn more about an unfamiliar topic related to the text, or ask a classmate or the teacher for assistance. These solutions are referred to as *fix-up strategies*, and teachers often post lists of these strategies in the classroom.

Setting a Purpose. Readers read for different reasons—for entertainment, to learn about a topic, for directions to accomplish a task, or to find the answer to a specific question, for instance—and the purposes they set direct their attention during reading (Tovani & Keene, 2000). Setting a purpose activates a mental blueprint to use while reading, which aids in determining how readers focus their attention and how they sort relevant from irrelevant information as they read (Blanton, Wood, & Moorman, 1990). Before they begin to read, children identify a single, fairly broad purpose that they sustain while reading the entire text. It must fit both children's reason for reading and the text. Children can ask themselves "Why am I going to read this text?" or "What do I need to learn from this book?" to help them set a purpose. It's important that children have a purpose when they read, because readers vary how they read and what they remember according to their purpose. When children don't set useful purposes, they misdirect their attention and remember unimportant ideas.

Summarizing. Readers pick out the most important ideas and the relationships among them and briefly restate them so they can be remembered (Harvey & Goudvis, 2007). It's crucial that children determine which ideas are the most important because if they focus on tangential ideas or details, their comprehension is compromised. To create effective summaries, children need to paraphrase, or restate ideas in their own words.

Summarizing is a difficult task, but instruction and practice improve children's ability to summarize as well as their overall comprehension (Duke & Pearson, 2002). One way to teach children to summarize folk tales and other brief stories is by using the Somebody-Wanted-But-So (Macon, Bewell, & Vogt, 1991) summarizing frame. Children create a sentence or two to identify who wanted something, what they wanted, the problem that arose, and how it was resolved. Figure 8–5 shows how a first-grade teacher used this frame to create a summary of "The 3 Billy Goats Gruff": The 3 billy goats Gruff **wanted** to eat grass up on the hill, **but** the mean troll wouldn't let them cross the bridge, **so** the biggest goat attacked and killed him.

Visualizing. Readers use the visualizing strategy when they create mental images of what they're reading (Harvey & Goudvis, 2007; Keene & Zimmermann, 2007). They often place themselves in the images they create, becoming a character in the story they're reading, traveling to that setting, or facing the conflict situations the characters face. Sometimes teachers ask children to close

Figure 8-5 ◆ The Somebody-Wanted-But-So Summarizing Frame

Frame	Question	Example
Somebody	Who is the character?	the 3 billy goats Gruff
Wanted	What does the character want?	to eat grass up on the hill
But	What is the problem?	the mean troll wouldn't let them cross the bridge
So	How does the character solve it?	the biggest goat attacked and killed him

their eyes to help visualize the story or to draw pictures of the scenes and characters they visualize. A second grader's poster about the visualizing strategy is shown in Figure 8–6. How well children use visualization often becomes clear when they view film versions of books they've read: Children who are good visualizers are usually disappointed with the film version and the actors who portray the characters; however, children who don't visualize are often amazed by the film and prefer it to the book.

Figure 8-6 ◆ A Visualization Poster

Visualizing

WIZ AR DS

I make pictures in my mind when I read.

Comprehension Skills

Even though there's controversy regarding the differences between comprehension strategies and skills, it's possible to identify some comprehension skills that children need to learn to become successful readers. These skills are related to strategies, but the big difference is that skills involve literal thinking; they're like questions to which there's one correct answer. One group of skills focus on big ideas and details. Children use the determining importance strategy to identify big ideas, and they use these related skills:

Recognizing details

Noticing similarities and differences

Comparing and contrasting big ideas and details

Sequencing details

In contrast, when big ideas and relationships among them aren't explicitly stated in the text, children draw inferences to comprehend them because higher-level thinking is required.

Another group of comprehension skills are related to the evaluating strategy:

Recognizing the author's bias

Detecting propaganda

Distinguishing between fact and opinion

Teachers teach these skills and children practice them until they become automatic procedures that don't require conscious thought or interpretation.

TEACHING ABOUT READER FACTORS

Comprehension instruction involves teaching children about comprehension and the strategies readers use to understand what they're reading and providing opportunities for children to practice what they're learning using authentic books (Duke & Pearson, 2002). Researchers emphasize the need to establish the expectation that the books children read will make sense (Duke & Pearson, 2002; Owocki, 2003). Teachers create an expectation of comprehension in these ways:

- Involving children in authentic reading activities every day
- Providing children access to well-stocked classroom libraries
- Teaching children to use comprehension strategies
- Ensuring that children become fluent readers
- Providing opportunities for children to talk about the books they read
- Linking vocabulary instruction to underlying concepts

Teachers can't assume that children will learn to comprehend simply by doing lots of reading; instead, children develop an understanding of comprehension and what readers do to be successful through a combination of instruction, opportunities for authentic reading, and comprehension activities (Block & Pressley, 2007). Guidelines for teaching comprehension are presented on page 216.

Guidelines
for Teaching Comprehension

▶ Teach children about both reader and text factors.

▶ Teach comprehension strategies using a combination of explanations, demonstrations, think-alouds, and authentic practice activities.

▶ Demonstrate how to use strategies through interactive read-alouds.

▶ Have children apply strategies in literacy activities and in thematic units.

▶ Combine strategies into routines so children learn to orchestrate their use.

▶ Ask children to reflect on their use of strategies.

▶ Display charts about the strategies children are learning.

▶ Differentiate between strategies and skills so children understand that strategies are problem-solving tactics and skills are automatic behaviors.

Explicit Instruction

The fact that comprehension is an invisible mental process makes it difficult to teach; however, through explicit instruction, teachers can make it more visible. They explain what comprehension is and why it's important, and they model how to do it. When teachers are reading aloud or doing shared reading, they use the think-aloud procedure to talk about their predictions, connections, and use of other strategies.

Teachers teach individual comprehension strategies and then show children how to integrate several strategies (Block & Pressley, 2007). They introduce each comprehension strategy in a series of minilessons in which they describe the strategy, model it as they read a book aloud, use it collaboratively with children, and then provide opportunities for guided and independent practice (Duke & Pearson, 2002). The minilesson feature on page 217 shows how Mrs. Macadangdang teaches her third graders to use the questioning strategy.

To teach comprehension strategies, teachers use stories they're reading aloud, books being featured in literature focus units, chapter books children are reading in literature circles, and leveled books children are reading in guided reading lessons. Almost any book can be used to teach at least several comprehension strategies. Figure 8–7 illustrates how *Officer Buckle and Gloria* (Rathmann, 1995), an award-winning story about a police officer and his dog who work as a team, can be used to teach any comprehension strategy, even though teachers wouldn't use the same book to teach more than one or two strategies. Other recommended books for teaching comprehension strategies are listed in Figure 8–8.

Developing Comprehension Through Reading

Children reinforce their awareness that reading is a meaning-making process and they refine their ability to apply comprehension strategies when they read books at their reading level and listen to teachers read aloud grade-level appropriate stories, informational

TOPIC: Teaching Children to Ask Self-Questions
GRADE: Third Grade
TIME: Three 30-minute periods

Mrs. Macadangdang (the children call her Mrs. Mac) introduced questioning by talking about why people ask questions and by asking questions about stories the third graders were reading. She encouraged them to ask questions, too. They made a list of questions for each chapter of *Chang's Paper Pony* (Coerr, 1993), a story set in the California gold rush era, as she read it aloud, and then they evaluated their questions, choosing the ones that focus on the big ideas and that helped them understand the story better. Now all of her children can generate questions, so she's ready to introduce the questioning strategy.

1 Introduce the Topic

Mrs. Mac reads the list of comprehension strategies posted in the classroom that they've learned to use and explains, "Today, we're going to learn a new thinking strategy—questioning. Readers ask themselves questions while they're reading to help them think about the book." She adds "Questioning" to the list.

2 Share Examples

The teacher introduces *The Josefina Story Quilt* (Coerr, 1989), the story of a pioneer family going to California in a covered wagon. She reads aloud the first chapter, thinking aloud and generating questions about the story. Each time she says a question, she places in a pocket chart a sentence strip on which the question has already been written. Here are the questions: Why is Faith excited? Why are they going in a covered wagon? Who is Josefina? Can a chicken be a pet? Can Josefina do anything useful? Why is Faith crying?

3 Provide Information

Mrs. Mac explains, "Questions really turn your thinking on! I know it's important to think while I'm reading because it helps me understand. I like to ask questions about things I think are important and things that don't make sense to me." They reread the questions in the pocket chart and talk about the most helpful questions. Many children thought the question about the covered wagon was important, but as they continue reading, they'll learn that Josefina does indeed do something useful—she turns out to be a "humdinger of a watch dog" (p. 54)! Then Mrs. Mac reads aloud the second chapter, stopping often for children to generate questions. The children write their questions on sentence strips and add them to the pocket chart.

4 Guide Practice

The following day, Mrs. Mac reviews the questioning strategy and children reread the questions for chapters 1 and 2. Then the children form pairs, get copies of the book, and read the next two chapters of *The Josefina Story Quilt* together, generating questions as they read. They write their questions on small self-stick notes and place them in the book. Mrs. Mac monitors children, noticing which ones need additional practice. Then the class comes together to share their questions and talk about the chapters they've read. On the third day, they read the last two chapters and generate more questions.

5 Assess Learning

As she monitored the children, Mrs. Mac made a list of children who needed more practice generating questions, and she will work with them as they read another book together.

Figure 8-7 ◆ Teaching Comprehension Strategies Using *Officer Buckle and Gloria*

Strategy	Activity
Activating Background Knowledge	Teachers talk about how police officers protect people, and sometimes they invite a police officer to visit the class and talk about safety.
Connecting	Children talk about their connections to their experiences with police officers, safety rules, dogs, and school assemblies. They also make text-to-text connections by comparing this book to *Make Way for Ducklings* (McCloskey, 2001), another story involving a police officer.
Determining Importance	Teachers use discussion and make graphic organizers to help children identify the characters, organize the story into the beginning-middle-end, and deduce the story's message or theme.
Drawing Inferences	Teachers scaffold children's thinking about whether Officer Buckle will appreciate Gloria's antics and about the story's message concerning teamwork.
Evaluating	Children evaluate the quality of the story and its award-winning illustrations as well as their comprehension of the story and its theme.
Monitoring	Teachers use think-alouds to demonstrate how they monitor their understanding of the story, and they invite one or two children to share their thinking.
Predicting	Teachers encourage children to make predictions about whether Gloria will make a good partner and what Officer Buckle will do once he learns about Gloria's antics.
Questioning	Teachers have children brainstorm questions after reading each page or two to demonstrate engagement, suggest predictions, and clarify any confusions.
Repairing	Teachers normally share this book using the interactive read-aloud procedure so children don't use fix-up strategies; however, they do monitor their understanding and ask questions when they're confused.
Setting a Purpose	This complex story can be approached in different ways: Teachers might ask children to focus on the safety lessons Officer Buckle teachers, consider how Officer Buckle faces his problems, or examine Gloria's role as a sidekick.
Summarizing	Children summarize the story by making a story map and drawing a picture or writing a sentence about the beginning, middle, and end. They also sequence story boards and use them to briefly retell the story.
Visualizing	Teachers focus on the characters, especially at the high point, when Officer Buckle learns about Gloria's antics. Children can role-play the characters or draw pictures to show each character's thoughts at specific points in the story.

books, and poems that they can't read themselves. They practice the comprehension strategies that they're learning and use higher levels of thinking to make predictions, notice clues in the text, draw inferences, and evaluate the book's quality. Teachers provide a combination of independent, small-group, and whole-class reading opportunities every day.

Independent Reading. Children need to spend lots of time reading authentic texts independently and talking about their reading with classmates and teachers. Having children read interesting books written at their reading level is the best way for them to apply comprehension strategies. As they read and discuss their reading, children are practicing what they're learning about comprehension. Reading a selection in a basal textbook each week isn't enough; instead, children need to read many, many books representing a range of genres during reading workshop or another daily independent reading time.

Interactive Read-Alouds. Teachers read books aloud using the interactive read-aloud procedure every day, even after children have learned to read. They share high-quality, grade-level-appropriate books that interest children and challenge them to think. As they listen, children build background knowledge and expand their vocabulary, watch their teacher demonstrate comprehension strategies, and practice the strategies they're learning. Afterward, they talk about the book in a grand conversation and other discussions, using comprehension strategies to ask questions, make connections, draw inferences, and evaluate the book.

Shared Reading. As teachers read big books aloud using shared reading, they demonstrate how to use comprehension strategies and provide opportunities for children to practice activating background knowledge, predicting, connecting, questioning, and other strategies. Because children can see the text in big books, teachers can also demonstrate how to monitor their reading, use the repairing strategy, and decode unfamiliar words more effectively than when they're reading regular-size books to children.

PreK Practices

How do 4-year-olds learn to comprehend?

Teachers nurture young children's comprehension by sharing picture books using interactive read-alouds and big books using shared reading (Morrow, Freitag, & Gambrell, 2009). As they read, teachers emphasize concepts about written language; build children's background knowledge and vocabulary; and model how to use comprehension strategies, including activating background knowledge, predicting what will happen next, and making connections to their own lives. Children listen attentively and engage in the reading experience, repeating refrains, clapping or pointing as the teacher directs, and talking about the book. They participate in response activities, such as using puppets to retell stories and drawing pictures to share information. Children demonstrate their budding knowledge about comprehension as they do "pretend reading," talk about books, and retell stories.

Figure 8–8 ◆ Books to Use in Teaching Comprehension Strategies

Allard, H. (1985). *Miss Nelson is missing!* New York: Sandpiper. (grades 1–2)

Brett, J. (2003). *Town mouse, country mouse.* New York: Putnam. (1–3)

Bunting, E. (1997). *A day's work.* New York: Sandpiper. (1–3)

Bunting, E. (1999). *Smoky night.* New York: Sandpiper. (2–4)

Cronin, D. (2000). *Click, clack, moo: Cows that type.* New York: Simon & Schuster. (1–3)

Demi. (1996). *Empty pot.* New York: Henry Holt. (2–4)

Galdone, P. (2008). *The gingerbread boy.* New York: Sandpiper. (preK–1)

Henkes, K. (1996). *Chrysanthemum.* New York: Mulberry Books. (K–1)

Henkes, K. (1996). *Lilly's purple plastic purse.* New York: Greenwillow. (K–1)

Long, M. (2003). *How I became a pirate.* Orlando: Harcourt. (preK–1)

McCloskey, R. (2001). *Make way for ducklings.* New York: Viking. (preK–1)

Munson, D. (2000). *Enemy pie.* San Francisco: Chronicle Books. (K–2)

Scieszka, J. (1996). *The true story of the 3 little pigs!* New York: Puffin Books. (1–3)

Steig, W. (1990). *Dr. DeSoto.* New York: Farrar, Straus & Giroux. (2–4)

Steig, W. (2006). *Sylvester and the magic pebble.* New York: Aladdin Books. (2–4)

Van Allsburg, C. (1986). *The stranger.* Boston: Houghton Mifflin. (3–4)

Van Allsburg, C. (1991). *The wretched stone.* Boston: Houghton Mifflin. (3–4)

Willems, M. (2004). *Knuffle bunny.* New York: Hyperion Books. (preK–K)

Woodson, J. (2001). *The other side.* New York: Putnam. (K–2)

Yorinks, A. (1989). *Hey, Al.* New York: Farrar, Straus & Giroux. (K–2)

Activities That Promote Comprehension

Teachers use a variety of activities to support children's comprehension of stories and other books they're reading. Figure 8–9 presents a list of comprehension activities. Second graders practice questioning by asking questions instead of giving answers during a grand conversation, for example, and fourth graders practice connecting when they write favorite quotes in one column of a reading log and then explain in the second column why each quote is meaningful. These activities help children review story events, clarify misconceptions, and deepen their comprehension.

NURTURING ENGLISH LEARNERS

Comprehension is often very difficult for English learners, and there are a number of reasons why (Bouchard, 2005). ELs often lack one or more of the three prerequisites for comprehension—background knowledge, vocabulary, and fluency. Many children who haven't had middle-class American experiences or who lack mainstream cultural knowledge can be at a disadvantage when they read or listen to a book read aloud because they don't have crucial background knowledge. First graders who listen to *Ira Sleeps Over* (Waber, 2008), for example, but who have never stayed overnight at a friend's house will have difficulty comprehending this story, and fourth graders who read *Molly's Pilgrim* (Cohen, 1998) but don't know about the Pilgrims who came to America in 1620 or about European Jewish immigrants will have difficulty grasping the story's theme.

ELs' limited background knowledge is typically reflected in their lack of familiarity with Tier 2 vocabulary. It isn't surprising that children have difficulty identifying and understanding words when they aren't familiar with a topic. Even if children seem to be aware of a topic, however, they may have difficulty with the vocabulary. For example, second graders who seem to know about football may have difficulty reading and comprehending *Kick, Pass, and Run!* (Kessler, 1996) because they don't understand the sports lingo, even though the book is at their reading level. Even when children are familiar with a topic, they can become so overwhelmed while trying to wade through unfamiliar Tier 2 vocabulary words in nearly every sentence that they don't understand what they're reading.

There can be a mismatch, too, between children's English proficiency and the book's reading level. Books with sophisticated sentence structures, including poetry, books with a great deal of dialogue, and books with unusual page layouts are more difficult. Like all readers, ELs can't read fluently and won't comprehend what they're reading if the book's too difficult.

Choosing Books. When teachers choose books for English learners, they consider the three prerequisites for comprehension and children's level of English language development. They ask themselves these questions:

- **Topic.** Do children have adequate background knowledge about the topic?
- **Vocabulary.** Do children know the meanings of most of the words related to the topic?
- **Linguistic Style.** Are the book's sentence patterns and language features familiar?
- **Page Layout.** Does the book have an unusual or confusing format?
- **Reading Level.** Is the book's reading level appropriate?

Figure 8-9 ◆ Comprehension Activities

Activity	Description
Dramatizations	Children assume roles as characters and dramatize story events. The teacher narrates the story or reads it aloud as younger children act it out, but with more experience, children can add dialogue and tell the story as they dramatize it.
Grand Conversations	The teacher and children talk about the story, sharing their ideas and asking questions. Sometimes children draw pictures or write in reading logs and then share their work during the conversation.
Hot Seat	One child assumes the role of a character from the story and is interviewed by classmates. Several children can assume the roles of all characters and discuss the story while classmates observe the interactions.
Open-Mind Portraits	Children use pictures and words to show what a character is thinking at the beginning, middle, and end of a story. They choose a characters and then draw a portrait of the character's face and cut it out. They attach additional pages and describe the character's thoughts at pivotal points in the story.
Reading Logs	Children write entries and draw pictures about books they're reading. Sometimes teachers provide prompts; at other times, children choose topics they're interested in exploring. They often write about connections, make predictions, draw inferences, construct summaries, and evaluate their reading.
Story Boards	Children sequence the illustrations that have been cut from a picture book and use them to retell the story. Children can also use "nonfiction" boards from an informational book to identify the big ideas.
Storytelling	Children retell a story, sometimes using illustrations, props, or puppets to guide them. They also can retell the story from a particular character's viewpoint.
Text Sets	Children read related books, including other versions and sequels and books by the same author or on the same topic. They can also examine online resources including author websites, interactive storybooks, and games.
Word Sorts	Children sort a pack of word cards related to a story according to characters, beginning-middle-end, or other categories. They work with partners or in small groups and talk about the story as they sort the cards.
Writing	Children write books and other compositions about stories they've read. They retell the story, often writing the beginning, middle, and end in chapters. They also craft scripts for readers theatre, create sequels, and write poems.

Teachers address these concerns by choosing books that are suitable for children at their level of English proficiency, and by providing extra support. They commonly build background knowledge and introduce key vocabulary words before children read; they can also read aloud part or all of the book before children read it, if the linguistic style is unfamiliar, or demonstrate how to read the first few pages, if the format's unusual.

Teaching Comprehension Strategies. English learners use the same comprehension strategies that native English speakers do, and they learn them the same way (Garcia, 2003). Teachers provide explicit instruction, and during the lessons, they demonstrate a strategy and explain how and when to use it and why it will help children become better readers. Teachers have to be creative to make strategies—invisible thought processes—more concrete. Some teachers put on hats they call *thinking caps*, and others draw quick sketches of their thinking, for example. They spend more time modeling how to apply the strategy and doing think alouds to share their thoughts as they read big books using shared reading and during interactive read-alouds. Next, teachers provide guided practice, often in guided reading groups, with children work-ing with partners and in small groups, and they guide children as they apply the strat-egy. Teachers often have children mark codes on small self-stick notes and place them next to the text that prompted their strategy use in the books they're reading. Once children understand how and when use a strategy, they read independently, applying the strategy as they read.

Active Engagement With Books. Peregoy and Boyle (2008) point out that many ELs read texts passively, as if they were waiting for the information to organize itself and highlight the big ideas. To help these children become more active readers and thinkers, teachers use these activities:

Share objects related to the book to introduce it

Read the book using the interactive read-aloud procedure

Provide puppets and other props for children to use for story retelling

Guide children as they dramatize a story

Encourage children to retell stories with a series of drawings or in writing

Have children draw pictures about the book and share them with classmates

Take children's dictation about the book using the Language Experience Approach

Encourage children to use story boards to explore a picture book or retell it

Have children create a story board for each chapter in a novel

Prepare a graphic organizer about the book for children to complete

Make a class poster about the book using interactive writing

Have children construct open-mind portraits

Add important words from the book to the word wall

Do a word sort using words from the word wall

Have children reread familiar books with partners or at the listening center

Use choral reading to reread a pattern book or a poem

These activities nurture children's ability to use higher-level thinking and apply the com-prehension strategies they're learning.

Go to the Assignments and Activities section of the Topic *Comprehension* in the MyEducationLab for the literacy course and complete the activity enti-tled *Assessing Reading Comprehension*. As you watch the video and an-swer the accompanying questions, note the com-prehension strategies Jimmy uses when reading.

Assessing Children's Knowledge of Reader Factors

Teachers assess children's comprehension informally every day. They listen to the com-ments children make during grand conversations, confer with children about books they're reading, and examine their entries in reading logs, for example. Children's interest in a book is sometimes an indicator, too: When children dismiss a book as "boring," they may mean that it's confusing or too difficult.

Teachers use these informal assessment procedures to monitor children's use of comprehension strategies and their understanding of books they're reading:

Assessment Tools

Comprehension

Teachers use a combination of informal assessment procedures, including story retellings and think-alouds, and commercially available tests to measure children's comprehension. These tests are often used in preK through fourth-grade classrooms:

◆ **Comprehension Thinking Strategies Assessment** (Keene, 2006)

The Comprehension Thinking Strategies Assessment examines first through eighth graders' ability to use these strategies to think about fiction and nonfiction texts: activating background knowledge, determining importance, drawing inferences, noticing text structure, questioning, setting a purpose, and visualizing. As children read a passage, they pause and reflect on their strategy use. Teachers score children's responses using a rubric. This 30-minute test can be administered to individuals or to the class, depending on whether children's responses are oral or written. This flexible assessment tool can be used to evaluate children's learning after teaching a strategy, to survey progress at the beginning of the school year, or to document achievement at the end of the year. It's available from Shell Education.

◆ **Developmental Reading Assessment, Grades K–3 (DRA)** (Beaver, 2006)
Developmental Reading Assessment, Grades 4–8 (Beaver & Carter, 2005)

Teachers use the DRA to determine children's reading levels, assess their strengths and weaknessnesses in fluency and comprehension, and make instructional decisions. Children read a leveled book and then retell what they've read. Their retellings are scored using a 4-point rubric. Both DRA tests are available from Pearson.

◆ **Informal Reading Iventories (IRIs)**

Teachers use individually administered IRIs to assess children's comprehension of narrative and informational texts. Comprehension is measured by children's ability to retell what they've read and to answer questions about the passage. The questions examine how well children use literal and higher-level thinking and their knowledge about word meanings. A number of commercially published IRIs are available:

Analytical Reading Inventory (Woods & Moe, 2007)
Comprehensive Reading Inventory (Cooter, Flynt, & Cooter, 2007)
Critical Reading Inventory (Applegate, Quinn & Applegate, 2008)
Qualitative Reading Inventory-4 (Leslie & Caldwell, 2006)

These IRIs can be purchased from Pearson. Other IRIs accompany basal reading series. IRIs are typically designed for grades 1–8, but first- and second-grade teachers often find that running records provide more useful information about beginning readers.

These tests provide valuable information about whether children meet grade-level comprehension standards.

Cloze Procedure. Teachers examine children's understanding of a text using the cloze procedure, in which children supply the deleted words in a passage taken from a book they've read. Although filling in the blanks may seem like a simple activity, it isn't, because children need to consider the content of the passage, vocabulary words, and sentence structure to choose the exact word that was deleted.

Story Retellings. Teachers often have children retell stories they've read or listened to read aloud to assess their literal comprehension (Morrow, 2002). Children's story retellings should be coherent and well organized and should include the big ideas and important details. When teachers prompt children with questions and encourage them to "tell me more," they're known as *aided retellings*; otherwise they're *unaided retellings*. Teachers often use checklists and rubrics to score children's story retellings.

Running Records. Teachers use running records (Clay, 2007a) to examine children's oral reading behaviors, analyze their comprehension, and determine their reading levels. Children read a book aloud, and afterward they retell it orally. Teachers encourage children to recall as much detail as possible, ask questions to prompt their recall when necessary, and sometimes pose other questions to probe the depth of their understanding. Finally, they evaluate the completeness of the retelling.

Think-Alouds. Teachers assess children's ability to apply comprehension strategies by having them think aloud and share their thinking as they read a passage (Wilhelm, 2001). Children usually think aloud orally, but they can also write their thoughts on small self-stick notes that they place beside sections of text or write entries in reading logs.

Teachers also use other assessment tools, including tests, to evaluate comprehension; the Assessment Tools feature on page 223 presents more information about comprehension tests. No matter whether teachers are using informal assessments or tests to examine comprehension, they need to consider whether they're assessing literal, inferential, critical, or evaluative thinking. The emphasis in both assessment and instruction should be on higher-level comprehension.

IF CHILDREN STRUGGLE...

The most important reason why children struggle with comprehension is that they don't apply comprehension strategies. Again and again, researchers have concluded that struggling readers don't read strategically (Cooper, Chard, & Kiger, 2006). These children read passively, without using comprehension strategies to think about the words they're reading. Sometimes children simply need to transfer the strategies they use for listening to reading, but more often they haven't learned to use comprehension strategies to think about what they're reading, or they're ignoring the strategies they've been taught. These children must understand how essential strategic reading is and learn to actively engage in reading; otherwise, it's unlikely that their comprehension will improve very much. The good news is that teachers can help children become more thoughtful readers by teaching them how and why to use comprehension strategies (Allington, 2006).

The second reason why children struggle with comprehension is that they lack one or more of the three prerequisites for comprehension—background knowledge, vocabulary, and fluency. Teachers take these prerequisites into account as they plan for reading instruction. They match children to books by choosing suitable books whenever they can, and they differentiate instruction and provide scaffolding so children can be successful. Children, too, need to learn how to choose appropriate books for independent reading because when they regularly read books that are too easy or too difficult, they don't become capable and confident readers.

How Effective Teachers Facilitate Children's Comprehension

▶ Teachers recognize that comprehension is a process involving both reader and text factors.

▶ Teachers ensure that children have adequate background knowledge, vocabulary, and fluency so that they can comprehend what they're reading.

▶ Teachers understand how comprehension strategies support children's understanding of books they're reading.

▶ Teachers teach children to use comprehension strategies and skills.

Chapter 9

Facilitating Children's Comprehension: Text Factors

Fourth Graders Learn About Frogs

The fourth graders in Mr. Abrams's class are studying frogs. They began by making a class **K-W-L chart** (Ogle, 1986), listing what they already know about frogs in the "K: What We Know" column and things they want to learn in the "W: What We Wonder" column. At the end of the unit, students will finish the chart by listing what they've learned in the "L: What We Have Learned" column. The fourth graders want to know how frogs and toads are different and if it's true that you get warts from frogs. Mr. Abrams assures them that they will learn the answers to many of their questions and makes a mental note to find the answer to their question about warts.

Aquariums with frogs and frog spawn are arranged in one area in the classroom. Mr. Abrams has brought in five aquariums and filled them with frogs he collected in his backyard and others he "rented" from a local pet store, and he has also brought in frog spawn from a nearby pond. The fourth graders are observing the frogs and the frog spawn daily and drawing diagrams and making notes in their learning logs.

Mr. Abrams sets out a text set with books about frogs representing the three genres—stories, informational books, and poetry—on a special shelf in the classroom library. He reads many of the books aloud to the class. When he begins, he reads the title and shows students several pages and asks them whether the book is a story, an informational book, or a poem. After determining the genre, they talk about their purpose for listening. For an informational book, the teacher writes a question or two on the chalkboard to guide their listening. After reading, the students answer the questions as part of their discussion. Students also read and reread many of these books during an independent reading time.

Mr. Abrams also has a class set of *Amazing Frogs and Toads* (Clarke, 1990), a nonfiction book with striking photograph illustrations and well-organized presentations of information. He reads it once with the whole class using shared reading, and they discuss the interesting information in the book. He divides the class into small groups, and each group chooses a question about frogs to research. Students reread the book, hunting for the answer to their question. Mr. Abrams has already taught the class to use the table of contents and the index to locate facts in an informational book. After students locate and reread the information, they use the writing process to develop a poster to answer the question and share what they've learned. He meets with each group to help them organize their posters and revise and edit their writing.

From the vast amount of information in *Amazing Frogs and Toads*, Mr. Abrams chooses nine questions, which he designs to address some of the questions on the "W: What We Wonder" section of the K-W-L chart, to highlight important information in the text, and to focus on the five expository text structures, the organizational patterns used for nonfiction texts. He is teaching the fourth graders that informational books, like stories, have special organizational elements. Here are his questions organized according to the expository structures:

What are amphibians? (Description)

What do frogs look like? (Description)

What is the life cycle of a frog? (Sequence)

How do frogs eat? (Sequence)

How are frogs and toads alike and different? (Comparison)

Why do frogs hibernate? (Cause and Effect)

How do frogs croak? (Cause and Effect)

How do frogs use their eyes and eyelids? (Problem and Solution)

How do frogs escape from their enemies? (Problem and Solution)

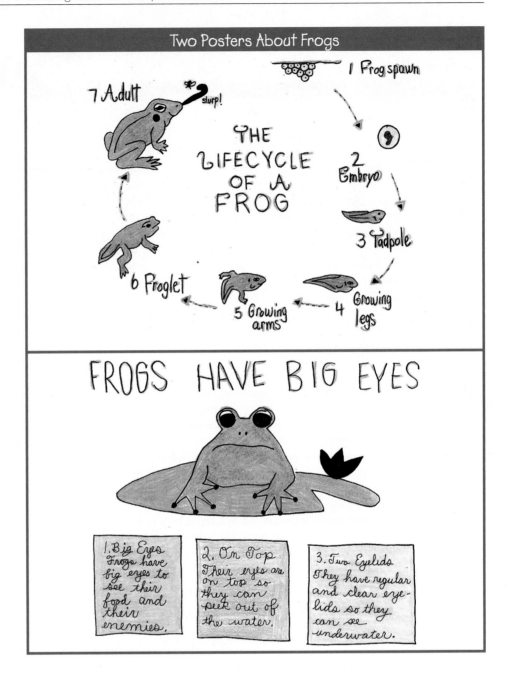

After the students complete their posters, they share them with the class through brief presentations, and the posters are displayed in the classroom. Two of the posters are shown above the life cycle poster emphasizes the sequence structure, and the "Frogs Have Big Eyes" poster explains that the frog's eyes help it solve problems—finding food, hiding from enemies, and seeing underwater.

Mr. Abrams's students use the information in the posters to write books about frogs. Students choose three posters and write one- to three-paragraph chapters to report the information from the poster. Students meet in writing groups to revise their rough drafts and then edit them with a classmate and with Mr. Abrams. Finally, students word process their final copies and add illustrations, a title page, and a table of contents. Then they compile their books and "publish" them by sharing them with classmates from the author's chair.

Armin wrote this chapter on "Hibernation" in his book:

> Hibernation means that an animal sleeps all winter long. Frogs hibernate because they are cold blooded and they might freeze to death if they didn't. They find a good place to sleep like a hole in the ground, or in a log, or under some leaves. They go to sleep and they do not eat, or drink, or go to the bathroom. They sleep all winter and when they wake up it is spring. They are very, very hungry and they want to eat a lot of food. Their blood warms up when it is spring because the temperature warms up and when they are warm they want to be awake and eat. They are awake in the spring and in the summer, and then in the fall they start to think about hibernating again.

Jessica wrote this chapter on "The Differences Between Frogs and Toads" for her book:

> You might think that frogs and toads are the same but you would be wrong. They are really different but they are both amphibians. I am going to tell you three ways they are different.
> First of all, frogs really love water so they stay in the water or pretty close to it. Toads don't love water. They usually live where it is dry. This is a big difference between frogs and toads.
> Second, you should look at frogs and toads. They look different. Frogs are slender and thin but toads are fat. Their skin is different, too. Frogs have smooth skin and toads have bumpy skin. I would say that toads are not pretty to look at.
> Third, frogs have long legs but toads have short legs. That probably is the reason why frogs are wonderful jumpers and toads can't. They move slowly. They just hop. When you watch them move, you can tell that they are very different.
> Frogs and toads are different kinds of amphibians. They live in different places, they look different, and they move in different ways. You can see these differences when you look at them and it is very interesting to study them.

Mr. Abrams helps his students develop a **rubric** to assess their books. It addresses the following points about the chapters:

- The title describes the chapter.
- The information in each chapter is presented clearly.
- Vocabulary from the **word wall** is used in each chapter.
- The information in each chapter is written in one or more indented paragraphs.
- The information in each chapter has very few spelling, capitalization, and punctuation errors.
- There is a useful illustration in each chapter.

Other points on the rubric consider the book as a whole:

- The title page lists the title and the author's name.
- All pages in the book are numbered.
- The table of contents lists the chapters and the pages for each chapter.
- The title is written on the cover of the book.
- The illustrations on the cover of the book relate to frogs.

The students evaluate their books using a 4-point scale; Mr. Abrams also uses the rubric to assess their writing. He conferences with students and shares his scoring with them. Also, he helps the students set goals for their next writing project.

To end the unit, the students finish the K-W-L chart. In the third column, "L: What We Have Learned," they list some of the information they have learned:

Tadpoles breathe through gills, but frogs breathe through lungs.

Tadpoles are vegetarians, but frogs eat worms and insects.

Snakes, rats, birds, and foxes are the frogs' enemies.

Some frogs in the rainforest are brightly colored and poisonous, too.

Some frogs are hard to see because they have camouflage coloring.

Male frogs puff up their air sacs to croak and make sounds.

Frogs have teeth, but they swallow their food whole.

Frogs have two sets of eyelids, and one set is clear so frogs can see when they are underwater.

Frogs can jump ten times their body length, but toads can't—they're hoppers.

Mr. Abrams stands back to reread the fourth graders' comments. "I can tell how much you've learned when I read the detailed information you've added in the L column," he remarks with a smile. He knows that one reason why his students are successful is because he taught them to use text structure as a tool for learning.

What readers know and do during reading has a tremendous impact on how well they comprehend, but comprehension involves more than just reader factors: It also involves text factors. Stories, informational books, and poems can be easier or more difficult to read depending on factors that are inherent in them (Harvey & Goudvis, 2007). These three types of text factors are the most important:

Genres. The three broad categories of literature are stories, informational books or nonfiction, and poetry, and there are subgenres within each category. For example, folktales, fantasies, and historical fiction are subgenres of stories.

Text Structures. Authors use text structures to organize texts and emphasize the big ideas. Sequence, comparison, and cause and effect, for example, are internal patterns used to organize nonfiction texts.

Text Features. Authors use text features to achieve a particular effect in their writing. Narrative devices include foreshadowing and dialogue in stories, headings and indexes are nonfiction features in informational books, and repetition and rhyme are poetic devices.

When children understand how authors organize and present their ideas in texts, this knowledge about text factors serves as a scaffold, making comprehension easier (Meyer & Poon, 2004; Sweet & Snow, 2003). Text factors make a similar contribution to writing: Children apply what they've learned about genres, text structures, and text features when they're writing (Mooney, 2001).

DEVELOPMENTAL CONTINUUM Comprehension: Text Factors

PreK	K	1	2	3	4
Four-year-olds know that texts differ according to genre, and they can identify examples of stories, informational books, and poems.	Kindergartners tell well-organized stories, identify big ideas in nonfiction books, and notice poetic devices in poems.	First graders apply what they've learned about text factors when crafting brief stories, informational books, and poems.	Children classify books by sub-genre and pick out examples of text structures and text features in books they're reading.	Children draw diagrams to highlight story elements and expository text structures, and they identify poetic forms or devices.	Fourth graders analyze story elements, use expository text structures in writing, and apply poetic forms in poems they write.

TEXT FACTORS OF STORIES

Stories are narratives about characters trying to overcome problems or deal with difficulties. They've been described as "waking dreams" that people use to find meaning in their lives. Children develop an understanding of what constitutes a story beginning in the preschool years when their parents read aloud to them, and they refine and expand their understanding through literacy instruction at school (Applebee, 1978). They learn about the subgenres of stories and read stories representing each one, examine the structural patterns that authors use to organize stories, and point out the narrative devices that authors use to breathe life into their stories.

Formats of Stories

Stories are available in picture-book and chapter-book formats. Picture books have brief texts, usually spread over 32 pages, in which text and illustrations combine to tell a story. The text is minimal, and the illustrations extend the sparse text. These popular picture books illustrate a variety of artistic styles and media:

Smoky Night (Bunting, 1999)

Kitten's First Full Moon (Henkes, 2004)

Officer Buckle and Gloria (Rathmann, 1995)

The House in the Night (Swanson, 2008)

Knuffle Bunny: A Cautionary Tale (Willems, 2004)

Owl Moon (Yolen, 2007)

Each year, the American Library Association honors the best illustrated children's book with its Caldecott Award. The books just listed received this prestigious award or were designated as honor books.

In some books, the illustrations tell the story without any text; these books are called *wordless picture books*. Some are appropriate for preschoolers' and kindergartners, such as *Have You Seen My Cat?* (Carle, 1997) and *Freight Train* (Crews, 2008); some for first and second graders, such as *Hogwash* (Geisert, 2008) and *The Red Book* (Lehman, 2004); and others for third and fourth graders, such as *Time Flies* (Rohmann, 1997) and *Flotsam* (Wiesner, 2006).

Novels are longer stories organized into chapters. They have only a few illustrations because pictures don't play an integral role in the story. The first novels that beginning readers read include Barbara Park's Junie B. Jones stories about the antics of a sassy primary-grade student, Marc Brown's chapter-book stories of a lovable aardvark named Arthur, and Dan Greenburg's adventure series, The Zack Files. Popular novels for third and fourth graders include *Flat Stanley* (Brown, 2003a). *Sideways Stories From Wayside School* (Sachar, 2004), *Tales of a Fourth Grade Nothing* (Blume, 2007), and *Because of Winn-Dixie* (DiCamillo, 2009).

Narrative Genres

Stories can be categorized in different ways, one of which is according to genre (Buss & Karnowski, 2000). Three general categories are folklore, fantasies, and realistic fiction. Figure 9–1 presents an overview of these narrative genres.

Folklore. Stories that began hundreds of years ago and were passed down from generation to generation by storytellers before being written down are *folk literature*. These stories, including fables, folktales, and myths, are an important part of our cultural heritage. Fables are brief narratives designed to teach a moral. The story format makes the lesson easier to understand, and the moral is usually stated at the end. Fables exemplify these characteristics:

- They are short, often less than a page long.
- The characters are usually animals.
- The characters are one-dimensional: strong or weak, wise or foolish.
- The setting is barely sketched; the stories could take place anywhere.
- The theme is usually stated as a moral at the end of the story.

The best-known fables, including "The Hare and the Tortoise" and "The Ant and the Grasshopper," are believed to have been written by a Greek slave named Aesop in the 6th century B.C. Individual fables hare been retold as picture-book stories, including *The Hare and the Tortoise* (Ward, 1999) and *The Lion and the Rat* (Wildsmith, 2007).

Folktales began as oral stories, told and retold by medieval storytellers as they traveled from town to town. The problem in a folktale usually revolves around one of four situations: a journey from home to perform a task, a journey to confront a monster, the miraculous change from a harsh home to a secure home, or a confrontation between a wise beast and a foolish beast. Here are other characteristics:

- The story often begins with the phrase "Once upon a time . . . "
- The setting is generalized and could be located anywhere.
- The plot structure is simple and straightforward.
- Characters are one-dimensional: good or bad, stupid or clever, industrious or lazy.
- The end is happy, and everyone lives "happily ever after."

Figure 9–1 ◆ Narrative Genres

Category	Genres	Description
Folklore	Fables	Brief tales told to point out a moral. For example: *Town Mouse, Country Mouse* (Brett, 2003) and *The Boy Who Cried Wolf* (Hennessy, 2006).
	Folktales	Stories in which heroes demonstrate virtues to triumph over adversity. For example: *Goldilocks and the Three Bears* (Marshall, 1998) and *Rumpelstiltskin* (Zelinsky, 1996).
	Myths	Stories created by ancient peoples to explain natural phenomena. For example: *Why Mosquitoes Buzz in People's Ears* (Aardema, 2004) and *Raven* (McDermott, 2001).
	Legends	Stories, including hero tales and tall tales, that recount the courageous deeds of people who struggled against each other or against gods and monsters. For example: *John Henry* (J. Lester, 1999) and *Johnny Appleseed* (Kellogg, 1988).
Fantasy	Modern Literary Tales	Stories written by modern authors that are similar to folktales. For example: *The Ugly Duckling* (Mitchell, 2007) and *Sylvester and the Magic Pebble* (Steig, 2006).
	Fantastic Stories	Imaginative stories that explore alternate realities and contain elements not found in the natural world. For example: *Inkheart* (Funke, 2003) and *Poppy* (Avi, 2005).
	Science Fiction	Stories that explore scientific possibilities. For example: *Moo Cow Kaboom!* (Hurd, 2003) and *Commander Toad in Space* (Yolen, 1996).
	High Fantasy	Stories that focus on the conflict between good and evil and often involve quests. For example: the Harry Potter series.
Realistic Fiction	Contemporary Stories	Stories that portray today's society. For example: *Going Home* (Bunting, 1998) and *Because of Winn-Dixie* (DiCamillo, 2009).
	Historical Stories	Realistic stories set in the past. For example: *Sarah, Plain and Tall* (MacLachlan, 2004) and *Henry's Freedom Box* (Levine, 2007).

Some folktales are cumulative tales, such as *The Gingerbread Boy* (Galdone, 2008); these stories are built around the repetition of words and events. Others are talking animal stories; in these stories, such as *The Three Little Pigs* (Kellogg, 2002), animals act and talk like humans. The best-known folktales are fairy tales. They have motifs or small recurring elements, including magical powers, transformations, enchantments, magical objects, trickery, and wishes that are granted, and they feature witches, giants, fairy godmothers, and other fantastic characters. Well-known examples are *Cinderella* (Ehrlich, 2004) and *Jack and the Beanstalk* (Kellogg, 1997).

People around the world have created myths to explain natural phenomena. Some explain the seasons, the sun, the moon, and the constellations, and others tell how the mountains and other physical features of the earth were created. Ancient peoples used myths to explain many things that have since been explained by scientific investigations. Myths exemplify these characteristics:

- Myths explain creations.
- Characters are often heroes with supernatural powers.
- The setting is barely sketched.
- Magical powers are required.

For example, the Native American myth *The Legend of the Bluebonnet* (dePaola, 1996) recounts how these flowers came to beautify the countryside. Other myths tell how animals came to be or why they look the way they do. Legends are myths about heroes such as Robin Hood and King Arthur, who have done things important enough to be remembered in a story; they may have some basis in history but aren't verifiable. American legends about Johnny Appleseed, Paul Bunyan, and Pecos Bill are known as *tall tales.*

Fantasies. Fantasies are imaginative stories. Authors create new worlds for their characters, but these worlds must be based in reality so that readers will believe they exist. One of the most beloved fantasies is *Charlotte's Web* (White, 2006). Fantasies include modern literary tales, fantastic stories, science fiction, and high fantasy.

Modern literary tales are related to folktales and fairy tales because they often incorporate many characteristics and conventions of traditional literature, but they've been written more recently and have identifiable authors. The best-known author of modern literary tales is Hans Christian Andersen, a Danish writer of the 1800s who wrote *The Snow Queen* (Ehrlich, 2006) and *The Ugly Duckling* (Mitchell, 2007). Other examples of modern literary tales include *Alexander and the Wind-Up Mouse* (Lionni, 2006) and *The Wolf's Chicken Stew* (Kasza, 1996).

Fantastic stories are realistic in most details, but some events require readers to suspend disbelief. They exemplify these characteristics:

- The events in the story could not happen in today's world.
- The setting is realistic.
- Main characters are people or personified animals.
- Themes often deal with the conflict between good and evil.

Some are animal fantasies, such as *Babe: The Gallant Pig* (King-Smith, 2005). The main characters in these stories are animals endowed with human traits. Readers often realize that the animals symbolize human beings and that these stories explore human relationships. Some are toy fantasies, such as *The Miraculous Journey of Edward Tulane* (DiCamillo, 2008). Toy fantasies are similar to animal fantasies except that the main characters are talking toys, usually stuffed animals or dolls. Other fantasies involve enchanted journeys during which wondrous things happen. The journey must have a purpose, but it's usually overshadowed by the thrill and delight of the fantastic world, as in Roald Dahl's *Charlie and the Chocolate Factory* (2007).

In science fiction stories, authors create a world in which science interacts with society. Many stories involve traveling through space to distant galaxies or meeting alien societies. Authors hypothesize scientific advancements and imagine technology of the future to create the plot. Science fiction exemplifies these characteristics:

- The story is set in the future.
- Conflict is usually between the characters and natural or mechanical forces.
- The characters believe in the advanced technology.
- A detailed description of scientific facts is provided.

Time-warp stories in which the characters move forward and back in time are also classified as science fiction. Jon Scieszka's Time Warp Trio stories, including *Knights of the Kitchen Table* (2004), are popular with third and fourth graders.

Heroes confront evil for the good of humanity in high fantasy. The primary characteristic is the focus on the conflict between good and evil, as in C. S. Lewis's *The Lion, the*

Witch and the Wardrobe (2005) and J. K. Rowling's Harry Potter stories. High fantasy is related to folk literature in that it's characterized by motifs and themes. Most stories include magical kingdoms, quests, tests of courage, magical powers, and superhuman characters.

Realistic Fiction.   These stories are lifelike and believable. The outcome is reasonable, and the story is a representation of action that seems truthful. Realistic fiction helps children discover that their problems aren't unique and that they aren't alone in experiencing certain feelings and situations. Realistic fiction also broadens children's horizons and allows them to experience new adventures. Two types are contemporary stories and historical stories.

Readers identify with characters who are their own age and have similar interests and problems in contemporary stories. In Paula Danziger's *Amber Brown Is Not a Crayon* (2006) and other books in the series, children read about a feisty girl with a colorful name who adjusts to contemporary life changes as her best friend since preschool moves away, her parents divorce, and her mom remarries. Here are the characteristics of contemporary fiction:

- Characters act like real people or like real animals.
- The setting is in the world as we know it today.
- Stories deal with everyday occurrences or "relevant subjects."

Other contemporary stories include *Knuffle Bunny: A Cautionary Tale* (Willems, 2004) and *Ramona the Pest* (Cleary, 1992).

In contrast, historical stories are set in the past. Details about food, clothing, and culture must be typical of the era in which the story is set because the setting influences the plot. These are the characteristics of this genre:

- The setting is historically accurate.
- Conflict is often between characters or between a character and society.
- The language is appropriate to the setting.
- Themes are universal, both for the historical period of the book and for today.

Examples of historical fiction include *Chang's Paper Pony* (Coerr, 1993) and *Follow the Drinking Gourd* (Winter, 2008). In these stories, readers are immersed in historical events, they appreciate the contributions of people who have lived before them, and they learn about human relationships.

Elements of Story Structure

Stories have unique structural elements that distinguish them from other genres. The most important story elements are plot, characters, setting, point of view, and theme. They work together to structure a story, and authors manipulate them to develop their stories.

Plot.   Plot is the sequence of events involving characters in conflict situations. It's based on the goals of one or more characters and the processes they go through to attain them (Lukens, 2006). The main characters want to achieve the goal, and other characters are introduced to prevent them from being successful. The story events are set in motion by characters as they attempt to overcome conflict and solve their problems. Figure 9–2 presents a list of stories with well-developed plots and other elements of story structure.

The most basic aspect of plot is the division of the main events into the beginning, middle, and end. In *The Tale of Peter Rabbit* (Potter, 2006), for instance, the three story parts are easy to pick out. As the story begins, Mrs. Rabbit sends her children out to play after warning them not to go into Mr. McGregor's garden. In the middle, Peter goes to Mr. McGregor's garden and is almost caught. Then Peter finds his way out of the garden and gets home safely—the end of the story. Children can make a beginning-middle-end story map using words and pictures, as the story map for *The Tale of Peter Rabbit* in Figure 9–3 shows.

Specific types of information are included in each part. In the beginning, the author introduces the characters, describes the setting, and presents a problem. Together, the characters, setting, and events develop the plot and sustain the theme through the story. In the middle, the plot unfolds, with each event preparing readers for what follows. Conflict heightens as the characters face roadblocks that keep them from solving their problems; how the characters tackle these problems adds suspense to keep readers interested. In the end, all is reconciled, and readers learn whether the characters' struggles are successful.

Conflict is the tension or opposition between forces in the plot, and it's what interests readers enough to continue reading the story (Lukens, 2006). Conflict occurs in these four ways:

Figure 9–2 ◆ Stories Illustrating the Elements of Story Structure

PLOT

Fleming, D. (2003). *Buster*. New York: Henry Holt. (grades preK–1)

Marshall, J. (1998). *Goldilocks and the three bears*. New York: Puffin Books. (preK–1)

Rathmann, P. (1995). *Officer Buckle and Gloria*. New York: Putnam. (K–2)

Steig, W. (2006). *Sylvester and the magic pebble*. New York: Aladdin Books. (1–3)

Willems, M. (2004). *Knuffle bunny: A cautionary tale*. New York: Hyperion Books. (preK–1)

CHARACTERS

Cleary, B. (1992). *Ramona the pest*. New York: HarperCollins. (3–4)

Dahl, R. (2007). *James and the giant peach*. New York: Puffin Books. (3–4)

Henkes, K. (1996). *Lilly's purple plastic purse*. New York: Greenwillow. (K–2)

Levine, E. (2007). *Henry's freedom box*. New York: Scholastic. (3–4)

SETTING

Bunting, E. (2006). *Pop's bridge*. San Diego: Harcourt. (1–3)

Coerr, E. (1993). *Chang's paper pony*. New York: HarperCollins. (3–4)

DiCamillo, K. (2009). *Because of Winn-Dixie*. Cambridge, MA: Candlewick Press. (3–4)

Hurd, T. (2003). *Moo cow kaboom!* New York: HarperCollins. (K–2)

Yorinks, A. (1989). *Hey, Al*. New York: Farrar, Straus & Giroux. (K–2)

POINT OF VIEW

Bunting, E. (2006). *One green apple*. New York: Clarion Books. (2–3)

Long, M. (2003). *How I became a pirate*. Orlando: Harcourt. (K–2)

MacLachlan, P. (2004). *Sarah, plain and tall*. New York: HarperTrophy. (3–4)

Pinkney, J. (2006). *The little red hen*. New York: Dial Books. (K–1)

Scieszka, J. (1996). *The true story of the 3 little pigs!* New York: Puffin Books. (1–3)

THEME

Bunting, E. (1999). *Smoky night*. San Diego: Harcourt Brace. (2–4)

DiCamillo, K. (2008). *The miraculous journey of Edward Tulane*. New York: Walker. (3–4)

Henkes, K. (1996). *Lilly's purple plastic purse*. New York: Greenwillow. (K–2)

Naylor, P. R. (2000). *Shiloh*. New York: Aladdin Books. (3–4)

Woodson, J. (2001). *The other side*. New York: Putnam. (K–1)

Figure 9–3 ◆ A Beginning-Middle-End Story Map for *The Tale of Peter Rabbit*

Between a Character and Nature. Conflict between a character and nature occurs in stories in which severe weather plays an important role and in stories set in isolated geographic locations.

Between a Character and Society. Sometimes the main character's activities and beliefs differ from those of others, and conflict arises between the character and society.

Between Characters. In this most common type of conflict, characters with different goals interact as the story progresses, and tension grows.

Within a Character. The main character struggles to overcome challenges in his or her own life.

Plot is developed through conflict that's introduced at the beginning, expanded in the middle, and finally resolved at the end. The development of the plot involves these components:

- A problem that introduces conflict is presented at the beginning of the story.
- Characters face roadblocks in attempting to solve the problem in the middle.
- The high point in the action occurs when the problem is about to be solved. This high point separates the middle and the end.
- The problem is solved and the roadblocks are overcome at the end of the story.

Figure 9–4 presents a plot diagram shaped like a mountain that incorporates these four components, which fourth graders completed after reading *Esperanza Rising* (Ryan, 2002). The problem in *Esperanza Rising* is that Esperanza and her mother must create a new life for themselves in California because they can't remain at their Mexican ranch home any longer. Certainly, there's conflict between characters here and conflict with society, too, but the most important conflict is within Esperanza as she leaves her comfortable life in Mexico to become a migrant laborer in California. Esperanza and her mother face many roadblocks. They become farm laborers, and the work is very difficult. Esperanza wants to bring her grandmother to join them, but they don't have enough money for her travel expenses. Then Esperanza's mother becomes ill, and Esperanza takes over her mother's work. Finally, Esperanza saves enough money to bring her grandmother to California, but her money disappears. The high point of the action occurs when Esperanza's mother recovers enough to return to the farm labor camp, and it turns out that her money wasn't stolen after all:

Figure 9-4 ◆ A Plot Diagram for *Esperanza Rising*

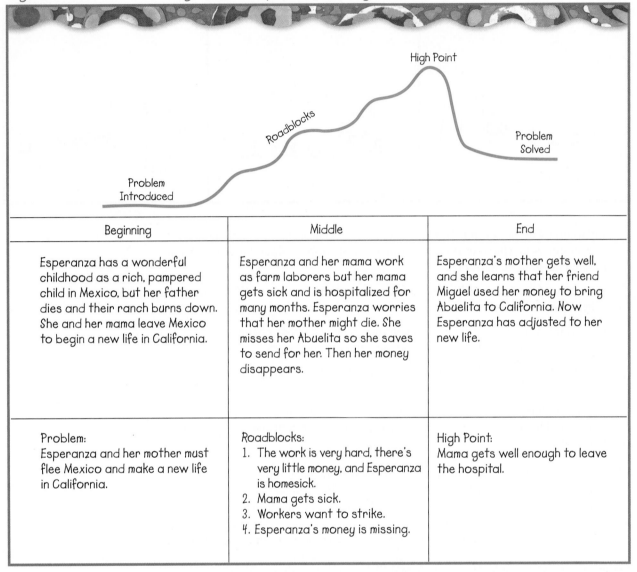

Beginning	Middle	End
Esperanza has a wonderful childhood as a rich, pampered child in Mexico, but her father dies and their ranch burns down. She and her mama leave Mexico to begin a new life in California.	Esperanza and her mama work as farm laborers but her mama gets sick and is hospitalized for many months. Esperanza worries that her mother might die. She misses her Abuelita so she saves to send for her. Then her money disappears.	Esperanza's mother gets well, and she learns that her friend Miguel used her money to bring Abuelita to California. Now Esperanza has adjusted to her new life.
Problem: Esperanza and her mother must flee Mexico and make a new life in California.	Roadblocks: 1. The work is very hard, there's very little money, and Esperanza is homesick. 2. Mama gets sick. 3. Workers want to strike. 4. Esperanza's money is missing.	High Point: Mama gets well enough to leave the hospital.

Esperanza's friend Miguel used it to bring her grandmother to California. As the story ends, the problem is solved: Esperanza adjusts to her new life in California with her mother and grandmother. *Esperanza* means "hope" in Spanish, and readers have reason to be optimistic that the girl and her family will create a good life for themselves.

Characters. Characters are the people or personified animals in the story. They're the most important structural element when stories are centered on a character or group of characters. Main characters have many personality traits, both good and bad; that is to say, they have all the characteristics of real people. Inferring a character's traits is an important part of comprehension: Through character traits, readers get to know a character well, and the character seems to come to life. A list of stories with fully developed main characters is included in Figure 9–2. Characters are developed in four ways:

Appearance. Readers learn about characters by the description of their facial features, body shapes, habits of dress, mannerisms, and gestures.

Action. The best way to learn about characters is through their actions.

Dialogue. Authors use dialogue to breathe life into characters, develop their personalities, and spark reader interest. Also, dialogue is an effective way to move a story forward.

Monologue. Authors provide insight into characters by revealing their thoughts.

Authors often use more than one of these techniques to develop their characters.

Setting. The setting is generally thought of as the location where the story takes place, but it's only one of four aspects of setting:

Location. Many stories take place in predictable settings that don't contribute to a story's effectiveness, but sometimes the location is integral.

Weather. Severe weather, such as a blizzard, rainstorm, or tornado, is crucial in some stories, but in others, the weather isn't mentioned because it doesn't affect the outcome of the story. Many stories take place on warm, sunny days.

Time Period. For stories set in the past or in the future, the time period is important. If *Riding Freedom* (Ryan, 1999) and *The Bracelet* (Uchida, 1996) were set in different eras, for example, they would lose much of their impact. Today, young women in the United States don't have to masquerade as men to work or vote, and Japanese Americans aren't sent to internment camps.

Time. This dimension involves both the time of day and the passage of time. Most stories take place during the day, except for scary stories that are set after dark. Many stories span a brief period of time, but others span as much as a year—long enough for the main character to grow to maturity.

In some stories, the setting is barely sketched; these are called *backdrop settings*. The setting in many folktales, for instance, is relatively unimportant, and the convention "Once upon a time . . ." is enough to set the stage. In other stories, the setting is elaborated and essential to the story's effectiveness; these settings are called *integral settings* (Lukens, 2006). Stories with integral settings also are listed in Figure 9–2.

Children can draw maps to show the setting of a story; these maps might show the path a character traveled or the passage of time in a story. Figure 9–5 shows a map for *Tulip Sees America* (Rylant, 1998). In this story, a man and his dog, named Tulip, take a trip across the United States and decide to stay in Oregon, where they can see the Pacific Ocean.

Point of View. Stories are written from a particular viewpoint, and this perspective determines to a great extent readers' understanding of the characters and events of the story (Lukens, 2006). Stories written from different viewpoints are presented in Figure 9–2. Here are the points of view:

First-Person Viewpoint. This point of view is used to tell a story through the eyes of one character using the first-person pronoun "I." The narrator, usually the main character, speaks as an eyewitness and a participant in the events.

Figure 9–5 ◆ A Second Grader's Story Map for *Tulip Sees America*

Omniscient Viewpoint. The author is godlike, seeing and knowing all. The author tells readers about the thought processes of each character without worrying about how the information is obtained.

Limited Omniscient Viewpoint. This viewpoint is used so that readers know the thoughts of one character. It's told in third person, and the author concentrates on the thoughts, feelings, and experiences of the main character or another important character.

Objective Viewpoint. Readers are eyewitnesses to the story and are confined to the immediate scene. They learn only what is visible and audible and are not aware of what any characters think. Most fairy tales are told from the objective viewpoint. The focus is on recounting events, not on developing the personalities of the characters.

Theme. Theme is the underlying meaning of a story; it embodies general truths about human nature (Lukens, 2006). Themes usually deal with the characters' emotions and values, and can be stated either explicitly or implicitly: Explicit themes are expressed clearly in the story, but implicit themes must be inferred. In a fable, the theme is often stated explicitly at the end, but in most stories, the theme emerges through the thoughts, speech, and actions of the characters as they try to overcome the obstacles that prevent them from reaching their goals. In *A Chair for My Mother* (V. Williams, 1993), for example, a young girl demonstrates the importance of sacrificing personal wants for her family's welfare as she and her mother collect money to buy a new chair after they lose all of their belongings in a fire.

Stories usually have more than one theme, and the themes generally can't be articulated with a single word. *Charlotte's Web* (White, 2006), for example, has several "friendship" themes, one explicitly stated and others that must be inferred. Friendship is a multidimensional theme—qualities of a good friend, unlikely friends, and sacrificing for a friend, for instance. Teachers probe children's thinking as they work to construct a theme and move beyond simplistic one-word labels.

Narrative Devices

Authors use narrative devices to make their writing more vivid and memorable (Lukens, 2006):

- **Dialogue.** Written conversations in which characters speak to each other
- **Flashbacks.** An interruption, often taking readers back to the beginning of the story
- **Foreshadowing.** Hints about events to come later in the story to build readers' expectations
- **Imagery.** Descriptive words and phrases used to create a picture in readers' minds
- **Suspense.** An excited uncertainty about the outcome of conflict in a story
- **Symbol.** A person, place, or thing used to represent something else, such as a lion to imply courage

Flashbacks, for example, are commonly used in stories, such as the Time Warp Trio series by Jon Scieszka and the Magic Tree House series by Mary Pope Osborne, where readers travel back in time for adventures.

Examining Text Factors in a Story

Jan Brett's *The Mitten* (2009) is an adaptation of a Ukrainian folktale. While walking through a snowy forest, a boy named Nicki unknowingly drops one of the new white mittens his grandmother knitted for him. A mole discovers it and crawls inside. One by one, a rabbit, a badger, and other woodland animals crawl inside, too, each bigger than the one before. Even a brown bear squeezes in and everyone sleeps snuggly in the mitten until a tiny mouse joins them, curling up on the bear's nose. The mouse tickles the bear's nose, and the bear sneezes, causing the mitten to shoot up into the air. The animals scatter, and Nicki sees a white shape in the distance floating to the ground—it's his lost mitten, stretched out of shape.

This story is a cumulative tale that's built through the repetition of events—animals crawling into the white mitten. It's similar in structure to other folktales, such as "The

Check the Compendium of Instructional Procedures, which follows Chapter 12, for more information on highlighted terms.

Little Red Hen" and "The Three Little Pigs," and the repetitive structure makes it easy for children to retell, especially when they're using story boards or stuffed animals. The plot is simple and straightforward: In the beginning, Nicki loses the mitten; in the middle, animals crawl into it; and at the end, Nicki recovers his stretched-out mitten. Nicki and the other characters are one dimensional, and the story's told from the objective viewpoint. *The Mitten* is most appropriate for prekindergartners through first graders.

Jan Brett is a talented author-illustrator. Her distinctive style is what makes this picture book special. Her illustrations are inspired by Ukrainian folk art, and they create the story's mood. Jan Brett incorporates border illustrations in most of her books, and here she creates mitten-shaped windows at the edge of each page. On left-facing pages, readers look through the windows to see Nicki walking through the woods, unaware of the woodland animals crawling into his mitten, and the windows on right-facing pages provide hints about what will happen next. She uses foreshadowing very effectively, and children quickly learn to check the mitten-shaped windows on each page.

TEXT FACTORS OF INFORMATIONAL BOOKS

Stories have been the principal genre for reading and writing instruction in prekindergarten to fourth grade because it's been assumed that constructing stories is a fundamental way of learning; however, many children—especially boys—prefer to read informational books (Stead & Duke, 2005). Certainly, children are interested in learning about their world—about the difference between dolphins and whales, how a road is built, threats to the environment, or the Apollo 11 moon landing—and informational books provide this knowledge.

Nonfiction Genres

Informational books provide facts about just about any topic you can think of. Consider, for example: *Flick a Switch: How Electricity Gets to Your Home* (Seuling, 2003), *Taj Mahal* (Arnold & Comora, 2007), *Martin's Big Words: The Life of Dr. Martin Luther King, Jr.* (Rappaport, 2007), *Saguaro Moon: A Desert Journal* (Pratt-Serafini, 2002), and *Groundhog Day!* (Gibbons, 2007). These books are picture books that use a combination of text and illustrations to present information.

Other books present information within a story context; the Magic School Bus series is perhaps the best known. In *The Magic School Bus and the Science Fair Expedition* (Cole, 2006), for example, Ms. Frizzle and her class travel through time to learn how scientific thinking developed. The page layout is innovative, with charts and reports containing factual information presented at the outside edges of most pages.

Alphabet Books. Many alphabet books are designed for young children who are learning to identify the letters of the alphabet. Some are predictable, featuring a letter and an illustration of a familiar object on each page, but others, such as *Alphabet Adventure* (Wood, 2001), *The Alphabet Room* (Pinto, 2003), and *Fancy Nancy's Favorite Fancy Words: From Accessories to Zany* (O'Connor, 2008), are more imaginative presentations. In these books, words representing each letter are highlighted and sometimes used in sentences.

Biographies. Children read biographies to learn about a person's life. A wide range of biographies are available for children today, from those featuring well-known personalities, such as *Neil Armstrong* (Rau, 2003), *Marco Polo* (Demi, 2008), and *Wilma Unlimited: How Wilma Rudolph Became the World's Fastest Woman* (Krull, 2000). Only a few autobiographies are available for children, but the Meet the Author series of autobiographies for kindergarten through fourth-grade students from Richard C. Owen Publisher is interesting to children who have read these authors' books. These autobiographies of contemporary authors, including Laura Numeroff's *If You Give an Author a Pencil* (2003) and Eve Bunting's *Once Upon a Time* (1995), include information about their lives and insights into their writing.

Expository Text Structures

Informational books are organized in particular ways called *expository text structures* (McGee & Richgels, 1985). Figure 9–6 describes these patterns, presents sample passages and cue words that signal the use of each pattern, and suggests a graphic organizer for each structure. When readers are aware of these patterns, it's easier to understand what they're reading, and when writers use these structures to organize their writing, it's easier to understand. Sometimes the pattern is signaled through the title, a topic sentence, or cue words, but sometimes it isn't. These are the most common expository text structures:

LITERACY PORTRAITS
Viewing Guide
Ms. Janusz's classroom is filled with stories and informational books. She uses these books for instructional purposes, and plenty of books are available for children to read independently. These second graders know about genres. They can identify books representing each genre and talk about the differences between them. Ms. Janusz teaches minilessons on genres and points out the genre of books she's reading aloud; she doesn't call all books "stories." Go to the Literacy Profiles section of the MyEducationLab for the Literacy Course and click on Rhiannon's Student Interview to watch her compare fiction and nonfiction. As you listen to Rhiannon, think about the information provided in this chapter. What conclusions can you draw about what Ms. Janusz has taught about text factors? Also, look at other video clips of Rhiannon to see how she applies her knowledge about genres in both reading and writing.

myeducationlab

Description. The author describes a topic by listing characteristics, features, and examples. Phrases such as *for example* and *characteristics are* cue this structure. When children delineate any topic, such as reptiles or the solar system, they use description.

Sequence. The author lists or explains items or events in numerical, chronological, or alphabetical order. Cue words for sequence include *first, second, third, next, then,* and *finally.* Children use this pattern to write directions for completing a math problem or the stages in an animal's life cycle. The events in a biography are often written in the sequence pattern, too.

Comparison. The author compares two or more things. *Different, in contrast, alike,* and *on the other hand* are cue words and phrases that signal this structure. When children compare and contrast book and movie versions of a story or reptiles and amphibians, they use this organizational pattern.

Cause and Effect. The author explains one or more causes and the resulting effect or effects. *Reasons why, if . . . then, as a result, therefore,* and *because* are words and phrases that cue this structure. Explanations of why dinosaurs became extinct or the effects of pollution use this pattern.

Problem and Solution. The author states a problem and offers one or more solutions. A variation is the question-and-answer format, in which the writer poses a question and then answers it. Cue words and phrases include *the problem is, the puzzle is, solve,* and *question . . . answer.* Children use this structure when they write about why money was invented or why endangered animals should be saved.

Figure 9–7 lists books exemplifying each of the expository text structures.

Figure 9–6 ◆ The Five Expository Text Structures

Pattern	Graphic Organizer	Sample Passage
Description The author describes a topic by listing characteristics and examples. Cue words include *for example* and *characteristics are*.		The Olympic symbol consists of five interlocking rings. The rings represent the five continents from which athletes come to compete in the games. The rings are colored black, blue, green, red, and yellow. At least one of these colors is found in the flag of every country sending athletes to compete in the Olympic games.
Sequence The author lists items or events in numerical or chronological order. Cue words include *first, second, third, next, then*, and *finally*.	1. _____ 2. _____ 3. _____ 4. _____ 5. _____	The Olympic games began as athletic festivals to honor the Greek gods. The most important festival honored Zeus, the king of the gods, and this festival became the Olympic games in 776 B.C. They ended in A.D. 394, and no games were held for more than 1,500 years. Then the modern Olympics began in 1896. Almost 300 male athletes competed in the first modern Olympics. In the 1900 games, female athletes also competed. The games have continued every four years since 1896 except during World War II.
Comparison The author explains how two or more things are alike and/or how they're different. Cue words include *different, in contrast, alike, same as*, and *on the other hand*.	Alike _____ Different _____	The modern Olympics is very different than the ancient games. While there were no swimming races, for example, there were chariot races. There were no female contestants, and all athletes competed in the nude. Of course, the ancient and modern Olympics are also alike in many ways. Some events, such as the javelin and discus throws, are the same. Some people say that cheating, professionalism, and nationalism in the modern games are a disgrace to the Olympic tradition, but according to ancient Greek writers, cheating, nationalism, and professionalism existed in their Olympics, too.
Cause and Effect The author lists one or more causes and the resulting effect or effects. Cue words include *reasons why, if . . . then, as a result, therefore*, and *because*.	Cause → Effect #1 Cause → Effect #2 Cause → Effect #3	There are several reasons why so many people attend the Olympic games or watch them on television. One reason is tradition. The name *Olympics* and the torch and flame remind people of the ancient games. People escape the ordinariness of daily life by attending or watching the Olympics. They like to identify with someone else's accomplishment. National pride is another reason, and an athlete's hard-earned victory becomes a nation's victory. There are national medal counts, and people keep track of how many medals their country's team has won.
Problem and Solution The author states a problem and lists one or more solutions. A variation is the question-and-answer format. Cue words include *problem is, dilemma is, puzzle is, solved*, and *question . . . answer*.	Problem → Solution	One problem with the modern Olympics games is that they're very expensive to operate. A stadium, pools, and playing fields must be built for the athletic events, and housing is needed for the athletes. And these facilities are used for only 2 weeks! In 1984, Los Angeles solved these problems by charging a fee for companies to be official sponsors. Many buildings that were already built in the Los Angeles area were also used. The Coliseum where the 1932 games were held was used again, and many local colleges became playing and living sites.

Figure 9–7 ◆ Informational Books Illustrating the Expository Text Structures

DESCRIPTION

Crews, D. (2008). *Freight train*. New York: Greenwillow. (preK)

Gibbons, G. (2007). *Groundhog day!* New York: Holiday House. (K–2)

SEQUENCE

Cole, J. (2006). *The magic school bus and the science fair expedition*. New York: Scholastic. (2–4)

Kelly, I. (2007). *It's a butterfly's life*. New York: Holiday House. (K–3)

Minor, W. (2006). *Yankee Doodle America: The spirit of 1776 from A to Z*. New York: Putnam. (3–4)

Royston, A. (2006). *The life and times of a drop of water: The water cycle*. Chicago: Raintree. (1–4)

COMPARISON

Bidner, J. (2007). *Is my cat a tiger? How your cat compares to its wild cousins*. New York: Lark Books. (2–4)

Thomas, I. (2006). *Scorpion vs. tarantula*. Chicago: Raintree. (3–4)

CAUSE-EFFECT

Brown, C. L. (2006). *The day the dinosaurs died*. New York: HarperCollins. (1–3)

Collins, A. (2006). *Violent weather: Thunderstorms, tornadoes, and hurricanes*. Washington, DC: National Geographic. (3–4)

Rockwell, A. (2006). *Why are the ice caps melting? The dangers of global warming*. New York: HarperCollins. (1–4)

PROBLEM-SOLUTION

Berger, M., Berger, G. (1999). *Do stars have points?* New York: Scholastic. (2–4)

Calmenson, S. (2007). *May I pet your dog? The how-to guide for kids meeting dogs (and dogs meeting kids)*. New York: Clarion Books. (1–4)

Morrison, M. (2006). *Mysteries of the sea: How divers explore the ocean depths*. Washington, DC: National Geographic. (2–4)

Thimmesh, C. (2006). *Team moon: How 400,000 people landed Apollo 11 on the moon*. Boston: Houghton Mifflin. (3–4)

Nonfiction Features

Informational books have unique text features that stories and books of poetry normally don't have, such as margin notes and glossaries. The purpose of these features is to make text easier to read and to facilitate children's comprehension. Here's a list of nonfiction text features:

- Headings and subheadings to direct readers' attention to the big ideas
- Photographs and drawings to illustrate the big ideas
- Figures, maps, and tables to provide detailed information visually
- Margin notes that provide supplemental information or direct readers to additional information on a topic
- Highlighted vocabulary words to identify key terms
- A glossary to assist readers in pronouncing and defining key terms
- An index to assist readers in locating specific information

PreK Practices

Do preschoolers recognize different genres?

When you think about the best books for young children, you probably think of stories, but 4-year-olds also enjoy nonfiction and poetry, and they do notice differences among genres (Bennett-Armistead, Duke, & Moses, 2005). As preK teachers share books during interactive read-alouds, it's important to identify the genre and talk about how it differs from other genres. Prekindergarten literacy standards state that young children should learn to identify genres, recognize their differences, and understand basic text structures. For instance, 4-year-olds apply beginning-middle-end to organize the stories they tell, use sequence to structure the information they share, and incorporate rhyme in the ditties they sing (Vukelich & Christie, 2009).

It's important that children understand these nonfiction text features so they can use them to make their reading more effective and improve their comprehension (Harvey & Goudvis, 2007).

Examining Text Factors in an Informational Book

What Do You Do With a Tail Like This? (Jenkins & Page, 2008) is a stunning informational book that was named a Caldecott Honor Book in recognition of its vibrant cut-paper collage illustrations. The book teaches that animals use their eyes, mouths, feet, and other body parts in very different ways. It's organized around these six questions:

What do you do with a nose like this?

What do you do with ears like this?

What do you do with a tail like this?

What do you do with eyes like this?

What do you do with feet like this?

What do you do with a mouth like this?

Each question is presented on a double-page spread with pictures of that feature belonging to five animals. Readers turn the page to see pictures of entire animals with sentence-long explanations of how each animal uses the feature. Each explanation predictably begins, "If you're a . . . " For instance, on the spread asking "What do you do with ears like this?" there's a picture of a cricket's knees. Turn the page, and there's a picture of the entire cricket with this sentence: "If you're a cricket, you hear with ears that are on your knees" (n.p.).

This question-and-answer book uses a problem-solution structure, and the predictable format and limited text makes it appropriate for K–3 students. At the back of the book, there's a special section, like a glossary, that provides more detailed information about each animal's special adaptation. The interactive quality makes this book unique: Children try to identify the animals based on picture clues and eagerly turn the page to learn amazing facts about alligators, skunks, hyenas, scorpions, monkeys, pelicans, snakes, and other animals.

TEXT FACTORS OF POETRY

It's easy to recognize a poem because the text looks different than a page from a story or an informational book. Layout, or the arrangement of words on a page, is an important text factor. Poems are written in a variety of poetic forms, ranging from free verse to haiku, and poets use poetic devices to make their writing more effective. Janeczko (2003) explains that it's important to point out poetic forms and devices to establish a common vocabulary for talking about poems, and because poems are shorter than other types of text, it's often easier for children to examine the text, notice differences in poetic forms, and find examples of poetic devices that authors have used.

Formats of Poetry Books

Three types of poetry books are published for children. Picture-book versions of *The Midnight Ride of Paul Revere* (Longfellow, 2001) and other classic poems are the first type. In these books, each line or stanza is presented and illustrated on a page. Others are specialized collections of poems, either written by a single poet or related to a single theme, such as *Tour America: A Journey Through Poems and Art* (Siebert, 2006). Comprehensive anthologies are the third type, and these books feature 50 to 500 or more poems arranged by category. One of the best is Jack Prelutsky's *The Random House Book of Poetry for Children* (2000). A list of poetry books with examples of each format is presented in Figure 9–8.

Poetic Forms

Poets who write for children employ a variety of poetic forms; some are conventional, but others are innovative. These are the more commonly used poetic forms:

Rhymed Verse. The most common type of poetry is rhymed verse, as in *My Parents Think I'm Sleeping* (Prelutsky, 2007) and *Today at the Bluebird Café: A Branchful of Birds* (Ruddell, 2007). Poets use various rhyme schemes, including limericks, and the effect of the rhyming words is a poem that's fun to read and listen to when it's read aloud.

Narrative Poems. Poems that tell a story are *narrative poems*. Perhaps our best-known narrative poem is Clement Moore's classic, "The Night Before Christmas."

Haiku. Haiku is a Japanese poetic form that contains just 17 syllables arranged in three lines of 5, 7, and 5 syllables. It's a concise form, much like a telegram, and the poems normally deal with nature, presenting a single clear image. Books of haiku to share with children include *Dogku* (Clements, 2007) and *Cool Melons—Turn to Frogs! The Life and Poems of Issa* (Gollub, 2004). The artwork in these picture books may give children ideas for illustrating their own haiku poems.

Figure 9–8 ◆ Collections of Poetry

PICTURE-BOOK VERSIONS OF SINGLE POEMS

Bates, K. L. (2002). *America the beautiful*. New York: Aladdin Books. (1–4)

Hoberman, M. A. (2004). *Eensy-weensy spider*. Boston: Little, Brown. (preK–K)

Scholastic. (2001). *The pledge of allegiance*. New York: Author. (K–2)

Westcott, N. B. (2003). *The lady with the alligator purse*. New York: Little, Brown. (preK–1)

SPECIALIZED COLLECTIONS

Florian, D. (2007). *Comets, stars, the moon, and Mars: Space poems and paintings*. Orlando: Harcourt. (3–4)

Havill, J. (2006). *I heard it from Alice Zucchini: Poems about the garden*. San Francisco: Chronicle Books. (K–3)

Kuskin, K. (2003). *Moon, have you met my mother? The collected poems of Karla Kuskin*. New York: HarperCollins. (2–4)

Larios, J. (2006). *Yellow elephant: A bright bestiary*. Orlando: Harcourt. (preK–2)

Prelutsky, J. (2005). *It's raining pigs and noodles*. New York: Greenwillow. (2–4)

Prelutsky, J. (2006). *Behold the bold umbrellaphant and other poems*. New York: Greenwillow. (preK–2)

Yolen, J., & Peters, A. F. (2007). *Here's a little poem: A very first book of poetry*. Cambridge, MA: Candlewick Press. (preK–K)

COMPREHENSIVE ANTHOLOGIES

Martin, B., Jr., & Sampson, M. (Sels.). (2008). *The Bill Martin Jr. big book of poetry*. New York: Simon & Schuster. (all)

Paschen, E., & Raccah, D. (Sels.). (2005). *Poetry speaks to children*. Naperville, IL: Sourcebooks MediaFusion. (2–4)

Prelutsky, J. (Sel.). (2000). *The Random House book of poetry for children*. New York: Random House. (all)

Rosen, M. (Sel.). (1993). *Poems for the very young*. Boston: Kingfisher. (preK–1)

Free Verse.   Unrhymed poetry is *free verse*. Word choice and visual images take on greater importance in free verse, and rhythm is less important than in other types of poetry. *The Friendly Four* (Greenfield, 2006) and *Next Stop Grand Central* (Kalman, 2001) are two collections of free verse. Poems for two voices are a unique form of free verse written in two side-by-side columns, and the columns are read simultaneously by two readers. The best-known collection is Paul Fleischman's Newbery Award–winning *Joyful Noise: Poems for Two Voices* (2004).

Concrete Poems.   The words and lines in concrete poems are arranged on the page to help convey the meaning. When the words and lines form a picture or outline the objects they describe, they're called *shape poems*. Sometimes the layout of words, lines, and stanzas is spread across a page or two to emphasize the meaning. *A Poke in the I: A Collection of Concrete Poems* (Janeczko, 2005) and *Doodle Dandies: Poems That Take Shape* (J. P. Lewis, 2002) are two collections of concrete poems.

To learn about other poetic forms, check *Handbook of Poetic Forms* (Padgett, 2007). Children use some of these forms when they write their own poems, including concrete poems.

Poetic Devices

Poetic devices are especially important tools because poets express their ideas very concisely. Every word counts! Here are some of the poetic devices they use:

- **Alliteration.** Repetition of sounds in nearby words
- **Imagery.** Words and phrases that appeal to the senses and evoke mental pictures
- **Metaphor.** A comparison between two unlikely things, without using *like* or *as*
- **Onomatopoeia.** Words that imitate sounds
- **Repetition.** Words, phrases, or lines that are repeated for special effect
- **Rhyme.** Words ending with similar sounds used at the end of the lines
- **Rhythm.** The internal beat in a poem that's felt when poetry is read aloud
- **Simile.** A comparison incorporating the word *like* or *as*

Narrative and poetic devices are similar, and many of them, such as imagery and metaphor, are important in both genres.

Poets use other conventions, too. Capitalization and punctuation are used differently; poets choose where to use capital letters and whether or when to add punctuation marks. They think about the meaning they're conveying and the rhythm of their writing as they decide how to break poems into lines and whether to divide the lines into stanzas. Layout is another consideration: The arrangement of lines on the page is especially important in concrete poems, but it matters for all poems.

Examining Text Factors in a Book of Poetry

Poetry Speaks to Children (Paschen & Raccah, 2005) is a comprehensive anthology for second through fourth graders that's accompanied by a CD of poets reading their poems. This richly illustrated picture book makes poetry fun and accessible. The anthology contains 95 classic and contemporary poems written by 73 poets on topics ranging from silly to serious: Nikki Giovanni tells why she likes chocolate, Billy Collins remembers turning 10, Ogden Nash recounts the story of brave little Isabel, and X. J. Kennedy reveals the secret of how to stay up late. Although most classic poems were written by white men, the contemporary poets contribute multicultural voices—Janet S. Wong, Naomi Shihab Nye, Gwendolyn Brooks, and Sandra Cisneros, for example.

The hour-long CD presents 50 poems read by 34 readers, many of them poets reading their own work. Several are slightly scratchy archival recordings, including Robert Frost reading his "Stopping by Woods on a Snowy Evening" and Basil Rathbone sharing Edgar Allan Poe's "The Raven." The readers display a variety of voices with unique accents, including James Berry, who speaks with a Jamaican-British lilt. For each poem that's included on the CD, the track number is shown next to the poem in the book.

Rhymed verse, narrative poems, and free-verse forms are represented in *Poetry Speaks to Children*. Lewis Carroll's "Jabberwocky" and Karla Kuskin's "Knitted Things" are rhymed verse, and Roald Dahl's "The Dentist and the Crocodile" and Ernest Thayer's "Casey at the Bat" are narrative poems. Contemporary poets often use free verse, and in this collection, James Berry's "Okay, Brown Girl, Okay," Sandra Cisneros's "Good Hot Dogs," and James Stevenson's "Why?" are written in free verse.

Rhyme is the most commonly used poetic device: X. J. Kennedy's "Flashlight," Jane Yolen's "Dinosaur Diet," and John Ciardi's "About the Teeth of Sharks" are examples. Gwendolyn Brooks uses rhyme, alliteration, and repetition in "The Tiger Who Wore White Gloves, or, What You Are You Are." Other poets use repetition, too: David McCord repeats the title in "Every Time I Climb a Tree," and Mary Ann Hoberman repeats the word *bit* in "Rabbit." Most of the poems are formatted in stanzas, but Nikki Giovanni's "Knoxville, Tennessee," a poem that explains why she likes summer, is formatted as a list without any punctuation or capitalization.

TEACHING ABOUT TEXT FACTORS

Researchers have documented that when teachers teach about text factors, children's comprehension increases (Fisher, Frey, & Lapp, 2008; Sweet & Snow, 2003). In addition, when children are familiar with the genres, organizational patterns, and text features in books they're reading, they're better able to create those text factors in their own writing (Buss & Karnowski, 2002). It's not enough to focus on stories, however; children need to learn about a variety of genres. In the vignette at the beginning of the chapter, Mr. Abrams used text factors to scaffold his students' learning about frogs. He taught them about the unique characteristics of informational books, emphasized text structures through the questions he asked, and used graphic organizers to help children visualize big ideas.

Go to the Building Teaching Skills and Dispositions section of the Topic *Comprehension* in the MyEducationLab for the literacy course and complete the activity entitled *Teaching Comprehension Skills and Strategies.* As you work through the learning unit, note the reader factors being examined in the classrooms.

Explicit Instruction

Teachers teach about text factors directly—often through minilessons (Simon, 2005). They highlight a genre, explain its characteristics, and then read aloud books representing that genre, modeling their thinking about text factors. Later, children make charts of the information they're learning and hang them in the classroom. Similarly, teachers introduce structural patterns and have children examine how authors use them to organize a book or an excerpt from a book they're reading. Children often create graphic organizers to visualize the structure of informational books they're reading and appreciate how the organization emphasizes the big ideas (Opitz, Ford, & Zbaracki, 2006). Teachers also focus on the literary devices that authors use to make

TOPIC: The Middle of a Story
GRADE: First Grade
TIME: One 30-minute period

Ms. Tomas is teaching a series of minilessons to her first-grade class about the characteristics of the beginning, middle, and end of stories. Several days ago, she taught a lesson about story beginnings, and the children analyzed the beginnings of several familiar stories. In this minilesson, Ms. Tomas uses the same stories to analyze the characteristics of story middles.

1 Introduce the Topic

Ms. Tomas begins by asking her first graders to name the three parts of a story, and they respond "beginning, middle, and end" in unison. She invites Kevin to read aloud the chart about the characteristics of story beginnings that they made previously. Then Ms. Tomas explains that in today's minilesson, they will examine the middle part of a story.

2 Share Examples

Ms. Tomas shows the children three familiar books: *Hey, Al* (Yorinks, 1989), *The Wolf's Chicken Stew* (Kasza, 1996), and *Tacky the Penguin* (H. Lester, 2008). She reminds them that several days ago, she read aloud the beginnings of these stories and explains that today she'll read aloud the middle parts. She briefly summarizes *Hey, Al* and reads the middle part aloud, then she repeats the procedure with the other two stories.

3 Provide Information

The teacher asks the children to think about the middle of the stories. Alexi replies that the problem is getting worse in the middle of each story: "It looks like the hunters will get the penguins in *Tacky the Penguin*, and the wolf looks like he is getting ready to eat the little chicks in *The Wolf's Chicken Stew*, and something bad is happening to Al and Eddie in *Hey, Al*." Ms. Tomas explains that authors add roadblocks to keep characters from solving their problems too quickly. The first graders identify the roadblocks in each story. Jack mentions another characteristic of story middles: "You meet other characters." Clara offers still another characteristic: "I think it's important that you get a little hint about how the story is going to end. I mean, Mr. Wolf is beginning to like the little chicks—you can tell." The teacher also points out that the middle is the longest part of the story, and children count the pages to assure themselves that she's right.

4 Guide Practice

Ms. Tomas uses interactive writing to develop a chart about the middle of stories. Their chart lists these characteristics:

1. The problem gets worse.   4. You get a hint about the ending.
2. There are roadblocks.   5. It is the longest part.
3. You meet new characters.

5 Assess Learning

After Ms. Tomas teaches a minilesson on the end of stories, she will read *Martha Speaks* (Meddaugh, 1995). Afterward, the children will make flip booklets and retell the beginning on the first page, the middle on the second page, and the end on the third page. Ms. Tomas will monitor their understanding of beginning, middle, and end through their retellings.

their writing more vivid and the conventions that make a text more reader-friendly. Children often collect sentences with narrative devices from stories they're reading and lines of poetry with poetic devices from poems to share with classmates, and they create charts with nonfiction features they've found in books to incorporate in reports they're writing. The minilesson on page 250 shows now Ms. Tomas teaches her first graders about the beginning, middle, and end of stories.

Comprehension Strategies

It's not enough that children can name the characteristics of a myth, identify cue words that signal expository text structures, or define *metaphor* or *assonance*. The goal is for them to actually use what they've learned about text factors when they're reading and writing. The comprehension strategy they use to apply what they've learned is called *noticing text factors*; it involves considering genre, recognizing text structure, and attending to literary devices. Lattimer (2003) explains the strategy this way: Children need to think about "what to expect from a text, how to approach it, and what to take away from it" (p. 12). Teachers teach about text factors through minilessons and other activities, but the last step is to help children internalize the information and apply it when they're reading and writing. One way teachers do this is by demonstrating how they use the strategy as they read books aloud using **think-alouds** (Harvey & Goudvis, 2007). Teachers also use the think-aloud procedure to demonstrate this strategy as they do modeled and shared writing.

Activities That Emphasize Text Factors

Instructional activities provide opportunities for children to examine text genres, text structures, and text features in the stories, informational books, and poems they're reading. These activities offer guided practice where children apply what they've learned through minilessons and deepen their comprehension, often in collaboration with classmates and with teacher guidance. Many teachers use these activities to differentiate instruction.

Stories. Children examine text factors as they participate in grand conversations and write and draw entries in reading logs, and they also learn more about stories as they participate in these oral, dramatic, and visual activities:

Story Boards. Children manipulate story boards, the cut-apart pages of a picture-book story, for a variety of activities. They can sequence story events, explore characters or setting, reread dialogue, and locate examples of other narrative devices. Teachers often have children line up around the classroom to sequence the pages, retell their page, or group themselves in the beginning, middle, and end parts.

Hot Seat. Children assume the role of a character and participate in a hot seat activity where they talk about the story from the character's point of view and answer classmates' questions. Sometimes several characters from a story get together to talk, sharing their perspectives and asking each other questions. This comprehension activity deepens children's understanding of the story as well as their awareness of plot, characters, and point of view and often leads to writing journal entries and letters from the character's perspective.

Drawings and Diagrams.　As they analyze story elements, children draw pictures of the beginning, middle, and end of stories, design plot diagrams and setting maps, and make posters about the characteristics of an element of story structure or charts about the text factors used in a particular story. These visual representations highlight important concepts about stories and reinforce children's learning.

Story Retelling.　Children retell stories, often using puppets, story boards, or collections of objects related to the story. As they participate in a story retelling activity, children apply their knowledge of plot, especially beginning-middle-end, and other elements of story structure, and they experiment with foreshadowing, dialogue, and other narrative devices. Sometimes children pretend to be a character and retell a story from that character's point of view; for example, they can retell *Officer Buckle and Gloria* (Rathmann, 1995), the story of a police officer and his dog who learn to work as a team, from an objective viewpoint or from either Officer Buckle's or Gloria's perspective. As children retell stories from different points of view, they learn that a character's perspective influences the story and its theme.

Open-Mind Portraits.　Children create multipage open-mind portraits to explore a character's appearance and thoughts. They use the information that the author provides about the character's appearance for the "portrait" page, and they infer the character's thoughts at pivotal points in the story and represent his or her thinking using words and pictures on the "thinking" pages. This activity helps children grapple with theme, the most difficult story element, because the character's thoughts as the story ends often address theme.

Through these activities, teachers have opportunities to emphasize the importance of text factors in comprehending stories.

Nonfiction.　After children read informational books, they explore them through the following activities that emphasize both the information children are learning and the books' unique text factors:

Semantic Feature Analysis.　When children do a semantic feature analysis, they're examining a big idea in a thematic unit and applying what they know about nonfiction, especially expository text structures. As they complete the semantic feature analysis chart, they think about relationships among the components listed in the left column. Word sorts are a similar classification activity, and as children organize words into categories, they're emphasizing relationships among the concepts represented by the words.

Story Boards.　Teachers also cut apart nonfiction picture books to make story boards for children to examine; however, to avoid confusion about genres, it might be better to call these cut-apart picture books "information" or "nonfiction" boards. In addition to locating the big ideas and key vocabulary words, children notice cue words the author used to emphasize the text structure and pick out text features, including headings, margin notes, illustrations, and highlighted vocabulary. Once children are aware of these features, they begin to insert them into the informational books they write.

Writing Informational Books. As children write informational books to share what they've learned in a thematic unit, they incorporate what they know about the nonfiction genre, expository text structures, and nonfiction features into their books to make them more reader-friendly. They create alphabet books, counting books, and question-and-answer books and use other formats that are similar to those in books they've read. They organize their writing into one-page chapters, and the chapter titles often hint at the structural patterns they're using. For example, second graders writing about plants used these chapter titles:

> The Parts of a Plant (description)
>
> A Plant's Life Cycle (sequence)
>
> Is It a Plant? (comparison)
>
> What Plants Need to Grow (cause and effect)
>
> Why People Need Plants (problem and solution)

Children also add a table of contents, illustrations and diagrams, margin notes, a glossary, an index, and other nonfiction features to their books.

Through these activities, children apply what they're learning about nonfiction in meaningful ways.

Poetry. Children deepen their understanding of poetry text factors as they read and listen to poems being read aloud, talk about poems, examine individual lines in a poem, and write their own poetry:

Interactive Read-Alouds. As teachers encourage children to participate in the reading experience by repeating lines, echoing rhyming words, or adding sound effects during interactive read-alouds, they're emphasizing the poem's text factors, and children develop an implicit understanding of poetic forms and devices that teachers can build on during minilessons.

Choral Reading. Children apply what they're learning about text features as they arrange poems and participate in choral reading activities. The power of the poet's words becomes clearer as children experiment with different ways of reading a poem. Not surprisingly, the most effective choral readings highlight the poem's structure and the poetic devices the poet used. Rhyming verse, for example, is read differently than free verse or poems with repeated lines or a refrain.

Poetry Picture Books. Children create picture-book versions to celebrate favorite poems. Each child chooses one line to write on a page and illustrate. Then the pages are compiled and made into a book, and the published book is placed in the classroom library for children to read. As they copy their line and draw their illustration, children think about the words and the images the poet has created. This close examination of one line and how it contributes to the entire poem provides an opportunity for children to think about text factors.

Writing Poems. Children write poems imitating the form of poems they've read, and they experiment with poetic devices, including alliteration, rhyme, and repetition, in their poems. For example, third-grade Jeremy wrote this poem, titled "Jeremy's Favorite Pizza," using poems from Georgia Heard's *Falling Down the Page: A Book of List Poems* (2009) as his model:

> crispy crust
> tomato sauce
> Italian seasoning
> pepperoni slices
> sausage meatballs
> mushrooms—OK
> NO olives
> mozzarella cheese
> PIPING HOT!

Jeremy proudly pointed out that each of the lines in his poem has exactly two words, and he used capital letters to indicate which words should be emphasized when the poem is read aloud.

Teachers often use these comprehension activities to provide guided practice as part of literature focus units and thematic units.

Assessing Children's Knowledge of Text Factors

Although there aren't formal tests to assess children's knowledge of text factors, they demonstrate their knowledge in a variety of ways:

- Talk about the characteristics of the genre in book talks and grand conversations
- Use their understanding of story elements to explain themes in reading log entries
- Apply their knowledge of genre when writing in response to prompts for district and state writing assessments
- Document their understanding of text structures as they make graphic organizers
- Write poems that are patterned after poems they've read
- Choose sentences with literary devices when asked to share favorite sentences with the class from a book they're reading
- Incorporate literary devices in their own writing

It's up to teachers to notice how children are applying their knowledge about text factors, and to find new ways for them to share their understanding.

IF CHILDREN STRUGGLE...

There's a good chance that children who are struggling to understand text factors don't have adequate background knowledge about literature. Daily experiences with books—reading and listening to stories, nonfiction, and poems read aloud—is essential for building children's familiarity with books; otherwise, they can't relate information about text factors to their background knowledge. Teachers intervene to expand children's knowledge about literature in these ways:

- Increase read-aloud experiences using both new and familiar books
- Provide opportunities for children to read both new and familiar books independently

- Invite children to talk about books in grand conversations, other discussions, and conferences
- Encourage children to use *genre*, *poem*, and other vocabulary related to text factors as they talk and write about books they're reading
- Ask children to compare books they're reading with others read previously

Reading new books and rereading familiar books are both worthwhile activities because struggling readers need to broaden their experiential base and dig deeper into familiar books. Children focus on the plot in the first reading, but they examine text factors through repeated readings.

Teachers intervene to teach children about text factors through minilessons and during guided reading lessons. They follow these guidelines:

- Use very familiar books to teach about text factors
- Incorporate vocabulary about text factors, including *genre*, *setting*, *expository text structures*, *sequence*, and *alliteration*, into lessons
- Have children create charts about text factors to display in the classroom

Most struggling readers benefit from additional explicit instruction.

When children aren't learning about text factors, teachers assess their teaching to ensure that they're providing enough attention to genres, text structures, and text features, because children's ability to comprehend depends on both reader and text factors. For example, they ask themselves which text factors they've taught during literature focus units. Have they taught genre units or chosen books for literature circles according to genre? They also check that they're talking about text factors as they do interactive read-alouds and are asking children to reflect on the author's use of text structures and narrative devices during grand conversations.

How Effective Teachers Facilitate Children's Comprehension

▶ Teachers teach children that stories have unique text factors: narrative genres, story elements, and narrative devices.

▶ Teachers teach children that informational books have unique text factors: nonfiction genres, expository text structures, and nonfiction features.

▶ Teachers teach children that poems have unique text factors: book formats, poetic forms, and poetic devices.

▶ Teachers encourage children to apply their knowledge of text factors when they're reading and writing.

Chapter 10

Scaffolding Children's Reading Development

Mrs. Ohashi Uses the Reading Process

Mrs. Ohashi's third graders are reading "The Great Kapok Tree," a selection in their basal reading program. This story, which is set in the Amazon rain forest, was originally published as a trade book. In the basal reader version, the text is unabridged, but because text from several pages has been printed on a single page, some illustrations from the original version have been deleted.

The children spend a week reading "The Great Kapok Tree" and participating in related literacy activities. Mrs. Ohashi's language arts block lasts 2 1/2 hours. During the first hour, she works with reading groups while other children work independently at centers. During the second hour, she teaches spelling, grammar, and writing. The last half hour is independent reading time when children read books from the classroom library.

The skills that Mrs. Ohashi teaches each week are determined by the basal reading program. She'll focus on cause and effect as children read and think about the selection. The vocabulary words she'll highlight are *community, depend, environment, generations, hesitated, ruins, silent,* and *squawking.* The third graders will learn about persuasive writing, and they'll write a persuasive letter to their parents. Mrs. Ohashi will teach **minilessons** on irregular past-tense verbs, and children will study the list of spelling words provided by the basal reading program.

Mrs. Ohashi's class is divided into four reading groups, and all but the group reading at the first-grade level can read the basal reader with her support. Her district's policy is that in addition to reading books at their instructional level, all children should be exposed to the grade-level textbooks. Mrs. Ohashi involves all children in most instructional activities, but she reads the story to the children in the lowest group and then these children read books at their instructional level.

To choose names for the groups at the beginning of the school year, Mrs. Ohashi put crayons into a basket. A child from each group chose a crayon, and the crayon's name became the name of the group. The children who read at or almost at grade level are heterogeneously grouped into the Wild Watermelon, Electric Lime, and Blizzard Blue groups. The six remaining children form the Atomic Tangerine group.

On Monday, Mrs. Ohashi begins the reading process with the first stage, prereading. She builds the children's background knowledge about the rain forest by reading aloud *Nature's Green Umbrella* (Gibbons, 1997). Children talk about rain forests and together compile a list of information they've learned, including the fact that each year, more than 200 inches of rain fall in the rain forest. Next, she introduces the selection of the week and children "picture walk" through it, looking at the illustrations, connecting with what they already know about rain forests, and predicting what the story is about.

The second stage is reading. Most of the third graders read the story with buddies, but the Atomic Tangerine group reads the selection with Mrs. Ohashi. These children join her at the reading group table, and she uses shared reading. She reads the story aloud while they follow along in their books. The teacher stops periodically to explain a word, invite predictions, clarify any confusions, and think aloud about the story.

Responding is the third stage. After everyone finishes reading the selection, children come together to talk about the story in a grand conversation. They talk about why the rain forests must be preserved. Ashley explains, "I know why the author wrote the story. On page 71, it tells about her. Her name is Lynne Cherry and it says that she wants to 'try to make the world a better place.' That's the message of this story." Then Katrina compares this story to *Miss Rumphius* (Cooney, 1985), the selection they read the previous week: "I think this story is just like the one we read before. It was about making the world more beautiful with flowers, and that's almost the same."

Mrs. Ohashi asks what would happen if there were no more rain forests. Children mention that animals in the rain forest might become extinct because they wouldn't have homes, and that there would be more air pollution because the trees wouldn't be able to clean the air. Then Mrs. Ohashi introduces a basket of foods, spices, and other products that come from the rain forest, including chocolate, coffee, tea, bananas, cashews, cinnamon, ginger, vanilla, bamboo, and rubber. The children are amazed at the variety of things that come from the rain forest.

Mrs. Ohashi moves on to the fourth stage, exploring. She introduces the grammar skill of the week: the past tense of irregular verbs. She has prepared 10 sentence strips with sentences about "The Great Kapok Tree," leaving blanks for the past-tense verbs, as suggested in the teacher's guide. On separate cards, she's written correct and incorrect verb forms on each side, for example: *The birds comed/came down from their trees.* She puts the sentence strips and verb cards in a pocket chart. She begins by talking about the past-tense form of regular verbs. The children understand that *-ed* marks the past tense, as in this sentence: *The man walked into the rain forest.* Other verbs, she explains, have different forms for present and past tense; for example, *The man sleeps/slept in the rain forest.* Then children read the sentences in the pocket chart and choose the correct form of each irregular verb.

Next, she explains that many irregular verbs have three forms—present tense, past tense, and past participle—as in *sing–sang–sung.* She puts word cards with these 10 present-tense forms in another pocket chart: *go, give, come, begin, run, do, eat, grow, see,* and *sing.* Then she passes out additional word cards listing the two past-tense forms of each verb. As they talk about each verb, children holding word cards with the past-tense forms add them to the pocket chart.

For the last 20 minutes of the language arts block, Mrs. Ohashi introduces this week's literacy centers and explains what to do at each one:

Comprehension Center. Children write a letter to Mrs. Ohashi in response to a question posted at the center or complete page 108 in their Practice Book.

Computer Center. Children play a phonics game on *r*-controlled vowels.

Grammar Center. Children sort word cards, putting present, past, and part participle forms of a verb together, and then complete page 56 in their Grammar Practice Book.

Listening Center. Children listen to "The Great Kapok Tree" or another of Lynne Cherry's books.

Reading Center. Children read books from the text set on rain forests.

Spelling Center. Children complete page 86 in their Spelling Activity Book.

Vocabulary Center. Children complete a word sort using words about rain forests.

These centers are arranged next to bulletin boards, on tables, or in corners of the classroom.

During the rest of the week, Mrs. Ohashi meets with reading groups during the first hour of the language arts block while other children work at centers. She meets with each group several times during the week and uses guided reading procedures as children reread the selection and supplemental or other leveled books. She also teaches vocabulary and comprehension as directed in the teacher's guide.

Mrs. Ohashi likes to begin with the Atomic Tangerine group each morning because she believes that it gets them off to a more successful start. She uses guided reading with these children. They begin by rereading several familiar leveled books, and Mrs. Ohashi listens to the children as they read. Next, she reviews one- and two-syllable words with *ar*, and they decode these words: *car, carpet, mark, bookmark, sharp, sharpest,* and *sharks.* Mrs. Ohashi introduces their new book, *Hungry, Hungry Sharks* (Cole, 1986). Children text walk through the first 11 pages, looking at illustrations and making predictions. They put a bookmark at page 11 to remember where to stop reading. Mrs. Ohashi asks them to read to find out if sharks are dinosaurs, and they eagerly begin. Children mumble-read so that Mrs. Ohashi can listen to them read. When children don't know a word, Mrs. Ohashi helps them sound it out or, if necessary, pronounces it for them. She writes the words on cards to review after reading. As soon as they finish, children discuss possible answers to her question. Several believe that sharks were dinosaurs, but others disagree. So, Mrs. Ohashi rereads page 10, which says, "There are no more dinosaurs left on earth. But there are plenty of sharks." After they agree that sharks aren't dinosaurs, they practice reading the word cards that Mrs. Ohashi prepared while they were reading.

Next, the children compose this sentence using **interactive writing**: *There are more than three hundred kinds of sharks today*. Children write on individual whiteboards as they take turns writing on chart paper. Then they reread the five sentences they wrote last week. During the rest of the week, children in the Atomic Tangerine group will continue reading *Hungry, Hungry Sharks* and participating in phonics, spelling, vocabulary, and writing activities.

Mrs. Ohashi meets with the Wild Watermelon group to reread "The Great Kapok Tree." The children read silently, but Mrs. Ohashi asks individual children to read a page aloud so that she can conduct **running records** to check their fluency. Afterward, the children talk about what the man might have been thinking as he walked away from the kapok tree on the last page of the story.

Next she focuses on cause and effect. She asks what's causing a problem in the story, and the children respond that cutting down the rain forest is the problem. When she asks about the effects of cutting down the trees, children mention several, including air pollution and destroying animal habitats. Then she passes out cards, each with a picture of an animal from the story, and asks children to scan the story to find the effect each animal mentioned to the sleeping man. Children reread and then share what they found.

Then Mrs. Ohashi repeats these activities with the other two reading groups. On the fourth and fifth days, she focuses on vocabulary words from the selection with the three on-grade-level reading groups.

In the second hour, Mrs. Ohashi begins a persuasive writing project. She explains that people read and write for three purposes—to entertain, to inform, and to persuade. "Which purpose," she asks, "do you think Lynne Cherry had for writing 'The Great Kapok Tree'?" The children respond that she had all three purposes, but that perhaps the most important purpose was to persuade. Then Mrs. Ohashi explains that in persuasive writing, authors use cause and effect. They explain a problem and tell how to solve it. They also provide reasons why it must be solved and tell what will happen if it isn't.

The fifth stage of the reading process is applying, and in this stage, readers create projects to extend their learning. The children talk about environmental problems in their community and decide to write letters to their parents and grandparents urging them to take good care of the environment. This is the format they'll use:

Sentence 1: Urge their parents to conserve and recycle.

Sentence 2: Tell how to conserve and recycle.

Sentence 3: Tell another way.

Sentence 4: Tell why it's important.

Sentence 5: Urge their parents to conserve and recycle.

Mrs. Ohashi and the third graders brainstorm many ideas and words on the chalkboard before they begin to write their rough drafts. On Wednesday and Thursday, they revise and edit their letters, and Mrs. Ohashi meets with children to work on their

A Third Grader's Persuasive Letter

Dear Nana and Pappa,

I want you to take very good care of the earth and it a more beautiful place. I want you to recycle paper. Like old newspaper and cardboard and bags from Savemart. You shuold put it in the blue RECYCLE can and it will be made into new paper. Don't burn it !! That means more air pollution. I love you and you love me so help me to have a good life on a healthy planet.

Love,
Rachel

letters. By Friday, most children are writing their final copies and addressing envelopes so their letters can be mailed. Before they begin recopying, Mrs. Ohashi reviews the friendly letter form so children will be sure to format their letters correctly. Rachel's letter to her grandparents is shown above.

Mrs. Ohashi ends the language arts block on Friday by showing the video version of "The Great Kapok Tree," which appeared on PBS's Reading Rainbow series.

Teachers use the reading process for literacy instruction. The reading process involves a series of stages during which readers develop their comprehension of a text by reading, responding, and applying what they've read. The term *text* refers to all reading materials—stories, maps, newspapers, cereal boxes, textbooks, e-mail, and so on; it's not limited to basal reading textbooks. In the vignette, Mrs. Ohashi guided her children through the reading process to scaffold their comprehension. Her instruction demonstrated that she knows that meaning doesn't exist on the pages of a book; instead, readers create comprehension through their interaction with the texts they're reading.

Teachers use a variety of programs for reading instruction; four of the most commonly used are basal reading programs, literature focus units, literature circles, and reading workshop. Each of these programs incorporates the reading process. In the balanced approach, teachers often combine two or three programs or supplement one program with additional literacy activities. Their goal is to provide explicit instruction, guided practice, and authentic application.

THE READING PROCESS

Reading is a constructive process of creating meaning that involves the reader, the text, and the purpose within social and cultural contexts. The goal is comprehension, understanding the text and being able to use it for the intended purpose. Readers don't simply look at the words on a page and grasp the meaning; rather, it's a complex process involving these essential components:

Phonemic Awareness and Phonics. As they read, children use their knowledge about the phonological system, including how to manipulate sounds in spoken words and apply phoneme–grapheme correspondences and phonics rules. They develop these abilities through phonemic awareness and phonics instruction.

Word Identification. Children recognize high-frequency words automatically and use their knowledge of phonics and word parts to decode unfamiliar words. Until children can recognize most of the words they're reading, they're slow, word-by-word readers.

Fluency. Children become fluent readers once they recognize most words automatically and read quickly and with expression. This is a milestone because children have limited cognitive resources to devote to reading, and beginning readers use most of this energy to decode words. Fluent readers, in contrast, devote most of their cognitive resources to comprehension.

Vocabulary. Children think about the meaning of words they're reading, choosing appropriate meanings, recognizing figurative uses, and relating them to their background knowledge. Knowing the meaning of words influences comprehension because it's difficult to understand when the words being read don't make sense.

Comprehension. Children use a combination of reader and text factors to understand what they're reading. They predict, connect, monitor, repair, and use other comprehension strategies as well as their knowledge of genres, organizational patterns, and literary devices to create meaning.

These components are supported by scientifically based reading research (National Reading Panel, 2000).

Teachers use the reading process to involve children in activities to teach, practice, and apply these components. The reading process is organized into five stages: prereading, reading, responding, exploring, and applying. This process is used, no matter which instructional program teachers have chosen, even though some of the activities at each stage differ. Figure 10–1 presents an overview of the reading process.

Stage 1: Prereading

The reading process begins before readers even open a book: The first stage, prereading, occurs as readers prepare to read. In the vignette, Mrs. Ohashi developed her children's background knowledge and stimulated their interest in "The Great Kapok Tree" as they learned about the rain forest. As readers get ready to read, they activate background knowledge, set purposes, and make plans for reading.

Activating Background Knowledge. Children have both world and literary background knowledge (Braunger & Lewis, 2006). World knowledge is what children have

---

Figure 10-1 ◆ Key Features of the Reading Process

Stage 1: Prereading
- Activate or build background knowledge and related vocabulary.
- Set purposes.
- Introduce key vocabulary words.
- Make predictions.
- Do a picture walk to preview the text.

Stage 2: Reading
- Read independently, with a partner, or using shared or guided reading, or listen to the text read aloud.
- Apply reading strategies and skills.
- Examine illustrations, charts, and diagrams.

Stage 3: Responding
- Write and draw pictures in reading logs.
- Participate in grand conversations or other discussions.

Stage 4: Exploring
- Reread all or part of the text.
- Learn new vocabulary words.
- Participate in minilessons on reading strategies and skills.
- Examine the author's craft.

Stage 5: Applying
- Construct projects.
- Read related books.
- Use information in thematic units.
- Value the reading experience.

---

acquired through life experiences and learning in their home communities and at school; in contrast, literary knowledge is the information about reading, genres, and text structures that children need to read and comprehend a text. Children activate their world and literary background knowledge in this stage, but when they lack the knowledge to read a text, teachers must build their knowledge base; otherwise, children won't be successful.

Teachers build children's knowledge about a topic by sharing a text set of related books, engaging children in discussions, sharing artifacts, and introducing key vocabulary words. Sometimes they collect objects related to the book and create a book box to use in introducing the book. In the vignette, Mrs. Oashi collected rain forest products to share with her third graders to build their background knowledge and engage them in the selection. Once children pick up a book, they think about its title, look at the illustration on the cover, and take a "picture walk" through the book to trigger this activation. Those who read novels often read the first paragraph or two to activate their world knowledge.

Teachers build children's literary knowledge by teaching about reading strategies and skills and studying different genres. Children read books representing a genre, examine structural patterns, and chart the characteristics. Through these activities, children learn how to vary their reading according to genre. It's not enough just to build children's knowledge about the topic; literary knowledge is also essential!

Setting Purposes.   The purpose guides children's reading: It provides motivation and direction for reading, as well as a mechanism for children to monitor their reading to see if they're fulfilling their purpose. Sustaining a single purpose is more effective than presenting children with a series of purposes (Blanton, Wood, & Moorman, 1990). Teachers often set purposes for reading, but children also need to set their own purposes. In literature circles and reading workshop, for example, readers choose texts they want to read and sat their own purposes. With lots of small-group and independent reading experiences, children become more effective at choosing books and setting their own purposes.

Planning for Reading. Once children activate their background knowledge and identify their purpose, they plan for reading. They vary how they make plans according to the type of selection they're preparing to read. For stories, they make predictions about the characters and events in the story, often basing them on the book's title or the cover illustration. If children have read other stories by the same author or in the same genre, they also use this information in making their predictions. Young children usually share their predictions orally, but more experienced readers write predictions in **reading logs**.

When children are preparing to read informational books, they preview the selection by flipping through the pages and noting section headings, illustrations, and diagrams. Sometimes they examine the table of contents to see how the book is organized, or they consult the index to locate specific information they want to read. They also notice highlighted terminology, which often triggers their background knowledge.

> Check the Compendium of Instructional Procedures, which follows Chapter 12, for more information on highlighted terms.

Stage 2: Reading

Children read the book or other selection during the reading stage using one of these types of reading:

◆ Independent reading
◆ Partner reading
◆ Guided reading
◆ Shared reading
◆ Teacher read-alouds

These types of reading vary in the amount of teacher scaffolding: Teachers provide very little support during independent reading, and the most support when they read aloud. As they decide which type of reading to use, teachers consider the purpose, children's reading levels, and the number of available copies of the text.

Independent Reading. When children read independently, they read quietly, by themselves, at their own pace, and often for their own purposes. Fluent readers usually read silently, but emergent and beginning readers typically read aloud softly to themselves. Because children generally choose the books they want to read independently, they need to learn how to choose books at an appropriate level of difficulty. Ohlhausen and Jepsen (1992) developed a procedure for choosing books that they called the "Goldilocks Strategy." These teachers created three categories—"too easy" books, "too hard" books, and "just right" books—using "The Three Bears" folktale as their model. The books in the "too easy" category are those children have read before or books without any unknown words; books in the "too hard" category are unfamiliar and confusing; and books in the "just right" category are interesting, with just a few new words. Figure 10–2 presents a Goldilocks Strategy chart made by a third-grade class. Children at every grade level can develop their own charts, using similar characteristics.

Independent reading is an important part of a balanced reading program because it's the most authentic type of reading. It's the way children develop a love of reading and come to think of themselves as readers. The reading selection, however, must be

Figure 10-2 ◆ Third Graders' Goldilocks Strategy Chart

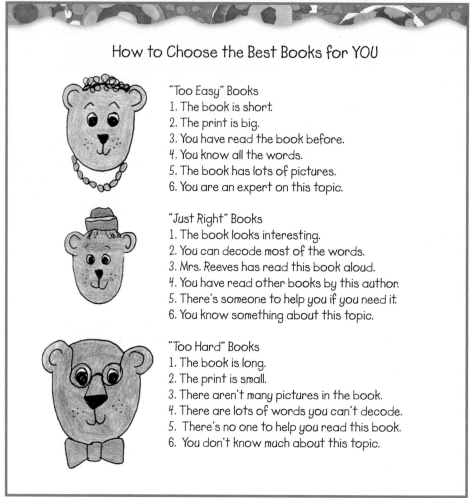

How to Choose the Best Books for YOU

"Too Easy" Books
1. The book is short.
2. The print is big.
3. You have read the book before.
4. You know all the words.
5. The book has lots of pictures.
6. You are an expert on this topic.

"Just Right" Books
1. The book looks interesting.
2. You can decode most of the words.
3. Mrs. Reeves has read this book aloud.
4. You have read other books by this author.
5. There's someone to help you if you need it.
6. You know something about this topic.

"Too Hard" Books
1. The book is long.
2. The print is small.
3. There aren't many pictures in the book.
4. There are lots of words you can't decode.
5. There's no one to help you read this book.
6. You don't know much about this topic.

at an appropriate level of difficulty so that children can read it independently. Otherwise, teachers use another type of reading to scaffold children and make it possible for them to be successful.

Partner Reading.   Children read or reread a selection with a classmate or sometimes with an older "buddy" (Friendland & Truesdell, 2004). Partner reading is an enjoyable social activity, and children can often read selections together that neither one could read individually. It's a good alternative to independent reading, and by working together, children are often able to figure out unfamiliar words and talk out confusions.

As teachers introduce partner reading, they show children how to read together and how to support each other. Children take turns reading aloud to each other or read in unison. They often stop and help each other identify an unfamiliar word or take a minute or two at the end of each page to talk about what they've read. Partner reading is a valuable way of providing the practice the beginning readers need to become fluent; it's also an effective way to work with children with special learning needs. However, unless the teacher has explained the technique and taught children how to work collaboratively, partner reading often deteriorates into the stronger of the two children reading aloud to the other child.

Teachers often organize cross-age partner reading programs with upper-grade students. The older children pair up with younger children and read books aloud or listen to the younger children read. Teachers prepare upper-grade students by teaching them how to choose books, read aloud, encourage children to make predictions and connections, and respond to books. The effectiveness of cross-age reading programs is supported by research, and teachers report that both younger and older children's reading improves; these activities have social benefits, too (Whang, Samway, & Pippitt, 1995).

Another way to encourage partner reading is with traveling bags of books. Teachers collect text sets with three or four books on a particular topic for children to take home and read with their parents (Reutzel & Fawson, 1990). For example, teachers might collect copies of *Good Dog, Paw!* (Lee, 2004), *Martha Speaks* (Meddaugh, 1995), and *McDuff's Wild Romp* (Wells, 2005) for a traveling bag of dog stories. Then children and their parents read the books and write a response in a reading log that is included in the bag. Children keep the bag at home for a week and then return it to school so that another child can borrow it. Teachers often add small toys or stuffed animals to the bags. If children are English learners whose parents don't read English, teachers send home small cassette tape players with audiotapes of the books.

Guided Reading. Teachers use guided reading to work with small groups of children who read at the same level. They select a book at children's instructional level and support children's use of reading strategies while they read (Fountas & Pinnell, 1996). Children do the actual reading themselves, although the teacher may read aloud to get them started on the first page. Fluent readers usually read silently, but beginning readers often murmur the words softly as they read, which helps the teacher keep track of children's reading and the strategies they're using.

Guided reading lessons usually last 20 to 30 minutes. To begin, children often reread, either individually or with a partner, familiar books used in previous lessons. For the new lesson, children read books that they haven't read before. Beginning readers generally read small picture books at one sitting, but more fluent readers take several days to a week or two to read novels.

Teachers observe children as they read. They spend a few minutes with each reader, sitting either in front of or beside the child. When they're working with beginning readers, teachers watch for evidence that the child is using these strategies to identify words, comprehend the book, and solve reading problems:

- Self-monitoring
- Checking predictions
- Decoding unfamiliar words
- Determining if the word makes sense
- Checking that the word is appropriate in the syntax of the sentence
- Using all sources of information
- Chunking phrases to read more fluently

Teachers take notes about their observations and use the information to decide which minilessons to teach and which book to choose for that child to read next.

Shared Reading. Teachers use shared reading to read aloud texts that are appropriate for children's interest level but too difficult for them to read on their own

> Go to the Assignments and Activities section of the Topic *Organization and Management* in the MyEducationLab for the literacy course and complete the activity entitled *Managing Guided Reading Groups*.

(Holdaway, 1979; Parkes, 2000). They use enlarged picture books known as *big books* so that children can see the text and read along. As they read, teachers model what fluent readers do (Fountas & Pinnell, 1996). After reading the book several times, teachers use it to teach phonics, high-frequency words, and other literacy concepts. Children can also read small versions of the book independently or with partners and use the text's pattern or structure for writing activities.

Predictable books are often used for shared reading because these books have rhyme, repetition, and patterns that enable young children to read them more easily. For example, preschoolers can remember and read the repeated questions and answers in *Where's Spot?* (Hill, 2003), and the circular structure of *This Is the House That Jack Built* (Taback, 2004) and the repetitive sentence patterns make this book easier for beginning readers to read. These and other predictable books are listed in Figure 10–3.

Shared reading is best known as part of a balanced literacy program in kindergarten and first-grade classrooms. It differs from reading aloud because children view the text as the teacher reads, and they often join in the reading of predictable refrains and rhyming words. After listening to the text read several times, they often remember enough of it to read along with the teacher.

PreK Practices

Which reading activities are best for young children?

Interactive read-alouds are the single most important reading activity for young children (Vukelich & Christie, 2009). As teachers read aloud picture books and involve children in a variety of participation activities, they model what good readers do. The children acquire positive attitudes about reading, develop concepts about written language, build background knowledge, and expand their vocabularies. In addition to reading aloud at least twice daily, teachers read big books using shared reading procedures, encourage children to look at books that have been read aloud, and have children read calendars, signs, children's names, and other environmental print in the classroom.

Teacher Read-Alouds. Teachers use the *interactive read-aloud* procedure as they read aloud books that are developmentally appropriate but written above children's reading levels (Fisher, Flood, Lapp, & Frey, 2004). As they read, teachers engage children in the experience rather than postponing their involvement until after reading. Children become active participants, for example, as they make predictions, repeat refrains, ask questions, identify big ideas, and make connections. In addition, when teachers read aloud, they model how good readers use reading strategies and *think aloud* about their use of reading strategies (Cappellini, 2005).

Read-alouds are an important component of literacy instruction at all grade levels, not just for emergent readers who can't read many books on their own. Teachers read books aloud during literature focus units, reading and writing workshop, and thematic units. There are many benefits of reading aloud: introducing vocabulary, modeling comprehension strategies, and increasing children's motivation (Rasinski, 2003).

The types of reading are compared in Figure 10–4. As teachers plan their instructional programs, they include reading aloud to children, teacher-led reading lessons, and independent reading each day.

Stage 3: Responding

Children respond to what they've read and continue to negotiate the meaning after reading. This stage reflects Rosenblatt's (2005) transactive theory. Two ways that children make tentative and exploratory comments immediately after reading are by writing in reading logs and participating in grand conversations or other discussions.

Figure 10–3 ◆ Predictable Books

Type	Description	Books
Rhymes	Rhyming words and refrains are repeated.	Martin, B., Jr., & Archambault, J. (2009). *Chicka chicka boom boom.* New York: Beach Lane Books. Seuss, Dr. (1963). *Hop on pop.* New York: Random House. Shaw, N. (1988). *Sheep in a jeep.* Boston: Houghton Mifflin. Kuskin, K. (2005). *So, what's it like to be a cat?* New York: Atheneum.
Repetitive Sentences	A sentence is repeated throughout the book.	Carle, E. (1991). *Have you seen my cat?* New York: Simon & Schuster. Ho, M. (2000). *Hush! A Thai lullaby.* New York: Scholastic. Rathmann, P. (2000). *Good night, gorilla.* New York: Puffin Books. Rosen, M. (2004). *We're going on a bear hunt.* New York: Candlewick Press.
Sequential Patterns	The book is organized using numbers, days of the week, or other familiar patterns.	Carle, E. (1997). *Today is Monday.* New York: Puffin Books. Christelow, E. (1998). *Five little monkeys jumping on the bed.* Boston: Houghton Mifflin. Moss, L. (2000). *Zin! Zin! Zin! A violin.* New York: Aladdin Books. Peek, M. (1991). *Roll over: A counting song.* New York: Clarion Books.
Pattern Stories	Episodes are repeated with new characters or other variations.	Brett, J. (1989). *The mitten.* New York: Putnam. Carle, E. (1987). *A house for hermit crab.* Saxonville, MA: Picture Book Studio. Taback, S. (1997). *There was an old lady who swallowed a fly.* New York: Viking. Carle, E. (1996). *Grouchy ladybug.* New York: HarperCollins.
Circular Stories	The plot is organized so that the ending leads back to the beginning.	Aardema, V. (1992). *Why mosquitoes buzz in people's ears.* New York: Puffin Books. Numeroff, L. J. (1987). *If you give a mouse a cookie.* New York: HarperCollins. Wood, A. (1984). *The napping house.* San Diego: Harcourt Brace.
Cumulative Stories	As each new episode is introduced, the previous episodes are repeated.	Cole, H. (1997). *Jack's garden.* New York: HarperCollins. Taback, S. (2004). *This is the house that Jack built.* New York: Puffin Books. West, C. (1996). *"Buzz, buzz, buzz," went bumblebee.* New York: Candlewick Press. Dunphy, M. (1995). *Here is the southwestern desert.* New York: Hyperion Books.
Questions and Answers	The same question is repeated on each page.	Guarino, D. (1989). *Is your mama a llama?* New York: Scholastic. Hill, E. (2003). *Where's Spot?* New York: Puffin Books. Martin, B., Jr. (2007). *Brown bear, brown bear, what do you see?* New York: Henry Holt.
Songs	Familiar songs with repetitive patterns are presented with one line or verse on each page.	Galdone, P. (1988). *Cat goes fiddle-I-fee.* New York: Clarion Books. Raffi. (1988). *Wheels on the bus.* New York: Crown. Westcott, N. B. (2003). *The lady with the alligator purse.* New York: Little, Brown. Cabrera, J. (2005). *If you're happy and you know it!* New York: Holiday House.

Figure 10-4 ◆ Types of Reading

Type	Strengths	Limitations
Independent Reading Children read a text on their own without teacher scaffolding.	Children develop responsibility. Children learn to select texts. Experience is authentic.	Children may not choose texts that they can read independently. Teacher has little involvement or control.
Partner Reading Two children take turns as they read a text together.	Children collaborate and assist each other. Children become more fluent readers. Children talk to develop comprehension.	One child may simply read to the other. Teacher has little involvement or control.
Guided Reading Teacher supports children as they apply reading strategies and skills to read a text.	Teacher teaches reading strategies and skills. Teacher provides scaffolding. Teacher monitors children's reading.	Multiple copies of texts at the appropriate reading level are needed. Teacher controls the reading experience.
Shared Reading Teacher reads aloud while children follow along using a big book or individual copies.	Teacher teaches concepts about print. Teacher models fluent reading and reading strategies. Children become a community of readers.	Big books or a class set of books are needed. Text may not be appropriate for everyone.
Teacher Read-Alouds Teacher reads aloud and provides opportunities for children to be actively involved in the experience.	Children have access to books they can't read themselves. Teacher models fluent reading and reading strategies. Children build background knowledge and vocabulary.	Children have no opportunity to read. Children may not be interested in the text.

Go to the Assignments and Activities section of the Topic *Organization and Management* in the MyEducationLab for the literacy course and complete the activity entitled *Analyzing Reading Logs to Support Student Learning.*

Reading Logs. Children write and draw their thoughts and feelings about what they've read in reading logs. As children write about what they've read, they unravel their thinking and elaborate on and clarify their responses. Children usually write in reading logs when they're reading stories and poems; sometimes they also do so when they're reading informational books, but during thematic units, they make notes of important information or draw charts and diagrams in learning logs.

Grand Conversations and Other Discussions. Children also talk about stories and poems with classmates in grand conversations, and have other discussions about informational books. Peterson and Eeds (2007) explain that in grand conversations, children share their personal responses and tell what they liked about the text. After sharing personal reactions, they shift the focus to "puzzle over what the author has written and . . . share what it is they find revealed" (p. 61). Often children make connections between the text and their own lives or between the text and other literature they've read. If they're reading a novel, they also make predictions about what might happen in the next chapter.

Teachers often share their ideas in grand conversations, but they act as interested participants, not leaders. The talk is primarily among the children, but teachers ask questions regarding things they're genuinely interested in learning more about and share information in response to questions that children ask. In the past, many discussions were "gentle inquisitions" during which children recited answers to factual questions that teachers asked to determine whether children read and understood an assignment. Although teachers can still judge comprehension, the focus in grand conversations is on deepening children's understanding of the story they've read.

Teachers and children also have discussions after reading informational books. Children talk about what interested them and what they learned about the topic, but teachers also focus their attention on the big ideas, ask clarifying questions, share information, and reread brief excerpts to explore an idea.

These discussions can be held with the whole class or with small groups. Young children usually meet as a class, but older children often prefer to talk in small groups. When children meet as a class, there's a feeling of community, and the teacher can be part of the group. When children meet in small groups, they have more opportunities to share their interpretations, but fewer viewpoints are expressed in each group and teachers move around, spending only a few minutes with each group. Teachers often compromise by having children begin their discussions in small groups and then come together as a class so that the groups can share what they discussed.

Stage 4: Exploring

Children go back into the text to examine it more analytically. This stage is more teacher directed than the others; it reflects the teacher-centered theory. Children reread the selection or excerpts from it, examine the author's craft, and focus on words and sentences from the text. Teachers also teach minilessons on strategies and skills.

Rereading the Selection. As children reread the selection or excerpts from it, they think about what they've read. Each time they reread a selection, children benefit in specific ways (Yaden, 1988): They deepen their comprehension by moving beyond their initial focus on the events or the big ideas to understanding the theme of a story or the relationships among the big ideas in a nonfiction text.

Examining the Author's Craft. Teachers plan exploring activities to focus children's attention on the genres, text structures, and literary devices that authors use. For example, they have children use **story boards** to sequence the events in the story, or make graphic organizers to highlight the plot, characters, and other elements of story structure. Children also learn about the structure of stories and informational books by writing books based on the selection they've read.

Teachers share information about the author of the featured selection and introduce other books by the same author. Sometimes children read several books by the same author and compare them. To focus on literary devices, children often reread excerpts to locate examples of onomatopoeia, similes and metaphors, and other types of figurative language.

Focusing on Words and Sentences. Teachers and children add "important" words to the **word wall** posted in the classroom. Children refer to it when they write and use the words the word-study activities, including drawing word clusters and posters to highlight particular words and doing **word sorts** to categorize words. Children also locate "important" sentences in books they read; these sentences are worthy of examination because they contain figurative language, employ an interesting sentence structure, express a theme, or illustrate a character trait. Children often copy the sentences onto sentence strips to display in the classroom, and sometimes they copy the sentences in their **reading logs** and use them to begin their entries.

Teaching Minilessons. Teachers present **minilessons** on procedures, concepts, strategies, and skills (Angelillo, 2008). They introduce the topic and make connections between the topic and examples in the featured selection children have read.

Figure 10-5 ◆ Application Projects

Visual Projects
- Design a graphic organizer or model about a book.
- Create a collage to represent the theme or big ideas in a book.
- Prepare illustrations of a story's events to use in retelling the story.
- Make a book box and fill it with objects and pictures representing the book.
- Construct a paper quilt about a book.
- Create an open-mind portrait to probe the thoughts of a character.

Writing Projects
- Rewrite a story from a different point of view.
- Write another episode or a sequel for a book.
- Write letters from one character to another.
- Create a found poem using words and phrases from a book.
- Write a poem on a topic related to a book.
- Keep a journal from one character's viewpoint.
- Create a multigenre project about a book.

Talk and Drama Projects
- Give a readers theatre presentation of an excerpt from a book.
- Create a choral reading using an excerpt from a book and have classmates present it.
- Dress as a book character and sit on the "hot seat" to answer classmates' questions.
- Present a rap, song, or poem about a book.

Internet Projects
- Write a book review and post it online.
- Investigate an author's website and share information from it with classmates.
- Create a multimodal project about the book using text, images, and sounds.
- Search the Web for information on a topic related to the book and share the results with classmates.
- Create a PowerPoint presentation about the book.

Stage 5: Applying

Readers extend their comprehension, reflect on their understanding, and value the reading experience in this final stage. Often they create projects to apply what they've learned; these projects take many forms, including open-mind portraits, readers theatre performances, and PowerPoint presentations. A list of projects is presented in Figure 10–5. Usually children choose which project they want to do and work independently, with a classmate, or in a small group, but sometimes the class decides to work together on a project.

Reading Strategies and Skills

Reading is a complex process involving both strategies and skills. Strategies represent the thinking that readers do as they read, in contrast, skills are quick, automatic behaviors that don't require any thought. For example, readers use the connecting strategy to compare the story they're reading to their own lives, the world around them, and other books they've read. They're actively thinking as they make connections. In contrast, noticing quotation marks that signal a character's dialogue is a skill; children don't have to think about what these punctuation marks show because they recognize their meaning automatically. The terms *strategy* and *skill* can be confusing; sometimes they're considered synonyms, but they're not. It's important to clarify the distinctions between the two.

Strategies are deliberate, goal-directed actions (Afflerbach, Pearson, & Paris, 2008). Readers exercise control in choosing appropriate strategies, using them flexibly, and monitoring their effectiveness. Strategies are linked with motivation: Afflerbach and his colleagues explain that "strategic readers feel confident that they can monitor and improve their own reading so they have both knowledge and motivation to succeed" (p. 370). Strategies reflect information-processing theory. In contrast, skills are automatic actions that occur without deliberate control or conscious awareness. The emphasis is on their effortless and accurate use. Skills reflect the behavioral theory, and they're used in the same way, no matter the reading situation. It's crucial that children become both strategic and skilled readers.

Strategies. Comprehension strategies are probably the best-known type, but readers use strategies throughout the reading process:

Phonemic Awareness Strategies. Children manipulate sounds in words using the blending and segmenting strategies.

Word-Identification Strategies. Children use strategies such as decoding by analogy to decode unfamiliar words.

Word-Learning Strategies. Children apply strategies such as context clues to figure out the meaning of unfamiliar words.

Comprehension Strategies. Children make predictions, draw inferences, monitor their progress, and use other strategies to understand what they're reading.

Learning about strategies begins when children are preschoolers. They learn to blend and segment sounds in words and to make predictions about stories teachers are reading to them. During the primary grades, children continue to learn more complex strategies, including drawing inferences and syllabic analysis.

Skills. Children also learn skills that they use when they're reading. Phonics skills are probably the best-known type, but a variety are used throughout the reading process. Skills can be grouped into much the same categories as reading strategies.

Phonemic Awareness Skills. Children break one-syllable words into onsets and rimes, identify beginning, middle, and ending sounds in words, and notice rhyming words.

Phonics Skills. Children use their knowledge of sound–symbol correspondences and phonics rules to decode words.

Word-Identification Skills. Children apply their knowledge of phonics, word families, syllabication rules, and root words and affixes to identify unfamiliar words.

Word-Learning Skills. Children identify synonyms, recognize metaphors and similes, and notice capital letters signaling proper nouns and adjectives as clues to the meaning of words.

Comprehension Skills. Children recognize details and connect them to main ideas, separate fact and opinion, and use other comprehension skills.

Guidelines
for Strategy Instruction

▶ Teach strategies in minilessons using explanations, demonstrations, think-alouds, and practice activities.

▶ Provide step-by-step explanations and modeling so that children understand what the strategy does, and how and when to use it.

▶ Provide both guided and independent practice opportunities so that children can apply the strategy in new situations.

▶ Have children apply the strategy in content-area activities as well as in literacy activities.

▶ Ask children to reflect on their use of strategies.

▶ Hang charts of strategies children are learning in the classroom, and encourage children to refer to them when reading and writing.

▶ Differentiate between strategies and skills so that children understand that strategies are problem-solving tactics and skills are automatic behaviors.

Children often use these skills in connection with strategies; the big difference is that strategies are used thoughtfully and skills are automatic.

Minilessons.   Children need explicit instruction about reading strategies because they don't acquire the knowledge through reading (Dowhower, 1999). Teachers need to provide three types of information about a strategy for children to learn to use it:

◆ Declarative knowledge—what the strategy does
◆ Procedural knowledge—how to use the strategy
◆ Conditional knowledge—when to use the strategy

For example, let's examine the declarative, procedural, and conditional knowledge for questioning, a comprehension strategy that children use to ask themselves questions while they're reading. They apply it to direct their reading, monitor whether they're understanding, and construct meaning (declarative knowledge). They ask themselves questions such as "What's going to happen next?" "How does this relate to what I know about _____?" and "Does this make sense?" (procedural knowledge). Children use this strategy again and again while they're reading (conditional knowledge).

Teachers use minilessons to teach children about strategies. They explain the strategy and model its use, and then children practice using it with teacher guidance and supervision before using it independently. Through this instruction, children develop metacognitive awareness, their ability to think about their strategy use. The guidelines for strategy instruction are presented in the box above.

Teachers demonstrate the thought processes readers use as they read by doing think-alouds (Wilhelm, 2001). Teachers think aloud or explain what they're thinking while they're reading so that children become more aware of how capable readers think; in the process, children also learn to think aloud about their use of strategies. They set a purpose for reading, predict what will happen next, make connections, ask questions, summarize what's happened so far, draw inferences, evaluate the text, and make other comments that reflect their thinking. Think-alouds are valuable both when teachers model them for children and when children engage in them themselves. When children use think-alouds, they're more thoughtful, strategic readers who improve the way they monitor their comprehension.

Children often record their strategy use with small self-stick notes. Teachers distribute pads of notes and explain how to use them. Children can focus on applying a single strategy or integrating a group of strategies. They write comments about their thinking on the self-stick notes while they're reading and place them in the margin of the pages so they can locate them when the book is closed. Afterward, children share their notes and talk about the strategies they used in a discussion with classmates.

ORGANIZING FOR INSTRUCTION

There's no one best way to teach reading. Instead, teachers create a balanced literacy approach using two or more programs. Four of the most commonly used literacy programs for prekindergarten through fourth grade are basal readers, literature focus units, literature circles, and reading workshop. By combining several approaches, teachers ensure that children receive explicit instruction to meet state literacy standards, differentiated instruction to meet their instructional needs, and opportunities for authentic literacy experiences. Figure 10–6 shows how each of these programs incorporates the reading process.

Basal Reading Programs

Commercial reading programs, commonly called *basal readers*, have been a staple in reading instruction for 150 years. Before 1850, William Holmes McGuffey wrote the McGuffey Readers, the first textbooks with increasingly challenging books designed for each grade level. The lessons featured selections that emphasized religious and patriotic values. Children used phonics to sound out words, studied vocabulary words in the context of stories, and practiced proper enunciation as they read aloud to classmates. These books were widely used until the beginning of the 20th century. The Scott Foresman basal reading program, introduced in 1930 and used through the 1960s, is probably the most famous; the first-grade textbooks featured stories about two children named Dick and Jane; their little sister, Sally; their pets, Puff and Spot; and their parents. The first-grade texts relied on the repetition of words through contrived sentences such as "See Jane. See Sally. See Jane and Sally," to practice reading words. Children were expected to memorize words rather than use phonics to decode them; this whole-word method was known as "look and say." The Scott Foresman program, which is no longer used, has been criticized for its lack of phonics instruction as well as for centering stories on an "ideal" middle-class white family.

Today's basal readers include more literature selections, celebrate diverse cultures, and emphasize an organized presentation of strategies and skills, especially phonics. Walsh (2003) reviewed five widely used series and found that they all present visually stimulating artwork to engage children's interest, employ similar methods of teaching decoding and comprehension, and provide detailed lesson plans in the teacher's guide. She also uncovered a common problem: None of the programs provided for the sustained development of background knowledge. Ignoring background knowledge is a problem because beginning in fourth grade, children who don't have a strong foundation of world and literary knowledge have difficulty reading and

Figure 10-6 ◆ How Instructional Programs Apply the Reading Process

Stage	Basal Reading Programs	Literature Focus Units
Prereading	Teachers activate children's background knowlege, introduce vocabulary, and preview the selection.	Teachers involve children in activities to build background knowledge and interest them in reading the book.
Reading	Children read the selection; if it's too difficult, teachers read it aloud before children read it themselves.	Children read the book independently or with a partner, or the teacher reads it aloud or uses shared reading.
Responding	Teachers ask comprehension questions, and children complete workbook assignments that focus on comprehension.	Children participate in grand conversations to talk about the book and write entries in reading logs.
Exploring	Teachers teach phonics, spelling, and grammar skills, and children practice the skills by completing workbook assignments.	Teachers teach vocabulary, phonics, and comprehension in minilessons. Children also research the book's author or related topics.
Applying	Children read related selections in the basal reader or in supplemental books.	Children create oral and written projects and share them with their classmates.

understanding conceptually demanding books; this drop in achievement is known as the "fourth-grade slump." Children from economically disadvantaged families are more likely to fall behind their classmates because they often have less background knowledge and are less proficient readers (Chall, Jacobs, & Baldwin, 1991).

Publishers of basal reading programs tout their textbooks as complete literacy programs containing all the materials needed for children to become successful readers. The accessibility of reading materials is one advantage: Teachers have copies of grade-level textbooks for every child. Another plus is that the instructional program is already planned: Teachers follow step-by-step directions to teach reading, and assign practice materials found in workbooks that accompany the textbook. It's unrealistic, however, to assume that a textbook could be a complete literacy program. Children who read above or below grade level need reading materials at their level. In addition, children need many more opportunities to listen to books read aloud and to read and reread books than are provided in a basal reading program. An overview of basal reading programs is presented on page 276.

Teachers usually have strong feelings about textbooks—they either love or hate them. Advocates highlight these benefits:

- Instructional materials and lesson plans are supplied, which makes the teacher's job easier.
- The program is closely aligned with grade-level literacy standards.
- Children are prepared for high-stakes achievement tests because instruction focuses on grade-level standards.
- Strategies and skills are clearly identified to make them easier to teach, test, and reteach.
- These programs are especially beneficial for inexperienced teachers who are less familiar with state standards and grade-level instructional materials and procedures.

Literature Circles	Reading Workshop
Children choose books to read, form groups, and get ready to read by making schedules and choosing roles.	Children choose books at their reading level and activate background knowledge by examining the cover.
Children read the book independently or with a partner according to the schedule, and prepare for the group meetings.	Children read the book independently, at their own pace.
Children complete their role assignments and participate actively in discussions about the book.	Children talk about the book they're reading in conferences with the teacher and sometimes write in reading logs.
Teachers teach minilessons about literature circle procedures, comprehension strategies, and text factors.	Teachers teach minilessons about text factors, authors, and comprehension strategies.
Children give brief presentations to the class about the books they've read.	Children give a book talk about the book they've read and pass it off to a classmate.

What some people tout as benefits, however, others criticize as drawbacks. Detractors argue these points:

- The instructional materials are less authentic than trade books.
- Children aren't as engaged in reading textbook selections as they are in reading trade books.
- Textbook programs don't produce in-depth learning or an appreciation of literature.
- Instruction focuses on teaching isolated strategies and skills.
- Children often spend more time completing worksheets than reading.
- Textbooks aren't appropriate for all children.

Despite these criticisms, many teachers like Mrs. Ohashi use textbooks as part of their literacy programs.

Components of Basal Reading Programs. Basal readers are recognized for their strong skills component: Teachers teach skills in a predetermined sequence, and children apply what they're learning as they read textbook selections and complete workbook assignments. They have these components:

Selections. Basal reading programs are organized into units on topics such as challenges, folktales, and friends. Each unit consists of four to six weeklong lessons, each with a featured selection. The selections in first-grade textbooks contain decodable text so children can apply the phonics skills they're learning, but as children become fluent readers, textbooks transition to literature selections that were originally published as trade books. Everyone reads the same selection, no matter their reading level; publishers argue that all children should be exposed to grade-level instruction because minority children have been denied equal access in the past.

Instruction. Teachers use basal reading programs to deliver explicit and systematic instruction that's aligned with state literacy standards. Most textbooks include instruction in phonemic awareness, phonics, high-frequency words, word-identification skills, spelling, grammar, and writing mechanics (capitalization and punctuation). The programs also emphasize comprehension strategies, including predicting, questioning, summarizing, and monitoring. These programs claim that it's their explicit, systematic instruction that ensures success.

Workbook Assignments. Children complete workbook pages before, during, and after reading each selection to reinforce instruction, 10 to 12 workbook pages that focus on phonics, vocabulary, comprehension, grammar, spelling, and writing accompany each selection. On these pages, children write words, letters, or sentences; match words and sentences; or complete graphic organizers as they apply the concepts, strategies, and skills they're learning. Teachers vary how they use the workbook pages. Once children know how to complete a workbook page, such as the pages that focus on practicing spelling words, they work independently or with partners. For more challenging assignments, however, such as those dealing with a comprehension strategy or a newly introduced skill, teachers guide children as the whole class works together.

Books for Independent Reading. Most basal reading programs include a collection of easy, on-grade-level, and challenging paperback books for children to read

OVERVIEW OF THE INSTRUCTIONAL APPROACH

Basal Reading Programs

TOPIC	DESCRIPTION
Purpose	To teach the strategies and skills that successful readers need using an organized program that includes grade-level reading selections, workbook practice assignments, and frequent testing.
Components	Basal reading programs involve five components: reading the selections in the grade-level textbook, instruction on strategies and skills, workbook assignments, independent reading opportunities, and a management plan that includes flexible grouping and regular assessment.
Theory Base	Basal reading programs are based on behaviorism because teachers provide explicit instruction and children are passive rather than active learners.
Applications	Basal reading programs organize instruction into units with weeklong lessons that include reading, strategy and skill instruction, and workbook activities. They should be used with other instructional approaches to ensure that children read books at their instructional levels and have opportunities to participate in authentic writing activities.
Strengths	• Textbooks are aligned with grade-level standards. • Children read selections at their grade level. • Teachers teach strategies and skills sequentially, and children practice them through reading and workbook assignments. • The teacher's guide provides detailed instructions for teaching reading. • Assessment materials are included in the program.
Limitations	• Selections may be too difficult for some children and too easy for others. • Selections may lack the authenticity of good literature or may not include a variety of genres. • Programs include many workbook assignments. • Most instruction is presented to the whole class.

independently. Multiple copies of each book are available, and teachers set out some of these books for children to read after finishing each selection. Certain books, especially in the primary grades, have been written to reinforce phonics skills and vocabulary words, but others are trade books. The goal is for the collection to meet the needs of all children, but sometimes teachers still need to supplement with easier books for English learners or struggling readers.

Assessment Tools. Basal reading programs provide a battery of tests that are aligned with state literacy standards. The tests include selection tests, unit tests, skill tests, and spelling tests that teachers administer to track children's achievement, diagnose reading problems, and report to parents and administrators. Increasingly, basal reading programs are using Web-based testing and reporting systems where teachers retrieve tests from the program's online test library and generate customized tests. Children can take these tests online, and teachers receive immediate results pinpointing standards that children have achieved and those requiring reteaching.

Program Materials. At the center of a basal reading program is the student textbook. It's colorful and inviting, often featuring fanciful pictures of children and exciting images of animals on the cover. The selections are grouped into units, and each unit presents stories, poems, and informational articles. Many multicultural selections have been included, and illustrations usually feature ethnically diverse people. Information about authors and illustrators is provided for many selections.

Commercial reading programs provide a variety of materials to support children's learning. Consumable workbooks are well known; children write letters, words, and sentences to practice phonics, comprehension, and vocabulary strategies and skills. Big books and kits with letter and word cards, wall charts, and manipulatives are available for preschool, kindergarten, and first-grade classrooms. CDs, DVDs, and online resources are included, and some programs offer online versions of their textbooks. First- and second-grade collections of paperback books have decodable text to provide practice on phonics skills and high-frequency words; supplemental paperbacks for third and fourth grades are related to unit topics.

Teachers receive multiple management tools along with basal reading programs. The teacher's guide is an oversize instructional manual that provides comprehensive information about how to plan lessons, teach the selections, differentiate instruction, and assess children's progress. The selections are shown in reduced size in the guidebook, and background information about the selection, instructions for reading the selection, and ideas for coordinating skill and strategy instruction are included. Online lesson planners are available that teachers download and use to develop schedules, organize instruction, and coordinate their lessons with state standards. Most programs include handbooks that provide in-depth information about differentiating instruction, strengthening home–school connections, and teaching test-taking skills. In addition, publishers of basal reading programs provide in-service training for teachers.

 REALITY CHECK!
Managing a Basal Reading Program

Many teachers find that basal reading programs make teaching easier because detailed lesson plans are available in the teacher's guide, and assessment is less time-consuming because of the tests available at the publisher's website. Teachers use online lesson planners to plan for instruction and coordinate their daily lessons with grade-level literacy standards. They check the teacher's guide for suggestions about pacing each unit, ideas for flexible grouping, and ways to monitor children's learning. Some teachers, however, are frustrated with basal readers because they provide few opportunities to customize instruction and because they reflect a teacher-centered approach to instruction.

Literature Focus Units

Teachers teach literature focus units featuring popular and award-winning stories, informational books, or books of poetry. Some literature focus units feature a single book, but others feature several books for an author study or a genre unit. Teachers guide children as they read and respond to a book; the emphasis is on teaching children about literature, but teachers include lessons on vocabulary and comprehension in the unit. An overview of this instructional approach is shown below.

Developing a Unit. Teachers develop a literature focus unit through a series of steps, beginning with choosing the literature and setting goals, then identifying and scheduling activities, and finally deciding how to assess children's learning. Effective teachers don't simply follow directions in literature focus unit planning guides available in school supply stores; rather, they do the planning themselves because they're the

OVERVIEW OF THE INSTRUCTIONAL APPROACH

Literature Focus Units

TOPIC	DESCRIPTION
Purpose	To teach reading through literature, using high-quality, grade-appropriate trade books.
Components	Teachers involve children in three activities: Children read and respond to a book together as a class; the teacher teaches minilessons on phonics, vocabulary, and comprehension using the book they're reading; and children create projects to extend their understanding.
Theory Base	Literature focus units represent a transition between teacher-centered and child-centered learning because the teacher guides children as they read a book. This approach reflects information-processing theory because teachers develop children's background knowledge, read aloud when children can't read fluently, and teach vocabulary and comprehension. It also reflects both Rosenblatt's transactive theory because children participate in grand conversations and write in reading logs, and critical literacy theory because issues of social justice often arise in the trade books.
Applications	Teachers teach units featuring a trade book, generally using books on a district-approved list, or units featuring a genre or author. Literature focus units are often alternated with another approach where children read books at their own reading levels.
Strengths	• Teachers select award-winning literature for these units. • Teachers scaffold children's comprehension as they read with the class or small groups. • Teachers teach minilessons on reading strategies and skills. • Children learn vocabulary through word walls and other activities. • Children learn about genres, story structure, and literary devices.
Limitations	• All children read the same book even if they don't like it and regardless of whether it's at their reading level. • Many activities are teacher directed.

ones who are most knowledgeable about their students, the time available, the strategies and skills they need to teach, and the activities they want to develop. Teachers follow these steps:

Step 1: Select the literature. Teachers select the book—a story, an informational book, or a book of poetry—for the unit and collect copies for each child. Many schools have class sets of books available; however, sometimes teachers have to ask administrators to purchase multiple copies or buy books themselves. They collect related books for the text set, too, including different versions of the story, sequels, additional books by the same author, or other books in the same genre. Teachers collect one or two copies of 10 or more books and place them on a special shelf in the classroom library. They introduce the text set and provide opportunities for children read them.

Teachers also assemble book boxes of artifacts to use in introducing the book, information about the author and the illustrator, and other supplemental materials. In addition, teachers locate multimedia resources, including CDs of the featured selection, DVDs to provide background knowledge, and author and illustrator websites.

Step 2: Set goals. Teachers decide what they want children to learn during the unit, and they connect their goals with grade-level literacy standards.

Step 3: Develop a unit plan. Teachers read the selected book and choose the focus for the unit—an element of story structure, the author or genre, or a related topic, such as weather or desert life, for example. Next, teachers choose activities to use at each stage, often jotting notes on a chart divided into sections for each stage; then they use the ideas they've brainstormed as they plan the unit. Generally, not all activities will be used, but teachers select the most appropriate ones according to their focus and the available time.

Step 4: Differentiate instruction. Teachers think about the activities they'll use to teach the unit and how to adapt them to ensure that every child can be successful. They decide how to use grouping, tiered activities, centers, and projects to accommodate children's learning differences.

Step 5: Create a time schedule. Teachers create a schedule that provides sufficient time for children to move through the reading process and to complete the activities planned for the unit. They also plan minilessons to teach the strategies and skills identified in their goals and those needed for children to be successful. Teachers usually have a set time for minilessons in their weekly schedule, but sometimes they arrange their schedules to teach minilessons just before they introduce specific activities.

Step 6: Assess children's learning. Teachers other distribute unit folders in which children store all their work; keeping all the materials together makes the unit easier for both children and teachers to manage. Teachers also plan ways to document children's learning and assign grades. One type of record keeping is an assignment checklist, which is developed with children and distributed at the beginning of the unit. Children keep track of their work and sometimes negotiate to change the checklist as the unit evolves. They file the checklists in their unit folders and mark off each item as it's completed. At the end of the unit, children turn in their assignment checklist and other completed work. Although this list doesn't include every activity, it identifies those that will be graded.

Figure 10-7 ◆ Recommended Authors for Author Studies

PreK and Kindergarten	First and Second Grades	Third and Fourth Grades
Ashley Bryan	Jan Brett	Eve Bunting
Eric Carle	Doreen Cronin	Joanna Cole
Donald Crews	Denise Fleming	Gail Gibbons
Tomie dePaola	Steven Kellogg	Patricia MacLachlan
Arthur Dorros	Patricia McKissack	Mary Pope Osborne
Dr. Seuss	Barbara Park	Jack Prelutsky
Lois Ehlert	Patricia Polacco	Pam Muñoz Ryan
Denise Fleming	Jon Scieszka	Jon Scieszka
Kevin Henkes	Janet Stevens	Chris Van Allsburg
Mo Willems	Jane Yolen	David Wiesner

Units Featuring a Book. Teachers choose award-winning and other high-quality books for literature focus units. Young children read predictable picture books or books with very little text, such as *Rosie's Walk* (Hutchins, 2005), a humorous story about a hen who walks leisurely around the barnyard, unwittingly leading the fox who is following her into one mishap after another. Other children read more sophisticated picture-book stories and novels, such as *Truth to Somewhere* (Bunting, 2000), a story about an orphan train taking children to adoptive families in the West in the late 1800s, and *Bunnicula: A Rabbit-Tale of Mystery* (Howe & Howe, 2006), a hilarious story about a bunny that might be a vampire.

Units Featuring a Genre or an Author. Teachers teach about a particular genre, such as folktales, science fiction, or biographies, in a genre unit. Children read several books illustrating the genre, participate in a variety of activities to deepen their knowledge about the genre's text factors, and sometimes apply what they've learned through a writing project. For example, after reading and comparing Cinderella tales from around the world, third graders often create picture books to retell their favorite version.

During an author study, children learn about an author's life and read one or more books he or she has written. Most contemporary authors have set up websites to share information about themselves and their books, and each year more authors are writing autobiographies. As children learn about authors, they develop a *concept of author*; this awareness is important so that children will think of them as real people who eat breakfast, ride bikes, and take out the garbage, just as they do. When children think of authors as real people, they view reading in a more personal way. This awareness also carries over to their writing: Children gain a new perspective as they realize that they, too, can write books. Figure 10–7 presents a list of recommended authors for author studies; the list is divided into grade levels, but many authors write books that are appropriate for children at more than one level.

REALITY CHECK!
Managing Literature Focus Units

Although many teachers love teaching their favorite books in literature focus units, this instructional approach requires them to invest time and energy to plan the unit. Teachers read and analyze the books they've chosen and plan for instruction, including minilessons, vocabulary activities, and writing assignments. They need to connect what they're teaching to grade-level standards and differentiate instruction so that all children can be successful.

Timing is another issue. Usually literature focus units featuring a picture book are completed in 1 week, and those featuring a chapter book are completed in 2 or 3 weeks. Genre and author units often last 3 or 4 weeks. Rarely, if ever, do literature focus units continue for more than a month; when teachers drag out a unit, they risk killing children's interest in that particular book or, worse yet, their interest in literature and reading.

In addition, teachers have to decide how to balance teaching literature with teaching reading, especially if some children can't read the books selected for the units. Teachers often hold daily **guided reading** lessons during a literature focus unit so that children receive instruction and have opportunities to read books at their level.

Literature Circles

One of the best ways to nurture children's love of reading and ensure that they become lifelong readers is through literature circles—small, student-led book discussion groups that meet regularly in the classroom (Daniels, 2001). The reading materials are quality books of children's literature, including stories, poems, biographies, and other informational books; what matters most is that children are reading something that interests them and it's manageable. Children choose the books to read and form temporary groups. Next, they set a reading and discussion schedule. Then they read independently or with partners and come together to talk about their reading in discussions that are like **grand conversations**. Sometimes the teacher meets with the group, and at other times, the group meets independently. A literature circle on one book may last from several days to a week or two, depending on the length of the book and the age of the children.

Features of Literature Circles. The key features of literature circles are choice, literature, and response:

Choice. Children make many choices in literature circles. They choose the books they'll read and the groups they'll participate in. They share in setting the schedule for reading and discussing the book, and they choose the roles they assume in the discussions. They also choose how they will share the book with classmates. Teachers structure literature circles so that children have these opportunities, but even more important, they prepare children for making choices by creating a community of learners in their classrooms in which children assume responsibility for their learning and can work collaboratively with classmates.

Literature. The books chosen for literature circles should be interesting to children and at their reading level. The books must seen manageable, especially during children's first literature circles. Samway and Whang (1996) recommend choosing shorter books or picture books at first so that children don't become bogged down. It's also important that teachers have read and liked the books because otherwise they won't be able to do convincing **book talks** when they introduce them. In addition, they won't be able to contribute to the book discussions.

Response. Children meet to discuss the book. Through these discussions, children summarize their reading, make connections, learn vocabulary, and explore the author's use of text factors. They learn that comprehension develops in layers. From an initial comprehension gained during reading, children deepen their understanding through the discussions. They learn to return to the text to reread sentences and paragraphs in order to clarify a point or state an opinion.

OVERVIEW OF THE INSTRUCTIONAL APPROACH

Literature Circles

TOPIC	DESCRIPTION
Purpose	To provide children with opportunities for authentic reading and response.
Components	Children form literature circles to read and discuss books that they choose themselves. They often assume roles for the book discussions.
Theory Base	Literature circles reflect sociolinguistic, transactive, and critical literacy theories because children work in small, supportive groups to read and discuss books, and the books they read often involve cultural and social issues that require children to think critically.
Applications	Teachers often use literature circles in conjunction with a basal reading program or with literature focus units so children have opportunities to do independent reading.
Strengths	• Books are available at a variety of reading levels. • Children are more strongly motivated because they choose the books they read. • Children have opportunities to work with their classmates. • Children participate in authentic literacy experiences. • Children learn how to respond to literature. • Teachers may participate in discussions to help children clarify misunderstandings and think more critically about the book.
Limitations	• Teachers often feel a loss of control because children are reading different books. • Children must be task oriented and use time wisely to be successful. • Sometimes children choose books that are too difficult or too easy for them.

Literature circles are effective because of these three key features. As children read and discuss books with classmates, they often become more engaged in reading and literature than they do in more teacher-directed approaches. An overview of literature circles is presented above.

Discussion Roles. Sometimes teachers have children assume roles and complete assignments in preparation for discussion group meetings (Daniels, 2001). One child is the discussion director; he or she assumes the leadership role and directs the discussion, choosing topics and formulating questions to guide the group. The other children prepare by selecting a passage to read aloud, drawing a picture or making a graphic related to the book, or investing a topic connected to the book. The roles are detailed in Figure 10–8. Although having children assume specific roles may seem artificial, it teaches them about the ways they can respond to literature.

Implementing Literature Circles. Teachers organize literature circles using a six-step series of activities.

Step 1: Select books.   Teachers prepare text sets with five or six related titles and collect copies of each book. They give a brief book talk to introduce the books, and then children sign up for the one they want to read. Children need time to preview the books, and then they decide what to read after considering the topic and the difficulty level.

Step 2: Form literature circles. Children get together to read each book; usually no more than four to six children participate in a group. They begin by setting a schedule for reading and discussing the book within the time limits set by the teacher. Children also choose discussion roles so that they can prepare for the discussion after reading.

Step 3: Read the book. Children read all or part of the book independently or with a partner, depending on the book's reading level. Afterward, children prepare for the discussion by doing the assignment for the role they assumed.

Step 4: Participate in a discussion. Children meet to talk about the book; these discussions usually last about 15 to 20 minutes. The discussion director or another child who's been chosen as the leader begins the discussion, and then classmates continue as they do in grand conversations. The talk is meaningful because children talk about what interests them in the book, and they share their responses according to their roles.

Step 5: Teach minilessons. Teachers teach minilessons before or after group meetings on various topics, including asking insightful questions, completing role sheets, using comprehension strategies, and examining text factors (Daniels & Steineke, 2004).

Step 6: Share with the class. Children in each literature circle share the book they've read with their classmates through a book talk or another presentation.

Figure 10-8 ◆ Roles Children Play in Literature Circles

Role	Responsibilities
Discussion Director	The discussion director guides the group's discussion and keeps the group on task. To get the discussion started or to redirect it, the child may ask: • What did the reading make you think of? • What questions do you have about the reading? • What do you predict will happen next?
Passage Master	The passage master focuses on the literary merits of the book. This child chooses several memorable passages to share with the group and tells why each one was chosen.
Word Wizard	The word wizard focuses on vocabulary. This child identifies several important or unfamiliar words from the reading, checks their meaning in a dictionary, and shares the information about the words with the group.
Connector	The connector makes links between the book and group members' lives, school and neighborhood happenings, historical events, or other books by the same author or on the same topic.
Summarizer	The summarizer prepares a brief summary of the reading to convey the big ideas. This child often begins the discussion by reading the summary aloud to the group.
Illustrator	The illustrator draws a picture or diagram related to the reading and shares it with the group.
Investigator	The investigator locates some information about the book, the author, or a related topic to share with the group.

Adapted from Daniels, 2001; Daniels & Bizar, 1998.

Using Literature Circles With Young Children. First and second graders can meet in small groups to read and discuss books, just as older, more experienced readers do (Frank, Dixon, & Brandts, 2001; Marriott, 2002; Martinez-Roldan & Lopez-Robertson, 1999/2000). These young children choose books at their reading levels, listen to the teacher read a book aloud, or participate in a shared reading activity. They benefit from listening to a book read aloud two times or reading it several times before participating in the discussion. In preparation for the literature circle, children often draw or write reading log entries to share with the group. Children meet with the teacher to talk about a book; the teacher guides the discussion at first and models how to share ideas and to participate in a discussion. The talk is meaningful because children share what interests them in the book; make text-to-self, text-to-world, and text-to-text connections; point out illustrations and other book features; ask questions; and discuss themes. Young children don't usually assume roles as older children do, but second and third graders are often ready to take on leadership roles. While one literature circle meets with the teacher, the other children in the classroom are usually reading books or preparing for their upcoming literature circle meeting with the teacher.

REALITY CHECK!
Managing Literature Circles

When teachers introduce literature circles, they teach children how to participate in small-group discussions and respond to literature. At first, many teachers participate in discussions, but they step back as children become comfortable with the procedures and engaged in the discussions. Unfortunately, groups don't always work well. Sometimes conversations get off track because children are disruptive, monopolize the discussion, or exclude certain classmates. If this happens, teachers must work to develop positive relationships among group members and build more effective discussion skills.

Reading Workshop

Nancy Atwell introduced reading workshop in 1987 as an alternative to traditional reading instruction. Children do authentic and independent reading, and teachers present minilessons on reading concepts, strategies, and procedures during reading workshop (Atwell, 1998). This approach represented a change in what teachers believe about how children learn and how literature should be used in the classroom. Whereas traditional reading programs emphasized dependence on a teacher's guide to determine how and when particular strategies and skills should be taught, reading workshop is an individualized reading program. Atwell developed reading workshop with her middle school children, but it's been adapted and used successfully at first through fourth grades. An overview of reading workshop is shown on page 285.

Reading workshop fosters real reading of self-selected books. Children read hundreds of books during reading workshop. At the first-grade level, children might read or reread three or four books each day, totaling close to a thousand books during the school year; older children read fewer, longer books. Even so, fourth-grade teachers report that their children read 20 to 25 books during the school year. Kindergarten teachers can also implement reading workshop in their classrooms (Cunningham & Shagoury, 2005); even though they do more of the reading themselves, teachers involve 5-year-olds in authentic literacy experiences and teach them about comprehension strategies and text factors.

OVERVIEW OF THE INSTRUCTIONAL APPROACH

Reading Workshop

TOPIC	DESCRIPTION
Purpose	To provide children with opportunities for authentic reading activities.
Components	Reading workshop involves reading, responding, sharing, teaching minilessons, and reading aloud to children.
Theory Base	The workshop approach reflects sociolinguistic and information-processing theories because children participate in authentic activities that encourage them to become lifelong readers.
Applications	Teachers often use reading workshop in conjunction with a basal reading program or with literature focus units so children have opportunities to do independent reading.
Strengths	• Children read books at their reading levels. • Children choose books that they want to read. • Activities are authentic and child directed. • Teachers have opportunities to work individually with children.
Limitations	• Teachers often feel a loss of control because children are reading different books. • Teachers have to design and teach minilessons on strategies and skills. • Children must be task oriented and use time wisely to be successful.

Components of Reading Workshop. There are several versions of reading workshop, but all of them contain five components—reading, responding, sharing, minilessons, and teacher read-alouds:

Reading. Children spend 30 to 60 minutes independently reading books. They choose the books they read, often reading series books or using recommendations from classmates. It's crucial that children be able to read the books they choose.

Responding. Children keep reading logs in which they write their initial impressions about the books they're reading. Sometimes they dialogue with the teacher about the book they're reading; journals allow for ongoing written conversation between the teacher and individual children. Responses often demonstrate children's reading strategies and offer insights into their thinking about literature; seeing how children think about their reading helps teachers guide their learning. Teachers collect children's reading logs periodically to monitor their responses. They write back and forth with children; however, because responding to children's journals is very time-consuming, teachers keep their responses brief and don't respond to every entry.

Sharing. For the last 15 minutes of reading workshop, the class gathers together to discuss books they've finished reading. Children talk about a book and why they liked it. Sometimes they read a brief excerpt aloud or formally pass the book to a classmate who wants to read it. Sharing is important because it helps children become a community to value and celebrate each other's accomplishments.

Minilessons. The teacher also spends 5 to 15 minutes teaching minilessons on reading workshop procedures, comprehension strategies, and text factors. Sometimes minilessons are taught to the whole class, and at other times, they're taught to small groups. At the beginning of the school year, teachers teach mini-lessons to the whole class on choosing books to read and other reading workshop procedures; later in the year, they teach minilessons on drawing inferences and other comprehension strategies and text factors. Teachers teach minilessons on particular authors when they introduce their books to the whole class, and on literary genres when they set out collections of books representing a genre in the classroom library.

Teacher Read-Alouds. Teachers use the interactive read-aloud procedure to read picture books and chapter books to the class as part of reading workshop. They choose high-quality literature that children might not be able to read themselves, award-winning books that they believe every child should be exposed to, or books that relate to a thematic unit. After reading, children talk about the book and share the reading experience. This activity is important because children listen to a book read aloud and respond to it together as a community of learners, not as individuals.

Figure 10-9 ◆ Schedules for Reading Workshop

First Grade

10 min.	The teacher rereads several familiar big books and then reads aloud a new big book.
15 min.	Children read matching small books independently and reread other familiar books.
10 min.	Children choose one of the books they've read or reread during independent reading to draw and write about.
10 min.	Several children share the favorite book.
15 min.	The teacher teaches a minilesson.

Second Grade

30 min.	Children read self-selected books and respond to them in reading logs.
10 min.	Children share with classmates books they have finished reading and do informal book talks about them. They often pass the "good" books to classmates who want to read them next.
20 min.	The teacher teaches a minilesson.
30 min.	The teacher reads aloud, and afterward, children participate in a grand conversation.

Fourth Grade

20 min.	Children read self-selected books independently.
20 min.	The teacher reads a novel aloud, and children talk about it in a grand conversation.
10 min.	The teacher teaches a minilesson using the read-aloud book as a mentor text.
20 min.	Children read self-selected books independently, applying the strategy or skill the teacher taught in the minilesson.
10 min.	Children talk about the books they're reading and how they used the strategy or skill taught in the minilesson.

REALITY CHECK!
Managing a Workshop Classroom

Teachers establish the workshop environment in their classrooms, beginning on the first day of the school year. They provide time for children to read and teach them how to choose and respond to books. Through their interactions with children, the respect they show them, and the way they model reading, teachers establish a community of learners.

Teachers develop a schedule for reading workshop with time allocated for each component, as shown in Figure 10–9. In their schedules, teachers allot as much time as possible for children to read. After developing the schedule, teachers post it in the classroom and talk with children about the activities and their expectations. Teachers teach the workshop procedures and continue to model them until children become comfortable with the routines. As children gain experience with the workshop approach, their enthusiasm grows and the workshop is successful.

Teachers take time during reading workshop to observe children as they work together in small groups. Researchers who have observed in reading workshop classrooms report that some children, even as young as first graders, are excluded from group activities because of gender, ethnicity, or socioeconomic status (Henkin, 1995); the socialization patterns in classrooms seem to reflect society's. For example, teachers should be alert to the possibility that boys might share books only with other boys. If teachers see instances of discrimination, they should confront the situation directly and work to foster a classroom environment where children treat each other equitably.

CHAPTER Review

How Effective Teachers Scaffold Children's Reading Development

▶ Teachers use the reading process—prereading, reading, responding, exploring, and applying—to ensure that children comprehend books they read.

▶ Teachers use independent reading, partner reading, guided reading, shared reading, and interactive read-alouds to share books with children.

▶ Teachers teach reading strategies and skills to ensure that children become capable readers.

▶ Teachers organize for instruction using a combination of explicit instruction, guided practice, and authentic application activities.

▶ Teachers use a combination of instructional approaches to provide effective literacy instruction, because they understand that no single approach is a complete program.

Chapter 11

Scaffolding Children's Writing Development

First Graders Participate in Writing Workshop

The 20 first graders in Mrs. Ockey's class participate in writing workshop from 10:20 to 11:30. Here is the schedule:

10:20–10:40 Shared reading/Minilesson

10:40–11:15 Writing and conferencing with Mrs. Ockey

11:15–11:30 Author's chair

Mrs. Ockey devotes more than an hour each morning to writing workshop because she wants her children to have time to talk about their experiences, extend their vocabulary, and manipulate basic English syntactic patterns through writing and talking. Many of these 5- and 6-year-olds are English learners whose parents or grandparents immigrated to the United States from southeast Asia and who speak Hmong, Khmer, or Lao at home. They're learning to speak English as they learn to read and write in English.

Writing workshop begins with a 20-minute whole-class meeting. Mrs. Ockey either reads a big book using the shared reading procedures or teaches a minilesson, often using as an example something from the big book she has read previously. Yesterday, Mrs. Ockey read *An Egg Is an Egg* (Weiss, 1990), an informational book about egg-laying animals. After reading the big book twice, Mrs. Ockey and the children participated in an instructional conversation and talked about animals that lay eggs and those that don't.

Today, Mrs. Ockey rereads *An Egg Is an Egg*, and the children join in to read familiar words. Afterward, she reads the book again, asking the children to look for words on each page with *ou* and *ow* spellings. In a previous minilesson, Mrs. Ockey explained that usually these spellings are pronounced /ou/ as in *ouch*, but sometimes *ow* is pronounced /ō/ as in *snow*, and they began a chart of words with each spelling or pronunciation. The first graders locate several more words to add to their chart. After they add the new words from the big book, Shaqualle suggests *hour* and Leticia suggests *found*, words they noticed in books they were reading. The children practice reading the lists of words together, and Der reads the lists by himself. He smiles proudly as his classmates clap. Now the chart looks like this:

ou	ow	ow (long o)
loud	clown	low
sound	brown	blowing
cloud	down	tow
outside	town	slowly
flour	flower	sown
around	tower	snows
shout	now	
hour		
found		

Mrs. Ockey quickly reviews the class's guidelines for writing because two children have recently joined the class, and she has noticed that some of the other children aren't on task during the writing and conferencing period. The class's guidelines for writing are posted on a chart that the children wrote using interactive writing earlier in the school year. Mrs. Ockey rereads each guideline and then asks a child to explain it in his or her own words. Here is the class's list:

1. Think about your story.
2. Draw pictures on a storyboard.
3. Write words by the pictures.
4. Tell your story to 1 editor.
5. Write your story.
6. Read your story to 2 editors.
7. Illustrate your story.
8. Publish your story.

The second part of writing workshop is writing and conferencing. The children use a process approach to write personal narratives, stories about their families, pets, and events in their lives. To begin, the children plan their stories using storyboards, sheets of paper divided into four, six, or eight blocks. (Note that these are different from **story boards** described in the Compendium.) They sketch a drawing in each numbered block and then add a word or two to describe the picture. Next, they use their storyboards to tell their stories to one of five first graders serving as editors that day; today's editors are Pauline, Lily, Mai, Destiny, and Khammala. It's easy to recognize the editors in Mrs. Ockey's classroom because they're wearing neon-colored plastic visors with the word "Editor" printed on them.

After this rehearsal, the children write their stories using one sheet of paper for each block on their planning sheets. Next, they read their writing to two editors, who often ask the child to add more detail or to insert a word or phrase that has been omitted. Then the children draw and color a picture to complement and extend the words on each page. Sometimes they add a cover and title page and staple their stories together, and at other times, they turn in their drafts for the bilingual aide in the classroom to word process.

Children complete an editing sheet when they share their writing with the two classmates who are serving as editors; a copy of the editing sheet is shown on page 291. The author writes his or her name and the title of the story at the top of the sheet. The editors check off each box as they read their classmate's story and then sign their names at the bottom of the page. Mrs. Ockey often calls herself their third editor, and the children know that they must complete this editing sheet with two classmates before they ask her to review their writing.

Mrs. Ockey has divided the class into five conference groups, and she meets with one group each day while the other children are working on their stories. The children bring their writing folders to the conference table and talk with Mrs. Ockey about their work. They are working at different stages of the writing process.

The teacher begins by asking the children to each explain what they're writing about and where they are in the writing process. Then she examines each child's storyboard or writing and offers compliments, asks questions, and provides feedback about their work. She also makes notes about each child's progress.

Today, she's meeting with Lily, Der, Dalany, and Matthew. Lily begins by showing Mrs. Ockey her storyboard for a story about her cousin's birthday. She has developed eight blocks for her story, and she talks about each one, working to express her ideas in a sentence or two. Mrs. Ockey praises Lily for tackling such a long story and for including a beginning, middle, and end. She encourages Lily to begin writing, and a week later, Lily completes her book and shares it with her classmates. Here is Lily's published story, "My Cousin's Birthday":

Page 1	This is my cousin's birthday.
Page 2	I bought her a present.
Page 3	I have clothes for her present.
Page 4	She makes a wish on her birthday cake.
Page 5	We eat cake.
Page 6	We play games.
Page 7	My cousin is happy.
Page 8	We went to sleep.

Mrs. Ockey's Editing Sheet

Check Your Work!

Does the story make sense?	☐	☐
Punctuation marks	☐	☐
Capital letters	☐	☐
Spelling	☐	☐

My editors are:

_____   _____

Next, Mrs. Ockey turns to Der, who thinks that he's working on a storyboard for a story about his grandmother's cat, but he can't find it. Mrs. Ockey checks her notes and recalls that Der couldn't find his storyboard for the same story last week, so she asks him to get a new storyboard and start again. They talk out the story together. Der wants to describe what his grandmother's cat looks like and then tell all the things that she can do. He begins drawing a picture in the first block while Mrs. Ockey watches. After he draws the picture, Mrs. Ockey will help him add one or two key words in the block. Then she'll help him do a second block. Mrs. Ockey plans to keep Der close to her for a few days to ensure that he completes the storyboard and writes his story.

Next Mrs. Ockey turns her attention to Matthew, who is finishing his ninth book, "The Soccer Game." He reads it to Mrs. Ockey:

Page 1   Me and my friends play soccer.

Page 2   I won a trophy.

Page 3   I won another point.

Page 4   I played at the soccer field.

Page 5   I won again.

Page 6   I went home.

Then they read it over again, and Mrs. Ockey helps him correct the spelling of *trophy* and *soccer* and correct several letters that were printed backward. He also shows her his editing sheet, which indicates that he had already edited his story with Pauline and Sammy serving as his editors. Matthew says that he wants to finish the book today so that he can share it at the author's chair. Mrs. Ockey sends him over to write his name on the sharing list posted beside the author's chair.

Dalany is next. She reminds Mrs. Ockey that she finished her book, "The Apple Tree," last week, and she's waiting for it to be word processed. Mrs. Ockey tells her that it's done and gives her the word-processed copy. They read it over together and Dalany returns to her desk to draw the illustrations. Here is Dalany's book, "The Apple Tree":

Page 1	I see the apple tree.
Page 2	I picked the apple up.
Page 3	I ate the apple.
Page 4	I see another girl pick up the apple.
Page 5	The girl ate the apple.
Page 6	We are friends.

Page 5 from Dalany's word-processed book with hand-drawn illustrations is shown below.

After the children write their stories, an aide word-processes them in Standard English, adding a title page, a dedication page, and a "Readers' Comments" page. The child draws an illustration on each page. Then Mrs. Ockey laminates the title page and adds a back cover and the child staples the book together. The author shares the book

A Page From Dalany's Story About "The Apple Tree"

The girl ate the apple.

at that day's author's chair, and then the book is placed in the classroom library. Children take turns reading each other's books and adding comments on the back page. They take great pride in reading their classmates' comments in their books. Mrs. Ockey and the first graders have written these comments in Matthew's book about playing soccer:

I have a trophy. Der

I like Matthew play soccer. Pauline

You are a good soccer player! Mrs. Ockey

Nice story. Rosemary

You good soccer play. Jesse

Do you win and win? Lily

I like play soccer. Michael

Although not all comments are grammatically correct, Matthew can read them, and he has walked around and thanked each person for his or her comment. It's important to him that lots of friends read his book and write comments.

The third part of writing workshop is author's chair. Each day, three children sit in the author's chair and share their published stories. After children read their stories, their classmates offer comments and ask clarifying questions. Then they clap for the author, and the published book is ceremoniously placed in a special section of the classroom library for everyone to read.

The writing process, like the reading process, involves a series of five recursive stages. Children participate in a variety of activities as they gather and organize ideas, draft their compositions, revise and edit their drafts, and finally, publish their writings (Dorn & Soffos, 2001). Some teachers have thought that young children weren't ready for writing, but the first graders in Mrs. Ockey's class demonstrated that beginning writers can learn about the writing process and move beyond single-draft compositions.

Reading and writing have been thought of as opposites: Readers decoded or deciphered written language, and writers encoded or produced written language. Then researchers began to notice similarities between reading and writing and talked of both of them as processes. Now reading and writing are viewed as parallel processes of meaning construction, and we understand that readers and writers use similar strategies for making meaning with text.

THE WRITING PROCESS

The focus in the writing process is on what children think about and do as they write. The five stages are prewriting, drafting, revising, editing, and publishing. The labeling and numbering of the stages don't mean that the writing process is a linear series of neatly packaged categories. Rather, the process involves recurring cycles, and

Go to the Assignments and Activities section of the Topic *Writing* in the MyEducationLab for the literacy course and complete the activity entitled *Revising to Add Details.* As you watch the video and answer the accompanying questions, note the recursive nature of the writing process.

labeling is simply an aid for identifying and discussing writing activities. In the classroom, the stages merge and recur as children write. The key features of each stage are shown in Figure 11–1.

Stage 1: Prewriting

Prewriting is the "getting ready to write" stage. The traditional notion that writers have a topic completely thought out and ready to flow onto the page is ridiculous: If writers wait for ideas to fully develop, they may wait forever. Instead, writers begin tentatively—talking, reading, writing—to see what they know and in what direction they want to go. Prewriting has probably been the most neglected stage in the writing process; however, it's as crucial to writers as a warm-up is to athletes. Murray (1982) believes that at least 70% of writing time should be spent in prewriting. During the prewriting stage, children choose a topic, consider purpose and form, and gather and organize ideas for writing.

Choosing a Topic.   Children should choose their own topics for writing—topics that they're interested in and know about—so that they'll be more engaged, but that isn't always possible. Sometimes teachers provide the topics, especially in connection with literature focus units and content-area units. It's best when teacher-selected topics are broad so children can narrow them in the way that's best for them. Asking children to choose their own topics for writing doesn't mean that teachers never give writing assignments; teachers do provide general guidelines. They may specify the writing form, and at other times they may establish the function, but children should choose their own content.

Considering Purpose.   As children prepare to write, they need to think about the purpose of their writing: Are they writing to entertain? to inform? to persuade? Setting the purpose for writing is just as important as setting the purpose for reading, because purpose influences decisions children make about form.

Considering Genre.   Children make decisions about the genre or form their writing will take: a story? a letter? a poem? a report? Figure 11–2 describes the genres that children learn to use. The genre they choose relates to their purpose for writing: If they're

---

Figure 11-1 ◆ Key Features of the Writing Process

Stage 1: Prewriting
- Choose a topic.
- Consider the purpose for writing.
- Identify the genre the writing will take.
- Gather and organize ideas using words, pictures, diagrams, and talk.

Stage 2: Drafting
- Write a rough draft.
- Emphasize ideas rather than mechanical correctness.

Stage 3: Revising
- Reread the rough draft.
- Share writing in writing groups.

- Make substantive changes that reflect classmates' comments.
- Conference with the teacher.

Stage 4: Editing
- Proofread the revised rough draft.
- Identify and correct spelling, capitalization, punctuation, and grammar errors.
- Conference with the teacher.

Stage 5: Publishing
- Make the final copy.
- Share the writing with an authentic audience.

Figure 11-2 ◆ Writing Genres

Genre	Description	Activities
Descriptive Writing	Descriptive writing paints vivid pictures of people, places, events, and things. Writers use sensory details to breathe life into their writing.	descriptive paragraphs descriptive sentences poems
Expository Writing	Expository writing presents information. Writers use the expository text structures to organize their presentation of information and cue words to guide readers.	alphabet books directions posters
Journals and Letters	Journals and letters are personal writing. Writers use this genre to share news and explore new ideas. They also learn the special formats that letters and envelopes require.	e-mail messages friendly letters learning logs
Narrative Writing	Narratives are accounts of experiences, either true or imaginary. Writers create a world for readers to imagine, tell a story, and explain why it's memorable.	innovations personal narratives retellings of stories
Persuasive Writing	Persuasion is winning someone to your viewpoint. Writers state their position and support it with examples and evidence.	advertisements book and movie reviews persuasive letters
Poetry Writing	Poetry is a concise form that evokes an emotional response. Writers use figurative language, poetic forms, and poetic devices.	acrostics color poems "I Am . . . " poems

writing to share information, a report might be the most appropriate genre, but if they're writing to convince someone to do something, a persuasive letter may be the best choice.

Rehearsal Activities. Children engage in a variety of activities to gather and organize ideas for writing. They brainstorm words, draw pictures, and talk with classmates as they gather ideas, and they create graphic organizers to visually display their words and images. Their choice of diagram varies according to genre. For example, children often draw a series of three boxes for the beginning, middle, and end when they're planning a story and use a Venn diagram to compare two ideas.

Stage 2: Drafting

Children get their ideas down on paper and write a first draft of their compositions in this stage. Because they don't begin writing with their pieces already composed in their minds, writers begin tentatively with the ideas they've developed through prewriting activities. Their drafts are usually messy, reflecting the outpouring of ideas with cross-outs, lines, and arrows as they think of better ways to express ideas. Children write quickly, with little concern about legible handwriting, correct spelling, or careful use of capitalization and punctuation.

When they write rough drafts, children skip every other line to leave space for revisions and write only on one side of a sheet of paper. Wide spacing between lines is crucial. At first, teachers make small *x*'s on every other line as a reminder to skip lines, but once children understand the importance of leaving space, they skip lines automatically. Children write *Rough Draft* on their drafts; this label indicates to

classmates, parents, and administrators that the emphasis is on content, not mechanics. It also explains why the draft hasn't been graded.

Instead of writing drafts by hand, many children, even kindergartners and first graders, use computers to compose rough drafts, polish their writing, and print out final copies. There are many benefits of using computers for word processing. Children are often more motivated to write, and they tend to write longer pieces. Their writing looks neater, and they use spell-check programs to identify and correct misspelled words.

Stage 3: Revising

After writers have completed their rough drafts, they work to refine their presentation of ideas. Children often break the writing process cycle as soon as they complete a draft, believing that once they've jotted down their ideas, the writing task is complete. Experienced writers, however, know they must turn to others for reactions and revise on the basis of these comments. Revision is not just polishing; it's meeting the needs of readers by adding, substituting, deleting, and rearranging material. *Revision* means "seeing again," and in this stage, writers see their compositions again with the help of classmates and the teacher. Revising consists of three activities: rereading the rough draft, sharing the rough draft with classmates, and revising on the basis of feedback.

Rereading the Rough Draft. Writers need to distance themselves from their rough drafts for a day or two and then reread it from a fresh perspective, as a reader might. As they reread, children make changes—adding, substituting, deleting, and moving words, sentences, and paragraphs—and place question marks by sections that need work; children ask for help with these trouble spots when they meet with classmates in writing groups.

Sharing in Writing Groups. Children meet in small writing groups to share their rough drafts with classmates, who respond and suggest possible revisions. Sometimes teachers participate in these groups, and sometimes they meet separately with children, as Mrs. Ockey did in the vignette at the beginning of the chapter. Writing groups provide a scaffold in which teachers and classmates talk about plans and strategies for writing and revising.

In some classrooms, writing groups form whenever four or five children finish their rough drafts and want to get feedback. The children gather around a conference table or sit on the floor in a corner of the classroom and take turns reading their rough drafts aloud; classmates listen and respond, offering compliments and revision suggestions. But in other classrooms, writing groups are assigned, and children get together when everyone in the group has finished writing and is ready to share. Sometimes the teacher participates in the writing group; however, if the teacher is involved in something else, children work independently and conference with the teacher afterward.

Making Revisions. Children make four types of changes as they revise their drafts:

Additions. Writers insert words and sentences to provide additional information and improve the flow of ideas. Children like to use the caret symbol (∧) to indicate where they're inserting new words and sentences.

Substitutions. Writers replace words and sentences to express their ideas more effectively. As children learn about synonyms, alternatives for tired words such as *good* and *said*, and how to use a thesaurus, they become more interested in making substitutions.

Deletions. Writers cross out redundant, unnecessary, or inappropriate words and sentences. Deletions are particularly difficult for writers to make, especially those who think longer compositions are better than shorter ones.

Moves. Writers change the location of words and sentences to improve their presentation of ideas or heighten the lyrical quality of their writing. This is the most sophisticated type of revision, and children make fewer moves than additions, substitutions, or deletions. (Faigley & Witte, 1981)

Children often use a blue pen to cross out words, draw arrows, and write between the double-spaced lines of their rough drafts so that revisions will show clearly; this way, teachers can easily check the types of revisions they make. Revisions are an important gauge of children's growth as writers.

Revising Centers. Teachers often set up revising centers to give children revision options: They can talk with a classmate about the ideas in their rough draft, examine the organization of their writing, consider their word choice, or check that they've included all required components in the composition. A list of revising centers is shown in Figure 11–3. Teachers introduce these centers as they teach about the writing process, and then children work at them before or after participating in a writing group. Teachers usually provide a checklist of center options that children put in their writing folders, and then they check off the centers that they complete. Through these center activities, children develop a repertoire of revising strategies and personalize their writing process.

Stage 4: Editing

Editing is putting the piece of writing into its final form. Until this stage, the focus has been primarily on ideas. Now the focus changes to mechanics, and children polish their writing by correcting spelling mistakes and other mechanical errors. Mechanics are the commonly accepted conventions of written Standard English; they consist of capitalization, punctuation, spelling, sentence structure, usage, and formatting considerations specific to poems, scripts, letters, and other writing genres. The use of these commonly accepted conventions is a courtesy to those who will read the composition.

Children are more efficient editors if they set the composition aside for a few days before beginning to edit. After working so closely with a piece of writing during drafting and revising, they're too familiar with it to notice many mechanical errors; but with the distance gained by waiting a few days, children are better able to approach editing with a fresh perspective and gather the enthusiasm necessary to finish the writing process. Then children move through two activities in the editing stage: proofreading to locate errors and correcting the ones they find.

Proofreading. Children proofread their compositions to locate and mark possible errors. Proofreading is a unique type of reading in which children read word by word, hunting for errors rather than reading for meaning. Errors are highlighted with

special proofreader's marks; children enjoy using these marks, the same ones adult authors and editors use. Figure 11–4 presents a list of proofreaders' marks that children use when they're proofreading their writing. Concentrating on mechanics is difficult because of our natural inclination to read for meaning; even experienced proofreaders often find themselves focusing on comprehension and thus overlook errors that don't inhibit meaning. It's important, therefore, to take time to explain proofreading and demonstrate how it differs from regular reading.

To demonstrate proofreading, teachers copy a piece of writing on the chalkboard or display it on an overhead projector. The teacher reads it aloud several times, each time hunting for a particular type of error, such as spelling, capitalization, or paragraph indentation. During each reading, the teacher reads the composition slowly, softly pro-

Figure 11-3 ◆ Revising and Editing Centers

Type	Centers	Activities
Revising	Rereading	Children reread their rough drafts with a partner and the partner offers compliments and asks questions.
	Word Choice	Children choose three to five words in their rough drafts and look for more-specific or more-powerful synonyms using a thesaurus, word walls in the classroom, or suggestions from classmates.
	Graphic Organizer	Children draw a chart or diagram to illustrate the organization of their compositions, and they revise their rough drafts if the organization isn't effective or the writing isn't complete.
	Sentence Combining	Children choose a section of their drafts with too many short sentences and combine some of them to improve the flow of their writing.
Editing	Spelling	Children work with a partner to proofread their writing. They locate misspelled words and use a dictionary to correct them. Children may also check for specific errors in their application of recently taught skills.
	Homonyms	Children check their rough drafts for homonym errors, and after consulting a chart posted in the center, they correct the errors.
	Punctuation	Children proofread their writing to check for punctuation marks. They make corrections as needed and then highlight all punctuation marks in their drafts.
	Capitalization	Children check that each sentence begins with a capital letter, the word "I" is capitalized, and proper nouns and adjectives are capitalized. After the errors are corrected, children highlight all capital letters in their drafts.

Figure 11-4 ◆ Proofreaders' Marks

Correction	Mark	Example
Delete	ℯ	Most whales are big and huge creatures.
Insert	∧	A baby whale is ᵃᶜᵃˡˡᵉᵈ a calf.
Indent paragraph	¶	¶ Whales look a lot like fish, but the two are quite different.
Capitalize	≡	In the United states it is illegal to hunt whales.
Change to lower case	/	Why do beached Whales die?
Add period	⊙	Baleen whales do not have any teeth⊙
Add comma	∧	Some baleen whales are blue whales, gray whales and humpback whales.
Add apostrophe	∨	People are the whales only enemy.

nouncing each word and touching it with a pen to focus attention on it. The teacher marks possible errors as they're located.

Editing checklists help children focus on particular types of errors. Teachers develop checklists with two to six items that are appropriate for their grade level. A first-grade checklist, for example, might have only two items—perhaps one about capital letters at the beginning of sentences and a second about periods at the end. In contrast, a fourth-grade checklist might contain items such as using commas in a series, indenting paragraphs, and spelling homonyms correctly. Teachers revise the checklist during the school year to focus attention on skills that have recently been taught.

A third-grade editing checklist is presented in Figure 11–5. The writer and a classmate work as partners to edit their drafts. First, children proofread their own compositions, searching for errors in each category on the checklist, and after proofreading, check off the item. After completing the checklist, children sign their names and trade checklists and compositions: Now they become editors and complete each other's checklist. Having both the writer and the editor sign the checklist helps them take the activity seriously.

Correcting Errors. After children proofread their compositions and locate as many errors as they can, they use red pens to correct the errors independently or with an editor's assistance. Some errors are easy to correct, some require a dictionary, and others involve instruction from the teacher. It's unrealistic to expect children to locate and correct every mechanical error in their compositions; published books aren't always error-free!

Figure 11–5 ◆ A Third-Grade Editing Checklist

Author   Editor

1. I have circled the words that might be misspelled.

2. I have checked that all sentences begin with capital letters.

3. I have checked that all sentences end with punctuation marks.

4. I have checked that all proper nouns begin with a capital letter.

Signatures:

Author: _____   Editor: _____

Once in a while, children may change a correct spelling or punctuation mark and make it incorrect, but they catch far more errors than they create.

Children work at editing centers to check for and correct specific types of errors. A list of editing centers is also shown in Figure 11–3. Teachers often vary the activities at a center to reflect the types of errors children are making. For example, children who continue to misspell common words can check for these words on a chart posted in the center, or after a series of lessons on contractions or punctuation marks, one or more centers can focus on applying the newly taught skill.

Editing can end after children and their editors correct as many mechanical errors as possible, or after children meet with the teacher for a final editing conference; when mechanical correctness is crucial, this conference is important. Teachers proofread the composition with the child, and they identify and make the remaining corrections together, or the teacher makes checkmarks in the margin to note errors for the child to correct independently.

Stage 5: Publishing

When children publish their compositions, they bring their writing to life. They make the final copy and share it orally with a real audience of classmates, parents, and others. In this way, children come to think of themselves as authors. Publication is a powerful motivator: Children want to continue writing and to improve the quality of their writing through revising and editing (Weber, 2002).

Making Books. The most popular way for children to publish their writing is by making books. Simple booklets can be made by folding a sheet of paper into quarters, like a greeting card. Children write the title on the front and use the three remaining sides for their composition. They can also construct booklets by stapling sheets of writing paper together and adding covers made out of construction paper. Sheets of wallpaper cut from old sample books also make sturdy covers. These stapled booklets can be cut into various shapes, too. Children can make more sophisticated books by wrapping cardboard covers with contact paper, wallpaper samples, or cloth. Pages are sewn or stapled together, and the first and last pages (endpapers) are glued to the cardboard covers to hold the book together.

Sharing Writing. Children share their writing by sitting in a special chair called the *author's chair* and reading their writing aloud to classmates. Afterward, classmates ask questions, offer compliments, and celebrate the completion of the writing project. Sharing writing is a social activity that helps writers develop sensitivity to their audience and confidence in themselves as authors. Beyond just providing the opportunity for children to share writing, teachers need to teach children how to make appropriate comments as they respond to their classmates' writing. Teachers also serve as a model for responding to children's writing without dominating the sharing.

Here are some other ways for children to share their writing:

- Read it to their families
- Share it at a back-to-school event
- Place it in the class library
- Post it on the class website
- Display it at a school or community event
- Submit it to a children's literary magazine

Through this sharing, children communicate with genuine audiences who respond to their writing in meaningful ways.

Adapting the Writing Process for Young Children

Young children do learn to use the five-stage writing process, but at first, teachers often simplify it by abbreviating the revising and editing stages. Children's revising is limited to reading the text to themselves or to the teacher to check that they've written all that they wanted to say. Revising becomes more elaborate as children learn about audience and decide to "add more" or "fix" their writing to make it appeal to their classmates. Some emergent and beginning writers ignore editing altogether—as soon as they have dashed off their drafts, they're ready to publish or share their writing. Others, however, change a spelling, fix a poorly written letter, or add a period to the end of the text as they read over their writing. When children begin writing, teachers accept their work as it's written and focus on the message. Then as children gain experience with writing, teachers encourage them to fix more and more of their errors.

TEACHING WRITING

Writing instruction involves three components. First, writing strategies and skills: Children learn to apply writing strategies and skills as they use the writing process. Second, the six traits: Children learn about the traits of effective writing and use this knowledge to improve the quality of their writing. Third, writing genres: Children examine writing genres and then apply what they're learning in their own writing.

Guidelines
for Writing Instruction

▶ Cultivate a community of writers.

▶ Provide daily opportunities for children to write.

▶ Guide children as they apply the writing process, with particular emphasis on revising.

▶ Model and teach writing strategies and skills.

▶ Teach the six traits so children can incorporate these qualities into their own writing.

▶ Train children to use rubrics to assess their own writing.

▶ Collect children's writing in portfolios.

Teachers use an apprenticeship model of writing, where they cultivate a community of writers and children learn to use the writing process. Like Mrs. Ockey, they combine explicit instruction with authentic practice as children apply what they're learning about writing strategies, the traits of effective writing, and genres in their own compositions. The guidelines of effective writing instruction are shown above.

Writing Strategies and Skills

Writing strategies are like reading strategies: They're tools that children use deliberately to craft effective compositions. Children apply many of the same strategies for both reading and writing, such as activating background knowledge, questioning, repairing, and evaluating, and they also use some specific writing strategies. They use strategies purposefully as they plan, revise, and edit their writing. Writers also draw on other, more specific strategies at each stage of the writing process and for varied types of writing activities (Dean, 2006). Children learn to apply these writing strategies:

Elaborating. Writers expand their ideas by adding details, examples, and quotes; it's the opposite of narrowing. Sometimes children brainstorm additional words and ideas; at other times, however, they have to do more research to elaborate their ideas.

Formatting. Writers design the layout of the final copies of their compositions. Formatting plays a more important role in some genres than in others; for example, children spend a great deal of time formatting the poems they write and digital compositions of information, including PowerPoint presentations.

Generating. Writers brainstorm ideas and the words to express them. Sometimes they activate their background knowledge and brainstorm lists, but at other times, they read books or research a topic.

Narrowing. Writers limit the scope of their topic to make it more manageable. When children attempt to write about a broad topic, they're often so overwhelmed with information that they can't complete the composition.

Organizing. Writers impose an order on their presentation of ideas using their knowledge of narrative elements, expository structures, or poetic forms. Outlining is the traditional form of organizing, but clusters and other graphic organizers are usually more effective.

Proofreading. Writers proofread to identify mechanical errors in their compositions, including spelling, capitalization, punctuation, and grammar mistakes. It's a special type of reading where children focus on the physical details of words rather than on their meaning.

Rereading. Writers often stop writing to read what they've written. They use this strategy for a number of reasons: to check that they're achieving their purpose, to monitor their flow of ideas, or to appreciate the voice they're creating. After a break, children reread to remember where they left off so they can begin to write again.

Revising. Revising isn't just a stage in the writing process; it's also a strategy writers use to improve the quality of their compositions. The four most important aspects are adding, deleting, substituting, and moving words, sentences, and longer pieces of text. For example, children add dialogue, delete redundant sentences, substitute more vivid verbs, or move paragraphs to improve the organization.

Be Strategic!

Writing Strategies

Children use these strategies to draft and refine their writing:

- ▶ Elaborate   ▶ Organize
- ▶ Format   ▶ Proofread
- ▶ Generate   ▶ Reread
- ▶ Narrow   ▶ Revise

They learn to apply writing strategies through a combination of explicit instruction and authentic writing activities.

Children use these writing strategies purposefully as they draft and refine their writing.

In contrast, writing skills are knowledge-based, automatic actions that children learn to apply during the writing process. Writers use these skills:

Content Skills. Children apply skills such as crafting topic sentences to arrange information into paragraphs. These skills are most important during the drafting and revising stages.

Word Skills. Children use skills such as adding synonyms and figurative language during drafting and revising to make their writing clearer.

Sentence Skills. Children apply skills such as varying the type of sentences to make their writing more interesting. They use these skills during drafting and revising.

Grammar Skills. Children use skills such as monitoring subject–verb agreement to correct any nonstandard English errors during editing.

Mechanical Skills. Children apply spelling, capitalization, and punctuation skills to make their compositions more readable, especially during the editing stage.

Teachers use minilessons with demonstrations and think-alouds to teach writing strategies and skills, and then children apply what they're learning during guided practice and independent writing projects. These strategies and skills are often reflected in rubrics that teachers and children use to assess writing.

Check the Compendium of Instructional Procedures, which follows Chapter 12, for more information on highlighted terms.

The Six Traits

What makes a piece of writing good? Spandel (2008) has identified these six qualities, which she calls *traits*:

Ideas. The ideas are the essence of a composition. Children choose an interesting idea during prewriting, and as they draft and revise, they narrow and develop it using main ideas and details.

Organization. The organization is the skeleton of the composition. Children hook the reader in the beginning, identify the purpose, present ideas logically, provide transitions between ideas, and end with a satisfying conclusion so that the important questions are answered. Children organize their writing during prewriting and follow their plans as they draft.

Voice. The writer's distinctive style is voice; it's what breathes life into a piece of writing. Culham (2003) calls voice "the writer's music coming out through the words" (p. 102). During the drafting and revising stages, children create voice in their writing through the words they choose, the sentences they craft, and the tone they adopt.

Word Choice. Careful word choice makes the meaning clear and the composition more interesting to read. Children learn to choose lively verbs and specific nouns, create word pictures, and use idiomatic expressions as they craft their pieces. They focus on word choice as they draft and revise their writing.

Sentence Fluency. Sentence fluency is the rhythm and flow of language. Children vary the length and structure of their writing so that it has a natural cadence and is easy to read aloud. They develop sentence fluency as they draft, revise, and edit their writing.

Mechanics. The term mechanics refers to correct spelling, conventional capitalization and punctuation, and standard English grammar. In the editing stage, children proofread their compositions and correct mechanical errors to make the writing easier to read.

As children learn about these traits, they apply their knowledge and find ways to make their writing more effective.

Teaching Procedure. Teachers teach a series of minilessons about each trait. They explain the trait, share examples from books they've read aloud and from children's own writing, involve children in activities to investigate and experiment with the trait, and have children apply what they've learned in their own writing. Figure 11–6 presents a list of books and activities that teachers can use in teaching the six traits.

As children study the six traits, they internalize what good writers do. They learn to recognize good writing, develop a vocabulary for talking about writing, get better at evaluating their own writing, and acquire strategies to improve the quality of their writing.

Writing Genres

The forms of writing are called *genres*. That's the same term used for the types of literature, and some literature and writing genres are the same, such as poetry, but others are different. Children learn to use a variety of writing genres, and they're often expected to apply their knowledge of writing genres on state- and district-mandated writing assessments. Through reading and examining writing samples, children become knowledgeable about these genres and how they're structured (Donovan & Smolkin, 2002).

Descriptive Writing. Children describe something by painting a word picture. They use sensory words and comparisons so that readers can imagine people, places, and things; they don't explain or tell a story about it. Sometimes writers add descriptive

Figure 11-6 ◆ Teaching the Six Traits

Trait	Books	Ways to Teach
Ideas	Baylor, B. (1995). *I'm in charge of celebrations*. New York: Aladdin Books. (grades 1–4) Moss, T. (1998). *I want to be*. New York: Puffin Books. (K–3) Van Allsburg, C. (1996). *The mysteries of Harris Burdick*. Boston: Houghton Mifflin. (4) Wyeth, S. D. (2002). *Something beautiful*. New York: Dragonfly. (K–3)	• Read aloud books with well-developed ideas. • Choose photos, pictures, or objects to write about. • Make graphic organizers to develop an idea.
Organization	Brown, M. W. (2006). *Another important book*. New York: HarperTrophy. (K–2) Fanelli, S. (2007). *My map book*. New York: Walker. (1–3) Fleischman, P. (2004). *Seedfolks*. New York: HarperTrophy. (3–4) Ryan, P. M. (2001). *Mice and beans*. New York: Scholastic. (1–2)	• Analyze the structure of a book using a graphic organizer. • Collect effective leads from books. • Find examples of effective transitions in books. • Collect effective endings from books.
Voice	Erickson, J. R. (1999). *The original adventures of Hank the cowdog*. New York: Puffin Books. Long, M. (2003). *How I became a pirate*. Orlando: Harcourt. Pennypacker, S. (2008). *Clementine*. New York: Hyperion Books. (1–3) Sceiszka, J. (1996). *The true story of the 3 little pigs!* New York: Puffin Books. (2–4)	• Read aloud books with strong voices. • Have children describe the voice in a text. • Personalize a story by telling it from one character's viewpoint. • Add emotion to a voiceless piece of writing.
Word Choice	Barrett, J. (2001). *Things that are the most in the world*. New York: Aladdin Books. (1–3) Leedy, L., & Street, P. (2003). *There's a frog in my throat! 440 animal sayings a little bird told me*. New York: Holiday House. (K–4) O'Connor, J. (2008). *Fancy Nancy's favorite fancy words*. New York: HarperCollins. (K–3) Scieszka, J. (2001). *Baloney (Henry P)*. New York: Viking. (2–4)	• Listen to or read books with good word choice. • Collect lively and precise words. • Learn to use a thesaurus. • Craft metaphors and similes.
Sentence Fluency	Aylesworth, J. (1995). *Old black fly*. New York: Henry Holt. (K–2) Grimes, N. (2002). *My name blue*. New York: Puffin Books. (3–4) Grossman, B. (1998). *My little sister ate one hare*. New York: Dragonfly. (1–3) Locker, T. (2003). *Cloud dance*. San Diego: Voyager. (2–4)	• Do choral readings of books with sentence fluency. • Collect favorite sentences on sentence strips. • Practice writing alliterative sentences. • Reread favorite books.
Mechanics	Pattison, D. (2003). *The journey of Oliver K. Woodman*. San Diego: Harcourt Brace. (2–4) Pulver, R. (2003). *Punctuation takes a vacation*. New York: Holiday House. (1–3) Truss, L. (2006). *Eats, shoots & leaves: Why commas really do make a difference!* New York: Putnam. (3–4) Truss, L. (2008). *Twenty-odd ducks: Why every punctuation mark counts!* New York: Henry Holt. (3–4)	• Proofread excerpts from books to find mechanical errors that have been added. • Add capital letters to excerpts that have had them removed. • Add punctuation marks to excerpts that have had them removed. • Correct grammar errors that have been added to excerpts from books.

Adapted from Culham (2003); Spandel (2008).

words and sentences to their writing, but they also do descriptive writing, including descriptive sentences and paragraphs, and poems. Teachers teach descriptive writing by having children examine something—an apple or a maple tree, for instance—or look at a photo or a piece of art, and brainstorm lists of words about the object or picture using each of the five senses. Later, children use the words they've collected for a writing project.

Expository Writing. Children use expository writing to explain something, present information, or specify how to make or do something. They use the writing process to draft and refine alphabet books, informational books, and other types of reports to share information they've learned during thematic units and about their hobbies and special interests.

Journals and Letters. Young children compose daily entries about themselves and topics that interest them in personal journals; this type of journal is especially beneficial for emergent and beginning writers who are learning to print letters, spell high-frequency words, and develop writing fluency. Children also write entries in reading logs to explore books they're reading and in learning logs to examine big ideas they're studying in thematic units. In addition, children learn the format used in letters and write friendly letters, courtesy letters (thank-you notes, invitations, get well cards), and e-mail messages.

Narrative Writing. Children write stories about true and imaginary experiences. They focus on a single event and apply what they've learned about story elements and narrative devices. In particular, they organize their stories into three parts—beginning, middle, and end. Children often write about events in their own lives; these stories are called *personal narratives*. They also write innovations that are modeled on books they've read and retellings of familiar stories, often from a different viewpoint.

Persuasive Writing. Children use persuasive writing to share their opinions and convince others to agree with them. They make posters and advertisements, write persuasive letters, and prepare book and movie reviews. When children write persuasively, they use logical arguments: They clearly state their position and support it with examples and evidence. Older children also identify opposing viewpoints and refute them.

Poetry. Poetry is a unique genre: Poets create word pictures, powerful images, and stirring stories using very few words. Poetry is meant to be read aloud so that readers and listeners can appreciate the sounds of language as well as its meaning. Children use poetic forms to structure their poems and choose their words carefully, often using wordplay and poetic devices. They organize the words they write into lines, not sentences, and arrange the lines creatively on the page to visually enhance the meaning. Some children use capitalization and punctuation, but others ignore these conventions.

Children often write powerful poems, especially when they use poetic forms to structure their writing. Here are four poetic forms that children use successfully:

Color Poems. Children begin each line or every other line of their poems with a color; the same color may be repeated, or different colors may be used (Koch, 2000). For example, kindergartners dictated this poem about America's colors:

Red, white, and blue are America's colors.
Red is for love:
We love America.
We say, "America is the best!"
White is for patriotism:
We salute the flag.
We say the Pledge of Allegiance.
Blue is for honor:
We honor our brave soldiers.
We say, "thank you!"
Hurray for the red, white, and blue!

The repetition of colors and beginning the two lines that follow with *we* provide the structure for the poem.

"I Am . . . " Poems. Children assume the perspective of another person and repeat the "*I am* . . ." line at the beginning and end of each stanza. They begin the other lines with *I* followed by an active-voice verb, not a form of "to be." Fourth-grade Madison wrote this poem about Neil Armstrong:

I am the First Man to walk on the moon.
I flew in a landing craft named Eagle.
I landed in the Sea of Tranquility.
I climbed down the ladder.
I put my left foot on the ground.
I said some famous words—
"That's one small step for a man,
one giant leap for mankind."
I collected soil samples.
I planted the American flag.
I am Neil Armstrong.

Madison repeats the *I* pattern to recount the events of the astronaut's famous moon walk.

"If I Were . . . " Poems. As in "I am . . ." poems, children write from the perspective of other people or things (Koch, 2000). In this poem, second-grade David writes about what he would do if he were a giant:

If I were a giant
I would drink up the seas
and I would touch the sun.
I would eat the world
and stick my head in space.

Children can also write poems from the perspective of characters in books they're reading, historical personalities, or things related to thematic units, for instance, a whale or a saguaro cactus.

List Poems. Children brainstorm a list about a topic, with each line following the same structure (Heard, 2009); the last line presents a twist or sums up the poem. See the examples on pages 254 and 332.

Children use the writing process to draft and refine their poems. During revising, they learn to "unwrite," or delete unnecessary words in the poems, and as they make their final copies, children decide how to arrange the lines in their poems and how to use capitalization and punctuation.

NURTURING ENGLISH LEARNERS

Writing can be a daunting task for English learners. Children need to know English vocabulary, sentence structure, and spelling to communicate effectively in writing, but Mrs. Ockey's first graders in the vignette at the beginning of the chapter showed that young English learners can become good writers when their teacher sets high expectations, teaches them how to write, and involves them in daily writing activities.

Teachers must be mindful of the increased linguistic demands placed on English learners and take into account these considerations as they teach writing:

Topics. At first, children write about personal topics—their families, afterschool activities, friends, and family trips, for example—but with experience, they move on to writing about books they're reading and topics they're learning in thematic units. To nudge ELs toward new writing topics, teachers offer suggestions about content-related topics, demonstrate how to write a book on a topic related to a book or unit, and create a collaborative book where each child contributes a page. Making this switch is especially important because English learners need to take advantage of writing as a tool for learning academic vocabulary and understanding the big ideas they're studying.

Talk. All children need to talk before they begin writing to activate background knowledge and develop ideas, but conversation is even more important for English learners because they're learning English vocabulary and sentence structures, too. Teachers often make a list of academic words that they call a *word bank* as they talk with ELs during prewriting so the children will have the words available when they're writing. Sometimes teachers include a few phrases they've practiced for children to use when they're writing.

Models. English learners often use a pattern book as a model for their writing. Pattern books help children move beyond personal writing, and they're useful in teaching new sentence structures. For example, children learn to write questions and answers as they make their own versions or innovations of Bill Martin Jr.'s *Brown Bear, Brown Bear, What Do You See?* (2008) and three of his books that follow the same pattern: *Panda Bear, Panda Bear, What Do You See?* (2007b) about endangered animals; *Baby Bear, Baby Bear, What Do You See?* (2007a), about animal babies; and *Polar Bear, Polar Bear, What Do You Hear?* (1992), about animal sounds. Children write innovations using *If You Give a Mouse a Cookie* (Numeroff, 1985), *The Cow Who Clucked* (Fleming, 2006), and other pattern books, too.

Focus on Ideas. Many young writers value correctly spelled words and neat handwriting over the clear communication of ideas; but as they learn to use the writing process, most children gradually understand that the focus is on developing ideas before they reach the editing stage, and that messy rough drafts are a good thing because they reflect thoughtful drafting and revising. English learners, however, often struggle to accept the notion that developing ideas precedes mechanical correctness. Teachers demonstrate the writing process using interactive writing to nurture ELs' appreciation of the concept that writers often make their papers messy as they improve them.

If teachers address these considerations, ELs are better able to grow as writers along with their classmates.

Teachers also vary the instructional procedures they use with emergent, beginning, and fluent EL writers. Teachers use the Language Experience Approach to demonstrate how speech is recorded (Rothenberg & Fisher, 2007). They help children organize their ideas into words and into one or more sentences, write the sentences, saying each word as they write it, and read the sentences. Later, children often copy the text underneath the teacher's writing and practice rereading it.

Beginning writers learn writing strategies and skills through interactive writing. As children take turns doing the writing, they learn to form letters correctly, spell high-frequency words and phonetically regular words, capitalize words, and add punctuation marks correctly. Teachers guide children, help them correct errors, and take advantage of teachable moments to provide instruction when children are most likely to learn from it. Children often practice what they've seen demonstrated when they're writing at writing centers or during writing workshop.

Once children become fluent writers, they still benefit from teacher scaffolding because they're continuing to deal with their limited knowledge of English vocabulary and linguistic structures. Teachers provide assistance by meeting with these children during prewriting and by conferencing with them while they're revising and editing their writing.

Assessing Children's Writing

Teachers assess both the process children use as they write and the quality of their compositions. They observe as children use the writing process to develop their compositions and conference with children as they revise and edit their writing. Teachers notice, for example, whether children use writing strategies to organize ideas for writing and whether they take into account feedback from classmates when they revise. So that children can document their writing process activities, teachers also have them keep all drafts, checklists, and rubrics in writing folders.

Teachers develop rubrics, or scoring guides, to assess the quality of children's writing (Farr & Tone, 1994). Rubrics make the analysis of writing simpler and the assessment process more reliable and consistent. They may have 4, 5, or 6 levels, with descriptors related to ideas, organization, language, and mechanics at each level. Some rubrics are general and are appropriate for almost any writing assignment, while others are designed for a specific writing assignment. Figure 11–7 presents a kindergarten writing rubric that teachers use to document young children's growth as writers. The Assessment Tools feature on page 311 presents information about locating rubrics on the Internet.

Children, too, can learn to create rubrics to assess the quality of their writing. To be successful, they need to analyze examples of other children's writing and determine the qualities that demonstrate strong, average, and weak papers; teachers need to model how to address the qualities at each level in the rubric. Skillings and Ferrell (2000) taught second and third graders to develop the criteria for evaluating their writing, and the children moved from using the rubrics their teachers prepared to creating their own 3-level rubrics, which they labeled as the "very best" level, the "okay" level, and the "not so good" level. Perhaps the most important outcome of teaching children to create rubrics, according to Skillings and Ferrell, is that they develop metacognitive strategies and the ability to think abut themselves as writers.

On-Demand Writing Tests. In most school districts, children take on-demand writing tests every year, and most states have implemented writing assessments, beginning

Figure 11-7 ◆ Kindergarten Writing Rubric

Exceptional Writer
4
- Writes several complete sentences or one more sophisticated sentence.
- Spaces between words and sentences consistently.
- Spells some high-frequency words correctly.
- Spells some consonant-vowel-consanant words correctly.
- Uses capital letters to begin some sentences.
- Uses periods and other punctuation marks to end some sentences.

Developing Writer
3
- Writes a complete sentence.
- Spaces between some words.
- Spells one or more high-frequency words correctly.
- Spells beginning and ending sounds in most words.
- Uses both upper- and lowercase letters.

Beginning Writer
2
- Writes from left to right and top to bottom.
- Spells one or more words using one or more letters that represent beginning or other sounds in the word.
- Rereads the writing with one-to-one matching of words.

Emergent Writer
1
- Uses random letters that do not correspond to sounds.
- Uses scribbles to represent writing.
- Draws a picture insted of writing.
- Dictates words or sentences.

in third or fourth grade. These writing tests present a prompt for children to respond to within a set time period, and they're scored using a 4- or 6-point scale. Good writing instruction is the best way to prepare children for on-demand writing assessments (Angelillo, 2005). Children who use writing strategies and skills, apply the six traits, and vary their writing according to genre will do well on almost any type of writing assignment. Nevertheless, writing tests place additional demands on children:

The Prompt. Children need to know how to read and interpret the prompt. They must identify the genre and the audience and look for clue words, such as *describe* and *convince*, to figure out what they're expected to do. Prompts usually have several parts, so children must consider the entire prompt carefully without jumping to conclusions.

The Topic. Children need to get used to writing on assigned topics that may not interest them, because they're accustomed to choosing their own.

Time Restrictions. Children need to practice writing under test conditions so they'll know how to allocate their time for planning, writing, and proofreading.

Teachers teach children about prompts, model how to write in response to a prompt, and have children practice taking writing tests.

Teachers use a four-step procedure with these steps to help practice for on-demand writing tests:

1. **Analyze the prompt.** Children read and analyze the prompt to determine what it's really asking them to do.
2. **Develop ideas.** Children brainstorm a list of ideas about the topic.
3. **Plan their writing.** Children create a graphic organizer with their plan for writing.
4. **Proofread.** Children take a minute or two at the end of the writing time to proofread their compositions and correct errors in spelling, capitalization, punctuation, and grammar.

Through these steps, children become familiar with the test-taking procedure. Shelton and Fu (2004) describe how a fourth-grade teacher interrupted her students' writing workshop to provide an intensive 6-week test preparation before the state on-demand writing assessment. During the preparation, children learned to read prompts, studied the two genres that might be tested, and practiced writing under test conditions. These fourth graders scored higher than the state average, but even though they did well, they disliked writing for the test and eagerly returned to writing workshop, where they chose their own topics, collaborated with classmates, and didn't have to adhere to time restrictions.

Assessment Tools

Writing

Teachers use rubrics to assess children's writing. Sometimes they create their own rubrics, but at other times, they use rubrics developed by the school district or state department of education. These rubrics are often used for yearly or quarterly mandated writing assessments. Basal reading programs and supplemental writing programs also provide rubrics.

In addition, teachers access writing rubrics that are posted online. Teachers often use Google or another search engine to locate an online rubric that's appropriate for their grade level or for a specific writing assignment. They also check these websites that offer collections of rubrics:

◆ **NWREL**
www.nwrel.org/assessmetn/scoring.php
Rubrics to assess the six traits of effective writing from the Northwest Regional Educational Laboratory, the group that developed this approach to writing instruction.

◆ **Read • Write • Think**
www.thinkfinity.org
Search for rubrics using the Thinkfinity Search Engine. Hundreds of rubrics, organized by grade level, for specific writing assignments are available.

◆ **Rubrician.com**
www.rubrician.com
This website has links to hundreds of writing rubrics at all grade levels.

◆ **Writing With Writers**
http://teacher.scholastic.com
Scholastic's collection of genre-related writing rubrics, including descriptive writing, biography, and poetry scoring guides.

Before they use any writing rubric, teachers should examine it, checking that it addresses the characteristics or qualities they've taught, varies the achievement of characteristics at each level, and is written in child-friendly language.

IF CHILDREN STRUGGLE...

When children aren't making adequate progress in writing, teachers step in to determine the problem and then intervene to address it. Emergent, beginning, and fluent writers exhibit different problems that reflect what they know about writing, so teachers start by identifying children's stage of writing development. They observe children as they write independently and with classmates, examine samples of children's writing, and talk with children about their writing as they analyze their problems.

If the children are emergent writers, teachers ask themselves these questions:

- Do children use pencils to print letters and letterlike forms?
- Do children print their names and other letters of the alphabet?
- Do children demonstrate an awareness of concepts about written language, including the direction of print on a page?
- Do children dictate words and sentences for the teacher to write?
- Do children write a few high-frequency words?
- Do children choose letters to represent words according to beginning sound?

Some children struggle because they don't understand how written language works and haven't developed concepts about print. Some aren't focusing on letters and words, and others aren't applying phonemic awareness and phonics concepts they're being taught to represent words with letters signifying beginning sounds. Teachers use shared reading and the Language Experience Approach in their interventions, and they also provide daily opportunities for children to write independently and with teacher guidance.

When children are beginning writers, teachers consider these questions:

- Do children write single-draft, multisentence compositions on a topic?
- Do children reread their writing and try to make it better?
- Do children sit in the author's chair to share their writing?
- Do children spell some high-frequency words correctly?
- Do children apply phonics and spelling strategies to spell other words?
- Do children use capitalization and punctuation?
- Do children use legible handwriting?

Beginning writers who struggle have developed concepts about written language, but they aren't aware of audience and haven't learned to develop ideas, spell words conventionally, and write legibly. Teachers design interventions that include using minilessons and interactive writing to teach writing strategies and skills, introduce the writing process, and provide daily guided and independent writing opportunities.

If children are fluent writers, teachers ask themselves these questions:

- Do children use the writing process to draft and refine their writing?
- Do children use writing strategies to solve problems?
- Do children apply their knowledge of the six traits when they revise their writing?
- Do children vary their writing according to genre?

Fluent writers' problems are difficult to identify and solve because as children get older, their problems become more complex. Teachers usually begin with the writing process and observe as children complete a writing project. Many struggling writers don't spend enough time gathering and organizing ideas before they begin writing, and they revise only superficially, if at all. Editing is another stumbling point because many struggling writers are poor spellers who can't catch the words they've misspelled during proofreading.

Ensuring that children understand and use the writing process goes a long way toward improving their writing. Teachers also provide time every day for these struggling children to write with teacher guidance and independently.

THE WRITING PROCESS IN ACTION

Teachers use an apprenticeship model of writing where they cultivate a community of writers, and children use the writing process to draft and refine their writing, as the first graders did in Mrs. Ockey's classroom in the vignette. Teachers use interactive writing to model how to apply the writing process, and they use writing centers and writing workshop to provide opportunities for children to do their own writing.

Interactive Writing

Children and the teacher create a text together in interactive writing and "share the pen" as they write it on chart paper (Button, Johnson, & Furgerson, 1996; McCarrier, Pinnell, & Fountas, 2000). The teacher guides children as they write the words and sentences on chart paper, taking advantage of opportunities to demonstrate how to form letters and think aloud about remembering the sentence they're writing. The teacher also explains about capitalizing names, using apostrophes in contractions, and adding quotation marks. As children learn more about written language, the teacher releases more and more responsibility to them, and they write longer texts.

Teachers use interactive writing to write class news, predictions before reading, retellings of stories, thank-you letters, math story problems, and many other group writings (Tompkins & Collom, 2004). Two interactive writing samples are shown in Figure 11–8 on page 315; the top one was written by a kindergarten class during a health unit, and the second sample is a first-grade class's interactive writing of a math story problem. After writing this story problem, children wrote other subtraction problems individually. The boxes drawn around some of the letters and words represent correction tape that was used to correct misspellings or poorly formed letters. In the kindergarten sample, children took turns writing individual letters, and in the first-grade sample, the children took turns writing entire words, and the teacher wrote the letters written in black.

Teachers help children spell all words conventionally. They teach high-frequency words, assist children in segmenting sounds and syllables in other words, point out unusual spelling patterns, and teach other conventions of print. Whenever children misspell a word or form a letter incorrectly, teachers use correction tape to cover the mistake and help them make the correction. For example, when a child wrote the numeral *8* to spell *ate* in the second sample in Figure 11–7, the teacher explained that *eight* and *ate* are homonyms, covered the numeral with correction tape, and helped the child "think out" the spelling of the word, including the silent *e*. Teachers emphasize the importance of using conventional spelling as a courtesy to readers; in contrast to the emphasis on conventional spelling in interactive writing, children are encouraged to use invented spelling when writing independently at writing centers or during writing workshop.

Writing Centers

Teachers set up writing centers in preschool and kindergarten classrooms so that children have a special place to write. The center should be located at a table with chairs and equipped with a box of supplies containing pencils, crayons, a date stamp, different kinds

PreK Practices

Can 4-year-olds learn to write?

Preschoolers aren't too young to be writers (Schickedanz & Casbergue, 2009). They understand that print carries a message and that it's different than drawing. Many 4-year-olds incorporate writing into play activities; for example, they create signs for block constructions and write grocery lists in the housekeeping center. Others staple together booklets of paper and write books using a combination of drawing and scribbles to convey a message (Ray & Glover, 2008). Sometimes they remember the text long enough to reread it; at other times, however, it's forgotten as quickly as it's written. Once they learn to write their names, preschoolers acquire a stock of familiar letters to use in writing other words, and they begin to write simple messages that adults can decipher.

of paper, journal notebooks, a stapler, blank books, notepaper, and envelopes. The alphabet, printed in upper- and lowercase letters, should be available for children to refer to as they write. In addition, a crate with files for each child is needed so writers can store their work. They also send their completed writings to classmates using the classroom mail delivery system. Writers often place their messages in a box or bag at the center and each day one child delivers the mail.

When children come to the writing center, they draw and write in journals, compile books, and write messages to classmates. At first, they write single-draft compositions, but the social interaction that's part of life at a center encourages children to consider their audience and make revisions and editing changes. Teachers should be available to encourage and assist children at the center. They can observe children as they invent spellings and can provide information about letters, words, and sentences, as needed. If the teacher can't be at the writing center, perhaps an aide, a parent volunteer, or an older student might be able to assist.

Figure 11–9 on page 316 presents two compositions created by 5-year-olds at a writing center. The top sample shows an emergent writer's response to *If You Give a Mouse a Cookie* (Numeroff, 1985). The child read his writing this way: "I love chocolate chip cookies." The second sample was written by a beginning writer after listening to his teacher read *Are You My Mother?* (Eastman, 1966). The child wrote, "The bird said, 'Are you my mother, you big old Snort?'" After the child shared his writing, he added, "The mommy said, 'Here is a worm. I am here. I'm here.'" Notice that the words the mother said are written as though they're coming out of her mouth and going up into the air.

Young children also make books at the writing center based on books they've read. For example, they use the same patterns in *Polar Bear, Polar Bear, What Do You Hear?* (Martin, 1991), *The Very Hungry Caterpillar* (Carle, 1994), *No David!* (Shannon, 1998), and *Is Your Mama a Llama?* (Guarino, 2004) to create new versions called *innovations*. Beginning writers often use invented spelling as they write innovations, but they're encouraged to spell high-frequency and other familiar words correctly so that their writing is easier to read.

Writing Workshop

Writing workshop is the best way to implement the writing process (Fletcher & Portalupi, 2007). Children write on topics that they choose themselves and assume ownership of their writing. At the same time, the teacher's role changes from provider of knowledge to guide, and the classroom becomes a community of writers who write and share their writing.

Children have writing folders in which they keep all papers related to the writing project they're working on. Different kinds of paper, some lined and some unlined, are available, as are writing instruments, including pencils and red and blue pens. Children also have access to the classroom library because their writing often grows out of books they've read; they may write a pattern story or retell a story from a different viewpoint, for example.

Figure 11-8 ◆ Two Interactive Writing Samples

As they write, children sit at desks or tables arranged in small groups. The teacher cir-culates, conferencing briefly with everyone, and the classroom atmosphere is free enough that children converse quietly with classmates and move around to assist each other or share ideas. There's space for children to meet for writing groups, and often a sign-up sheet for writing groups is posted in the classroom. A table is available for the teacher to meet with individual children or small groups for conferences, writing groups, proofreading, and mini-lessons.

Writing workshop is a 60-minute period scheduled each day. During this time, chil-dren are involved in three components: writing, sharing, and minilessons. Sometimes teacher read-alouds are added when they're not used in conjunction with reading work-shop. The feature on page 317 presents an overview of the workshop approach.

Minilessons. Teachers teach minilessons on writing workshop procedures, writing strategies and skills, such as organizing ideas, proofreading, and using quotation marks, the six traits, and writing genres (Fletcher & Portalupi, 2007). Teachers often display an anonymous piece of writing (from a child in another class or from a previous year) for chil-dren to read and use it in teaching the lesson. Teachers also select excerpts from read-aloud books and mentor texts to show how published authors use writing strategies and skills.

Figure 11–9 ◆ Five-Year-Olds' Writing Samples

Writing. Children spend 30 minutes or longer working on writing projects. Just as children in reading workshop read at their own pace, in writing workshop, they usually work independently on writing projects they've chosen themselves. They move through the writing process as they plan, draft, revise, edit, and, finally, publish their writing:

Prewriting. Children choose topics and set their own purposes for writing. Then they gather and organize ideas, often drawing pictures, making graphic organizers, or talking out their ideas with classmates.

Drafting. Children work independently to write rough drafts using the ideas they developed during prewriting.

Revising. Children participate in small groups to share their rough drafts and get feedback to help them revise their writing.

Editing. Children work with classmates to proofread and correct mechanical errors in their writing, and they also meet with the teacher for a final editing.

Publishing. Children prepare a final copy of their writing, and they sit in the author's chair to share it with classmates.

At first children may use an abbreviated writing process, but once they've learned to revise and edit, they move through all five stages of the writing process.

Teachers conference with children as they write. Many teachers prefer moving around the classroom to meet with children rather than having writers come to a table to meet with them: too often, a line forms, and children lose precious writing time. Some teachers move around the classroom in a regular pattern, meeting with one-fifth of the class each day so that they're sure to conference with everyone during the week.

Other teachers spend the first 15 minutes of writing time stopping briefly to check on 10 or more children. Many use a zigzag pattern to reach all areas of the classroom each day. These teachers often kneel down beside each child, sit on the edge of the child's chair, or carry their own stool around to each child's desk. During the 1- or 2-minute conferences, teachers ask children what they're writing, listen to them read a paragraph or a page or two, and ask what they plan to do next. Then these teachers use the remaining time to conference more formally with children who are revising and editing their compositions. They identify strengths in children's writing, ask questions, and discover possibilities during revising conferences. Some teachers like to read the pieces themselves, and others like to listen to children read their drafts aloud. As they interact with children, teachers model the kinds of responses that children are learning to give to each other.

Children work with classmates to revise and edit their writing. They share their rough drafts in writing groups composed of three or four classmates. Sometimes teachers join in, but children normally run the groups themselves. They take turns

OVERVIEW OF THE INSTRUCTIONAL APPROACH

Writing Workshop

TOPIC	DESCRIPTION
Purpose	To provide children with opportunities for authentic writing activities.
Components	Writing workshop consists of writing, sharing, teaching minilessons, and teacher read-alouds to children.
Theory Base	The workshop approach reflects sociolinguistic and information-processing theories because children participate in authentic activities that encourage them to enjoy writing.
Applications	Teachers often add writing workshop to other instructional approaches so children have opportunities to use the writing process to develop and refine compositions.
Strengths	• Children learn to work through the stages of the writing process. • Activities are child directed, and children work at their own pace. • Teachers have opportunities to work individually with children during conferences.
Limitations	• Teachers often feel a loss of control because children are working at different stages of the writing process. • Teachers have the responsibility to teach minilessons on strategies and skills, both to the whole class and to children working in small groups. • Children must learn to be task oriented and to use time wisely to be successful.

reading their rough drafts to each other and listen as classmates offer compliments and suggestions for revision. Children also participate in revising and editing centers. They know how to work at each center and understand the importance of working with classmates to make their writing better.

After proofreading their drafts with a classmate and then meeting with the teacher for a final editing, children make the final copy of their writing. They often want to word process their writing so that it looks professional. Many times, children compile their final copies to make books, but sometimes they attach their writing to artwork, make posters, write letters that will be mailed, or perform scripts. Not every piece is necessarily published; sometimes children decide not to continue with a piece of writing, and they file that piece in their writing folders and start something new.

Sharing. For the last 10 minutes, children share their new publications (Mermelstein, 2007). Children take turns sitting in the author's chair to read their published writing aloud. After each sharing, classmates clap and offer compliments. They may also make other comments and suggestions, but the focus is on celebrating completed writing projects, not on revising them.

REALITY CHECK!
Managing Writing Workshop

It takes time to implement the workshop approach because children have to learn how to use the writing process to develop and refine a piece of writing and other workshop procedures (Gillet & Beverly, 2001). Some children expect to write single-draft compositions because that's what they're used to doing, or they complain that they don't know what to write about because they're used to having their teachers supply the topics. But with careful instruction and clear guidelines, even young children can learn to use writing workshop, as Mrs. Ockey's first graders demonstrated in the vignette at the beginning of the chapter.

Teachers develop a schedule for writing workshop, allocating as much time as possible for writing. The writing workshop schedule in first- and second-grade classrooms often looks like this:

8:45–9:05   Minilesson

9:05–9:35   Writing

9:35–9:45   Sharing

After developing the schedule, teachers post it in the classroom and talk to children about the activities and their expectations. Teachers teach the workshop procedures and continue to model them until children become comfortable with the routines. As children gain experience with the workshop approach, their enthusiasm grows and the workshop approach is successful.

Teachers monitor children's progress on their writing projects using a classroom chart that Nancie Atwell (1998) calls "status of the class"; a third-grade class chart is

Figure 11-10 ◆ Status of the Class Chart

Names	Dates 3/15	3/16	3/17	3/18	3/19	3/22	3/23	3/24
Antonio	4	5	5	5	5	1	1	1 2
Bella	2	2	2 3	2	2	4	5	5
Charles	3	3 1	1	2	2 3	4	5	5
Dina	4 5	5	5	1	1	1	1	2 3
Dustin	3	3	4	4	4	5	5 1	1
Eddie	2 3	2	2 4	5	5	1	1 2	2 3
Elizabeth	2	3	3	4	4	4 5	5	1 2
Elsa	1 2	3 4	4 5	5	5	1	2	2

Code:

1 = Prewriting   2 = Drafting   3 = Revising   4 = Editing   5 = Publishing

shown in Figure 11–10. At the beginning of each writing workshop session, children identify the stage of the writing process they're involved in and write it on the chart. If they move to another stage during the writing period, they also write in that number. This chart provides a quick way for teachers to assess whether children are moving through the writing process at a reasonable pace, determine if any one is "stuck," decide who is ready for a revising or editing conference, and choose children to sit in the author's chair to share their writing.

CHAPTER Review

How Effective Teachers Scaffold Children's Writing Development

▶ Teachers teach children to use the writing process—prewriting, drafting, revising, editing, and publishing—to write and refine their compositions.

▶ Teachers adapt the writing process so that young children can become authors.

▶ Teachers teach children about the six traits of effective writing—ideas, organization, voice, word choice, sentence fluency, and mechanics.

▶ Teachers involve children in writing workshop and other authentic writing activities.

Chapter 12

Integrating Literacy Into Thematic Units

Third Graders Create Multigenre Projects

Mrs. Zumwalt's third graders are studying ocean animals, and her focus is adaptation: How do animals adapt to survive in the ocean? As the children learn about ocean life, they take special notice of how individual animals adapt. For example, Alyssa learns that whelks have hard shells to protect them, Aidan knows that some small fish travel together in schools, Cody reports that clams burrow into the sand to be safe, and Christopher read that sea otters have thick fur to keep them warm in cold ocean water. Children add what they learn about adaptation to a chart in the classroom.

A month ago, Mrs. Zumwalt began the unit by passing out informational books from the text set on ocean animals for children to peruse. After they examined the books for 30 minutes or so, she brought them together to begin a K-W-L chart. This huge chart covers half of the back wall of the classroom; three sheets of poster paper hang vertically, side by side. The first sheet is labeled "K—What We Know About Ocean Animals." The middle sheet is labeled "W—What We Wonder About Ocean Animals," and the one on the right is labeled "L—What We've Learned About Ocean Animals." Mrs. Zumwalt asked children what they already knew about ocean animals, and they offered many facts, including "sea stars can grow a lot of arms," "sharks have three rows of teeth," and "jellyfish and puffer fish are poisonous," which Mrs. Zumwalt recorded in the K column. They also asked questions, including "How can an animal live inside a jellyfish?" "Is it true that father seahorses give birth?" and "How do some fish light up?" which she wrote in the W column. The children continued to think of questions for several days, and Mrs. Zumwalt added them to the W column. At the end of the unit, they'll complete the L column.

Mrs. Zumwalt talked about the six ocean habitats—seashore, open ocean, deep ocean, seabed, coral reefs, and polar seas—and the animals living in each one. She began with the seashore, and the class took a field trip to the Monterey Bay Aquarium to learn about animals that live at the seashore. She focused on several animals in each habitat, reading aloud books and emphasizing how animals have adapted. For each habitat, they made a class chart about it, and children recorded information in their learning logs. They hung the charts in the classroom, and after all six habitats were introduced, Mrs. Zumwalt set out a pack of cards with names of animals and pictures of them for children to sort according to habitat. The box on page 322 shows the word sort.

Children have learning logs with 20 sheets of lined paper for writing, 10 sheets of unlined paper for drawing and charting, and 15 information sheets about ocean animals. There's also a page for a personal word wall that's divided into nine boxes and labeled with letters of the alphabet; children record words from the class word wall on their personal word walls. Mrs. Zumwalt introduces new words during her presentations and as she reads aloud books from the text set on ocean animals; then she adds them to the word wall.

Eight of her 20 third graders come from homes where Spanish is spoken, and these children struggle with oral and written English. Mrs. Zumwalt brings them together most days for an extra lesson while their classmates work on other activities; she either previews the next lesson she'll teach or the next book she'll read, or she reviews her last lesson or the last book she read. In this small-group setting, children talk about what they're learning, ask questions, examine artifacts and pictures, and practice vocabulary. They often create interactive writing charts to share what they've discussed with their classmates. Here is their chart about schools of fish:

> There are two kinds of schools. Kids go to school to be smart and little fish travel in groups that are called "schools." Fish are safer when they stick together in schools.

Once the class became familiar with a variety of ocean animals, each child picked an animal to study; they chose sting rays, dolphins, squids, sea anemones, sand dollars, great white sharks, seals, penguins, sea turtles, jellyfish, octopuses, seahorses, pelicans, killer whales, barracudas, tunas, electric eels, lobsters, manatees, and squid. They researched their animals using books in the text set and online resources. After they became experts, Mrs. Zumwalt introduced the idea of developing multigenre projects about the animals they'd studied. For this multigenre project, children will create items representing different genres and package them in a box. Earlier in the year, the children worked collaboratively to develop a class multigenre project, so they were familiar with the procedure and the format.

Ocean Habitat Sort

Seashore	Open Ocean	Deep Ocean	Seabed	Coral Reefs	Polar Seas
shrimp	puffer fish	nautilus	sting ray	sea fan	penguin
sea gull	swordfish	sperm whale	nurse shark	coral	narwhal
sea otter	sea turtles		clam	barracuda	elephant seal
crab	manta ray		scallop		walrus
lobster	porpoise		sponge		leopard seal
octopus	dolphin		whelk		krill
pelican	squid				

The children decided to create four items for their multigenre projects: an informational book with chapters about their animal's physical traits, diet, habitat, and enemies and three other items. Possible items included an adaptation poster, a life-cycle chart, a poem, an alliterative sentence, a diagram of the animal, and a pack of true/false cards about the animal. They plan to package their projects in cereal boxes brought from home and decorated with pictures, interesting information, and a big idea statement about how that animal has adapted to ocean life.

The third graders used the writing process to develop their informational books. For prewriting, they used large, multicolored index cards to jot notes: green for "Physical Traits," yellow for "Diet," blue for "Habitat," purple for "Enemies," and pink for other interesting information. After they took notes using book and online resources, they shared the information they'd gathered one-on-one with classmates, who asked questions about things that confused them and encouraged the children to add more information about incomplete topics. Next, children wrote rough drafts and shared them with the partners they worked with earlier. Then they met in writing groups with Mrs. Zumwalt and several classmates and refined their drafts using the feedback they received from their group.

Now children are proofreading and correcting their revised drafts and publishing their books. Once they correct the mechanical errors and meet with Mrs. Zumwalt for an editing conference, they recopy their drafts in their best handwriting, add illustrations, and compile the pages into a hardbound book. They're also preparing their boxes and the other items for their multigenre projects.

Christian researched pelicans; his informational book is shown on page 323. In addition, he drew a life-cycle chart showing a pelican egg, a newly hatched bird in the nest, a young adult bird flapping its wings, and an older adult diving into the ocean for food; he made a Venn diagram comparing white and brown pelicans; and he wrote an alliterative sentence about pelicans using only words that begin with *p*. His multi-genre project box is decorated with pictures of pelicans and interesting information he collected, including "their wings are nine feet long" and "pelicans can live to be 25 years old." The adaptation statement on his multigenre box reads, "Pelicans have web feet and they can dive underwater to catch their food to eat. That's how they can survive at the seashore."

Today, the children finish the K-W-L chart by adding comments about what they've learned about ocean animals. Cody offers that "octopuses can change shape and color to camouflage themselves," Hernan reports that "dolphins' tails go up and down and fishes' tails go side to side," and Carlos adds that "jellyfish are related to sea anemones because neither one has teeth."

Next Monday afternoon, the third graders will share their completed multigenre boxes one-on-one with second graders, and that evening, they'll share them with their parents at back-to-school night. To prepare, the children have been sharing their projects in the classroom: Each day, three children sit in the author's chair to explain their projects and read their informational books aloud to the class.

Christian's Book About Pelicans

Chapter 1—Introduction
Pelicans are birds that live on the seashore. They have web feet for walking on sand and swimming. They can dive underwater to catch their food. That's how they live near the ocean.

Chapter 2—Physical Traits
Pelicans have some interesting physical traits. The pelican is easy to identify. They have big pouches and you can tell them by their big necks and plump bodies. The pelican has big legs and colors brown and white.

Chapter 3—Diet
Diet is what an animal eats. The pelican swallows a lot of fish. Pelicans gobble up meat. Pelicans attack sea stars and they chomp on seahorses.

Chapter 4—Habitat
A habitat is where an animal lives. The pelican lives in many countries. Pelicans are found where there's air and where it's warm. Some pelicans are now living in Monterey. Pelicans live by water, too.

Chapter 5—Enemies
Most animals are both prey and predator. That means animals are usually both the hunted and the hunter. The pelican eats seahorses and sea stars. Pelicans are hunted by sharks and people. Why do people hurt these birds? People dump waste into the water and it kills the fishes that the pelicans eat!

Chapter 6—Conclusion
I hope pelicans will always live in Monterey Bay but they could die if people dump pollution into the ocean and that would be very sad.

hildren read and write all through the school day as they learn science, social studies, and other content areas in thematic units. Just as Mrs. Zumwalt's third graders learned about ocean animals through reading and writing, children at all grade levels—even kindergartners and first graders—use reading and writing as tools to learn about insects, the water cycle, pioneers, space, the rain forest, and other topics. Teachers integrate the curriculum, breaking down barriers between subjects to make learning more meaningful, and organize content-area study into thematic units (Bredekamp, 1990). They identify big ideas to investigate because teachers can't try to cover every topic; if they do, children will learn very little. Units are time-consuming because child-centered learning takes time (Harvey, 1998). Teachers must make careful choices as they plan units, because only a relatively few topics can be presented in depth during a school year.

During thematic units, children have authentic opportunities to question, discuss, explore, and apply what they're learning. They use talking, reading, and writing as tools for learning and to demonstrate their learning as they give oral reports, create posters, write books, and develop projects. Thematic units are an important part of balanced literacy programs because they provide opportunities for real-world application of what children are learning about reading and writing.

ONNECTING READING AND WRITING

Reading and writing should be connected because reading has a powerful impact on writing, and vice versa (Tierney & Shanahan, 1996): When children read about a topic before writing, their writing is enhanced because of what they learn about the topic, and when they write about the ideas in a book they're reading, their comprehension is deepened because they're exploring big ideas and relationships among them. Making this connection is especially important when children are learning content-area information because of the added challenges that unfamiliar topics and technical vocabulary present.

There are other reasons for connecting reading and writing, too. Making meaning is the goal of both reading and writing: Children activate background knowledge, set purposes, and use many of the same strategies for reading and writing. In addition, the reading and writing processes are remarkably similar.

Reading Trade Books

A wide variety of high-quality picture books and chapter books are available today for teachers to use in teaching thematic units. Two outstanding science-related trade books, for example, are *Team Moon: How 400,000 People Landed Apollo 11 on the Moon* (Thimmesh, 2006), a stunning book that highlights the contributions of the people working behind the scenes on that space mission, and *Owen and Mzee: The True Story of a Remarkable Friendship* (Hatkoff, Hatkoff, & Kahumbu, 2006), a photo essay about a friendship between a giant tortoise and a baby hippo orphaned during a tsunami. Two notable trade books on social studies topics are *Freedom on the Menu: The Greensboro Sit-Ins* (Weatherford, 2007), a powerful book that tells the story of desegregation through the eyes of an 8-year-old, and *One Thousand Tracings: Healing the Wounds of World War II* (Judge, 2007), a moving picture-book story of an American family who started a relief effort that reached 3,000 people in war-ravaged Europe. Other informational books, such as *Martin's Big Words: The Life of Martin Luther King, Jr.* (Rappaport, 2007), *Through Georgia's Eyes* (Rodriguez, 2006), and *Wilma Unlimited: How Wilma Rudolph Became the World's Fastest Woman* (Krull, 2000), are biographies. These books are entertaining and informative, and the author's engaging writing styles and formats keep readers interested. They're relevant, too, because many children make connections to their own life experiences and background knowledge as they read these books, and teachers use them to build children's background knowledge at the beginning of a thematic unit.

Teachers share these trade books in many ways. They use **interactive read-alouds** to share some books that are too difficult for children to read on their own, and they feature others in literature focus units. They use related books at a range of reading levels for literature circles, and others for children to read independently during reading workshop. Because many books on social studies and science topics are available at a range of reading levels, teachers can find good books, many at their children's reading levels, to use in teaching in the content areas.

Check the Compendium of Instructional Procedures, which follows this chapter, for more information on highlighted terms.

Text Sets. Teachers collect text sets of books and other reading materials on topics to use in teaching thematic units, as Mrs. Zumwalt did in the vignette at the beginning of the chapter. Materials for text sets are carefully chosen to incorporate different genres, a range of reading levels to meet the needs of all children in the class, and multimedia resources that present a variety of perspectives. It's especially important to include plenty of books and other materials that English learners and struggling readers can read (Robb, 2003).

Teachers collect as many different types of materials as possible, for example:

- stories
- informational books
- poems and songs
- reference books
- websites

- videos and DVDs
- magazines
- photographs
- artifacts and models
- maps

Too often, teachers don't think about using magazines to teach social studies and science concepts, but excellent magazines are available, including *Click* and *National Geographic Explorer*. Some magazines are also available online, including *Time for Kids*. Figure 12–1 presents a list of print and online magazines.

Figure 12–1 ◆ Children's Magazines

Format	Magazines
Print	*Appleseeds* (social studies) (grades 3–4)
	Click (science) (preK–2)
	Faces: People, Places, Cultures (multicultural) (3–4)
	Kids Discover (science and history) (2–4)
	Ladybug (stories, poems, and songs) (preK–K)
	National Geographic Explorer (social studies) (3–4)
	Odyssey (science) (3–4)
	Ranger Rick (nature) (1–4)
	Spider (stories and poems) (K–3)
	Your Big Backyard (nature) (preK–1)
Online	*Odyssey*, odysseymagazine.com (science) (3–4)
	National Geographic Kids, kids.nationalgeographic.com (social studies) (3–4)
	Time for Kids, www.timeforkids.com (current events) (K–4)
	Ranger Rick, www.nwf.org/rangerrick (nature) (1–4)
	Your Big Backyard, www.nwf.org/kidzone (nature) (preK–1)

Mentor Texts. Teachers use stories, informational books, and poems that children are familiar with to model writing concepts (Dorfman & Cappelli, 2007, 2009). Picture books are especially useful mentor texts because they're short enough to be reread quickly. Teachers begin by rereading a mentor text and pointing out a specific feature such using a repetitive pattern, adding punch with strong verbs, or writing from a different perspective. Then children imitate the feature in brief collaborative compositions and in their own writing so that they have opportunities to experiment with literary devices, imitate sentence and book structures, try out new genres, or explore different page arrangements.

Informational books are often used as mentor texts to teach children about new genres, organizational structures, and page formats. One excellent mentor text is Margaret Wise Brown's classic, *The Important Book* (1990), which describes significant associations with common words. Children use Brown's text pattern to describe associations related to words and concepts they're learning. For example, a kindergarten class studying frogs composed this description, "The Important Things About Frogs":

> The most important thing about frogs
> is that they're amphibians.
> Frogs are cold blooded,
> and they hibernate during the winter.
> Frogs eat insects,
> and they're strong jumpers.
> But the most important thing about frogs
> is that they're amphibians—
> First they live in the water
> and then they live on land.

Another nonfiction mentor text is *Gone Wild: An Endangered Animal Alphabet* (McLimans, 2006), a graphic masterpiece where letters of the alphabet are transformed into vulnerable animals, and text boxes accompanying each letter provide information about the animal. Children can use this format to write a class alphabet book during a science or social studies unit.

Teachers use mentor texts in minilessons to teach children how to make their writing more powerful, and children use these books as springboards for writing as part of thematic units. Dorfman and Cappelli (2007) explain that "mentor texts serve as snapshots into the future. They help children envision the kind of writers they can become" (p. 3).

Writing as a Learning Tool

Children use writing as a tool for learning during thematic units to record information, categorize ideas, draw graphic organizers, and write summaries. The focus is on using writing to help children think and learn, not on spelling every word correctly. Nevertheless, children should use classroom resources, such as word walls, to spell most words correctly and write as neatly as possible so that they can reread their own writing. Armbruster, McCarthey, and Cummins (2005) point out that writing to learn serves two other purposes as well: When children write about what they're learning, it helps them become better writers, and teachers can use children's writing to assess their learning.

Figure 12-2 ◆ Two Pages From a Second Grader's Learning Log

Learning Logs. Children use learning logs to record and react to what they're learning. Robb (2003) explains that learning logs are "a place to think on paper" (p. 60). Children write in these journals to discover gaps in their knowledge and to explore relationships between what they're learning and their past experiences. They make notes of important concepts, reinforce the meaning and spelling of new vocabulary words, discover gaps in their knowledge, and explore relationships between what they're learning and their past experiences.

Teachers also have children keep observation logs in which they make daily entries to track the growth of plants or animals. A class of second graders took a walk in the woods wearing old socks over their shoes to collect seeds, in much the same way that animals pick up seeds on their fur coats and transport them. To simulate winter, the teacher placed the children's socks in the freezer for several weeks. Then they "planted" one child's sock in the class terrarium and watched it each day as they waited for the seeds to sprout. Two pages from a child's log documenting the experiment are presented in Figure 12–2. In the left entry, the child wrote, "No plants so far and still dirt!" In the second entry, he wrote, "I see a leaf with a point on it."

Quickwriting. Children use quickwriting to review what they're learning. This type of impromptu writing was popularized by Peter Elbow (1998) as a way to help children focus on content rather than mechanics. Children choose a topic and reflect on what they're learning about the topic on paper. They generate ideas and the words to express them, make connections among ideas, and draw conclusions. Emergent writers often do "quickdraws" in which they draw pictures and add a few words. During a thematic unit on the solar system, for example, fourth graders each chose a word from the word wall for a quickwrite. One child wrote about the red planet:

> Mars is known as the red planet. Mars is Earth's neighbor. Mars is a lot like Earth. On Mars one day lasts 24 hours. It is the fourth planet in the solar system. Mars may have life forms. Two Viking ships landed on Mars. It has a dusty and rocky surface. The Viking ships found no life forms. Mars' surface shows signs of water from long ago. It has now water now. And Mars has no rings either.

Quickwrites take only 5–10 minutes to complete, and they provide a good way of checking on what children are learning.

Graphic Organizers. Children make charts called *graphic organizers* to arrange information to highlight big ideas and relationships among them. These charts take many forms, and the form reflects the information being provided: When children chronicle the life cycle of a penguin, for example, they make a circle flow chart; when they compare penguins with other birds, they make a Venn diagram; when they identify a penguin's body parts, they draw and label a picture; when they brainstorm what makes a penguin unique, they make a cluster; and when they research penguins and other animals that live in Antarctica, they use a data chart to record information. Figure 12–3 presents a second grader's chart about penguins. The chart shows that penguins have three enemies—leopard seals, skua gulls, and people. Sometimes teachers want to prepare the diagram for children to fill in, but it's important that children learn to choose

Figure 12-3 ◆ A Second Grader's Chart About Penguins

the most appropriate format for themselves. Children in the primary grades need to learn to recognize text structures and how to represent them in charts.

DEMONSTRATING LEARNING

Children use writing and talking to demonstrate their learning when they write books and poems and make oral presentations to their classmates. Through these demonstrations, they synthesize their knowledge and apply it in new ways. In addition, children celebrate and bring closure to their study during a thematic unit.

Writing Projects

Children research topics and then use writing to demonstrate their learning. Because this writing is more formal, children use the writing process to revise and edit their rough drafts before making a final copy. They demonstrate learning by making reports, poems, and multigenre projects.

Reports. Reports are the best known type of writing to demonstrate learning; children write many types of reports, ranging from posters to collaborative books and individual reports. Too often, children aren't exposed to report writing until they are faced with writing a term paper in high school, and then they're overwhelmed with learning how to take notes on note cards, organize information, write the paper, and compile a bibliography. There's no reason to postpone report writing; early, successful experiences with nonfiction reinforce children's learning about content-area topics as well as enhance their writing abilities (Tompkins, 2008). Children often prepare these types of reports:

> **Posters.** Children combine visual and verbal elements when they make posters (Moline, 1995). They draw pictures and diagrams and write labels and commentary. For example, children draw diagrams of the inner and outer planets in the solar system, identify the parts of a complex machine, label the parts of a covered wagon and the essential provisions pioneers carried, identify important events of a person's life on a life line, or chart the explorers' voyages to America and around the world on a map. Children plan the information they want to include in the poster and consider how to devise an attention-getting display using headings, illustrations, captions, boxes, and rules. They prepare a rough draft of their posters, section by section, and then revise and edit each section. Then they make a final copy of each section, glue the sections onto a sheet of posterboard, and share their posters with classmates as they would share finished pieces of writing.

> **"All About . . . " Books.** The first reports that young children write are "All About . . . " books, in which they provide information about familiar topics, such as "Going to the Beach" and "Meat-Eating Dinosaurs." Young children write an entire booklet on a single topic; usually one piece of information and an illustration appear on each page. A page from a first grader's "All About Penguins" book is shown in Figure 12–4.

> **Alphabet Books.** Children use the letters of the alphabet to organize the information they want to share in an alphabet book. These collaborative books incorporate the sequence structure, because the pages are arranged in alphabetical order. Alphabet books such as *Z Is for Zamboni: A Hockey Alphabet* (Napier, 2002) can be

Figure 12-4　◆　A Page From a First Grader's "All About Penguins" Book

Penguins lay eggs and keep them worm with ther feets and ther stomechs.

used as models. Children begin by brainstorming information related to the topic being studied and identify a word or fact for each letter of the alphabet. Then they work individually, in pairs, or in small groups to compose pages for the book. The format for the pages is similar to the one used in alphabet books written by professional authors: Children write the letter in one corner of the page, draw an illustration, and write a sentence or paragraph to describe the word or fact. The text usually begins "_____ is for _____," and then a sentence or paragraph description follows. The "U" page from a fourth-grade class's alphabet book on the California missions is shown in Figure 12–5.

Class Collaborations. Children work together to write collaborative books. Sometimes children each write one page for the report, or they can work together in small groups to write chapters. Children create collaborative reports on almost any science or social studies topic. For example, they write collaborative biographies where each child or small group writes about one event or accomplishment in the subject's life, and then the pages are assembled in chronological order. Or, children work in small groups to write chapters for a report on the planets in the solar system or the Oregon Trail.

Individual Reports. Children write their own reports during thematic units. They do "authentic" research, in which they explore topics that interest them or hunt for answers to questions that puzzle them (Harvey, 1998; Stead, 2002). Children read books and interview people with special knowledge to learn about their topics, and increasingly they're turning to the Internet for information. After learning about their topics, children write reports to share their new knowledge.

Poetry. Children often write poems to demonstrate their learning. They write formula poems by beginning each line or stanza with a word or line, they create free-form poems, and they follow the structure of model poems as they create their own poems. Children use to these poetry forms to demonstrate content-area learning:

"I Am . . . " Poems. Children assume the role of a person and write a poem from that person's viewpoint. They begin and end the poem (or each stanza) with "I am _____" and begin all the other lines with "I." For example, a second grader wrote this "I am . . . " poem about Rosa Parks:

Figure 12-5 ◆ The "U" Page From a Fourth-Grade Class's Alphabet Book

I am Rosa Parks.
I didn't obey the bus driver.
I didn't want to sit in the back of the bus.
I said, "It's not fair!"
I want equal rights for everybody.
I am Rosa Parks.

List Poems. Children create a poem from a brainstormed list, following the models in Georgia Heard's (2009) book of list poems. Second graders collaborated on this list poem, "At the Aquarium," after a field trip; they worked with partners and in small groups to craft their lines, incorporating descriptive words and powerful verbs, and the teacher contributed the last two lines:

Gooey jellyfish floating by.
A blue lobster waving at us.
Seahorses holding tails.
Lionfish gobbling up shrimp.
Sharks circling round and round.
Electric eels shocking their prey.
A giant octopus changing colors.
Harbor seals catching fish.
Dolphins playing with their trainers.
Sea turtles swimming in slow motion.
Silly crabs walking sideways.
Kids pressing their faces against the glass,
wishing they were aquarists!

Found Poems. Children create poems by culling words and phrases from a book they're reading and arranging them into a free-form poem. Fourth graders created this poem about a Saguaro cactus after reading *Cactus Hotel* (Guiberson, 2007):

A young cactus sprouts up.
After 10 years only four inches high,
after 25 years two feet tall,
after 50 years 10 feet all.
A welcoming signal across the desert.
A Gila woodpecker,
a white-winged dove,
an elf owl
decide to stay.
After 60 years an arm grows,
the cactus hotel is 18 feet tall.
After 150 years 7 long branches
and holes of every size
in the cactus hotel.

Multigenre Projects. Children explore a science or social studies topic through several genres in a multigenre project (Allen, 2001), combining content-area study with writing in significant and meaningful ways. Romano (2000) explains that the benefit of this approach is that each genre offers ways of learning and understanding that the others don't; children gain different understandings, for example, by writing a simulated diary entry, an alphabet book, and a time line. Teachers or children identify a *repetend*, a common thread or unifying feature for the project, which helps children move beyond the level of remembering facts to a higher, more analytical level of understanding. In the vignette at the beginning of the chapter, Mrs. Zumwalt's repetend was adaptation, and in their multigenre projects, her children highlighted how the animal they studied adapted to life in the ocean.

Depending on the information they want to present and their repetend, children use a variety of genres such as these for their projects:

alphabet books	posters
biographical sketches	questions and answers
books	quotes
journals	reports
letters	riddles
maps	songs
photo galleries	Venn diagrams
poems	word sorts

Children generally use three or more genres in a multigenre project and include both textual and visual genres. What matters most is that the genres amplify and extend the repetend.

Not only can children create multigenre projects, but some authors use the technique in trade books; *The Magic School Bus and the Electric Field Trip* (Cole, 1999) and others in the Magic School Bus series are examples of multigenre books. Each book features a story about Ms. Frizzle and her children on a fantastic science adventure, and on the side panels of pages, a variety of explanations, charts, diagrams, and essays are presented. Together, the story and informational side panels present a more complete, multigenre presentation or project.

Oral Presentations

Teachers often have children develop and give brief oral presentations to demonstrate their learning. A good first oral presentation is to draw a picture to illustrate an important fact and share it with classmates. As children talk about the picture, teachers encourage them to use content-related vocabulary and to articulate the important facts. During a unit on the solar system, for example, children can draw a picture of a planet and then share their pictures with the class, pointing out several features of the planet that they included in their drawings.

A second quick and easy oral presentation is the question-and-answer report: Teachers and children generate a list of questions related to a unit, and then children develop very brief reports to answer the questions. For example, a child might prepare a report to answer one of these questions about the solar system: Is the sun a planet? What are the inner planets? Are there people living on other planets? A variation of the question-and-answer report is the true-false report: A child prepares a statement that could be either true or false, shares it with the class, tells whether it's true or false, and then gives a couple of reasons for his or her answer.

Another type of beginning presentation is the "three-things-I-know" report: Children choose a topic and develop a brief presentation to share three things that they know about it. For example, a first grader might share these three things about the moon:

The moon is the earth's satellite.

The moon reflects the sun's light.

Astronauts have walked on the moon.

When children give a three-things report, they often hold up three fingers and point to one finger as they talk about each thing.

As they gain experience, children develop the poise and confidence to give longer, more sophisticated oral reports. For these presentations, children follow several steps that are similar to the stages of the writing process. First, they focus their topics. For example, a presentation on the solar system is too broad, but one on whether life is possible on each planet is more specific and more interesting. Next, children identify several big ideas, gather information about each one, and decide how to organize the presentation. Third, children create a visual to support their presentation, such as a poster listing their big ideas, a chart with a diagram to help listeners visualize some information, or an illustration about their topic. Sometimes they also collect artifacts or prepare a costume to wear. Fourth, they rehearse their presentation, thinking about how they will share the information they've gathered succinctly and incorporate important vocabulary words. Finally, they give the presentation to their classmates.

Sometimes children give individual oral presentations, and at other times, they work in small groups and share the presentation. In a group presentation, each child is responsible for one part. For a presentation on whether life is possible on each planet, for instance, one child could delineate the qualities necessary for life and other children could explain whether each planet exhibits these qualities. In this way, children can tackle complex topics because they're sharing the responsibility.

Classmates who are the listeners also play an important role in successful oral presentations. Children should be attentive, listen to the speaker, ask questions, and applaud afterward. Young children are better listeners when they understand what's expected of them, when the presentations are brief and supported by visuals, and when only one or two are presented at a time.

THEMATIC UNITS

Thematic units are interdisciplinary units that integrate reading and writing with social studies, science, and other curricular areas. Children explore topics that interest them and find answers to questions they've posed and are genuinely interested in answering. Then children share their learning at the end of the unit, as Mrs. Zumwalt's children did in the vignette. They are assessed on what they've learned as well as on the processes they used in learning and working in the classroom.

How to Develop a Thematic Unit

To begin planning a thematic unit, teachers choose the general topic and determine the instructional focus using literacy and content-area standards. Next, they identify the resources they have available and develop their teaching plan, integrating content-area study with reading and writing activities. Teachers work through these steps in developing a thematic unit:

1. **Determine the focus.** Teachers identify three or four big ideas to emphasize in the unit because the goal isn't to teach a collection of facts but to help children grapple with several big understandings. Teachers also choose which literacy and content-area standards to teach during the unit.

2. **Collect a text set of books.** Teachers collect stories, informational books, and poems on topics related to the unit for the text set and place them in a special area in

the classroom library. Teachers will read some books aloud, and children will read others independently or in small groups. Other books are used for minilessons or as models or patterns for writing projects.

3. **Locate Internet and other multimedia materials.** Teachers locate websites, DVDs, maps, models, artifacts, and other materials for the unit. Some materials are used to build children's background knowledge, and others to teach the big ideas. Also, children create multimedia materials to display in the classroom.

4. **Plan instructional activities.** Teachers think about ways to teach the unit using reading and writing as learning tools, brainstorm possible activities, and then develop a unit plan with possible activities. They also make decisions about coordinating the thematic unit with a literature focus unit using one book related to the unit, literature circles featuring books from the text set, or reading and writing workshop.

5. **Identify topics for minilessons.** Teachers plan minilessons to teach strategies and skills related to reading and writing nonfiction as well as content-area topics related to the unit based on state standards and on needs they've identified from children's work.

6. **Consider ways to differentiate instruction.** Teachers devise ways to use flexible grouping to adjust instruction to meet children's developmental levels and language proficiency levels, provide appropriate books and other instructional materials for all children, and scaffold struggling children and challenge high achievers with tiered activities and projects.

7. **Brainstorm possible projects.** Teachers think about projects children can develop to apply and personalize their learning at the end of the unit. This planning makes it possible for teachers to collect needed supplies and have suggestions ready for children who need assistance in choosing a project. Children usually work independently or in small groups, but sometimes the whole class works together on a project.

8. **Plan for assessment.** Teachers consider how they'll monitor children's progress and evaluate learning at the end of the unit. In this way, they can explain to children at the beginning of the unit how they'll be evaluated and check to see that their assessment emphasizes children's learning of the big ideas.

After considering unit goals, standards to teach, the available resources, and possible activities, teachers are prepared to develop a time schedule, write lesson plans, and create rubrics and other assessment tools.

NURTURING ENGLISH LEARNERS

Teachers have two goals in mind as they consider how to accommodate English learners' instructional needs when they develop thematic units: to maximize children's opportunities to learn English and to develop content-area knowledge. They have to consider the instructional challenges facing ELs and how to adjust instruction and assessment to meet their needs (Peregoy & Boyle, 2008).

Challenges in Learning Content-Area Information. English learners often have more difficulty learning during thematic units than during literacy instruction because of the additional language demands of unfamiliar topics, vocabulary words, and informational books (Rothenberg & Fisher, 2007). Here are the most important challenges:

English Language Proficiency. Children's ability to understand and communicate in English has an obvious effect on their learning. Teachers address this challenge by teaching English and content-area information together. They use artifacts and visual materials to support children's understanding of the topics they're teaching and simplify the language, when necessary, in their explanations of the big ideas. They consider the reading levels of the stories and informational books they're using, and when children can't read these books themselves, they read them read them aloud. But if the books are still too difficult, they find others to use instead. Teachers also provide frequent opportunities for ELs to use the new vocabulary as they talk informally about the topics they're learning.

Background Knowledge. English learners often lack the necessary background knowledge about content-area topics, so teachers need to take time to expand children's knowledge base using artifacts, photos, models, picture books, videos, and field trips, and they need to make clear links between the topics and children's past experiences and previous thematic units; otherwise, the instruction won't be meaningful. Finding time to preteach this information isn't easy, but without it, English learners aren't likely to learn much during the unit. Teachers also involve all children, including ELs, in activities to activate their background knowledge.

Vocabulary. English learners are often unfamiliar with content-area vocabulary because these words aren't used in everyday conversation; they're technical terms, such as *pioneer, democracy, scavenger,* and *amphibian*. Because some words, such as *democracy,* are cognates, children who speak Spanish or another Latin-based language at home may be familiar with them, but other Tier 3 words entered English from other languages. Teachers address this challenge by preteaching key vocabulary words, posting words (with picture clues, if needed) on **word walls**, and using artifacts, photos, and picture books to introduce the words. They also involve children in vocabulary activities, including making word posters and doing **word sorts**.

Reading. Informational books are different than stories: Authors organize facts differently, incorporate special features, and use more sophisticated sentence structures. In addition, nonfiction text is dense, packed with facts and technical vocabulary. Teachers address the challenge of an unfamiliar genre in three ways. First, they teach children about informational books, including the expository text structures and the distinctive text features of this genre. Next, they teach the strategies that readers use to comprehend informational books, including determining the big ideas and summarizing. Third, they teach ELs to make graphic organizers to highlight the big ideas and the relationships among them. Through this instruction, English learners are equipped with the necessary tools to read informational books more effectively.

Writing. Writing is difficult for English learners because it reflects their English proficiency, but it also supports their learning of content knowledge and English. All children should use writing as a tool for learning during thematic units. As they draw graphic organizers, make charts, and write in learning logs, they're grappling with the big ideas and the vocabulary they're learning. Children also use writing to demonstrate learning. This more formal writing is much harder for English learners because of increased language demands, so teachers choose projects that require less writing or have children work with partners or in small groups.

These challenges are primarily the result of the children's limited knowledge of English, and when teachers differentiate instruction, ELs are more likely to be successful in learning content-area information and developing English language proficiency.

Adjusting Instruction. Teachers differentiate instruction to maximize children's learning. They encourage children's participation in instructional activities because many ELs avoid interacting with mainstream classmates or fear asking questions in class (Peregoy & Boyle, 2008; Rothenberg & Fisher, 2007). Teachers adjust their instruction in these ways:

- Use visuals and manipulatives, including artifacts, videos, photographs, and models
- Preteach big ideas and key vocabulary
- Teach children about expository text structures
- Use graphic organizers to highlight relationships among big ideas
- Organize children to work in small collaborative groups and with partners
- Include frequent opportunities for children to talk informally about big ideas
- Provide opportunities for children to use oral language, reading, and writing
- Collect text sets, including picture books and online resources
- Review big ideas and key vocabulary

These suggestions take into account children's level of English development, their limited background knowledge and vocabulary about many topics, and their reading and writing levels.

Choosing Alternative Assessments. Teachers monitor English learners' progress by observing them and asking questions. Too often, teachers ask ELs if they understand, but that usually isn't effective, because they tend respond positively, even when they're confused. It's more productive to interact with children, talking with them about the activity they're involved in or asking questions about the book they're reading.

Teachers also devise alternative assessments to learn more about English learners' achievement when they have difficulty on regular evaluations (Rothenberg & Fisher, 2007). For example, instead of writing a composition, children can draw pictures or graphic organizers about the big ideas and add words from the word wall to label them to demonstrate their learning, or they can talk about what they've learned in a conference. When it's important to have English learners create written projects, they'll be more successful if they work with partners and in small groups. Portfolios are especially useful in documenting ELs' achievement. Children place work samples in their portfolios to show what they've learned about content-area topics and how their English proficiency has developed.

Topics for Thematic Units

Teachers develop thematic units on a variety of topics. Figure 12–6 lists possible topics for thematic units at each grade level. The units teachers develop are organized to provide opportunities for children to apply what they're learning about reading and writing as well as to meet grade-level standards.

A First-Grade Unit on Trees. A 4-week unit plan on trees is shown on pages 340–341. In this unit, first graders learn about trees and their importance to people and animals. Children observe trees in their community and learn to identify the parts of a tree and types of trees. Teachers use the interactive read-aloud procedure to share books from the text set and list important words on the word wall. A collection of leaves, photos of trees, pictures of animals that live in trees, and products that come from trees is displayed in the classroom, and children learn about categorizing as they sort types of leaves, shapes of trees, foods that grow on trees and those that don't, and animals that live in trees and those that don't. Children learn how to use writing as a tool for

Figure 12–6 ◆ Topics for Thematic Units

Prekindergarten	Kindergarten	First Grade
Caring for Pets	Zoo Animals	Animals Around the World
Comparing Animals and Plants	Plants	How Plants Grow
Farm Animals	Water	Solids, Liquids, and Gases
Floating and Sinking	Being a Scientist	Energy
All About Me	Five Senses	Weather
My Family	Being Healthy	Trees
Celebrations and Traditions	My School	My Neighborhood
Houses	We Are Americans	Traditions
	Foods Around the World	Homes Around the World

Second Grade	Third Grade	Fourth Grade
Animal Life Cycles	Ecosystems (Deserts, Ponds,	Food Chains
Motion	Oceans, Rain Forests)	Electricity
Sound	Types of Animals (Mammals,	Light
Water Cycle	Birds, Fish, Reptiles,	Solar System
The Earth's Surface	Amphibians, Insects)	Rocks and Minerals
People Grow and Change	Properties of Matter	Ecology
Nutrition	My County	Archeology
My Town or City	American Indians	My State
Inventors and Inventions	Pioneers	Immigrants
Patriotism		Famous Americans

learning as they make entries in learning logs, and teachers use interactive writing to make charts about the big ideas. They also view information on bookmarked websites to learn more about trees. As a culminating activity, children plant a tree at their school or participate in a community tree-planting campaign.

In this unit, teachers differentiate instruction in several ways. First, teachers include books in the text set that match children's reading levels; if they can't find books for emergent readers, they collaborate with these young children to make pattern books that they can read. One adaptable pattern is "I see _____ tree":

- Children use the pattern to make a number book.

  I see 1 tree.
  I see 2 trees.
  I see 3 trees.

- Children add color words.

  I see a green tree.
  I see a purple tree.
  I see an orange tree.

- Children combine a number and a color on each page.

  I see 3 brown trees.
  I see 4 yellow trees.
  I see 5 red trees.

- Children name different species of trees.

  I see a maple tree.
  I see a pine tree.
  I see a dogwood tree.

- Children incorporate a more complex sentence pattern.

  I see a bird in a little tree.
  I see a squirrel in a big tree.
  I see 3 bees in an apple tree.

They illustrate the pages, usually with drawings, but for the tree species book, they use photos taken during a field trip.

Second, teachers vary the grouping patterns: Some instruction is presented to the whole class, but children are organized into small groups and pairs for other activities. Teachers use small groups for **shared reading** and interactive writing activities, and children read books from the text set and make posters with partners if they're more successful working with a classmate. Children also examine tree artifacts, read books, and write books independently.

Third, teachers adapt activities to accommodate children's instructional needs, checking children's background knowledge at the beginning of the unit and adjusting instruction accordingly. They focus their instruction on the big ideas using a combination of oral, visual, written, and digital activities; for example, children listen to books read aloud, participate in discussions, make charts and diagrams, post words on the **word wall**, participate in interactive writing, and visit websites as they learn about trees.

Teachers also differentiate children's culminating projects about trees. Some projects involve the whole class, and children work with partners or individually on others. The tree-planting project that grew out of a child's suggestion involves the whole class; children work together to make multigenre projects and class scrapbooks, and work individually or with partners to write "All About Trees" books. Teachers recognize that children's books will vary, because some first graders write three-page books with one sentence on each page, some craft seven- or eight-page books with several sentences and informative diagrams on each page, and others dictate a sentence or two that the teacher writes for them.

Teachers link assessment with instruction in this thematic unit. At the beginning of the unit, they survey children's background knowledge using a **K-W-L chart**. During the unit, teachers monitor children's progress as they observe children, listening to their comments during discussions and watching them participating in activities. At the end of the unit, teachers evaluate children's learning without using tests; instead, they ask children to demonstrate what they've learned by drawing and labeling a picture about one of the big ideas they've studied, or they examine the information that children include in their "All About Trees" books. Teachers also gauge children's learning as they finish the last column of the K-W-L chart.

A Fourth-Grade Unit on the Desert Ecosystem. A 3-week plan for a unit on desert life is presented on pages 342–343. In this unit, children investigate the plants, animals, and people that live in the desert and learn how they support each other. They write entries in learning logs to take notes, draw diagrams, record words they're learning, and write reactions to books they're reading. Children divide into book clubs during the first week to read books about the desert. During the second week, children participate in an author study of Byrd Baylor, a woman who lives in the desert and writes

A Plan for a First-Grade Unit on Trees

UNIT INTRODUCTION

- Take a walking field trip through the neighborhood to look at trees and take photos of them.
- Begin a K-W-L chart about trees.
- View websites about trees, including Trees Are Terrific (www.urbanext.uiuc.edu/trees1) and Exploring the Secret Life of Trees (www.urbanext.uiuc.edu/trees2).
- Read one or more books from the text set.
- Examine a collection of artifacts about trees.

TEXT SET

Brown, R. (2007). *The old tree*. Cambridge, MA: Candlewick Press.

Cherry, L. (2000). *The great kapok tree*. Orlando: Harcourt.

Ehlert, L. (1999). *Red leaf, yellow leaf*. Orlando: Harcourt.

Ganeri, A. (2006). *From seed to apple*. Portsmouth, NH: Heinemann.

Gibbons, G. (2002). *Tell me, tree: All about trees for kids*. Boston: Little, Brown.

Hiscock, B. (1999). *The big tree*. Honesdale, PA: Boyds Mills Press.

Iverson, D. (1999). *My favorite tree: Terrific trees of North America*. Nevada City, CA: Dawn.

Miller, D. S. (2002). *Are trees alive?* New York: Walker.

Pfeffer, E. W. (2007). *A log's life*. New York: Simon & Schuster.

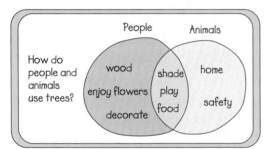

How do people and animals use trees?

People / Animals

wood, enjoy flowers, decorate / shade, play, food / home, safety

What Trees Need

Trees need 3 things to live. They need sunlight to shine on them. They need water because they get thirsty. They need good soil to grow strong. With these 3 things trees will be healthy.

Tree Shapes

1
2
3

USING THE TEXT SET

- Read books using interactive read-alouds.
- Use shared reading to read big books.
- Do book talks to interest children in looking at or reading some of the books.
- Have children read those books at their reading level at the reading center.
- Examine nonfiction text factors in informational books.
- Use books as mentor texts or models for writing.

DIGGING INTO THE BIG IDEAS

- Use interactive writing to create charts about the parts of a tree, how we use trees, or what trees need to live.
- Write a big book about the foods that come from trees.
- Do a semantic feature analysis to classify animals that live in trees.
- Draw a Venn diagram to compare the ways people and animals use trees.
- Create a poster about the shapes of trees or features of leaves.

WORD WALL

AB	CDEFGH	IJKLM
bark	fruit	leaf
branch	flower	leaves
birds	evergreen	kapok
acorn	chocolate	jagged
apples		maple syrup
beaver		

NO	PQR	STUVWYZ
nest	root	trunk
oak	paper	smooth
needle	rough	wood
nuts	palm	seed
owl	pine	squirrel
oxygen	rain forest	shade
		vein

VOCABULARY ACTIVITIES

- Add new words to the word wall.
- Make word posters.
- Highlight words in books children are reading and around the classroom.
- Do word sorts.
- Have children label pictures they draw with words on the word wall.

DIFFERENTIATION

- **Books:** Include books at children's reading levels in the text set.
- **Grouping:** Incorporate small-group, partner, individual, and whole-class activities into the unit.
- **Activities:** Use the Language Experience Approach and interactive writing to support emergent writers, and shared reading for emergent readers.
- **Projects:** Have children create collaborative projects.

CULMINATING PROJECTS

- Plant a tree at school or join with a community group to plant a tree in the neighborhood.
- Write "All About Trees" books.
- Develop a class multigenre project about trees.
- Make a class scrapbook of tree photos taken at the beginning of the unit with sentences to describe each one.

CENTERS

- **Reading:** Read books from the text set.
- **Listening:** Listen to a book from the text set.
- **Word Sort:** Do word sorts using vocabulary from the word wall.
- **Learning Logs:** Draw and write about trees in learning logs.
- **Art:** Paint a picture of a tree in each season, dictate or write a descriptive sentence to describe each one, and compile the pages to make a book.
- **Science:** Examine and sort leaves, bark, nuts, plastic fruits, and other artifacts related to trees.
- **Writing:** Write poems and riddles about trees.
- **Computers:** View bookmarked websites about trees.

ASSESSMENT

- **Survey:** Check children's background knowledge about trees using the K column of the K-W-L chart.
- **Monitor:** Ask children to choose one word from the word wall to talk, draw, or write about, and observe children as they participate in activities.
- **Evaluate:** Have children draw and label a picture about one big idea to demonstrate learning, check the information children include in their "All About Trees" books, and complete the K-W-L chart.

A Plan for a Fourth-Grade Unit on the Desert Ecosystem

UNIT INTRODUCTION

- Begin a K-W-L chart about the desert ecosystem.
- Share one or more books from the text set.
- Have children participate in a tea party activity.
- Visit theme-related websites, including Desert Biomes (www.desertusa.com) and A Virtual Museum of the Mojave Desert (http://score.rims.k12.ca.us/activity/mojave).

DIFFERENTIATION

- **Books:** Include books at all children's reading level in the text set.
- **Grouping:** Make available small-group and partner activities, including at centers, and provide small-group instruction.
- **Activities:** Include oral and visual activities, and provide plenty of opportunities for active involvement in activities.
- **Projects:** Design tiered projects and collaborative projects.

ASSESSMENT

- **Survey:** Use a K-W-L chart or have children write about what they know about this ecosystem in learning logs at the beginning of the unit.
- **Monitor:** Have children complete graphic organizers about big ideas, and write and draw pictures about big ideas in learning logs.
- **Evaluate:** Use rubrics to evaluate children's projects, and have children individually or with partners complete the L column of the K-W-L chart.

DIGGING INTO THE BIG IDEAS

- Create posters and graphic organizers about big ideas and relationships among them.
- Complete a semantic feature analysis comparing the desert to other ecosystems.
- Record information and explore ideas about deserts in learning logs.
- Research topics related to this ecosystem and share information in multigenre reports and other projects.

CENTERS

- **Data chart:** Record information about desert biomes on the ecosystem chart.
- **Listening:** Listen to a book from the text set.
- **Word sort:** Sort words from the word wall.
- **Visual literacy:** Create tabletop dioramas about various desert biomes.
- **Writing:** Prepare a page for the class alphabet book about deserts.

342

USING THE TEXT SET

- Use for interactive read-alouds.
- Read these books during reading workshop.
- Participate in literature circles using books from the text set.
- Do book talks to encourage independent reading.
- Use books in minilessons about genres, expository text structures, and nonfiction features.
- Use books as models or mentor texts for writing activities.

TEXT SET ON THE DESERT ECOSYSTEM

Bash, B. (2002). *Desert giant*. Boston: Little, Brown.
Baylor, B. (1993). *Desert voices*. New York: Scribner.
George, J. C. (1996). *One day in the desert*. New York: HarperTrophy.
Gibbons, G. (1999). *Deserts*. New York: Holiday House.
Gulberson, B. Z. (2007). *Cactus hotel*. New York: Holt
Jablonsky, A. (1994). *100 questions about desert life*. Tucson, AZ: Southwest Parks and Monuments Association.
Mora, P. (2008). *The desert is my mother*. Houston: Piñata Books.
Pratt-Serafini, K. J. (2002). *Saguaro moon: A desert journal*. Nevada City, CA: Dawn Publications.
Siebert, D. (1992). *Mojave*. New York: HarperTrophy.
Simon, S. (1990). *Deserts*. New York: Morrow.
Taylor, B. (1998). *Desert life*. New York: Dorling Kindersley.
Wright-Frierson, V. (2002). *A desert scrapbook*. New York: Aladdin Books.

VOCABULARY ACTIVITIES

- Post words on a ward wall.
- Make posters and diagrams to learn about key Tier 3 vocabulary.
- Use quickwrites to explore meanings of words.
- Do a word sort using words from the world wall.
- Create a class alphabet book about the desert using words from the word wall.

AUTHOR STUDY

- Share information about author Byrd Baylor, who lives in the Arizona desert.
- Read Byrd Baylor's books about the desert, including *The Desert is Theirs* (1987) and *Desert Voices* (1993).
- Write "I Am . . ." poems based on *Desert Voices*.
- Creates a multigenre project about the author and her books.
- Write letters to Byrd Baylor.

Byrd Baylor

I ♥ Deserts

CULMINATING PROJECTS

- Create a class multigenre project on deserts.
- Write a collaborative report about the desert ecosystem.
- Research a desert animal or plant and give an oral presentation about it.
- Design a chart to compare the desert ecosystem with another ecosystem.
- Develop a museum or online virtual museum about this ecosystem.

DESERT WORD WALL

ABC	DEFGH	UKL
biome	ecosystem	kangaroo rat
cactus	fragile	king snake
adaptation	gila monster	jackrabbit
coyote	dunes	Joshua tree
coral snake	endangered	lizard
camouflage	exoskeleton	javelina
burrow	hamster	
coyote	hawk	

MNO	PQRS	TVWXYZ
Mojave Desert	Sahara Desert	water
oasis	scorpion	tortoise
owl	Sonoran Desert	toad
	roadrunner	yucca
	sandgrouse	
	spiny	
	saguaro	
	sidewinder	

about desert life, and they read many of her books. During the third week, children participate in reading workshop to read other desert books and reread favorites. To apply their learning, children create projects, including writing desert riddles, making a chart of the desert ecosystem, and drawing a desert mural. Together as a class, children create a desert alphabet book.

Teachers differentiate instruction in this unit to allow for individual learning differences. They include books in the text set that match children's reading levels so everyone can participate in literature circles and reading workshop, and they emphasize learning in small groups through center activities, book clubs, and collaborative projects. Teachers include oral, visual, written, and computer activities in the unit. Children listen to book talks, participate in tea parties where they share cards about the desert ecosystem with classmates, do word sorts, complete semantic feature analysis charts, conduct research, write in learning logs, and view websites about deserts. Teachers also have children create culminating projects to share the results of their research about desert plants and animals; they incorporate individual, small-group, and whole-class projects, including multigenre projects, oral presentations, and virtual museums.

Assessment is an integral part of the desert ecosystem unit: Teachers survey children's knowledge about deserts when they start the unit, monitor their progress each week, and at the end evaluate their understanding of the big ideas they've studied. To begin, teachers survey children's background knowledge by creating a K-W-L chart and completing the K column. They monitor children's progress by listening to children's comments during discussions, reading their learning log entries, and reviewing the graphic organizers they complete. Teachers use rubrics to evaluate projects, and they have children use them to self-assess their own work. They also bring closure to the unit by completing the L column of the K-W-L chart.

CHAPTER Review

How Effective Teachers Integrate Literacy Into Thematic Units

▶ Teachers have children use reading and writing as learning tools.

▶ Teachers provide opportunities for children to use writing to demonstrate learning.

▶ Teachers organize content-area instruction into thematic units.

▶ Teachers focus on big ideas in thematic units.

Compendium of Instructional Procedures

Book talks are brief teasers that teachers give to introduce books and interest children in reading them. Teachers show the book, summarize it without giving away the ending, and read a short excerpt aloud to hook children's interest. Then they pass the book off to an interested reader or place it in the classroom library. Children use the same steps when they give book talks to share the books they've read during reading workshop. Here's a transcript of a third grader's book talk about Paula Danziger's *Amber Brown Is Not a Crayon* (2006):

> This is my book: *Amber Brown Is Not a Crayon.* It's about these two kids—Amber Brown, who is a girl, and Justin Daniels, who is a boy. See? Here is their picture. They are in third grade, too, and their teacher—his name is Mr. Cohen—pretends to take them on airplane trips to the places they study. They move their chairs so that it is like they are on an airplane and Amber and Justin always put their chairs side by side. I'm going to read you the very beginning of the book. [She reads the first three pages aloud to the class.] This story is really funny and when you are reading you think the author is telling you the story instead of you reading it. And there are more stories about Amber Brown. This is the one I'm reading now—*You Can't Eat Your Chicken Pox, Amber Brown* [1995].

There are several reasons why this child and others in her class are so successful in giving book talks. The teacher has modeled how to give a book talk, and children are reading books that they've chosen—books they really like. In addition, these children are experienced in talking with their classmates about books.

Procedure.   Teachers follow these steps in conducting a book talk:

1. Select a book to share.   Teachers choose a new book to introduce to children or a book that children haven't shown much interest in. They familiarize themselves with the book by reading or rereading it.

2. Plan a brief presentation.   Teachers plan how they will present the book to interest children in reading it. They usually begin with the title and author of the book, and they mention the genre or topic and briefly summarize the plot without giving away the ending. Teachers also decide why they liked the book and think about why children might be interested in it. Sometimes they choose a short excerpt to read and an illustration to show.

3. Show the book and present the planned book talk.   Teachers present the book talk and show the book. Their comments are usually enough so that at least one child will ask to borrow the book to read.

Teachers use book talks to introduce children to books in the classroom library. At the beginning of the school year, teachers take time to introduce many of the books in the library, and during the year, they introduce new books as they're added. They also introduce the books selected for a literature circle or a text set for a thematic unit.

Choral Reading

Children use choral reading to orally share poems and other brief texts. This group reading activity provides children, especially struggling readers, with valuable oral reading practice. They learn to read more expressively and increase their reading fluency. In addition, it's a great activity for English learners because they practice reading aloud with classmates in a nonthreatening group setting. As they read with English-speaking classmates, they hear and practice English pronunciation of words, phrasing of words in a sentence, and intonation patterns.

Many arrangements for choral reading are possible: Children read the text together as a class or divide it and read sections in small groups. Or, individual children read particular lines or stanzas while the class reads the rest of the text. Here are four arrangements:

- **Echo Reading.** A leader reads each line and the group repeats it.
- **Leader and Chorus Reading.** A leader reads the main part, and the group reads the refrain in unison.
- **Small-Group Reading.** The class divides into two or more groups, and each group reads part of the text.
- **Cumulative Reading.** One child reads the first line or stanza, and another child joins in as each line or stanza is read to create a cumulative effect.

Children read the text aloud several times, experimenting with different arrangements until they decide which one conveys the meaning most effectively.

Procedure. Here are the steps in this instructional procedure:

1. Select a text to use for choral reading. Teachers choose a poem or other short text and copy it onto a chart or make multiple copies for children to read.

2. Arrange the text for choral reading. Teachers work with children to decide how to arrange the text. They add marks to the chart, or they have children mark individual copies so that they can follow the arrangement.

3. Rehearse the text. Teachers read the text with children several times at a natural speed, pronouncing words carefully.

4. Have children read the text aloud. Teachers emphasize that children pronounce words clearly and read with expression. They can tape-record children's reading. Children can hear themselves, and sometimes they want to rearrange the choral reading after hearing a recording of their reading.

Choral reading makes children active participants in the poetry experience, and it helps them appreciate the magic of poetry. Many poems can be arranged for choral reading, and poems with repetitions, echoes, refrains, or questions and answers work well. Try these poems, for example:

"My Parents Think I'm Sleeping," by Jack Prelutsky (2007)

"I Woke Up This Morning," by Karla Kuskin (2003)

"Ode to La Tortilla," by Gary Soto (2005)

"The New Kid on the Block," by Jack Prelutsky (2000)

"A Circle of Sun," by Rebecca Kai Dotlich (Yolen & Peters, 2007)

Poems written specifically for two readers are very effective, including the book-length poem *I Am the Dog/I Am the Cat* (Hall, 1994). In addition, songs, such as Woody Guthrie's *This Land Is Your Land* (2002), work well.

Grand Conversations

Grand conversations are discussions about stories in which children explore the big ideas and reflect on their feelings (Peterson & Eeds, 2007). They're different than traditional discussions because they're child centered: Children do most of the talking as they voice their opinions and support their views with examples from the story. They talk about what puzzles them, what they find interesting, and their connections to the story. Children usually don't raise their hands to be called on by the teacher; instead, they take turns and speak when no one else is speaking, much as adults do when they talk with friends. They also encourage their classmates to contribute to the conversation. Even though teachers participate, the talk is primarily among the children.

Grand conversations have two parts. The first part is open ended: Children talk about their reactions to the book, and their comments determine the direction of the conversation; teachers share their responses, ask questions, and provide information. Later, teachers focus children's attention on one or two topics that they didn't talk about in the first part of the conversation.

Procedure.   Teachers follow these steps in using this instructional procedure:

1. Read the book.   Children read a story or part of story, or they listen to the teacher read it aloud.

2. Prepare for the grand conversation.   Children think about the story by drawing pictures or writing in reading logs. This step is especially important when children don't talk much, because with this preparation, they're more likely to have ideas to share with classmates.

3. Have small-group conversations.   Children form small groups to talk about the story before getting together as a class. This step is optional and is generally used when children are uncomfortable about sharing with the whole class or when they need more time to talk about the story.

4. Begin the grand conversation.   Children form a circle for the class conversation so that everyone can see each other. Teachers begin by asking, "Who would like to begin?" or "What are you thinking about?" One child makes a comment, and classmates take turns talking about the idea the first child introduced.

5. Continue the conversation.   A child introduces a new idea and classmates talk about it, sharing ideas, asking questions, and reading excerpts to make a point. Children limit their comments to the idea being discussed, and after children finish discussing this idea, a new one is introduced. To ensure that everyone participates, teachers often ask that no one make no more than three comments until everyone has spoken at least once.

6. Ask questions.   Teachers ask questions to direct children to aspects of the story that have been missed; for example, they might focus on an element of story structure or the author's craft. Or they may ask children to compare the book to others by the same author.

7. Conclude the conversation. After exploring all of the big ideas, teachers end the conversation by summarizing and drawing conclusions about the story or part of the story.

8. Reflect on the conversation. Children write (or write again) in reading logs to reflect on the ideas they've discussed.

During literature circles, children meet in small groups because they're reading different books, but when they're participating in literature focus units, children usually get together as a class.

Guided Reading

Guided reading is a small-group instructional procedure that teachers use to read a book with a small group of children who read at approximately the same level. They select a book at children's instructional level, that is, they can read it with approximately 90% accuracy (Fountas & Pinnell, 1996). Children do the actual reading themselves, usually reading quietly at their own pace through the entire book. Beginning readers often mumble the words softly as they read, which helps the teacher keep track of their reading and the beginning reading strategies they're using. Teachers use guided reading with young English learners just as they do with their native English-speaking classmates. Peregoy and Boyle (2008) point out that guided reading is effective because ELs experience success as they read interesting books in small, comfortable groups with teacher guidance.

Procedure. Teachers adapt the procedure for guided reading to meet their students' needs, but they generally follow these steps:

1. Choose an appropriate book. Teachers choose a book that children can read with 90% accuracy. They collect copies of the book for each child.

2. Introduce the book. Teachers set the purpose for reading and show the book's cover, reading the title and the author's name. Next, they activate children's background knowledge on a topic related to the book, often introducing key vocabulary as they talk. Children "picture walk" through the book, looking at the illustrations, talking about them, and making predictions. And finally, teachers review one or more of the reading strategies they've already taught and remind children to apply them as they read.

3. Have children read the book. Teachers provide support with decoding and reading strategies as children read. They observe children as they read and assess their use of word-identification and comprehension strategies. Whenever assistance is required, they help individual children decode unfamiliar words, deal with unfamiliar sentence structures, and comprehend ideas presented in the text. They offer prompts, such as "Look at how that word ends" or "Does that make sense?"

4. Encourage children to respond. Children talk about the book, ask questions, and relate it to others they've read. Teachers also compliment children on the strategies they used during reading.

5. Have children revisit the text. Teachers use the text that children have just read to demonstrate a comprehension strategy, teach a phonics concept or word-identification skill, or review new vocabulary words.

6. Provide opportunities for independent reading. Teachers place the book in a book basket or in the classroom library so that children can reread it.

Teachers teach guided reading lessons using leveled books while the other children are involved in other literacy activities; classmates are often reading independently, writing books, and doing phonics and spelling activities at centers. Teachers rotate the groups every 20–30 minutes so that children participate in a variety of teacher-directed and independent activities each day.

Hot Seat

Hot seat is a role-playing activity that builds children's comprehension. Children assume the persona of a character from a story, the featured person from a biography they're reading, or an author whose books they've read, and they sit in a chair designated as the "hot seat" to be interviewed by classmates. It's called *hot seat* because children have to think quickly to respond to their classmates' questions and comments. Children aren't intimidated by performing for classmates; in fact, in most classrooms, the activity is very popular. Children often wear a costume they've created when they assume the character's persona and share objects they've collected and artifacts they've made.

Procedure. Here are the steps in the hot seat activity:

1. **Learn about the character.** Children prepare for the hot seat activity by reading a story or a biography to learn about the character they'll impersonate.

2. **Create a costume.** Children design a costume appropriate for their character. In addition, they often collect objects or create artifacts to use in their presentations.

3. **Prepare opening remarks.** Children think about the most important things they'd like to share about the character and plan what they'll say at the beginning of the activity.

4. **Introduce the character.** One child sits in front of classmates in a chair designated as the "hot seat," tells a little about the character he or she is role-playing using a first-person viewpoint (e.g., "I was the first person to step onto the moon's surface"), and shares artifacts.

5. **Ask questions and make comments.** Classmates ask questions to learn more about the character and offer advice, and the child remains in the role to respond to them.

6. **Summarize the ideas.** The child doing the role-play selects a classmate to summarize the important ideas that were presented about the character. The child in the hot seat clarifies any misunderstandings and adds any big ideas that classmates don't mention.

When children participate in the hot seat activity, they deepen their understanding of the book they're reading. They explore the characters, analyze story events, draw inferences, and try out different interpretations.

Interactive Read-Alouds

Teachers use interactive read-alouds to share books with children. The focus is on enhancing children's comprehension by engaging them in the reading process before, during, and after reading. Teachers introduce the book and activate children's background knowledge before beginning to read. Next, they include children during reading through conversation and other activities. Afterward, children respond to the book. What's most important is how teachers engage children while they're reading aloud (Fisher, Flood, Lapp, & Frey, 2004).

Teachers often involve children by pausing periodically to talk about what's just been read. The timing is crucial: When reading stories, it's more effective to stop where children can make predictions and connections, after episodes that children

Interactive Techniques	
Stories	• Make and revise predictions at pivotal points. • Share personal, world, and literary connections. • Draw a picture of a character or an event. • Assume the persona of a character and share the character's thoughts. • Reenact a scene from the story.
Informational Books	• Ask questions or share information. • Raise hands when specific information is read. • Restate the headings as questions. • Take notes. • Complete graphic organizers.
Poetry	• Add sound effects. • Mumble read along with the teacher. • Repeat lines after the teacher. • Clap when rhyming words, alliteration, or other poetic devices are heard.

might find confusing, and just before the ending becomes clear. When reading informational books, teachers stop to talk about big ideas as they're presented, briefly explain technical terms, and emphasize connections between the ideas. Teachers often read a poem from beginning to end once, and then stop as they're rereading it for children to play with words, notice poetic devices, and repeat favorite words and lines. The box above lists interactive techniques. Deciding how often to pause for an activity and knowing when to continue reading develop through practice and vary from one group of children to another.

Procedure.　Teachers follow these steps to conduct interactive read-alouds:

1. Pick a book.　Teachers choose award-winning and other high-quality books that are appropriate for children and that fit into their instructional programs.

2. Prepare to share the book.　Teachers practice reading the book to ensure that they can read it fluently and to decide where to pause and engage children with the text; they write prompts on self-stick notes to mark these pages. Teachers also think about how they'll introduce the book and highlight difficult vocabulary words.

3. Introduce the book.　Teachers activate children's background knowledge, set a clear purpose for listening, and preview the text.

4. Read the book interactively.　Teachers read the book aloud, modeling fluent reading. They stop periodically to ask questions to focus children's attention on specific points in the text and involve them in other activities.

5. Involve children in after-reading activities.　Children participate in discussions and other response activities.

Teachers use this instructional procedure whenever they're reading aloud, no matter whether it's an after-lunch read-aloud period or during a literature focus unit or a thematic unit. Reading aloud has always been an important activity in preschool and kindergarten classrooms, but sometimes teachers think they should read to children only until they learn to read; however, reading aloud to share the excitement of books, especially those that children can't read themselves, should remain an important part of the literacy program at all grade levels.

Interactive Writing

Teachers use interactive writing to compose a message with children and write it on chart paper (Button, Johnson, & Furgerson, 1996). The text is created by the group, and the teacher guides children as they write it word by word. Children take turns writing known letters and familiar words, adding punctuation marks, and marking spaces between words. As children participate in creating and writing the text on chart paper, they also write it on small whiteboards. Afterward, children read and reread the text using shared reading at first, and then read it independently.

Interactive writing is used to demonstrate how writing works and show children how to construct words using their knowledge of sound–symbol correspondences and spelling patterns, and it's a powerful instructional procedure to use with English learners, no matter their age (Tompkins & Collom, 2004). It was developed by the well-known British educator Moira McKenzie, who based it on Don Holdaway's work in shared reading (Fountas & Pinnell, 1996).

Procedure. Teachers follow these steps to do interactive writing with small groups or the entire class:

1. Collect materials for interactive writing. Teachers collect chart paper, colored marking pens, white correction tape, an alphabet chart, magnetic letters or letter cards, and a pointer. They also collect small whiteboards, pens, and erasers for individual children's writing.

2. Set a purpose. Teachers present a stimulus activity. Often they read or reread a trade book, but children also share daily news or summarize information they're learning during a thematic unit.

3. Choose a sentence to write. Teachers negotiate the text—often a sentence or two—with children. Children repeat the sentence several times and segment it into words.

4. Pass out writing supplies. Teachers distribute individual whiteboards, pens, and erasers for children to use to write the text individually as it's being written on chart paper. They periodically ask children to hold their boards up to check their work.

5. Write the first sentence. The teacher and children slowly pronounce the first word of the sentence, "stretching" it out; children identify the sounds and the letters that represent them, and they write the letters on chart paper. The teacher chooses children to write letters and words, depending on their knowledge of phonics and spelling. They use a colored pen, and the teacher uses another color to write words children can't spell to keep track of how much writing children are able to do. Teachers have an alphabet poster with upper- and lowercase letters available for children to refer to when they're unsure how to form a letter, and white correction tape (sometimes called "boo-boo" tape) to correct poorly formed letters and misspellings. After writing each word, one child serves as the "spacer" and uses his or her hand to mark the space between words. This procedure is repeated to write each word in the sentence, and children reread the sentence from the beginning after each new word is completed. When appropriate, teachers point out capital letters, punctuation marks, and other conventions of print.

First Graders' Prediction About *Rosie's Walk* Written Interactively

6. Write additional sentences. Teachers follow the procedure described in the fifth step to write the remaining sentences to finish the text.

7. Display the completed text. After completing the message, teachers post the chart in the classroom and have children reread it, first using shared reading, and then independent reading. Children often reread interactive charts when they "read the room," and teachers use the charts in teaching high-frequency words and phonics concepts.

When teachers introduce interactive writing in preschool or kindergarten, they ask children to write letters to represent the beginning sounds in words and familiar words such as *the*, *a*, and *is*. As children learn more about phoneme–grapheme correspondences, they do more of the writing. The box above shows first graders' prediction about what will happen to a hen named Rosie that was written before reading *Rosie's Walk* (Hutchins, 2005). The children wrote the red letters and the teacher wrote blue ones; the rectangles represent correction tape used to cover errors. Once children write words fluently, they do interactive writing in small groups. Each group member uses a different color pen and takes turns writing words. They also sign their names in color on the page so that the teacher can track who wrote each word.

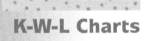

K-W-L Charts

Teachers use K-W-L charts during thematic units to activate children's background knowledge about a topic and to scaffold them as they ask questions and organize the information they're learning (Ogle, 1986). Teachers create a K-W-L chart by hanging up three sheets of butcher paper and labeling them *K*, *W*, and *L*; the letters stand for "What We **K**now," "What We **W**onder," and "What We **L**earned." A K-W-L chart developed by a second-grade class as they were studying the water cycle is shown on page 353. The teacher did the actual writing on the K-W-L chart, but the children generated the ideas and questions. It often takes several weeks to complete this activity because teachers introduce the K-W-L chart at the beginning of a unit and use it to identify what children already know and what they want to learn. At the end of the unit, children complete the last section of the chart, listing what they've learned.

Second-Grade K-W-L Chart on the Water Cycle		
K What We Know	W What We Wonder	L What We Learned
Water is very important. Animals and plants need water to drink. People need water, too. Water comes from the water pipes and the faucet in the kitchen. Water comes from oceans and rivers and ponds. We get water from the rain. Water sinks into the ground when it rains.	Where does water come from? Is snow like rain? How does rain get in the clouds? Why are clouds white? What is the water cycle? Why does it rain? What would happen if it never rained?	Water goes up into the air and makes clouds. The water cycle happens over and over. Water vapor goes up into the clouds. Another word for rain is precipitation. Water goes up, makes a cloud, comes down, and it starts all over. Evaporation is when water changes from a liquid to a gas. Condensation is the opposite of evaporation. Condensation is when water vapor changes into a liquid—water. You can't see water vapor because it is invisible.

Procedure. Teachers follow these steps to create K-W-L charts:

1. Post a K-W-L chart. Teachers post a large chart on the classroom wall, divide it into three columns, and label them *K* (What We **K**now), *W* (What We **W**onder), and *L* (What We **L**earned).

2. Complete the K column. At the beginning of a thematic unit, teachers ask children to brainstorm what they know about the topic and write this information in the K column. Sometimes children suggest information that isn't correct; these statements are turned into questions and added to the W column.

3. Complete the W column. Teachers write the questions that children suggest in the W column. They continue to add questions to the W column during the unit.

4. Complete the L column. At the end of the unit, children reflect on what they've learned, and teachers record this information in the L column.

Children also make individual K-W-L charts by folding a legal-size sheet of paper in half, lengthwise, cutting the top flap into thirds, and labeling the flaps *K*, *W*, and *L*. Then children lift the flaps to write in each column, as shown on page 354. Checking how children complete their L columns is a good way to monitor their learning.

A Fourth Grader's Flip Chart on Spiders

Language Experience Approach

The Language Experience Approach (LEA) is a reading and writing procedure that's based on children's language and experiences (Ashton-Warner, [1963], 1986). A child dictates words and sentences about an experience, and the teacher writes them. As the words and sentences are written, the teacher models how written language works. The text becomes the child's reading material. Because the language comes from the child and the content is based on his or her experiences, the child is usually able to read the text. A kindergartner's LEA writing is shown on page 355. The child drew this picture and dictated the accompanying sentence after listening to her teacher read Jan Brett's *Gingerbread Baby* (1999), a recent version of "The Gingerbread Man" story. This shared reading activity is an effective way to help children begin reading; even those who haven't been successful with other reading activities can read what they've dictated.

Procedure. This flexible procedure can be used with the entire class, with small groups, and with individual children, depending on the teacher's purpose. Teachers follow these steps when working with individual children:

A Kindergartner's LEA Writing Sample About *Gingerbread Baby*

The Gingerbread Baby runs and runs into the gingerbread house.

1. Provide an experience. The writing stimulus can be an experience shared in school, a book read aloud, a field trip, or something else, such as having a pet or playing in the snow.

2. Talk about the experience. The teacher and the child talk about the experience to review it and generate words so that the child's dictation will be more complete. Teachers often begin with an open-ended question, such as "What are we going to write about?" The child talks about the experience to clarify and organize ideas and use more specific vocabulary.

3. Record the child's dictation. The teacher takes the child's dictation. If the child hesitates, the teacher rereads what's been written and encourages him or her to continue. Teachers print neatly and spell words correctly, but they preserve children's language as much as possible. It's a great temptation to change the child's language to their own, in either word choice or grammar, but editing should be kept to a minimum so that children don't get the impression that their language is inferior or inadequate.

4. Read the text aloud. The teacher reads the text aloud, pointing at each word as it's read; this reading reminds the child of the content and demonstrates how to read the text aloud with appropriate intonation. Then the child reads along with the teacher, and after several joint readings, he or she reads it alone.

5. Make sentence strips. The teacher rewrites the text on sentence strips that the child keeps in an envelope attached to the back of the paper. The child reads and sequences the sentence strips, and once he or she can read them smoothly, the child cuts the strips into individual words and arranges the words into the familiar sentence. Later, the child creates new sentences with the word cards.

6. Add word cards to word bank. The child adds the word cards to his or her word bank (a small box that holds the word cards) after working with this text. These word cards can be used for a variety of activities, including word sorts.

LEA is often used to create texts children can read and use as a resource for writing. For example, during a thematic unit on insects, first graders learned about ladybugs and created a big book with this dictated text:

Part 1: What Ladybugs Do

Ladybugs are helper insects. They help people because they eat aphids. They make the earth pretty. They are red and they have 7 black spots. Ladybugs keep their wings under the red wing cases. Their wings are transparent and they fly with these wings. Ladybugs love to eat aphids. They love them so much that they can eat 50 aphids in one day!

Part 2: How Ladybugs Grow

Ladybugs live on leaves in bushes and in tree trunks. They lay eggs that are sticky and yellow on a leaf. The eggs hatch and out come tiny and black larvae. They like to eat aphids, too. Next the larva becomes a pupa and then it changes into a ladybug. When the ladybugs first come out of the pupa, they are yellow but they change into red and their spots appear. Then they can fly.

Part 3: Ladybugs Are Smart

Ladybugs have a good trick so that the birds won't eat them. If a bird starts to attack, the ladybug turns over on her back and squeezes a stinky liquid from her legs. It smells terrible and makes the bird fly away.

Each part was written on a poster, and they were bound into a book. After reading the book, children each chose a sentence to be written on a sentence strip. Some wrote their own sentences, and the teacher wrote them for others. After they practiced reading their sentences, they cut the sentences apart and rearranged the words, and finally they used the sentences in writing their own "All About Ladybugs" books.

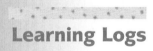

Learning Logs

Children write in learning logs during thematic units. Like other journals, learning logs are booklets in which children record information, write questions, summarize big ideas, draw diagrams, and reflect on their learning. Their writing is impromptu, and the emphasis is on using writing as a learning tool rather than creating polished products. Even so, children work carefully and spell content-related words posted on the word wall correctly. As teachers monitor learning logs, they quickly see how well the children understand the big ideas they're learning.

Procedure. Children construct learning logs at the beginning of a thematic unit and then write entries in them. Here are the steps in this instructional procedure:

1. Prepare learning logs. Children construct learning logs using a combination of lined and unlined paper that's stapled into booklets with cardboard or laminated construction-paper covers.

2. Have children write entries. Children take notes, draw diagrams and illustrations, list vocabulary words, and write summaries.

3. Monitor children's entries. Teachers read children's entries, answer their questions, and sometimes write responses.

4. Have children write reflections. Teachers often have children review their entries at the end of the unit and write about what they've learned.

Children use writing as a tool for learning as they write entries, and these journals document children's learning during a thematic unit.

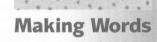

Making Words

Making words is a teacher-directed spelling activity in which children arrange letter cards to spell words (Cunningham & Cunningham, 1992). Teachers choose a key word from a book children are reading and then prepare a set of letter cards that children manipulate to spell words. The teacher leads children as they create a variety of words using the letters. For example, after reading *Diary of a Spider* (Cronin, 2005), a group of first graders built these short-*i* and long-*i* words using the letters in the word *spider*: *is*, *sip*, *rip*, *dip*, *drip*, *side*, *ride*, and *ripe*. After spelling these words, children used all of the letters to spell the key word—*spider*. As children make words, they're practicing what they know about phoneme–grapheme correspondences and spelling patterns, and teachers get feedback on what children understand, correct confusions, and review phonics and spelling concepts when necessary.

Teachers often use this activity with small groups of English learners to practice spelling strategies and skills. It's effective because ELs collaborate with classmates, and the activity is both nonthreatening and hands-on. Sometimes teachers bring together a group of ELs to do a making words activity as a preview before doing it with the whole class (or afterward as a review), and sometimes a different word is used to reinforce a spelling pattern that they're learning.

Procedure.   Here are the steps in making words:

1. Make letter cards. Teachers prepare a set of small letter cards with multiple copies of each letter, especially common letters such as *a*, *e*, *i*, *r*, *s*, and *t*, printing the lowercase letterform on one side and the uppercase form on the reverse. They package the cards by letter in small plastic bags or partitioned plastic boxes.

2. Choose a word. Teachers choose a word to use in the word-making activity, and without disclosing it, have a child distribute the needed letter cards to classmates.

3. Name the letter cards. Teachers ask children to name the letter cards and arrange them on their desks, with consonants in one group and vowels in another.

4. Make words. Children use the letter cards to spell words containing two, three, four, five, six, or more letters, and they list the words they can spell on a chart. Teachers monitor children's work and encourage them to fix any misspelled words.

5. Share words. Teachers have children identify two-letter words they made with the letter cards and continue to report longer and longer words until they identify the chosen word made using every letter card. After children share all of the words, teachers suggest any words they missed and point out recently taught spelling patterns.

Teachers choose words for word-making lessons from books children are reading. For example, the key word *hermit crabs* from Carle's *A House for Hermit Crab* (2005) offers many word-making possibilities. For additional ideas, teachers can check the collection of grade-level word-making books by Patricia Cunningham and Dorothy Hall (2008a, 2008b, 2008c, 2008d, 2008e).

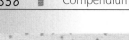

Minilessons

Teachers teach short, focused lessons called *minilessons* on literacy strategies and skills (Hoyt, 2000). Topics include how to write an entry in a reading log, make connections, insert quotation marks, and add inflectional endings. Teachers introduce a topic and connect it to the reading or writing children are involved in, provide information, and supervise as children practice the topic. Minilessons usually last 15 to 30 minutes, and sometimes teachers extend the lesson over several days as children apply the topic in reading and writing activities. It's not enough to simply explain strategies and skills or remind children to use them. Minilessons are an effective way to teach strategies and skills so that children actually do learn to use them. Teachers must actively engage children, encourage and scaffold them while they're learning, and then gradually withdraw their support.

Procedure. Teachers follow these steps to teach minilessons to small groups and to the whole class:

1. Introduce the topic. Teachers introduce the strategy or skill by naming it and making a connection between the topic and ongoing classroom activities.

2. Share examples. Teachers explain how to use the topic with examples from children's writing or from books children are reading.

3. Provide information. Teachers provide information about the topic and demonstrate how they use the strategy or skill.

4. Supervise practice. Children practice applying the strategy or skill with teacher supervision.

5. Assess learning. Teachers monitor children's progress and evaluate their use of newly learned strategies or skills.

Teachers teach minilessons on literacy strategies and skills as a part of literature focus units, reading and writing workshop, and other instructional approaches. Other minilessons focus on instructional procedures, such as how to use a dictionary or share writing from the author's chair, and concepts, such as homophones or adjectives.

Open-Mind Portraits

Children draw open-mind portraits to help them think more deeply about a character, reflect on story events from the character's viewpoint, and analyze the theme (McLaughlin & Allen, 2001). The portraits have two parts: the character's face on the top, "portrait" page, and several "thinking" pages revealing the character's thoughts at pivotal points in the story. The two pages of a second grader's open-mind portrait depicting the piglet who tells a hilarious tale about how she outwits a big, bad wolf in *Hog-Eye* (Meddaugh, 1998) are shown on page 359.

Procedure. Children follow these steps to make open-mind portraits while they're reading a story or immediately afterward:

1. Make a portrait of a character. Children draw and color a large portrait of the head and neck of a character in a story they're reading.

2. Cut out the "portrait" and "thinking" pages. Children cut out the portrait and attach it with a brad or staple on top of several more sheets of drawing paper. It's important that children place the fastener at the top of the portrait so that there's space available to draw and write on the "thinking" pages.

An Open-Mind Portrait of the Piglet in *Hog-Eye*

Portrait Page   Thinking Page

I am in big trubul. Oh yes, I know a good trick. I will call it Green 3 Leaf but it is itchy Poisun Ivy!!!

3. Design the "thinking" pages. Children lift the portrait page and draw and write about the character's thoughts at key points in the story.

4. Share the completed open-mind portraits. Children share their portraits with classmates and talk about the words and pictures they chose to include on the "thinking" pages.

Children create open-mind portraits to think more deeply about a character in a story they're reading in literature focus units and literature circles. They often reread parts of the story to recall specific details about the character's appearance before they draw the portrait, and they write several entries in a simulated journal to start thinking from that character's viewpoint before making the "thinking" pages. In addition to using this activity with stories, children can make open-mind portraits of historical figures as part of social studies units.

Readers Theatre

Readers theatre is a dramatic performance of a script by a group of readers (Black & Stave, 2007). Children assume parts, rehearse by reading their characters' lines in the script, and then do a performance for their classmates. Children interpret the story with their voices, without using much action. Readers theatre is an effective instructional procedure because children have opportunities to read good literature, and through this procedure they engage with text, interpret characters, and bring the text to life (Keehn, Martinez, & Roser, 2005). Moreover, English learners and readers who aren't fluent gain valuable oral reading practice in a relaxed small-group setting. The box on page 360 lists books of narrative and informational scripts for primary-grade students.

Readers Theatre Scripts

Barchers, S. I. (1997). *50 fabulous fables: Beginning readers theatre*. Portsmouth, NH: Teacher Ideas Press.

Barchers, S. I., & Pfeffinger, C. R. (2006). *More readers theatre for beginning readers*. Portsmouth, NH: Teacher Ideas Press.

Fredericks, A. D. (2007). *Nonfiction readers theatre for beginning readers*. Portsmouth, NH: Teacher Ideas Press.

Laughlin, M. K., Black, P. T., & Loberg, M. K. (1991). *Social studies readers theatre for children: Scripts and script development*. Portsmouth, NH: Teacher Ideas Press.

Martin, J. M. (2002). *12 fabulously funny fairy tale plays*. New York: Scholastic.

Pugliano-Martin, C. (1999). *25 just-right plays for emergent readers*. New York: Scholastic.

Shepard, A. (2005). *Stories on stage: Children's plays for reader's theater with 15 play scripts from 15 authors*. Olympia, WA: Shepard.

Wolf, J. M. (2002). *Cinderella outgrows the glass slipper and other zany fractured fairy tale plays*. New York: Scholastic.

Wolfman, J. (2004). *How and why stories for readers theatre*. Portsmouth, NH: Teacher Ideas Press.

Worthy, J. (2005). *Readers theatre for building fluency: Strategies and scripts for making the most of this highly effective, motivating, and research-based approach to oral reading*. New York: Scholastic.

Procedure. Teachers follow these steps as they work with a small group or the whole class:

1. Select a script. Children select a script and then read and discuss it as they would any story. Afterward, they volunteer to read each part.

2. Rehearse the reading. Children decide how to use their voice, gestures, and facial expressions to interpret the characters they're reading. They read the script several times, striving for accurate pronunciation, voice projection, and appropriate inflections. Less rehearsal is needed for an informal, in-class presentation than for a more formal production; nevertheless, interpretations should always be developed as fully as possible.

3. Stage the reading. Readers theatre can be presented on a stage or in a corner of the classroom. Children stand or sit in a row and read their lines. They stay in position through the production or enter and leave according to the characters' appearances "onstage." If readers are sitting, they stand to read their lines; if they're standing, they step forward to read. The emphasis isn't on production quality; rather, it's on the interpretive quality of readers' voices and expressions. Costumes and props aren't necessary; however, adding a few small props enhances interest as long as they don't interfere with the interpretive quality of the reading.

Readers theatre avoids many of the restrictions inherent in theatrical productions: Children don't memorize their parts or spend long hours rehearsing, and elaborate props, costumes, and backdrops aren't needed.

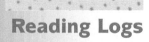

Reading Logs

Reading logs are journals in which children write their reactions to books they're reading or listening to the teacher read aloud. In these entries, children clarify misunderstandings, explore ideas, and deepen their comprehension (Hancock, 2008). They also add diagrams about story elements and information about authors and genres. Children usually write single entries after reading picture books, but they write after reading every chapter or two when they're reading novels. They often write a series of entries about a collection of books written by the same author or about versions of the same folktale.

Sometimes children choose topics for entries, and at other times, they respond to questions or prompts that teachers have prepared. Both student-choice and teacher-directed entries are useful: When children choose their own topics, they delve into their own ideas, sharing what's important to them, and when teachers provide prompts, they direct children's thinking to topics that they might otherwise miss.

Procedure. Children follow these steps as they write in reading logs:

1. Prepare reading logs. Children make reading logs by stapling paper into booklets and write the title of the book on the cover.

2. Write entries. Children write their reactions and reflections, make diagrams, and draw illustrations. Sometimes they choose their own topics, and at other times, teachers provide topics. Children also jot down memorable quotes, and take notes about characters, plot, or other story elements.

3. Share entries. Teachers monitor children's work by reading and responding to their entries. They ask questions and write comments back to children.

Children write and draw reading log entries to help them understand stories they're reading and those the teacher is reading aloud during literature focus units and literature circles (Daniels, 2001).

Rubrics

Rubrics are scoring guides that teachers use to assess oral language, reading, and writing projects (Spandel, 2009). These guides usually have levels, ranging from high to low, with assessment criteria at each level. Rubrics are distributed when children begin a project so that they know what's expected and how they'll be assessed. Teachers mark the assessment criteria either while they're reading the composition or immediately afterward and then determine the overall score. The assessment criteria on some rubrics describe the traits or qualities children are expected to demonstrate. No matter which assessment criteria are used, the same criteria are addressed at each level.

Rubrics can be constructed with any number of levels, but it's easier to show growth when the rubric has more levels. Much more improvement is needed to move to the next level if the rubric has 4 levels than if it has 6 levels. A rubric with 10 levels would be even more sensitive, but rubrics with many levels are harder to construct and more time-consuming to use. Researchers recommend that teachers use rubrics with 4 or 6 levels so that there's no middle score—each level is either above or below the middle—because teachers are inclined to rely on the middle level, when there is one. Rubrics are often used for determining proficiency levels and assigning grades. The level that is above the midpoint is usually designated as "proficient," or "passing"—that's a 3 on a 4-point rubric and a 4 on a 5- or 6-point rubric. The levels on a 6-point rubric can be described this way:

1 = minimal level   4 = proficient level
2 = beginning or limited level   5 = excellent level
3 = developing level   6 = superior level

Teachers also equate levels to letter grades.

Scoring guides help children become better speakers, readers, and writers because they lay out the qualities that constitute excellence and clarify teachers' expectations so children understand how their projects will be assessed. Children, too, can use rubrics to improve their work. When they're involved in a writing project, for instance, they can examine their rough drafts and decide how to revise to make their writing more effective.

Procedure.   Teachers follow these steps:

1. Choose a rubric. Teachers choose a rubric that's appropriate to the project or create one that reflects the assignment.

2. Introduce the rubric. Teachers distribute copies of the rubric and talk about the criteria used at each level, focusing on the requirements at the proficient level.

3. Have children self-assess their work. Children use the rubric to self-assess their work. They highlight phrases in the rubric or check off items that best describe their writing. Then they determine which level has the most highlighted words or checkmarks; that level is the overall score, and children circle it.

4. Assess children's projects. Teachers assess children's oral language, reading, or writing projects by highlighting phrases in the rubric or checking off items that best describe the work. Then they assign the overall score by determining which level has the most highlighted words or checkmarks and circle it.

5. Conference with children. Teachers talk with children about the assessment, identifying strengths and weaknesses. Then children set goals for the next project.

Many commercially prepared rubrics are currently available, especially for writing. State departments of education post rubrics for mandated writing tests on their websites, and school districts hire teams of teachers to develop writing rubrics. Spandel (2009) provides rubrics that assess the six traits, rubrics accompany basal reading programs, and others are available on the Internet. Even though ready-to-use rubrics are convenient, they're not appropriate for all children or every project. Rubrics may have only 4 levels when 6 would be better, or they may have been written for teachers, not in kid-friendly language. Because of these limitations, teachers often adapt commercial rubrics or develop their own.

Running Records

In this reading-stage activity, teachers observe individual children as they read aloud and record information to analyze their reading fluency (Clay, 2000c). They calculate the percentage of words the child reads correctly and then analyze the miscues. Teachers mark a copy of the text as the child reads to indicate which words are read correctly and which the child can't identify.

Procedure.   Teachers conduct running records with individual children using these steps:

1. Choose a book. Teachers have the child read aloud a leveled book or other text.

2. Take the running record. As the child reads aloud, the teacher records information about the words read correctly as well as those misread by making checkmarks on a copy of the text for each word read correctly and uses other marks for miscues. The box on page 363 shows how to mark miscues.

How to Mark Miscues

Miscue	Explanation	Marking
Incorrect word	If the child reads a word incorrectly, the teacher writes the incorrect word above the correct word.	take / taken
Self-correction	If the child self-corrects an error, the teacher writes SC (for "self-correction") following the incorrect word.	for SC / from
Unsuccessful attempt	If the child attempts to pronounce a word, the teacher records each attempt above the correct text.	be-bef-before / before
Skipped word	If the child skips a word, the teacher marks the error with a dash.	— / the
Inserted word	If the child says words that aren't in the text, the teacher writes an insertion symbol (caret) and records the inserted words.	Not / ^
Supplied word	If the child can't identify a word, the teacher supplies it and writes T above the word.	T / which
Repetition	If the child repeats a word or phrase, it isn't scored as a miscue, but the teacher notes it by making a checkmark for each repetition.	✓✓✓ / so

3. Calculate the percentage of miscues. Teachers calculate the percentage of miscues by dividing the number of miscues by the total number of words read. When the child makes 5% or fewer miscues, the book is considered to be at his or her independent level. When there are 6–10% miscues, the book is at the child's instructional level, and when there are more than 10% miscues, the book is too difficult—the child's frustration level.

4. Analyze the miscues. Teachers look for patterns in the miscues to determine how the child is growing as a reader and what strategies and skills should be taught next.

Many teachers conduct running records on all children at the beginning of the school year and at the end of each grading period. In addition, teachers do running records more often during guided reading lessons and with children who aren't making expected progress to diagnose their reading problems and make instructional decisions.

Semantic Feature Analysis

Teachers create a semantic feature analysis to help children examine the characteristics of content-area concepts (Rickelman & Taylor, 2006). They draw a grid for the analysis with characteristics or components of the concept listed on one axis and examples listed on the other. Children reading a novel, for example, can do a semantic feature analysis with vocabulary words listed on one axis and the characters' names on the other; they decide which words relate to which characters and use pluses and minuses to mark the relationships on the grid. Teachers often do a semantic feature analysis with the whole class, but children can work in small groups or individually to complete the grid. The examination should be done as a whole-class activity, however, so that children can share their insights.

Semantic Feature Analysis on Pond Life					
Type	Lives on or in water	Lives near water	Is a food consumer	Is a plant	Produces oxygen
algae	+	−	−	+	+
catfish	+	−	+	−	−
cattail	+	−	−	+	+
crayfish	+	−	+	−	−
dragonfly	$\frac{1}{2}$	$\frac{1}{2}$	+	−	−
duckweed	+	−	−	+	+
frog	$\frac{1}{2}$	$\frac{1}{2}$	+	−	−
great blue heron	−	+	+	−	−
mallard duck	−	+	+	−	−
mosquito	$\frac{1}{2}$	$\frac{1}{2}$	+	−	−
mussel	+	−	+	−	−
pond skater	+	−	+	−	−
pond snail	+	−	+	−	−
raccoon	−	+	+	−	−
salamander	$\frac{1}{2}$	$\frac{1}{2}$	+	−	−
snapping turtle	$\frac{1}{2}$	$\frac{1}{2}$	+	−	−
water boatman	+	−	+	−	−
waterlily	+	−	−	+	+

Procedure.   Teachers follow these steps to do a semantic feature analysis:

1. Create a grid. Teachers create a grid with characteristics or components of the concept listed on the horizontal axis and examples on the vertical axis.

2. Complete the grid. Children complete the grid, cell by cell, by considering the relationship between each item on the vertical axis and the items on the horizontal axis. Then they mark the cell with a plus to indicate a relationship, a minus to indicate no relationship, and a question mark when they're unsure.

3. Examine the grid. Children and the teacher examine the grid for patterns and then draw conclusions based on the patterns.

Children do a semantic feature analysis as part of literature focus units and thematic units. For example, during a unit on pond life, children completed the semantic feature analysis shown above. By doing this semantic feature analysis, the children learned that animals living in or near ponds are food consumers, and that aquatic plants are food producers and they oxygenate the water.

Shared Reading

Teachers use shared reading to read authentic literature with children who can't read those books independently (Holdaway, 1979). Teachers read the book aloud, modeling fluent reading, and then they read the book again and again for several days. The focus for the first reading is children's enjoyment. Teachers draw children's attention to concepts about print, comprehension, and interesting words and sentences during the next couple of readings. Finally, children focus on decoding particular words during the last reading or two.

Children are actively involved in shared reading. Teachers encourage them to make predictions and to chime in on reading repeated words and phrases. Individual children or small groups take turns reading brief parts once they begin to recognize words and phrases. Children examine interesting features that they notice in the book—punctuation marks, illustrations, tables of contents, for example—and teachers point out others. They also talk about the book, both while they're reading and afterward. Shared reading builds on children's experience listening to their parents read bedtime stories (Fisher & Medvic, 2000).

Procedure. Teachers follow these steps to use shared reading with the whole class or small groups of children:

1. Introduce the text. Teachers talk about the book or other text by activating or building background knowledge on topics related to the book and by reading the title and the author's name aloud.

2. Read the text aloud. Teachers read the story aloud to children, using a pointer (a dowel rod with a pencil eraser on the end) to track the text as they read. They invite children to be actively involved by making predictions and by joining in the reading, if the story is repetitive.

3. Have a grand conversation. Children talk about the story, ask questions, and share their responses.

4. Reread the story. Children take turns using the pointer to track the reading and turning pages. Teachers invite children to join in reading familiar and predictable words. Also, they take opportunities to teach and use graphophonic cues and reading strategies while reading. Depending on children's reading expertise, teachers vary the support that they provide.

5. Continue the process. Teachers continue to reread the story with children over a period of several days, again having children turn pages and take turns using the pointer to track the text while reading. They encourage children who can read the text to read along with them.

6. Have children read independently. After children become familiar with the text, teachers distribute individual copies for children to read independently and use for a variety of activities.

Teachers use shared reading during literature focus units, literature circles, and thematic units. Teachers usually choose big books for shared reading but they also use poems written on charts, Language Experience stories, and interactive writing charts so that children can see the text and read along.

Story Boards

Story boards are cards on which the illustrations and text from a picture book have been attached. Teachers make story boards by cutting apart two copies of a picture book and gluing the pages on pieces of cardboard. The most important use of story boards is to sequence the events of a story by lining the cards up on a chalkboard tray or hanging them on a clothesline. Once the pages have been laid out, children visualize the story and its structure in new ways and examine the illustrations more closely. For example, children arrange story boards from *How I Became a Pirate* (Long, 2003) to retell the story and pick out the beginning, middle, and end. They use story boards to identify the dream sequences in the middle of *Abuela* (Dorros, 1997) and compare versions of folktales, such as *The Mitten* (Brett, 2009; Tresselt, 1989) and *The Woodcutter's Mitten* (Koopmans, 1995).

Teachers use this instructional procedure because it allows children to manipulate and sequence stories and examine illustrations more carefully. Story boards are especially useful tools for English learners who use them to preview a story before reading or to review the events in a story after reading. ELs also draw story boards because they can often share their understanding better through art than through language. In addition, story boards present many opportunities for teaching comprehension when only one copy of a picture book is available.

Procedure. Teachers generally use story boards with a small group of children or with the whole class, but individual children can reexamine them as part of center activities. Here are the steps:

1. Collect two copies of a book. Teachers use two copies of a picture book for the story boards. Paperback copies are preferable because they're less expensive. In a few picture books, all the illustrations are on right-hand or left-hand pages, so only one copy is needed.

2. Cut the books apart. Teachers remove the covers and separate the pages, evening out the cut edges.

3. Attach the pages to pieces of cardboard. Teachers glue each page or double-page spread to a piece of cardboard, making sure that pages are alternated so that each illustration is included.

4. Laminate the cards. Teachers laminate the cards so that they can withstand use by children.

5. Use the cards in sequencing activities. Teachers use the story board cards for a number of activities, including sequencing, story structure, rereading, and word-study activities.

Children use story boards for a variety of activities during literature focus units. For a sequencing activity, teachers pass out the cards in a random order, and children line up around the classroom to sequence the story events. Story boards can also be used when only a few copies of a picture book are available so that children can identify words for the word wall, notice literary language, examine an element of story structure, or study the illustrations.

Story Retelling

Teachers use story retelling to monitor children's comprehension (Morrow, 1985). Teachers sit one-on-one with individual children and ask them to retell a story they've just read or listened to read aloud. Children organize the information they remember to provide a personalized summary that reveals their level of comprehension (Hoyt, 1999). Teachers can't assume that children already know how to retell stories, even though many do. Through explanations and demonstrations of the retelling procedure, children learn what's expected of them. Children also need to practice retelling stories before they'll be good at it.

Once teachers begin listening to children retell stories, they notice that those who understand a story retell it differently than those who don't. Good comprehenders' retellings make sense: They reflect the organization of the story and include all of the important story events. In contrast, weak comprehenders often recall events haphazardly or omit important events, especially those in the middle of the story.

Procedure. Teachers follow these steps to have children retell a story:

1. Introduce the story. Teachers introduce the story by reading the title, examining the cover of the book, or talking about a topic related to the story. They also explain that children will be asked to retell the story afterward.

2. Read and discuss the story. Children read the story or listen to it read aloud. When children are reading the story themselves, it's essential that the story is at their reading level. Afterward, they talk about the story, sharing ideas and clarifying confusions.

3. Create a graphic organizer. Children create a graphic organizer or a series of drawings to guide their retelling. (This step is optional, but it's especially helpful for children who have difficulty retelling stories.)

4. Have a child retell the story. Teachers ask children to individually retell the story in their own words, asking questions, if necessary, to elicit more information:

Who was the story about?

What happened next?

Where did the story take place?

What did the character do next?

How did the story end?

5. Mark the scoring guide. Teachers mark a scoring guide as the child retells the story. The scoring guide lists important information about characters and events in the story, usually organized into beginning, middle, and end sections. As they listen to the child's retelling, teachers place checkmarks by each piece of information that the child recalls. If the child omits important information, teachers ask questions to prompt his or her recall, and they write *P* beside information that was recalled with prompting.

Retelling is an instructional tool as well as an assessment tool. McKenna and Stahl (2003) explain that through story retelling, children expand their oral language, enhance their use of comprehension strategies, and deepen their knowledge of story structure. When children participate regularly in retelling activities, their comprehension improves as they learn to focus on the big ideas in the story, and their oral language abilities are enhanced as they incorporate sentence patterns, vocabulary, and phrases from stories into their own talk.

Think-Alouds

Teachers use the think-aloud procedure to teach children how to direct and monitor their thinking during reading (Wilhelm, 2001). By making their thinking explicit, teachers are demonstrating what capable readers do implicitly (Keene & Zimmerman, 2007). After they watch teachers think aloud, children practice the procedure by thinking aloud about the literacy strategies they're learning. As they think aloud, children respond to the text, identify big ideas, ask self-questions, make connections, figure out how to solve problems that arise, and reflect on their use of strategies. This procedure is valuable because children learn to be more active readers. They learn how to think metacognitively and to regulate their own cognitive processes.

Procedure. Teachers use these steps to teach children to think aloud:

1. Choose a book. Teachers choose a text, often a big book, that children are familiar with to demonstrate how to think aloud.

2. Plan the think-aloud. Teachers decide which strategy they want to demonstrate, where they'll pause, and the kinds of thinking they want to share.

3. Demonstrate a think-aloud. Teachers read the text, pausing to think aloud, explaining what they're thinking and how they're using a strategy or solving a reading problem. They often use these "I" sentence starters to talk about their thinking:

I wondered if . . .

I was confused by . . .

I didn't understand why . . .

I think the big idea is . . .

I reread this part because . . .

4. Annotate the text. Teachers write a small self-stick note about their thinking and attach it next to the text that prompted the think-aloud. They often use a word or phrase, such as *picture in my mind* or *reread*, to quickly document their thinking.

5. Continue thinking aloud. Teachers continue reading the book, pausing to think aloud again and annotate the text with additional notes about their thinking.

6. Reflect on the procedure. Teachers review their annotations, talk about their strategy use, and reflect on the usefulness of think-alouds as a tool for comprehending what they're reading.

7. Repeat the procedure. Teachers read another book and have children take turns thinking aloud and annotating the text. Once children are familiar with the procedure, they practice doing think-alouds in small groups and with partners.

After children know how to think aloud, teachers can use this procedure as an assessment tool. During student–teacher conferences, children reflect on their reading and evaluate how well they use particular strategies, and they think about what they could do differently to comprehend more effectively. Children can also refer to their annotations and write reflections about their use of particular strategies.

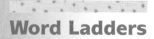

Word Ladders

Word ladders are games where children change one word into another through a series of steps, altering one letter at each step; the goal is to use as few steps as possible to change the first word into the last word. This type of puzzle was invented by Lewis Carroll, author of *Alice in Wonderland*. Typically, the first and last words are related in some way, such as *fall–down*, *slow–fast*, and *trick–treat*, and all the middle words must be real words. A well-known word ladder, shown on page 369, is *cat–dog*, and it can be solved in three steps: *cat–cot–dot–dog*.

A Cat-Dog Word Ladder

The teacher says:	Children write:
Begin with the word *cat*.	cat
Change the vowel to form another word for *bed*, sometimes the kind of bed you use when you're camping.	cot
Change one letter to form a word that means "a tiny, round mark."	dot
Finally, change the final consonant to make a word that goes with the first word, *cat*.	dog

Teachers can create a variation of word ladders to practice phonics, spelling, and vocabulary skills (Rasinski, 2006). They guide children to build a series of words as they provide graphophonemic and semantic clues about the words. As for traditional word ladder puzzles, each word comes from the previous one, but children may be asked to add, delete, or change one or more letters to make the next word. Children write the words in a list so they can see what they've written. Teachers make their own word ladders to reinforce the phonics concepts and spelling patterns; in this case, it's not necessary to relate the first and last words as in traditional word ladders. A word ladder to practice words with the short and long sounds of /oo/ is shown on page 370.

Procedure. Here's the procedure for using word ladders:

1. Create the word ladder. Teachers create a word ladder with 5 to 15 words, choosing words from spelling lists or phonics lessons, and they write clues for each word, incorporating a combination of graphophonemic and semantic clues.

2. Pass out supplies. Teachers often have children use whiteboards and marking pens for this activity, but they can also use blank paper or paper with word ladders already drawn on them.

3. Do the word ladder. Teachers read the clues they've prepared and have children write the words. Children take turns identifying the words and spelling them correctly. When necessary, teachers provide additional clues and explain any unfamiliar words, phonics rules, or spelling patterns.

4. Review the word ladder. Once children complete the word ladder, they reread the words and talk about any that they had difficulty writing. They also volunteer other words they can write using these letters.

Word ladders are a fun way for children to practice the phonics and spelling skills they're learning and, at the same time, think about the meanings of words. The activity's gamelike format makes it engaging for both children and teachers. To see more word ladders, check Rasinski's (2005a, 2005b) books of word ladder games for second through fourth graders; other word ladder games are also available on the Internet.

An / oo / Word Ladder	
The teacher says:	**Children write:**
Write the word *good*. We're practicing words with *oo* today.	good
Change the beginning sound to write the past tense of *stand*. The word is *stood*.	stood
Change the ending sound to write a word that means "a seat without arms or a back."	stool
Change the beginning sound to write a word that means the opposite of *warm*.	cool
Add two letters—one before and one after the *c*—to spell where we are right now.	school
Change the beginning sound to spell *tool*.	tool
Drop a letter to make a word that means *also*.	too
Change the first letter to write a word that means "a place where people can go to see wild animals."	zoo
Add a letter to *zoo* to spell the sound a car makes.	zoom
Change the beginning sound—use two letters for this blend—to spell something we use for sweeping.	broom
Change one letter to spell a word that means *creek*.	brook
Change the beginning sound to make a word that means "a dishonest person."	crook

Word Sorts

Children use word sorts to examine and categorize words according to their meanings, phoneme–grapheme correspondences, or spelling patterns (Bear, Invernizzi, Templeton, & Johnston, 2008). The purpose of word sorts is to help children focus on conceptual and phonological features of words and identify recurring patterns. For example, as children sort cards with words such as *stopping, eating, hugging, running,* and *raining,* they discover the rule for doubling the final consonant in short vowel words before adding an inflectional ending.

Word sorts are effective for English learners because children build skills to understand how English differs from their native language, and they develop knowledge to help them predict meaning through spelling (Bear, Helman, Templeton, Invernizzi, & Johnston, 2007). Because word sorts can be done in small groups, teachers can choose words for the sorts that are appropriate for children's developmental levels.

Procedure. Here are the steps for conducting a word sort:

1. Choose a topic. Teachers choose a language skill or content-area topic for the word sort and decide whether it will be an open or closed sort. In an open sort, children determine the categories themselves based on the words they're sorting. In a closed sort, teachers present the categories as they introduce the sorting activity.

2. Compile a list of words. Teachers compile a list of 6 to 20 words, depending on grade level, that exemplify particular categories, and they write the words on small cards. Or, small picture cards can be used.

3. Introduce the sorting activity. If it's a closed sort, teachers present the categories and have children sort word cards into these categories. If it's an open sort, children identify the words and look for possible categories. Children arrange and rearrange the cards until they're satisfied with the sorting. Then they add category labels.

4. Make a permanent record. Children make a permanent record of their sort by gluing the word cards onto a large sheet of construction paper or poster board or by writing the words on a sheet of paper.

5. Share word sorts. Children share their word sorts with classmates, explaining the categories they used (for open sorts).

Teachers use word sorts to teach phonics, spelling, and vocabulary. During literature focus units, children sort vocabulary words according to the beginning, middle, or end of the story or according to character. During thematic units, children sort vocabulary words according to big ideas.

Word Walls

Word walls are collections of words posted in the classroom that children use for word-study activities and refer to when they're writing (Wagstaff, 1999). Teachers make word walls using construction-paper squares or sheets of butcher paper that have been divided into alphabetized sections. For one type of word wall, children and the teacher write important words from books they're reading or about big ideas they're learning during thematic units. Usually children choose the words to write on the word wall, and they may even do the writing themselves, but teachers add any Tier 2 words that children haven't chosen. These word walls are taken down after each book or unit is completed.

A second type of word wall features high-frequency words children are learning. Teachers hang large sheets of construction paper, one for each letter of the alphabet, on a wall of the classroom, and then post high-frequency words as they're introduced (Cunningham, 2005; Lynch, 2005). This word wall remains on display all year, and additional words are added during the year. In kindergarten classrooms, teachers begin the school year by placing word cards with children's names on the wall chart and add common environmental print, such as *K-Mart* and *McDonald's*. Later in the year, they add words such as *I, love, the, you, Mom, Dad, good*, and other words that children want to read and write.

Procedure. Teachers usually create word walls with the whole class, and they follow these steps:

1. Prepare the word wall. Teachers prepare a blank word wall in the classroom from sheets of construction paper or butcher paper, dividing it into 12 to 24 boxes and labeling the boxes with letters of the alphabet.

2. Introduce the word wall. Teachers introduce the word wall and write several key words on it when they're beginning a new book or a thematic unit.

3. Add words to the word wall. Children suggest "important" words for the word wall as they're reading a book or participating in thematic-unit activities. Children and the teacher write the words in the alphabetized blocks, making sure to write large enough so the words are visible. If a word is misspelled, it's corrected, because children will be using the words in various activities. Sometimes the teacher adds a small picture or writes a synonym for a difficult word, puts a box around the root word, or writes the plural form or other related words nearby.

4. Use the word wall. Teachers use the word wall for a variety of word-study activities, and children refer to the word wall when they're writing.

Teachers use word walls during literature focus units and thematic units, and to teach high-frequency words. They involve children in a variety of word-study activities, including making words, word ladders, and word sorts. In addition, teachers use words from high-frequency word walls for word-study activities. One example is a popular word hunt game: Teachers distribute small whiteboards and have children identify and write words from the word wall on their boards according to the clues they provide. For example, teachers say "Find the word that begins like _____," "Look for the word that rhymes with _____," "Find the word that alphabetically follows _____," or "Think of the word that means the opposite of _____," depending on what children are learning. Children read and reread the words, apply phonics and word-study concepts, and practice spelling high-frequency words as they play this game.

GLOSSARY

Affix A syllable added to the beginning (prefix) or end (suffix) of a word to change the word's meaning (e.g., *il-* in *illiterate* and *-al* in *national*).

Alphabetic principle The assumption underlying alphabetical language systems that each sound has a corresponding graphic representation (or letter).

Antonyms Words with opposite meanings (e.g., *good–bad*).

Automaticity Identifying words accurately and quickly.

Basal readers Reading textbooks that are leveled according to grade.

Big books Enlarged versions of picture books that teachers read with children.

Blend To combine the sounds represented by letters to pronounce a word.

Bound morpheme A morpheme that is not a word and cannot stand alone (e.g., *-s, tri-*).

Closed syllable A syllable ending in a consonant sound (e.g., *make, duck*).

Cloze An activity in which children replace words that have been deleted from a text.

Comprehension The process of constructing meaning using both the author's text and the reader's background knowledge for a specific purpose.

Concepts about print Basic understandings about the way print works, including the direction of print, spacing, punctuation, letters, and words.

Consonant A speech sound characterized by friction or stoppage of the airflow as it passes through the vocal tract; usually any letter except *a, e, i, o,* and *u*.

Consonant digraph Two adjacent consonants that represent a sound not represented by either consonant alone (e.g., *th–this, ch–chin, sh–wash, ph–telephone*).

Context clue Information from the words or sentences surrounding a word that helps to clarify the word's meaning.

Cueing systems The phonological, semantic, syntactic, and pragmatic information that children rely on as they read.

Decoding Using word-identification strategies to pronounce and attach meaning to an unfamiliar word.

Differentiated instruction Procedures for assisting children in learning, providing options, challenging them, and matching books to readers to maximize their learning.

Diphthong A sound produced when the tongue glides from one sound to another; it's represented by two vowels (e.g., *oy–boy, ou–house, ow–how*).

Elkonin boxes A strategy for segmenting sounds in a word that involves drawing a box to represent each sound.

Emergent literacy Children's early reading and writing development before conventional reading and writing.

Environmental print Signs, labels, and other print found in the community.

Explicit instruction Systematic instruction of concepts, strategies, and skills that builds from simple to complex.

Fluency Reading smoothly, quickly, and with expression.

Free morpheme A morpheme that can stand alone as a word (e.g., *book, cycle*).

Frustration level The level of reading material that is too difficult for a child to read successfully.

Genre A category of literature such as folklore, science fiction, biography, or historical fiction, or a writing form.

Goldilocks principle A strategy for choosing "just right" books.

Grapheme A written representation of a sound using one or more letters.

Graphophonemic Referring to sound–symbol relationships.

Guided reading Children work in small groups to read as independently as possible a text selected and introduced by the teacher.

High-frequency word A common English word, usually a word among the 100 or 300 most common words.

Homographic homophones Words that sound alike and are spelled alike but have different meanings (e.g., baseball *bat* and the animal *bat*).

Homographs Words that are spelled alike but are pronounced differently (e.g., a *present* and to *present*).

Homonyms Words that sound alike but are spelled differently (e.g., *there–their–they're*); also called *homophones*.

Independent reading level The level of reading material that a child can read independently with high comprehension and an accuracy level of 95–100%.

Inflectional endings Suffixes that express plurality or possession when added to a noun (e.g., *girls, girl's*), tense when added to a verb (e.g., *walked, walking*), or comparison when added to an adjective (e.g., *happier, happiest*).

Informal reading inventory (IRI) An individually administered reading test used to determine children's independent, instructional, and frustration levels.

Instructional reading level The level of reading material that a child can read with teacher support and instruction with 90–94% accuracy.

Intervention Intense, individualized instruction for struggling readers to solve reading problems and accelerate their growth.

Invented spelling Children's attempts to spell words that reflect their developing knowledge about the spelling system.

Leveling books A method of estimating the difficulty level of a text.

Lexile scores A method of estimating the difficulty level of a text.

Listening capacity level The highest level of graded passage that can be comprehended well when read aloud to the child.

Literal comprehension The understanding of what is explicitly stated in a text.

Long vowels The vowel sounds that are also names of the alphabet letters: /ā/ as in *make*, /ē/ as in *feet*, /ī/ as in *ice*, /ō/ as in *coat*, and /ū/ as in *rule*.

Metacognition Children's awareness of their own thought and learning processes.

Minilesson Explicit instruction about literacy procedures, concepts, strategies, and skills that are taught to small groups or the whole class.

Miscue analysis A strategy for categorizing and analyzing a child's oral reading errors.

Morpheme The smallest meaningful part of a word; sometimes it's a word (e.g., *cup*, *hope*), and sometimes it's not a whole word (e.g., *-ly*, *bi-*).

Onset The part of a syllable (or one-syllable word) that comes before the vowel (e.g., *str* in *string*).

Open syllable A syllable ending in a vowel sound (e.g., *sea*).

Orthography The spelling system.

Phoneme A sound; it's represented in print with slashes (e.g., /s/ and /th/).

Phoneme–grapheme correspondence The relationship between a sound and the letter that represents it.

Phonemic awareness The ability to manipulate the sounds in words orally.

Phonics Predictable relationships between phonemes and graphemes.

Phonogram A rime used for word-family decoding and spelling activities.

Phonological awareness The ability to identify and manipulate phonemes, onsets and rimes, and syllables; it includes phonemic awareness.

Phonology The sound system of language.

Pragmatics The social use system of language.

Prefix A syllable added to the beginning of a word to change the word's meaning (e.g., *re-* in *reread*).

Proofreading Reading a composition to identify spelling and other mechanical errors.

Prosody The ability to orally read sentences expressively, with appropriate phrasing and intonation.

Readability formula A method of estimating the difficulty level of a text.

Rhyming Words with the same rime sound (e.g., *white*, *bright*).

Rime The part of a syllable (or one-syllable word) that begins with the vowel (e.g., *ing* in *string*).

Scaffolding The support a teacher provides to children as they read and write.

Segment To pronounce a word slowly, saying each sound distinctly.

Semantics The meaning system of language.

Shared reading The teacher reads a book aloud as a group of children follow along in the text, often using a big book.

Short vowels The vowel sounds represented by /ă/ as in *cat*, /ĕ/ as in *bed*, /ĭ/ as in *big*, /ŏ/ as in *hop*, and /ŭ/ as in *cut*.

Skill An automatic processing behavior that children use in reading and writing, such as sounding out words, recognizing antonyms, and capitalizing proper nouns.

Strategy A problem-solving behavior that children use in reading and writing, such as predicting, monitoring, visualizing, and summarizing.

Suffix A syllable added to the end of a word to change the word's meaning (e.g., *-y* in *hairy*, *-ful* in *careful*).

Syllable An uninterrupted segment of speech that includes a vowel sound (e.g., *get*, *a-bout*, *but-ter-fly*, *con-sti-tu-tion*).

Synonyms Words that mean nearly the same thing (e.g., *road–street*).

Syntax The structural system of language or grammar.

Trade book A published book that isn't a textbook; the type of books in bookstores and libraries.

Vowel A voiced speech sound made without friction or stoppage of the airflow as it passes through the vocal tract; the letters *a*, *e*, *i*, *o*, *u*, and sometimes *w* and *y*.

Vowel digraph Two or more adjacent vowels in a syllable that represent a single sound (e.g., *bread*, *eight*, *pain*, *saw*).

Word families Groups of words that rhyme (e.g., *ball*, *call*, *fall*, *hall*, *mall*, *tall*, and *wall*).

Word sort A word-study activity in which children group words into categories.

Word wall An alphabetized chart posted in the classroom listing words children are learning.

Zone of proximal development The distance between a child's actual developmental level and his or her potential level that can be reached with teacher scaffolding.

REFERENCES

Aardema, V. (2004). *Why mosquitoes buzz in people's ears*. New York: Puffin Books.

Adams, M. J. (1990). *Beginning to read: Thinking and learning about print*. Cambridge, MA: MIT Press.

Afflerbach, P. (2007a). Best practices in literacy assessment. In L. B. Gambrell, L. M. Morrow, & M. Pressley (Eds.), *Best practices in literacy instruction* (3rd ed., pp. 264–282). New York: Guilford Press.

Afflerbach, P. (2007b). *Understanding and using reading assessment, K–12*. Newark, DE: International Reading Association.

Afflerbach, P., Pearson, P. D., & Paris, S. G. (2008). Clarifying differences between reading skills and strategies. *The Reading Teacher, 61*, 364–373.

Allen, C. A. (2001). *The multigenre research paper: Voice, passion, and discovery in grades 4–6*. Portsmouth, NH: Heinemann.

Allen, J. (1999). *Words, words, words*. Portsmouth, NH: Heinemann.

Allen, J. (2007). *Inside words: Tools for teaching academic vocabulary, grades 4–12*. Portland, ME: Stenhouse.

Allington, R. L. (2006). *What really matters for struggling readers: Designing research-based programs* (2nd ed.). Boston: Allyn & Bacon/Pearson.

Allington, R. L. (2009). *What really matters in fluency: Research-based best practices across the curriculum*. Boston: Allyn & Bacon/Pearson.

Angelillo, J. (2005). *Making revision matter*. New York: Scholastic.

Angelillo, J. (2008). *Whole-class teaching: Minilessons and more*. Portsmouth, NH: Heineman.

Applebee, A. N. (1978). *Child's concept of story: Ages 2–17*. Chicago: University of Chicago Press.

Applegate, M. D., Quinn, K. B., & Applegate, A. J. (2008). *The critical reading inventory: Assessing students' reading and thinking* (2nd ed.). Upper Saddle River, NJ: Merrill/Prentice Hall.

Armbruster, B. B., Lehr, F., & Osborn, J. (2001). *Put reading first: The research building blocks for teaching children to read*. Urbana, IL: Center for the Improvement of Early Reading Achievement.

Armbruster, B. B., McCarthey, S. J., & Cummins, S. (2005). Writing to learn in elementary classrooms. In R. Indrisano & J. R. Paratore (Eds.), *Learning to write, writing to learn: Theory and research in practice* (pp. 71–96). Newark, DE: International Reading Association.

Arnold, C., & Comora, M. (2007). *Taj Mahal*. Minneapolis: Carolrhoda.

Ashton-Warner, S. (1965). *Teacher*. New York: Simon & Schuster.

Ashton-Warner, S. ([1963]1986). *Teacher*. New York: Simon & Schuster.

Aston, D. H. (2008). *The moon over Star*. New York: Dial Books.

Atwell, N. (1998). *In the middle: New understandings about reading and writing with adolescents* (2nd ed.). Upper Montclair, NJ: Boynton/Cook.

Avi. (2005). *Poppy*. New York: HarperTrophy.

Baker, L. (2002). Metacognition in comprehension instruction. In C. C. Block & M. Pressley (Eds.), *Comprehension instruction: Research-based best practices* (pp. 77–95). New York: Guilford Press.

Bandura, A. (1997). *Self-efficacy: The exercise of control*. New York: W. H. Freeman.

Banks, K. (2006). *Max's words*. New York: Farrar, Straus & Giroux.

Barretta, G. (2007). *Dear deer: A book of homophones*. New York: Holt.

Baumann, J. F., Kame'enui, E. J., & Ash, G. (2003). Research on vocabulary instruction: Voltaire redux. In J. Flood, D. Lapp, J. R. Squire, & J. M. Jensen (Eds.), *Handbook of research on teaching the English language arts* (2nd ed., pp. 752–785). Mahwah, NJ: Erlbaum.

Bean, R. M., & Swan, A. (2006). Vocabulary assessment: A key to planning vocabulary instruction. In C. C. Block & J. N. Mangieri (Eds.), *The vocabulary-enriched classroom: Practices for improving the reading performance of all children in grades 3 and up* (pp. 164–187). New York: Scholastic.

Bear, D. R., Helman, L., Templeton, S., Invernizzi, M., & Johnston, F. (2007). *Words their way with English learners: Word study for phonics, vocabulary, and spelling instruction*. Upper Saddle River, NJ: Merrill/Prentice Hall.

Bear, D. R., Invernizzi, M., Templeton, S., & Johnston, F. (2008). *Words their way: Word study for phonics, vocabulary, and spelling instruction* (4th ed.). Upper Saddle River, NJ: Merrill/ Prentice Hall.

Beaver, J. (2006). *Developmental reading assessment, grades K–3* (2nd ed.). Upper Saddle River, NJ: Celebration Press/ Pearson.

Beaver, J., & Carter, M. (2005). *Developmental reading assessment, grades 4–8* (2nd ed.). Upper Saddle River, NJ: Celebration Press/Pearson.

Beck, I. L., McKeown, M. G., & Kucan, L. (2002). *Bringing words to life: Robust vocabulary instruction*. New York: Guilford Press.

Bennett-Armistead, V. S., Duke, N. K., & Moses, A. M. (2005). *Literacy and the youngest learner: Best practices for educators of children from birth to 5*. New York: Scholastic.

Blachowicz, C. L. Z., & Fisher, P. J. (2007). Best practices in vocabulary instruction. In L. B. Gambrell, L. M. Morrow, & M. Pressley (Eds.), *Best practices in literacy instruction* (3rd ed., pp. 178–203). New York: Guilford Press.

Black, A., & Stave, A. M. (2007). *A comprehensive guide to readers theatre: Enhancing fluency and comprehension in middle school and beyond.* Newark, DE: International Reading Association.

Blanton, W. E., Wood, K. D., & Moorman, G. B. (1990). The role of purpose in reading instruction. *The Reading Teacher, 43,* 486–493.

Block, C. C., & Pressley, M. (2007). Best practices in teaching comprehension. In L. B. Gambrell, L. M. Morrow, & M. Pressley (Eds.), *Best practices in literacy instruction* (3rd ed., pp. 220–242). New York: Guilford Press.

Blume, J. (2007). *Tales of a fourth grade nothing.* New York: Puffin Books.

Bollard, J. K. (2006). *Scholastic children's thesaurus.* New York: Scholastic.

Bouchard, M. (2005). *Comprehension strategies for English language learners.* New York: Scholastic.

Boyd-Batstone, P. (2004). Focused anecdotal records assessment: A tool for standards-based, authentic assessment. *The Reading Teacher, 58,* 230–239.

Bracey, G. W. (2004). *Setting the record straight: Responses to misconceptions about public education in the United States.* Portsmouth, NH: Heinemann.

Brady, E. W. (1989). *Toliver's secret.* New York: Knopf.

Braunger, J., & Lewis, J. P. (2006). *Building a knowledge base in reading* (2nd ed.). Newark, DE: International Reading Association/National Council of Teachers of English.

Bredekamp, S. (Ed.). (1990). *Developmentally appropriate practice in early childhood programs serving children from birth through age 8.* Washington, DC: National Association for the Education of Young Children.

Brennan-Nelson, D. (2004). *My teacher likes to say.* Chelsea, MI: Sleeping Bear Press.

Brett, J. (1999). *Gingerbread baby.* New York: Putnam.

Brett, J. (2003). *Town mouse, country mouse.* New York: Putnam.

Brett, J. (2009). *The mitten* (20th anniversary ed.). New York: Putnam.

Brown, J. (2003a). *Flat Stanley.* New York: HarperCollins.

Brown, J. (2003b). *Stanley in space.* New York: HarperCollins.

Brown, J. S., Collins, A., & Duguid, S. (1989). Situated cognition and the culture of learning. *Educational Researcher, 18*(1), 32–42.

Brown, M. W. (1990). *The important book.* New York: HarperCollins.

Bunting, E. (1995). *Once upon a time.* Katonah, NY: Richard C. Owen.

Bunting, E. (1998). *Going home.* New York: HarperTrophy.

Bunting, E. (1999). *Smoky night.* San Diego: Voyager.

Bunting, E. (2000). *Train to somewhere.* New York: Clarion Books.

Bus, A. G., van Ijzendoorn, M. H., & Pellegrini, A. D. (1995). Joint book reading makes for success in learning to read: A meta-analysis on intergenerational transmission of literacy. *Review of Educational Research, 65,* 1–21.

Buss, K., & Karnowski, L. (2000). *Reading and writing literary genres.* Newark, DE: International Reading Association.

Button, K., Johnson, M. J., & Furgerson, P. (1996). Interactive writing in a primary classroom. *The Reading Teacher, 49,* 446–454.

Calderon, M. (2007). *Teaching reading to English language learners, grades 6–12.* Thousand Oaks, CA: Corwin Press.

Caldwell, J. S., & Leslie, L. (2005). *Intervention strategies to follow informal reading inventory assessment: So what do I do now?* Boston: Allyn & Bacon/Pearson.

Cappellini, M. (2005). *Balancing reading and language learning: A resource for teaching English language learners, K–5.* York, ME: Stenhouse.

Carle, E. (1994). *The very hungry caterpillar.* New York: Scholastic.

Carle, E. (1997). *Have you seen my cat?* New York: Aladdin Books.

Carle, E. (2000). *Does a kangaroo have a mother, too?* New York: Harper Collins.

Carle, E. (2002). *The very hungry caterpillar.* New York: Puffin Books.

Carle, E. (2005). *A house for hermit crab.* New York: Aladdin Books.

Casbarro, J. (2005, February). The politics of high-stakes testing. *Education Digest, 70*(6), 20–23.

Chall, J. S. (1967). *Learning to read: The great debate.* New York: McGraw-Hill.

Chall, J. S., Jacobs, V. A., & Baldwin, L. E. (1991). *The reading crisis: Why poor children fall behind.* Cambridge, MA: Harvard University Press.

Clarke, B. (1990). *Amazing frogs and toads.* New York: Knopf.

Clay, M. M. (2000a). *Concepts about print: What have children learned about the way we print language?* Portsmouth, NH: Heinemann.

Clay, M. M. (2000b). *Follow me, moon.* Portsmouth, NH: Heinemann.

Clay, M. M. (2000c). *Running records for classroom teachers.* Portsmouth, NH: Heinemann.

Clay, M. M. (2005a). *Literacy lessons: Designed for individuals (Part 1: Why? When? And how?).* Portsmouth, NH: Heinemann.

Clay, M. M. (2005b). *Literacy lessons: Designed for individuals (Part 2: Teaching procedures).* Portsmouth, NH: Heinemann.

Clay, M. M. (2007a). *An observation survey of early literacy achievement* (rev. ed.). Portsmouth, NH: Heinemann.

Clay, M. M. (2007b). *No shoes.* Portsmouth, NH: Heinemann.

Clay, M. M. (2007c). *Sand.* Portsmouth, NH: Heinemann.

Clay, M. M. (2007d). *Stones.* Portsmouth, NH: Heinemann.

Cleary, B. (1992). *Ramona the pest.* New York: HarperCollins.

Cleary, B. (2000). *Henry Huggins* (50th anniversary ed.). New York: HarperCollins.

Cleary, B. P. (2009). *Skin like milk, hair of silk: What are similes and metaphors?* Minneapolis: Millbrook Press.

Clements, A. (2007). *Dogku.* New York: Simon & Schuster.

Clymer, T. (1963). The utility of phonic generalizations in the primary grades. *The Reading Teacher, 16,* 252–258.

Coerr, E. (1989). *The Josefina story quilt.* New York: HarperCollins.

Coerr, E. (1993). *Chang's paper pony.* New York: HarperCollins.

Cohen, B. (1998). *Molly's pilgrim.* New York: HarperCollins.

Cole, H. (1997). *Jack's garden.* New York: Greenwillow.

Cole, J. (1986). *Hungry, hungry sharks.* New York: Random House.

Cole, J. (1993). *The magic school bus lost in the solar system.* New York: Scholastic.

Cole, J. (1996). *The magic school bus inside a beehive.* New York: Scholastic.

Cole, J. (1999). *The magic school bus and the electric field trip.* New York: Scholastic.

Cole, J. (2006). *The magic school bus and the science fair expedition.* New York: Scholastic.

Cooney, B. (1985). *Miss Rumphius.* New York: Puffin Books.

Cooper, J. D., & Pikulski, J. J. (2003). *Houghton Mifflin reading* (California ed.). Boston: Houghton Mifflin.

Cooper, J. D., Chard, D. J., & Kiger, N. D. (2006). *The struggling reader: Interventions that work.* New York: Scholastic.

Cooter, R. B., Jr., Flynt, E. S., & Cooter, K. S. (2007). *Comprehensive reading inventory.* Upper Saddle River, NJ: Merrill/Prentice Hall.

Cramer, R. L. (1998). *The spelling connection: Integrating reading, writing, and spelling instruction.* New York: Guilford Press.

Crews, D. (2008). *Freight train.* New York: Greenwillow.

Cronin, D. (2005). *Diary of a spider.* New York: HarperCollins.

Cronin, D. (2007). *Diary of a fly.* New York: HarperCollins.

Culham, R. (2003). *6 + 1 traits of writing.* New York: Scholastic.

Cummins, J. (1979). Linguistic interdependence and the educational development of bilingual children. *Review of Educational Research, 49,* 222–251.

Cunningham, A., & Shagoury, R. (2005). *Starting with comprehension: Reading strategies for the youngest learners.* Portland, ME: Stenhouse.

Cunningham, P. M. (2005). *Phonics they use: Words for reading and writing* (4th ed.). New York: HarperCollins.

Cunningham, P. M. (2007). Best practices in teaching phonological awareness and phonics. In L. B. Gambrell, L. M. Morrow, & M. Pressley (Eds.), *Best practices in literacy instruction* (pp. 159–177). New York: Guilford Press.

Cunningham, P. M. (2008). *Phonics they use: Words for reading and writing* (5th ed.). Boston: Allyn & Bacon/Pearson.

Cunningham, P. M. (2009). *What really matters in vocabulary: Research-based practices across the curriculum.* Boston: Allyn & Bacon/Pearson.

Cunningham, P. M., & Allington, R. L. (2007). *Classrooms that work: They can all read and write* (4th ed.). Boston: Allyn & Bacon/Pearson.

Cunningham, P. M., & Cunningham, J. W. (1992). Making words: Enhancing the invented spelling-decoding connection. *The Reading Teacher, 46,* 106–115.

Cunningham, P. M., & Cunningham, J. W. (2002). What we know about how to teach phonics. In A. E. Farstrup & S. J. Samuels (Eds.), *What research has to say about reading instruction* (3rd ed., pp. 87–109). Newark, DE: International Reading Association.

Cunningham, P. M., & Hall, D. P. (2008a). *Making words: First grade.* Boston: Allyn & Bacon/Pearson.

Cunningham, P. M., & Hall, D. P. (2008b). *Making words: Fourth grade.* Boston: Allyn & Bacon/Pearson.

Cunningham, P. M., & Hall, D. P. (2008c). *Making words: Kindergarten.* Boston: Allyn & Bacon/Pearson.

Cunningham, P. M., & Hall, D. P. (2008d). *Making words: Second grade.* Boston: Allyn & Bacon/Pearson.

Cunningham, P. M., & Hall, D. P. (2008e). *Making words: Third grade.* Boston: Allyn & Bacon/Pearson.

D'Aoust, C. (1992). Portfolios: Process for students and teachers. In K. B. Yancy (Ed.), *Portfolios in the writing classroom* (pp. 39–48). Urbana, IL: National Council of Teachers of English.

Dahl, K. L., Scharer, P. L., Lawson, L. L., & Grogan, P. R. (2001). *Rethinking phonics: Making the best teaching decisions.* Portsmouth, NH: Heinemann.

Dahl, R. (2007). *Charlie and the chocolate factory.* New York: Puffin Books.

Daniels, H. (2001). *Literature circles: Voice and choice in book clubs and reading groups.* York, ME: Stenhouse.

Daniels, H., & Bizar, M. (1998). *Methods that matter: Six structures for best practice classrooms.* York, ME: Stenhouse.

Daniels, H., & Steineke, N. (2004). *Mini-lessons for literature circles.* Portsmouth, NH: Heinemann.

Danzinger, P. (1995). *You can't eat your children pox, Amber Brown.* New York: Putnam.

Danziger, P. (1998). *Amber Brown sees red.* New York: Scholastic.

Danziger, P. (1999). *Amber Brown is feeling blue.* New York: Scholastic.

Danziger, P. (2004). *Amber Brown is green with envy.* New York: Scholastic.

Danziger, P. (2006). *Amber Brown is not a crayon.* New York: Scholastic.

Danziger, P. (2007). *Amber Brown goes fourth.* New York: Puffin Books.

Dean, D. (2006). *Strategic writing: The writing process and beyond in the secondary English classroom.* Urbana, IL: National Council of Teachers of English.

Demi. (2008). *Marco Polo.* Tarrytown, NY: Marshall Cavendish.

dePaola, T. (1996). *The legend of the bluebonnet.* New York: Putnam.

Dewey, J. (1997). *Experience and education.* New York: Free Press.

DiCamillo, K. (2008). *The miraculous journey of Edward Tulane*. New York: Walker.

DiCamillo, K. (2009). *Because of Winn-Dixie*. Cambridge, MA: Candlewick Press.

Donovan, C. A., & Smolkin, L. B. (2002). Children's genre knowledge: An examination of K–5 children's performance on multiple tasks providing differing levels of scaffolding. *Reading Research Quarterly 37*, 428–465.

Dooley, C. M., & Maloch, B. (2005). Exploring characters through visual representations. In N. L. Roser & M. G. Martinez (Eds.), *What a character! Character study as a guide to literary meaning making in grades K–8* (pp. 111–123). Newark, DE: International Reading Association.

Dorfman, L. R., & Cappelli, R. (2007). *Mentor texts: Teaching writing through children's literature, K–6*. Portland, ME: Stenhouse.

Dorfman, L. R., & Cappelli, R. (2009). *Nonfiction mentor texts*. Portland, ME: Stenhouse.

Dorn, L. J., & Soffos, C. (2001). *Shaping literate minds: Developing self-regulated learners*. York, ME: Stenhouse.

Dorros, A. (1997). *Abuela*. New York: Puffin Books.

Dowhower, S. L. (1991). Speaking of prosody: Fluency's unattended bedfellow. *Theory Into Practice, 30*, 165–173.

Dowhower, S. L. (1999). Supporting a strategic stance in the classroom: A comprehension framework for helping teachers help children to be strategic. *The Reading Teacher, 52*, 672–688.

Duke, N. K., & Pearson, P. D. (2002). Effective practices for developing reading comprehension. In A. E. Farstrup & S. J. Samuels (Eds.), *What research has to say about reading instruction* (3rd ed., pp. 205–242). Newark, DE: International Reading Association.

Dunn, D. M., Dunn, L. W., & Dunn, L. M. (2006). *Peabody picture vocabulary test-4*. Bloomington, MN: American Guidance Service/Pearson.

Durant, A. (2004). *Dear tooth fairy*. Cambridge, MA: Candlewick Press.

Eastman, P. D. (1966). *Are you my mother?* New York: Random House.

Edwards, P. A. (2004). *Children's literacy development: Making it happen through school, family, and community involvement*. Boston: Allyn & Bacon/Pearson.

Ehlert, L. (1992). *Planting a rainbow*. Orlando: Voyager.

Ehrlich, A. (2004). *Cinderella*. New York: Dutton.

Ehrlich, A. (2006). *The snow queen*. New York: Dutton.

Elbow, P. (1998). *Writing without teachers* (2nd ed.). New York: Oxford University Press.

Eldredge, J. L. (2005). *Teach decoding: How and why* (2nd ed.). Upper Saddle River, NJ: Merrill/Prentice Hall.

Faigley, L., & Witte, S. (1981). Analyzing revision. *College Composition and Communication, 32*, 400–410.

Falwell, C. (2006). *Word wizard*. New York: Clarion Books.

Farr, R., & Tone, B. (1994). *Portfolio and performance assessment*. Orlando: Harcourt Brace.

Fay, K., & Whaley, S. (2004). *Becoming one community: Reading and writing with English language learners*. Portland, ME: Stenhouse.

Fisher, B. & Medvic E. F. (2000). *Perspectives on shared reading: Planning and practice*. Portsmouth, NH: Heinemann.

Fisher, D., Flood, J., Lapp, D., & Frey, N. (2004). Interactive read-alouds: Is there a common set of implementation practices? *The Reading Teacher, 58*, 8–17.

Fisher, D., Frey, N., & Lapp, D. (2008). Shared readings: Modeling comprehension, vocabulary, text structures, and text features for older readers. *The Reading Teacher, 61*, 548–556.

Fleischman, P. (2004). *Joyful noise: Poems for two voices*. New York: HarperCollins.

Fleming, D. (1995). *In the tall, tall grass*. New York: Henry Holt.

Fleming, D. (2006). *The cow who clucked*. New York: Henry Holt.

Fletcher, R., & Portalupi, J. (2007). *Craft lessons: Teaching writing K–8* (2nd ed.). York, ME: Stenhouse.

Fountas, I. C., & Pinnell, G. S. (1996). *Guided reading: Good first teaching for all children*. Portsmouth, NH: Heinemann.

Fountas, I. C., & Pinnell, G. S. (2006a). *The Fountas and Pinnell leveled book list, K–8* (2006–2008 ed.). Portsmouth, NH: Heinemann.

Fountas, I. C., & Pinnell, G. S. (2006b). *Leveled books, K–8: Matching texts to readers for effective teaching*. Portsmouth, NH: Heinemann.

Fountas, I. C., & Pinnell, G. S. (2007). *The Fountas and Pinnell benchmark assessment system*. Portsmouth, NH: Heinemann.

Frank, C. R., Dixon, C. N., & Brandts, L. R. (2001). Bears, trolls, and pagemasters: Learning about learners in book clubs. *The Reading Teacher, 54*, 448–462.

Frasier, D. (2007). *Miss Alaineus: A vocabulary disaster*. New York: HarperCollins/Voyager.

Freire, P. (2000). *Pedagogy of the oppressed* (30th anniversary ed.). New York: Continuum.

Friedland, E. S., & Truesdell, K. S. (2004). Kids reading together. *The Reading Teacher, 58*, 76–83.

Fry, E. (1968). A readability formula that saves time. *Journal of Reading, 11*, 587.

Funke, C. (2003). *Inkheart*. New York: Scholastic.

Galdone, P. (2008). *The gingerbread boy*. New York: Clarion Books.

Gambrell, L. B., Malloy, J. A., & Mazzoni, S. A. (2007). Evidence-based best practices for comprehensive literacy instruction. In L. B. Gambrell, L. M. Morrow, & M. Pressley (Eds.), *Best practices in literacy instruction* (3rd ed., pp. 11–29). New York: Guilford Press.

Ganske, K. (2000). *Word journeys: Assessment-guided phonics, spelling, and vocabulary instruction*. New York: Guilford Press.

Garcia, G. E. (2000). Bilingual children's reading. In M. Kamil, P. Mosenthal, P. D. Pearson, & R. Barr (Eds.),

Handbook of reading research (Vol. 3, pp. 813–834). Newark, DE: International Reading Association.

Garcia, G. E. (2003). Comprehension development and instruction of English-language learners. In A. P. Sweet & C. E. Snow (Eds.), *Rethinking reading comprehension* (pp. 30–50). New York: Guilford Press.

Gaskins, R. W., Gaskins, J. W., & Gaskins, I. W. (1991). A decoding program for poor readers—and the rest of the class, too! *Language Arts, 68,* 213–225.

Gay, G. (2000). *Culturally responsive teaching: Theory, research, and practice.* New York: Teachers College Press.

Geisert, A. (2008). *Hogwash.* Boston: Houghton Mifflin.

Genesee, F., & Riches, C. (2006). Literacy: Instructional issues. In F. Genesee, K. Lindholm-Leary, W. M. Saunders, & D. Christian (Eds.), *Educating English language learners: A synthesis of research evidence* (pp. 109–175). New York: Cambridge University Press.

Gentry, J. R., & Gillet, J. W. (1993). *Teaching kids to spell.* Portsmouth, NH: Heinemann.

Gibbons, G. (1993). *From seed to plant.* New York: Holiday House.

Gibbons, G. (1997). *Nature's green umbrella.* New York: HarperCollins.

Gibbons, G. (2007). *Groundhog Day!* New York: Holiday House.

Gillet, J. W., & Beverly, L. (2001). *Directing the writing workshop: An elementary teacher's handbook.* New York: Guilford Press.

Gillon, G. T. (2004). *Phonological awareness: From research to practice.* New York: Guilford Press.

Gollub, M. (2004). *Cool melons—turn to frogs! The life and poems of Issa.* New York: Lee & Low.

Graham, S., Weintraub, N., & Berninger, V. W. (1998). The relationship between handwriting style and speed and legibility. *Journal of Educational Research, 91,* 290–296.

Graves, M. F. (2006). *The vocabulary book: Learning and instruction.* New York: Teachers College Press.

Gray, L. M. (2001). *My mama had a dancing heart.* New York: Scholastic.

Greenburg, D. (1997). *Never trust a cat who wears earrings.* New York: Grosset & Dunlap.

Greenburg, D. (2003). *Just add water . . . and scream!* New York: Grosset & Dunlap.

Greene, A. H., & Melton, G. D. (2007). *Test talk: Integrating test preparation into reading workshop.* Portsmouth, ME: Stenhouse.

Greenfield, E. (2006). *The friendly four.* New York: HarperCollins.

Griffin, J. B. (2002). *Phoebe the spy.* New York: Putnam.

Griffith, F., & Olson, M. (1992). Phonemic awareness helps beginning readers break the code. *The Reading Teacher, 45,* 516–523.

Griffith, L. W., & Rasinski, T. V. (2004). A focus on fluency: How one teacher incorporated fluency with her reading curriculum. *The Reading Teacher, 58,* 126–137.

Guarino, D. (2004). *Is your mama a llama?* New York: Scholastic.

Guiberson, B. Z. (2007). *Cactus hotel.* New York: Henry Holt.

Guthrie, J. T. (2004). Teaching for literacy engagement. *Journal of Literacy Research, 36*(1), 1–28.

Guthrie, J. T., & Wigfield, A. (2000). Engagement and motivation in reading. In M. L. Kamil, P. B. Mosenthal, P. D. Pearson, & R. Barr (Eds.), *Handbook of reading research* (Vol. 3, pp. 403–422). Mahwah, NJ: Erlbaum.

Guthrie, W. (2002). *This land is your land.* Boston: Little, Brown.

Gwynne, F. (2005). *A chocolate moose for dinner.* New York: Aladdin Books.

Gwynne, F. (2006). *The king who rained.* New York: Aladdin Books.

Halfmann, J. (2007). *Hermit crab's home: Safe in a shell.* Norwalk, CT: Soundprints.

Hall, D. (1994). *I am the dog/I am the cat.* New York: Dial Books.

Halliday, M. A. K. (1978). *Language as social semiotic: The social interpretation of language and meaning.* Baltimore: University Park Press.

Hancock, M. R. (2008). *A celebration of literature and response: Children, books, and teachers in K–8 classrooms* (3rd ed.). Upper Saddle River, NJ: Merrill/Prentice Hall.

Harste, J., Woodward, V., & Burke, C. (1984). *Language stories and literacy lessons.* Portsmouth, NH: Heinemann.

Hart, B., & Risley, T. (2003). The early catastrophe: The 30 million word gap. *American Educator, 27* (1), 4–9.

Harvey, S. (1998). *Nonfiction matters: Reading, writing, and research in grades 3–8.* York, ME: Stenhouse.

Harvey, S., & Goudvis, A. (2007). *Strategies that work: Teaching comprehension for understanding and engagement* (2nd ed.). Portland, ME: Stenhouse.

Hatkoff, I., Hatkoff, C., & Kahumbu, P. (2006). *Owen and Mzee: The true story of a remarkable friendship.* New York: Scholastic.

Hayes, J. R. (2004). A new framework for understanding cognition and affect in writing. In R. B. Ruddell & N. J. Unrau (Eds.), *Theoretical models and processes of reading* (5th ed., pp. 1399–1430). Newark, DE: International Reading Association.

Heard, G. (Ed.). (2009). *Falling down the page: A book of list poems.* New York: Roaring Brook Press.

Hebert, E. A. (2001). *The power of portfolios: What children can teach us about learning and assessment.* San Francisco: Jossey-Bass.

Hellweg, P. (2009). *The American Heritage children's thesaurus.* Boston: Houghton Mifflin.

Henkes, K. (1996). *Chrysanthemum.* New York: HarperTrophy.

Henkes, K. (2004). *Kitten's first full moon.* New York: Greenwillow.

Henkin, R. (1995). Insiders and outsiders in first-grade writing workshops: Gender and equity issues. *Language Arts, 72,* 429–434.

Hennessy, B. G. (2006). *The boy who cried wolf*. New York: Simon & Schuster.

Hill, E. (2003). *Where's Spot?* New York: Puffin Books.

Hoff, S. (2000a). *Oliver*. New York: HarperTrophy.

Hoff, S. (2000b). *Sammy the seal*. New York: HarperTrophy.

Hoffman, J. V., Assaf, L. C., & Paris, S. G. (2005). High-stakes testing in reading: Today in Texas, tomorrow? In S. J. Barrentine & S. M. Stokes (Eds.), *Reading assessment: Principles and practices for elementary teachers* (2nd ed., pp. 108–120). Newark, DE: International Reading Association.

Holdaway, D. (1979). *The foundations of literacy*. Portsmouth, NH: Heinemann.

Hollingworth, L. (2007). Five ways to prepare for standardized tests without sacrificing best practice. *The Reading Teacher, 61*, 339–342.

Howe, D., & Howe, J. (2006). *Bunnicula: A rabbit-tale of mystery*. New York: Aladdin Books.

Hoyt, L. (1999). *Revisit, reflect, retell: Strategies for improving reading comprehension*. Portsmouth, NH: Heinemann.

Hoyt, L. (2000). *Snapshots*. Portsmouth, NH: Heinemann.

Huerta-Macías, A. (1995). Alternative assessment: Responses to commonly asked questions. *TESOL Journal, 5*, 8–10.

Hurd, T. (2003). *Moo cow kaboom!* New York: HarperCollins.

Hutchins, P. (1989). *Don't forget the bacon!* New York: HarperCollins.

Hutchins, P. (2005). *Rosie's walk*. New York: Aladdin Books.

International Reading Association (IRA). (1999). *High-stakes assessments in reading: A position statement*. Newark, DE: Author.

Invernizzi, M. (2003). Concepts, sounds, and the ABCs: A diet for a very young reader. In D. M. Barone & L. M. Morrow (Eds.), *Literacy and young children: Research-based practices* (pp. 140–156). New York: Guilford Press.

Invernizzi, M., Meier, J. D., & Juel, C. (2003). *Phonological Awareness Literacy Screening System*. Charlottesville: University of Virginia Press.

Irwin, J. W. (1991). *Teaching reading comprehension processes* (2nd ed). Boston: Allyn & Bacon.

Ivey, G., & Baker, M. I. (2004). Phonics instruction for older students? Just say no. *Educational Leadership, 61*(6), 35–39.

Janeczko, P. B. (2003). *Opening a door: Reading poetry in the middle school classroom*. New York: Scholastic.

Janeczko, P. B. (2005). *A poke in the I: A collection of concrete poems*. Cambridge, MA: Candlewick Press.

Jenkins, S., & Page, R. (2008). *What do you do with a tail like this?* New York: Sandpiper.

Johns, J. L., & Berglund, R. L. (2006). *Fluency: Strategies and assessments* (3rd ed.). Newark, DE: International Reading Association and Kendall/Hunt.

Johnson, H., & Freedman, L. (2005). *Developing critical awareness at the middle level*. Newark, DE: International Reading Association.

Judge, L. (2007). *One thousand tracings: Healing the wounds of World War II*. New York: Hyperion Books.

Juel, C. (1991). Beginning reading. In R. Barr, M. L. Kamil, P. Mosenthal, & P. D. Pearson (Eds.), *Handbook of reading research* (Vol. 2, pp. 759–788). New York: Longman.

Juel, C., Griffith, P. L., & Gough, P. B. (1986). Acquisition of literacy: A longitudinal study of children in first and second grade. *Journal of Educational Psychology, 78*, 243–255.

Kalman, M. (2001). *Next stop Grand Central*. New York: Putnam.

Kame'enui, E., Simmons, D., & Cornachione, C. (2000). *A practical guide to reading assessments*. Newark, DE: International Reading Association.

Kaminski, R. A., & Good, R. H., III. (1996). *Dynamic Indicators of Basic Early Literacy Skills (DIBELS)*. Eugene: University of Oregon Center on Teaching and Learning.

Kaplan, R. (1996). *Moving day*. New York: Greenwillow.

Kasza, K. (1996). *The wolf's chicken stew*. New York: Putnam.

Keehn, S., Martinez, M. G., & Roser, N. L. (2005). Exploring character through readers theatre. In N. L. Roser & M. G. Martinez (Eds.), *What a character! Character study as a guide to literary meaning making in grades K–8* (pp. 96–110). Newark, DE: International Reading Association.

Keene, E. (2006). *Assessing comprehension thinking strategies*. Huntington Beach, CA: Shell Education.

Keene, E. O., & Zimmermann, S. (2007). *Mosaic of thought: The power of comprehension strategy instruction* (2nd ed.). Portsmouth, NH: Heinemann.

Keller, L. (1998). *The scrambled states of America*. New York: Henry Holt.

Keller, L. (2003). *Open wide: Tooth school inside*. New York: Owlet.

Kellogg, S. (1985). *Paul Bunyan*. New York: HarperCollins.

Kellogg, S. (1988). *Johnny Appleseed*. New York: HarperCollins.

Kellogg, S. (1997). *Jack and the beanstalk*. New York: HarperTrophy.

Kellogg, S. (2002). *The three little pigs*. New York: HarperTrophy.

Kessler, L. (1996). *Kick, pass, and run!* New York: HarperCollins.

King-Smith, D. (2005). *Babe the gallant pig*. New York: Knopf.

Kintsch, W. (2004). The construction-integration model and its implications for instruction. In R. B. Ruddell & N. J. Unrau (Eds.), *Theoretical models and processes of reading* (5th ed., pp. 1270–1328). Newark, DE: International Reading Association.

Klesius, J. P., Griffith, P. L., & Zielonka, P. (1991). A whole language and traditional instruction comparison: Overall effectiveness and development of the alphabetic principle. *Reading Research and Instruction, 30*, 47–61.

Kline, S. (1998). *Horrible Harry's secret*. New York: Puffin Books.

Koch, K. (2000). *Wishes, lies, and dreams: Teaching children to write poetry*. New York: HarperCollins.

Koopmans, L. (1995). *The woodcutter's mitten*. New York: Crocodile Books.

Krull, K. (2000). *Wilma unlimited: How Wilma Rudolph became the world's fastest woman.* New York: Sandpiper.

Kuhn, M. R., & Rasinski, T. (2007). Best practices in fluency instruction. In L. B. Gambrell, L. M. Morrow, & M. Pressley (Eds.), *Best practices in literacy instruction* (3rd ed., pp. 204–219). New York: Guilford Press.

Kuhn, M. R., & Stahl, S. A. (2004). Fluency: A review of developmental and remedial practices. In R. B. Ruddell & N. J. Unrau (Eds.), *Theoretical models and processes of reading* (5th ed., pp. 412–453). Newark, DE: International Reading Association.

Kuhs, T. M., Johnson, R. L., Agruso, S. A., & Monrad, D. M. (2001). *Put to the test: Tools and techniques for classroom assessment.* Portsmouth, NH: Heinemann.

Kuskin, K. (2003). *Moon, have you met my mother? The collected poems of Karla Kuskin.* New York: HarperCollins.

Lapp, D., & Flood, J. (2003). Understanding the learner: Using portable assessment. In R. L. McCormack & J. R. Paratore (Eds.), *After early intervention, then what? Teaching struggling readers in grades 3 and beyond* (pp. 10–24). Newark, DE: International Reading Association.

Lareau, A. (2000). *Home advantage: Social class and parental intervention in elementary education* (2nd ed.). Lanham, MD: Rowman & Littlefield.

Lattimer, H. (2003). *Thinking through genre.* Portland, ME: Stenhouse.

Lave, J., & Wenger, E. (1991). *Situated learning: Legitimate peripheral participation.* Cambridge, England: Cambridge University Press.

Lee, C. (2004). *Good dog, Paw!* Cambridge, MA: Candlewick Press.

Leedy, L. (2009). *Crazy like a fox: A simile story.* New York: Holiday House.

Leedy, L., & Street, P. (2003). *There's a frog in my throat! 440 animal sayings a little bird told me.* New York: Holiday House.

Lehman, B. (2004). *The red book.* Boston: Houghton Mifflin.

Leslie, L., & Caldwell, J. (2006). *Qualitative reading inventory* (4th ed.). Boston: Allyn & Bacon/Pearson.

Lester, H. (2008). *Tacky the penguin.* New York: Houghton Mifflin.

Lester, J. (1999). *John Henry.* New York: Puffin Books.

Levine, E. (2007). *Henry's freedom box.* New York: Scholastic.

Lewis, C. S. (2005). *The lion, the witch and the wardrobe.* New York: HarperCollins.

Lewis, J. P. (2002). *Doodle dandies! Poems that take shape.* New York: Aladdin Books.

Lewison, M., Leland, C., & Harste, J. C. (2008). *Creating critical classrooms: K–8 reading and writing with an edge.* New York: Erlbaum.

Lewkowicz, N. K. (1994). The bag game: An activity to heighten phonemic awareness. *The Reading Teacher, 47,* 508–509.

Lionni, L. (2006). *Alexander and the wind-up mouse.* New York: Knopf.

Long, M. (2003). *How I became a pirate.* Orlando: Harcourt.

Longfellow, H. W. (2001). *The midnight ride of Paul Revere* (C. Bing, Illus.). Brooklyn, NY: Handprint Books.

Lukens, R. J. (2006). *A critical handbook of children's literature* (8th ed.). Boston: Allyn & Bacon.

Lynch, J. (2005). *High frequency word walls.* New York: Scholastic.

MacLachlan, P. (2004). *Sarah, plain and tall.* New York: HarperTrophy.

Macon, J. M., Bewell, D., & Vogt, M. E. (1991). *Responses to literature.* Newark, DE: International Reading Association.

Mariotti, A. S., & Homan, S. P. (2005). *Linking reading assessment to instruction.* London: Routledge.

Marriott, D. (2002). *Comprehension right from the start: How to organize and manage book clubs for young readers.* Portsmouth, NH: Heinemann.

Marshall, J. (1998). *Goldilocks and the three bears.* New York: Puffin Books.

Martin, B., Jr. (1992). *Polar bear, polar bear, what do you hear?* New York: Henry Holt.

Martin, B., Jr. (2007a). *Brown bear, brown bear, what do you see?* New York: Henry Holt.

Martin, B., Jr. (2007b). *Baby bear, baby bear, what do you see?* New York: Henry Holt.

Martin, B., Jr. (2007c). *Panda bear, panda bear, what do you see?* New York: Henry Holt.

Martin, B., Jr., & Archambault, J. (1988). *Barn dance!* New York: Henry Holt.

Martinez, M., Roser, N. L., & Strecker, S. (1998/1999). "I never thought I could be a star": A readers theatre ticket to fluency. *The Reading Teacher, 52,* 326–334.

Martinez-Roldan, C. M., & Lopez-Robertson, J. M. (1999/2000). Initiating literature circles in a first grade bilingual classroom. *The Reading Teacher, 53,* 270–281.

Mathis, S. B. (2006). *The hundred penny box.* New York: Puffin Books.

McCabe, P. P. (2003). Enhancing self-efficacy for high-stakes reading tests. *The Reading Teacher, 57,* 12–20.

McCarrier, A., Pinnell, G. S., & Fountas, I. C. (2000). *Interactive writing: How language and literacy come together, K–2.* Portsmouth, NH: Heinemann.

McCloskey, R. (2001). *Make way for ducklings.* New York: Viking.

McDermott, G. (2001). *Raven.* San Diego: Voyager.

McGee, L. M. (2007). *Transforming literacy practices in preschool: Research-based practices that give all children the opportunity to reach their potential as learners.* New York: Scholastic.

McGee, L. M., & Richgels, D. J. (1985). Teaching expository text structures to elementary students. *The Reading Teacher, 38,* 739–745.

McGee, L. M., & Richgels, D. J. (2003). *Designing early literacy programs: Strategies for at-risk preschool and kindergarten children.* New York: Guilford Press.

McGee, L. M., & Richgels, D. J. (2008). *Literacy's beginnings: Supporting young readers and writers* (5th ed.). Boston: Allyn & Bacon.

McKenna, M. C., & Dougherty Stahl, K. A. (2009). *Assessment for reading instruction* (2nd ed.). New York: Guilford Press.

McKenna, M. C., & Stahl, S. A. (2003). *Assessment for reading instruction*. New York: Guilford Press.

McKeown, M. G., & Beck, I. L. (2004). Direct and rich vocabulary instruction. In J. F. Baumann & E. B. Kame'enui (Eds.), *Vocabulary instruction: Research to practice* (pp. 13–27). New York: Guilford Press.

McKissack, P. (2001). *Goin' somewhere special*. New York: Atheneum.

McLaughlin, M., & Allen, M. B. (2001). *Guided comprehension: A teaching model for grades 3–8*. Newark, DE: International Reading Association.

McLimans, D. (2006). *Gone wild: An endangered animal alphabet*. New York: Walker.

McQuillan, J. (1998). *The literacy crisis: False claims, real solutions*. Portsmouth, NH: Heinemann.

Meddaugh, S. (1995). *Martha speaks*. Boston: Houghton Mifflin.

Meddaugh, S. (1998). *Hog-eye*. New York: Sandpiper.

Mellard, D. F., & Johnson, E. (2008). *RTI: A practitioner's guide to implementing Response to Intervention*. Thousand Oaks, CA: Corwin Press and the National Association of Elementary School Principals.

Mermelstein, L. (2007). *Don't forget to share: The crucial last step in the writing workshop*. Portsmouth, NH: Heinemann.

Mesmer, H. A. E., & Griffith, P. L. (2005). Everybody's selling it—But just what is explicit, systematic phonics instruction? *The Reading Teacher, 59*, 366–376.

Meyer, B. J. F., & Poon, L. W. (2004). Effects of structure strategy training and signaling on recall of text. In R. B. Ruddell & N. J. Unrau (Eds.), *Theoretical models and processes of reading* (5th ed., pp. 810–850). Newark, DE: International Reading Association.

Mitchell, S. (2007). *The ugly duckling*. Cambridge, MA: Candlewick Press.

Moline, S. (1995). *I see what you mean: Children at work with visual information*. York, ME: Stenhouse.

Moll, L. (1994). Literacy research in community and classrooms: A sociocultural approach. In R. R. Ruddell, M. R. Ruddell, & H. Singer (Eds.), *Theoretical models and processes of reading* (4th ed., pp. 197–207). Newark, DE: International Reading Association.

Moll, L. C., & Gonzales, N. (2004). Engaging life: A funds of knowledge approach to multicultural education. In J. A. Banks & C. A. M. Banks (Eds.), *Handbook of research on multicultural education* (2nd ed., pp. 699–715). San Francisco: Jossey-Bass.

Mooney, M. E. (2001). *Text forms and features: A resource for intentional teaching*. Katonah, NY: Richard C. Owen.

Morrow, L. M. (1985). Retelling stories: A strategy for improving children's comprehension, concept of story structure, and oral language complexity. *Elementary School Journal, 85*, 647–661.

Morrow, L. M. (2002). *Organizing and managing the language arts block*. New York: Guilford Press.

Morrow, L. M., & Tracey, D. H. (2007). Best practices in early literacy development in preschool, kindergarten, and first grade. In L. B. Gambrell, L. M. Morrow, & M. Pressley (Eds.), *Best practices in literacy instruction* (3rd ed., pp. 57–82). New York: Guilford Press.

Morrow, L. M., Freitag, E., & Gambrell, L. B. (2009). *Using children's literature in preschool to develop comprehension* (2nd ed.). Newark, DE: International Reading Association.

Moses, W. (2008). *Raining cats and dogs*. New York: Philomel.

Most, B. (1996). *Cock-a-doodle-moo!* San Diego: Harcourt Brace.

Murray, D. M. (1982). *Learning by teaching*. Montclair, NJ: Boynton/Cook.

Murray, D. M. (2003). *A writer teaches writing* (2nd ed.). Belmont, CA: Wadsworth.

Nagy, W. E. (1988). *Teaching vocabulary to improve reading comprehension*. Urbana, IL: ERIC Clearinghouse on Reading and Communication Skills and the National Council of Teachers of English and the International Reading Association.

Nagy, W. E., Anderson, R. C., & Herman, P. A. (1987). Learning word meanings from context during normal reading. *American Educational Research Journal, 24*, 237–270.

Napier, M. (2002). *Z is for Zamboni: A hockey alphabet*. Chelsea, MI: Sleeping Bear Press.

National Commission on Excellence in Education. (1983). *A nation at risk: The imperative for educational reform*. Washington, DC: US Government Printing Office.

National Reading Panel. (2000). *Teaching children to read: An evidence-based assessment of the scientific research literature on reading and its implications for reading instruction*. Washington, DC: National Institute of Child Health and Human Development.

Nieto, S. (2002). *Language, culture, and teaching: Critical perspectives for a new century*. Mahwah, NJ: Erlbaum.

Nilsson, N. L. (2008). A critical analysis of eight informal reading inventories. *The Reading Teacher, 61*, 526–536.

Norman, K. A., & Calfee, R. C. (2004). Tile Test: A hands-on approach for assessing phonics in the early grades. *The Reading Teacher 58*, 42–52.

Norton, M. (2003a). *The borrowers*. New York: Sandpiper.

Norton, M. (2003b). *The borrowers aloft*. New York: Sandpiper.

Numeroff, L. J. (1985). *If you give a mouse a cookie*. New York: HarperCollins.

Numeroff, L. J. (2003). *If you give an author a pencil*. Katonah, NY: Richard C. Owen.

O'Connor, J. (2008). *Fancy Nancy's favorite fancy words: From accessories to zany*. New York: HarperCollins.

O'Donohue, W., & Kitchener, R. F. (Eds.). (1998). *Handbook of behaviorism*. New York: Academic Press.

O'Malley, J. M., & Pierce, L. V. (1996). *Authentic assessment for English language learners: Practical approaches for teachers*. Boston: Addison-Wesley.

Ogle, D. M. (1986). K-W-L: A teaching model that develops active reading of expository text. *The Reading Teacher, 39,* 564–570.

Ohlhausen, M. M., & Jepsen, M. (1992). Lessons from Goldilocks: "Somebody's been choosing my books but I can make my own choices now!" *The New Advocate, 5,* 31–46.

Opitz, M. F., Ford, M. P., & Zbaracki, M. D. (2006). *Books and beyond: New ways to reach readers.* Portsmouth, NH: Heinemann.

Osborne, M. P. (2003). *High tide in Hawaii.* New York: Random House.

Owocki, G. (2003). *Comprehension: Strategic instruction for K–3 students.* Portsmouth, NH: Heinemann.

Owocki, G., & Goodman, Y. M. (2002). *Kidwatching: Documenting children's literacy development.* Portsmouth, NH: Heinemann.

Padgett, R. (2007). *Handbook of poetic forms* (2nd ed.). New York: Teachers & Writers Collaborative.

Papandropoulou, I., & Sinclair, H. (1974). What is a word? Experimental study of children's ideas on grammar. *Human Development, 17,* 241–258.

Paratore, J. R. (2001). *Opening doors, opening opportunities: Family literacy in an urban community.* Boston: Allyn & Bacon.

Park, B. (2003). *Junie B., first grader: Boss of lunch.* New York: Random House.

Parkes, B. (2000). *Read it again! Revisiting shared reading.* Portland, ME: Stenhouse.

Paschen, E., & Raccah, D. (Sels.). (2005). *Poetry speaks to children.* Naperville, IL: Sourcebooks MediaFusion.

Payne, C. D., & Schulman, M. B. (1999). *Getting the most out of morning messages and other shared writing lessons.* New York: Scholastic.

Pearson, P. D., Raphael, T. E., Benson, V. L., & Madda, C. L. (2007). Balance in comprehensive literacy instruction: Then and now. In L. B. Gambrell, L. M. Morrow, & M. Pressley (Eds.), *Best practices in literacy instruction* (3rd ed., pp. 31–54). New York: Guilford Press.

Peregoy, S. F., & Boyle, O. F. (2008). *Reading, writing and learning in ESL: A resource book for K–12 teachers* (5th ed.). Boston: Allyn & Bacon/Pearson.

Peterson, R., & Eeds, M. (2007). *Grand conversations: Literature groups in action.* New York: Scholastic.

Piaget, J. (1969). *The psychology of intelligence.* Paterson, NJ: Littlefield, Adams.

Pikulski, J. J., & Chard, D. J. (2005). Fluency: Bridge between decoding and reading comprehension. *The Reading Teacher, 58,* 510–519.

Pinnell, G. S., & Fountas, I. C. (1998). *Word matters: Teaching phonics and spelling in the reading/writing classroom.* Portsmouth, NH: Heinemann.

Pinto, S. (2003). *The alphabet room.* New York: Bloomsbury.

Piven, H. (2007). *My dog is as smelly as dirty socks.* New York: Schwartz & Wade.

Potter, B. (2006). *The tale of Peter Rabbit.* New York: Warne.

Pratt-Serafini, K. J. (2002). *Saguaro moon: A desert journal.* Nevada City, CA: Dawn.

Prelutsky, J. (2007). *My parents think I'm sleeping.* New York: Greenwillow.

Prelutsky, J. (Sel.). (2000). *The Random House book of poetry for children.* New York: Random House.

Pressley, M. (2002a). Comprehension strategies instruction: A turn-of-the-century status report. In C. C. Block & M. Pressley (Eds.), *Comprehension instruction: Research-based best practices* (pp. 11–27). New York: Guilford Press.

Pressley, M. (2002b). Metacognition and self-regulated comprehension. In A. E. Farstrup & S. J. Samuels (Eds.), *What research has to say about reading instruction* (3rd ed., pp. 291–309). Newark, DE: International Reading Association.

Prince, S. (1999). *Playing.* Littleton, MA: Sundance.

Rappaport, D. (2007). *Martin's big words: The life of Dr. Martin Luther King, Jr.* New York: Hyperion Books.

Rasinski, T. (2005a). *Daily word ladders: Grades 2–3.* New York: Scholastic.

Rasinski, T. (2005b). *Daily word ladders: Grades 4–6.* New York: Scholastic.

Rasinski, T. (2006). Developing vocabulary through word building. In C. C. Block & J. N. Mangieri (Eds.), *The vocabulary-enriched classroom: Practices for improving the reading performance of all students in grades 3 and up* (pp. 36–53). New York: Scholastic.

Rasinski, T. V. (2003). *The fluent reader.* New York: Scholastic.

Rasinski, T. V., & Padak, N. D. (2008). *From phonics to fluency: Effective teaching of decoding and reading fluency in the elementary school* (2nd ed.). Boston: Allyn & Bacon/Pearson.

Rathmann, P. (1995). *Officer Buckle and Gloria.* New York: Putnam.

Rau, D. M. (2003). *Neil Armstrong.* Chicago: Children's Press.

Ray, K. W., & Glover, M. (2008). *Already ready: Nurturing writers in preschool and kindergarten.* Portsmouth, NH: Heinemann.

Read, C. (1975). *Children's categorization of speech sounds in English* (NCTE Research Report No. 17). Urbana, IL: National Council of Teachers of English.

Read, C. (1986). *Children's creative spelling.* London: Routledge & Kegan Paul.

Reutzel, D. R., & Fawson, P. C. (1990). Traveling tales: Connecting parents and children in writing. *The Reading Teacher, 44,* 222–227.

Richardson, A. (2006). *Caring for your hermit crab.* Mankato, MN: Capstone Press.

Riches, C., & Genesee, F. (2006). Literacy: Crosslinguistic and crossmodal issues. In F. Genesee, K. Lindholm-Leary, W. M. Saunders, & D. Christian (Eds.), *Educating English language learners: A synthesis of research evidence* (pp. 64–108). New York: Cambridge University Press.

Rickelman, R. J., & Taylor, D. B. (2006). Teaching vocabulary by learning content-area words. In C. C. Block & J. N. Mangieri (Eds.), *The vocabulary-enriched classroom: Practices for improving the reading performance of all students in grades 3 and up* (pp. 54–73). New York: Scholastic.

Robb, L. (2003). *Teaching reading in social studies, science, and math*. New York: Scholastic.

Rodriguez, R. V. (2006). *Through Georgia's eyes*. New York: Henry Holt.

Rohmann, E. (1997). *Time flies*. New York: Dragonfly.

Romano, T. (2000). *Blending genre, alternating style: Writing multiple genre papers*. Portsmouth, NH: Heinemann/ Boynton/Cook.

Root, P. (2004). *Rattletrap car*. Cambridge, MA: Candlewick Press.

Rosenblatt, L. (2005). *Making meaning with texts: Selected essays*. Portsmouth, NH: Heinemann.

Rosenblatt, L. M. (2004). The transactional theory of reading and writing. In R. B. Ruddell & N. J. Unrau (Eds.), *Theoretical models and processes of reading* (5th ed., pp. 1363–1398). Newark, DE: International Reading Association.

Roskos, K. A., Tabors, P. O., & Lenhart, L. A. (2009). *Oral language and early literacy in preschool* (2nd ed.). Newark, DE: International Reading Association.

Roth, F. P., Speece, D. L., & Cooper, D. H. (2002). A longitudinal analysis of the connection between oral language and early reading. *Journal of Educational Research, 95*, 259–274.

Roth, S. (2001). *Happy birthday Mr. Kang*. Washington, DC: National Geographic Children's Books.

Rothenberg, C., & Fisher, D. (2007). *Teaching English language learners: A differentiated approach*. Upper Saddle River, NJ: Merrill/Prentice Hall.

Ruddell, D. (2007). *Today at the Bluebird Café: A branchful of birds*. New York: McElderry.

Ruddell, R. B., & Unrau, N. J. (2004). Reading as a meaning-construction process: The reader, the text, and the teacher. In R. B. Ruddell & N. J. Unrau (Eds.), *Theoretical models and processes of reading* (5th ed., pp. 1462–1521). Newark, DE: International Reading Association.

Rumelhart, D. E. (2004). Toward an interactive model of reading. In R. B. Ruddell & N. J. Unrau (Eds.), *Theoretical models and processes of reading* (5th ed., pp. 1149–1179). Newark, DE: International Reading Association.

Ryan, P. M. (1999). *Riding Freedom*. New York: Scholastic.

Ryan, P. M. (2002). *Esperanza rising*. New York: Scholastic/ Blue Sky Press.

Rylant, C. (1998). *Tulip sees America*. New York: Blue Sky Press.

Rylant, C. (2007). *Henry and Mudge and the big sleepover*. New York: Aladdin Books.

Sachar, L. (1988). *There's a boy in the girls' bathroom*. New York: Yearling.

Sachar, L. (2000). *Marvin Redpost: A magic crystal?* New York: Random House.

Sachar, L. (2004). *Sideways stories from Wayside School*. New York: HarperCollins.

Samuels, S. J. (2002). Reading fluency: Its development and assessment. In A. E. Farstrup & S. J. Samuels (Eds.), *What research has to say about reading instruction* (3rd ed., pp. 166–185). Newark, DE: International Reading Association.

Samuels, S. J. (2004). Toward a theory of automatic information processing in reading, revisited. In R. B. Ruddell & N. J. Unrau (Eds.), *Theoretical models and processes of reading* (5th ed., pp. 1127–1148). Newark, DE: International Reading Association.

Samway, K. D., & McKeon, D. (2007). *Myths and realities: Best practices for English language learners* (2nd ed.). Portsmouth, NH: Heinemann.

Samway, K. D., & Whang, G. (1996). *Literature study circles in a multicultural classroom*. York, ME: Stenhouse.

Santoro, L. E., Chard, D. J., Howard, L., & Baker, S. K. (2008). Making the *very* most of classroom read-alouds to promote comprehension and vocabulary. *The Reading Teacher, 61*, 396–408.

Schickedanz, J. A., & Casbergue, R. M. (2009). *Writing in preschool: Learning to orchestrate meaning and marks* (2nd ed.). Newark, DE: International Reading Association.

Scieszka, J. (2004). *Knights of the kitchen table*. New York: Puffin Books.

Scieszka, J. (2005). *Baloney (Henry P.)*. New York: Puffin Books.

Scott, J. A., & Nagy, W. E. (2004). Developing word consciousness. In J. F. Baumann & E. J. Kame'enui (Eds.), *Vocabulary instruction: Theory to practice* (pp. 210–217). New York: Guilford Press.

Seeger, L. V. (2007). *First the egg*. New York: Roaring Brook Press.

Seuling, B. (2003). *Flick a switch: How electricity gets to your home*. New York: Holiday House.

Seuss, Dr. (1963). *Hop on pop*. New York: Random House.

Seuss, Dr. (1965). *Fox in socks*. New York: Random House.

Shanahan, T., & Beck, I. (2006). Effective literacy teaching for English-language learners. In D. August & T. Shanahan (Eds.), *Developing literacy in second-language learners: Report of the National Literacy Panel on Language-Minority Children and Youth* (pp. 415–488). Mahwah, NJ: Erlbaum.

Shannon, D. (1998). *No, David!* New York: Blue Sky Press.

Shefelbine, J. (1995). *Learning and using phonics in beginning reading* (Literacy research paper; volume 10). New York: Scholastic.

Shelton, N. R. & Fu, D. (2004). Creating space for teaching writing and for test preparation. *Language Arts, 82*, 120–128.

Short, K. G., & Harste, J. (1996). *Creating classrooms for authors and inquirers*. Portsmouth, NH: Heinemann.

Siebert, D. (2006). *Tour America: A journey through poems and art*. San Francisco: Chronicle Books.

Simon, L. (2005). *Write as an expert: Explicit teaching of genres*. Portsmouth, NH: Heinemann.

Simont, M. (2001). *The stray dog*. New York: HarperCollins.

Skillings, M. J., & Ferrell, R. (2000). Student-generated rubrics: Bringing children into the assessment process. *The Reading Teacher, 53*, 452–455.

Skinner, B. F. (1974). *About behaviorism*. New York: Random House.

Sluss, D. J. (2005). *Supporting play: Birth through age eight*. Clifton Park, NY: Thomson/Delmar Learning.

Snow, C. E., Burns, M. S., & Griffin, P. (Eds.). (1998). *Preventing reading difficulties in young children*. Washington, DC: National Academy Press.

Snow, C. E., Griffin, P., & Burns, M. S. (Eds.). (2005). *Knowledge to support the teaching of reading: Preparing teachers for a changing world*. San Francisco: Jossey-Bass.

Soto, G. (2005). *Neighborhood odes*. San Diego: Harcourt.

Spandel, V. (2008). *Creating young writers: Using the six traits to enrich writing process in primary classrooms* (2nd ed.). Boston: Allyn & Bacon.

Spandel, V. (2009). *Creating writers through 6-trait writing assessment and instruction* (5th ed.). Boston: Allyn & Bacon/Pearson.

Stahl, S. A., & Nagy, W. E. (2006). *Teaching word meanings*. Mahwah, NJ: Erlbaum.

Stanovich, K. E. (1986). Matthew effects in reading: Some consequences of individual differences in the acquisition of literacy. *Reading Research Quarterly, 21*, 360–406.

Stanovich, K. E. (1992). Speculations on the causes and consequences of individual differences in early reading acquisition. In P. B. Gough, L. C. Ehri, & R. Treiman (Eds.), *Reading acquisition* (pp. 307–342). Hillsdale, NJ: Erlbaum.

Stead, T. (2002). *Is that a fact? Teaching nonfiction writing K–3*. Portland, ME: Stenhouse.

Stead, T., & Duke, N. K. (2005). *Reality checks: Teaching reading comprehension with nonfiction, K–5*. York, ME: Stenhouse.

Steig, W. (2006). *Sylvester and the magic pebble*. New York: Aladdin Books.

Stires, S. (1991). Thinking through the process: Self-evaluation in writing. In B. M. Power & R. Hubbard (Eds.), *The Heinemann reader: Literacy in process* (pp. 295–310). Portsmouth, NH: Heinemann.

Strickland, D. S. (2002). The importance of effective early intervention. In A. E. Farstrup & S. J. Samuels (Eds.), *What research has to say about reading instruction* (3rd ed., pp. 261–290). Newark, DE: International Reading Association.

Strickland, D. S., & Schickedanz, J. A. (2009). *Learning about print in preschool* (2nd ed.). Newark, DE: International Reading Association.

Swanborn, M. S. W., & de Glopper, K. (1999). Incidental word learning while reading: A meta-analysis. *Review of Educational Research, 69*, 261–285.

Swanson, S. M. (2008). *The house in the night*. Boston: Houghton Mifflin.

Sweet, A. P., & Snow, C. E. (2003). Reading for comprehension. In A. P. Sweet & C. E. Snow (Eds.), *Rethinking reading comprehension* (pp. 1–11). New York: Guilford Press.

Taback, S. (2004). *This is the house that Jack built*. New York: Puffin Books.

Tabors, P. O. (2008). *One child, two languages: A guide for early childhood educators of children learning English as a second language* (2nd ed.). Baltimore: Paul H. Brookes.

Terban, M. (2006). *Scholastic dictionary of idioms*. New York: Scholastic.

Terban, M. (2007a). *Eight ate: A feast of homonym riddles*. New York: Clarion Books.

Terban, M. (2007b). *Mad as a wet hen!: And other funny idioms*. New York: Sandpiper.

The pot of gold (an Irish folk tale). (2001). Upper Saddle River, NJ: Celebration Press/Pearson.

Thimmesh, C. (2006). *Team moon: How 400,000 people landed Apollo 11 on the moon*. Boston: Houghton Mifflin.

Tierney, R. J. (1990). Redefining reading comprehension. *Educational Leadership, 47*, 37–42.

Tierney, R. J., & Shanahan, T. (1996). Research on the reading-writing relationship: Interactions, transactions, and outcomes. In R. Barr, M. L. Kamil, P. Mosenthal, & P. D. Pearson (Eds.), *Handbook of reading research* (Vol. 2, pp. 246–280). Mahwah, NJ: Erlbaum.

Tomlinson, C. A. (2004). *How to differentiate instruction in mixed-ability classrooms* (2nd ed.). Alexandria, VA: Association for Supervision and Curriculum Development.

Tompkins, G. E. (2008). *Teaching writing: Balancing process and product* (5th ed.). Upper Saddle River, NJ: Merrill/Prentice Hall.

Tompkins, G. E., & Collom, S. (Eds.). (2004). *Sharing the pen: Interactive writing with young children*. Upper Saddle River, NJ: Merrill/Prentice Hall.

Torgesen, J. K., & Bryant, B. R. (2004). *Test of Phonological Awareness* (2nd ed.). East Moline, IL: LinguiSystems.

Tovani, C. (2000). *I read it, but I don't get it: Comprehension strategies for adolescent readers*. Portland, ME: Stenhouse.

Tracey, D. H., & Morrow, L. M. (2006). *Lenses on reading: An introduction to theories and models*. New York: Guilford Press.

Tresselt, A. (1989). *The mitten*. New York: HarperTrophy.

Uchida, Y. (1996). *The bracelet*. New York: Putnam.

Van Allsburg, C. (1993). *The garden of Abdul Gasazi*. Boston: Houghton Mifflin.

Van Den Broek, P., & Kremer, K. E. (2000). The mind in action: What it means to comprehend during reading. In B. M. Taylor, M. F. Graves, & P. Van Den Broek (Eds.), *Reading for meaning: Fostering comprehension in the middle grades* (pp. 1–31). New York: Teachers College Press.

Venezky, R. L. (1999). *The American way of spelling: The structure and origins of American English orthography*. New York: Guilford Press.

Viorst, J. (2009). *Alexander and the terrible, horrible, no good, very bad day*. New York: Atheneum.

Vukelich, C., & Christie, J. (2009). *Building a foundation for preschool literacy* (2nd ed.). Newark, DE: International Reading Association.

Vygotsky, L. S. (1978). *Mind in society.* Cambridge, MA: Harvard University Press.

Vygotsky, L. S. (1986). *Thought and language.* Cambridge, MA: MIT Press.

Waber, B. (2008). *Ira sleeps over.* New York: Sandpiper.

Wagstaff, J. (1999). *Teaching reading and writing with word walls.* New York: Scholastic.

Walsh, K. (2003, Spring). Basal readers: The lost opportunity to build the knowledge that propels comprehension. *American Educator, 27,* 24–27.

Ward, C. (1999). *The hare and the tortoise.* New York: Millbrook Press.

Weatherford, C. B. (2007). *Freedom on the menu: The Greensboro sit-ins.* New York: Dial Books.

Weber, C. (2002). *Publishing with students: A comprehensive guide.* Portsmouth, NH: Heinemann.

Weiss, N. (1990). *An egg is an egg.* New York: Putnam.

Wells, R. (2005). *McDuff's wild romp.* New York: Hyperion Books.

Whang, G., Samway, K. D., & Pippitt, M. (1995). *Buddy reading: Cross-age tutoring in a multicultural school.* Portsmouth, NH: Heinemann.

White, E. B. (2006). *Charlotte's web.* New York: HarperCollins.

White, T. G. (2005). Effects of systematic and strategic analogy-based phonics on grade 2 students' word reading and reading comprehension. *Reading Research Quarterly, 40,* 234–255.

Whitin, P. E. (2002). Leading into literature circles through the sketch-to-sketch strategy. *The Reading Teacher, 55,* 444–450.

Wiesner, D. (2006). *Flotsam.* New York: Clarion Books.

Wildsmith, B. (2007). *The lion and the rat.* New York: Oxford University Press.

Wilhelm, J. D. (2001). *Improving comprehension with think-aloud strategies.* New York: Scholastic.

Wilkinson, P. (1998). *Spacebusters.* New York: DK Children's Books.

Willems, M. (2004). *Knuffle bunny: A cautionary tale.* New York: Hyperion Books.

Williams, K. T. (2006). *Expressive vocabulary test-2.* Bloomington, MN: American Guidance Service/Pearson.

Williams, V. B. (1993). *A chair for my mother.* New York: HarperTrophy.

Winograd, P., & Arrington, H. J. (1999). Best practices in literacy assessment. In L. B. Gambrell, L. M. Morrow, S. B. Neuman, & M. Pressley (Eds.), *Best practices in literacy instruction* (pp. 210–241). New York: Guilford Press.

Winter, J. (2008). *Follow the drinking gourd.* New York: Knopf.

Wisniewski, D. (1999). *Tough cookie.* New York: Lothrop, Lee & Shepard.

Wittels, H. (2001). *A first thesaurus.* New York: Golden Books.

Wood, A. (1984). *The napping house.* San Diego: Harcourt Brace.

Wood, A. (1997). *Quick as a cricket.* London: Child's Play.

Wood, A. (2001). *Alphabet adventure.* New York: Blue Sky Press.

Woods, M. L., & Moe, A. J. (2007). *Analytical reading inventory* (8th ed.). Upper Saddle River, NJ: Merrill/Prentice Hall.

Wylie, R. E., & Durrell, D. D. (1970). Teaching vowels through phonograms. *Elementary English, 47,* 787–791.

Yaden, D. B., Jr. (1988). Understanding stories through repeated read-alouds: How many does it take? *The Reading Teacher, 41,* 556–560.

Yolen, J. (1996). *Commander Toad in space.* New York: Putnam.

Yolen, J. (2007). *Owl moon.* New York: Philomel.

Yolen, J., & Peters, A. F. (Eds.). (2007). *Here's a little poem.* Cambridge, MA: Candlewick Press.

Yopp, H. K. (1988). The validity and reliability of phonemic awareness tests. *Reading Research Quarterly, 23,* 159–177.

Yopp, H. K. (1992). Developing phonemic awareness in young children. *The Reading Teacher, 45,* 696–703.

Yopp, H. K. (1995). Read-aloud books for developing phonemic awareness: An annotated bibliography. *The Reading Teacher, 48,* 538–542.

Yopp, H. K., & Yopp, R. H. (2000). Supporting phonemic awareness development in the classroom. *The Reading Teacher, 54,* 130–143.

Yorinks, A. (1986). *Hey, Al.* New York: Farrar, Straus & Giroux.

Zelinsky, P. O. (1996). *Rumpelstiltskin.* New York: Puffin Books.

Zimmermann, S., & Hutchins, C. (2003). *Seven keys to comprehension: How to help your kids read it and get it!* New York: Three Rivers Press.

INDEX

Academic vocabulary, 176
Accelerated Reader® Program, 34
Affixes, 155, 157, 171, 172, 189, 190
"All About..." books, 329, 356
Alliteration, 248
Alphabet books, 44, 45, 242, 329–330
Alphabetic principle, 108
Antonyms, 180–181
Assessment
    alternative assessment, 84
    anecdotal notes, 76
    checklists, 78
    children's work samples, 64–69
    classroom, 30
    cloze procedure, 196, 197, 223
    comprehension, 222–224
    comprehension: text factors, 254
    conferences, 77, 196
    diagnostic assessments, 80
    documenting student's learning, 84–85
    high-stakes testing, 31, 87–90
    informal reading inventories, 195, 223
    miscue analysis, 363
    monitoring students progress, 76–79
    observations, 76, 195
    on-demand writing tests, 309–311
    oral language, 39–40
    phonemic awareness, 105–106
    phonics, 117–118
    portfolios, 85–87
    reading, 83–84
    reading fluency, 160–162
    rubrics, 77–79, 161, 196, 309, 361–362
    running records, 161, 163, 224,
        362–363
    self-assessment, 86
    spelling development, 140–143
    "status of the class," 318–319
    story retelling, 224, 366–367
    tests, 48, 80, 196
    thematic units, 337
    think-alouds, 224, 367–368
    vocabulary, 194–196
    vs. evaluation, 69
    weekly spelling tests, 139–140
    writing, 84
    writing fluency, 167–168
    written language concepts, 48–49

Authenticity, 14, 22, 25
Author's chair, 292, 293, 301, 318–319
Author units, 280–281
Automaticity
    reading fluency, 150, 151–158,
        160–161
    writing fluency, 163, 164–165, 167

Background knowledge, 205, 261–262
Balanced approach, 14–16, 118
Basal reading programs, 93–96, 170–172
    components, 275–277
    description, 20–22
    management, 277–278
    materials, 277
    pros and cons, 20, 274–276
    and the reading process, 273–274
    workbooks, 276–277
Basic Interpersonal Communication
    Skills (BICS), 38
Beginning-middle-end of stories,
    236–238
Beginning readers, 50, 51, 54–57
Beginning writers, 50, 51, 54–57
Behaviorism, 5, 6
BICS (Basic Interpersonal
    Communication Skills), 38
Big books, 32, 33, 41, 51, 265–266, 268,
    277
Book talks, 345–346

CALP (Cognitive Academic Language
    Proficiency), 38
CAP (Concepts About Print), 48–49
Chant and clap procedure, 153
Characters, 236, 238–239
Checklists, 77, 78
Choral reading, 159, 253, 346–347
Cloze procedure, 196, 197, 223
Cognitive Academic Language
    Proficiency (CALP), 38
Cognitive strategies, 9, 206
Collaborative books, 47
Color poems, 306–307
Community of learners, 12–14
Comprehension
    activities, 220, 221
    assessment, 222–224

definition of, 203
developmental continuum, 203
English learners, 220–222
explicit instruction, 216
grand conversations, 347–348
guidelines, 216
hot seat, 349
interactive read-alouds, 349–351
minilesson, 217
open-mind portraits, 358–359
prerequisites for, 205–206
reader factors, 204, 215–220
reading logs, 360–361
shared reading, 365
skills, 215
story boards, 366
story retelling, 366–367
strategies (*See* Comprehension
    strategies)
text factors, 204
think-alouds, 367–368
through reading, 216, 218–219
Comprehension strategies, 199, 221–222,
    271
    activating background knowledge, 206,
        207
    connecting, 206, 207, 208, 209
    determining importance, 207, 209
    drawing inferences, 207, 209–210
    evaluating, 207, 210–211
    monitoring, 207, 211–212
    predicting, 207, 212
    questioning, 207–208, 212
    repairing, 207, 212–213
    setting a purpose, 207, 213
    summarizing, 207, 213
    text factors, 251
    visualizing, 207, 213–214
Concepts About Print (CAP), 48, 49
Concrete poems, 248
Conditional knowledge, 272
Conferences, 77
Connecting
    as comprehension strategy, 206–209
    reading and writing, 38–39, 324–329
Consonants, 108–109
Constructivism, 5–7
Context clues, 190

387